ADVENTURES
FOR READERS
BOOK ONE

The ADVENTURES IN LITERATURE Program

ADVENTURES FOR READERS: BOOK ONE
Teacher's Manual
Tests
Reading/Writing Workshop A

ADVENTURES FOR READERS: BOOK TWO
Teacher's Manual
Tests
Reading/Writing Workshop B

ADVENTURES IN READING
Teacher's Manual
Tests
Reading/Writing Workshop C

ADVENTURES IN APPRECIATION
Teacher's Manual
Tests
Reading/Writing Workshop D

ADVENTURES IN AMERICAN LITERATURE
Teacher's Manual
Tests

ADVENTURES IN ENGLISH LITERATURE
Teacher's Manual
Tests

CURRICULUM AND WRITING

Fannie Safier
Formerly teacher of English
New York City Schools, New York, New York

Secondary English Editorial Staff
Harcourt Brace Jovanovich, Publishers

ADVENTURES
FOR READERS
BOOK ONE

HERITAGE EDITION REVISED

 Harcourt Brace Jovanovich, Publishers
Orlando   New York   Chicago   San Diego   Atlanta   Dallas

Acknowledgments

For permission to reprint copyrighted material, grateful acknowledgment is made to the following sources:

The Atlantic Monthly Company, Boston, Mass. and John Cushman Associates, Inc.: "The Erne from the Coast" by T. O. Beachcroft from *Atlantic Monthly*, 1938. Copyright 1938, renewed © 1966 by T. O. Beachcroft.

Bobbs-Merrill Company, Inc.: "When the Frost Is on the Punkin" by James Whitcomb Riley from *The Complete Works of James Whitcomb Riley*, published by Bobbs-Merrill in 1916.

The Christian Science Monitor: The poem "Unfolding Bud" by Naoshi Koriyama from *The Christian Science Monitor* of July 13, 1957. Copyright © 1957 by The Christian Science Publishing Society. All rights reserved.

B. J. Chute: "The Brain and I" by B. J. Chute.

The Borden Deal Family Trust (Borden Deal, Trustee): "Antaeus" by Borden Deal. Copyright © 1961 by Southern Methodist University Press.

The Devin-Adair Company, Inc. and Michael McLaverty: "The Wild Duck's Nest" from *The Game Cock and Other Stories* by Michael McLaverty. Copyright 1947, © 1975 by The Devin-Adair Company.

The Dial Press: "The Reward of Baucis and Philemon" excerpted from *Stories of the Gods and Heroes* by Sally Benson. Copyright 1940, © 1968 by Sally Benson. Excerpt from *Tell Me How Long the Train's Been Gone* (retitled: "Those Saturday Afternoons") by James Baldwin. Copyright © 1968 by James Baldwin.

Dodd, Mead & Company, Inc.: "A School for Foxes" (retitled: "Animals Go to School") from *The Lost Woods* by Edwin Way Teale. Copyright 1945, 1973 by Edwin Way Teale.

Doubleday & Company, Inc.: Excerpt from *The Story of My Life* (retitled: "The Two Faces of Nature") by Helen Keller. Excerpt from *Roots* by Alex Haley. Copyright © 1976 by Alex Haley. "Dogs That Have Known Me" from *Please Don't Eat the Daisies* by Jean Kerr. Copyright © 1957 by Conde Nast Publications, Inc.

Doubleday & Company, Inc. and Curtis Brown Ltd., London, on behalf of Daphne du Maurier: Excerpt from "The Birds" from *Kiss Me Again, Stranger* by Daphne du Maurier. Copyright © 1952 by Daphne du Maurier.

Doubleday & Company, Inc. and Jonathan Cape Ltd.: "All You've Ever Wanted" from *All and More* by Joan Aiken, illustrated by Pat Marriott.

Doubleday & Company, Inc. and The National Trust: "Rikki-Tikki-Tavi" from *The Jungle Book* by Rudyard Kipling.

Norma Millay Ellis: "The Courage That My Mother Had" by Edna St. Vincent Millay from *Collected Poems*, Harper & Row. Copyright 1954 by Norma Millay Ellis.

Esquire Associates: "Mind over Water" by Diana Nyad from *Esquire*, October 1975. Copyright © 1975 by Esquire Associates. "The Tiger's Heart" by Jim Kjelgaard from *Esquire*, April 1951. Copyright © 1951 by Esquire Associates.

Farrar, Straus & Giroux, Inc.: "Bad Characters" from *The Collected Stories of Jean Stafford*. Copyright © 1954, 1969 by Jean Stafford. This selection originally appeared in *The New Yorker*.

Farrar, Straus & Giroux, Inc. and Granada Publishing Ltd.: "Arachne" from *Men and Gods* by Rex Warner, originally published in the United States by Farrar, Straus & Young in 1951.

Dorothy R. Geiger, 9515 Van Alden Avenue, Northridge, California, 91324: "In the Fog" by Milton Geiger.

Harcourt Brace Jovanovich, Inc.: "Fog" and "Lost" from *Chicago Poems* by Carl Sandburg. Copyright 1916 by Holt, Rinehart and Winston, Inc., renewed 1944 by Carl Sandburg. "Park Pigeons" from *So That It Flower* by Melville Cane. Copyright 1930, 1958 by Melville Cane. "The Boy and the Wolf" adapted from the Greek of Aesop

Design and Production: Kirchoff/Wohlberg, Inc.

Cover: Frederic E. Church, *Mount Desert Island, Maine,* 1865.
Washington University Gallery of Art, St. Louis, Missouri

Critical Readers

We wish to thank the following people, who helped to evaluate materials in this book:

Vicki Hartman, Clinton High School, Clinton, Mississippi

Dorothy D. Hendry, Huntsville High School, Huntsville, Alabama

Virginia Irwin, Simonsen Junior High School, Jefferson City, Missouri

Carol Kuykendall, Houston Independent School District, Houston, Texas

Suzanne Mitoraj, Mark Sheehan High School, Wallingford, Connecticut

Genevieve Murguia, South Pasadena Junior High School, South Pasadena, California

Bette B. Perlmutter, Arlington Junior High School, Poughkeepsie, New York

Eva-Lynn Powell, Educational Specialist, Hialeah, Florida

Robert Rosenberger, Walter A. Teague Middle School, Altamont Springs, Florida

Jerome Smiley, Alva T. Stanforth Junior High School, Elmont, New York

Russell Thompson, Olle Middle School, Houston, Texas

John Malcolm Brinnin, Boston University, Boston, Massachusetts

Francelia Butler, University of Connecticut, Storrs, Connecticut

W. T. Jewkes, University of Arizona, Tucson, Arizona

Richard J. Smith, University of Wisconsin, Madison, Wisconsin

David Thorburn, Massachusetts Institute of Technology, Cambridge, Massachusetts

Special Acknowledgment

Irene M. Reiter, Northeast High School, Philadelphia, Pennsylvania

We also wish to thank

Madeline Hendrix, Librarian, Alva T. Stanforth Junior High School, Elmont, New York, for assistance in compiling bibliographies

Lee A. Jacobus, University of Connecticut, Storrs, Connecticut, for developing the Guide to Literary Terms and Techniques.

Contents

See page xv for the contents of *Reading and Writing About Literature*

Part One   Themes in Literature

FACES IN THE MIRROR

THE FAMILY

THE EARTH IS HOME

Part Two   Forms of Literature

SHORT STORIES

DRAMA

Part Three   Myths and Fables

MYTHS OF THE GREEKS AND ROMANS

It is natural for you to respond to the characters in a story as you would to real people. As you read, you gather impressions and form opinions of them. You may decide you like certain characters and dislike others. You may find yourself judging the characters' actions, approving or disapproving of what they do.

All the stories in this unit are about young people who are forming an idea of themselves as individuals. Sometimes the characters are moody and confused, and uncertain of how to handle their problems. At other times they show insight into themselves and others, and act with courage and determination.

Some of the experiences you read about in this unit may be familiar to you. You may even recognize yourself in some of the characters you meet.

FACES IN THE MIRROR

It was a fine spring day,
perfect for fishing at the pool
below the dam.

Stolen Day   *Sherwood Anderson*

It must be that all children are actors. The whole thing started with a boy on our street named Walter, who had inflammatory rheumatism.[1] That's what they called it. He didn't have to go to school.

Still he could walk about. He could go fishing in the creek or the waterworks pond. There was a place up at the pond where in the spring the water came tumbling over the dam and formed a deep pool. It was a good place. Sometimes you could get some good big ones there.

I went down that way on my way to school one spring morning. It was out of my way but I wanted to see if Walter was there.

He was, inflammatory rheumatism and all. There he was, sitting with a fish pole in his hand. He had been able to walk down there all right.

It was then that my own legs began to hurt, My back too. I went on to school but, at the recess time, I began to cry. I did it when the teacher, Sarah Suggett, had come out into the schoolhouse yard.

She came right over to me.

"I ache all over," I said. I did, too.

I kept on crying and it worked all right.

"You'd better go on home," she said.

So I went. I limped painfully away. I kept on limping until I got out of the schoolhouse street.

Then I felt better. I still had inflammatory rheumatism pretty bad but I could get along better.

I must have done some thinking on the way home.

"I'd better not say I have inflammatory rheumatism," I decided. "Maybe if you've got that you swell up."

I thought I'd better go around to where Walter was and ask him about that, so I did—but he wasn't there.

"They must not be biting today," I thought.

I had a feeling that, if I said I had inflammatory rheumatism, Mother or my brothers and my sister Stella might laugh. They did laugh at me pretty often and I didn't like it at all.

"Just the same," I said to myself, "I have got it." I began to hurt and ache again.

I went home and sat on the front steps of our house. I sat there a long time. There wasn't anyone at home but Mother and the two little ones. Ray would have been four or five then and Earl might have been three.

It was Earl who saw me there. I had got tired sitting and was lying on the porch. Earl was always a quiet, solemn little fellow.

---

1. **inflammatory rheumatism** (rōō′mə-tīz′əm): a painful disease affecting the joints and muscles.

He must have said something to Mother for presently she came.

"What's the matter with you? Why aren't you in school?" she asked.

I came pretty near telling her right out that I had inflammatory rheumatism but I thought I'd better not. Mother and Father had been speaking of Walter's case at the table just the day before. "It affects the heart," Father had said. That frightened me when I thought of it. "I might die," I thought. "I might just suddenly die right here; my heart might stop beating."

On the day before I had been running a race with my brother Irve. We were up at the fairgrounds after school and there was a half-mile track.

"I'll bet you can't run a half-mile," he said. "I bet you I could beat you running clear around the track."

And so we did it and I beat him, but afterwards my heart did seem to beat pretty hard. I remembered that lying there on the porch. "It's a wonder, with my inflammatory rheumatism and all, I didn't just drop down dead," I thought. The thought frightened me a lot. I ached worse than ever.

"I ache, Ma," I said. "I just ache."

She made me go in the house and upstairs and get into bed.

It wasn't so good. It was spring. I was up there for perhaps an hour, maybe two, and then I felt better.

I got up and went downstairs. "I feel better, Ma," I said.

Mother said she was glad. She was pretty busy that day and hadn't paid much attention to me. She had made me get into bed upstairs and then hadn't even come up to see how I was.

I didn't think much of that when I was up there but when I got downstairs where she was, and when, after I had said I felt better and she only said she was glad and went right on with her work, I began to ache again.

I thought, "I'll bet I die of it. I bet I do."

I went out to the front porch and sat down. I was pretty sore at Mother.

"If she really knew the truth, that I have the inflammatory rheumatism and I may just drop down dead any time, I'll bet she wouldn't care about that either," I thought.

I was getting more and more angry the more thinking I did.

"I know what I'm going to do," I thought; "I'm going to go fishing."

I thought that, feeling the way I did, I might be sitting on the high bank just above the deep pool where the water went over the dam, and suddenly my heart would stop beating.

And then, of course, I'd pitch forward, over the bank into the pool and, if I wasn't dead when I hit the water, I'd drown sure.

They would all come home to supper and they'd miss me.

"But where is he?"

Then Mother would remember that I'd come home from school aching.

She'd go upstairs and I wouldn't be there. One day during the year before, there was a child got drowned in a spring. It was one of the Wyatt children.

Right down at the end of the street there was a spring under a birch tree and there had been a barrel sunk in the ground.

Everyone had always been saying the spring ought to be kept covered, but it wasn't.

So the Wyatt child went down there, played around alone, and fell in and got drowned.

Mother was the one who had found the drowned child. She had gone to get a pail of water and there the child was, drowned and dead.

This had been in the evening when we were all at home, and Mother had come running up the street with the dead, dripping child in her arms. She was making for the Wyatt house as hard as she could run, and she was pale.

She had a terrible look on her face, I remembered then.

"So," I thought, "they'll miss me and there'll be a search made. Very likely there'll be someone who has seen me sitting by the pond fishing, and there'll be a big alarm and all the town will turn out and they'll drag the pond."

I was having a grand time, having died. Maybe, after they found me and had got me out of the deep pool, Mother would grab me up in her arms and run home with me as she had run with the Wyatt child.

I got up from the porch and went around the house. I got my fishing pole and lit out for the pool below the dam. Mother was busy—she always was—and didn't see me go. When I got there I thought I'd better not sit too near the edge of the high bank.

By this time I didn't ache hardly at all, but I thought.

"With inflammatory rheumatism you can't tell," I thought.

"It probably comes and goes," I thought.

"Walter has it and he goes fishing," I thought.

I had got my line into the pool and suddenly I got a bite. It was a regular whopper. I knew that. I'd never had a bite like that.

I knew what it was. It was one of Mr. Fenn's big carp.

Mr. Fenn was a man who had a big pond of his own. He sold ice in the summer and the pond was to make the ice. He had bought some big carp and put them into his pond and then, earlier in the spring when there was a freshet,[2] his dam had gone out.

So the carp had got into our creek and one or two big ones had been caught—but none of them by a boy like me.

The carp was pulling and I was pulling and I was afraid he'd break my line, so I just tumbled down the high bank, holding onto the line and got right into the pool. We had it out, there in the pool. We struggled. We

---

2. **freshet:** a sudden overflowing of a stream from a heavy rain or thaw.

wrestled. Then I got a hand under his gills and got him out.

He was a big one all right. He was nearly half as big as I was myself. I had him on the bank and I kept one hand under his gills and I ran.

I never ran so hard in my life. He was slippery, and now and then he wriggled out of my arms; once I stumbled and fell on him, but I got him home.

So there it was. I was a big hero that day. Mother got a washtub and filled it with water. She put the fish in it and all the neighbors came to look. I got into dry clothes and went down to supper—and then I made a break that spoiled my day.

There we were, all of us, at the table, and suddenly Father asked what had been the matter with me at school. He had met the teacher, Sarah Suggett, on the street and she had told him how I had become ill.

"What was the matter with you?" Father asked, and before I thought what I was saying I let it out.

"I had the inflammatory rheumatism," I said—and a shout went up. It made me sick to hear them, the way they all laughed.

It brought back all the aching again, and like a fool I began to cry.

"Well, I *have* got it—I *have*, I *have*," I cried, and I got up from the table and ran upstairs.

I stayed there until Mother came up. I knew it would be a long time before I heard the last of the inflammatory rheumatism. I was sick all right, but the aching I now had wasn't in my legs or in my back.

SEEKING MEANING

1. Why do you suppose the narrator's "symptoms" develop after he sees Walter fishing at the pond?
2. How do you know that the narrator wants his mother to pay more attention to him?
3. Why does he insist that he had "the inflammatory rheumatism"?
4. Explain the title of the story.

DEVELOPING SKILLS IN READING

Understanding a Character's Motivation
In order for a character in a short story to be believable, there must be a purpose, or *motivation*, for the character's actions. What do you think motivates the narrator in this story to "steal" a day? Find passages in the story that reveal the reasons for the narrator's behavior.

ABOUT THE AUTHOR

Sherwood Anderson (1876–1941) was born in Camden, Ohio, and spent much of his youth in Clyde. He left school when he was fourteen and worked at a variety of odd jobs. He became successful as a businessman and organized a paint-manufacturing company. He was not happy, however, and gave up his business in order to devote himself to writing. Anderson is best known for his stories of small-town life in America. His stories, like "Stolen Day," are often told by a narrator who is recalling some incident from the past. Anderson developed a style based on the spoken American language. His style and subject matter have strongly influenced other twentieth-century writers.

maggie and milly and molly and may

E. E. Cummings

maggie and milly and molly and may
went down to the beach(to play one day)

and maggie discovered a shell that sang
so sweetly she couldn't remember her troubles,and

milly befriended a stranded star   5
whose rays five languid fingers were;

and molly was chased by a horrible thing
which raced sideways while blowing bubbles:and

may came home with a smooth round stone
as small as a world and as large as alone.   10

For whatever we lose(like a you or a me)
it's always ourselves we find in the sea

SEEKING MEANING

1. The poet tells us that *maggie* "discovered a shell that sang." What kind of music does a seashell make? How do you know that *maggie* tends to daydream?

2. How do you know that the "star" in line 5 is a starfish? What clues does the poet give you? What does *milly*'s discovery tell you about her?

3. What is the "horrible thing" that races with a sidewise motion? What does *molly*'s reaction reveal about her?

4. In what way can a stone be both small and large? Explain the meaning of line 10. Do you think *may* is imaginative?

5. The poet says in the last line that we always find ourselves in the sea. How does each girl's personality determine what she sees?

6. E. E. Cummings' poetry looks unusual on the page. He experiments with capitalization and punctuation. His purpose, in part, is to make readers approach his poems as original and fresh works. Can you suggest a reason for *not* capitalizing the names in this poem? What do you think is the purpose of closing up spaces before parenthetical expressions? How do these visual devices add a sense of fun?

Harvey said they could earn
a hundred dollars a week.
All that was needed was
a little snappy advertising.

The Brain and I   *B. J. Chute*

"About a hundred dollars a week," said Harvey, crossing his ankles and looking admiringly at his white shoes.

Ostentatiously[1] white, they were. Anyone else would be wearing grubby sneakers, but grubby sneakers are not Harvey Baines' way of life. The year he wore water-buffalo sandals to school, he got elected class president and made his acceptance speech in Latin. So, if Harvey said we could earn a hundred dollars a week, maybe it was true. I said respectfully, "How do you arrive at that figure, Mr. Rockefeller?"

"Five dollars a project, four projects a day, five days a week." He rolled over on the lawn and intercepted a beetle. "By September, we should be in a very satisfactory position."

Very satisfactory indeed, I thought, and my mind wandered to the sailboat I would own some day, the movie camera, the printing press, the Taj Mahal[2] . . . "What will we call our business?" I asked happily.

Harvey dismissed the beetle, observing that it was only *Coccinella novemnotata.*[3] "Enterprises, Inc.," he said. "Inc. stands for Incredible."

"Or Incompetent."

"Don't be a pessimist," he said. " 'A man's reach should exceed his grasp, or what's a Heaven for?'[4] Robert Browning, 1812–1889." I murmured my thanks, and he nodded graciously. "We'll run an ad in the *Elmville Herald.* . . ."

"They're going to want money." I warned.

"I'm earning the money," he said. "I'm mowing the lawn." I looked at him, lying flat on his back, but he only smiled and added, "You finish the lawn, Chip, while I create the ad.—Division of labor. We use my head and your feet."

I snarled, and he looked sympathetic and said I could wear his sun visor. Who but Harvey Baines would wear a sun visor to mow a lawn? However, I put the silly thing on, and right away I felt like one of those guys who run roulette games, whatever they're called.

---

1. **Ostentatiously** (ŏs'tĕn-tā'shəs-lē): very noticeably.
2. **Taj Mahal** (täzh' mə-häl'): a famous white marble building at Agra, India, built by an emperor to house tombs for himself and his wife.

3. *Coccinella novemnotata:* the scientific name (in Latin) for a North American ladybug.
4. **"A man's . . . for?"**: a quotation from Browning's poem "Andrea del Sarto."

"What do you call them?" I said to Harvey. "Those guys who——"

"Croupiers," said Harvey, and handed me his notepad. "See what you think of this."

It looked neat, boxed in with black lines:

> **RELAX! Let us solve your problems, share your troubles, run your errands. No job too large, no job too small. Call ENTERPRISES, INC., any hour, day or night, at Sycamore 3787.**

"Hey," I said, "that's *my* phone number."

"I know," said Harvey, "but I'm a heavy sleeper. Don't worry, Chip. Your family will understand."

I tried to picture my father, taking down telephone messages, while Harvey and I galloped across the countryside, hunting the wild boar in Patagonia[5] and threading needles for little old ladies. No job too large, no job too small, eh? I pulled my sun visor down over my nose, shouted "Damn the torpedoes! Full speed ahead!" and launched the lawnmower into outer space. Harvey's calm voice followed me down the track amid flying grass. "Admiral Farragut," he said. "Battle of Mobile Bay,[6] August fifth, 1864."

I needn't have worried about my family. We went three days without a nibble, and Harvey undertook to teach me chess. My king, as usual, was in check, and I had two pawns in the outfield and a bishop coming up to bat, when the phone rang.

The voice in my ear said, "Enterprises, Inc.?" I could feel myself turning pale, sort of a microbe color, and Harvey took the phone away from me. "Yes, sir," he said, and then

"No, sir," and then, "Certainly, sir, ten dollars will be quite satisfactory," and he sounded like an executive with a $20,000-a-week payroll. Man, that's living!

He hung up crisply. "Gent way out on Chester Street. Wants us to deliver a coat to Brook Avenue."

"Ten dollars? Just to deliver a *coat?*"

"He says it's valuable and he's in a hurry. Come on, pal, pick up your feet." He shot out the door, and I picked up my feet and shot after him.

We made good time to Chester Street, parked our bikes outside our customer's house, and Harvey pushed the doorbell. A thin man in shirtsleeves popped out and glared at us. "About time!" he snapped, wounding me to the quick because we had come lippety-lippety like a flock of busy bunnies. Harvey said something about the press of business, and the man said "Argh" (I think that's how you spell it) and then "It's in the backyard."

"The *backyard?*"

The man said "Argh" again, repeating himself, added, "Here's the address it goes to, and here's your ten dollars," and closed the door in our faces. Harvey's left eyebrow rose. I took the ten-dollar bill out of his hand and studied it carefully. Alexander Hamilton seemed to have an honest face, and after a moment I said "Argh." Quoting, of course.

"Come on," Harvey said. "If he wants to keep his coat in the backyard, he has every right to do so. A man's house is his castle, *et domus sua cuique tutissimum refugium.*"[7]

I said approvingly, "You took the words right out of my mouth," stuffed Alexander H.

---

5. **Patagonia** (pǎt'ə-gō'nē-ə): a region at the southern tip of South America, including parts of Argentina and Chile.

6. **torpedoes . . . Mobile Bay:** The "torpedoes" were mines that had been anchored in the bay.

7. **A man's . . . *refugium*:** a quotation from the writings of Sir Edward Coke (1552–1634), an English judge. The second half of the sentence is Latin for "and one's own home is the most secure place of refuge to everyone."

into my pocket, and fell into step behind my gallant leader. The backyard was small, weedy and rubbishy, with a broken-down shed in one corner. Standing near the shed, chewing grass, was a . . .

"Goat!" Harvey shouted. "He said *goat*, not coat." We stared at each other, and then I said numbly, "So that's why he was willing to pay ten dollars."

It was a sizable goat with a long beard and a menacing pair of horns. "What do you know about goats?" I inquired in a thin voice.

"Just that they're hollow-horned ruminants[8] of the mammalian order Artiodactyla."[9] He pulled up a handful of grass, added "*Capra hircus hircus,*[10] I believe," and advanced confidently. *Capra hircus hircus* stopped chewing, said something vindictive, and charged, head down.

I gave a cry and started to sprint backwards. Harvey the Lionhearted stood his ground. With inches to go for a first down, the goat uttered a wild bleat and skidded to a stop. For a moment, I was overcome with awe by Harvey's mesmeric[11] eye, but then I realized the goat was tethered. "Perfect," said Harvey smoothly, meaning he'd planned it that way. "You grab the rope at your end, Chip, and I'll keep him interested at my end. Take it easy."

It seemed like the kind of thing Julius Caesar would work out for his troops. I moved off delicately. Unfortunately, the goat at once abandoned its hard-nosed confrontation with Harvey and spun around on its little ball-bearing hooves. I dived forthrightly for the nearest shelter, which happened to be a wooden wheelbarrow. There was a solid thunk—

horns hitting wood—and I hunkered down and thought about my misspent youth.

The horns thunked again, and I was just beginning to feel like an African drum when I heard Harvey say it was okay to come out. Having a trusting nature, I crawled forth, to be greeted by an arresting tableau. Harvey had collared the goat and was wrestling it, and the goat was rearing and ducking and shaking its head, while the rope larruped[12] and looped in the grass. I grabbed for one end, causing the goat to forget Harvey and remember me.

I went, and the goat came. Harvey jerked on the collar and went over backwards, with the goat on top. I hurled myself into the fray, and we all thrashed around wildly, churning up the yard. Eventually, the majority ruled, the goat gave up, and we sat astride it. "What do we do now?" I panted.

"Tie up our package," said Harvey, and forthwith began to wrap the goat up with the rope, a clothesline and a knot he called a sheet bend (or was it a sheep bend?). "We'll cart it to Brook Avenue in the wheelbarrow, and then come back here for our bikes."

I wailed, "You mean we *walk*?" and he said heartlessly, "I ain't wheeling you, bud." Sighing pitifully, I helped him load our horned package, and we set forth on our journey. The goat kept muttering in its beard, the wheelbarrow lurched from side to side, and motorists shouted rude remarks, but the ten dollars in my pocket soothed my jangled nerves.

When we finally arrived at the Brook Avenue house, a large woman was standing on its steps, a broom in her fists and her eyebrows

---

8. **ruminants** (rōō′mə-nənts): cud-chewing animals.
9. **Artiodactyla** (är′tē-ō-dăk′tə-lə): the order of hoofed animals having two or four toes on each foot.
10. *Capra hircus hircus:* the scientific name (in Latin) for the common goat.
11. **mesmeric** (mĕz-mĕr′ĭk): hypnotic.

12. **larruped** (lăr′əpt): whipped about.

beetling. "Get out of here," she said by way of welcome.

"But, madam," Harvey protested, "the gentleman told us . . ."

"Ha!" she said. "The *gentleman,* as you call him, sold me that goat, and I made him take it back. Now he's trying to dump it on me again. I won't have it!" Her voice rose dangerously. "Do you hear me? I WON'T HAVE IT!"

Harvey said yes, he heard her, and she quieted down to a shriek. "It ate my rosebushes, and it scared my neighbors, and it —" She speared the three of us with one look. "Take that thing out of here!"

Harvey folded his arms. "Madam, we undertook to deliver . . ."

Somewhat hampered by her broom, she folded her arms right back at him. "I refuse to accept delivery," she announced. "You can keep the goat. I *give* it to you." She hurled herself into the house, and the door slammed. We stood there, gazing at our newly acquired property, and I said, not for the first time, "What do we do now?"

"Sell it," good old Never-at-a-loss Baines said tersely. "We've already got ten dollars, so the rest is pure profit." He then added, "We'd better find out what the encyclopedia says about goats. We're going to need something brilliant in the way of a sales pitch."

I am not the type to consult an encyclopedia for a sales pitch, but I grunted in resignation. Mine not to reason why, mine but to do and die.[13]

---

13. **Mine . . . die:** Chip is thinking of these lines from the poem "The Charge of the Light Brigade" by Alfred, Lord Tennyson: "Theirs not to reason why,/Theirs but to do and die."

"Yours but to do and die," said Harvey, picking my brains.

"Longfellow," I said cleverly.

"Tennyson," said Harvey.

My house was nearest, so while Harvey and goat waited outside, I went in for the encyclopedia. My mother saw me passing and reminded me that my room was a mess, but I thought fast like Harvey and told her I couldn't tidy it up because everything was in alphabetical order. "In your *room?*" said my mother. "Yes," I said, and then I hissed, "Sssh, I can't stop now, I'm on jury duty," and she just said, "Oh, in that case——" and let me go. That's what I like about my mother. She's very fair-minded.

Outside, I joined my partner and opened the volume. Harvey had been right about the Latin names and the hollow horns, so I read on. "Goats have been mentioned by Confucius[14] and Zoroaster. Who's Zoroaster?"

"Persian religious leader, sometime around 1000 B.C." He shook his head. "The public won't identify with Zoroaster. They'll think he's a soft drink."

I tried again. "They make intelligent and affectionate pets. They clear the fields of weeds and brush. And they carry small burdens."

Harvey said "Ha!" and snapped his fingers. He can snap his fingers louder than anyone I ever knew, and it makes me very nervous. When I had resettled, he said, "That's it. We won't sell the goat. We'll just start a delivery service." I came unstuck all over again, but he went on perfectly calmly. "We'll rig up a basket arrangement that it can carry on its back . . ."

"A howdah,"[15] I said wanly. "Howdah you do."

"Pannier,"[16] said Harvey. "Howdahs are for elephants."

I choked back a sob of disappointment and asked him why he thought anyone would want their packages carried by a goat. "Prestige," he said. "Snappy advertising. 'Don't let bad service get your goat. Use ours.' " He added dreamily, "We could charge double," and the thought appealed to me, as he knew it would.

He got to his feet briskly and began to untie our goat, checking the knot at the collar and handing the end of the rope to me. I accepted it doubtfully and wound it three times around my wrist. That was my second mistake. My first mistake was ever to get mixed up with Harvey Baines.

I realized this at the exact moment that the goat realized it was no longer tied. It gave a single wild "Me-e-eh!" and a bronco heave, catapulted out of the wheelbarrow, and headed for freedom. Devotedly attached to it as I was, I had no choice but to follow.

"Wait for me, you silly ass!" cried Harvey.

"I can't wait, you silly ass!" cried myself.

I think that was the point at which the goat and I went through the privet[17] hedge at 90 mph. At the first corner, the goat whirled left, and I whirled after it. We missed two lampposts and a fire hydrant, shot down a back alley, dodged an absolutely astounded cat, and exploded into Elmville's main street. Amid minced oaths and squealing brakes, we bounced against a baby carriage and ricocheted off an elderly gentleman in a straw hat. (I think he cried "Bravo!") Hurtling onwards, we zoomed past Larue's Dry Cleaners, took a coat of paint off Joe Dinker's Repair Shop, and scared the daylights out of the Happy Corner

---

14. **Confucius** (kən-fyōō'shəs): a famous Chinese philosopher and teacher who lived about 500 B.C.
15. **howdah** (hou'də): a seat for riders on an elephant or a camel, often sheltered by a canopy.

16. **Pannier** (păn'yər): a basket slung over the back of an animal.
17. **privet** (prĭv'ĭt): a shrub with pointed leaves and white flowers.

Eatery's Irish setter, who up to then had just been setting.

I began to think we would go straight on into the sunset, but, just as I abandoned hope, Old Whiskers gave a terrific jerk on the rope, uttered that familiar battle cry, and cannonballed straight across the street and up onto the sidewalk. The two of us—me and that highly motivated hollow-horned ruminant—dived head over hooves into as fine a display of fresh garden vegetables as any grocer ever set up outside his shop.

Happiness is a goat being rained on by falling cabbages. Unhappiness is a grocer whose cabbages are doing the raining. The grocer shot forth, took one look at the wreckage and stood there, stunned, mouth open and smoke coming out of his ears. Until that moment, I had not had the pleasure of meeting the grocer, whose name was Mr. Bullins and who was new in town, having just purchased the shop from Mr. Miles, who had retired to Florida. I found myself wishing that I, too, had retired to Florida.

There was a long and exquisitely painful silence. I shifted a juicy tomato from my ear to my shoulder, took my elbow out of a lettuce, gave Mr. Bullins a weak smile, and looked around for Harvey. He was nowhere in sight. Abandoned to my fate, I lay there, surrounded by a grocer who was vibrating like a beehive, a sea of vegetables, a munching goat, and half a dozen fascinated bystanders. "Mr. Bullins," I said feebly, "I can explain. . . ."

Mr. Bullins found his voice. "Get that animal out of here!" he yelled. "Look what you've done to my vegetables—they're ruined!"

I winced, and a cucumber slid down and smote me on my nose. "Mr. Bullins," I squeaked, "it was an accident. I was only —we were——" My message was not getting through. It became suddenly clear to me that the only thing to do was to pay up before I got sued for damages and jailed for life. If I gave him the ten dollars in my pocket, I could then creep home quietly and pull the roof over my head. I struggled to sit up, and the goat

promptly butted me in the chest and knocked me down. Nothing personal. It just wanted my cucumber.

I pushed the animal away, sat up again, and extracted my ten-dollar bill. With one wistful look at Alexander Hamilton's fine face, I held it out wordlessly. I hoped that Mr. Bullins' better nature might rise to the occasion and he would give me back some change, but he merely grunted. He then pocketed Enterprises, Inc.'s total cash assets and told me that, if I knew what was good for me, I had better get out of his sight.

I was outraged, and my mouth began to open and close like a frog's. A voice behind me said pleasantly, "Spot of trouble, old boy?" and I craned my neck around and there was Harvey. Harvey the Brain himself, hands in pockets, cool, sunny, relaxed. I could have clobbered him.

I started to say bitterly, "Where were you in my hour of need?" but my bosom pal, Mr. Bullins, interrupted with another of his yells. Our goat, having rejected the cucumber, had reared up on its hind legs and was checking through some tomatoes that had somehow escaped the Last Days of Pompeii.[18] Mr. Bullins' howl soared skyward. "Get that thing out of here!"

Harvey raised that left eyebrow of his, strolled over and said something to the goat. "Get it out of here," said Mr. Bullins, "before I call the police."

"Harvey!" I said urgently. "I gave him our ten dollars, because I thought——" I could hear my voice turning into a bleat, and I stopped. One goat was enough.

Harvey shook his head at me soothingly, and turned to the grocer. "Mr. Bullins, I believe?" he said cordially. "My name is Baines, Harvey Baines." He extended his hand. Mr. Bullins declined it. "I can see you're in a bit of trouble, sir," Harvey went on, not a ruffle on his brow. "Can I be of service?"

Mr. Bullins glared at him, then at me. "*He's* the one in trouble," he said. "If he's your friend, take him away with you. *And* that goat of yours!"

"I think not," said Harvey, very politely. He stood there for a moment, surveying the scene and whistling softly to himself. Then, hands in pockets, he paced six steps to the curb and six steps back to the vegetable stand. Shaking his head, he whipped a tape measure out of his pocket, made a few quick measurements, frowned slightly, and straightened up. "Just as I thought, Mr. Bullins," he said sternly. "You are four inches over the property line."

Mr. Bullins made a sound like a strangled question mark.

"Your vegetable stand, Mr. Bullins," Harvey said patiently, "extends beyond your legal limits. You are infringing on town property, and, as I am a citizen of this town, as is my friend here——" He waved at me, and I waved back, courteous if a bit feeble. "As we are both citizens," he continued, "you are, in a strict sense, infringing on *our* property, rather than we on yours."

Mr. Bullins gurgled.

"Our goat, therefore," said Harvey, "was not trespassing, but was only observing the ancient law of trover and conversion.[19] Your cabbages and tomatoes, so to speak, were in the public domain.[20] I seem to recall a legal precedent for this, relative to cauliflowers."

---

18. **Last Days of Pompeii** (pŏm-pā'): In A.D. 79, Mount Vesuvius, in southern Italy, erupted and destroyed the city of Pompeii. Chip humorously exaggerates in referring to the destruction of Mr. Bullins' vegetable stand as a disaster.

19. **trover and conversion:** an action to recover property used illegally by another person.
20. **in the public domain:** open to anyone's use.

He paused weightily. *"Fitzhugh* vs. *Fitzhugh,* was it not? *Flora caulis publica est. . . ."* [21]

Mr. Bullins yelped as if an elephant had trod on his toes.

"Circa[22] 1898," said Harvey, concluding his little lecture. "Now, under the circumstances, I believe that your acceptance of ten dollars to redress your wrongs was completely illegal. *We* are the ones who have been wronged." He paused eloquently. "I suggest," he said, "that you return our money." He extended his right hand, this time not for shaking. There was a short, sharp silence, during which Mr. Bullins seemed about to explode.

"Thank you," said Harvey firmly, hand still outstretched. I thought he was being premature, but he had not misjudged his man. The ten-dollar bill emerged slowly from Mr. Bullins' pocket. "Thank you," said Harvey again, tweaked it lightly out of the grocer's reluctant fingers, and sailed it over to me. I put it tenderly into my own pocket and wiped my brow.

"And now," Harvey said cheerfully, "as a matter of equity, perhaps you would like us to tidy up for you? We would not want a good citizen like yourself—a newcomer in town— to receive a summons for littering. Right?" He set a large cabbage on the stand, festooned[23] it with tomatoes, and stepped back to admire the effect.

"Please," said Mr. Bullins faintly. "Get lost."

Harvey added a cucumber and said "Very nice" approvingly. "As a matter of fact, Mr. Bullins, for a modest sum, Chip and I will be happy to arrange a special display for you. . . ."

"Get," said Mr. Bullins, "out."

"Later, then," Harvey said courteously. "You can call on us at any time." He turned to me. "Come on, Chip, we don't want to outstay our welcome. Come on, goat." I got rockily to my feet. The goat, who had been tasting my shoelaces, gave a sort of surfeited snuffle. With Harvey leading the way, we made a dignified exit, and behind us I heard a single cheer. I do not think it came from Mr. Bullins.

We walked two blocks before I said anything. We still had the goat and the ten dollars, and, apart from contusions and lacerations, I felt pretty good. I did, however, have one question to ask. "Tell me, O Sage," I said, "how did you happen to know about the Fitzhughs?"

"Who?" said Harvey.

"The Fitzhughs. *Fitzhugh* vs. *Fitzhugh.* Circa 1898."

He gave me a gentle smile. "Nobody I know," he said. "Friends of yours?"

Light began to dawn. "You mean—?"

Harvey nodded. " 'Necessity,' " he observed mildly, " 'is the mother of invention.' William Wycherley, 1640–1716." He then quickened his pace and added, "Come on, Chip, we have work to do. I want to get a harness for our goat and a basket, so we can inaugurate the Enterprises, Inc., Special Delivery Service."

I started to say, "No one will ever hire us," but Harvey held up his hand, and I shut up. "Our first customer," said Harvey, rather grandly, "will be Mr. Bullins."

And, of course, he was.

---

21. *Flora . . . est:* Latin for "The cauliflower belongs to the public."
22. **Circa** (sûr′kə): about (used before approximate dates or figures).
23. **festooned:** decorated with a ring of flowers or leaves (here, a ring of tomatoes).

SEEKING MEANING

1. This story tells of a business partnership between two boys and the humorous events that grow out of that partnership. What plan do the boys have for making money? How do they set that plan into action?

2. How does Enterprises, Inc., come into possession of a goat? What sales pitch does Harvey invent for using the goat?

3. When the boys untie the goat, it leaps from the wheelbarrow and heads for freedom. What comic confusion does the goat cause before diving into Mr. Bullins' vegetable display?

4. How does Harvey get Chip out of trouble with Mr. Bullins?

5. Early in the story, Chip lets the reader know that no one but Harvey Baines would wear a sun visor to mow a lawn. In what other ways does Harvey show himself to be an unusual character?

6. Harvey supplies the brains of the partnership. What role would you say Chip plays? Give evidence from the story to support your answer.

DEVELOPING VOCABULARY

Using the Glossary

At the back of this book, you will find a list of words, together with their pronunciations and meanings, called a *glossary*. The words in this glossary are found in the selections that appear throughout the book. You can use this glossary as you would a dictionary—to find the pronunciations and meanings of words that are unfamiliar to you.

For example, take the word *intercepted* in this sentence from "The Brain and I":

He rolled over on the lawn and *intercepted* a beetle.

If you consult the glossary, you will find this entry for the word *intercept:*

> **intercept** (ĭn′tər-sĕpt′) *v.* To seize or stop on the way; cut off.

The abbreviation *v.* tells you that the word *intercept* is a verb. You probably know that the ending *-ed* indicates past tense. To get the meaning of *intercepted,* change the definition to past tense: "seized or stopped on the way."

To show how a word is pronounced, a dictionary uses special marks called *diacritical marks.* Accent marks show you which syllables are stressed. Other marks show how vowels are pronounced. In the glossary, the pronunciation of a word is given in parentheses. You can use the pronunciation key at the bottom of each right-hand page to determine which sounds the marks stand for.

Use the glossary to find the pronunciation and meaning of each italicized word in the following sentences from the story.

> Having a trusting nature, I crawled forth, to be greeted by an arresting *tableau.*
>
> "Sell it," good old Never-at-a-loss Baines said *tersely.*
>
> "I seem to recall a legal *precedent* for this, relative to cauliflowers."
>
> I thought he was being *premature,* but he had not misjudged his man.
>
> "I want to get a harness for our goat and a basket so we can *inaugurate* the Enterprises, Inc., Special Delivery Service."

For more information about the words in the glossary, consult a dictionary.

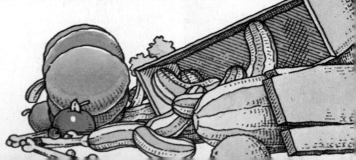

DEVELOPING SKILLS OF EXPRESSION

Using Verbs in Description

Harvey *had collared* the goat and *was wrestling* it, and the goat *was rearing* and *ducking* and *shaking* its head, while the rope *larruped* and *looped* in the grass.

This description is made vivid through the use of effective verbs, which are indicated in italics.

Here are six verbs that appear in the story. Choose the best verb for each of the following sentences.

glared	skidded	dodged
snapped	thrashed	craned

1. The little boy stood on tiptoe and ____ his neck to see over the fence.
2. The bicycle ____ when the front wheel hit a patch of ice on the road.
3. The bird ____ its wings violently.
4. The quarterback ____ reporters and fans by slipping out the back door.
5. The motorist ____ at the car up ahead that was blocking traffic.
6. Because I had a headache, I ____ at people all morning for the slightest things.

Use each of the six verbs in a sentence of your own.

ABOUT THE AUTHOR

B. J. Chute (1913–   ), whose full name is Beatrice Joy Chute, was born and raised in Minnesota, but has made her home in New York City for many years. She has written hundreds of sports and adventure stories. Many of her stories, like "The Brain and I," are about the humorous experiences of teenagers. Besides writing, she has taught at Barnard College, done volunteer work for the New York City Police Department, and raised six foster children.

Sister Opal walked past the shops on Essex Street, looking for something really good and fine. Then she saw the very thing she wanted in the window of an antique shop.

The Baroque° Marble

E. A. Proulx

Late autumn rain again. Sister Opal woke up in a Polaroid yellow light with her head hanging off the bed all sideways. Down in the street children's voices slid under the window, muffled and changed by the damp morning. Sister Opal thought the children sounded as if they were speaking Russian or Basque[1]— some queer, garbled language. She pretended she was in another country where she didn't know a word of the language and where she would have to make signs to get breakfast in a few minutes when she went downstairs. False panic began to rise in her, then subsided. From her position of suspension over the edge of the bed, the furniture looked darker, and the unfamiliar angle gave it a sinister look. The bureau loomed, a skyscraper in dull, dark varnish. Perhaps there were tiny people and offices inside. The chair arms seemed to have clenched hands at their ends, like brown old men sitting anxiously in the doctor's office waiting to hear the bad news.

Sister Opal twisted her head around toward the yellow window. On the sill was a square glass jar of marbles, reddish-brown, yellow and white glassies and a very large blue one.

° **Baroque** (bǝ-rōk′): irregularly shaped.
1. **Basque** (băsk): the language of the Basque people, who live in the western Pyrenees, a mountain range on the border between Spain and France.

Most of them were mob marbles, as much alike as the faces of the crowd to a dictator on his balcony. Off to one side of the jar there was a white marble, deformed and not a true round—a lopsided freak of a marble—her favorite one. When this marble sat alone on the splendor of Sister Opal's blue velvet best dress, it took on a silver, translucent glow. In the jar, it was dirty-white, opaque and with more space around it than the other marbles, as if they avoided getting too close to it.

The jar of marbles was a kind of wealth. It was the most Sister Opal owned. Eight hundred and forty-three marbles. She took a miser's satisfaction in pouring them out onto

the bed, watching them roll into the valleys, gathering up their heavy, glassy weight, cold but soon warming in her hand. Each marble was individually beautiful. A kind of classic Greek perfection shone in their roundness. Under Sister Opal's father's magnifying glass the perfect marbles disclosed blemishes, pits and scratches. Sister Opal liked them unmagnified; in their smallness she found their greatest value.

She touched the shade and it leaped up, startled, to the top of the wooden roller, where it chattered a few seconds in fright, and then clung, tightly wound. Her warm breath made a milky fog on the window glass and her

warm finger wrote, "All the sailors have died of scurvy, yours truly, Opal Foote."

Downstairs, Sister Opal's family sat at the table. Dark and sullen, they crunched toast, stabbed at their eggs and made whirlpools in their coffee with spoons. Except for Sister Opal, it was a bad-tempered family in the mornings and the only conversations were mumbles to each other to pass the sugar or salt. By noontime the family would be chatty and warm, and by suppertime everyone was in high spirits. Sister Opal's four brothers (except for Roy, who worked on the night shift at GE) were very jovial at suppertime when Sister Opal was weary. This morning Sister

Opal's father asked about homework. Sister Opal thought of homework as yellow leaves dropping softly down, like the yellow blank pages she had dropped into the wastepaper basket last night. Guilty, Sister Opal went outside with jammy toast, hearing something from her father about being home right after school to make up Roy's dinner pail and to start supper because Mama had to work late. Sister Opal sang a private song as she walked along the wet sidewalk, hopping the shallow puddles which were out to ruin her good shoes.

> Sailors died of scurvy, oh,
> They threw them in the sea.
> Pack Roy's dinner pail tonight
> With a thermos bottle of tea.

At three thirty Sister Opal was not on her way back home to pack up Roy's dinner pail. Instead, she was walking thoughtfully down Essex Street, peering into all the windows of the silver and antique shops. Art class that afternoon had completely enthralled Sister Opal. Mrs. Grigson had shown a film about ordinary people who started art collections with inexpensive things that became rare and valuable as time went by. Sister Opal envisioned herself someday in her own apartment with rare *objets d'art* in glass cases and white walls hung with glowing works of great artists which she, Sister Opal, had picked up years before for just a song. Even though she had only a few dollars in her savings account (a birthday present from her grandmother), and little hope of getting more, she was looking for something really good and fine on Essex Street. The film had indicated that all the people who built up enviable art collections had started off with the things they really liked. This was Sister Opal's primary mission: to find something she really liked.

Then she would face the money problem. She had quite forgotten about Roy's empty dinner pail, the cold stove, and Mama working late.

As she splashed through the puddles of Essex Street, she dismissed old silver, all lumpy with twisted roses and crests, and dark with tarnish. She rejected the idea of collecting glass — too space-consuming and bothersome. She didn't really like sculpture, and she didn't know where she could buy real paintings or prints. The rain began again and Sister Opal's shoes were sodden and squishy. Past shops with small, dirty windows she went, discarding ceramics, carved wooden figures, vases, chandeliers, toy soldiers, andirons, dog grates,[2] lacquerware and crystal.

Then, in the window of R. Sonnier's, she saw *it*. On a piece of blue velvet, quite like Sister Opal's best dress, there lay a large, glowing, misshapen marble. Sister Opal drew in her breath and exhaled slowly. This was it. She would collect marbles, rare ones from China, ancient ones from Peru, Roman marbles, marbles Genghis Khan[3] had played with, marbles from Napoleon's[4] cabinets, from Istanbul and Alexandria, marbles of solid gold, of azure, of lapis lazuli,[5] of wood and stone and jewel. And she would begin with the marble in this very window! In she marched, a thin black girl with wet shoes, whose older brother was going to go supperless on the night shift.

The shop inside was crowded with objects stacked on shelves, in corners or looming down from the ceiling, crumpled, dusty dark things. A fat, middle-aged white man was

---

2. **andirons** (ănd′ī′ərnz), **dog grates:** metal supports and frames for fireplaces.
3. **Genghis Khan** (jĕng′gĭs kän): a Mongol ruler of the late twelfth and early thirteenth centuries.
4. **Napoleon** (nə-pō′lē-ən): Napoleon Bonaparte, a general who became emperor of France from 1804 to 1815.
5. **lapis lazuli** (lăp′ĭs lăz′yoō-lē): a blue, semiprecious stone.

reading a book in a leather chair behind the counter. He looked up when the door opened and then back to his book. Sister Opal did not waste time looking around the shop. She marched briskly up to R. Sonnier, or as briskly as one can march with wet shoes.

"Excuse me, how much is that marble in the window, and do you have any other kinds?"

looked her up and down, seeing the wet shoes, the cotton dress in late October, the brown skin and thinness that was Sister Opal. "It is for sale for four hundred and fifty dollars. A bargain for those who can afford such things. Marbles I believe you'll find at Woolworth's."

Sister Opal felt a horrible combination of shame, embarrassment, anger, pride and sadness rise in her. She carried as a memory

"*What* marble in the window? I haven't got any marble that I know of in there. This is an antique shop, not a toy store." Sister Opal went to the curtain that hung behind the window to give a background for the objects displayed and pulled it aside.

"There," she said simply, pointing to the fat, lucent sphere.

"Young lady," said R. Sonnier, highly amused, "that is *not* a marble. That is a baroque pearl, an antique baroque pearl, and even though I am letting it go at an unbelievably low price, I doubt you could afford it." He

for the rest of her life R. Sonnier's knowing look that dismissed her as a person of no importance at all. Sister Opal, in a burst of pride and fantasy, said in a haughty voice, "*I* prefer to think of baroque pearls as marbles. And I would definitely like *that* marble. Please save it for me because it might be quite a while before I can pick it up. My name is Opal Foote."

R. Sonnier digested this information and repeated, "Then you want me to save this baroque pearl for you? You intend to buy it?"

"Yes," said Sister Opal. "Opal Foote is the

name." She gave him her address and then left with her shoes squelching softly. She was committed to the baroque marble which R. Sonnier was saving for her. Suddenly she remembered Roy's dinner pail and the gloomy apartment without one picture or really nice thing in it. There were only the family photographs kept in an old candy box and a plastic vase filled with plastic flowers. She ran home hoping that Roy hadn't left for work yet.

At the table that night Sister Opal's father looked on her with disfavor. His cheerful supper face was cloudy, and Sister Opal knew the storm would break before she poured out his coffee. Roy had had to go to work without any dinner, supper had been late and Opal had broken three eggs by slamming the old refrigerator door so hard that the eggs had shot out of their aluminum nest and run all over everything inside. Sister Opal's father finished the last bit of mashed potato on his plate and leaned back, glaring at Sister Opal.

"Well, girl, how come you didn't get home to fix your brother's dinner pail or start the supper? Everybody in this family's got to do his part. Now I'm waiting to hear."

There was no escape. Sister Opal took a deep breath and began telling about the art class and Essex Street and the baroque pearl in R. Sonnier's shop. Her father's face was first incredulous, then angry, then sad. He said nothing for a long time. Opal sat miserably, waiting for the lecture. Her brother Andrew got up and poured the coffee and patted Opal's shoulder as he passed behind her chair. Her father began to speak, slowly at first.

"Well, Sister, I think for a family in the kind of situation we got, where we all work to keep some kind of decency in our lives, and where we are trying to work toward an education for all you kids, an education of *some*

kind, that any ideas about collecting art are just plain *crazy*. We are poor people and it's no use you pretending otherwise. Maybe someday your children, or more likely, grandchildren can collect art, but right now, girl, we can't gather enough money together to collect milk bottles! Wait!" (Sister Opal had uttered a furious "But!")

"Now just wait! I don't want to crush you down like a pancake. I *know* how you felt when that antique man looked you up and down and made his remarks. Every person in this family knows how you felt. And I understand how you answered him back pridefully about how you'd *get* that pearl or marble or whatever it is. But now, Opal, you got to swallow your pride and forget that marble, or else you got to do something about it. You got any ideas? Because I personally do not."

"I am old enough and able enough to get a job after school in the evenings and earn enough money to *buy* that baroque pearl myself, and I am going to do it!" Opal spoke slowly.

Her father looked at Opal, sadder than ever, and said, "If you are old enough to get a job, Sister Opal, you are old enough to save that job money for college or for helping this big family to get along. How would it be if I decided to save the money I make at Quadrant for buying myself a Picasso[6] or something? Or suppose Roy decided not to kick in money for groceries and things but to buy himself a—a—harpsichord[7] or a statue?" The idea of big, quiet Roy, clumsy and inarticulate,[8] buying himself a harpsichord or a statue sent half the table snorting with laughter.

6. **Picasso** (pĭ-kä′sō): a work of art by Pablo Picasso (1881–1973), a Spanish painter and sculptor.
7. **harpsichord** (härp′sĭ-kôrd′): a keyboard instrument, related to the piano.
8. **inarticulate** (ĭn′är-tĭk′yə-lĭt): unable to express himself effectively.

"Besides," continued her father, "who's going to pack up Roy's dinner pail and start the supper while you are at some job?"

Sister Opal's brother Andrew stood up. "I am sick and tired of hearing about Roy's dinner pail. I expect the sun isn't going to come up and set any more—no, it's going to be Roy's dinner pail! I say that if Sister Opal sees more in life than groceries and trying to get along, she should at least have the chance to try. I can get home a little earlier and start supper myself, and Roy can pack up his *own* dinner pail. You've told us yourself, Papa, that if a person wants something bad enough, and works hard enough *for* it, he'll get it. I'm willing to see Opal get that baroque pearl. I wouldn't mind seeing a few nice things around here myself."

The great argument broke out and raged around the supper table and took on fresh vigor when Sister Opal's mother came in, tired and with a sharp edge to her tongue. The final resolution, near midnight, was that if Sister Opal got a job, she could save half the money for the baroque pearl and half for college. Sister Opal felt triumphant and like a real art collector.

It took her three days to find a job. She was to work at Edsall's drugstore after school until ten thirty from Monday to Friday and all day Saturday. She dipped out ice cream, made sodas and cherry Cokes, mixed Alka-Seltzer for gray-faced men, sold cigars and newspapers, squeezed her homework in between customers and wiped off the sticky counter with a yellow sponge (Mr. Edsall had bought five hundred yellow sponges at a bargain sale the year before and Sister Opal got to despise those yellow sponges). She made change for people to use in the phone booth, she cleaned out the Pyrex coffeepots and made fresh coffee a thousand times a day, sold cough drops and throat lozenges all through the winter

and dispensed little plastic hats to ladies when the spring rains came. She got home at eleven o'clock each night with aching legs and red eyes, and Sunday mornings she slept late, catching up. In little ways, her mother showed an extra tenderness for her only daughter's great desire for a beautiful object. Her father surprised Sister Opal by Scotch-taping a reproduction of a Picasso painting over the kitchen calendar. He had cut *The Three Musicians* out of an old magazine. When Roy said, "What's that!?" Sister Opal's father remarked loftily, "I always did like Picasso."

"Yeah," said Andrew to Roy, "at least he doesn't go in for harpsichords and statues." This joke about harpsichords and statues was one that Roy had never quite fathomed, and he eventually grew so confused on the matter that he was convinced that he really did take an extraordinary interest in keyboard music and sculpture. It was even suspected by the family that on his night off he had once gone, not to a night baseball game, but to a concert.

Sister Opal's weeks turned into months, and the long drugstore nights dragged through winter into spring. She had two bank accounts, one for college money and one for the baroque pearl. In March on a Friday night, she had four hundred dollars in the school account, and four hundred fifty in the pearl account. It was enough. She got permission from Mr. Edsall to take the next day off to go to R. Sonnier's to buy the pearl.

Early in the morning Sister Opal woke to pale yellow spring sun. She leaped up with her heart beating hard and dressed the part of a baroque pearl buyer. Something special was needed. Her blue velvet best dress had been outgrown and remade during the winter into a blue velvet best skirt. She put it on and borrowed her mother's white silk blouse. She shined her shoes until the cracks didn't show

and rushed downstairs to breakfast. Everybody knew she was going to buy the pearl that day but nobody said anything. The whole family was shy and quiet with anticipation. Andrew sat breathing quietly on his coffee.

At nine o'clock Sister Opal was walking along Essex Street. She went past the dusty windows displaying lumpy silverware, ceramic mugs with gold decorations, wooden candelabra from Spain, and then she came to R. Sonnier's shop. In his window there was a display of silver and gold watches and clocks under glass bells. Sister Opal smiled, thinking of the baroque pearl hidden secretly in a box, waiting for Sister Opal all those long months. She went inside. R. Sonnier sat in his chair behind the counter, reading a book. Nothing had changed. Stuff was still stacked to the ceiling, stuff still hung down to the floor. R. Sonnier looked up. His eyes were flat, incurious.

"Can I help you?"

"It's me, Mr. Sonnier. Opal Foote. I've come to get my baroque marble that you've been saving for me."

"What marble? I don't have any marbles."

Patiently Sister Opal explained about the baroque pearl she had asked him to save for her last fall, and then she expectantly waited for the shock of recognition, the rummaging in a desk drawer and the uncovering of the baroque pearl. She hadn't even yet seen it up close or held it. R. Sonnier looked annoyed.

"Listen, young lady, I had a baroque pearl last fall, and I sold it to a very nice lady who comes in here often to buy things. I never save anything except for my good customers. This lady paid me by check right away. I don't run any layaway plan here, and that baroque pearl was priced at almost five hundred dollars."

"You sold it? But it was supposed to be *mine!* I worked after school all fall and winter long, and I earned the money for it!" Sister Opal pulled out her wad of money. R. Sonnier looked astounded.

"Little lady, how was I to know you were serious? We get people in here every day saying they like something and they'll be back the next day or next week. They never show up, never! So when somebody comes in and says I'll take that ring or that vase, here, here's the money, why, I *sell* it to them. I'd go out of business if I believed everything people tell me. But since you've worked all that time, maybe you'd like to see some nice earrings I've got, jade and . . ."

"No. I was starting a famous marble collection. I don't want anything else." Sister Opal tucked her worthless money away in her old purse and went out with her back straight and stiff.

She walked around downtown all day long, looking into bookstores, department stores, stationery shops, jewelry stores, boutiques, but nothing seemed attractive to her. She thought it was strange that all the times she hadn't had any money hundreds and hundreds of things in the store windows had looked so great and she had really wanted them. Now that she had a lot of money nothing interested her. She stared at the most exotic clothes without even a twinge of desire. Her beautiful baroque pearl belonged to somebody else; she didn't want any other thing. She put off going home as long as possible, but when the lights began to come on she knew it was time to go back.

The family was at supper. Every head turned to Sister Opal as she came in and slumped into her chair.

"Well!" boomed Roy, who didn't work Saturday nights. "Let's see that solid gold marble you got!" Sister Opal's mother, who saw something was wrong, said, "Well, what's the trouble, Sister? Was the store closed?" Sister Opal, who had not cried, or even felt much of anything except emptiness and loss, burst into a howl she didn't even know was inside her.

"He sold it to somebody else a long time ago-o-oo-o!" Between sobs, hiccups and tears dripping into her plate, Sister Opal told the family about R. Sonnier and how he had sold the pearl. Andrew was indignant and declared that if he was ever in the market for a baroque pearl, he would rather die in the gutter than buy it from R. Sonnier. But Sister Opal's father said judiciously, "Well, Sister, he didn't do it out of spite and meanness. He was just being businesslike. If you were a store man and somebody breezed in and said, 'Here, you hold on to that stuffed elephant for me, I'll be back someday and pay for it,' and a week later somebody else came in and said, 'Here, here's a thousand dollars for that stuffed elephant,' you *know* you are going to sell that elephant right there and then. Sister Opal, you should have checked back with that R. Sonnier every week or so, so that he'd know you were really serious about buying it. I know you're disappointed. I'm disappointed myself. I was looking forward to seeing that baroque pearl and knowing somebody in our family owned it." This brought a fresh howl from Sister Opal which her father silenced by continuing.

"As I see it, Sister, you can either curl up and die because you didn't get your fancy marble, or you can hurry up and quit crying and think about the future. Probably you should take that pearl money and put it with the college money so that you can study up on baroque pearls when you get to college. So you got to adopt a long-range plan now and think about education and a career. . . ."

Sister Opal heard her father talking on in a kindly way about his favorite subject, education and getting knowledge and getting ahead and having a career. She knew that most of what he was saying was sensible, but she had heard it all so many times she didn't want to hear it again. Her father didn't *know* how it felt to be a girl and to want a beautiful thing very badly. Sister Opal excused herself from the table and went up to her room. She flung herself on the bed sideways and dangled her head off the edge, looking at the pale rectangle of the window. The marble jar was dark in the twilight and it glittered along one side from the reflected light of the streetlamp. Sister Opal reached out for the marble jar, tipped the contents onto the bed with a rich, sensuous, rolling sound. Her thin hand slid through the marble pile in the darkening room until she touched the familiar lopsided marble. Warming it in the hollow of her hand, she could just make out its ephemeral[9] glow, its waxy luster against the darkness of her hand and the darkness of the oncoming night. She rolled it slightly in her palm and said softly to the warmed, heavy marble, "Oh, what a beautiful baroque pearl."

---

9. **ephemeral** (ĭ-fĕm′ər-əl): lasting only a short time.

SEEKING MEANING

1. At the opening of the story, you learn that Sister Opal considers her marbles a kind of wealth. In what way are they valuable to her? Which marble is her favorite one? Why?

2. What decision does Sister Opal reach after she sees a film about art collectors? Why do you think she wants the baroque pearl so much?

3. In what ways do the members of Sister Opal's family help her achieve her goal? How do you know that they are pleased by her desire to own a beautiful object?

4. How does Sister Opal's father help her deal with her disappointment after she learns that the pearl has been sold?

DEVELOPING SKILLS IN READING

Noting Details That Reveal Character
Sometimes a writer tells you directly what a character is like. For example, on page 22 E. A. Proulx describes Roy as *big, quiet, clumsy,* and *inarticulate.* More often, however, a writer reveals character indirectly. Instead of telling you what a character is like, the writer *shows* you what that character does, says, and thinks, and how other figures in the story react to that character, allowing you to draw your own *inferences,* or conclusions.

In the opening paragraphs of "The Baroque Marble," the author does not tell you directly that Sister Opal is a highly imaginative girl who is very sensitive to beautiful things. However, she shows you these qualities through Sister Opal's thoughts and actions. Which details in the first three paragraphs of the story reveal the power of Sister Opal's imagination? Which details reveal her love of beautiful things? Which details later in the story reveal that she is also persistent?

DEVELOPING VOCABULARY

Finding Synonyms and Antonyms

In this story, the word *deformed* is used to describe Sister Opal's white marble. When Sister Opal sees the baroque pearl, she takes it for a *misshapen* marble. The words *deformed* and *misshapen* both mean "badly shaped." Words that have the same or nearly the same meaning are called *synonyms*. The words *haughty* and *prideful,* used to describe Sister Opal, are another pair of synonyms.

Words that are opposite in meaning are called *antonyms*. Against Sister Opal's dress, the white marble has a *translucent* glow. *Translucent* means "letting light through." Inside the jar, the white marble is *opaque*. The words *translucent* and *opaque* are antonyms. What, then, does *opaque* mean?

Dictionaries often list synonyms and antonyms of a word. The abbreviation *Syn.* is used for synonyms, and *Ant.* for antonyms.

List a synonym and an antonym for each italicized word in these sentences from the story. Use your dictionary if necessary.

The bureau loomed, a skyscraper in *dull,* dark varnish.

Dark and *sullen,* they crunched toast, stabbed at their eggs and made whirlpools in their coffee with spoons.

Mrs. Grigson had shown a film about ordinary people who started art collections with inexpensive things that became *rare* and valuable as time went by.

DEVELOPING SKILLS OF EXPRESSION

Using Modifiers in Description

Look at the italicized words in this passage. Which of these words describe color? Which describe size? Which describe shape? Which describe other characteristics?

Sister Opal twisted her head around toward the *yellow* window. On the sill was a *square glass* jar of marbles, *reddish-brown, yellow* and *white* glassies and a very *large blue* one. . . . Off to one side of the jar there was a *white* marble, *deformed* and not a *true* round—a *lopsided* freak of a marble—her *favorite* one. When this marble sat alone on the splendor of Sister Opal's *blue velvet best* dress, it took on a *silver, translucent* glow. In the jar, it was *dirty-white, opaque* and with more space around it than the other marbles, as if they avoided getting too close to it.

Each italicized word in this passage is used as an adjective, which is one kind of modifier. A *modifier* is a word that gives another word a more exact meaning. When the modifier *white* is added to the noun *marble,* you have a more precise picture of the marble. With the additional modifiers *deformed* and *lopsided,* you have an even more definite picture.

Use two or more modifiers to describe each of the following objects:

book   scarf   stone   table

The Medicine Bag

Virginia Driving Hawk Sneve

My kid sister Cheryl and I always bragged about our Sioux grandpa, Joe Iron Shell. Our friends, who had always lived in the city and only knew about Indians from movies and TV, were impressed by our stories. Maybe we exaggerated and made Grandpa and the reservation sound glamorous, but when we'd return home to Iowa after our yearly summer visit to Grandpa we always had some exciting tale to tell.

We always had some authentic Sioux article to show our listeners. One year Cheryl had new moccasins that Grandpa had made. On another visit he gave me a small, round, flat, rawhide drum which was decorated with a painting of a warrior riding a horse. He taught me a real Sioux chant to sing while I beat the drum with a leather-covered stick that had a feather on the end. Man, that really made an impression.

We never showed our friends Grandpa's picture. Not that we were ashamed of him, but because we knew that the glamorous tales we told didn't go with the real thing. Our friends would have laughed at the picture, because Grandpa wasn't tall and stately like TV Indians. His hair wasn't in braids, but hung in stringy, gray strands on his neck and he was old. He was our great-grandfather, and he didn't live in a tepee, but all by himself in a part log, part tar-paper shack on the Rosebud Reservation in South Dakota. So when Grandpa came to visit us, I was so ashamed and embarrassed I could've died.

There are a lot of yippy poodles and other fancy little dogs in our neighborhood, but they usually barked singly at the mailman from the safety of their own yards. Now it sounded as if a whole pack of mutts were barking together in one place.

I got up and walked to the curb to see what the commotion was. About a block away I saw a crowd of little kids yelling, with the dogs yipping and growling around someone who was walking down the middle of the street.

I watched the group as it slowly came closer and saw that in the center of the strange procession was a man wearing a tall black hat. He'd pause now and then to peer at something in his hand and then at the houses on either side of the street. I felt cold and hot at the same time as I recognized the man. "Oh, no!" I whispered. "It's Grandpa!"

I stood on the curb, unable to move even though I wanted to run and hide. Then I got mad when I saw how the yippy dogs were growling and nipping at the old man's baggy pant legs and how wearily he poked them away with his cane. "Stupid mutts," I said as I ran to rescue Grandpa.

When I kicked and hollered at the dogs to get away, they put their tails between their legs and scattered. The kids ran to the curb where they watched me and the old man.

"Grandpa," I said and felt pretty dumb when my voice cracked. I reached for his beat-up old tin suitcase, which was tied shut with a rope. But he set it down right in the street and shook my hand.

"*Hau, Takoza*, Grandchild," he greeted me formally in Sioux.

All I could do was stand there with the whole neighborhood watching and shake the hand of the leather-brown old man. I saw how his gray hair straggled from under his big black hat, which had a drooping feather in its crown. His rumpled black suit hung like a sack over his stooped frame. As he shook my hand, his coat fell open to expose a bright-red, satin shirt with a beaded bolo tie[1] under the collar. His get-up wasn't out of place on the reservation, but it sure was here, and I wanted to sink right through the pavement.

"Hi," I muttered with my head down. I tried to pull my hand away when I felt his bony hand trembling, and looked up to see fatigue in his face. I felt like crying. I couldn't think of anything to say so I picked up Grandpa's suitcase, took his arm, and guided him up the driveway to our house.

Mom was standing on the steps. I don't know how long she'd been watching, but her hand was over her mouth and she looked as if she couldn't believe what she saw. Then she ran to us.

"Grandpa," she gasped. "How in the world did you get here?"

She checked her move to embrace Grandpa and I remembered that such a display of affection is unseemly to the Sioux and would embarrass him.

"*Hau*, Marie," he said as he shook Mom's hand. She smiled and took his other arm.

As we supported him up the steps the door banged open and Cheryl came bursting out of the house. She was all smiles and was so obviously glad to see Grandpa that I was ashamed of how I felt.

_____

1. **bolo tie:** a string tie held together by a sliding device.

"Grandpa!" she yelled happily. "You came to see us!"

Grandpa smiled and Mom and I let go of him as he stretched out his arms to my ten-year-old sister, who was still young enough to be hugged.

"*Wicincala*, little girl," he greeted her and then collapsed.

He had fainted. Mom and I carried him into her sewing room, where we had a spare bed.

After we had Grandpa on the bed Mom stood there helplessly patting his shoulder.

"Shouldn't we call the doctor, Mom?" I suggested, since she didn't seem to know what to do.

"Yes," she agreed with a sigh. "You make Grandpa comfortable, Martin."

I reluctantly moved to the bed. I knew Grandpa wouldn't want to have Mom undress him, but I didn't want to, either. He was so skinny and frail that his coat slipped off easily. When I loosened his tie and opened his shirt collar, I felt a small leather pouch that hung from a thong around his neck. I left it alone and moved to remove his boots. The scuffed old cowboy boots were tight and he moaned as I put pressure on his legs to jerk them off.

I put the boots on the floor and saw why they fit so tight. Each one was stuffed with money. I looked at the bills that lined the boots and started to ask about them, but Grandpa's eyes were closed again.

Mom came back with a basin of water. "The doctor thinks Grandpa is suffering from heat exhaustion," she explained as she bathed Grandpa's face. Mom gave a big sigh, "*Oh hinh*, Martin. How do you suppose he got here?"

We found out after the doctor's visit. Grandpa was angrily sitting up in bed while Mom tried to feed him some soup.

"Tonight you let Marie feed you, Grandpa,"

spoke my dad, who had gotten home from work just as the doctor was leaving. "You're not really sick," he said as he gently pushed Grandpa back against the pillows. "The doctor said you just got too tired and hot after your long trip."

Grandpa relaxed, and between sips of soup he told us of his journey. Soon after our visit to him Grandpa decided that he would like to see where his only living descendants lived and what our home was like. Besides, he admitted sheepishly, he was lonesome after we left.

I knew everybody felt as guilty as I did—especially Mom. Mom was all Grandpa had left. So even after she married my dad, who's a white man and teaches in the college in our city, and after Cheryl and I were born, Mom made sure that every summer we spent a week with Grandpa.

I never thought that Grandpa would be lonely after our visits, and none of us noticed how old and weak he had become. But Grandpa knew and so he came to us. He had ridden on buses for two and a half days. When he arrived in the city, tired and stiff from sitting for so long, he set out, walking, to find us.

He had stopped to rest on the steps of some building downtown and a policeman found him. The cop, according to Grandpa, was a good man who took him to the bus stop and waited until the bus came and told the driver to let Grandpa out at Bell View Drive. After Grandpa got off the bus, he started walking again. But he couldn't see the house numbers on the other side when he walked on the sidewalk so he walked in the middle of the street. That's when all the little kids and dogs followed him.

I knew everybody felt as bad as I did. Yet I was proud of this eighty-six-year-old man, who had never been away from the reservation, having the courage to travel so far alone.

"You found the money in my boots?" he asked Mom.

"Martin did," she answered, and roused herself to scold. "Grandpa, you shouldn't have carried so much money. What if someone had stolen it from you?"

Grandpa laughed. "I would've known if anyone tried to take the boots off my feet. The money is what I've saved for a long time—a hundred dollars—for my funeral. But you take it now to buy groceries so that I won't be a burden to you while I am here."

"That won't be necessary, Grandpa," Dad said. "We are honored to have you with us and you will never be a burden. I am only sorry that we never thought to bring you home with us this summer and spare you the discomfort of a long trip."

Grandpa was pleased. "Thank you," he answered. "But do not feel bad that you didn't bring me with you, for I would not have come then. It was not time." He said this in such a way that no one could argue with him. To Grandpa and the Sioux, he once told me, a thing would be done when it was the right time to do it and that's the way it was.

"Also," Grandpa went on, looking at me, "I have come because it is soon time for Martin to have the medicine bag."

We all knew what that meant. Grandpa thought he was going to die and he had to follow the tradition of his family to pass the medicine bag, along with its history, to the oldest male child.

"Even though the boy," he said still looking at me, "bears a white man's name, the medicine bag will be his."

I didn't know what to say. I had the same hot and cold feeling that I had when I first saw Grandpa in the street. The medicine bag was the dirty leather pouch I had found around his neck. "I could never wear such a thing," I almost said aloud. I thought of having my friends see it in gym class, at the swimming pool, and could imagine the smart things they would say. But I just swallowed hard and took a step toward the bed. I knew I would have to take it.

But Grandpa was tired. "Not now, Martin," he said, waving his hand in dismissal, "it is not time. Now I will sleep."

So that's how Grandpa came to be with us for two months. My friends kept asking to come see the old man, but I put them off. I told myself that I didn't want them laughing at Grandpa. But even as I made excuses I knew it wasn't Grandpa that I was afraid they'd laugh at.

Nothing bothered Cheryl about bringing her friends to see Grandpa. Every day after school started there'd be a crew of giggling little girls or round-eyed little boys crowded around the old man on the patio, where he'd gotten in the habit of sitting every afternoon.

Grandpa would smile in his gentle way and patiently answer their questions, or he'd tell them stories of brave warriors, ghosts, animals, and the kids listened in awed silence. Those little guys thought Grandpa was great.

Finally, one day after school, my friends came home with me because nothing I said stopped them. "We're going to see the great Indian of Bell View Drive," said Hank, who was supposed to be my best friend. "My brother has seen him three times so he oughta be well enough to see us."

When we got to my house Grandpa was sitting on the patio. He had on his red shirt, but today he also wore a fringed leather vest that was decorated with beads. Instead of his usual cowboy boots he had solidly beaded moccasins on his feet that stuck out of his black trousers. Of course, he had his old black hat on—he was seldom without it. But it had been brushed and the feather in the beaded

headband was proudly erect, its tip a brighter white. His hair lay in silver strands over the red shirt collar.

I started just as my friends did and I heard one of them murmur, "Wow!"

Grandpa looked up and when his eyes met mine they twinkled as if he were laughing inside. He nodded to me and my face got all hot. I could tell that he had known all along I was afraid he'd embarrass me in front of my friends.

"*Hau, hoksilas,* boys," he greeted and held out his hand.

My buddies passed in a single file and shook his hand as I introduced them. They were so polite I almost laughed. "How, there, Grandpa," and even a "How-do-you-do, sir."

"You look fine, Grandpa," I said as the guys sat on the lawn chairs or on the patio floor.

"*Hanh,* yes," he agreed. "When I woke up this morning it seemed the right time to dress in the good clothes. I knew that my grandson would be bringing his friends."

"You guys want some lemonade or something?" I offered. No one answered. They were listening to Grandpa as he started telling how he'd killed the deer from which his vest was made.

Grandpa did most of the talking while my friends were there. I was so proud of him and amazed at how respectfully quiet my buddies were. Mom had to chase them home at suppertime. As they left they shook Grandpa's hand again and said to me:

"Martin, he's really great!"

"Yeah, man! Don't blame you for keeping him to yourself."

"Can we come back?"

But after they left, Mom said, "No more visitors for a while, Martin. Grandpa won't admit it, but his strength hasn't returned. He likes having company, but it tires him."

That evening Grandpa called me to his room before he went to sleep. "Tomorrow," he said, "when you come home, it will be time to give you the medicine bag."

I felt a hard squeeze from where my heart is supposed to be and was scared, but I answered, "OK, Grandpa."

All night I had weird dreams about thunder and lightning on a high hill. From a distance I heard the slow beat of a drum. When I woke up in the morning I felt as if I hadn't slept at all. At school it seemed as if the day would never end and, when it finally did, I ran home.

Grandpa was in his room, sitting on the bed. The shades were down and the place was dim and cool. I sat on the floor in front of Grandpa, but he didn't even look at me. After what seemed a long time he spoke.

"I sent your mother and sister away. What you will hear today is only for a man's ears. What you will receive is only for a man's hands." He fell silent and I felt shivers down my back.

"My father in his early manhood," Grandpa began, "made a vision quest to find a spirit guide for his life. You cannot understand how it was in that time, when the great Teton Sioux were first made to stay on the reservation. There was a strong need for guidance from *Wakantanka,* the Great Spirit. But too many of the young men were filled with despair and hatred. They thought it was hopeless to search for a vision when the glorious life was gone and only the hated confines of a reservation lay ahead. But my father held to the old ways.

"He carefully prepared for his quest with a purifying sweat bath and then he went alone to a high butte top to fast and pray. After three days he received his sacred dream—in which he found, after long searching, the white man's iron. He did not understand his vision of finding something belonging to the white people, for in that time they were the enemy.

When he came down from the butte to cleanse himself at the stream below, he found the remains of a campfire and the broken shell of an iron kettle. This was a sign which reinforced his dream. He took a piece of the iron for his medicine bag, which he had made of elk skin years before, to prepare for his quest.

"He returned to his village, where he told his dream to the wise old men of the tribe. They gave him the name Iron Shell, but neither did they understand the meaning of the dream. This first Iron Shell kept the piece of iron with him at all times and believed it gave him protection from the evils of those unhappy days.

"Then a terrible thing happened to Iron Shell. He and several other young men were taken from their homes by the soldiers and sent far away to a white man's boarding school. He was angry and lonesome for his parents and the young girl he had wed before he was taken away. At first Iron Shell resisted the teachers' attempts to change him and he did not try to learn. One day it was his turn to work in the school's blacksmith shop. As he walked into the place he knew that his medicine had brought him there to learn and work with the white man's iron.

"Iron Shell became a blacksmith and worked at the trade when he returned to the reservation. All of his life he treasured the medicine bag. When he was old, and I was a man, he gave it to me, for no one made the vision quest anymore."

Grandpa quit talking and I stared in disbelief as he covered his face with his hands. His shoulders were shaking with quiet sobs and I looked away until he began to speak again.

"I kept the bag until my son, your mother's father, was a man and had to leave us to fight in the war across the ocean. I gave him the

bag, for I believed it would protect him in battle, but he did not take it with him. He was afraid that he would lose it. He died in a faraway place."

Again Grandpa was still and I felt his grief around me.

"My son," he went on after clearing his throat, "had only a daughter and it is not proper for her to know of these things."

He unbuttoned his shirt, pulled out the leather pouch, and lifted it over his head. He held it in his hand, turning it over and over as if memorizing how it looked.

"In the bag," he said as he opened it and removed two objects, "is the broken shell of the iron kettle, a pebble from the butte, and a piece of the sacred sage."[2] He held the pouch upside down and dust drifted down.

"After the bag is yours you must put a piece of prairie sage within and never open it again until you pass it on to your son." He replaced the pebble and the piece of iron, and tied the bag.

---

2. **sage:** a plant with aromatic leaves, believed to have healing powers.

I stood up, somehow knowing I should. Grandpa slowly rose from the bed and stood upright in front of me, holding the bag before my face. I closed my eyes and waited for him to slip it over my head. But he spoke.

"No, you need not wear it." He placed the soft leather bag in my right hand and closed my other hand over it. "It would not be right to wear it in this time and place where no one will understand. Put it safely away until you are again on the reservation. Wear it then, when you replace the sacred sage."

Grandpa turned and sat again on the bed. Wearily he leaned his head against the pillow. "Go," he said, "I will sleep now."

"Thank you, Grandpa," I said softly and left with the bag in my hands.

That night Mom and Dad took Grandpa to the hospital. Two weeks later I stood alone on the lonely prairie of the reservation and put the sacred sage in my medicine bag.

SEEKING MEANING

1. Martin says that he and his sister always bragged about Grandpa. Why, then, is Martin embarrassed when Grandpa comes to visit the family?

2. Grandpa explains that the purpose of his visit is to pass along the medicine bag and its history to Martin. Why is Martin miserable at the thought of wearing the medicine bag?

3. Martin is concerned about how his friends will react to Grandpa. What actually happens when they come to visit Grandpa?

4. When he feels it is time, Grandpa tells Martin the history of the medicine bag. Why does Grandpa treasure it?

5. Martin's feelings toward Grandpa begin to change after he sees how much his friends admire the old man. When do his feelings about the medicine bag change? How do you know at the end of the story that he understands and respects the tradition it represents?

DEVELOPING VOCABULARY

Recognizing Words of American Indian Origin

Many words in our language are *loan words*, or words that have been borrowed from other languages. For example, the word *butte* comes from French, the word *patio* from Spanish, and the word *Indian* from Latin.

A number of words in English have been borrowed from American Indian languages. The word *moccasin* comes from a family of languages called Algonquian. The word *tepee* comes from a word in the Siouan language family.

Many place names come from Indian words. The state names Iowa and South Dakota, both mentioned in the story, are Indian names. What other state names can you think of that are American Indian names? What cities and rivers carry Indian names?

All the words in the following list come from American Indian languages. Give the meaning of each word, using a dictionary if necessary.

hogan	manitou	succotash
kayak	pemmican	terrapin
mackinaw	sagamore	totem

DEVELOPING SKILLS OF EXPRESSION

Using Specific Details

When Martin and his friends come home from school, they find Grandpa sitting on the patio. The author uses specific details to give the reader a clear picture of Grandpa.

> He had on his red shirt, but today he also wore a fringed leather vest that was decorated with beads. Instead of his usual cowboy boots he had solidly beaded moccasins on his feet that stuck out of his black trousers. Of course, he had his old black hat on—he was seldom without it. But it had been brushed and the feather in the beaded headband was proudly erect, its tip a brighter white. His hair lay in silver strands over the red shirt collar.

What details help you visualize Grandpa's vest? His hat?

Write a short description telling what some person looks like. If you wish, you may choose someone whose picture appears in a book, newspaper, or magazine. Use specific details in your description.

ABOUT THE AUTHOR

Virginia Driving Hawk Sneve (1933–   ), who grew up on the Rosebud Sioux reservation in South Dakota, draws upon her personal experiences in creating the people and situations in her stories. In addition to her career as a writer, she has worked as a teacher and guidance counselor. Her books about Indian life include *Jimmy Yellow Hawk, High Elk's Treasure,* and *When Thunders Spoke.*

One way or another, Aunt Polly was going to cure Tom of what ailed him. She tried every remedy she could think of without success. Then she heard of Pain Killer.

The Cat and the Pain Killer

Mark Twain

One of the reasons why Tom's mind had drifted away from its secret troubles was that it had found a new and weighty matter to interest itself about. Becky Thatcher had stopped coming to school. Tom had struggled with his pride a few days and tried to "whistle her down the wind,"[1] but failed. He began to find himself hanging around her father's house, nights, and feeling very miserable. She was ill. What if she should die! There was distraction in the thought. He no longer took an interest in war, nor even in piracy. The charm of life was gone; there was nothing but dreariness left. He put his hoop away, and his bat; there was no joy in them any more. His aunt was concerned. She began to try all manner of remedies on him. She was one of those people who are infatuated with patent medicines and all newfangled methods of producing health or mending it. She was a constant experimenter in these things. When something fresh in this line came out she was in a fever, right away, to try it, not on herself, for she was never ailing, but on anybody else that came handy. She was a subscriber for all the "health" periodicals, and the solemn ignorance they were inflated with was breath to

---

1. **"whistle . . . wind":** forget about her.

her nostrils. All the "rot" they contained about ventilation, and how to go to bed, and how to get up, and what to eat, and what to drink, and how much exercise to take, and what frame of mind to keep oneself in, and what sort of clothing to wear, was all gospel to her; and she never observed that her health journals of the current month customarily upset everything they had recommended the month before. She was as simple-hearted and honest as the day was long, and so she was an easy victim. She gathered together her quack periodicals and her quack medicines, and thus armed with death, went about on her pale horse, metaphorically speaking,[2] with "hell following after." But she never suspected that she was not an angel of healing and the balm of Gilead[3] in disguise, to the suffering neighbors.

The water treatment was new, now, and Tom's low condition was a windfall to her. She had him out at daylight every morning, stood him up in the woodshed, and drowned him with a deluge of cold water; then she scrubbed him down with a towel like a file, and so brought him to; then she rolled him up in a wet sheet and put him away under blankets till she sweated his soul clean and "the yellow stains of it came through his pores" — as Tom said.

Yet notwithstanding all this, the boy grew more and more melancholy and pale and dejected. She added hot baths, sitz baths,[4] shower baths, and plunges. The boy remained as dismal as a hearse. She began to assist the water with a slim oatmeal diet and blister plasters. She calculated his capacity as she would a jug's, and filled him up every day with quack cure-alls.

Tom had become indifferent to persecution by this time. This phase filled the old lady's heart with consternation.[5] This indifference must be broken up at any cost. Now she heard of Pain Killer for the first time. She ordered a lot at once. She tasted it and was filled with gratitude. It was simply fire in a liquid form. She dropped the water treatment and everything else and pinned her faith to Pain Killer. She gave Tom a teaspoonful and watched with the deepest anxiety for the result. Her troubles were instantly at rest, her soul at peace again; for the "indifference" was broken up. The boy could not have shown a wilder, heartier interest if she had built a fire under him.

Tom felt that it was time to wake up; this sort of life might be romantic enough, in his blighted condition, but it was getting to have too little sentiment and too much distracting variety about it. So he thought over various plans for relief and finally hit upon that of professing to be fond of Pain Killer. He asked for it so often that he became a nuisance, and his aunt ended by telling him to help himself and quit bothering her. But since it was Tom, she watched the bottle clandestinely.[6] She found that the medicine did really diminish, but it did not occur to her that the boy was mending the health of a crack in the sitting-room floor with it.

---

2. **metaphorically** (mĕt'ə-fôr'ĭk-lē) **speaking:** to use a comparison. Twain humorously compares Aunt Polly to Death, who traditionally rides a pale horse. He is referring to a passage in the Bible (Revelation 6:8).
3. **balm** (bäm) **of Gilead** (gĭl'ē-əd): a reference to a passage in Jeremiah 8:22. In ancient times, the people of Gilead, a region in what is now Jordan, produced balm, an ointment used for healing.
4. **sitz** (sĭts) **baths:** baths taken sitting in shallow water.

5. **consternation** (kŏn'stər-nā'shən): alarm.
6. **clandestinely** (klăn-dĕs'tən-lē): secretly.

One day Tom was in the act of dosing the crack when his aunt's yellow cat came along, purring, eyeing the teaspoon avariciously, and begging for a taste. Tom said: "Don't ask for it unless you want it, Peter."

But Peter signified that he did want it.

"You better make sure."

Peter was sure.

"Now you've asked for it, and I'll give it to you, because there ain't anything mean about *me*; but if you find you don't like it you mustn't blame anybody but your own self."

Peter was agreeable. So Tom pried his mouth open and poured down the Pain Killer. Peter sprang a couple of yards in the air and then delivered a war whoop and set off round and round the room, banging against furniture, upsetting flowerpots, and making general havoc. Next he rose on his hind feet and pranced around, in a frenzy of enjoyment, with his head over his shoulder and his voice proclaiming his happiness. Then he went tearing around the house again, spreading chaos and destruction in his path. Aunt Polly entered in time to see him throw a few double somersaults, deliver a final mighty hurrah, and sail through the open window, carrying the rest of the flowerpots with him. The old lady stood petrified with astonishment, peering over her glasses; Tom lay on the floor expiring with laughter.

"Tom, what on earth ails that cat?"

"*I* don't know, Aunt," gasped the boy.

"Why, I never see anything like it. What *did* make him act so?"

"'Deed I don't know, Aunt Polly; cats always act so when they're having a good time."

"They do, do they?" There was something in the tone that made Tom apprehensive.

"Yes'm. That is, I believe they do."

"You *do?*"

"Yes'm."

The old lady was bending down, Tom watching with interest emphasized by anxiety. Too late he divined her "drift." The handle of the telltale teaspoon was visible under the bed valance.[7] Aunt Polly took it, held it up. Tom winced and dropped his eyes. Aunt Polly raised him by the usual handle—his ear—and cracked his head soundly with her thimble.

"Now, sir, what did you want to treat that poor dumb beast so for?"

"I done it out of pity for him—because he hadn't any aunt."

"Hadn't any aunt!—you numskull. What has that got to do with it?"

"Heaps. Because if he'd 'a' had one she'd 'a' burned him out herself! She'd 'a' roasted his bowels out of him 'thout any more feeling than if he was a human!"

Aunt Polly felt a sudden pang of remorse. This was putting the thing in a new light; what was cruelty to a cat *might* be cruelty to a boy, too. She began to soften; she felt sorry. Her eyes watered a little, and she put her hand on Tom's head and said gently: "I was meaning for the best, Tom. And, Tom, it *did* do you good."

Tom looked up in her face with just a mere

twinkle peeping through his gravity:[8] "I know you was meaning for the best, Auntie, and so was I with Peter. It done *him* good, too. I never see him get around so since——"

"Oh, go 'long with you, Tom, before you aggravate me again. And you try and see if you can't be a good boy, for once, and you needn't take any more medicine."

Tom reached school ahead of time. It was noticed that this strange thing had been occurring every day latterly. And now, as usual of late, he hung about the gate of the schoolyard instead of playing with his comrades. He was sick, he said, and he looked it. He tried to seem to be looking everywhere but whither he was looking—down the road. Pres-

---

7. **valance** (văl'əns): drapery hanging from the edge of the bed.

8. **gravity:** here, seriousness.

ently Jeff Thatcher hove in sight,[9] and Tom's face lighted; he gazed a moment and then turned sorrowfully away. When Jeff arrived, Tom accosted him and "led up" warily to opportunities for remarks about Becky, but the giddy lad never could see the bait. Tom watched and watched, hoping whenever a frisking frock came in sight and hating the owner of it as soon as he saw she was not the right one. At last frocks ceased to appear, and he dropped hopelessly into the dumps; he entered the empty schoolhouse and sat down to suffer. Then one more frock passed in at the gate, and Tom's heart gave a great bound. The next instant he was out and "going on," yelling, laughing, chasing boys, jumping over the fence at risk of life and limb, throwing handsprings, standing on his head—doing all the heroic things he could conceive of, and keeping a furtive eye out, all the while, to see if Becky Thatcher was noticing. But she seemed to be unconscious of it all; she never looked. Could it be possible that she was not aware that he was there? He carried his exploits to her immediate vicinity, came war-whooping around, snatched a boy's cap, hurled it to the roof of the schoolhouse, broke through a group of boys, tumbling them in every direction, and fell sprawling, himself, under Becky's nose, almost upsetting her—and she turned, with her nose in the air, and he heard her say: "Mf! Some people think they're mighty smart—always showing off!"

Tom's cheeks burned. He gathered himself up and sneaked off, crushed and crestfallen.

9. **hove in sight:** came into view, like a ship on the horizon.

SEEKING MEANING

1. Tom's condition might be described as "lovesickness." What are his symptoms?

2. A pain killer is supposed to relieve pain. What is unusual about the Pain Killer in this story? In what way is it "good" for Tom?

3. Tom's explanation of his treatment of Peter makes Aunt Polly see her own treatment of Tom in a "new light." Why does Aunt Polly suddenly become gentle with Tom?

4. Tom recovers as soon as Becky Thatcher returns to school. How does he show that he is cured?

5. Why do you suppose Tom doesn't tell Becky that he is glad to see her? Do you believe Becky is really annoyed by Tom's behavior? Give reasons to support your answers.

DEVELOPING VOCABULARY

Getting Meaning from Context

When you come across an unfamiliar word in your reading, you may be able to work out its meaning by looking at the *context,* that is, the sentence or paragraph in which the word appears. For example, you can probably guess the meaning of the word *avariciously* from its use in this sentence:

> One day Tom was in the act of dosing the crack when his aunt's yellow cat came along purring, eyeing the teaspoon *avariciously,* and begging for a taste.

The word *avariciously* means "greedily." What other words in the sentence give clues to this meaning?

Look at the passage on page 39 in which Twain describes Peter's reaction to Pain Killer. Can you guess the meaning of the words *havoc* and *chaos* from the context? Check your answers in the glossary. How close did you come to the precise meanings of these words? What is the difference in meaning between them?

DEVELOPING SKILLS OF EXPRESSION

Describing Action

Here is the passage describing Peter's reaction to Pain Killer. Twain makes his description vivid by using a number of lively action words.

Peter *sprang* a couple of yards in the air and then delivered a war whoop and set off round and round the room, *banging* against furniture, *upsetting* flowerpots, and making general havoc. Next he rose on his hind feet and *pranced* around, in a frenzy of enjoyment, with his head over his shoulder and his voice proclaiming his happiness. Then he went *tearing* around the house again, spreading chaos and destruction in his path. Aunt Polly entered in time to see him *throw* a few double somersaults, deliver a final mighty hurrah, and *sail* through the open window, carrying the rest of the flowerpots with him.

Write a paragraph describing an action-filled event that you have seen or taken part in recently. You may use a sports event, such as a track race, a basketball game, or a swimming contest. You may choose to describe an exciting scene in a movie or a television show. Use words that help the reader see and hear the action.

ABOUT THE AUTHOR

You may know that Mark Twain (1835-1910) was the pen name of Samuel Langhorne Clemens. He began using the name Mark Twain after working as a steamboat pilot on the Mississippi River. He took the name from a cry of the riverboatmen, "By the mark, twain!" This cry meant that the depth of the river was two fathoms (twelve feet or about four meters), a depth that was safe for the riverboats.

Twain grew up in Hannibal, Missouri, a small town on the Mississippi River. Many of his own experiences as a boy are re-created in *The Adventures of Tom Sawyer* and *The Adventures of Huckleberry Finn*, two of the best-known and best-loved books in American literature. When Twain was twelve, his father died. He had to leave school and go to work. After working for five years as a printer's apprentice, he left Missouri to see the world. He spent the next four years as an apprentice to a steamboat pilot. He later wrote about his experiences as a cub pilot in *Life on the Mississippi*.

When the Civil War broke out, he headed west and supported himself by writing for newspapers. Much of Twain's writing grew out of his experiences in the West. Some of his best stories are tall tales of the frontier, such as "The Celebrated Jumping Frog of Calaveras County." A number of humorous sketches about life in mining camps are contained in *Roughing It*, an autobiographical account of his years in the West. As his writing became well known, he began to give lecture tours throughout America and abroad, entertaining audiences with his wonderful stories.

Mark Twain is generally thought to be one of the greatest humorists this country has produced.

*The class had to have
a victim, and the teacher
decided that Ruth was
the perfect guinea pig.*

Guinea Pig   *Ruth McKenney*

I was nearly drowned, in my youth, by a Red Cross Lifesaving Examiner, and I once suffered, in the noble cause of saving human life from a watery grave, a black eye which was a perfect daisy and embarrassed me for days. Looking back on my agonies, I feel that none of my sacrifices, especially the black eye, were in the least worthwhile. Indeed, to be brutally frank about it, I feel that the whole modern school of scientific lifesaving is a lot of hogwash.

Of course, I've had rather bad luck with lifesavers, right from the beginning. Long before I ever had any dealings with professional lifesavers my sister nearly drowned me, quite by mistake. My father once took us to a northern Michigan fishing camp, where we found the life very dull. He used to go trolling for bass on our little lake all day long, and at night come home to our lodge, dead beat and minus any bass. In the meantime Eileen and I, who were nine and ten at the time, used to take an old rowboat out to a shallow section of the lake and, sitting in the hot sun, feed worms to an unexciting variety of small, undernourished fish called gillies. We hated the whole business.

Father, however, loved to fish, even if he didn't catch a single fish in three weeks, which on this trip he didn't. One night, however, he carried his enthusiasm beyond a de-

cent pitch. He decided to go bass fishing after dark, and rather than leave us alone in the lodge and up to heaven knows what, he ordered us to take our boat and row along after him.

Eileen and I were very bored rowing around in the dark, and finally, in desperation, we began to stand up and rock the boat, which resulted, at last, in my falling into the lake with a mighty splash.

When I came up, choking and mad as anything, Eileen saw me struggling, and, as she always says with a catch in her voice, she only meant to help me. Good intentions, however, are of little importance in a situation like that. For she grabbed an oar out of the lock, and with an uncertain gesture hit me square on the chin.

I went down with a howl of pain. Eileen, who could not see much in the darkness, was now really frightened. The cold water revived me after the blow and I came up to the surface, considerably weakened but still able to swim over to the boat. Whereupon Eileen, in a noble attempt to give me the oar to grab, raised it once again, and socked me square on the top of the head. I went down again, this time without a murmur, and my last thought was a vague wonder that my own sister should want to murder me with a rowboat oar.

As for Eileen, she heard the dull impact of the oar on my head and saw the shadowy figure of her sister disappear. So she jumped in the lake, screeching furiously, and began to flail around in the water, howling for help and looking for me. At this point I came to the surface and swam over to the boat, with the intention of killing Eileen.

Father, rowing hard, arrived just in time to pull us both out of the water and prevent me from attacking Eileen with the rowboat anchor. The worst part about the whole thing, as far as I was concerned, was that Eileen was considered a heroine and Father told everybody in the lake community that she had saved my life. The postmaster put her name in for a medal.

After what I suffered from amateur lifesaving, I should have known enough to avoid even the merest contact with the professional variety of water mercy. I learned too late that being socked with an oar is as nothing compared to what the Red Cross can think up.

From the very beginning of that awful lifesaving course I took the last season I went to a girls' camp, I was a marked woman. The rest

of the embryo[1] lifesavers were little, slender maidens, but I am a peasant type, and I was monstrously big for my fourteen years. I approximated, in poundage anyway, the theoretical adult we energetic young lifesavers were scheduled to rescue, and so I was, for the teacher's purpose, the perfect guinea pig.

The first few days of the course were unpleasant for me, but not terribly dangerous. The elementary lifesaving hold, in case you haven't seen some hapless victim being rescued by our brave beach guardians, is a snakelike arrangement for supporting the drowning citizen with one hand while you paddle him in to shore with the other. You are supposed to wrap your arm around his neck and shoulders, and keep his head well above water by resting it on your collarbone.

This is all very well in theory, of course, but the trick that none of Miss Folgil's little pupils could master was keeping the victim's nose and mouth above the waterline. Time and again I was held in a viselike[2] grip by one of the earnest students with my whole face an inch or two under the billowing waves.

"No, no, Betsy," Miss Folgil would scream through her megaphone, as I felt the water rush into my lungs. "No, no, you must keep the head a little higher." At this point I would begin to kick and struggle, and generally the pupil would have to let go while I came up for air. Miss Folgil was always very stern with me.

"Ruth," she would shriek from her boat, "I insist! You must allow Betsy to tow you all the way in. We come to Struggling in Lesson 6."

This was but the mere beginning, however. A few lessons later we came to the section of the course where we learned how to undress

under water in forty seconds. Perhaps I should say we came to the point where the *rest* of the pupils learned how to get rid of shoes and such while holding their breaths. I never did.

There was quite a little ceremony connected with this part of the course. Miss Folgil, and some lucky creature named as timekeeper and armed with a stopwatch, rowed the prospective victim out to deep water. The pupil, dressed in high, laced tennis shoes, long stockings, heavy bloomers, and a middy blouse, then stood poised at the end of the boat. When the timekeeper yelled "Go!" the future boon to mankind dived into the water and, while holding her breath under the surface, unlaced her shoes and stripped down to her bathing suit. Miss Folgil never explained what connection, if any, this curious rite had with saving human lives.

I had no middy of my own, so I borrowed one of my sister's. My sister was a slender little thing and I was, as I said, robust, which puts it politely. Eileen had some trouble

---

1. **embryo** (ĕm′brē-ō): here, beginning.
2. **viselike** (vīs′līk′): like a vise, or clamping device.

wedging me into that middy, and once in it I looked like a stuffed sausage. It never occurred to me how hard it was going to be to get that middy off, especially when it was wet and slippery.

As we rowed out for my ordeal by undressing, Miss Folgil was snappish and bored.

"Hurry up," she said, looking irritated. "Let's get this over with quick. I don't think you're ready to pass the test, anyway."

I was good and mad when I jumped off the boat, and determined to Make Good and show that old Miss Folgil, whom I was beginning to dislike thoroughly. As soon as I was under water, I got my shoes off, and I had no trouble with the bloomers or stockings. I was just beginning to run out of breath when I held up my arms and started to pull off the middy.

Now, the middy, in the event you don't understand the principle of this girl-child garment, is made with a small head opening, long sleeves, and no front opening. You pull it on and off over your head. You do if you are

lucky, that is. I got the middy just past my neck, so that my face was covered with heavy linen cloth, when it stuck.

I pulled frantically and my lungs started to burst. Finally I thought the heck with the test, the heck with saving other people's lives, anyway. I came to the surface, a curious sight, my head enfolded in a water-soaked middy blouse. I made a brief sound, a desperate glub-glub, a call for help. My arms were stuck in the middy and I couldn't swim. I went down. I breathed in large quantities of water and linen cloth.

I came up again, making final frantic appeals. Four feet away sat a professional lifesaver, paying absolutely no attention to somebody drowning right under her nose. I went down again, struggling with last panic-stricken feverishness, fighting water and a middy blouse for my life. At this point the timekeeper pointed out to Miss Folgil that I had been under water for eighty-five seconds, which was quite a time for anybody. Miss

Folgil was very annoyed, as she hated to get her bathing suit wet, but, a thoughtful teacher, she picked up her megaphone, shouted to the rest of the class on the beach to watch, and dived in after me.

If I say so myself, I gave her quite a time rescuing me. I presented a new and different problem, and probably am written up in textbooks now under the heading "What to Do When the Victim Is Entangled in a Tight Middy Blouse." Miss Folgil finally towed my still-breathing body over to the boat, reached for her bowie knife, which she carried on a ring with her whistle, and cut Eileen's middy straight up the front. Then she towed me with Hold No. 2 right in to the shore and delivered me up to the class for artificial respiration. I will never forgive the Red Cross for that terrible trip through the water, when I might have been hoisted into the boat and rowed in except for Miss Folgil's overdeveloped sense of drama and pedagogy.

I tried to quit the lifesaving class after that, but the head counselor at the camp said I must keep on, to show that I was the kind of girl who always finished what she planned to do. Otherwise, she assured me, I would be a weak character and never amount to anything when I grew up.

So I stayed for Lesson 6: "Struggling." After that I didn't care if I never amounted to anything when I grew up. In fact, I hoped I wouldn't. It would serve everybody right, especially Miss Folgil. I came a little late to the class session that day and missed the discussion of theory, always held on the beach before the actual practice in the lake. That was just my hard luck. I was always a child of misfortune. I wonder that I survived my youth at all.

"We were waiting for you, Ruth," Miss Folgil chirped cheerily to me as I arrived, sullen and downcast, at the little group of ear-nest students sitting on the sand.

"What for?" I said warily. I was determined not to be a guinea pig any more. The last wave had washed over my helpless face.

"You swim out," Miss Folgil went on, ignoring my bad temper, "until you are in deep water—about twelve feet will do. Then you begin to flail around and shout for help. One of the students will swim out to you."

All of this sounded familiar and terrible. I had been doing that for days, and getting water in my nose for my pains.

"But when the student arrives," Miss Folgil went on, "you must not allow her to simply tow you away. You must struggle, just as hard as you can. You must try to clutch her by the head, you must try to twine your legs about her, and otherwise hamper her in trying to save you."

Now, *this* sounded something like.[3] I was foolishly fired by the attractive thought of getting back at some of the fiends who had been ducking me in the name of science for the past two weeks. Unfortunately, I hadn't studied Chapter 9, entitled "How to Break Holds the Drowning Swimmer Uses." Worse, I hadn't heard Miss Folgil's lecture on "Be Firm with the Panic-Stricken Swimmer—Better a Few Bruises Than a Watery Grave." This last was Miss Folgil's own opinion, of course.

So I swam out to my doom, happy as a lark. Maybelle Anne Pettijohn, a tall, lean girl who ordinarily wore horn-rimmed spectacles, was Miss Folgil's choice to rescue Exhibit A, the panic-stricken swimmer.

I laughed when I saw her coming. I thought I could clean up Maybelle Anne easily enough, but alas, I hadn't counted on Maybelle Anne's methodical approach to life. She had read Chapter 9 in our textbook, and she had listened carefully to Miss Folgil's inspir-

---

3. **something like:** the way it should be.

ing words. Besides, Maybelle Anne was just naturally the kind of girl who ran around doing people dirty for their own good. "This may hurt your feelings," she used to say mournfully, "but I feel I have to tell you . . ."

When Maybelle Anne got near me, I enthusiastically lunged for her neck and hung on with both hands while getting her around her waist with my legs. Maybelle Anne thereupon dug her fingernails into my hands with ferocious force, and I let go and swam away, hurt and surprised. This was distinctly not playing fair.

"What's the idea?" I called out.

"It says to do that in the book," Maybelle Anne replied, treading water.

"Well, you lay off of that stuff," I said, angered, book or no book. Maybelle Anne was a Girl Scout, too, and I was shocked to think she'd go around using her fingernails in a fair fight.

"Come on, struggle," Maybelle Anne said, getting winded from treading water. I swam over, pretty reluctant and much more wary. Believe it or not, this time Maybelle Anne, who was two medals from being a Beaver or whatever it is Girl Scouts with a lot of medals get to be, bit me.

In addition to biting me, Maybelle Anne swung her arm around my neck, with the intention of towing me in to the shore. But I still had plenty of fight left and I had never been so mad in my life. I got Maybelle Anne underwater two or three times, and I almost thought I had her when suddenly, to my earnest surprise, she hauled off and hit me as hard as she could, right in the eye. Then she towed me in, triumphant as anything.

Maybelle Anne afterward claimed it was all in the book, and she wouldn't even apologize for my black eye. Eileen and I fixed her, though. We put a little garter snake in her bed and scared the daylights out of her. Maybelle Anne was easy to scare anyway, and really a very disagreeable girl. I used to hope that she would come to a bad end, which, from my point of view, at least, she did. Maybelle Anne grew up to be a Regional Red Cross Lifesaving Examiner.

I'll bet she just loves her work.

SEEKING MEANING

1. What two surprising events revealed in the first sentence tell you that this is a humorous story?

2. Ruth tells you that her sister once nearly drowned her. Which details of the "rescue" are particularly funny?

3. Why does Miss Folgil consider Ruth to be the perfect guinea pig for the lifesaving course?

4. Reread Ruth's description of being helped into Eileen's middy blouse (page 46). How does this passage prepare you for Ruth's underwater struggle with the middy?

5. Why does Ruth agree to be the guinea pig for the lesson on struggling?

6. Ruth expects a "fair fight" from Maybelle Anne. What kind of fight do you think she considers "fair"? What is "unfair" about Maybelle Anne's methods?

7. Although Ruth says that she was nearly drowned on several occasions, how do you know that she is a good swimmer? Why does this knowledge make the story even funnier?

DEVELOPING SKILLS IN READING

Recognizing Humor in Situations

"Guinea Pig" begins like a serious story about a near-fatal accident: "I was nearly drowned, in my youth . . . ." Before you are midway through the first sentence, however, you realize that the author is going to treat the subject humorously. After all, who ever heard of being drowned by a Lifesaving Examiner, an expert in saving lives? And what a reward for serving a noble cause—a black eye! These unlikely events are surprising and funny.

Some of the funniest situations in the story occur when people's intentions misfire. Instead of helping, a character ends up hindering. Instead of winning, a character winds up losing. How is this humor shown when Eileen attempts to help Ruth back into the rowboat? How do Ruth's plans for Maybelle Anne misfire?

Some of the situations in the story are funny because they are exaggerated. Reread the description of the underwater test on page 46. Which details in this test are particularly silly?

You often enjoy a comic situation more if you know that it is coming. Before Ruth appears for the test, you know that she will have trouble with the middy blouse. How do you know that Maybelle Anne has some surprises in store for Ruth?

DEVELOPING VOCABULARY

Analyzing Words with *dis-*

Many words in our language are made up of individual elements or parts. For example, the word *disagreeable* has three parts. The root, or main part of the word, is *agree.* The part that follows the root, *-able,* is a suffix that means "capable of" or "tending to." The part that stands in front of the root, *dis-,* is a prefix meaning "not" or "the lack of" or "the opposite of." When you put these meanings together, you get the definition of *disagreeable:* "not tending to agree." Ruth thinks Maybelle Anne is disagreeable because she is hard to get along with.

You can sometimes figure out the meaning of an unfamiliar word by analyzing its structure. Using the definitions of the prefix *dis-* given above, work out the meanings of the following words. Then check your answers in a dictionary.

discontent	displease	disservice
disorder	disregard	disunion

*He was no good at baseball
and no good at music either—
until a famous composer
became his coach.*

The Captive Outfielder

Leonard Wibberley

The boy was filled with anxiety which seemed to concentrate in his stomach, giving him a sense of tightness there, as if his stomach were all knotted up into a ball and would never come undone again. He had his violin under his chin and before him was the music stand and on the walls of the studio the pictures of the great musicians were frowning upon him in massive disapproval. Right behind him on the wall was a portrait of Paganini,[1] and he positively glowered down at the boy, full of malevolence and impatience.

That, said the boy to himself, *is because he could really play the violin and I can't and never will be able to. And he knows it and thinks I'm a fool.*

Below Paganini was a portrait of Mozart,[2] in profile. He had a white wig tied neatly at the back with a bow of black ribbon. Mozart should have been looking straight ahead, but his left eye, which was the only one visible, seemed to be turned a little watching the boy.

Detail from *Red Violin* (1948). Oil painting by Raoul Dufy.
Musée des Beaux-Arts, Le Havre

---

1. **Paganini** (păg'ə-nē'nē): Nicolò Paganini (1782–1840), an Italian violinist and composer.
2. **Mozart** (mōt'särt'): Wolfgang Amadeus Mozart (1756–1791), an Austrian composer. His extraordinary musical gifts were apparent when he was very young.

The look was one of disapproval. When Mozart was the boy's age—that is, ten—he had already composed several pieces and could play the violin and the organ. Mozart didn't like the boy either.

On the other side of the Paganini portrait was the blocky face of Johann Sebastian Bach.[3] It was a grim face, bleak with disappointment. Whenever the boy was playing it

seemed to him that Johann Sebastian Bach was shaking his head in resigned disapproval of his efforts. There were other portraits around the studio—Beethoven, Brahms, Chopin.[4] Not one of them was smiling. They were all in agreement that this boy was certainly the poorest kind of musician and never would learn his instrument, and it was painful to them to have to listen to him while he had his lesson.

Of all these great men of music who surrounded him the boy hated Johann Sebastian Bach the most. This was because his teacher, Mr. Olinsky, kept talking about Bach as if without Bach there never would have been any music. Bach was like a god to Mr. Olinsky, and he was a god the boy could never hope to please.

"All right," said Mr. Olinsky, who was at the grand piano. "The 'Arioso.' And you will kindly remember the time. Without time no one can play the music of Johann Sebastian Bach." Mr. Olinsky exchanged glances with the portrait of Bach, and the two seemed in perfect agreement with each other. The boy was quite sure that the two of them carried on disheartened conversations about him after his lesson.

There was a chord from the piano. The boy put the bow to the string and started. But it was no good. At the end of the second bar Mr. Olinsky took his hands from the piano and covered his face with them and shook his head, bending over the keyboard. Bach shook his head too. In the awful silence all the portraits around the studio expressed their disapproval, and the boy felt more wretched than ever and not too far removed from tears.

---

3. **Johann Sebastian Bach** (bäкн): a German composer (1685–1750).

Bach. Painting by Elias Gottlieb Haussman. Library of Congress

---

4. **Beethoven** (bā′tō-vən), **Brahms** (brämz), **Chopin** (shō′pǎn′): Ludwig van Beethoven (1770–1827), a German composer; Johannes Brahms (1833–1897), a German composer; Frédéric François Chopin (1810–1849), a Polish composer and pianist.

"The *time*," said Mr. Olinsky eventually. "The time. Take that first bar. What is the value of the first note?"

"A quarter note," said the boy.

"And the next note?"

"A sixteenth."

"Good. So you have one quarter note and four sixteenth notes making a bar of two quarters. Not so?"

"Yes."

"But the first quarter note is tied to the first sixteenth note. They are the same note. So the first note, which is C sharp, is held for five sixteenths, and then the other three sixteenths follow. Not so?"

"Yes," said the boy.

"THEN WHY DON'T YOU PLAY IT THAT WAY?"

To this the boy made no reply. The reason he didn't play it that way was that he couldn't play it that way. It wasn't fair to have a quarter note and then tie it to a sixteenth note. It was just a dirty trick like Grasshopper Smith pulled when he was pitching in the Little League. Grasshopper Smith was on the Giants, and the boy was on the Yankees. The Grasshopper always retained the ball for just a second after he seemed to have thrown it and struck the boy out. Every time. Every single time. The boy got a hit every now and again from other pitchers. Once he got a two-base hit. The ball went joyously through the air, bounced and went over the center-field fence. A clear, good two-base hit. But it was a relief pitcher. And whenever Grasshopper Smith was in the box, the boy struck out. Him and Johann Sebastian Bach. They were full of dirty tricks. They were pretty stuck-up too. He hated them both.

Meanwhile he had not replied to Mr. Olinsky's question, and Mr. Olinsky got up from the piano and stood beside him, looking at him, and saw that the boy's eyes were

Beethoven (1870). Lithograph by Prang. Library of Congress

bright with frustration and disappointment because he was no good at baseball and no good at music either.

"Come and sit down a minute, boy," said Mr. Olinsky, and led him over to a little wickerwork sofa.

Mr. Olinsky was in his sixties, and from the time he was this boy's age he had given all his life to music. He loved the boy, though he had known him for only a year. He was a good boy, and he had a good ear. He wanted him to get excited about music, and the boy was not excited about it. He didn't practice properly. He didn't apply himself. There was something lacking, and it was up to him, Mr. Olinsky, to supply whatever it was that was lacking so that the boy would really enter into the magic world of music.

How to get to him then? How to make a real contact with this American boy when he himself was, though a citizen, foreign-born?

He started to talk about his own youth. It had been a very grim youth in Petrograd.[5] His parents were poor. His father had died when he was young, and his mother had, by a very great struggle, got him into the conservatory. She had enough money for his tuition only. Eating was a great problem. He could afford only one good meal a day at the conservatory cafeteria so that he was almost always hungry and cold. But he remembered how the great Glazunov[6] had come to the cafeteria one day and had seen him with a bowl of soup and a piece of bread.

"This boy is thin," Glazunov had said. "From now on he is to have two bowls of soup, and they are to be big bowls. I will pay the cost."

There had been help like that for him—occasional help coming quite unexpectedly—in those long, grinding, lonely years at the conservatory. But there were other terrible times. There was the time when he had reached such an age that he could no longer be boarded at the conservatory. He had to give up his bed to a smaller boy and find lodgings somewhere in the city.

He had enough money for lodgings, but not enough for food. Always food. That was the great problem. To get money for food he had taken a room in a house where the family had consumption. They rented him a room cheaply because nobody wanted to board with them. He would listen to the members of the family coughing at nighttime—the thin, shallow, persistent cough of the consumptive. He was terribly afraid—afraid that he would contract consumption himself, which was incurable in those days, and die. The thought of death frightened him. But he was equally frightened of disappointing his mother, for if he died he would not graduate and all her efforts to make him a musician would be wasted.

Then there was the time he had had to leave Russia after the Revolution.[7] And the awful months of standing in line to get a visa[8] and then to get assigned to a train. It had taken seven months. And the train to Riga[9]— what an ordeal that had been. Normally it took eighteen hours. But this train took three weeks. Three weeks in cattle cars in midwinter, jammed up against his fellow passengers, desperately trying to save his violin from being crushed. A baby had died in the cattle car, and the mother kept pretending it was only asleep. They had had to take it from her by force eventually and bury it beside the tracks out in the howling loneliness of the coutryside.

And out of all this he had got music. He had become a musician. Not a concert violinist, but a great orchestral violinist, devoted to his art.

He told the boy about this, hoping to get him to understand what he himself had gone through in order to become a musician. But when he was finished, he knew he had not reached the boy.

That is because he is an American boy, Mr. Olinsky thought. *He thinks all these things happened to me because I am a foreigner, and*

---

5. **Petrograd:** the capital of the Russian Empire; now called Leningrad.
6. **Glazunov** (glä′zōō-nôf′): Aleksandr Konstantinovich Glazunov (1865–1936), a Russian composer.

7. **the Revolution:** the Russian Revolution of 1917.
8. **visa** (vē′zə): an official permit added to a passport, permitting entry into or travel through a particular country.
9. **Riga** (rē′gə): the capital of Latvia, which was an independent country at this time.

these things don't happen in America. And maybe they don't. But can't he understand that if I made all these efforts to achieve music—to be able to play the works of Johann Sebastian Bach as Bach wrote them—it is surely worth a little effort on his part?

But it was no good. The boy, he knew, sympathized with him. But he had not made a real contact with him. He hadn't found the missing something that separated this boy from him and the boy from music. He tried again. "Tell me," he said, "what do you do with your day?"

"I go to school," said the boy flatly.

"But after that? Life is not all school."

"I play ball."

"What kind of ball?" asked Mr. Olinsky. "Bouncing a ball against a wall?"

"No," said the boy. "Baseball."

"Ah," said Mr. Olinsky. "Baseball." And he sighed. He had been more than thirty years in the United States and he didn't know anything about baseball. It was an activity beneath his notice. When he had any spare time, he went to a concert. Or sometimes he played chess. "And how do you do at baseball?" he said.

"Oh—not very good. That Grasshopper Smith. He always strikes me out."

"You have a big match coming up soon perhaps?"

"A game. Yes. Tomorrow. The Giants against the Yankees. I'm on the Yankees. It's the play-off. We are both tied for first place." For a moment he seemed excited, and then he caught a glimpse of the great musicians around the wall and the bleak stare of Johann Sebastian Bach, and his voice went dull again. "It doesn't matter," he said. "I'll be struck out."

"But that is not the way to think about it," said Mr. Olinsky. "Is it inevitable that you be struck out? Surely that cannot be so. When I

was a boy——" Then he stopped, because when he was a boy he had never played anything remotely approaching baseball, and so he had nothing to offer the boy to encourage him.

Here was the missing part then—the thing that was missing between him and the boy and the thing that was missing between the boy and Johann Sebastian Bach. Baseball. It was just something they didn't have in common, and so they couldn't communicate with each other.

"When is this game?" said Mr. Olinsky.

"Three in the afternoon," said the boy.

"And this Grasshopper Smith is your *bête noire*[10]—your black beast, huh?"

"Yeah," said the boy. "And he'll be pitching. They've been saving him for this game."

Mr. Olinsky sighed. This was a long way from the "Arioso." "Well," he said, "we will consider the lesson over. Do your practice and we will try again next week."

The boy left, conscious that all the musicians were watching him. When he had gone, Mr. Olinsky stood before the portrait of Johann Sebastian Bach.

"Baseball, maestro," he said. "Baseball. That is what stands between him and you and him and me. You had twenty children and I had none. But I am positive that neither of us knows anything about baseball."

He thought about this for a moment. Then he said, "Twenty children—many of them boys. Is it possible, maestro—is it just possible that with twenty children and many of them boys? . . . You will forgive the thought, but is it just possible that you may have played something like baseball with them

---

10. *bête noire* (bĕt nwär'): a French expression (translated above) meaning someone or something feared and disliked. In English the equivalent is *bugbear* or *bugaboo*.

sometimes? And perhaps one of those boys always being—what did he say?—struck out?''

He looked hard at the blocky features of Johann Sebastian Bach, and it seemed to him that in one corner of the grim mouth there was a touch of a smile.

Mr. Olinsky was late getting to the Clark Stadium Recreation Park in Hermosa Beach for the play-off between the Giants and the Yankees because he had spent the morning transposing the ''Arioso'' from A major into C major to make it simpler for the boy. Indeed, when he got there the game was in the sixth and last inning and the score was three to nothing in favor of the Giants.

The Yankees were at bat, and it seemed that a moment of crisis had been reached.

''What's happening?'' Mr. Olinsky asked a man seated next to him who was eating a hot dog in ferocious bites.

''You blind or something?'' asked the man. ''Bases loaded, two away and if they don't get a hitter to bring those three home, it's good-bye for the Yankees. And look who's coming up to bat. That dodo!''

Mr. Olinsky looked and saw the boy walking to the plate.

Outside the studio and in his baseball uniform he looked very small. He also looked frightened, and Mr. Olinsky looked savagely at the man who had called the boy a dodo and was eating the hot dog, and he said the only American expression of contempt he had learned in all his years in the United States. ''You don't know nothing from nothing,'' Mr. Olinsky snapped.

''That so?'' said the hot-dog man. ''Well, you watch. Three straight pitches and the Grasshopper will have him out. I think I'll go home. I got a pain.''

But he didn't go home. He stayed there

while the Grasshopper looked carefully around the bases and then, leaning forward with the ball clasped before him, glared intently at the boy. Then he pumped twice and threw the ball, and the boy swung at it and missed, and the umpire yelled, ''Strike one.''

''Two more like that, Grasshopper,'' yelled somebody. ''Just two more and it's in the bag.''

The boy turned around to look at the crowd and passed his tongue over his lips. He looked directly at where Mr. Olinsky was sitting, but the music teacher was sure the boy had not seen him. His face was white and his eyes glazed so that he didn't seem to be seeing anybody.

Mr. Olinsky knew that look. He had seen it often enough in the studio when the boy had made an error and knew that however much he tried he would make the same error over and over again. It was a look of pure misery— a fervent desire to get an ordeal over with.

The boy turned again, and the Grasshopper threw suddenly and savagely to third base. But the runner got back on the sack in time, and there was a sigh of relief from the crowd.

Again came the cool examination of the bases and the calculated stare at the boy at the plate. And again the pitch with the curious whip of the arm and the release of the ball one second later. Once more the boy swung and missed, and the umpire called, ''Strike two.'' There was a groan from the crowd.

''Oh and two the count,'' said the score-keeper, but Mr. Olinsky got up from the bench and, pushing his way between the people on the bleachers before him, he went to the backstop fence.

''You,'' he shouted to the umpire. ''I want to talk to that boy there.''

The boy heard his voice and turned and looked at him aghast. ''Please, Mr. Olinsky,'' he said. ''I can't talk to you now.''

"Get away from the back fence," snapped the umpire.

"I insist on talking to that boy," said Mr. Olinsky. "It is very important. It is about Johann Sebastian Bach."

"Please go away," said the boy, and he was very close to tears. The umpire called for time out while he got rid of this madman, and the boy went to the netting of the backstop.

"You are forgetting about the 'Arioso'!" said Mr. Olinsky urgently. "Now you listen to me, because I know what I am talking about. You are thinking of a quarter note, and it should be five sixteenths. It is a quarter note—C sharp—held for one sixteenth more. *Then* strike. You are too early. It must be exactly on time."

"What the heck's he talking about?" asked the coach, who had just come up.

The boy didn't answer right away. He was looking at Mr. Olinsky as if he had realized for the first time something very important which he had been told over and over again, but had not grasped previously.

"He's talking about Johann Sebastian Bach," he said to the coach. "Five sixteenths. Not a quarter note."

"Bach had twenty children," said Mr. Olinsky to the coach. "Many of them were boys. He would know about these things."

"Let's get on with the game," said the coach.

Mr. Olinsky did not go back to the bleachers. He remained behind the backstop and waited for the ceremony of the base inspection and the hard stare by the pitcher. He saw the Grasshopper pump twice, saw his hand go back behind his head, saw the curiously delayed flick of the ball, watched it speed to the boy and then he heard a sound which afterward he thought was among the most beautiful and satisfying he had heard in all music.

It was a clean, sharp "click," sweet as birdsong.

The ball soared higher and higher into the air in a graceful parabola.[11] It was fifteen feet over the center fielder's head, and it cleared the fence by a good four feet.

Then pandemonium broke loose. People were running all over the field, and the boy was chased around the bases by half his teammates, and when he got to home plate he was thumped upon the back and his hair ruffled, and in all this Mr. Olinsky caught one glimpse of the boy's face, laughing and yet with tears pouring down his cheeks.

A week later the boy turned up at Mr. Olinsky's studio for his violin lesson. He looked around at all the great musicians on the wall, and they no longer seemed to be disapproving and disappointed in him.

Paganini was almost kindly. There was a suggestion of a chuckle on the noble profile of Mozart, and Beethoven no longer looked so forbidding. The boy looked at the portrait of Johann Sebastian Bach last.

He looked for a long time at the picture, and then he said two words out loud — words that brought lasting happiness to Mr. Olinsky. The words were: "Thanks, coach."

The "Arioso" went excellently from then on.

---

11. **parabola** (pə-răb′ə-lə): a high-peaked curve.

SEEKING MEANING

1. What two reasons does the boy have for feeling that he is a failure?
2. What reason does the boy have for disliking Bach more than the other "great men of music"?
3. Why does Mr. Olinsky tell the boy about his own youth? Why is he unable to reach the boy?
4. At the stadium, Mr. Olinsky helps the boy realize the importance of timing in music and in baseball. How does this new understanding help the boy solve both his problems?
5. At the end of the story, the boy looks at the portrait of Bach and says, "Thanks, coach." Why does he feel that the composer has helped him?

DEVELOPING VOCABULARY

Acquiring Special Vocabularies

People with the same jobs often use a special vocabulary. Here are some musicians' terms that appear in the story. Use a dictionary to help you define each one. If more than one definition is given, be sure to choose the meaning that applies to music.

bar	quarter note
chord	sixteenth note
keyboard	transpose
C sharp (Look under *sharp*.)	

Here are some baseball terms that appear in the story. Do you know the precise meaning of each one? Use a dictionary to look up any words you don't know.

backstop	play-off
bleachers	relief pitcher
plate	sack

Tell in your own words what this sentence means: "Bases loaded, two away and if they don't get a hitter to bring those three home, it's goodbye for the Yankees."

ABOUT THE AUTHOR

Leonard Wibberley (1915–1983) said that "the desire to become an author is born in childhood and has its birth in childhood reading." This statement is certainly true in his case. *Treasure Island*, a book he read when he was very young, inspired him to become a writer. He wrote more than a hundred books, including *The Mouse That Roared*.

Wibberley was born in Dublin, Ireland. When he was eight, his family moved to London. After his father died, Wibberley had to leave school. He went to work as a stockroom apprentice for a publisher and later became a reporter. In 1943 he moved to the United States.

"The Captive Outfielder" grew out of Wibberley's own experiences and those of his son Kevin, who was at one time active in the Little League. Kevin missed many games because he had violin lessons. His teacher was concerned that Kevin would injure himself playing ball and spoil his violin playing. Wibberley said, "Out of this conflict—the violin teacher, very dedicated, and the boy, very keen on baseball—I evolved the story."

Every day he thought about a project for science class.
He wanted to do something unusual and worthwhile.
Then the idea came to him like a flash.

A Ribbon for Baldy   *Jesse Stuart*

The day Professor Herbert started talking about a project for each member of our general science class, I was more excited than I had ever been. I wanted to have an outstanding project. I wanted it to be greater, to be more unusual than those of my classmates. I wanted to do something worthwhile, and something to make them respect me.

I'd made the best grade in my class in general science. I'd made more yardage, more tackles and carried the football across the goal line more times than any player on my team. But making good grades and playing rugged football hadn't made them forget that I rode a mule to school, that I had worn my mother's shoes the first year and that I slipped away at the noon hour so no one would see me eat fat pork between slices of corn bread.

Every day I thought about my project for the general science class. We had to have our project by the end of the school year and it was now January.

In the classroom, in study hall and when I did odd jobs on my father's 50 acres, I thought about my project. But it wouldn't come to me like an algebra problem or memorizing a poem. I couldn't think of a project that would help my father and mother to support us. One that would be good and useful.

"If you set your mind on something and keep on thinking about it, the idea will eventually come," Professor Herbert told us when Bascom Wythe complained about how hard it was to find a project.

One morning in February I left home in a white cloud that had settled over the deep

valleys. I could not see an object ten feet in front of me in this mist. I crossed the pasture into the orchard and the mist began to thin. When I reached the ridge road, the light thin air was clear of mist. I looked over the sea of rolling white clouds. The tops of the dark winter hills jutted up like little islands.

I have to ride a mule, but not one of my classmates lives in a prettier place, I thought, as I surveyed my world. Look at Little Baldy! What a pretty island in the sea of clouds. A thin ribbon of cloud seemed to envelop cone-shaped Little Baldy from bottom to top like the new rope Pa had just bought for the wind-lass¹ over our well.

Then, like a flash—the idea for my project came to me. And what an idea it was! I'd not tell anybody about it! I wouldn't even tell my father, but I knew he'd be for it. Little Baldy wrapped in the white coils of mist had given me the idea for it.

I was so happy I didn't care who laughed at me, what anyone said or who watched me eat fat meat on corn bread for my lunch. I had an idea and I knew it was a wonderful one.

"I've got something to talk over with you," I told Pa when I got home. "Look over there at that broom sedge² and the scattered pines on Little Baldy. I'd like to burn the broom sedge and briers and cut the pines and farm that this summer."

We stood in our barnlot and looked at Little Baldy.

"Yes, I've been thinkin' about clearin' that hill up someday," Pa said.

"Pa, I'll clear up all this south side and you clear up the other side," I said. "And I'll plow all of it and we'll get it in corn this year."

"Now this will be some undertakin'," he said. "I can't clear that land up and work six days a week on the railroad section. But if you will clear up the south side, I'll hire Bob Lavender to do the other side."

"That's a bargain," I said.

That night while the wind was still and the broom sedge and leaves were dry, my father and I set fire all the way around the base. Next morning Little Baldy was a dark hill jutting high into February's cold, windy sky.

Pa hired Bob Lavender to clear one portion and I started working on the other. I worked early of mornings before I went to school. I hurried home and worked into the night.

Finn, my ten-year-old brother, was big enough to help me saw down the scattered

---

1. **windlass** (wĭnd′ləs): a device for raising and lowering a bucket on a rope.

2. **broom sedge**: a grass used in making brooms.

pines with a crosscut.[3] With a handspike[4] I started the logs rolling and they rolled to the base of Little Baldy.

By middle March, I had my side cleared. Bob Lavender had finished his too. We burned the brush and I was ready to start plowing.

By April 15th I had plowed all of Little Baldy. My grades in school had fallen off some. Bascom Wythe made the highest mark in general science and he had always wanted to pass me in this subject. But I let him make the grades.

If my father had known what I was up to, he might not have let me do it. But he was going early to work on the railway section and he never got home until nearly dark. So when I laid Little Baldy off to plant him in corn, I started at the bottom and went around and around this high cone-shaped hill like a corkscrew. I was three days reaching the top. Then, with a hand planter, I planted the corn on moonlit nights.

When I showed my father what I'd done, he looked strangely at me. Then he said, "What made you do a thing like this? What's behind all of this?"

"I'm going to have the longest corn row in the world," I said. "How long do you think it is, Pa?"

"That row is over 20 miles," Pa said, laughing.

Finn and I measured the corn row with a rod pole and it was 23.5 miles long.

When it came time to report on our projects and I stood up in class and said I had a row of corn on our hill farm 23.5 miles long, everybody laughed. But when I told how I got the idea and how I had worked to accomplish my project, everybody was silent.

Professor Herbert and the general science class hiked to my home on a Saturday in early May when the young corn was pretty and green in the long row. Two newspapermen from a neighboring town came too, and a photographer took pictures of Little Baldy and his ribbon of corn. He took pictures of me, of my home and parents and also of Professor Herbert and my classmates.

When the article and pictures were published, a few of my classmates got a little jealous of me but not one of them ever laughed at me again. And my father and mother were the proudest two parents any son could ever hope to have.

SEEKING MEANING

1. The boy telling this story is a good student as well as a good athlete. Why does he feel that his classmates don't respect him?

2. One of the boy's goals is to change the way his classmates feel about him. What is his other goal?

3. What does the ribbon in the title of the story refer to? How does the boy get the idea for his project?

4. What qualities of character help the boy succeed in his plan?

5. When the boy begins to tell the class about his project, everybody laughs. However, as his classmates listen to his report, they become silent. Why do you think their mood changes?

6. How do you know by the end of the story that the boy has achieved both his goals?

DEVELOPING SKILLS OF EXPRESSION

Reporting on a Project

To the boy in this story, the science project represented a challenge—an opportunity to

---

3. **crosscut:** a saw that cuts across the grain of wood.
4. **handspike:** a bar or pole used as a lever to move heavy objects.

achieve something that would make others proud of him. Think of some projects you have worked on. Have you ever created an original costume for a Halloween party? Built a radio? Designed a piece of furniture? Made the decorations for a room in your house? Tell the class how you got your idea and how you accomplished your project.

ABOUT THE AUTHOR

Jesse Stuart (1907–1984) was born in Kentucky, where he grew up on a small farm. He went to a one-room country school, but he could not attend regularly because he had to help his family with the farm. He struggled to get an education, working his way through high school and college. After graduation, he taught school, then returned to farm work. His first book of poetry, *Man with the Bull Tongue Plow*, was published in 1934. Many of these poems had been written on leaves, tobacco sacks, and scraps of paper.

Most of Stuart's writing is about the Kentucky hill country and its people. "A Ribbon for Baldy" is based on one of the author's experiences while he was a student at Greenup High School. Here he tells how he came to write the story:

As I grow older, I constantly rediscover the beauty of the land where I was born and where I still live today. This valley becomes more valuable and precious to me every day. It has been and still is the source of my work as a writer. . . .

One day, as I stood by the W-Hollow stream, listening to its sound, I thought of Old Baldy. Old Baldy is one of three cone-shaped hills that you can see if you stand on the ridge overlooking the valley. These three hills are independent of the other hills that enclose the valley; they are separate formations and very unusual.

The highest of these hills looked like a giant wigwam. It was part of the first fifty acres my father ever bought. Since much of his farm was pastureland, we needed to use as much land as we could for farming. We had to grow feed for our domestic animals and corn and wheat for our meal and flour. So we had to use the cone-shaped hill. We called it Old Baldy. We cleared Old Baldy from bottom to top. Then I plowed it, breaking the roots with a bull-tongue plow. I drove my team of mules around and around the hill like a corkscrew until I reached the top. Then, when I laid off a furrow in which to plant the corn, I began at the bottom and went around and around again all the way to the top, making one long row of corn. It was the longest row of corn in this valley, the longest row in eastern Kentucky, and maybe in the whole country.

When we were asked by our teacher in general science in Greenup High School to write about the most unusual thing we had ever done or seen, I wrote about this row of corn. And I had the most unusual paper in my class. This was one of my themes that I never kept. And now, I went back to this cone-shaped hill which we used to call Baldy and memories of high school days came back to me. Now Baldy and I had time to renew our friendship; I thought about this paper I had written. And one day I sat on a mossy stone under a poplar tree near the base of Baldy and rewrote that theme. Later, my wife Naomi gave it the title of "A Ribbon for Baldy," and I sent it to a magazine where it was accepted as a story. This factual article, which became a story, was written in a day. It was written of experiences I had lived in my association with this piece of earth while I was a student in Greenup High.

Emily didn't really enjoy solitude, but sometimes— without warning— she would be seized with the urge to be alone.

Bad Characters   *Jean Stafford*

Up until I learned my lesson in a very bitter way, I never had more than one friend at a time, and my friendships, though ardent, were short. When they ended and I was sent packing in unforgetting indignation, it was always my fault; I would swear vilely in front of a girl I knew to be pious and prim (by the time I was eight, the most grandiloquent[1] gangster could have added nothing to my vocabulary—I had an awful tongue), or I would call a Tenderfoot Scout a sissy or make fun of athletics to the daughter of the high school coach. These outbursts came without plan; I would simply one day, in the middle of a game of Russian bank[2] or a hike or a conversation, be possessed with a passion to be by myself, and my lips instantly and without warning would accommodate me. My friend was never more surprised than I was when this irrevocable slander, this terrible, talented invective, came boiling out of my mouth.

Afterward, when I had got the solitude I had wanted, I was dismayed, for I did not like it. Then I would sadly finish the game of cards as if someone were still across the table from me; I would sit down on the mesa and through a glaze of tears would watch my friend departing with outraged strides; mournfully, I would talk to myself. Because I had already alienated everyone I knew, I then had nowhere to turn, so a famine set in and I would have no companion but Muff, the cat, who loathed all human beings except, significantly, me—truly. She bit and scratched the hands that fed her, she arched her back like a Halloween cat if someone kindly tried to pet her, she hissed, laid her ears flat to her skull, growled, fluffed up her tail into a great bush and flailed it like a bullwhack.[3] But she purred for me, she patted me with her paws, keeping her claws in their velvet scabbards. She was not only an ill-natured cat, she was also badly dressed. She was a calico, and the distribution of her colors was a mess; she looked as if she had been left out in the rain and her paint had run. She had a Roman nose[4] as the result of some early injury, her tail was skinny, she had a perfectly venomous look in her eye. My

---

1. **grandiloquent** (grăn-dĭl′ə-kwənt): speaking in a grand and highflown manner (here used sarcastically).
2. **Russian bank:** a card game for two players.

3. **bullwhack:** a long whip used to drive a team of animals.
4. **Roman nose:** a nose with a high, curved bridge.

family said—my family discriminated against me—that I was much closer kin to Muff than I was to any of them. To tease me into a tantrum, my brother Jack and my sister Stella often called me Kitty instead of Emily. Little Tess did not dare, because she knew I'd chloroform her if she did. Jack, the meanest boy I have ever known in my life, called me Polecat and talked about my mania for fish, which, it so happened, I despised. The name would have been far more appropriate for *him*, since he trapped skunks up in the foothills—we lived in Adams, Colorado—and quite often, because he was careless and foolhardy, his clothes had to be buried, and even when that was done, he sometimes was sent home from school on the complaint of girls sitting next to him.

Along about Christmastime when I was eleven, I was making a snowman with Virgil Meade in his backyard, and all of a sudden, just as we had got around to the right arm, I had to be alone. So I called him a son of a sea cook, said it was common knowledge that his mother had bedbugs and that his father, a dentist and the deputy marshal, was a bootlegger on the side. For a moment, Virgil was too aghast to speak—a little earlier we had agreed to marry someday and become millionaires—and then, with a bellow of fury, he knocked me down and washed my face in snow. I saw stars, and black balls bounced before my eyes. When finally he let me up, we were both crying, and he hollered that if I didn't get off his property that instant, his father would arrest me and send me to Canon City. I trudged slowly home, half frozen, critically sick at heart. So it was old Muff again for me for quite some time. Old Muff, that is, until I met Lottie Jump, although "met" is a euphemism[5] for the way I first encountered her.

I saw Lottie for the first time one afternoon in our own kitchen, stealing a chocolate cake. Stella and Jack had not come home from school yet—not having my difficult disposition, they were popular, and they were at their friends' houses, pulling taffy, I suppose, making popcorn balls, playing cassino,[6] having fun—and my mother had taken Tess with her to visit a friend in one of the TB sanitariums. I was alone in the house, and making a funny-looking Christmas card, although I had no one to send it to. When I heard someone in the kitchen, I thought it was Mother home early, and I went out to ask her why the green pine tree I had pasted on a square of red paper looked as if it were falling down. And there, instead of Mother and my baby sister, was this pale, conspicuous child in the act of lifting the glass cover from the devil's-food my mother had taken out of the oven an hour before and set on the plant shelf by the window. The child had her back to me, and when she heard my footfall, she wheeled with an amazing look of fear and hatred on her pinched and pasty face. Simultaneously, she put the cover over the cake again, and then she stood motionless as if she were under a spell.

I was scared, for I was not sure what was happening, and anyhow it gives you a turn to find a stranger in the kitchen in the middle of the afternoon, even if the stranger is only a skinny child in a moldy coat and sopping-wet basketball shoes. Between us there was a lengthy silence, but there was a great deal of noise in the room: the alarm clock ticked smugly; the teakettle simmered patiently on the back of the stove; Muff, cross at having been waked up, thumped her tail against the side of the terrarium in the window where she had been sleeping—contrary to orders—among the geraniums. This went on, it seemed to me, for hours and hours while that tall, sickly girl and I confronted each other. When, after a long time, she did open her mouth, it was to tell a prodigious[7] lie. "I came to see if you'd like to play with me," she said. I think she sighed and stole a sidelong and regretful glance at the cake.

Beggars cannot be choosers, and I had been missing Virgil so sorely, as well as all those other dear friends forever lost to me, that in spite of her flagrance[8] (she had never clapped eyes on me before, she had had no way of knowing there was a creature of my age in the house—she had come in like a hobo to steal my mother's cake), I was flattered and consoled. I asked her name and, learning it, believed my ears no better than my eyes: Lottie Jump. What on earth! What on earth—you surely will agree with me—and yet when I told her mine, Emily Vanderpool, she laughed until she coughed and gasped. "Beg pardon," she said. "Names like them always hit my funny bone. There was this towhead boy in school named Delbert Saxonfield." I saw no connection and I was insulted (what's so funny about Vanderpool, I'd like to know), but Lottie Jump was, technically, my guest and I *was* lonesome, so I asked her, since she had spoken of playing with me, if she knew

---

5. **euphemism**(yo͞o′fə-mĭz′əm): a mild word substituted for a harsher word.
6. **cassino:** a card game.

7. **prodigious** (prə-dĭj′əs): enormous.
8. **flagrance** (flā′grəns): shocking behavior (here referring to the girl's glaring lie).

how to play Andy-I-Over.[9] She said "Naw." It turned out that she did not know how to play any games at all; she couldn't do anything and didn't want to do anything; her only recreation and her only gift was, and always had been, stealing. But this I did not know at the time.

As it happened, it was too cold and snowy to play outdoors that day anyhow, and after I had run through my list of indoor games and Lottie had shaken her head at all of them (when I spoke of Parcheesi, she went "Ugh!" and pretended to be sick), she suggested that we look through my mother's bureau drawers.

This did not strike me as strange at all, for it was one of my favorite things to do, and I led the way to Mother's bedroom without a moment's hesitation. I loved the smell of the lavender she kept in gauze bags among her chamois gloves and linen handkerchiefs and filmy scarves; there was a pink fascinator[10] knitted of something as fine as spider's thread, and it made me go quite soft—I wasn't soft as a rule, I was as hard as nails and I gave my mother a rough time—to think of her wearing it around her head as she waltzed on the ice in the bygone days. We examined stockings, nightgowns, camisoles, strings of

9. **Andy-I-Over:** a game in which a ball is tossed over a building or bounced against its side.

10. **fascinator:** a woman's scarf.

beads and mosaic pins, keepsake buttons from dresses worn on memorial occasions, tortoiseshell combs, and a transformation[11] made from Aunt Joey's hair when she had racily had it bobbed.[12] Lottie admired particularly a blue cloisonné[13] perfume flask with ferns and peacocks on it. "Hey," she said, "this sure is cute. I like thing-daddies like this here." But very abruptly she got bored and said. "Let's talk instead. In the front room." I agreed, a little perplexed this time, because I had been about to show her a remarkable powder box that played "The Blue Danube."[14] We went into the parlor, where Lottie looked at her image in the pier glass[15] for quite a while and with great absorption, as if she had never seen herself before. Then she moved over to the window seat and knelt on it, looking out at the front walk. She kept her hands in the pockets of her thin dark-red coat; once she took out one of her dirty paws to rub her nose for a minute and I saw a bulge in that pocket, like a bunch of jackstones. I know now that it wasn't jackstones, it was my mother's perfume flask; I thought at the time her hands were cold and that that was why she kept them put away, for I had noticed that she had no mittens.

Lottie did most of the talking, and while she talked, she never once looked at me but kept her eyes fixed on the approach to our house. She told me that her family had come to Adams a month before from Muskogee,[16] Oklahoma, where her father, before he got tuberculosis, had been a brakeman on the Frisco.[17] Now they lived down by Arapahoe[18]

Creek, on the west side of town, in one of the cottages of a wretched settlement made up of people so poor and so sick — for in nearly every ramshackle house someone was coughing himself to death — that each time I went past I blushed with guilt because my shoes were sound and my coat was warm and I was well. I wished that Lottie had not told me where she lived, but she was not aware of any pathos[19] in her family's situation, and, indeed, it was with a certain boastfulness that she told me her mother was the short-order[20] cook at the Comanche Café (she pronounced this word in one syllable), which I knew was the dirtiest, darkest, smelliest place in town, patronized by coal miners who never washed their faces and sometimes had such dangerous fights that the sheriff had to come. Laughing, Lottie said that her brother didn't have any brains and had never been to school. She herself was eleven years old, but she was only in the third grade, because teachers had always had it in for her — making her go to the blackboard and all like that when she was tired. She hated school — she went to Ashton, on North Hill, and that was why I had never seen her, for I went to Carlyle Hill — and she especially hated the teacher, Miss Cudahy, who had a head shaped like a pine cone and who had killed several people with her ruler. Lottie loved the movies ("Not them Western ones or the ones with apes in," she said. "Ones about hugging and kissing. I love it when they die in that big old soft bed with the curtains up top, and he comes in and says 'Don't leave me, Marguerite de la Mar' "), and she loved to ride

---

11. **transformation:** a hairpiece.
12. **bobbed:** cut short.
13. **cloisonné** (kloi′zə-nā′): decorative enamelware.
14. **"The Blue Danube":** a waltz by Johann Strauss.
15. **pier glass:** a tall mirror set between windows.
16. **Muskogee** (mŭs-kō′gē).
17. **Frisco:** a railroad line.
18. **Arapahoe** (ə-răp′ə-hō).

19. **pathos** (pā′thŏs′): something that moves people to feel pity.
20. **short-order:** food that is prepared and served quickly.

in cars. She loved Mr. Goodbars, and if there was one thing she despised worse than another it was tapioca. ("Pa calls it fish eyes. He calls floating island[21] horse spit. He's a big piece of cheese.") She did not like cats (Muff was now sitting on the mantelpiece, glaring like an owl); she kind of liked snakes — except cottonmouths and rattlers — because she found them kind of funny; she had once seen a goat eat a tin can. She said that one of these days she would take me downtown — it was a slow-poke town, she said, a one-horse burg (I had never heard such gaudy, cynical talk and was trying to memorize it all) — if I would get some money for the trolley fare; she hated to walk, and I ought to be proud that she had walked all the way from Arapahoe Creek today for the sole solitary purpose of seeing me.

Seeing our freshly baked dessert in the window was a more likely story, but I did not care, for I was deeply impressed by this bold, sassy girl from Oklahoma and greatly admired the poise with which she aired her prejudices. Lottie Jump was certainly nothing to look at. She was tall and made of skin and bones; she was evilly ugly, and her clothes were a disgrace, not just ill-fitting and old and ragged but dirty, unmentionably so; clearly she did not wash much or brush her teeth, which were notched like a saw, and small and brown (it crossed my mind that perhaps she chewed tobacco); her long, lank hair looked as if it might have nits. But she had personality. She made me think of one of those self-contained dogs whose home is where his handout is and who travels alone but, if it suits him to, will become the leader of a pack. She was aloof, never looking at me, but amiable in the way she kept calling me "kid." I liked her enormously, and presently I told her so.

---

21. **floating island:** a custard dessert.

At this, she turned around and smiled at me. Her smile was the smile of a jack-o'-lantern — high, wide, and handsome. When it was over, no trace of it remained. "Well, that's keen, kid, and I like you, too," she said in her downright Muskogee accent. She gave me a long, appraising look. Her eyes were the color of mud. "Listen, kid, how much do you like me?"

"I like you loads, Lottie," I said. "Better than anybody else, and I'm not kidding."

"You want to be pals?"

"Do I!" I cried. So *there*, Virgil Meade, you big fat hootenanny, I thought.

"All right, kid, we'll be pals." And she held out her hand for me to shake. I had to go and get it, for she did not alter her position on the window seat. It was a dry, cold hand, and the grip was severe, with more a feeling of bones in it than friendliness.

Lottie turned and scanned our path and scanned the sidewalk beyond, and then she said, in a lower voice, "Do you know how to lift?"

"Lift?" I wondered if she meant to lift *her*. I was sure I could do it, since she was so skinny, but I couldn't imagine why she would want me to.

"Shoplift, I mean. Like in the five-and-dime."

I did not the know the term, and Lottie scowled at my stupidity.

"*Steal,* for crying in the beer!" she said impatiently. This she said so loudly that Muff jumped down from the mantel and left the room in contempt.

I was thrilled to death and shocked to pieces. "Stealing is a sin," I said. "You get put in jail for it."

"Ish ka bibble! I should worry if it's a sin or not," said Lottie, with a shrug. "And they'll never put a smart old whatsis like *me* in jail. It's fun, stealing is — it's a picnic. I'll teach you

if you want to learn, kid." Shamelessly she winked at me and grinned again. (That grin! She could have taken it off her face and put it on the table.) And she added, "If you don't, we can't be pals, because lifting is the only kind of playing I like. I hate those dumb games like Statues. Kick-the-Can — phooey!"

I was torn between agitation (I went to Sunday school and knew already about morality; Judge Bay, a crabby old man who loved to punish sinners, was a friend of my father's and once had given Jack a lecture on the criminal mind when he came to call and found Jack looking up an answer in his arithmetic book) and excitement over the daring invitation to misconduct myself in so perilous a way. My life, on reflection, looked deadly prim; all I'd ever done to vary the monotony of it was to swear. I knew that Lottie Jump meant what she said — that I could have her

friendship only on her terms (plainly, she had gone it alone for a long time and could go it alone for the rest of her life) — and although I trembled like an aspen[22] and my heart went pitapat, I said, "I want to be pals with you, Lottie."

"All right, Vanderpool," said Lottie, and got off the window seat. "I wouldn't go braggin' about it if I was you. I wouldn't go telling my ma and pa and the next-door neighbor that you and Lottie Jump are going down to the five-and-dime next Saturday aft[23] and lift us some nice rings and garters and things like that. I mean it, kid." And she drew the back of her forefinger across her throat and made a dire face.

---

22. **aspen:** a tree whose leaves flutter in the slightest breeze.
23. **aft:** afternoon.

"I won't, I promise, I won't. My *gosh*, why would I?"

"That's the ticket," said Lottie, with a grin. "I'll meet you at the trolley shelter at two o'clock. You have the money. For both down and up. I ain't going to climb up that ornery hill after I've had my fun."

"Yes, Lottie," I said. Where was I going to get twenty cents? I was going to have to start stealing before she even taught me how. Lottie was facing the center of the room, but she had eyes in the back of her head, and she whirled around back to the window; my mother and Tess were turning in our front path.

"Back way," I whispered, and in a moment Lottie was gone; the swinging door that usually squeaked did not make a sound as she vanished through it. I listened and I never heard the back door open and close. Nor did I hear her, in a split second, lift the glass cover and remove that cake designed to feed six people.

I was restless and snappish between Wednesday afternoon and Saturday. When Mother found the cake was gone, she scolded me for not keeping my ears cocked. She assumed, naturally, that a tramp had taken it, for she knew I hadn't eaten it; I never ate anything if I could help it (except for raw potatoes, which I loved) and had been known as a problem feeder from the beginning of my life. At first it occurred to me to have a tantrum and bring her around to my point of view: my tantrums scared the living daylights out of her because my veins stood out and I turned blue and couldn't get my breath. But I rejected this for a more sensible plan. I said, "It just so happens I didn't hear anything. But if I had, I suppose you wish I had gone out in the kitchen and let the robber cut me up into a million little tiny pieces with his sword. You wouldn't even bury me. You'd just put me on the dump. *I* know who's wanted in this family and who isn't." Tears of sorrow, not of anger, came in powerful tides and I groped blindly to the bedroom I shared with Stella, where I lay on my bed and shook with big, silent *weltschmerzlich*[24] sobs. Mother followed me immediately, and so did Tess, and both of them comforted me and told me how much they loved me. I said they didn't; they said they did. Presently, I got a headache, as I always did when I cried, so I got to have an aspirin and a cold cloth on my head, and when Jack and Stella came home, they had to be quiet. I heard Jack say, "Emily Vanderpool is the biggest polecat in the U.S.A. Whyn't she go in the kitchen and say, 'Hands up'? He woulda lit out." And Mother said, "Sh-h-h! You don't want your sister to be sick, do you?" Muff, not realizing that Lottie had replaced her, came in and curled up at my thigh, purring lustily; I found myself glad that she had left the room before Lottie Jump made her proposition to me, and in gratitude I stroked her unattractive head.

Other things happened. Mother discovered the loss of her perfume flask and talked about nothing else at meals for two whole days. Luckily, it did not occur to her that it had been stolen—she simply thought she had mislaid it—but her monomania[25] got on my father's nerves and he lashed out at her and at the rest of us. And because I was the cause of it all and my conscience was after me with red-hot pokers, I finally *had* to have a tantrum. I slammed my fork down in the middle of supper on the second day and yelled, "If you don't stop fighting, I'm going to kill myself. Yammer, yammer, nag, nag!" And I put my fingers in my ears and squeezed my eyes

24. *weltschmerzlich* (vĕlt′shmĕrts′lĭĸн): a German word meaning "sorrowful over the state of the world."
25. **monomania** (mŏn′ō-mā′nē-ə): exaggerated interest in one thing.

tight shut and screamed so the whole country could hear, "Shut *up!*" And then I lost my breath and began to turn blue. Daddy hastily apologized to everyone, and Mother said she was sorry for carrying on so about a trinket that had nothing but sentimental value—she was just vexed with herself for being careless, that was all, and she wasn't going to say another word about it.

I never heard so many references to stealing and cake, and even to Oklahoma (ordinarily no one mentioned Oklahoma once in a month of Sundays) and the ten-cent store as I did throughout those next days. I myself once made a ghastly slip and said something to Stella about "the five-and-dime." "The five and-*dime!*" she exclaimed. "Where'd you get *that* kind of talk? Do you by any chance have reference to the *ten-cent store?*"

The worst of all was Friday night—the very night before I was to meet Lottie Jump—when Judge Bay came to play two-handed pinochle[26] with Daddy. The Judge, a giant in intimidating haberdashery[27]—for some reason, the white piping on his vest bespoke, for me, handcuffs and prison bars—and with an aura of disapproval for almost everything on earth except what pertained directly to himself, was telling Daddy, before they began their game, about the infamous vandalism that had been going on among the college students. "I have reason to believe that there are girls in this gang as well as boys," he said. "They ransack vacant houses and take everything. In one house on Pleasant Street, up there by the Catholic church, there wasn't anything to take, so they took the kitchen sink. Wasn't a question of taking everything *but*—they took the kitchen sink."

"Whatever would they want with a kitchen sink?" asked my mother.

"Mischief," replied the Judge. "If we ever catch them and if they come within my jurisdiction,[28] I can tell you I will give them no quarter. A thief, in my opinion, is the lowest of the low."

Mother told about the chocolate cake. By now, the fiction was so factual in my mind that each time I thought of it I saw a funny-paper bum in baggy pants held up by rope, a hat with holes through which tufts of hair stuck up, shoes from which his toes protruded, a disreputable stubble on his face; he came up beneath the open window where the devil's-food was cooling, and he stole it and hotfooted it for the woods, where his companion was frying a small fish in a beat-up skillet. It never crossed my mind any longer that Lottie Jump had hooked that delicious cake.

Judge Bay was properly impressed. "If you will steal a chocolate cake, if you will steal a kitchen sink, you will steal diamonds and money. The small child who pilfers a penny from his mother's pocketbook has started down a path that may lead him to holding up a bank."

It was a good thing I had no homework that night, for I could not possibly have concentrated. We were all sent to our rooms, because the pinochle players had to have absolute quiet. I spent the evening doing cross-stitch. I was making a bureau runner for a Christmas present; as in the case of the Christmas card, I had no one to give it to, but now I decided to give it to Lottie Jump's mother. Stella was reading *Black Beauty*,[29] crying. It was an interminable evening. Stella went to bed first; I

---

26. **pinochle** (pē′nŭk′əl): a card game for two to four players.
27. **haberdashery** (hăb′ər-dăsh′ə-rē): men's clothing. The judge's appearance filled Emily with fear.
28. **jurisdiction** (jŏor′əs-dĭk′shən): authority or legal power.
29. ***Black Beauty:*** a well-known story about a horse by Anna Sewell.

saw to that, because I didn't want her lying there awake listening to me talking in my sleep. Besides, I didn't want her to see me tearing open the cardboard box—the one in the shape of a church, which held my Christmas Sunday-school offering. Over the door of the church was this shaming legend: "My mite[30] for the poor widow." When Stella had begun to grind her teeth in her first deep sleep, I took twenty cents away from the poor widow, whoever she was (the owner of the kitchen sink, no doubt), for the trolley fare, and secreted it and the remaining three pennies in the pocket of my middy. I wrapped the money well in a handkerchief and buttoned the pocket and hung my skirt over the middy. And then I tore the paper church into bits—the heavens opened and Judge Bay came toward me with a double-barreled shotgun—and hid the bits under a pile of pajamas. I did not sleep one wink. Except that I must have, because of the stupendous nightmares that kept wrenching the flesh off my skeleton and caused me to come close to perishing of thirst; once I fell out of bed and hit my head on Stella's ice skates. I would have waked her up and given her a piece of my mind for leaving them in such a lousy place, but then I remembered: I wanted *no* commotion of any kind.

I couldn't eat breakfast and I couldn't eat lunch. Old Johnny-on-the-spot Jack kept saying "*Poor* Polecat. Polecat wants her fish for dinner." Mother made an abortive[31] attempt to take my temperature. And when all that hullabaloo subsided, I was nearly in the soup because Mother asked me to mind Tess while she went to the sanitarium to see Mrs. Rogers, who, all of a sudden, was too sick to

have anyone but grown-ups near her. Stella couldn't stay with the baby, because she had to go to ballet, and Jack couldn't, because he had to go up to the mesa and empty his traps. ("No, they *can't* wait. You want my skins to rot in this hot-one-day-cold-the-next weather?") I was arguing and whining when the telephone rang. Mother went to answer it and came back with a look of great sadness; Mrs. Rogers, she had learned, had had another hemorrhage. So Mother would not be going to the sanitarium after all and I needn't stay with Tess.

By the time I left the house, I was as cross as a bear. I felt awful about the widow's mite and I felt awful for being mean about staying with Tess, for Mrs. Rogers was a kind old lady, in a cozy blue hug-me-tight[32] and an oldfangled boudoir cap,[33] dying here all alone; she was a friend of Grandma's and had lived just down the street from her in Missouri, and all in the world Mrs. Rogers wanted to do was go back home and lie down in her own big bedroom in her own big, high-ceilinged house and have Grandma and other members of the Eastern Star[34] come in from time to time to say hello. But they wouldn't let her go home; they were going to kill or cure her. I could not help feeling that my hardness of heart and evil of intention had had a good deal to do with her new crisis; right at the very same minute I had been saying "Does that old Mrs. Methuselah[35] *always* have to spoil my fun?" the poor wasted thing was probably coughing up her blood and saying to the nurse, "Tell Emily Vanderpool not to mind me, she can run and play."

I had a bad character, I know that, but my

---

30. **mite:** a small sum of money The reference to the widow is from Mark 12:42–44.
31. **abortive** (ə-bôr′tĭv): unsuccessful.

32. **hug-me-tight:** a close-fitting woman's jacket.
33. **boudoir** (bōō′dwär′) **cap:** a woman's nightcap.
34. **Eastern Star:** a Masonic order for women.
35. **Mrs. Methuselah** (mĕ-thōō′zə-lə): According to Genesis 5:27, Methuselah lived 969 years.

badness never gave me half the enjoyment Jack and Stella thought it did. A good deal of the time I wanted to eat lye. I was certainly having no fun now, thinking of Mrs. Rogers and of depriving that poor widow of bread and milk; what if this penniless woman without a husband had a dog to feed, too? Or a baby? And besides, I didn't want to go downtown to steal anything from the ten-cent store; I didn't want to see Lottie Jump again — not really, for I knew in my bones that that girl was trouble with a capital *T*. And still, in our short meeting she had mesmerized[36] me; I would think about her style of talking and the expert way she had made off with the perfume flask and the cake (how had she carried the cake through the streets without being noticed?) and be bowled over, for the part of me that did not love God was a black-hearted villain. And apart from these considerations, I had some sort of idea that if I did not keep my appointment with Lottie Jump, she would somehow get revenge; she had seemed a girl of purpose. So, revolted and fascinated, brave and lily-livered, I plodded along through the snow in my flopping galoshes up toward the Chautauqua,[37] where the trolley stop was. On my way, I passed Virgil Meade's house; there was not just a snowman, there was a whole snow family in the backyard, and Virgil himself was throwing a stick for his dog. I was delighted to see that he was alone.

Lottie, who was sitting on a bench in the shelter eating a Mr. Goodbar, looked the same as she had the other time except that she was wearing an amazing hat. I think I had expected her to have a black handkerchief over the lower part of her face or to be wearing a Jesse James waistcoat. But I had never thought of a hat. It was felt; it was the color of cooked meat; it had some flowers appliquéd[38] on the front of it; it had no brim, but rose straight up to a very considerable height, like a monument. It sat so low on her forehead and it was so tight that it looked, in a way, like part of her.

"How's every little thing, bub?" she said, licking her candy wrapper.

"Fine, Lottie," I said, freshly awed.

A silence fell. I drank some water from the drinking fountain, sat down, fastened my galoshes, and unfastened them again.

"My mother's teeth grow wrong way too," said Lottie, and showed me what she meant: the lower teeth were in front of the upper ones. "That so-called trolley car takes its own sweet time. This town is blah."

To save the honor of my hometown, the trolley came scraping and groaning up the hill just then, its bell clanging with an idiotic frenzy, and ground to a stop. Its broad, proud cow catcher[39] was filled with dirty snow, in the middle of which rested a tomato can, put there, probably, by somebody who was bored to death and couldn't think of anything else to do — I did a lot of pointless things like that on lonesome Saturday afternoons. It was the custom of this trolley car, a rather mysterious one, to pause at the shelter for five minutes while the conductor, who was either Mr. Jansen or Mr. Peck, depending on whether it was the A.M. run or the P.M., got out and stretched and smoked and spit. Sometimes the passengers got out, too, acting like sightseers whose destination was this sturdy stucco gazebo instead of, as it really was, the Piggly Wiggly or

---

36. **mesmerized** (mĕz′mə-rīzd′): fascinated.
37. **Chautauqua** (shə-tô′kwə): an annual program of educational assemblies, which flourished during the late nineteenth and early twentieth centuries; here applied to the meetinghouse.
38. **appliquéd** (ap′lə-kād′): attached as a decoration.
39. **cowcatcher:** a metal frame on the front of a street-car used to clear the tracks.

the Nelson Dry. You expected them to take snapshots of the drinking fountain or of the Chautauqua meetinghouse up on the hill. And when they all got back in the car, you expected them to exchange intelligent observations on the aborigines[40] and the ruins they had seen.

Today there were no passengers, and as soon as Mr. Peck got out and began staring at the mountains as if he had never seen them before while he made himself a cigarette, Lottie, in her tall hat (was it something like the Inspector's hat in the Katzenjammer Kids?),[41]

got into the car, motioning me to follow. I put our nickels in the empty box and joined her on the very last double seat. It was only then that she mapped out the plan for the afternoon, in a low but still insouciant[42] voice. The hat—she did not apologize for it, she simply referred to it as "my hat"—was to be the repository[43] of whatever we stole. In the future, it would be advisable for me to have one like it. (How? Surely it was unique. The flowers, I saw on closer examination, were tulips, but they were blue, and a very unsettling shade of blue.) I was to engage a clerk on one

40. **aborigines** (ăb′ə-rĭj′ə-nēz): the earliest inhabitants of a region.
41. **Katzenjammer Kids:** the name of a comic strip.

42. **insouciant** (ĭn-sōō′sē-ənt): carefree.
43. **repository** (rĭ-pŏz′ə-tôr′ē): place used for storage.

side of the counter, asking her the price of, let's say, a tube of Daggett & Ramsdell vanishing cream, while Lottie would lift a round comb or a barrette or a hair net or whatever on the other side. Then, at a signal, I would decide against the vanishing cream and would move on to the next counter that she indicated. The signal was interesting; it was to be the raising of her hat from the rear—"like I've got the itch and gotta scratch," she said. I was relieved that I was to have no part in the actual stealing, and I was touched that Lottie, who was going to do all the work, said we would "go halvers" on the take. She asked me if there was anything in particular I wanted— she herself had nothing special in mind and was going to shop around first—and I said I would like some rubber gloves. This request was entirely spontaneous; I had never before in my life thought of rubber gloves in one way or another, but a psychologist—or Judge Bay —might have said that this was most significant and that I was planning at that moment to go on from petty larceny to bigger game, armed with a weapon on which I wished to leave no fingerprints.

On the way downtown, quite a few people got on the trolley, and they all gave us such peculiar looks that I was chickenhearted until I realized it must be Lottie's hat they were looking at. No wonder. I kept looking at it myself out of the corner of my eye; it was like a watermelon standing on end. No, it was like a tremendous test tube. On this trip—a slow one, for the trolley pottered through that part of town in a desultory,[44] neighborly way, even going into areas where no one lived—Lottie told me some of the things she had stolen in Muskogee and here in Adams. They included a white satin prayer book (think of it!), Mr. Goodbars by the thousands (she had probably never paid for a Mr. Goodbar in her life), a dinner ring valued at two dollars, a strawberry emery, several cans of corn, some shoelaces, a set of poker chips, countless pencils, four spark plugs ("Pa had this old car, see, and it was broke, so we took 'er to get fixed; I'll build me a radio with 'em sometime— you know? Listen in on them earmuffs to Tulsa?"), a Boy Scout knife, and a Girl Scout folding cup. She made a regular practice of going through the pockets of the coats in the cloakroom every day at recess, but she had never found anything there worth a red cent and was about to give that up. Once, she had taken a gold pencil from a teacher's desk and had got caught—she was sure that this was one of the reasons she was only in the third grade. Of this unjust experience, she said, "The old hoot owl! If I was drivin' in a car on a lonesome stretch and she was settin' beside me, I'd wait till we got to a pile of gravel and then I'd stop and say, 'Git out, Miss Priss.' She'd git out, all right."

Since Lottie was so frank, I was emboldened at last to ask her what she had done with the cake. She faced me with her grin; this grin, in combination with the hat, gave me a surprise from which I have never recovered. "I ate it up," she said. "I went in your garage and sat on your daddy's old tires and ate it. It was pretty good."

There were two ten-cent stores side by side in our town. Kresge's and Woolworth's, and as we walked down the main street toward them, Lottie played with a yo-yo. Since the street was thronged with Christmas shoppers and farmers in for Saturday, this was no ordinary accomplishment; all in all, Lottie Jump was someone to be reckoned with. I cannot say that I was proud to be seen with her; the fact is that I hoped I would not meet anyone I

---

44. **desultory** (dĕs′əl-tôr′ē): aimless.

knew, and I thanked my lucky stars that Jack was up in the hills with his dead skunks, because if he had seen her with that lid and that yo-yo, I would never have heard the last of it. But in another way I *was* proud to be with her; in a smaller hemisphere, in one that included only her and me, I was swaggering—I felt like Somebody, marching along beside this lofty Somebody from Oklahoma who was going to hold up the dime store.

There is nothing like Woolworth's at Christmastime. It smells of peanut brittle and terrible chocolate candy, Djer-Kiss talcum powder and Ben Hur perfume—smells sourly of tinsel and waxily of artificial poinsettias.[45] The crowds are made up largely of children and women, with here and there a deliberative[46] old man; the women are buying ribbons and wrappings and Christmas cards, and the children are buying asbestos pot holders for their mothers and, for their fathers, suede bookmarks with a burnt-in design that says "A good book is a good friend" or "Souvenir from the Garden of the Gods." It is very noisy. The salesgirls are forever ringing their bells and asking the floorwalker to bring them change for a five; babies in go-carts are screaming as parcels fall on their heads; the women, waving rolls of red tissue paper, try to attract the attention of the harried girl behind the counter. ("Miss! All I want is this one batch of the red. Can't I just give you the dime?" And the girl, beside herself, mottled with vexation, cries back, "Has to be rung up, Moddom, that's the rule.") There is pandemonium[47] at the toy counter, where things are being tested by the customers—wound up, set off, tooted, pounded, made to say "Maaaah-Maaaah!" There is very little gaiety in the scene and, in fact, those baffled old men look as if they were walking over their own dead bodies, but there is an atmosphere of carnival, nevertheless, and as soon as Lottie and I entered the doors of Woolworth's golden-and-vermilion bedlam,[48] I grew giddy and hot—not pleasantly so. The feeling, indeed, was distinctly disagreeable, like the beginning of a stomach upset.

Lottie gave me a nudge and said softly, "Go look at the envelopes. I want some rubber bands."

This counter was relatively uncrowded (the seasonal stationery supplies—the Christmas cards and wrapping paper and stickers—were at a separate counter), and I went around to examine some very beautiful letter paper; it was pale pink and it had a border of roses all around it. The clerk here was a cheerful middle-aged woman wearing an apron, and she was giving all her attention to a seedy old man who could not make up his mind between mucilage and paste. "Take your time, Dad," she said. "Compared to the rest of the girls, I'm on my vacation." The old man, holding a tube in one hand and a bottle in the other, looked at her vaguely and said, "I want it for stamps. Sometimes I write a letter and stamp it and then don't mail it and steam the stamp off. Must have ninety cents' worth of stamps like that." The woman laughed. "I know what you mean," she said. "I get mad and write a letter and then I tear it up." The old man gave her a condescending look[49] and said, "That so? But I don't suppose yours are of a political nature." He bent his gaze again to the choice of adhesives.

This first undertaking was duck soup for Lottie. I did not even have to exchange a word

<hr/>

45. **poinsettias** (poin-sĕt′ē-əz): yellow flowers surrounded by red leaves.
46. **deliberative** (dĭ-lĭb′ə-rā′tĭv): deep in thought.
47. **pandemonium** (păn′də-mō′nē-əm): disorder.

48. **bedlam** (bĕd′ləm): noise and confusion.
49. **condescending** (kŏn′dĭ-sĕnd′ĭng) **look:** a look suggesting a low opinion of another person.

with the woman; I saw Miss Fagin[50] lift up *that hat* and give me the high sign, and we moved away, she down one aisle and I down the other, now and again catching a glimpse of each other through the throngs. We met at the foot of the second counter, where notions were sold.

"Fun, huh?" said Lottie, and I nodded, although I felt wholly dreary. "I want some crochet hooks," she said. "Price the rickrack."

This time the clerk was adding up her receipts and did not even look at me or at a woman who was angrily and in vain trying to buy a paper of pins. Out went Lottie's scrawny hand, up went her domed chimney. In this way for some time she bagged sitting birds: a tea strainer (there was no one at all at that counter), a box of Mrs. Carpenter's All-Purpose Nails, the rubber gloves I had said I wanted, and four packages of mixed seeds. Now you have some idea of the size of Lottie Jump's hat.

I was nervous, not from being her accomplice but from being in this crowd on an empty stomach, and I was getting tired—we had been in the store for at least an hour—and the whole enterprise seemed pointless. There wasn't a thing in her hat I wanted—not even the rubber gloves. But in exact proportion as my spirits descended, Lottie's rose; clearly she had only been target-practicing and now she was moving in for the kill.

We met beside the books of paper dolls, for reconnaissance.[51] "I'm gonna get me a pair of pearl beads," said Lottie. "You go fuss with the hairpins, hear?"

Luck, combined with her skill, would have stayed with Lottie, and her hat would have been a cornucopia[52] by the end of the afternoon if, at the very moment her hand went out for the string of beads, that idiosyncrasy[53] of mine had not struck me full force. I had never known it to come with so few preliminaries; probably this was so because I was oppressed by all the masses of bodies poking and pushing me, and all the open mouths breathing in my face. Anyhow, right then, at the crucial time, I *had to be alone.*

I stood staring down at the bone hairpins for a moment, and when the girl behind the counter said, "What kind does Mother want, hon? What color is Mother's hair?" I looked past her and across at Lottie and I said, "Your brother isn't the only one in your family that doesn't have any brains." The clerk, astonished, turned to look where I was looking and caught Lottie in the act of lifting up her hat to put the pearls inside. She had unwisely chosen a long strand and was having a little trouble; I had the nasty thought that it looked as if her brains were leaking out.

The clerk, not able to deal with this emergency herself, frantically punched her bell and cried, "Floorwalker! Mr. Bellamy! I've caught a thief!"

Momentarily there was a violent hush—then such a clamor as you have never heard. Bells rang, babies howled, crockery crashed to the floor as people stumbled in their rush to the arena.

Mr. Bellamy, nineteen years old but broad of shoulder and jaw, was instantly standing beside Lottie, holding her arm with one hand while with the other he removed her hat to reveal to the overjoyed audience that incredi-

---

50. **Miss Fagin** (fā′gən): Fagin is a character who runs a school for thieves in Charles Dickens' novel *Oliver Twist.* Like Fagin, Lottie gives lessons in stealing.
51. **reconnaissance** (rĭ-kŏn′ə-səns): a survey made in preparation for an attack.
52. **cornucopia** (kôr′nə-kō′pē-ə): a container overflowing with abundance.
53. **idiosyncrasy** (ĭd′ē-ō-sĭng′krə-sē): a personal peculiarity.

ble array of merchandise. Her hair all wild, her face a mask of innocent bewilderment, Lottie Jump, the scurvy thing, pretended to be deaf and dumb. She pointed at the rubber gloves and then she pointed at me, and Mr. Bellamy, able at last to prove his mettle, said "Aha!" and, still holding Lottie, moved around the counter to me and grabbed *my* arm. He gave the hat to the clerk and asked her kindly to accompany him and his red-handed catch to the manager's office.

I don't know where Lottie is now—whether she is on the stage or in jail. If her performance after our arrest meant anything, the first is quite as likely as the second. (I never saw her again, and for all I know she lit out of town that night on a freight train. Or perhaps her whole family decamped as suddenly as they had arrived; ours was the most transient population. You can be sure I made no attempt to find her again, and for months I avoided going anywhere near Arapahoe Creek or North Hill.) She never said a word but kept making signs with her fingers, ad-libbing[54] the whole thing. They tested her hearing by shooting off a popgun right in her ear and she never batted an eyelid.

They called up my father, and he came over from the Safeway on the double. I heard very little of what he said because I was crying so hard, but one thing I did hear him say was "Well, young lady, I guess you've seen to it that I'll have to part company with my good friend Judge Bay." I tried to defend myself, but it was useless. The manager, Mr. Bellamy, the clerk, and my father patted Lottie on the shoulder, and the clerk said, "Poor, afflicted child." For being a poor, afflicted child, they gave her a bag of hard candy, and she gave them the most fraudulent smile of gratitude,

and slobbered a little, and shuffled out, holding her empty hat in front of her like a beggarman. I hate Lottie Jump to this day, but I have to hand it to her—she was a genius.

The floorwalker would have liked to see me sentenced to the reform school for life, I am sure, but the manager said that considering this was my first offense, he would let my father attend to my punishment. The clerk, who looked precisely like Emmy Schmalz, clucked her tongue and shook her head at me. My father hustled me out of the office and out of the store and into the car and home, muttering the entire time; now and again I'd hear the words *morals* and *nowadays.*

What's the use of telling the rest? You know what happened. Daddy on second thoughts decided not to hang his head in front of Judge Bay but to make use of his friendship in this time of need, and he took me to see the scary old curmudgeon[55] at his house. All I remember of that long declamation, during which the Judge sat behind his desk never taking his eyes off me, was the warning "I want you to give this a great deal of thought, Miss. I want you to search and seek in the innermost corners of your conscience and root out every bit of badness." Oh, *him!* Why, listen, if I'd rooted out all the badness in me, there wouldn't have been anything left of me. My mother cried for days because she had nurtured an outlaw and was ashamed to show her face at the neighborhood store; my father was silent, and he often looked at me. Stella, who was a prig, said, "And to think you did it at *Christmas*time!" As for Jack—well, Jack a couple of times did not know how close he came to seeing glory when I had a butcher knife in my hand. It was Polecat this and Polecat that until I nearly went off my rocker. Tess, of course, didn't know what was going

---

54. **ad-libbing** (ăd-lĭb´ĭng): making up on the spot.

55. **curmudgeon** (kər-mŭj´ən): a bad-tempered person.

on, and asked so many questions that finally I told her to go to Helen Hunt Jackson[56] in a savage tone of voice.

Good old Muff.

It is not true that you don't learn by experience. At any rate, I did that time. I began immediately to have two or three friends at a time—to be sure, because of the stigma on me, they were by no' means the elite[57] of Carlyle Hill Grade—and never again when that terrible need to be alone arose did I let fly. I would say, instead, "I've got a headache. I'll have to go home and take an aspirin," or "Gosh all hemlocks, I forgot—I've got to go to the dentist."

After the scandal died down, I got into the Campfire Girls. It was through pull, of course, since Stella had been a respected member for two years and my mother was a friend of the leader. But it turned out all right. Even Muff did not miss our periods of companionship, because about that time she grew up and started having literally millions of kittens.

---

56. **Helen Hunt Jackson:** the author of *Ramona*, a love story.
57. **elite** (ĭ-lēt′): the most distinguished social group.

SEEKING MEANING

1. This story tells of the brief but eventful relationship of two girls who turn out to be the "bad characters" of the title. Are Lottie and Emily "bad" in the same way? How are their characters different?

2. Emily surprises Lottie Jump in the act of stealing a cake. However, when Lottie explains her presence with a lie, Emily accepts the explanation. Why?

3. Although Lottie is "nothing to look at," Emily is drawn to her. What does she find attractive in Lottie's personality?

4. Emily says she knows about *morality*, that is, the difference between right and wrong. Why, then, does she come under Lottie's harmful influence so easily? Why does she agree to help Lottie steal?

5. As Saturday afternoon draws near, Emily's conscience is troubled. What events occur on Friday night that increase her sense of guilt?

6. When she is standing at the counter in Woolworth's, Emily suddenly gets the urge to be alone. Do you think she wants to be caught? Explain your answer.

7. Lottie has the stolen merchandise in her hat, but it is Emily who is punished for stealing. How does Lottie manage to outwit everyone? Why do you think Emily is unable to defend herself?

8. How does Emily reform at the end of the story?

DEVELOPING SKILLS IN READING

Recognizing Clues to Later Actions

Very often a writer establishes the way a character behaves early in a story to prepare the reader for what that character will do later on. What you learn about Emily in the first few paragraphs prepares you for her actions later in the story. For example, you are told that Emily sometimes has a powerful need to be alone, a need that leads her to insult her friends. In what way does the incident with Virgil Meade prepare you for what happens later in Woolworth's? You also learn that Emily's brother and sister often tease her into a tantrum. How does this information prepare you for the scene that takes place later at the dinner table (pages 71–72)?

When you first meet Lottie, you learn certain things about her that signal what is to come. When she is caught stealing the cake, she makes up a monstrous lie. She then manages to steal a perfume flask under Emily's very nose. At the end of the story, how does Lottie use her talent for deceiving people?

DEVELOPING VOCABULARY

Learning Words That Come from Names

You probably know that the word *pasteurize* comes from the name of Louis Pasteur, the French bacteriologist who found a way of destroying harmful bacteria in milk and other liquids. A number of words in our language come from the names of persons and places.

The word *mesmerize* means "to hypnotize" or "to fascinate." It comes from the name of Franz Anton Mesmer, an Austrian physician who practiced hypnotism in connection with certain of his theories. When Emily says that she is *mesmerized* by Lottie, she means that she is unable to resist Lottie's influence.

Emily speaks of entering the *bedlam* of Woolworth's. The word *bedlam* now means any place of confusion. Use a dictionary to find the origin of this word.

Each of these words comes from the name of a person or place. Use a dictionary to find the origin of the word, what it means today, and how it came to have its modern meaning.

badminton	gerrymander	maverick
boycott	hamburger	tuxedo
derrick	macadam	watt

ABOUT THE AUTHOR

Jean Stafford (1915–1979) said that her roots were in the semifictitious town of Adams, Colorado, where her stories about Emily Vanderpool are set. Her short stories and articles appeared in *The New Yorker, Vogue, Harper's,* and other magazines. Among her novels are *Boston Adventure, The Mountain Lion,* and *The Catherine Wheel.* She also wrote a children's book with the intriguing title *Elephi, the Cat with the High IQ.* Elephi can turn on electric lights, drink from a faucet, and play games. Jean Stafford was awarded the Pulitzer Prize in 1970 for her book *Collected Stories.*

*Luke kept the promise he
had made to his dying father.
But there was another promise
he would keep — the promise
he made to himself.*

Luke Baldwin's Vow

Morley Callaghan

That summer when twelve-year-old Luke Baldwin came to live with his Uncle Henry in the house on the stream by the sawmill, he did not forget that he had promised his dying father he would try to learn things from his uncle; so he used to watch him very carefully.

Uncle Henry, who was the manager of the sawmill, was a big, burly man weighing more than two hundred and thirty pounds, and he had a rough-skinned, brick-colored face. He looked like a powerful man, but his health was not good. He had aches and pains in his back and shoulders which puzzled the doctor. The first thing Luke learned about Uncle Henry was that everybody had great respect for him. The four men he employed in the sawmill were always polite and attentive when he spoke to them. His wife, Luke's Aunt Helen, a kindly, plump, straightforward woman, never argued with him. "You should try and be like your Uncle Henry," she would say to Luke. "He's so wonderfully practical. He takes care of everything in a sensible, easy way."

Luke used to trail around the sawmill after Uncle Henry not only because he liked the fresh clean smell of the newly cut wood and the big piles of sawdust, but because he was impressed by his uncle's precise, firm tone when he spoke to the men.

Sometimes Uncle Henry would stop and explain to Luke something about a piece of lumber. "Always try and learn the essential facts, son," he would say. "If you've got the facts, you know what's useful and what isn't useful, and no one can fool you."

He showed Luke that nothing of value was ever wasted around the mill. Luke used to listen, and wonder if there was another man in the world who knew so well what was needed and what ought to be thrown away. Uncle Henry had known at once that Luke needed a bicycle to ride to his school, which was two miles away in town, and he bought him a good one. He knew that Luke needed good,

serviceable clothes. He also knew exactly how much Aunt Helen needed to run the house, the price of everything, and how much a woman should be paid for doing the family washing. In the evenings Luke used to sit in the living room watching his uncle making notations in a black notebook which he always carried in his vest pocket, and he knew that he was assessing the value of the smallest transaction that had taken place during the day.

Luke promised himself that when he grew up he, too, would be admired for his good, sound judgment. But, of course, he couldn't always be watching and learning from his

Uncle Henry, for too often when he watched him he thought of his own father; then he was lonely. So he began to build in another secret life for himself around the sawmill, and his companion was the eleven-year-old collie, Dan, a dog blind in one eye and with a slight limp in his left hind leg. Dan was a fat, slow-moving old dog. He was very affectionate and his eye was the color of amber. His fur was amber too. When Luke left for school in the morning, the old dog followed him for half a mile down the road, and when he returned in the afternoon, there was Dan waiting at the gate.

Sometimes they would play around the millpond or by the dam, or go down the stream to the lake. Luke was never lonely when the dog was with him. There was an old rowboat that they used as a pirate ship in the stream, and they would be pirates together, with Luke shouting instructions to Captain Dan and with the dog seeming to understand and wagging his tail enthusiastically. Its amber eye was alert, intelligent, and approving. Then they would plunge into the brush on the other side of the stream, pretending they were hunting tigers. Of course, the old dog was no longer much good for hunting; he was too slow and too lazy. Uncle Henry no longer used him for hunting rabbits or anything else.

When they came out of the brush, they would lie together on the cool, grassy bank being affectionate with each other, with Luke talking earnestly, while the collie, as Luke believed, smiled with the good eye. Lying in the grass, Luke would say things to Dan he could not say to his uncle or his aunt. Not that what he said was important; it was just stuff about himself that he might have told to his own father or mother if they had been alive. Then they would go back to the house for dinner, and after dinner Dan would follow him down the road to Mr. Kemp's house, where they would ask old Mr. Kemp if they could go with him to round up his four cows. The old man was always glad to see them. He seemed to like watching Luke and the collie running around the cows, pretending they were riding on a vast range in the foothills of the Rockies.

Uncle Henry no longer paid much attention to the collie, though once when he tripped over him on the veranda he shook his head and said thoughtfully, "Poor old fellow, he's through. Can't use him for anything. He just eats and sleeps and gets in the way."

One Sunday during Luke's summer holidays, when they had returned from church and had had their lunch, they had all moved out to the veranda where the collie was sleeping. Luke sat down on the steps, his back against the veranda post, Uncle Henry took the rocking chair, and Aunt Helen stretched herself out in the hammock, sighing contentedly. Then Luke, eyeing the collie, tapped the step with the palm of his hand, giving three little taps like a signal, and the old collie, lifting his head, got up stiffly with a slow wagging of the tail as an acknowledgment that the signal had been heard, and began to cross the veranda to Luke. But the dog was sleepy; his bad eye was turned to the rocking chair; in passing his left front paw went under the rocker. With a frantic yelp, the dog went bounding down the steps and hobbled around the corner of the house, where he stopped, hearing Luke coming after him. All he needed was the touch of Luke's hand. Then he began to lick the hand methodically, as if apologizing.

"Luke," Uncle Henry called sharply, "bring that dog here."

When Luke led the collie back to the veranda, Uncle Henry nodded and said, "Thanks, Luke." Then he took out a cigar, lit it, put his big hands on his knees, and began to rock in the chair while he frowned and eyed the dog steadily. Obviously he was making some kind of an important decision about the collie.

"What's the matter, Uncle Henry?" Luke asked nervously.

"That dog can't see any more," Uncle Henry said.

"Oh, yes, he can," Luke said quickly. "His bad eye got turned to the chair, that's all, Uncle Henry."

"And his teeth are gone, too," Uncle Henry went on, paying no attention to what Luke had said. Turning to the hammock, he called, "Helen, sit up a minute, will you?"

When she got up and stood beside him, he went on, "I was thinking about this old dog the other day, Helen. It's not only that he's about blind, but did you notice that when we drove up after church he didn't even bark?"

"It's a fact he didn't, Henry."

"No, not much good even as a watchdog now."

"Poor old fellow. It's a pity, isn't it?"

"And no good for hunting either. And he eats a lot, I suppose."

"About as much as he ever did, Henry."

"The plain fact is the old dog isn't worth his keep any more. It's time we got rid of him."

"It's always so hard to know how to get rid of a dog, Henry."

"I was thinking about it the other day. Some people think it's best to shoot a dog. I haven't had any shells for that shotgun for over a year. Poisoning is a hard death for a dog. Maybe drowning is the easiest and quickest way. Well, I'll speak to one of the mill hands and have him look after it."

Crouching on the ground, his arms around the old collie's neck, Luke cried out, "Uncle Henry, Dan's a wonderful dog! You don't know how wonderful he is!"

"He's just a very old dog, son," Uncle Henry said calmly. "The time comes when you have to get rid of any old dog. We've got to be practical about it. I'll get you a pup, son. A smart little dog that'll be worth its keep. A pup that will grow up with you."

"I don't want a pup!" Luke cried, turning his face away. Circling around him, the dog began to bark, then flick his long pink tongue at the back of Luke's neck.

Aunt Helen, catching her husband's eye, put her finger on her lips, warning him not to go on talking in front of the boy. "An old dog like that often wanders off into the brush and sort of picks a place to die when the time comes. Isn't that so, Henry?"

"Oh, sure," he agreed quickly. "In fact, when Dan didn't show up yesterday, I was sure that was what had happened." Then he yawned and seemed to forget about the dog.

But Luke was frightened, for he knew what his uncle was like. He knew that if his uncle had decided that the dog was useless and that it was sane and sensible to get rid of it, he would be ashamed of himself if he were diverted by any sentimental consideration. Luke knew in his heart that he couldn't move his uncle. All he could do, he thought, was keep the dog away from his uncle, keep him out of the house, feed him when Uncle Henry wasn't around.

Next day at noontime Luke saw his uncle walking from the mill toward the house with old Sam Carter, a mill hand. Sam Carter was a dull, stooped, slow-witted man of sixty with an iron-gray beard, who was wearing blue overalls and a blue shirt. He hardly ever spoke to anybody. Watching from the veranda, Luke noticed that his uncle suddenly gave Sam Carter a cigar, which Sam put in his pocket. Luke had never seen his uncle give Sam a cigar or pay much attention to him.

Then, after lunch, Uncle Henry said lazily that he would like Luke to take his bicycle and go into town and get him some cigars.

"I'll take Dan," Luke said.

"Better not, son," Uncle Henry said. "It'll take you all afternoon. I want those cigars. Get going, Luke."

His uncle's tone was so casual that Luke tried to believe they were not merely getting rid of him. Of course he had to do what he was told. He had never dared to refuse to obey an order from his uncle. But when he had taken his bicycle and had ridden down the path that followed the stream to the town road and had got about a quarter of a mile along the road, he found that all he could think of was his uncle handing old Sam Carter the cigar.

Slowing down, sick with worry now, he got off the bike and stood uncertainly on the sunlit road. Sam Carter was a gruff, aloof old man who would have no feeling for a dog.

Then suddenly Luke could go no farther without getting some assurance that the collie would not be harmed while he was away. Across the fields he could see the house.

Leaving the bike in the ditch, he started to cross the field, intending to get close enough to the house so Dan could hear him if he whistled softly. He got about fifty yards away from the house and whistled and waited, but there was no sign of the dog, which might be asleep at the front of the house, he knew, or over at the sawmill. With the saws whining, the dog couldn't hear the soft whistle. For a few minutes Luke couldn't make up his mind what to do, then he decided to go back to the road, get on his bike, and go back the way he had come until he got to the place where the river path joined the road. There he could leave his bike, go up the path, then into the tall grass and get close to the front of the house and the sawmill without being seen.

He had followed the river path for about a hundred yards, and when he came to the place where the river began to bend sharply toward the house his heart fluttered and his legs felt paralyzed, for he saw the old rowboat in the one place where the river was deep, and in the rowboat was Sam Carter with the collie.

The bearded man in the blue overalls was smoking the cigar; the dog, with a rope around its neck, sat contentedly beside him, its tongue going out in a friendly lick at the hand holding the rope. It was all like a crazy dream picture to Luke; all wrong because it looked so lazy and friendly, even the curling smoke from Sam Carter's cigar. But as Luke cried out, "Dan! Dan! Come on, boy!" and the dog jumped at the water, he saw that Sam Carter's left hand was hanging deep in the water, holding a foot of rope with a heavy stone at the end. As Luke cried out wildly, "Don't! Please don't!" Carter dropped the stone, for the cry came too late; it was blurred

by the screech of the big saws at the mill. But Carter was startled, and he stared stupidly at the riverbank, then he ducked his head and began to row quickly to the bank.

But Luke was watching the collie take what looked like a long, shallow dive, except that the hind legs suddenly kicked up above the surface, then shot down, and while he watched, Luke sobbed and trembled, for it was as if the happy secret part of his life around the sawmill was being torn away from him. But even while he watched, he seemed to be following a plan without knowing it, for he was already fumbling in his pocket for his jackknife, jerking the blade open, pulling off his pants, kicking his shoes off, while he muttered fiercely and prayed that Sam Carter would get out of sight.

It hardly took the mill hand a minute to reach the bank and go slinking furtively

around the bend as if he felt that the boy was following him. But Luke hadn't taken his eyes off the exact spot in the water where Dan had disappeared. As soon as the mill hand was out of sight, Luke slid down the bank and took a leap at the water, the sun glistening on his slender body, his eyes wild with eagerness as he ran out to the deep place, then arched his back and dived, swimming under water, his open eyes getting used to the greenish-gray haze of the water, the sandy bottom, and the imbedded rocks.

His lungs began to ache, then he saw the shadow of the collie floating at the end of the taut rope, rock-held in the sand. He slashed at the rope with his knife. He couldn't get much strength in his arm because of the resistance of the water. He grabbed the rope with his left hand, hacking with his knife. The collie suddenly drifted up slowly, like a water-soaked log. Then his own head shot above the surface, and, while he was sucking in the air, he was drawing in the rope, pulling the collie toward him and treading water. In a few strokes he was away from the deep place and his feet touched the bottom.

Hoisting the collie out of the water, he scrambled toward the bank, lurching and stumbling in fright because the collie felt like a dead weight.

He went on up the bank and across the path to the tall grass, where he fell flat, hugging the dog and trying to warm him with his own body. But the collie didn't stir; the good amber eye remained closed. Then suddenly Luke wanted to act like a resourceful, competent man. Getting up on his knees, he stretched the dog out on its belly, drew him between his knees, felt with trembling hands for the soft places on the flanks just above the hipbones, and rocked back and forth, pressing with all his weight, then relaxing the pressure as he straightened up. He hoped that he was working the dog's lungs like a bellows. He had read that men who had been thought drowned had been saved in this way.

"Come on, Dan. Come on, old boy," he pleaded softly. As a little water came from the collie's mouth, Luke's heart jumped, and he muttered over and over, "You can't be dead, Dan! You can't, you can't! I won't let you die, Dan!" He rocked back and forth tirelessly, applying the pressure to the flanks. More water dribbled from the mouth. In the collie's body he felt a faint tremor. "Oh, gee, Dan, you're alive," he whispered. "Come on, boy. Keep it up."

With a cough the collie suddenly jerked his head back, the amber eye opened, and there they were looking at each other. Then the collie, thrusting his legs out stiffly, tried to hoist himself up, staggered, tried again, then stood there in a stupor. Then he shook himself like any other wet dog, turned his head, eyed Luke, and the red tongue came out in a weak flick at Luke's cheek.

"Lie down, Dan," Luke said. As the dog lay down beside him, Luke closed his eyes, buried his head in the wet fur, and wondered why all the muscles of his arms and legs began to jerk in a nervous reaction, now that it was all over. "Stay there, Dan," he said softly, and he went back to the path, got his clothes, and came back beside Dan and put them on. "I think we'd better get away from this spot, Dan," he said. "Keep down, boy. Come on." And he crawled on through the tall grass till they were about seventy-five yards from the place where he had undressed. There they lay down together.

In a little while he heard his aunt's voice calling, "Luke. Oh, Luke! Come here, Luke!"

"Quiet, Dan," Luke whispered. A few minutes passed, and then Uncle Henry called, "Luke, Luke!" and he began to come down the path. They could see him standing there, massive and imposing, his hands on his hips as he looked down the path; then he turned and went back to the house.

As he watched the sunlight shine on the back of his uncle's neck, the exultation Luke had felt at knowing the collie was safe beside him turned to bewildered despair, for he knew that even if he should be forgiven for saving the dog when he saw it drowning, the fact was that his uncle had been thwarted.[1] His mind was made up to get rid of Dan, and in a few days' time, in another way, he would get rid of him, as he got rid of anything around the mill that he believed to be useless or a waste of money.

As he lay back and looked up at the hardly moving clouds, he began to grow frightened.

---

1. **thwarted** (thwôrt′ĭd): prevented from carrying out his plans.

He couldn't go back to the house, nor could he take the collie into the woods and hide him and feed him there unless he tied him up. If he didn't tie him up, Dan would wander back to the house.

"I guess there's just no place to go, Dan," he whispered sadly. "Even if we start off along the road, somebody is sure to see us."

But Dan was watching a butterfly that was circling crazily above them. Raising himself a little, Luke looked through the grass at the corner of the house, then he turned and looked the other way to the wide blue lake. With a sigh he lay down again, and for hours they lay there together, until there was no sound from the saws in the mill and the sun moved low in the western sky.

"Well, we can't stay here any longer, Dan," he said at last. "We'll just have to get as far away as we can. Keep down, old boy," and he began to crawl through the grass, going farther away from the house. When he could no longer be seen, he got up and began to trot across the field toward the gravel road leading to town.

On the road, the collie would turn from time to time as if wondering why Luke shuffled along, dragging his feet wearily, head down. "I'm stumped, that's all, Dan," Luke explained. "I can't seem to think of a place to take you."

When they were passing the Kemp place, they saw the old man sitting on the veranda, and Luke stopped. All he could think of was that Mr. Kemp had liked them both and it had been a pleasure to help him get the cows in the evening. Dan had always been with them. Staring at the figure of the old man on the veranda, he said in a worried tone, "I wish I could be sure of him, Dan. I wish he was a dumb, stupid man who wouldn't know or care whether you were worth anything. . . . Well, come on." He opened the gate bravely,

but he felt shy and unimportant.

"Hello, son. What's on your mind?" Mr. Kemp called from the veranda. He was a thin, wiry man in a tan-colored shirt. He had a gray, untidy mustache, his skin was wrinkled and leathery, but his eyes were always friendly and amused.

"Could I speak to you, Mr. Kemp?" Luke asked when they were close to the veranda.

"Sure. Go ahead."

"It's about Dan. He's a great dog, but I guess you know that as well as I do. I was wondering if you could keep him here for me."

"Why should I keep Dan here, son?"

"Well, it's like this," Luke said, fumbling the words awkwardly. "My uncle won't let me keep him any more . . . says he's too old." His mouth began to tremble, then he blurted out the story.

"I see, I see," Mr. Kemp said slowly, and he got up and came over to the steps and sat down and began to stroke the collie's head. "Of course, Dan's an old dog, son," he said quietly. "And sooner or later you've got to get rid of an old dog. Your uncle knows that. Maybe it's true that Dan isn't worth his keep."

"He doesn't eat much, Mr. Kemp. Just one meal a day."

"I wouldn't want you to think your uncle was cruel and unfeeling, Luke," Mr. Kemp went on. "He's a fine man . . . maybe just a little bit too practical and straightforward."

"I guess that's right," Luke agreed, but he was really waiting and trusting the expression in the old man's eyes.

"Maybe you should make him a practical proposition."

"I—I don't know what you mean."

"Well, I sort of like the way you get the cows for me in the evenings," Mr. Kemp said, smiling to himself. "In fact, I don't think you need me to go along with you at all. Now, supposing I gave you seventy-five cents a week. Would you get the cows for me every night?"

"Sure I would, Mr. Kemp. I like doing it, anyway."

"All right, son. It's a deal. Now I'll tell you what to do. You go back to your uncle, and before he has a chance to open up on you, you say right out that you've come to him with a business proposition. Say it like a man, just like that. Offer to pay him the seventy-five cents a week for the dog's keep."

"But my uncle doesn't need seventy-five cents, Mr. Kemp," Luke said uneasily.

"Of course not," Mr. Kemp agreed. "It's the principle of the thing. Be confident. Remember that he's got nothing against the dog. Go to it, son. Let me know how you do," he added, with an amused smile. "If I know your uncle at all, I think it'll work."

"I'll try it, Mr. Kemp," Luke said. "Thanks very much." But he didn't have any confidence, for even though he knew that Mr. Kemp was a wise old man who would not deceive him, he couldn't believe that seventy-five cents a week would stop his uncle, who was an important man. "Come on, Dan," he called, and he went slowly and apprehensively[2] back to the house.

When they were going up the path, his aunt cried from the open window, "Henry, Henry, in heaven's name, it's Luke with the dog!"

Ten paces from the veranda, Luke stopped and waited nervously for his uncle to come out. Uncle Henry came out in a rush, but when he saw the collie and Luke standing there, he stopped stiffly, turned pale, and his mouth hung open loosely.

"Luke," he whispered, "that dog had a stone around his neck."

---

2. **apprehensively** (ăp′rĭ-hĕn′sĭv-lē): fearfully.

"I fished him out of the stream," Luke said uneasily.

"Oh, oh, I see," Uncle Henry said, and gradually the color came back to his face. "You fished him out, eh?" he asked, still looking at the dog uneasily. "Well, you shouldn't have done that. I told Sam Carter to get rid of the dog, you know."

"Just a minute, Uncle Henry," Luke said, trying not to falter. He gained confidence as Aunt Helen came out and stood beside her husband, for her eyes seemed to be gentle, and he went on bravely, "I want to make you a practical proposition, Uncle Henry."

"A what?" Uncle Henry asked, still feeling insecure, and wishing the boy and the dog weren't confronting him.

"A practical proposition," Luke blurted out quickly. "I know Dan isn't worth his keep to you. I guess he isn't worth anything to anybody but me. So I'll pay you seventy-five cents a week for his keep."

"What's this?" Uncle Henry asked, looking bewildered. "Where would you get seventy-five cents a week, Luke?"

"I'm going to get the cows every night for Mr. Kemp."

"Oh, for heaven's sake, Henry," Aunt Helen pleaded, looking distressed, "let him keep the dog!" and she fled into the house.

"None of that kind of talk!" Uncle Henry called after her. "We've got to be sensible about this!" But he was shaken himself, and overwhelmed with a distress that destroyed all his confidence. As he sat down slowly in the rocking chair and stroked the side of his big face, he wanted to say weakly, "All right, keep the dog," but he was ashamed of being so weak and sentimental. He stubbornly refused to yield to this emotion; he was trying desperately to turn his emotion into a bit of good, useful common sense, so he could justify his distress. So he rocked and pondered. At last he smiled. "You're a smart little shaver, Luke," he said slowly. "Imagine you working it out like this. I'm tempted to accept your proposition."

"Gee, thanks, Uncle Henry."

"I'm accepting it because I think you'll learn something out of this," he went on ponderously.

"Yes, Uncle Henry."

"You'll learn that useless luxuries cost the smartest men hard-earned money."

"I don't mind."

"Well, it's a thing you'll have to learn sometime. I think you'll learn, too, because you certainly seem to have a practical streak in you. It's a streak I like to see in a boy. OK, son," he said, and he smiled with relief and went into the house.

Turning to Dan, Luke whispered softly, "Well, what do you know about that?"

As he sat down on the step with the collie beside him and listened to Uncle Henry talking to his wife, he began to glow with exultation. Then gradually his exultation began to change to a vast wonder that Mr. Kemp should have had such a perfect understanding of Uncle Henry. He began to dream of someday being as wise as old Mr. Kemp and knowing exactly how to handle people. It was possible, too, that he had already learned some of the things about his uncle that his father had wanted him to learn.

Putting his head down on the dog's neck, he vowed to himself fervently that he would always have some money on hand, no matter what became of him, so that he would be able to protect all that was truly valuable from the practical people in the world.

SEEKING MEANING

1. At the beginning of the story, Luke Baldwin wants to be like his Uncle Henry. Why does Luke admire his uncle?

2. Why does Uncle Henry believe that Luke's collie is worthless? What does the dog mean to Luke?

3. When his uncle sends him into town on an errand, Luke becomes worried about Dan. Why does he suspect that the collie will come to harm?

4. Mr. Kemp tells Luke that his uncle is not "cruel or unfeeling" but "maybe just a little bit too practical" (page 89). Do you agree with Mr. Kemp's judgment of Uncle Henry? Give evidence from the story to support your answer.

5. What is the "practical proposition" that Luke offers Uncle Henry? Why is Uncle Henry upset by the offer?

6. At the end of the story, Uncle Henry accepts Luke's proposition, claiming that it will teach Luke to be practical. Luke does learn an important lesson. How is it different from the lesson Uncle Henry intended to teach him?

7. A *vow* is a solemn promise. What is Luke's vow?

DEVELOPING SKILLS IN READING

Drawing Conclusions

Very often, after completing a story, the reader is left with certain thoughts or questions about the meaning of the story—those ideas that reach beyond the individual characters and events. "Luke Baldwin's Vow" tells how a boy manages to save his dog's life by appealing to his uncle's practical nature. The meaning of the story lies in what it tells about *values,* or the things or qualities that are important to people.

The story presents the reader with two very different sets of values. What is most important to Uncle Henry? By contrast, what is most important to Luke? How do these values clash during the course of the story?

Which of these statements do you think best describes the outcome of the story? Explain your answer.

Luke learns that only his own values matter.

Luke learns that he must have regard for his uncle's values even if he does not agree with them.

Luke convinces Uncle Henry to change his values.

DEVELOPING SKILLS OF EXPRESSION

Combining Details in Description
A good writer often combines two or more closely related ideas into a single longer sentence.

Uncle Henry, who was the manager of the sawmill, was a big, burly man weighing more than two hundred and thirty pounds, and he had a rough-skinned, brick-colored face.

In this sentence, Morley Callaghan tells the reader what Uncle Henry does and what he looks like. What characteristics of Uncle Henry's physical appearance are emphasized?

Compare the picture you have of Uncle Henry with this picture of Mr. Kemp:

He was a thin, wiry man in a tan-colored shirt. He had a gray, untidy mustache, his skin was wrinkled and leathery, but his eyes were always friendly and amused.

What details have been combined in the second sentence?

You can picture both characters clearly because the author uses specific details in describing them.

Observe people in a crowd—on a bus, in a store, or at a sports event. Write a description of one person, combining specific details into one or two sentences.

ABOUT THE AUTHOR

Morley Callaghan (1903–   ) is one of Canada's most distinguished novelists and short-story writers. He was born in Toronto and educated at the University of Toronto and at the Osgoode Hall Law School. While he was working as a reporter on the Toronto *Daily Star,* he met Ernest Hemingway, who took an interest in Callaghan's work and encouraged him to write. In a number of his stories, like "Luke Baldwin's Vow," Callaghan shows a keen understanding of young people and their problems. Some of his well-known stories are "The Snob," "A Cap for Steve," and "All the Years of Her Life."

Practice in Reading and Writing

DESCRIPTION

Reading Description

Description is an important element in almost every kind of writing. In stories, description helps the reader picture characters and settings. Look at the opening paragraph from "The Baroque Marble" by E. A. Proulx:

> Late autumn rain again. Sister Opal woke up in a Polaroid yellow light with her head hanging off the bed all sideways. Down in the street children's voices slid under the window, muffled and changed by the damp morning. Sister Opal thought the children sounded as if they were speaking Russian or Basque—some queer, garbled language. She pretended she was in another country where she didn't know a word of the language and where she would have to make signs to get breakfast in a few minutes when she went downstairs. False panic began to rise in her, then subsided. From her position of suspension over the edge of the bed, the furniture looked darker, and the unfamiliar angle gave it a sinister look. The bureau loomed, a skyscraper in dull, dark varnish. Perhaps there were tiny people and offices inside. The chair arms seemed to have clenched hands at their ends, like brown old men sitting anxiously in the doctor's office waiting to hear the bad news.

This passage helps you see, hear, and feel what Sister Opal experiences after she wakes up. You learn from this description that Sister Opal has a vivid imagination that can transform, or change, the real world into a fantasy world. What do the sounds in the street suggest to her? What does she imagine the furniture to be?

The passage also prepares you for what will be revealed about Sister Opal later in the story—her daydreaming, her long, solitary walks, and her ability to see beauty and wonder in ordinary objects.

A writer selects details that develop a single strong impression of a character. In this paragraph from "Luke Baldwin's Vow," Morley Callaghan describes Uncle Henry. Notice that every sentence in the paragraph supports the idea that Uncle Henry is a practical man.

He showed Luke that nothing of value was ever wasted around the mill. Luke used to listen, and wonder if there was another man in the world who knew so well what was needed and what ought to be thrown away. Uncle Henry had known at once that Luke needed a bicycle to ride to his school, which was two miles away in town, and he bought him a good one. He knew that Luke needed good, serviceable clothes. He also knew exactly how much Aunt Helen needed to run the house, the price of everything, and how much a woman should be paid for doing the family washing. In the evenings Luke used to sit in the living room watching his uncle making notations in a black notebook which he always carried in his vest pocket, and he knew that he was assessing the value of the smallest transaction that had taken place during the day.

How many specific details are used to emphasize Uncle Henry's concern with the price and value of things?

Here are some points to remember when you read description:

---

1. *Through description, a writer helps you to use your senses—to see, hear, smell, taste, and feel as you read.*
2. *By selecting details with care, a writer can communicate a single strong impression about a character or a setting.*

3. *A writer need not describe every aspect of a person or a scene. Effective description includes only significant details.*

Writing Description
When you write description, remember these points:

---

1. *Be familiar with what you are describing.*
2. *Select specific details that will create a picture in your reader's mind.*
3. *Use precise nouns, verbs, adjectives, and adverbs.*

4. *Use words that will appeal to your reader's senses.*
5. *It is often a good idea to state at the beginning of a descriptive paragraph the main impression you want your reader to get.*

Select one of the following sentences to open a paragraph of description, or write an opening sentence of your own. Then provide a paragraph to support the ideas in this sentence.

What I like about holiday dinners is the variety of smells that come from the kitchen.

One look told me that the shopper was completely exhausted.

The home of the future will be very different from the home of today.

Using Comparisons

In "The Cat and the Pain Killer," Mark Twain uses effective comparisons to help the reader understand what Tom is experiencing. Twain says that during one of Tom's treatments, Aunt Polly "scrubbed him down with a towel like a file." A *file* is an instrument with a rough surface. Imagine how that towel must have felt against Tom's skin!

Despite Aunt Polly's efforts, Tom "remained as dismal as a hearse." What does this comparison tell you about Tom's mood?

To help the reader appreciate how Pain Killer tasted to Tom, Twain says that it was "simply fire in a liquid form." What do you imagine the first swallow must have done to Tom?

In "A Ribbon for Baldy," Jesse Stuart compares the hills to islands in a sea of clouds. He helps you see and appreciate the beauty of his land:

I looked over the sea of rolling white clouds. The tops of the dark winter hills jutted up like little islands.

Write a sentence or two of comparison, using one of the following ideas or an idea of your own:

Imagine seeing your neighborhood from the window of an airplane. What would the houses, the automobiles, and the people look like from that height?

Imagine the different moods of the sea. What comparison could you use to describe the sea when it is gentle, when it is playful, and when it is angry?

In what way is a car like a human being? What comparisons in behavior could you make?

For Further Reading

Bagnold, Enid, *National Velvet* (Morrow, 1949; paperback, Grosset & Dunlap)
> Velvet Brown, a fourteen-year-old English girl, wins a horse in a village lottery and decides to race it in the Grand National Steeplechase.

Burch, Robert, *Queenie Peavy* (Viking, 1966)
> An imaginative, rebellious, and likable girl, growing up in Georgia during the 1930's, discovers her own values.

Byars, Betsy, *Summer of the Swans* (Viking, 1970)
> Fourteen-year-old Sara Godfrey forgets her own feelings of unhappiness in her frantic search for her ten-year-old retarded brother, who is lost.

Hamilton, Virginia, *M. C. Higgins, the Great* (Macmillan, 1974; paperback, Dell)
> While both his parents work, M. C. (which stands for Mayo Cornelius) takes care of his younger brothers and sisters on Sarah Mountain. Two strangers who come to the mountain—a wandering girl and a folk-song collector—make important changes in M.C.'s life.

Harris, Marilyn, *The Runaway's Diary* (Four Winds, 1971; paperback, Archway)
> A sensitive fifteen-year-old keeps a diary of her adventures as she journeys from her home in Pennsylvania to the Canadian wilderness, accompanied by an adopted German shepherd puppy.

Lee, Mildred, *The Rock and the Willow* (Lothrop, Lee & Shepard, 1963; paperback, Archway)
> Enie, entering high school in rural Alabama in the 1930's, faces her problems with courage and dignity, determined to make her life better.

L'Engle, Madeleine, *The Young Unicorns* (Farrar, Straus & Giroux, 1968)
> A gang called the Alphabats spell trouble and danger for Dave, a former member, who resists returning to the gang.

Mazer, Harry, *Snow Bound* (Delacorte, 1973; paperback, Dell)
> Cindy and Tom, running away from home for different reasons, find their lives in danger when they are lost in a blizzard.

McKenney, Ruth, *My Sister Eileen* (Harcourt Brace Jovanovich, 1968)
> The author recalls hilarious adventures with her younger sister in a small town in Ohio and later in New York City.

Neville, Emily, *It's Like This, Cat* (Harper & Row, 1963)
> Fourteen-year-old Dave tells about his life in New York City, his family, his friends, and the new people he comes to know—including his first girlfriend—when he adopts a stray cat.

Rawlings, Marjorie Kinnan, *The Yearling* (Scribner, 1961; paperback, Scribner)
> Jody Baxter grows up quickly when he must make a painful decision about his pet fawn, which has been destroying his parents' crops.

Twain, Mark, *The Adventures of Tom Sawyer* (many editions)
> This famous novel is set in a small town in Missouri in the nineteenth century. Tom's adventures include witnessing a murder, falling in love with Becky Thatcher, attending his own funeral, and being rescued from a cave.

West, Jessamyn, *Cress Delahanty* (Harcourt Brace Jovanovich, 1954; paperback, Avon)
> Cress is an amiable teen-ager growing up on a California ranch. The stories in the book cover her life from twelve to sixteen.

Wojciechowska, Maia, *Shadow of a Bull* (Atheneum, 1964; paperback, Atheneum)
> Manolo does not wish to become a bullfighter like his father, but he is expected to face his first bull in the ring when he is twelve.

Every family has its own stories to tell—of shared experiences—of special joys and sorrows. Each of the selections in this unit might be considered a page or a chapter from a different family book. Some selections are told from the point of view of a young person; others are told from the point of view of an adult looking back on childhood. What you will find are differences in attitudes, values, and judgments about family relationships.

THE FAMILY

Family Group (1949). Sculpture in bronze by Henry Moore.
Art Resource

The selection you are about to read is a chapter from a novel called To Kill a Mockingbird. *"Scout" Finch, the girl who tells the story, and her brother, Jem, think they know all there is to know about their father, Atticus. To their surprise, they discover something about him that other people have known all along.*

One-Shot Finch   *Harper Lee*

Atticus was feeble: he was nearly fifty. When Jem and I asked him why he was so old, he said he got started late, which we felt reflected upon his abilities and manliness. He was much older than the parents of our school contemporaries, and there was nothing Jem or I could say about him when our classmates said, "*My* father——"

Jem was football-crazy. Atticus was never too tired to play keep-away, but when Jem wanted to tackle him Atticus would say, "I'm too old for that, son."

Our father didn't do anything. He worked in an office, not in a drugstore. Atticus did not drive a dump truck for the county, he was not the sheriff, he did not farm, work in a garage, or do anything that could possibly arouse the admiration of anyone.

Besides that, he wore glasses. He was nearly blind in his left eye, and said left eyes were the tribal curse of the Finches. Whenever he wanted to see something well, he turned his head and looked from his right eye.

He did not do the things our schoolmates' fathers did: he never went hunting, he did not play poker or fish or drink or smoke. He sat in the living room and read.

With these attributes, however, he would not remain as inconspicuous as we wished him to: that year, the school buzzed with talk about him defending Tom Robinson,[1] none of which was complimentary. After my bout with Cecil Jacobs,[2] when I committed myself to a policy of cowardice, word got around that Scout Finch wouldn't fight any more, her daddy wouldn't let her. This was not entirely correct: I wouldn't fight publicly for Atticus, but the family was private ground. I would fight anyone from a third cousin upwards tooth and nail. Francis Hancock, for example, knew that.

When he gave us our air rifles Atticus wouldn't teach us to shoot. Uncle Jack instructed us in the rudiments thereof; he said Atticus wasn't interested in guns. Atticus said to Jem one day, "I'd rather you shot at tin

---

1. **Tom Robinson:** Atticus is a lawyer.
2. **Cecil Jacobs:** a boy who teased Scout about her father's defense of Tom Robinson. Scout fought him.

cans in the backyard, but I know you'll go after birds. Shoot all the bluejays you want, if you can hit 'em, but remember it's a sin to kill a mockingbird.''

That was the only time I ever heard Atticus say it was a sin to do something, and I asked Miss Maudie[3] about it.

''Your father's right,'' she said. ''Mockingbirds don't do one thing but make music for us to enjoy. They don't eat up people's gardens, don't nest in corncribs, they don't do one thing but sing their hearts out for us. That's why it's a sin to kill a mockingbird.''

''Miss Maudie, this is an old neighborhood, ain't it?''

''Been here longer than the town.''

''Nome, I mean the folks on our street are old. Jem and me's the only children around here. Mrs. Dubose is close on to a hundred and Miss Rachel's old and so are you and Atticus.''

''I don't call fifty very old,'' said Miss Maudie tartly. ''Not being wheeled around yet, am I? Neither's your father. But I must say Providence was kind enough to burn down that old mausoleum of mine, I'm too old to keep it up—maybe you're right, Jean Louise,[4] this is a settled neighborhood. You've never been around young folks much, have you?''

---

3. **Miss Maudie:** Maudie Atkinson, the family's neighbor.

4. **Jean Louise:** Scout's real name.

"Yessum, at school."

"I mean young grown-ups. You're lucky, you know. You and Jem have the benefit of your father's age. If your father was thirty you'd find life quite different."

"I sure would. Atticus can't do anything. . . ."

"You'd be surprised," said Miss Maudie. "There's life in him yet."

"What can he do?"

"Well, he can make somebody's will so airtight can't anybody meddle with it."

"Shoot. . . ."

"Well, did you know he's the best checker player in this town? Why, down at the Landing when we were coming up, Atticus Finch could beat everybody on both sides of the river."

"Good Lord, Miss Maudie, Jem and me beat him all the time."

"It's about time you found out it's because he lets you. Did you know he can play a jew's-harp?"[5]

This modest accomplishment served to make me even more ashamed of him.

"*Well . . .*" she said.

"Well what, Miss Maudie?"

"Well nothing. Nothing—it seems with all that you'd be proud of him. Can't everybody play a jew's-harp. Now keep out of the way of the carpenters. You'd better go home, I'll be in my azaleas and can't watch you. Plank might hit you."

I went to the backyard and found Jem plugging away at a tin can, which seemed stupid with all the bluejays around. I returned to the front yard and busied myself for two hours erecting a complicated breastworks at the side of the porch, consisting of a tire, an orange crate, the laundry hamper, the porch chairs, and a small U.S. flag Jem gave me from a popcorn box.

When Atticus came home to dinner he found me crouched down aiming across the street. "What are you shooting at?"

"Miss Maudie's rear end."

Atticus turned and saw my generous target bending over her bushes. He pushed his hat to the back of his head and crossed the street. "Maudie," he called, "I thought I'd better warn you. You're in considerable peril."

Miss Maudie straightened up and looked toward me. She said, "Atticus, you are a devil from hell."

When Atticus returned he told me to break camp. "Don't you ever let me catch you pointing that gun at anybody again," he said.

I wished my father was a devil from hell. I sounded out Calpurnia[6] on the subject. "Mr. Finch? Why, he can do lots of things."

"Like what?" I asked.

Calpurnia scratched her head. "Well, I don't rightly know," she said.

Jem underlined it when he asked Atticus if he was going out for the Methodists and Atticus said he'd break his neck if he did, he was just too old for that sort of thing. The Methodists were trying to pay off their church mortgage, and had challenged the Baptists to a game of touch football. Everybody in town's father was playing, it seemed, except Atticus. Jem said he didn't even want to go, but he was unable to resist football in any form, and he stood gloomily on the sidelines with Atticus and me watching Cecil Jacobs' father make touchdowns for the Baptists.

One Saturday Jem and I decided to go exploring with our air rifles to see if we could find a rabbit or a squirrel. We had gone about five hundred yards beyond the Radley Place

---

5. **jew's-harp:** a musical instrument held between the teeth and plucked with a finger.

6. **Calpurnia:** the family's housekeeper. The children's mother is dead.

when I noticed Jem squinting at something down the street. He had turned his head to one side and was looking out of the corners of his eyes.

"Whatcha looking at?"

"That old dog down yonder," he said.

"That's old Tim Johnson, ain't it?"

"Yeah."

Tim Johnson was the property of Mr. Harry Johnson, who drove the Mobile bus and lived on the southern edge of town. Tim was a liver-colored bird dog, the pet of Maycomb.

"What's he doing?"

"I don't know, Scout. We better go home."

"Aw Jem, it's February."

"I don't care, I'm gonna tell Cal."

We raced home and ran to the kitchen.

"Cal," said Jem, "can you come down the sidewalk a minute?"

"What for, Jem? I can't come down the sidewalk every time you want me."

"There's somethin' wrong with an old dog down yonder."

Calpurnia sighed. "I can't wrap up any dog's foot now. There's some gauze in the bathroom, go get it and do it yourself."

Jem shook his head. "He's sick, Cal. Something's wrong with him."

"What's he doin', trying to catch his tail?"

"No, he's doin' like this."

Jem gulped like a goldfish, hunched his shoulders and twitched his torso. "He's goin' like that, only not like he means to."

"Are you telling me a story, Jem Finch?" Calpurnia's voice hardened.

"No Cal, I swear I'm not."

"Was he runnin'?"

"No, he's just moseyin' along, so slow you can't hardly tell it. He's comin' this way."

Calpurnia rinsed her hands and followed Jem into the yard. "I don't see any dog," she said.

She followed us beyond the Radley Place and looked where Jem pointed. Tim Johnson was not much more than a speck in the distance, but he was closer to us. He walked erratically, as if his right legs were shorter than his left legs. He reminded me of a car stuck in a sand bed.

"He's gone lopsided," said Jem.

Calpurnia stared, then grabbed us by the shoulders and ran us home. She shut the wood door behind us, went to the telephone and shouted, "Gimme Mr. Finch's office!"

"Mr. Finch!" she shouted. "This is Cal. I swear . . . there's a mad dog down the street a piece—he's comin' this way, yes sir, he's—Mr. Finch, I declare he is—old Tim Johnson, yes sir . . . yessir . . . yes—"

She hung up and shook her head when we tried to ask her what Atticus had said. She rattled the telephone hook and said, "Miss Eula May—now ma'am, I'm through talkin' to Mr. Finch, please don't connect me no more—listen, Miss Eula May, can you call Miss Rachel and Miss Stephanie Crawford and whoever's got a phone on this street and tell 'em a mad dog's comin'? Please ma'am!"

Calpurnia listened. "I know it's February, Miss Eula May, but I know a mad dog when I see one. Please ma'am hurry!"

Calpurnia asked Jem, "Radleys got a phone?"

Jem looked in the book and said no. "They won't come out anyway, Cal."

"I don't care, I'm gonna tell 'em."

She ran to the front porch, Jem and I at her heels. "You stay in that house!" she yelled.

Calpurnia's message had been received by the neighborhood. Every wood door within our range of vision was closed tight. We saw no trace of Tim Johnson. We watched Calpurnia running toward the Radley Place, holding her skirt and apron above her knees. She went up to the front steps and banged on the door. She got no answer, and she shouted,

"Mr. Nathan, Mr. Arthur, mad dog's comin'! Mad dog's comin'!"

"She's supposed to go around in back," I said.

Jem shook his head. "Don't make any difference now," he said.

Calpurnia pounded on the door in vain. No one acknowledged her warning; no one seemed to have heard it.

As Calpurnia sprinted to the back porch a black Ford swung into the driveway. Atticus and Mr. Heck Tate got out.

Mr. Heck Tate was the sheriff of Maycomb County. He was as tall as Atticus, but thinner. He was long-nosed, wore boots with shiny metal eyeholes, boot pants and a lumber jacket. His belt had a row of bullets sticking in it. He carried a heavy rifle. When he and Atticus reached the porch, Jem opened the door.

"Stay inside, son," said Atticus. "Where is he, Cal?"

"He oughta be here by now," said Calpurnia, pointing down the street.

"Not runnin', is he?" asked Mr. Tate.

"Naw sir, he's in the twitchin' stage, Mr. Heck."

"Should we go after him, Heck?" asked Atticus.

"We better wait, Mr. Finch. They usually go in a straight line, but you never can tell. He might follow the curve — hope he does or he'll go straight in the Radley backyard. Let's wait a minute."

"Don't think he'll get in the Radley yard," said Atticus. "Fence'll stop him. He'll probably follow the road. . . ."

I thought mad dogs foamed at the mouth, galloped, leaped and lunged at throats, and I thought they did it in August. Had Tim Johnson behaved thus, I would have been less frightened.

Nothing is more deadly than a deserted, waiting street. The trees were still, the mockingbirds were silent, the carpenters at Miss Maudie's house had vanished. I heard Mr. Tate sniff, then blow his nose. I saw him shift his gun to the crook of his arm. I saw Miss Stephanie Crawford's face framed in the glass window of her front door. Miss Maudie appeared and stood beside her. Atticus put his foot on the rung of a chair and rubbed his hand slowly down the side of his thigh.

"There he is," he said softly.

Tim Johnson came into sight, walking dazedly in the inner rim of the curve parallel to the Radley house.

"Look at him," whispered Jem. "Mr. Heck said they walked in a straight line. He can't even stay in the road."

"He looks more sick than anything," I said.

"Let anything get in front of him and he'll come straight at it."

Mr. Tate put his hand to his forehead and leaned forward. "He's got it all right, Mr. Finch."

Tim Johnson was advancing at a snail's pace, but he was not playing or sniffing at foliage: he seemed dedicated to one course and motivated by an invisible force that was inching him toward us. We could see him shiver like a horse shedding flies; his jaw opened and shut; he was alist, but he was being pulled gradually toward us.

"He's lookin' for a place to die," said Jem.

Mr. Tate turned around. "He's far from dead, Jem, he hasn't got started yet."

Tim Johnson reached the side street that ran in front of the Radley Place, and what remained of his poor mind made him pause and seem to consider which road he would take. He made a few hesitant steps and stopped in front of the Radley gate; then he tried to turn around, but was having difficulty.

Atticus said, "He's within range, Heck. You

A still from the movie *To Kill a Mockingbird*.
© 1962 Universal Pictures Company, Inc.

better get him now before he goes down the side street—Lord knows who's around the corner. Go inside, Cal."

Calpurnia opened the screen door, latched it behind her, then unlatched it and held onto the hook. She tried to block Jem and me with her body, but we looked out from beneath her arms.

"Take him, Mr. Finch." Mr. Tate handed the rifle to Atticus; Jem and I nearly fainted.

"Don't waste time, Heck," said Atticus. "Go on."

"Mr. Finch, this is a one-shot job."

Atticus shook his head vehemently: "Don't just stand there, Heck! He won't wait all day for you——"

" . . . Mr. Finch, look where he is! Miss and you'll go straight into the Radley house! I can't shoot that well and you know it!"

"I haven't shot a gun in thirty years——"

Mr. Tate almost threw the rifle at Atticus. "I'd feel mighty comfortable if you did now," he said.

In a fog, Jem and I watched our father take the gun and walk out into the middle of the street. He walked quickly, but I thought he moved like an underwater swimmer: time had slowed to a nauseating crawl.

When Atticus raised his glasses Calpurnia murmured, "Sweet Jesus help him," and put her hands to her cheeks.

Atticus pushed his glasses to his forehead; they slipped down, and he dropped them in the street. In the silence, I heard them crack. Atticus rubbed his eyes and chin; we saw him blink hard.

In front of the Radley gate, Tim Johnson had made up what was left of his mind. He had finally turned himself around, to pursue his original course up our street. He made two steps forward, then stopped and raised his head. We saw his body go rigid.

With movements so swift they seemed si-multaneous, Atticus' hand yanked a ball-tipped lever as he brought the gun to his shoulder.

The rifle cracked. Tim Johnson leaped, flopped over and crumpled on the sidewalk in a brown-and-white heap. He didn't know what hit him.

Mr. Tate jumped off the porch and ran to the Radley Place. He stopped in front of the dog, squatted, turned around and tapped his finger on his forehead above his left eye. "You were a little to the right, Mr. Finch," he called.

"Always was," answered Atticus. "If I had my 'druthers I'd take a shotgun."

He stooped and picked up his glasses, ground the broken lenses to powder under his heel, and went to Mr. Tate and stood looking down at Tim Johnson.

Doors opened one by one, and the neighborhood slowly came alive. Miss Maudie walked along the steps with Miss Stephanie Crawford.

Jem was paralyzed. I pinched him to get him moving, but when Atticus saw us coming he called, "Stay where you are."

When Mr. Tate and Atticus returned to the yard, Mr. Tate was smiling. "I'll have Zeebo collect him," he said. "You haven't forgot much, Mr. Finch. They say it never leaves you."

Atticus was silent.

"Atticus?" said Jem.

"Yes?"

"Nothin'."

"I saw that, One-Shot Finch!"

Atticus wheeled around and faced Miss Maudie. They looked at one another without saying anything, and Atticus got into the sheriff's car. "Come here," he said to Jem. "Don't you go near that dog, you understand? Don't go near him, he's just as dangerous dead as alive."

"Yes, sir," said Jem. "Atticus——"

"What, son?"

"Nothing."

"What's the matter with you, boy, can't you talk?" said Mr. Tate, grinning at Jem. "Didn't you know your daddy's——"

"Hush, Heck," said Atticus, "let's go back to town."

When they drove away, Jem and I went to Miss Stephanie's front steps. We sat waiting for Zeebo to arrive in the garbage truck.

Jem sat in numb confusion, and Miss Stephanie said, "Uh, uh, uh, who'da thought of a mad dog in February? Maybe he wadn't mad, maybe he was just crazy. I'd hate to see Harry Johnson's face when he gets in from the Mobile run and finds Atticus Finch's shot his dog. Bet he was just full of fleas from some-where——"

Miss Maudie said Miss Stephanie'd be sing-ing a different tune if Tim Johnson was still coming up the street, that they'd find out soon enough, they'd send his head to Mont-gomery.

Jem became vaguely articulate: "'d you see him, Scout? 'd you see him just standin' there? . . . 'n' all of a sudden he just relaxed all over, an' it looked like that gun was a part of him . . . an' he did so quick, like . . . I hafta aim for ten minutes 'fore I can hit somethin'. . . ."

Miss Maudie grinned wickedly. "Well now, Miss Jean Louise," she said, "still think your father can't do anything? Still ashamed of him?"

"Nome," I said meekly.

"Forgot to tell you the other day that be-sides playing the jew's-harp, Atticus Finch was the deadest shot in Maycomb County in his time."

"Dead shot . . ." echoed Jem.

"That's what I said, Jem Finch. Guess you'll change *your* tune now. The very idea, didn't you know his nickname was Ol' One-Shot

when he was a boy? Why, down at the Land-ing when he was coming up, if he shot fifteen times and hit fourteen doves he'd complain about wasting ammunition."

"He never said anything about that," Jem muttered.

"Never said anything about it, did he?"

"No ma'am."

"Wonder why he never goes huntin' now," I said.

"Maybe I can tell you," said Miss Maudie. "If your father's anything, he's civilized in his heart. Marksmanship's a gift of God, a talent —oh, you have to practice to make it perfect, but shootin's different from playing the piano or the like. I think maybe he put his gun down when he realized that God had given him an unfair advantage over most living things. I guess he decided he wouldn't shoot till he had to, and he had to today."

"Looks like he'd be proud of it," I said.

"People in their right minds never take pride in their talents," said Miss Maudie.

We saw Zeebo drive up. He took a pitchfork from the back of the garbage truck and gingerly lifted Tim Johnson. He pitched the dog onto the truck, then poured something from a gallon jug on and around the spot where Tim fell. "Don't yawl come over here for a while," he called.

When we went home I told Jem we'd really have something to talk about at school on Monday. Jem turned on me.

"Don't say anything about it, Scout," he said.

"What? I certainly am. Ain't everybody's daddy the deadest shot in Maycomb County."

Jem said, "I reckon if he'd wanted us to know it, he'da told us. If he was proud of it, he'da told us."

"Maybe it just slipped his mind," I said.

"Naw, Scout, it's something you wouldn't understand. Atticus is real old, but I wouldn't care if he couldn't do anything—I wouldn't care if he couldn't do a blessed thing."

Jem picked up a rock and threw it jubilantly at the carhouse. Running after it, he called back: "Atticus is a gentleman, just like me!"

SEEKING MEANING

1. At the opening of the selection, Scout and Jem are disappointed that their father, Atticus, isn't more like their schoolmates' fathers. What are some of the things they wish their father could do?

2. Why are Scout and Jem surprised when they see Heck Tate, the sheriff, hand his rifle to Atticus? Why does the sheriff tell Atticus that this is a "one-shot job"?

3. How did Atticus get the nickname "Ol' One-Shot"?

4. After Atticus shoots the mad dog, Scout and Jem see their father in a new light. Scout wants to brag about Atticus' talent, but Jem has a different reaction. Why does he tell Scout not to mention the shooting? What has he learned to admire in Atticus?

5. Why do you think Atticus never told his children about his skill as a marksman? Consider what you have learned about his attitude toward guns throughout the selection.

DEVELOPING SKILLS IN READING

Noting Details That Reveal Character
At the opening of the story, you know what Scout and her brother think of their father. They believe that Atticus is "feeble" and has no accomplishments they can be proud of. By the end of the selection, however, you know how wrong they have been. You have been able to form a different opinion of Atticus from what he says and does and from what other characters say about him.

Atticus is not a "feeble" man, as Scout believes at first, but a *gentle* man who dislikes violence. How is this characteristic revealed through Atticus' speech and actions? How is it revealed by what other characters say about him? What does Atticus do that shows that he is brave? How do you learn that Atticus is modest about his accomplishments?

DEVELOPING VOCABULARY

Adding Different Meanings with *in-*

Scout says that she and her brother wanted Atticus to remain *inconspicuous*. Because they were not proud of Atticus' accomplishments, they did not want him to draw attention to himself.

Conspicuous people attract attention. People who are *inconspicuous* are just the opposite—they do not attract attention. Adding the negative prefix *in-* reverses the meaning of the word *conspicuous*.

See how the addition of *in-* changes the meaning of the following words.

activity	correct	secure
inactivity	incorrect	insecure

In these words, the prefix *in-* means "not" or "without." What pairs can you add to the list?

The prefix *in-* does not always add the meaning "not" or "without" to a word. The prefix *in-* can also mean "in." Decide which meaning the prefix has in each of these words:

inability	input	intake
incomplete	insane	invisible

DEVELOPING SKILLS OF EXPRESSION

Narrating Events in Order

Narrative is another word for *story*. A narrative relates a series of events. In most narratives, the events are presented in *chronological order*, or the order in which they happen. Scout tells the events that lead up to the shooting of the dog in chronological order. Notice how she builds up to the most exciting part of the narrative by reporting every detail she witnesses from the moment Atticus takes the gun until he raises it to shoot.

In a fog, Jem and I watched our father take the gun and walk out into the middle of the street. He walked quickly, but I thought he moved like an underwater swimmer: time had slowed to a nauseating crawl.

When Atticus raised his glasses Calpurnia murmured, "Sweet Jesus help him," and put her hands to her cheeks.

Atticus pushed his glasses to his forehead; they slipped down, and he dropped them in the street. In the silence, I heard them crack. Atticus rubbed his eyes and chin; we saw him blink hard.

In front of the Radley gate, Tim Johnson had made up what was left of his mind. He had finally turned himself around, to pursue his original course up our street. He made two steps forward, then stopped and raised his head. We saw his body go rigid.

With movements so swift they seemed simultaneous, Atticus' hand yanked a ball-tipped lever as he brought the gun to his shoulder.

Write a narrative based on a series of events you have witnessed or heard about. Narrate the events in chronological order.

ABOUT THE AUTHOR

Harper Lee (1926–   ), whose family is related to Robert E. Lee, lived in Alabama as a child. Her novel *To Kill a Mockingbird* was one of the most widely acclaimed books of the 1960's. It won many awards, including the 1961 Pulitzer Prize. The action of the book covers three years in the life of Scout Finch and her older brother, Jem, who live in a small Alabama town during the Depression of the 1930's. Scout's experiences are based on Harper Lee's recollections of life in the South.

Those Winter Sundays   *Robert Hayden*

Sundays too my father got up early
and put his clothes on in the blueblack cold,
then with cracked hands that ached
from labor in the weekday weather made
banked fires° blaze. No one ever thanked him.   5   **5. banked fires:** fires kept burning low.

I'd wake and hear the cold splintering, breaking.
When the rooms were warm, he'd call,
and slowly I would rise and dress,
fearing the chronic angers of that house,

Speaking indifferently to him,   10
who had driven out the cold
and polished my good shoes as well.
What did I know, what did I know
of love's austere and lonely offices?

SEEKING MEANING

1. Which lines tell you the father worked hard on weekdays?

2. As a child, the poet feared "the chronic angers" in his house. *Chronic* means "constant" or "recurring." What do you think the phrase "chronic angers" refers to?

3. The word *austere* in line 14 means "requiring sacrifice or self-denial." Which details in the poem explain why the father's "offices," or duties, could be called "austere"? Which details explain why they could be called "lonely"?

4. In the last two lines, the poet indicates that as a child he failed to understand his father's expressions of love. What might have happened in the course of time to make him understand and appreciate his father's sacrifices?

DEVELOPING SKILLS IN READING

Responding to Images in Poetry

In line 2 of "Those Winter Sundays," Hayden uses the phrase "blueblack cold." What does this phrase suggest to you about winter mornings?

The phrase "blueblack cold" is an *image.* An image represents something that you can experience through your senses. The image "blueblack cold" summons up dark, chilling winter mornings. You can *see* and even *feel* what such mornings are like. An image may also help you *smell, taste,* or *hear* something—in your imagination, of course.

In contrast to the image of "blueblack cold," Hayden uses an image of heat in line 5. We are told that the father made "banked fires blaze." What do you see happening to the low-burning fires?

Love is often described as "warmth," and lack of love or indifference as "coldness." In what way does the contrast between *warm* and *cold* also apply to the feelings of people in the poem?

ABOUT THE AUTHOR

Robert Hayden (1913–1980), a prize-winning poet and a teacher, grew up in Detroit. One summer when he was in high school, he began reading the works of the poets Edna St. Vincent Millay and Countee Cullen. It was then that he began applying himself seriously to writing poetry, spending hours struggling to get his own thoughts down on paper.

Hayden once said this about his poem "Those Winter Sundays": "It is a sad poem, and one that I had to write. . . . The last stanza —oh, it's full of regret. Many people have told me this poem expresses their own feelings exactly. . . . It seems to speak to all people, as I certainly want my poems to do."

*Katrin was sure of what
she wanted as a graduation
present until she discovered
that there was something
she valued much more.*

Mama and the Graduation Present

Kathryn Forbes

During the last week that Papa was in the hospital, we rented the big downstairs bedroom to two brothers, Mr. Sam and Mr. George Stanton.

The Stantons worked in the office of the Gas and Electric Company, and they paid a whole month's rent in advance, which was a very good thing for us. They were nice young men, and after dinner every night they would come out to the kitchen to tell Mama how much they enjoyed her cooking.

After they got better acquainted with Miss Durant,[1] they teased her about her "rabbit food" and made bets with each other as to which one of them would be the first to coax her to eat a big, thick steak—medium rare.

Mama was very proud of her three boarders; she listened to their chattering and laughter and said it was going to be fine when we had the hospital bills paid up and the money back to the Aunts. Then we would get more furniture and more boarders. Enough to fill all the chairs in the dining room. The Stanton

brothers said they knew two more men from their place who would like to board with us.

On the day that Papa came home from the hospital, it was like a big party. We all stayed home from school, and Mama let Dagmar[2] decorate the table real fancy.

Everything seemed all right again when Papa walked carefully into the kitchen and sat down in the rocking chair. His face was white, and he looked thinner, but his smile was just the same. He had a bandage on his head, and he made little jokes about how they shaved off his hair when he wasn't looking.

It was strange having Papa about the house during the day, but it was nice, too. He would be there in the kitchen when I came home from school, and I would tell him all that had happened.

Winford School had become the most important thing in life to me. I was finally friends with the girls, and Carmelita[3] and I were invited to all their parties. Every other Wednesday they came to my house, and we

---

1. **Miss Durant:** one of the family's boarders. She eats only raw vegetables.

2. **Dagmar:** Katrin has two younger sisters, Christine and Dagmar, and an older brother, Nels.
3. **Carmelita:** a friend of Katrin's.

would sit up in my attic, drink chocolate, eat cookies, and make plans about our graduation.

We discussed "High" and vowed that we would stay together all through the next four years. We were the only ones in our class going on to Lowell. Lowell, we told each other loftily, was "academic."

We were enthralled with our superiority. *We* were going to be the first class at Winford to have evening graduation exercises; *we* were having a graduation play; *we* were making our own graduation dresses in sewing class.

And when I was given the second lead in the play—the part of the Grecian boy—I found my own great importance hard to bear. I alone, of all the girls, had to go downtown to the costumer's to rent a wig. A coarse black wig that smelled of disinfectant, but made me feel like Geraldine Farrar.[4] At every opportunity, I would put it on and have Papa listen to my part of the play.

Then the girls started talking about graduation presents.

Madeline said that she was getting an onyx ring with a small diamond. Hester was getting a real honest-to-goodness wristwatch, and Thyra's family was going to add seven pearls to the necklace they had started for her when she was a baby. Even Carmelita was getting something special; her sister Rose was putting a dollar every payday onto an ivory manicure set.

I was intrigued, and wondered what great surprise my family had in store for me. I talked about it endlessly, hoping for some clue. It would be terrible if my present were not as nice as the rest.

"It is the custom, then," Mama asked, "the giving of gifts when one graduates?"

"My goodness, Mama," I said, "it's practically the most important time in a girl's life—when she graduates."

I had seen a beautiful pink celluloid dresser set at Mr. Schiller's drugstore, and I set my heart upon it. I dropped hint after hint, until Nels took me aside and reminded me that we did not have money for that sort of thing. Had I forgotten that the Aunts and the hospital must be paid up? That just as soon as Papa was well enough, he must do the Beauchamp job[5] for no pay?

"I don't care," I cried recklessly. "I *must* have a graduation present. Why, Nels, think how I will feel if I don't get any. When the girls ask me—"

Nels got impatient and said he thought I was turning into a spoiled brat. And I retorted that since he was a boy, he naturally couldn't be expected to understand certain things.

When Mama and I were alone one day, she asked me how I would like her silver brooch for a graduation present. Mama thought a lot of that brooch—it had been her mother's.

"Mama," I said reasonably, "what in the world would I want an old brooch for?"

"It would be like a—an heirloom, Katrin. It was your grandmother's."

"No, thank you, Mama."

"I could polish it up, Katrin."

I shook my head. "Look, Mama, a graduation present is something like—well, like that beautiful dresser set in Mr. Schiller's window."

There, now, I had told. Surely, with such a hint—

Mama looked worried, but she didn't say anything. Just pinned the silver brooch back on her dress.

---

4. **Geraldine Farrar:** a famous opera singer.

5. **Beauchamp job:** To help pay for his operation, Papa has arranged to work on Dr. Beauchamp's house.

I was so sure that Mama would find some way to get me the dresser set that I bragged to the girls as if it were a sure thing. I even took them by Schiller's window to admire it. They agreed with me that it was wonderful. There were a comb, a brush, a mirror, a pincushion, a clothes brush, and even something called a hair receiver.

Graduation night was a flurry of excitement.

I didn't forget a single word of my part in the play. Flushed and triumphant, I heard Miss Scanlon say that I was every bit as good as Hester, who had taken elocution lessons for years. And when I went up to the platform for my diploma, the applause for me was long and loud. Of course, the Aunts and Uncles were all there, and Uncle Ole and Uncle Peter could clap very loud, but I pretended that it was because I was so popular.

And when I got home—there was the pink celluloid dresser set!

Mama and Papa beamed at my delight, but Nels and Christine, I noticed, didn't say anything. I decided that they were jealous, and I felt sorry that they would not join me in my joy.

I carried the box up to my attic and placed the comb and brush carefully on my dresser. It took me a long while to arrange everything to my satisfaction. The mirror, so. The pincushion, here. The hair receiver, there.

Mama let me sleep late the next morning. When I got down for breakfast, she had already gone downtown to do her shopping. Nels was reading the want-ad section of the paper. Since it was vacation, he was going to try to get a job. He read the jobs aloud to Papa, and they discussed each one.

After my breakfast, Christine and I went upstairs to make the beds. I made her wait while I ran up to my attic to look again at my wonderful present. Dagmar came with me, and when she touched the mirror, I scolded her so hard she started to cry.

Christine came up then and wiped Dagmar's tears and sent her down to Papa. She looked at me for a long time.

"Why do you look at me like that, Christine?"

"What do you care? You got what you wanted, didn't you?" She pointed to the dresser set. "Trash," she said, "cheap trash."

"Don't you *dare* talk about my lovely present like that! You're jealous, that's what. I'll tell Mama on you."

"And while you're telling her," Christine said, "ask her what she did with her silver brooch. The one her very own mother gave her. Ask her that."

I looked at Christine with horror. "What? You mean— Did Mama—?"

Christine walked away.

I grabbed up the dresser set and ran down the stairs to the kitchen. Papa was drinking his second cup of coffee, and Dagmar was playing with her doll in front of the stove. Nels had left.

"Papa, oh, Papa!" I cried. "Did Mama— Christine says—" I started to cry then, and Papa had me sit on his lap.

"There now," he said, and patted my shoulder. "There now."

And he dipped a cube of sugar into his coffee and fed it to me. We were not allowed to drink coffee—even with lots of milk in it— until we were considered grown-up, but all of us children loved that occasional lump of sugar dipped in coffee.

After my hiccuping and sobbing had stopped, Papa talked to me very seriously. It was like this, he said. I had wanted the graduation present. Mama had wanted my happiness more than she had wanted the silver brooch. So she had traded it to Mr. Schiller for the dresser set.

"But I never wanted her to do that, Papa. If I had known—I would never have let her——"

"It was what Mama wanted to do, Katrin."

"But she *loved* it so. It was all she had of Grandmother's."

"She always meant it for you, Katrin."

I stood up slowly. I knew what I must do.

And all the way up to Mr. Schiller's drugstore, the graduation present in my arms, I thought of how hard it must have been for Mama to ask Mr. Schiller to take the brooch as payment. It was never easy for Mama to talk to strangers.

Mr. Schiller examined the dresser set with care. He didn't know, he said, about taking it back. After all, a bargain was a bargain, and he had been thinking of giving the brooch to his wife for her birthday next month.

Recklessly, I mortgaged my vacation.

If he would take back the dresser set, if he would give me back the brooch, I would come in and work for him every single day, even Saturdays.

"I'll shine the showcases," I begged. "I'll sweep the floor for you."

Mr. Schiller said that would not be necessary. Since I wanted the brooch back so badly, he would call the deal off. But if I was serious about working during vacation, he might be able to use me.

So I walked out of Mr. Schiller's drugstore not only with Mama's brooch, but also with a

job that started the next morning. I felt very proud. The dresser set suddenly seemed a childish and silly thing.

I put the brooch on the table in front of Papa.

He looked at me proudly. "Was it so hard to do, Daughter?"

"Not so hard as I thought." I pinned the brooch on my dress. "I'll wear it always," I said. "I'll keep it forever."

"Mama will be glad, Katrin."

Papa dipped a lump of sugar and held it out to me. I shook my head. "Somehow," I said, "I just don't feel like it, Papa."

"So?" Papa said. "So?"

And he stood up and poured out a cup of coffee and handed it to me.

"For me?" I asked wonderingly.

Papa smiled and nodded. "For my grown-up daughter," he said.

I sat up straight in my chair. And felt very proud as I drank my first cup of coffee.

SEEKING MEANING

1. When Katrin learns about the graduation presents her friends will receive, she chooses a pink celluloid dresser set as her gift. Why is this present so important to her?

2. Why does Katrin feel that the brooch is not a suitable graduation present?

3. How does Mama pay for the dresser set? What does she value more than the silver brooch?

4. How does Katrin get the brooch back? What does she value more than the dresser set?

5. At the end of the story, Papa offers Katrin a cup of coffee, a drink reserved for adults in their family. How has Katrin grown up?

DEVELOPING VOCABULARY

Analyzing Words from Latin

Katrin's friend Carmelita is promised a manicure set as a graduation present. The word *manicure* comes from the Latin words *manus,* meaning "hand," and *cura,* meaning "care." The word *manicure* refers to the care of hands and fingernails.

Several English words come from the Latin word *manus.* What is the connection of each word in the following list with the meaning "hand"? Use a dictionary to check your answers.

manifest   manipulate   manuscript

The word *graduation* is related to the Latin word *gradus,* which means "step" or "rank." How is each word in the following list related to the meaning "step"? Check your answers in a dictionary.

centigrade   degrade   graduation

DEVELOPING SKILLS OF EXPRESSION

Writing Dialogue

A writer frequently lets characters speak for themselves. Here is the scene in which Christine strikes out at Katrin:

"Why do you look at me like that, Christine?"

"What do you care? You got what you wanted, didn't you?" She pointed to the dresser set. "Trash," she said, "cheap trash."

"Don't you *dare* talk about my lovely present like that! You're jealous, that's what. I'll tell Mama on you."

"And while you're telling her," Christine said, "ask her what she did with her silver brooch. The one her very own mother gave her. Ask her that."

I looked at Christine with horror. "What? You mean— Did Mama—?"

This *dialogue,* or conversation, is realistic. The characters are speaking naturally. They do not always use complete sentences. Where do you find the characters using incomplete sentences or breaking off their own thoughts?

You are told on page 113 that Mama went to Mr. Schiller to exchange the brooch for the dresser set. This is an important point in the story, but you are not told what the characters said to each other. Write the dialogue that might have taken place between Mama and Mr. Schiller. Make the dialogue reveal what the two people are feeling. We know that this must have been a difficult and painful experience for Mama. How did Mr. Schiller react? Was he annoyed with Mama, or did he understand her?

The Courage That My Mother Had

Edna St. Vincent Millay

The courage that my mother had
Went with her, and is with her still:
Rock from New England quarried;°
Now granite in a granite hill.

The golden brooch my mother wore   5
She left behind for me to wear;
I have no thing I treasure more:
Yet, it is something I could spare.

Oh, if instead she'd left to me
The thing she took into the grave!—   10
That courage like a rock, which she
Has no more need of, and I have.

3. **quarried:** dug from a pit.

SEEKING MEANING

1. In what way is courage like a rock? What does this comparison suggest about the mother's character?

2. Which line suggests that the mother's character was formed by the land where she was born? Explain your answer.

3. The word *granite* appears twice in line 4. What is the granite that is now buried in a "granite hill"?

4. Why does the poet feel that her mother's courage would have been a greater gift than the golden brooch?

ABOUT THE AUTHOR

Edna St. Vincent Millay (1892–1950) began writing poetry in her childhood. She published "Renascence," a long poem that expressed delight in the world of nature, when she was only nineteen. Her first volume of poetry came out in 1917, the year she graduated from Vassar College. Readers were attracted to the intensity of feeling and highly personal tone in her work. By the 1920's she was recognized as a major American poet. Her volume *The Harp-Weaver and Other Poems* won the Pulitzer Prize in 1923.

Sled

Thomas E. Adams

All the adventure of the night and snow lay before him: if only he could get out of the house.

"You can't go out," his mother said, "until you learn how to act like a gentleman. Now apologize to your sister."

He stared across the table at his sister.

"Go on," his mother said.

His sister was watching her plate. He could detect the trace of a smile at the corners of her mouth.

"I won't! She's laughing at me!" He saw the smile grow more pronounced. "Besides, she *is* a liar!"

His sister did not even bother to look up, and he felt from looking at her that he had said exactly what she had wanted him to say. He grew irritated at his stupidity.

"That settles it," his mother said calmly, without turning from the stove. "No outs for you."

He stared at his hands, his mind in a panic. He could feel the smile on his sister's face. His hand fumbled with the fork on his plate. "No," he said meekly, prodding a piece of meat with the fork. "I'll apologize."

His sister looked up at him innocently.

"Well?" said his mother. "Go on."

He took a deep breath. "I'm . . ." He met his sister's gaze. "I'm sorry!" But it came out too loudly, he knew.

"He is not," his sister said.

He clenched his teeth and pinched his legs with his fingers. "I am too," he said. It sounded good, he knew; and it was half over.

He had control now, and he relaxed a bit and even said further: "I'm sorry I called you a liar."

"That's better," his mother said. "You two should love each other. Not always be fighting."

He paused strategically for a long moment.

"Can I go out now?"

"Yes," his mother said.

He rose from the table glaring at his sister with a broad grin, calling her a liar with his eyes.

His hand plucked his jacket from the couch and swirled it around his back. The buttons refused to fit through the holes, so he let them go in despair. He sat down just long enough to pull on his shiny black rubbers. Finally he put on his gloves. Then with four proud strides he arrived at the door and reached for the knob.

"Put your hat on," his mother said without looking at him.

His face toward the door, screwed and tightened with disgust. "Aw, Ma."

"Put it on."

"Aw, Ma, it's not that cold."

"Put it on."

"Honest, Ma, it's not that cold out."

"Are you going to put your hat on, or are you going to stay and help with the dishes?"

He sighed. "All right," he said. "I'll put it on."

The door to the kitchen closed on his back and he was alone in the cold gloom of the shed. Pale light streamed through the frosted window and fell against the wall where the

sled stood. The dark cold room was silent, and he was free. He moved into the shaft of light and stopped, when from the kitchen he heard the muffled murmur of his mother's voice, as if she were far away. He listened. The murmuring hushed, and he was alone again.

The sled. It was leaning against the wall, its varnished wood glistening in the moonlight. He moved closer to it and saw his shadow block the light, and he heard the cold cracking of the loose linoleum beneath his feet.

He picked it up. He felt the smooth wood slippery in his gloved hands. The thin steel runners shone blue in the light as he moved one finger along the polished surface to erase any dust. He shifted the sled in his hands and stood getting the feel of its weight the way he had seen his brother hold a rifle. He gripped the sled tightly, aware of the strength in his arms; and he felt proud to be strong and alone and far away with the sled in the dark cold silent room.

The sled was small and light. But strong. And when he ran with it, he ran very quickly, quicker than anyone, because it was very light and small and not bulky like other sleds. And when he ran with it, he carried it as if it were part of him, as if he carried nothing in his arms. He set the rear end on the floor, now, and let the sled lean against him, his hands on the steering bar. He pushed down on the bar and the thin runners curved gracefully because they were made of shiny blue flexible steel; and with them he could turn sharply in the snow, sharper than anyone. It was the best sled. It was his.

He felt a slight chill in the cold room, and in the moonlight he saw his breath in vapor rising like cigarette smoke before his eyes. His body shivered with excitement as he moved hurriedly but noiselessly to the door. He flung it open; and the snow blue and sparkling, and the shadows deep and mysterious, the air silent and cold, all awaited him.

gutters stood enormous heaps of snow, pale dark in the shadows, stretching away from him like a string of mountains. He moved out of the shadows, between two piles of snow, and into the center of the street, where he stood for a moment gazing down the white road that gradually grew darker until it melted into the gloom at the far end.

Then he started to trot slowly down the street. Slowly, slowly gaining speed without losing balance. Faster he went now, watching the snow glide beneath his shiny black rubbers. Faster and faster, but stiffly, don't slip. Don't fall, don't fall: now! And his body plunged downward, and the sled whacked in the quiet, and the white close to his eyes was flying beneath him as he felt the thrill of gliding alone along a shadowy street, with only the ski-sound of the sled in the packed snow. Then before his eyes the moving snow gradually slowed. And stopped. And he heard only the low sound of the wind and his breath.

Up again and start the trot. He moved to the beating sound of his feet along the ground. His breath came heavily and quickly, and matched the rhythm of his pumping legs, straining to carry the weight of his body without the balance of his arms. He reached a wild dangerous breakneck speed, and his leg muscles swelled and ached from the tension, and the fear of falling too early filled his mind: and down he let his body go. The white road rushed to meet him; he was off again, guiding the sled obliquely across the street toward a huge pile of snow near a driveway.

Squinting his eyes into the biting wind, he calculated when he would turn to avoid crashing. The pile, framed against the darkness of the sky, glistened white and shiny. It loomed larger and larger before him. He steered the sled sharply, bending the bar; and the snow flew as the sled churned sideways, and he heard suddenly a cold metallic snap.

"Joey!" From the kitchen came his mother's voice. He turned toward the kitchen door and refused to answer.

"Joseph!"

"What!" His tone was arrogant, and a chill of fear rushed through his mind.

There was a long awful silence.

"Don't you forget to be home by seven o'clock." She hadn't noticed, and his fear was gone.

"All right!" He answered, ashamed of his fear. He stepped across the threshold and closed the door. Then he removed the hat and dropped it in the snow beside the porch.

He plodded down the alley, thrilling in the cold white silence—the snow was thick. The gate creaked as he pushed it open, holding and guiding the sled through the portal. The street was white, and shiny were the icy tracks of automobiles in the lamplight above. While between him and the light the black branches of trees ticked softly, in the slight wind. In the

He and the sled went tumbling over in the hard wet snow. He rolled with it and the steering bar jarred his forehead. Then the dark sky and snow stopped turning, and all he felt was the cold air stinging the bump on his forehead.

The runner had snapped; the sled was broken. He stared at the shiny smooth runner and touched the jagged edge with his fingers. He sat in the middle of the driveway, the sled cradled in his lap, running his fingers up and down the thin runner until he came to the jagged edge where it had broken.

With his fingers he took the two broken edges and fitted them back into place. They stuck together with only a thin crooked line to indicate the split. But it was like putting a broken cup together. He stared at it, and wished it would be all right and felt like crying.

He got up and walked slowly back down to the street to his house. He sat down between the back bumper of a parked car and a pile of snowpile. Through his wet eyelids he saw the lamplight shimmering brightly against them. He felt a thickness in his throat, and he swallowed hard to remove it, but it did not go away.

He leaned back, resting his head against the snowpile. Through his wet eyelids he saw the lamplight shimmering brightly against the sky. He closed his eyes and saw again the shiny graceful curve of the runner. But it was broken now. He had bent it too far; too far. With his hand he rubbed his neck, then his eyes, then his neck again. He felt the snow coming wet through his pants. As he shifted to a new position, he heard the creaking of a gate. He turned toward the sound.

His sister was walking away from his house. He watched her move slowly across the street and into the grocery store. Through the plate-glass window he saw her talking with the storekeeper. He stared down at the runner. With his gloves off, he ran his fingers along the cold smooth surface and felt the thin breakline. He got up, brushed the snow off the seat of his pants, and walked to the gate to wait for his sister.

He saw her take a package from the man and come out of the store. She walked carefully on the smooth white, her figure dark in its own shadow as she passed beneath the streetlight, the package in her arm. When she reached the curb on his side, he rested his arms on the nose of the sled and exhaled a deep breath nervously. He pretended to be staring in the opposite direction.

When he heard her feet crunching softly in the snow, he turned: "Hi," he said.

"Hi," she said and she paused for a moment. "Good sledding?"

"Uh-huh," he said. "Just right. Snow's

packed nice and hard. Hardly any slush at all." He paused. "I'm just resting a bit now."

She nodded. "I just went for some milk."

His fingers moved slowly down the runner and touched the joined edges.

"Well . . ." she said, about to leave.

His fingers trembled slightly, and he felt his heart begin to beat rapidly: "Do you want to take a flop?" In the still night air he heard with surprise the calm sound of his voice.

Her face came suddenly alive. "Can I? I mean, will you let me? Really?"

"Sure," he said. "Go ahead." And he handed her the sled very carefully. She gave him the package.

He put the bag under his arm and watched her move out of the shadows of the trees and into the light. She started to trot slowly, awkwardly, bearing the sled. She passed directly beneath the light and then she slipped and slowed to regain her balance. The sled looked large and heavy in her arms, and seeing her awkwardness, he realized she would be hurt badly in the fall. She was moving away again, out of the reach of the streetlight, and into the gray haze farther down the road.

He moved to the curb, holding the bag tightly under his arm, hearing his heart pounding in his ears. He wanted to stop her, and he opened his mouth as if to call to her; but no sound came. It was too late: her dark figure was already starting the fall, putting the sled beneath her. Whack! And her head dipped with the front end jutting the ground, and the back of the sled and her legs rose like a seesaw and down they came with another muffled sound. The street was quiet, except for a low whimper that filled his ears.

He saw her figure rise slowly and move toward him. He walked out to meet her beneath the light. She held the sled loosely in one hand, the broken runner dangling, reflecting light as she moved.

She sobbed, and looking up he saw bright tears falling down her cheeks and a thin line of blood trickling down her chin. In the corner of her mouth near the red swelling of her lip, a little bubble of spit shone with the blood in the light.

He felt that he should say something, but he did not speak.

"I'm . . . I'm sorry," she said, and the bubble broke. "I'm sorry I . . . your sled." She looked down at the sled. "It'll never be the same."

"It'll be all right," he said. He felt that he ought to do something, but he did not move. "I can get it soldered. Don't worry about it." But he saw from her expression that she thought he was only trying to make her feel better.

"No," she said, shaking her head emphatically. "No, it won't! It'll always have that weak spot now." She began to cry very hard. "I'm sorry."

He made an awkward gesture of forgiveness with his hand. "Don't cry," he said.

She kept crying.

"It wasn't your fault," he said.

"Yes, it was," she said. "Oh, yes, it was."

"No!" he said. "No, it wasn't!" But she didn't seem to hear him, and he felt his words were useless. He sighed wearily with defeat, not knowing what to say next. He saw her glance up at him as if to see whether he were still watching her, then she quickly lowered her gaze and said with despair and anguish: "Oh . . . girls are so stupid!"

There was no sound. She was no longer crying. She was looking at the ground: waiting. His ears heard nothing; they felt only the cold silent air.

"No, they aren't," he said halfheartedly. And he heard her breathing again. He felt he had been forced to say that. In her shining eyes he saw an expression he did not understand. He wished she would go in the house.

But seeing the tears on her cheeks and the blood on her chin, he immediately regretted the thought.

She wiped her chin with her sleeve, and he winced, feeling rough cloth on an open cut. "Don't do that." His hand moved to his back pocket. "Use my handkerchief."

She waited.

The pocket was empty. "I haven't got one," he said.

Staring directly at him, she patted gingerly the swollen part of her lip with the tips of her fingers.

He moved closer to her. "Let me see," he said. With his hands he grasped her head and tilted it so that the light fell directly on the cut.

"It's not too bad," she said calmly. And as she said it she looked straight into his eyes, and he felt she was perfectly at ease; while standing that close to her, he felt clumsy and out of place.

In his hands her head was small and fragile, and her hair was soft and warm; he felt the rapid pulsing of the vein in her temple: his ears grew hot with shame.

"Maybe I better go inside and wash it off?" she asked.

With his finger he wiped the blood from her chin. "Yes," he said, feeling relieved. "You go

inside and wash it off." He took the sled and gave her the package.

He stared at the ground as they walked to the gate in silence. When they reached the curb he became aware that she was watching him.

"You've got a nasty bump on your forehead," she said.

"Yes," he said. "I fell."

"Let me put some snow on it," she said, reaching to the ground.

He caught her wrist and held it gently. "No," he said.

He saw her about to object: "It's all right. You go inside and take care of your lip." He said it softly, but with his grip and his eyes he told her more firmly.

"All right," she said after a moment, and he released his hold. "But don't forget to put your hat on."

He stared at her.

"I mean, *before* you go back in the house."

They both smiled.

"Thanks for reminding me," he said, and he dropped the sled in the snow and hurried to hold the gate open for her.

She hesitated, then smiled proudly as he beckoned her into the alley.

He watched her walk away from him down the dark alley in the gray snow. Her small figure swayed awkwardly as she stepped carefully in the deep snow, so as not to get her feet too wet. Her head was bowed, and her shoulders hunched, and he humbly felt her weakness. And he felt her cold. And he felt the snow running cold down her boots around her ankles. And though she wasn't crying now, he could still hear her low sobbing, and he saw her shining eyes and the tears falling and she trying to stop them and them falling even faster. And he wished he had never gone sledding. He wished that he had never even come out of the house tonight.

The back door closed. He turned and moved about nervously kicking at the ground. At the edge of the curb he dug his hands deep into the cold wet snow. He came up with a handful and absently began shaping and smoothing it. He stopped abruptly and dropped it as his feet.

He did not hear it fall. He was looking up at the dark sky, but he did not see it. He put his cold hands in his back pockets, but he did not feel them. He was wishing that he were some time a long time away from now and somewhere a long way away from here.

In the corner of his eye something suddenly dimmed. Across the street in the grocery store the light was out: it was seven o'clock.

SEEKING MEANING

1. At the opening of the story, Joey does not want to apologize to his sister. Why not? Why does he force himself to apologize?
2. Why does Joey feel that his sled is so special? After the runner breaks, Joey feels he is to blame. Why?
3. Why do you think Joey offers his sister a ride on the broken sled?
4. Joey's sister, believing she has broken the sled, wants her brother to forgive her. How does she apologize to Joey? Why does her behavior make her brother uncomfortable?
5. Early in the story, Joey's mother says, "You two should love each other. Not always be fighting." How do Joey and his sister show that they do care about each other after the accident with the sled? Find passages that support your answer.

DEVELOPING SKILLS IN READING

Inferring Character from Thoughts and Feelings

In addition to learning about Joey from what he says and does, you learn about him from his thoughts and feelings.

At the beginning of the story, you can tell that Joey feels humiliated. He has been forced to apologize to his sister, and he sees that she is laughing at him.

What passages reveal that the sled makes Joey feel strong and important?

When Joey breaks the sled, he feels miserable. What passage reveals his deep hurt?

At what point does Joey realize how seriously his sister might be hurt?

Where do you learn that Joey feels ashamed of tricking his sister?

How do you know that he understands his sister's feelings and sympathizes with her?

DEVELOPING VOCABULARY

Using Context Clues

While Joey was in the shed, "he heard the muffled *murmur* of his mother's voice, as if she were far away." If you were not familiar with the word *murmur*, you could use clues within the sentence to determine what it means. Other words in the sentence tell you that here the word *murmur* refers to a voice, that it is "muffled," and that it seems "far away." A *murmur* is a sound that is low and unclear.

Use context clues to figure out the meanings of the italicized words in these sentences from the story. Check your answers in a dictionary.

The gate creaked as he pushed it open, holding and guiding the sled through the *portal*.

She wiped her chin with her sleeve, and he *winced*, feeling rough cloth on an open cut.

Through his wet eyelids he saw the lamplight *shimmering* brightly against the sky.

Generally, Travis paid no attention to his brother Arliss'
screaming. Arliss would scream just to hear himself make
noise. This time was different, though. Travis knew that
Arliss was in real trouble.

Arliss and the Bear   *Fred Gipson*

That Little Arliss! If he wasn't a mess! From
the time he'd grown up big enough to get out
of the cabin, he'd made a practice of trying to
catch and keep every living thing that ran,
flew, jumped, or crawled.

Every night before Mama let him go to bed,
she'd make Arliss empty his pockets of whatever he'd captured during the day. Generally,
it would be a tangled-up mess of grasshoppers
and worms and praying bugs and little, rusty
tree lizards. One time he brought in a horned
toad that got so mad he swelled out round and
flat as a Mexican tortilla[1] and bled at the eyes.
Sometimes it was stuff like a young bird that
had fallen out of its nest before it could fly or
a green-speckled spring frog or a striped water
snake. And once he turned out of his pocket a
wadded-up baby copperhead that nearly
threw Mama into spasms. We never did figure
out why the snake hadn't bitten him, but
Mama took no more chances on snakes. She
switched Arliss hard for catching that
snake. . . .

Then, after the yeller dog came, Little
Arliss started catching even bigger game. Like
cottontail rabbits and chaparral birds[2] and a

baby possum that sulled[3] and lay like dead for
the first several hours until he finally decided
that Arliss wasn't going to hurt him.

Of course, it was Old Yeller that was doing
the catching. He'd run the game down and
turn it over to Little Arliss. Then Little Arliss
could come in and tell Mama a big fib about
how he caught it himself.

I watched them one day when they caught a
blue catfish out of Birdsong Creek. The fish
had fed out into water so shallow that his top
fin was sticking out. About the time I saw it,
Old Yeller and Little Arliss did, too. They
made a run at it. The fish went scooting away
toward deeper water, only Yeller was too fast
for him. He pounced on the fish and shut his
big mouth down over it and went romping to
the bank, where he dropped it down on the
grass and let it flop. And here came Little
Arliss to fall on it like I guess he'd been doing
everything else. The minute he got his hands
on it, the fish finned him and he went to crying.

But he wouldn't turn the fish loose. He just
grabbed it up and went running and squawl-
ing toward the house, where he gave the fish

1. **tortilla** (tôr-tē′yə): a cornmeal pancake.
2. **chaparral** (shăp′ə-răl′) **birds:** another name for road
runners. Chaparral is a thicket of thorny bushes and
small trees that grows in the Southwest.

3. **sulled:** played dead.

to Mama. His hands were all bloody by then, where the fish had finned him. They swelled up and got mighty sore; not even a mesquite[4] thorn hurts as bad as a sharp fish fin when it's run deep into your hand.

But as soon as Mama had wrapped his hands in a poultice of mashed-up prickly-pear root to draw out the poison, Little Arliss forgot all about his hurt. And that night when we ate the fish for supper, he told the biggest windy I ever heard about how he'd dived way down into a deep hole under the rocks and dragged that fish out and nearly got drowned before he could swim to the bank with it.

But when I tried to tell Mama what really happened, she wouldn't let me. "Now, this is Arliss' story," she said. "You let him tell it the way he wants to."

I told Mama then, I said: "Mama, that old yeller dog is going to make the biggest liar in Texas out of Little Arliss."

But Mama just laughed at me, like she always laughed at Little Arliss' big windies after she'd gotten off where he couldn't hear her. She said for me to let Little Arliss alone. She said that if he ever told a bigger whopper than the ones I used to tell, she had yet to hear it.

Well, I hushed then. If Mama wanted Little Arliss to grow up to be the biggest liar in Texas, I guessed it wasn't any of my business.

All of which, I figure, is what led up to Little Arliss' catching the bear. I think Mama had let him tell so many big yarns about catching live game that he'd begun to believe them himself.

When it happened, I was down the creek a ways, splitting rails to fix up the yard fence where the bulls had torn it down. I'd been down there since dinner, working in a stand of tall slim post oaks. I'd chop down a tree,

trim off the branches as far up as I wanted, then cut away the rest of the top. After that I'd start splitting the log.

I'd split the log by driving steel wedges into the wood. I'd start at the big end and hammer in a wedge with the back side of my ax. This would start a little split running lengthways of the log. Then I'd take a second wedge and drive it into this split. This would split the log further along and, at the same time, loosen the first wedge. I'd then knock the first wedge loose and move it up in front of the second one.

Driving one wedge ahead of the other like that, I could finally split a log in two halves. Then I'd go to work on the halves, splitting them apart. That way, from each log, I'd come out with four rails.

Swinging that chopping ax was sure hard work. The sweat poured off me. My back muscles ached. The ax got so heavy I could hardly swing it. My breath got harder and harder to breathe.

An hour before sundown, I was worn down to a nub. It seemed like I couldn't hit another lick. Papa could have lasted till past sundown, but I didn't see how I could. I shouldered my ax and started toward the cabin, trying to think up some excuse to tell Mama to keep her from knowing I was played clear out.

That's when I heard Little Arliss scream.

Well, Little Arliss was a screamer by nature. He'd scream when he was happy and scream when he was mad and a lot of times he'd scream just to hear himself make a noise. Generally, we paid no more mind to his screaming than we did to the gobble of a wild turkey.

But this time was different. The second I heard his screaming, I felt my heart flop clear over. This time I knew little Arliss was in real trouble.

I tore out up the trail leading toward the

---

4. **mesquite** (mĕs-kēt'): a thorny shrub.

cabin. A minute before, I'd been so tired out with my rail splitting that I couldn't have struck a trot. But now I raced through the tall trees in that creek bottom, covering ground like a scared wolf.

Little Arliss' second scream, when it came, was louder and shriller and more frantic-sounding than the first. Mixed with it was a whimpering crying sound that I knew didn't come from him. It was a sound I'd heard before and seemed like I ought to know what it was, but right then I couldn't place it.

Then, from way off to one side came a sound that I would have recognized anywhere. It was the coughing roar of a charging bear. I'd just heard it once in my life. That was the time Mama had shot and wounded a hog-killing bear, and Papa had had to finish it off with a knife to keep it from getting her.

My heart went to pushing up into my throat, nearly choking off my wind. I strained for every lick of speed I could get out of my running legs. I didn't know what sort of fix Little Arliss had got himself into, but I knew that it had to do with a mad bear, which was enough.

The way the late sun slanted through the trees had the trail all cross-banded with streaks of bright light and dark shade. I ran through these bright and dark patches so fast that the changing light nearly blinded me. Then suddenly, I raced out into the open where I could see ahead. And what I saw sent a chill clear through to the marrow of my bones.

There was Little Arliss, down in that spring hole again. He was lying half in and half out of the water, holding on to the hind leg of a little black bear cub no bigger than a small coon. The bear cub was out on the bank, whimpering and crying and clawing the rocks with all three of his other feet, trying to pull away. But

Little Arliss was holding on for all he was worth, scared now and screaming his head off. Too scared to let go.

How come the bear cub ever happened to prowl close enough for Little Arliss to grab him, I don't know. And why he didn't turn on him and bite loose, I couldn't figure out, either. Unless he was like Little Arliss, too scared to think.

But all of that didn't matter now. What mattered was the bear cub's mama. She'd heard the cries of her baby and was coming to save him. She was coming so fast that she had the brush popping and breaking as she crashed through and over it. I could see her black heavy figure piling off down the slant on the far side of Birdsong Creek. She was roaring mad and ready to kill.

And worst of all, I could see that I'd never get there in time!

Mama couldn't either. She'd heard Arliss, too, and she came from the cabin, running down the slant toward the spring, screaming at Arliss, telling him to turn the bear cub loose. But Little Arliss wouldn't do it. All he'd do was hang with that hind leg and let out one shrill shriek after another as fast as he could suck in a breath.

Now the she-bear was charging across the shallows in the creek. She was knocking sheets of water high in the bright sun, charging with her fur up and her long teeth bared, filling the canyon with that awful coughing roar. And no matter how fast Mama ran or how fast I ran, the she-bear was going to get there first!

I think I nearly went blind then, picturing what was going to happen to Little Arliss. I know that I opened my mouth to scream and not any sound came out.

Then, just as the bear went lunging up the creek bank toward Little Arliss and her cub, a flash of yellow came streaking out of the brush.

It was that big yeller dog. He was roaring like a mad bull. He wasn't one third as big and heavy as the she-bear, but when he piled into her from one side, he rolled her clear off her feet. They went down in a wild, roaring tangle of twisting bodies and scrambling feet and slashing fangs.

As I raced past them, I saw the bear lunge up to stand on her hind feet like a man while she clawed at the body of the yeller dog hanging to her throat. I didn't wait to see more. Without ever checking my stride, I ran in and jerked Little Arliss loose from the cub. I grabbed him by the wrist and yanked him up out of that water and slung him toward Mama like he was a half-empty sack of corn. I screamed at Mama. "Grab him, Mama! Grab him and run!" Then I swung my chopping ax high and wheeled, aiming to cave in the she-bear's head with the first lick.

But I never did strike. I didn't need to. Old Yeller hadn't let the bear get close enough. He couldn't handle her; she was too big and strong for that. She'd stand there on her hind feet, hunched over, and take a roaring swing at him with one of those big front claws. She'd slap him head over heels. She'd knock him so far that it didn't look like he could possibly get back there before she charged again, but he always did. He'd hit the ground rolling, yelling his head off with the pain of the blow, but somehow he'd always roll to his feet. And here he'd come again, ready to tie into her for another round.

I stood there with my ax raised, watching them for a long moment. Then from up toward the house, I heard Mama calling: "Come away from there, Travis. Hurry, Son! Run!"

That spooked me. Up till then, I'd been ready to tie into that bear myself. Now, suddenly, I was scared out of my wits again. I ran toward the cabin.

But like it was, Old Yeller nearly beat me there. I didn't see it, of course, but Mama said that the minute Old Yeller saw we were all in the clear and out of danger, he threw the fight to that she-bear and lit out for the house. The bear chased him for a little piece, but at the rate Old Yeller was leaving her behind, Mama said it looked like the bear was backing up.

But if the big yeller dog was scared or hurt in any way when he came dashing into the house, he didn't show it. He sure didn't show it like we all did. Little Arliss had hushed his

screaming, but he was trembling all over and clinging to Mama like he'd never let her go. And Mama was sitting in the middle of the floor, holding him up close and crying like she'd never stop. And me, I was close to crying, myself.

Old Yeller, though, all he did was come bounding in to jump on us and lick us in the face and bark so loud that there, inside the cabin, the noise nearly made us deaf.

The way he acted, you might have thought that bear fight hadn't been anything more than a rowdy romp that we'd all taken part in for the fun of it.

Till Little Arliss got us mixed up in that bear fight, I guess I'd been looking on him about like most boys look on their little brothers. I liked him, all right, but I didn't have a lot of use for him. What with his always playing in our drinking water and getting in the way of my chopping ax and howling his head off and chunking me with rocks when he got mad, it didn't seem to me like he was hardly worth the bother of putting up with.

But that day when I saw him in the spring, so helpless against the angry she-bear, I learned different. I knew then that I loved him as much as I did Mama and Papa, maybe in some ways even a little bit more.

So it was only natural for me to come to love the dog that saved him.

After that, I couldn't do enough for Old Yeller. What if he was a big, ugly meat-stealing rascal? What if he did fall over and yell bloody murder every time I looked crossways at him? What if he had run off when he ought to have helped with the fighting bulls? None of that made a lick of difference now. He'd pitched in and saved Little Arliss when I couldn't possibly have done it, and that was enough for me.

SEEKING MEANING

1. Arliss collects live things and puts them in his pockets. How do you know that he is too young to recognize that some creatures are dangerous?

2. Although he is cut badly by the fins of the catfish, Arliss does not let go of it. How does this incident prepare you for what later happens with the bear cub?

3. Travis is annoyed by Arliss' yarns. Why do you suppose Mama is amused rather than annoyed by Arliss' big fibs?

4. How does Old Yeller save Little Arliss?

5. When Travis sees how helpless Arliss is against the she-bear, he realizes how much he loves his brother. Why do you suppose he has been unaware of these feelings? How do Travis' feelings for Old Yeller change?

DEVELOPING SKILLS IN LANGUAGE

Using Context to Understand Expressions

The action of this story takes place more than a century ago in the Texas hill country. Travis uses a number of regional expressions that you can figure out by using context clues. For example, after he has split many logs, Travis says he feels "worn down to a nub" (page 126). When something is "worn down" it becomes smaller and smaller. Travis has been working hard and feels physically exhausted. You can guess that a "nub" must be something very small.

Locate and reread the passage in which each of the following quotations appears. Pay close attention to context. What do you think the italicized expressions mean?

"My heart *went to pushing up* into my throat, nearly choking off my wind."

". . . when he *piled into* her from one side, he rolled her clear off her feet."

". . . I'd been ready to *tie into* that bear myself."

". . . he threw the fight to that she-bear and *lit out* for the house."

". . . and howling his head off and *chunking* me with rocks when he got mad . . . ."

Caleb was expected to take care of his younger brother Leo, but he often preferred being with his own friends. He had no idea how much Leo dreaded spending those Saturday afternoons alone.

Those Saturday Afternoons

James Baldwin

I didn't like Caleb's friends because I was afraid of them. I came through the door, passing between my brother and his friends, down to the sidewalk, feeling, as they looked briefly at me and then continued joking with Caleb, what they felt: that here was Caleb's round-eyed, frail and useless sissy of a little brother. They pitied Caleb for having to take me out. On the other hand, they also wanted to go to the show, but didn't have the money. Therefore, in silence, I could crow over them even as they despised me. But this was always a terribly risky, touch-and-go business, for Caleb might always, at any moment, and with no warning, change his mind and drive me away, and, effectively, take their side against me. I always stood, those Saturday afternoons, in fear and trembling, holding on to the small shield of my bravado,[1] while waiting for Caleb to come down the steps of the stoop, to come down the steps, away from his friends, to me. I prepared myself, always, for the moment when he would turn to me, saying, "Okay, kid. You run along. I'll see you later."

---

1. **bravado** (brə-vä′dō): pretense of bravery or confidence where there is actually none.

This meant that I would have to go to the movies by myself and hang around in front of the box office, waiting for some grown-up to take me in. I could not go back upstairs, for this would be informing my mother and father that Caleb had gone off somewhere — after promising to take me to the movies. Neither could I simply hang around the block, playing with the kids on the block. For one thing, my demeanor,[2] as I came out of the house, those Saturdays, very clearly indicated that I had better things to do than play with *them;* for another, they were not terribly anxious to play with *me;* and, finally, my remaining on the block would have had exactly the same effect as my going upstairs. Someone would surely inform my father and mother, or they might simply look out of the window, or one of them would come downstairs to buy something they had forgotten while shopping. In short, to remain on the block after Caleb's dismissal was to put myself at the mercy of the block and to put Caleb at the mercy of our parents.

So I prepared myself, those Saturdays, to respond with a cool "Okay. See you later," and prepared myself then to turn indifferently away, and walk. This was surely the most terrible moment. The moment I turned away I was committed, I was trapped, and I then had miles to walk, so it seemed to me, before I would be out of sight, before the block ended and I could turn onto the avenue. I wanted to run out of that block, but I never did. I never looked back. I forced myself to walk very slowly, looking neither right nor left, trying to look neither up nor down — striving to seem at once distracted and offhand; concentrating on the cracks in the sidewalk, and

stumbling over them, trying to whistle, feeling every muscle in my body, feeling that all the block was watching me, and feeling — which was odd — that I deserved it. And then I reached the avenue, and turned, still not looking back, and was released from those eyes at least, but now faced other eyes, eyes coming toward me. These eyes were the eyes of children stronger than me, who would steal my movie money; these eyes were the eyes of cops, whom I feared; these eyes were the eyes of old folks who also thought I was a sissy and who might wonder what I was doing on this avenue by myself.

And then I got to the show. Sometimes, someone would take me in right away and sometimes I would have to wait. I looked at the posters which seemed magical indeed to me in those days. I was very struck, not altogether agreeably, by the colors. The faces of the movie stars were in red, in green, in blue, in purple, not at all like the colors of real faces and yet they looked more real than real. Or, rather, they looked like faces far from me, faces which I would never be able to decipher, faces which could be seen but never changed or touched, faces which existed only behind these doors. I don't know what I thought. Some great assault, certainly, was being made on my imagination, on my sense of reality. Caleb could draw, he was teaching me to draw, and I wondered if he could teach me to draw faces like these. I looked at the stills[3] from the show, seeing people in attitudes of danger, in attitudes of love, in attitudes of sorrow and loss. They were not like any people I had ever seen and this made them, irrevocably,[4] better. With one part of my mind, of course, I knew that here was James Cagney —

---

2. **demeanor** (dĭ-mē'nər): outward appearance.

3. **stills:** photographs taken from scenes of a film, used to attract customers.
4. **irrevocably** (ĭ-rĕv'ə-kə-blē): definitely.

holding his gun like a prize; and here was Clark Gable, all dimples, teeth, and eyes; here was Joan Crawford, gleaming with astonishment; and here was proud, quivering Katharine Hepburn, who could never be astonished; and here was poor, downtrodden Sylvia Sidney, weeping in the clutches of yet another gangster. But only the faces and the attitudes were real, more real than the lives we led, more real than our days and nights, and the names were merely brand names, like Campbell's baked beans or Kellogg's corn flakes. We went to see James Cagney because we had grown accustomed to that taste, we knew that we would like it.

But, then, I would have to turn my attention from the faces and the stills and watch the faces coming to the box office. And this was not easy, since I didn't, after all, want everyone in the neighborhood to know that I was loitering outside the movie house waiting for someone to take me in, exactly like an orphan. Eventually, I would see a face which looked susceptible[5] and which I did not know. I would rush up beside him or her—but it was usually a man, for they were less likely to be disapproving—and whisper, "Take me in," and give him my dime. Sometimes the man simply took the dime and disappeared into the movies, sometimes he gave my dime back to me and took me in, anyway. Sometimes I ended up wandering around the streets—but I couldn't wander into a strange neighborhood because I would be beaten up if I did—until I figured the show was out. It was dangerous to

5. **susceptible** (sə-sĕp′tə-bəl): likely to be sympathetic.

get home too early and, of course, it was practically lethal[6] to arrive too late. If all went well, I could cover for Caleb, saying that I had left him with some boys on the stoop. Then, if *he* came in too late and got a dressing down[7] for it, it could not be considered my fault.

Another time, it was raining and it was still too early for me to go home. I felt very, very low that day. It was one of the times that my tongue and my body refused to obey me—this happened often, when I was prey to my fantasies,[8] or overwhelmed by my real condition; and I had not been able to work up the courage to ask anyone to take me into the show. I stood there, watching people go in, watching people come out. Every once in a while, when the doors opened, I caught a glimpse of the screen—huge, black and silver, moving all the time. The ticket-taker was watching me, or so I thought, with a hostile suspicion, as though he were thinking, You just *try* to get somebody to take you in, I dare you! Actually, it's very unlikely he was thinking at all, and certainly not of me. But I walked away from the show because I could no longer bear his eyes, or anybody's eyes.

I walked the long block east from the movie house. The street was empty, black, and glittering. The globes of the streetlamps, with the water slanting both behind them and before, told me how hard the rain was falling. The water soaked through my coat at the shoulders and water dripped down my neck from my cap. I began to be afraid. I could not stay out here in the rain because then my father and mother would know I had been wandering the streets. I would get a beating, and, though Caleb was too old to get a beating, he

and my father would have a terrible fight and Caleb would blame it all on me and would not speak to me for days. I began to hate Caleb. I wondered where he was. If I had known where to find him, I would have gone to where he was and forced him, by screaming and crying even, to take me home or to take me wherever he was going. And I wouldn't have cared if he hit me, or even if he called me a sissy. Then it occurred to me that he might be in the same trouble as myself, since if I couldn't go home without *him*, he, even more surely, couldn't go home without *me*. Perhaps he was also wandering around in the rain. If he was, then, I thought, it served him right; it would serve him right if he caught pneumonia and died; and I dwelt pleasantly on this possibility for the length of the block. But at the end of the block I realized that he was probably *not* wandering around in the rain—*I* was; and I, too, might catch pneumonia and die. I started in the direction of our house only because I did not know what else to do. Perhaps Caleb would be waiting for me on the stoop.

The avenue, too, was very long and silent. Somehow, it seemed old, like a picture in a book. It stretched straight before me, endless, and the streetlights did not so much illuminate it as prove how dark it was. The familiar buildings were now merely dark, silent shapes, great masses of wet rock; men stood against the walls or on the stoops, made faceless by the light in the hallway behind them. The rain was falling harder. Cars sloshed by, sending up sheets of water and bobbing like boats; from the bars I heard music faintly, and many voices. Straight ahead of me a woman walked, very fast, head down, carrying a shopping bag. I reached my corner and crossed the wide avenue. There was no one on my stoop.

Now, I was not even certain what time it was; and everything was so abnormally,

---

6. **lethal** (lē′thəl): deadly.
7. **dressing down:** a scolding.
8. **prey to my fantasies:** upset by my imaginary fears.

wretchedly still that there was no way of guessing. But I knew it wasn't time yet for the show to be over. I walked into my hallway and wrung out my cap. I was sorry that I had not made someone take me into the show because now I did not know what to do. I *could* go upstairs and say that we had not liked the movie and had left early and that Caleb was with some boys on the stoop. But this would sound strange—I had never been known to dislike a movie; and if our father was home, he might come downstairs to look for Caleb, who would not know what story I had told and who would, therefore, in any case, be greatly handicapped[9] when he arrived. As far as Caleb knew, I was safely in the movies. That was our bargain, from which not even the rain released me. My nerve had failed me, but Caleb had no way of knowing that. I could not stay in my hallway because my father might not be at home and might come in. I could not go into the hallway of another building because if any of the kids who lived in the building found me they would have the right to beat me up. I could not go back out into the rain. I stood next to the big, cold radiator and I began to cry. But crying wasn't going to do me any good, either, especially as there was no one to hear me.

So I stepped out on my stoop again and looked carefully up and down the block. There was not a soul to be seen. The rain fell as hard as ever, with a whispering sound—like monstrous old gossips whispering together. The sky could not be seen. It was black. I stood there for a long time, wondering what to do. Then I thought of a condemned house, around the corner from us. We played there sometimes, though we were not supposed to, and it was dangerous. The front door

had been boarded up but the boards had been pried loose; and the basement windows had been broken and boys congregated in the basement and wandered through the rotting house. What possessed me to go there now I don't know, except that I could not think of another dry place in the whole world. I thought that I would just sit there, out of the rain, until I figured it was safe to come home. And I started running east, down our block. I turned two corners and I came to the house, with its black window sockets and garbage piled high around it and the rain moaning and whistling, clanging against the metal and drumming on the glass. The house stood by itself, for the house next to it had already been torn down. The house was completely dark. I had forgotten how afraid I was of the dark, but the rain was drenching me. I ran down the cellar steps and clambered into the house. I squatted there in a still, dry dread, in misery, not daring to look into the house but staring outward at the bright black area railing and the tempest[10] beyond. I was holding my breath. I heard an endless scurrying in the darkness, a perpetual busyness, and I thought of rats, of their teeth and ferocity and fearful size and I began to cry again. If someone had come up then to murder me, I don't believe I could have moved or made any other sound.

I don't know how long I squatted there this way, or what was in my mind—I think there was nothing in my mind, I was as blank as a toothache. I listened to the rain and the rats. Then I was aware of another sound; I had been hearing it for a while without realizing it. The sound came from the door which led to the backyard. I wanted to stand, but I crouched lower; wanted to run, but could not move. Sometimes the sound seemed to come

9. **handicapped** (hăn'dē-kăpt'): put at a disadvantage.

10. **tempest** (tĕm'pĭst): a violent storm.

closer and I knew that this meant my death; sometimes diminished or ceased altogether and then I knew that my assailant[11] was looking for me. Oh, how I hated Caleb for bringing my life to an end so soon! How I wished I knew where to find him! I looked toward the backyard door and I seemed to see, silhouetted against the driving rain, a figure, half bent, moaning, leaning against the wall. Then I heard a laugh, a low, happy, wicked laugh, and the figure turned in my direction and seemed to start toward me. Then I screamed and stood straight up, bumping my head on the window frame and losing my cap, and scrambled up the cellar steps, into the rain. I ran head down, like a bull, away from that house and out of that block and it was my great good luck that no person and no vehicle were in my path. I ran up the steps of my stoop and bumped into Caleb.

"Where have you been? Hey! What's the matter with you?"

For I had jumped up on him, almost knocking him down, trembling and sobbing.

"You're *soaked*. Leo, what's the matter with you? Where's your cap?"

But I could not say anything. I held him around the neck with all my might, and I could not stop shaking.

"Come on, Leo," Caleb said, in a different tone, "tell me what's the matter. Don't carry on like this." He pried my arms loose and held me away from him so that he could look into my face. "Oh, little Leo. Little Leo. What's the matter, baby?" He looked as though he were about to cry himself and this made me cry harder than ever. He took out his handkerchief and wiped my face and made me blow my nose. My sobs began to lessen, but I could not stop trembling. He thought that I was trembling from cold and he rubbed his hands roughly up and down my back and rubbed my hands between his. "What's the matter?"

I did not know how to tell him.

"Somebody try to beat you up?"

I shook my head. "No."

"What movie did you see?"

"I didn't go. I couldn't find nobody to take me in."

"And you just been wandering around in the rain all night?"

I shook my head. "Yes."

He looked at me and sat down on the hallway steps. "Oh, Leo." Then, "You mad at me?"

I said, "No. I was scared."

He nodded. "I reckon you were, man," he said. "I reckon you were." He wiped my face again. "You ready to go upstairs? It's getting late."

"Okay."

"How'd you lose your cap?"

"I went in a hallway to wring it out—and—I put it on the radiator and I heard some people coming—and—I ran away and I forgot it."

"We'll say you forgot it in the movies."

"Okay."

We started up the stairs.

"Leo," he said, "I'm sorry about tonight. I'm really sorry. I won't let it happen again. You believe me?"

"Sure. I believe you."

"Give us a smile, then."

I smiled up at him. He squatted down.

"Give us a kiss."

I kissed him.

"Okay. Climb up. I'll give you a ride—hold on, now."

He carried me piggyback up the stairs.

---

11. **assailant** (ə-sā′lənt): attacker.

SEEKING MEANING

1. This selection makes the reader aware of what is going on in the mind of a ten-year-old boy who often has to spend Saturday afternoons alone. How does Leo behave outwardly when Caleb sends him off on his own? Why doesn't he let Caleb know how he really feels?
2. Sometimes Leo can't find anyone to take him into the movie theater. Why doesn't he return home? Why doesn't he play with the children on his own block?
3. When Leo is wandering in the rain and feeling miserable, he is angry at his brother. Why does he feel that Caleb has let him down?
4. When Leo runs into Caleb on the stoop, he clings to him because he is frightened. How does Caleb react when he realizes how much Leo needs him?
5. Leo and Caleb do not reveal their true feelings for each other until there is a crisis. Do you think the brothers will become closer as a result of this experience? Tell why or why not.

ABOUT THE AUTHOR

James Baldwin (1924–   ) was born in New York City. After his graduation from high school, he supported himself by working at odd jobs and did his writing at night. Eventually he was able to devote himself full time to writing. He finished his first novel, *Go Tell It on the Mountain,* in 1953, while he was living in Paris. In addition to novels, he has written essays and plays. Two well-known collections of his essays are *Notes of a Native Son* and *The Fire Next Time.*

Baldwin has said that reading brings us closer to others: "You think your pain and your heartbreak are unprecedented in the history of the world, but then you read. It was books that taught me that the things that tormented me most were the very things that connected me with all the people who were alive, or who had ever been alive."

The Children's Hour

Henry Wadsworth Longfellow

Between the dark and the daylight,
  When the night is beginning to lower,
Comes a pause in the day's occupations,
  That is known as the Children's Hour.

I hear in the chamber above me   5
  The patter of little feet,
The sound of a door that is opened,
  And voices soft and sweet.

From my study I see in the lamplight,
  Descending the broad hall stair,   10
Grave Alice, and laughing Allegra,
  And Edith with golden hair.

A whisper, and then a silence:
  Yet I know by their merry eyes
They are plotting and planning together   15
  To take me by surprise.

A sudden rush from the stairway,
  A sudden raid from the hall!
By three doors left unguarded
  They enter my castle wall!   20

They climb up into my turret
  O'er the arms and back of my chair;
If I try to escape, they surround me;
  They seem to be everywhere.

They almost devour me with kisses,   25
  Their arms about me entwine,
Till I think of the Bishop of Bingen°
  In his Mouse Tower on the Rhine!

27. **Bishop of Bingen:** in legend, a
man who was devoured by mice
in his castle.

Do you think, O blue-eyed banditti,°
   Because you have scaled the wall,   30
Such an old mustache as I am
   Is not a match for you all!

I have you fast in my fortress,
   And will not let you depart,
But put you down into the dungeon   35
   In the round tower of my heart.

And there I will keep you forever,
   Yes, forever and a day,
Till the walls shall crumble to ruin,
   And molder in dust away.   40

29. **banditti:** Italian for "bandits."

SEEKING MEANING

1. What is "the Children's Hour"? When does it occur?

2. Longfellow compares himself to a castle and the children's entry into the study to the climbing of a castle wall. A *turret* is a tower on top of a castle. What is the "turret" referred to in line 21?

3. A *dungeon* is a prison. What does the word *dungeon* refer to in line 35? In what way does the poet intend to imprison the children?

4. In the last stanza, Longfellow appears to be talking about the destruction of the castle walls. Tell in your own words what he really means.

ABOUT THE AUTHOR

For many years, Henry Wadsworth Long-fellow (1807–1882) was one of the best-loved and most widely read of all American poets. He was one of a group of New England poets who became known as the "Fireside Poets." Their poetry had a large family audience. The members of a family would gather together, often before the fireside, and read poems aloud.

For a number of years, Longfellow combined a literary career with teaching. He was a professor of modern languages at Bowdoin College and later at Harvard University. Eventually he was able to leave teaching and devote himself to writing poetry full time. Two of his best-known poems are "The Children's Hour" and "The Wreck of the *Hesperus*," which appears on page 186.

Maud Martha and her family looked at the things they loved about their home. If only these things could last always!

Home *Gwendolyn Brooks*

What had been wanted was this always, this always to last, the talking softly on this porch, with the snake plant in the jardiniere[1] in the southwest corner, and the obstinate slip from Aunt Eppie's magnificent Michigan fern at the left side of the friendly door. Mama, Maud Martha, and Helen rocked slowly in their rocking chairs, and looked at the late afternoon light on the lawn and at the emphatic iron of the fence and at the poplar tree. These things might soon be theirs no longer. Those shafts and pools of light, the tree, the graceful iron, might soon be viewed possessively by different eyes.

Papa was to have gone that noon, during his lunch hour, to the office of the Home Owners' Loan. If he had not succeeded in getting another extension, they would be leaving this house in which they had lived for more than fourteen years. There was little hope. The Home Owners' Loan was hard. They sat, making their plans.

"We'll be moving into a nice flat[2] somewhere," said Mama. "Somewhere on South Park, or Michigan, or in Washington Park Court." Those flats, as the girls and Mama knew well, were burdens on wages twice the size of Papa's. This was not mentioned now.

"They're much prettier than this old house," said Helen. "I have friends I'd just as soon not bring here. And I have other friends that wouldn't come down this far for anything, unless they were in a taxi."

Yesterday, Maud Martha would have attacked her. Tomorrow she might. Today she said nothing. She merely gazed at a little hopping robin in the tree, her tree, and tried to keep the fronts of her eyes dry.

"Well, I do know," said Mama, turning her hands over and over, "that I've been getting tireder and tireder of doing that firing.[3] From October to April, there's firing to be done."

"But lately we've been helping, Harry and I," said Maud Martha. "And sometimes in

1. **jardiniere** (järd′n-îr′): an ornamental pot for plants.

2. **flat:** an apartment.
3. **firing:** starting a coal fire.

March and April and in October, and even in November, we could build a little fire in the fireplace. Sometimes the weather was just right for that.''

She knew, from the way they looked at her, that this had been a mistake. They did not want to cry.

But she felt that the little line of white, sometimes ridged with smoked purple, and all that cream-shot saffron[4] would never drift across any western sky except that in back of this house. The rain would drum with as sweet a dullness nowhere but here. The birds on South Park were mechanical birds, no better than the poor caught canaries in those ''rich'' women's sun parlors.

''It's just going to kill Papa!'' burst out Maud Martha. ''He loves this house! He *lives* for this house!''

''He lives for us,'' said Helen. ''It's us he loves. He wouldn't want the house, except for us.''

---

4. **saffron:** a yellow-orange color.

"And he'll have us," added Mama, "wherever."

"You know," Helen sighed, "if you want to know the truth, this is a relief. If this hadn't come up, we would have gone on, just dragged on, hanging out here forever."

"It might," allowed Mama, "be an act of God. God may just have reached down and picked up the reins."

"Yes," Maud Martha cracked in, "that's what you always say—that God knows best."

Her mother looked at her quickly, decided the statement was not suspect, looked away.

Helen saw Papa coming. "There's Papa," said Helen.

They could not tell a thing from the way Papa was walking. It was that same dear little staccato walk,[5] one shoulder down, then the other, then repeat, and repeat. They watched his progress. He passed the Kennedys', he passed the vacant lot, he passed Mrs. Blakemore's. They wanted to hurl themselves over the fence, into the street, and shake the truth out of his collar. He opened his gate—the gate —and still his stride and face told them nothing.

"Hello," he said.

Mama got up and followed him through the front door. The girls knew better than to go in too.

Presently Mama's head emerged. Her eyes were lamps turned on.

"It's all right," she exclaimed. "He got it. It's all over. Everything is all right."

The door slammed shut. Mama's footsteps hurried away.

"I think," said Helen, rocking rapidly, "I think I'll give a party. I haven't given a party since I was eleven. I'd like some of my friends to just casually see that we're homeowners."

_____

5. **staccato** (stə-kä′tō) **walk:** a walk of short, abrupt steps.

SEEKING MEANING

1. Why do the members of the family feel they are in danger of losing their home?

2. What reasons do Mama and Helen give for wanting to move? Are they telling the truth, or are they trying to prepare themselves for disappointment? Support your answer with passages from the selection.

3. When Mama returns from speaking to Papa, her eyes are described as "lamps turned on." What emotion do you think Mama is feeling?

DEVELOPING SKILLS IN READING

Drawing Conclusions

Gwendolyn Brooks never tells you directly that Maud Martha values the beauties of the natural world. However, you can draw this conclusion from what she tells you about Maud Martha's responses to nature. You are told of the pleasure Maud Martha takes in looking at the late afternoon light on the lawn, in watching a sunset, and in listening to the rain drumming on the roof. You also learn that she feels sorry for "mechanical" birds that are kept in cages.

To understand what an author tells you about characters, you often must read below the surface and draw your own conclusions. Read the following statements about the characters in the story. Do you agree with all of them? Support your answers with passages from the selection.

Maud Martha and Helen value different things in life.

Their home is in a wealthy neighborhood.

Maud Martha is not afraid to be honest about her feelings.

Papa has lost his job.

DEVELOPING VOCABULARY

Finding the Appropriate Meaning

Often the meaning and pronunciation of a word depend on how it is used in a sentence. The word *progress,* for example, may be used as a noun or a verb. Find the word in a dictionary and note the meaning and pronunciation for each part of speech. Look at the word *progress* in this sentence from "Home":

They watched his *progress.*

How is *progress* used here? How is it pronounced? Give its meaning.

The word *suspect* may be used as a noun, a verb, or an adjective. Find the meaning and pronunciation for each part of speech. How is *suspect* used in this sentence?

Her mother looked at her quickly, decided the statement was not *suspect,* looked away.

What does the word mean? How is it pronounced?

Look up the following words in a dictionary. In how many different ways can each word be used? Give the meaning and pronunciation for each part of speech.

excuse   perfect   record

ABOUT THE AUTHOR

Gwendolyn Brooks (1917–   ) recalls that as a child she was writing all the time: "My mother says I began rhyming at seven—but my notebooks date back to my eleventh year only."

In 1950 she won the Pulitzer Prize for *Annie Allen,* a collection of poems about a black girl growing up in Chicago. She returned to the same subject in her novel *Maud Martha,* from which "Home" is taken. Of that work, she has written: "My one novel is not autobiographical in the usual sense. . . . But it is true that much in the 'story' was taken out of my own life, and twisted, highlighted or dulled, dressed up or down. . . . 'Home' is indeed fact-bound. The Home Owners' Loan Corporation was a sickening reality."

In 1968, Gwendolyn Brooks succeeded Carl Sandburg as the poet laureate of Illinois.

Although the sentences in this poem do not begin with capital letters and end with periods, you will find that every stanza contains one or more complete thoughts.

My Grandmother Would Rock Quietly and Hum   *Leonard Adamé*

in her house
she would rock quietly and hum
until her swelled hands
calmed

in summer   5
she wore thick stockings
sweaters
and gray braids

(when el cheque° came
we went to Payless°   10
and I laughed greedily
when given a quarter)

mornings,
sunlight barely lit
the kitchen   15
and where
there were shadows
it was not cold

she quietly rolled
flour tortillas—   20
the papas°
cracking in hot lard
would wake me

she had lost her teeth
and when we ate   25
she had bread
soaked in café

always her eyes
were clear
and she could see   30
as I cannot yet see—
through her eyes
she gave me herself

she would sit
and talk   35
of her girlhood—
of things strange to me:
    México
    epidemics
    relatives shot   40
    her father's hopes
    of this country—
how they sank
with cement dust
to his insides   45

now
when I go
to the old house
the worn spots
by the stove   50
echo of her shuffling
and
México
still hangs in her
fading   55
calendar pictures

---

9. **el cheque** (ĕl chĕ′kā): the check.   10. **Payless:** a chain of food stores.   21. **papas** (pä′päs): potatoes.

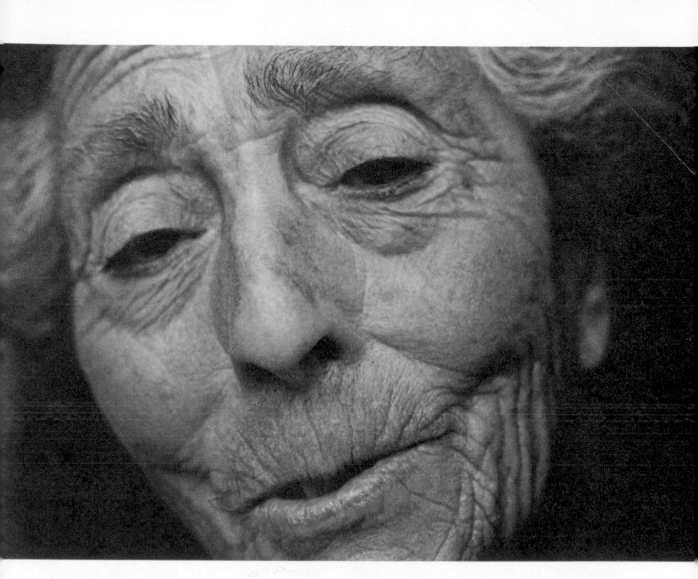

SEEKING MEANING

What images of his grandmother does the poet recall? In what ways did his grandmother enrich his life?

DEVELOPING VOCABULARY

Recognizing Words of Spanish Origin
The word *tortilla,* which appears in line 20 of Adamé's poem, is a Spanish word that has en-tered the English language. The word *cheque* in line 9 is an example of an English word that has entered Spanish. Many Spanish words have come into English, just as many English words have found their way into Spanish.

Here are several Spanish words that have become part of the English language. Tell what each one means. Use a dictionary to find the meanings of any unfamiliar words.

adios	fiesta	siesta
adobe	rodeo	sombrero

Some of the most hilarious stories in American literature are those that James Thurber has told about his family. Here is the story of one memorable night in the Thurber household.

The Night the Bed Fell

James Thurber

I suppose that the high-water mark of my youth in Columbus, Ohio, was the night the bed fell on my father. It makes a better recitation (unless, as some friends of mine have said, one has heard it five or six times) than it does a piece of writing, for it is almost necessary to throw furniture around, shake doors, and bark like a dog, to lend the proper atmosphere and verisimilitude[1] to what is admittedly a somewhat incredible tale. Still, it did take place.

It happened, then, that my father had decided to sleep in the attic one night, to be away where he could think. My mother opposed the notion strongly because, she said, the old wooden bed up there was unsafe; it was wobbly, and the heavy headboard would crash down on Father's head in case the bed fell, and kill him. There was no dissuading him, however, and at a quarter past ten he closed the attic door behind him and went up the narrow twisting stairs. We later heard ominous creakings as he crawled into bed. Grandfather, who usually slept in the attic bed when he was with us, had disappeared some days before. (On these occasions he was usually gone six or eight days and returned growling and out of temper, with the news that the Federal Union was run by a passel of blockheads and that the Army of the Potomac didn't have a chance.[2])

We had visiting us at this time a nervous first cousin of mine named Briggs Beall, who believed that he was likely to cease breathing when he was asleep. It was his feeling that if he were not awakened every hour during the night, he might die of suffocation. He had been accustomed to setting an alarm clock to ring at intervals until morning, but I persuaded him to abandon this. He slept in my room and I told him that I was such a light sleeper that if anybody quit breathing in the same room with me, I would wake instantly. He tested me the first night — which I had suspected he would — by holding his breath after my regular breathing had convinced him I was asleep. I was not asleep, however, and called to him. This seemed to allay his fears a little, but he took the precaution of putting a glass of spirits of camphor on a little table at the head of his bed. In case I didn't arouse him until he was almost gone, he said, he would

---

1. **verisimilitude** (vĕr′ə-sĭm-ĭl′ə-tood′): the appearance of truth.

2. **the Federal . . . chance:** Grandfather, who lives in the past, thinks the Civil War is still going on.

sniff the camphor, a powerful reviver.

Briggs was not the only member of his family who had his crotchets.[3] Old Aunt Melissa Beall (who could whistle like a man, with two fingers in her mouth) suffered under the premonition that she was destined to die on South High Street because she had been born on South High Street and married on South High Street. Then there was Aunt Sarah Shoaf, who never went to bed at night without the fear that a burglar was going to get in and blow chloroform under her door through a tube. To avert this calamity—for she was in greater dread of anesthetics than of losing her household goods—she always piled her money, silverware, and other valuables in a neat stack just outside her bedroom, with a note reading "This is all I have. Please take it and do not use your chloroform, as this is all I have." Aunt Gracie Shoaf also had a burglar phobia, but she met it with more fortitude. She was confident that burglars had been getting into her house every night for forty years. The fact that she never missed anything was to her no proof to the contrary. She always claimed that she scared them off before they could take anything, by throwing shoes down the hallway. When she went to bed, she piled, where she could get at them handily, all the shoes there were about her house. Five minutes after she had turned off the light, she would sit up in bed and say "Hark!" Her husband, who had learned to ignore the whole situation as long ago as 1903, would either be sound asleep or pretend to be sound asleep. In either case he would not respond to her tugging and pulling, so that presently she would arise, tiptoe to the door, open it slightly, and

---

3. **crotchets** (krŏch′ĭts): odd or fantastic ideas.

heave a shoe down the hall in one direction and its mate down the hall in the other direction. Some nights she threw them all, some nights only a couple of pairs.

But I am straying from the remarkable incidents that took place during the night that the bed fell on Father. By midnight we were all in bed. The layout of the rooms and the disposition of their occupants is important to an understanding of what later occurred. In the front room upstairs (just under Father's attic bedroom) were my mother and my brother Herman, who sometimes sang in his sleep, usually "Marching Through Georgia" or "Onward, Christian Soldiers." Briggs Beall and myself were in a room adjoining this one. My brother Roy was in a room across the hall from ours. Our bull terrier, Rex, slept in the hall.

My bed was an army cot, one of those affairs which are made wide enough to sleep on comfortably only by putting up, flat with the middle section, the two sides which ordinarily hang down like the sideboards of a drop-leaf table. When these sides are up, it is perilous to roll too far toward the edge, for then the cot is likely to tip completely over, bringing the whole bed down on top of one, with a tremendous banging crash. This, in fact, is precisely what happened about two o'clock in the morning. (It was my mother who, in recalling the scene later, first referred to it as "the night the bed fell on your father.")

Always a deep sleeper, slow to arouse (I had lied to Briggs), I was at first unconscious of what had happened when the iron cot rolled me onto the floor and toppled over on me. It left me still warmly bundled up and unhurt, for the bed rested above me like a canopy. Hence I did not wake up, only reached the edge of consciousness and went back. The racket, however, instantly awakened my mother, in the next room, who came to the

immediate conclusion that her worst dread was realized: the big wooden bed upstairs had fallen on Father. She therefore screamed, "Let's go to your poor father!" It was this shout, rather than the noise of my cot falling, that awakened Herman, in the same room with her. He thought that Mother had become, for no apparent reason, hysterical. "You're all right, Mamma!" he shouted, trying to calm her. They exchanged shout for shout for perhaps ten seconds: "Let's go to your poor father!" and "You're all right!" That woke up Briggs. By this time I was conscious of what was going on, in a vague way, but did

not yet realize that I was under my bed instead of on it. Briggs, awakening in the midst of loud shouts of fear and apprehension, came to the quick conclusion that he was suffocating and that we were all trying to "bring him out." With a low moan, he grasped the glass of camphor at the head of his bed and instead of sniffing it poured it over himself. The room reeked of camphor. "Ugf, ahfg," choked Briggs, like a drowning man, for he had almost succeeded in stopping his breath under the deluge of pungent spirits. He leaped out of bed and groped toward the open window, but he came up against one that was closed. With his hand, he beat out the glass, and I could hear it crash and tinkle on the alleyway below. It was at this juncture that I, in trying to get up, had the uncanny sensation of feeling my bed above me! Foggy with sleep, I now suspected, in my turn, that the whole uproar was being made in a frantic endeavor to extricate me from what must be an unheard-of and perilous situation. "Get me out of this!" I bawled. "Get me out!" I think I had the nightmarish belief that I was entombed in a mine. "Gugh," gasped Briggs, floundering in his camphor.

By this time my mother, still shouting,

pursued by Herman, still shouting, was trying to open the door to the attic, in order to go up and get my father's body out of the wreckage. The door was stuck, however, and wouldn't yield. Her frantic pulls on it only added to the general banging and confusion. Roy and the dog were now up, the one shouting questions, the other barking.

Father, farthest away and soundest sleeper of all, had by this time been awakened by the battering on the attic door. He decided that the house was on fire. "I'm coming, I'm coming!" he wailed in a slow, sleepy voice—it took him many minutes to regain full consciousness. My mother, still believing he was caught under the bed, detected in his "I'm coming!" the mournful, resigned note of one who is preparing to meet his Maker. "He's dying!" she shouted.

"I'm all right!" Briggs yelled to reassure her. "I'm all right!" He still believed that it was his own closeness to death that was worrying Mother. I found at last the light switch in my room, unlocked the door, and Briggs and I joined the others at the attic door. The dog, who never did like Briggs, jumped for him— assuming that he was the culprit in whatever was going on—and Roy had to throw Rex and hold him. We could hear Father crawling out of bed upstairs. Roy pulled the attic door open with a mighty jerk, and Father came down the stairs, sleepy and irritable but safe and sound. My mother began to weep when she saw him. Rex began to howl. "What in the name of heaven is going on here?" asked Father.

The situation was finally put together like a gigantic jigsaw puzzle. Father caught a cold from prowling around in his bare feet, but there were no other bad results. "I'm glad," said Mother, who always looked on the bright side of things, "that your grandfather wasn't here."

SEEKING MEANING

1. In his opening paragraph Thurber says that the story he is about to tell is a "somewhat incredible tale." After getting to know the members of his family, do you believe that the hilarious events he describes could have taken place? Why or why not?

2. "Crotchets" seem to run in Thurber's family. Which of the crotchets did you find most amusing? In what way did Rex, the bull terrier, have his crotchets?

3. During the night, Thurber's cot tipped over and fell on him with a loud crash. How did each member of the household interpret what he or she heard?

4. What do you think might have happened if Grandfather had been there the night the bed fell? Why?

5. Thurber claims that the story "makes a better recitation . . . than it does a piece of writing" (page 148). Suppose you were telling the story aloud. How would you lend it "proper atmosphere"?

DEVELOPING VOCABULARY

Analyzing Words with *-phobia* **and** *philo-*
Thurber tells us that his Aunt Gracie Shoaf had a "burglar phobia." A *phobia* is an unreasonable fear. It comes from the Greek word *phobos*, meaning "fear." Cousin Briggs also had a phobia, and so did Aunt Melissa Beall.

The word *phobia* can be used alone, as Thurber uses it, or it can be combined with other roots to name particular fears. Look up *hydrophobia* and *claustrophobia* in a dictionary. What specific fears do they name?

The root *philo-* (or *phil-*) comes from the Greek word *philos*, which means "loving." The Greek word *sophia* means "wisdom." What does *philosophy* mean? In Greek the word *adelphos* means "brother." What does the name *Philadelphia* mean?

How is *Anglophobia* different from *Anglophilia*? Use a dictionary to find the answer.

DEVELOPING SKILLS OF EXPRESSION

Using Exaggeration in a Humorous Story
Thurber makes his narrative funny by exaggerating the humorous characteristics of his family. For example, he says that his cousin Briggs Beall is afraid he will stop breathing in his sleep. Since there is no reason to believe that Briggs is physically ill, this peculiar fear is amusing. Thurber makes it even funnier by showing us what measures Briggs takes to keep from suffocating. He sets an alarm clock to ring at different times during the night. He keeps camphor on his night table to revive himself if he stops breathing. He even holds his breath in order to test whether Thurber is a light enough sleeper to hear him suffocating. These details exaggerate Briggs's "crotchets."

Write a humorous story of your own that is based on an actual event. Start with people and a setting that you know well. You may want to include an animal that has unusual habits. Consider inventing names for your characters. Then let your imagination go. Exaggerate as much as you want to.

ABOUT THE AUTHOR

James Thurber (1894–1961) is widely considered to be the finest American humorist since Mark Twain. Despite a childhood accident which resulted in the loss of one eye and the gradual weakening of the other, Thurber had a long and successful writing career. Over a period of thirty years, he contributed hundreds of stories, essays, and articles to *The New Yorker* magazine. Thurber was also a masterful cartoonist.

Thurber used material from his childhood in Columbus, Ohio, to create his most famous collection of stores, *My Life and Hard Times*. "The Night the Bed Fell" is taken from this collection.

Practice in Reading and Writing

NARRATION

Reading Narration

Narration is the kind of writing that tells a story. The following narrative passage is from the selection "Home." When this passage begins, the family is waiting nervously for Papa to return with the answer from the Home Owners' Loan.

> Helen saw Papa coming. "There's Papa," said Helen.
> They could not tell a thing from the way Papa was walking. It was that same dear little staccato walk, one shoulder down, then the other, then repeat, and repeat. They watched his progress. He passed the Kennedys', he passed the vacant lot, he passed Mrs. Blakemore's. They wanted to hurl themselves over the fence, into the street, and shake the truth out of his collar. He opened his gate—the gate—and still his stride and face told them nothing.
> "Hello," he said.
> Mama got up and followed him through the front door. The girls knew better than to go in too.
> Presently Mama's head emerged. Her eyes were lamps turned on.
> "It's all right," she exclaimed. "He got it. It's all over. Everything is all right."
> The door slammed shut. Mama's footsteps hurried away.

The author, Gwendolyn Brooks, has made good use of several skills basic to good narrative writing.

---

1. *A narrative tells about a series of events.*
What are the events that make up this narrative passage?

2. *To make a narrative clear, a writer must arrange the events in some kind of logical order—usually the order in which they occur.*

What order is used for the events in the model passage?

3. *A good narrative has unity. All the events deal with one main action.*

What is the main action of this passage?

Writing Narration

Here are some points to remember when you write a narrative:

---

1. *Provide your narrative with a beginning, a middle, and an end.*
2. *Include only those events that deal with the main action.*
3. *Arrange the events in a logical order.*

Writing Dialogue

Dialogue is often an important part of narrative writing. Remember these points:

---

1. *Begin a new paragraph for each speaker.*
2. *Use quotation marks to enclose each speaker's exact words.*
3. *Begin each quotation with a capital letter. If the sentence is divided into two parts, begin the second part with a small letter.*

 "We are ready," said the teacher, "to rehearse the play."

4. *Use commas to separate a quotation from the rest of the sentence.*
 He said, "Hello."
 "Hello," he said.
5. *Do not use quotation marks unless you are quoting a person's exact words.*
 Helen said that she would like to give a party.

Write a narrative, using one of these topics or a topic of your own:

> What happened during vacation
> A trip to the circus
> An episode at camp
> One night in the life of a baby sitter

For Further Reading

Alcott, Louisa May, *Little Women* (many editions)
This famous novel is about the four March sisters—Jo, Meg, Amy, and Beth—who grow up in New England at the time of the Civil War.

Armstrong, William, *Sounder* (Harper & Row, 1972; paperback, Harper)
A Southern family struggles to survive after the father is sent to prison for stealing food. This is a moving story about a mother's dignity, and the love between a boy and his dog.

Benary-Isbert, Margot, *The Ark* (Harcourt Brace Jovanovich, 1953)
A refugee family in postwar Germany rebuild their lives.

Blume, Judy, *Then Again, Maybe I Won't* (Bradbury, 1971; paperback, Dell)
Thirteen-year-old Tony experiences problems when his family moves to a wealthy suburban neighborhood.

Cleaver, Vera, and Bill Cleaver, *Where the Lilies Bloom* (Lippincott, 1969; paperback, New American Library)
When her father dies, fourteen-year-old Mary Call Luther becomes the head of the family, assuming responsibility for a ten-year-old brother and an older sister. The story takes place in the Appalachian hill country.

Corbin, William, *Smoke* (Coward-McCann, 1967)
Fourteen-year-old Chris reluctantly seeks his new stepfather's help to save the life of a stray German shepherd.

Forbes, Kathyrn, *Mama's Bank Account* (Harcourt Brace Jovanovich, 1968; paperback, Starline)
The oldest daughter of a Norwegian-American family describes her family's experiences in turn-of-the-century San Francisco.

Gilbreth, Frank B., and Ernestine Gilbreth Carey, *Cheaper by the Dozen* (Thomas Y. Crowell, 1963; paperback, Bantam)
The authors write humorously of growing up in a family of twelve children, with a remarkable mother and an efficiency expert for a father.

Gipson, Fred, *Old Yeller* (Harper & Row, 1956; paperback, Harper)
This story takes place on a Texas homestead more than a century ago. While his father is away on a cattle drive, fourteen-year-old Travis and an old yellow dog prove that they can take care of family emergencies.

Lindsay, Howard, and Russel Crouse, *Life with Father* and *Life with Mother* (Alfred A. Knopf, 1953)
These plays are based on Clarence Day's entertaining stories about his family.

Nash, Ogden, *Parents Keep Out: Elderly Poems for Youngerly Readers* (Little, Brown, 1951)
Here is a collection of humorous poems about family life.

Peck, Robert Newton, *A Day No Pigs Would Die* (Alfred A. Knopf, 1973; paperback, Dell)
Thirteen-year-old Rob raises a prizewinning pig on a Vermont farm during the 1920's. Rob's parents help him accept a painful decision.

Ruark, Robert, *The Old Man and the Boy* (Holt, Rinehart & Winston, 1957; paperback, Fawcett)
The author is the boy and his understanding grandfather is the old man in this memoir of a happy boyhood spent along the North Carolina seacoast.

Taylor, Sydney, *All-of-a-Kind Family* (Follett Publishing, 1951; paperback, Dell)
Five sisters grow up on New York's Lower East Side in the early 1900's.

Trapp, Maria August, *The Story of the Trapp Family Singers* (Lippincott, 1949; paperback, Doubleday)
The author tells how her family fled from Austria during World War II and settled in Vermont. *The Sound of Music*, a Broadway musical and also a film, was based on this book.

Wyss, Johann David, *Swiss Family Robinson* (many editions)
A family, shipwrecked on an island in the South Seas, survive by working together.

About three thousand years ago, in Biblical times, a poet named David composed sacred songs called *psalms* in praise of God. In these lines from Psalm 8, David celebrates the splendor of the universe. He also tells how humble he feels in the presence of such wonders.

> When I consider thy heavens, the work of thy fingers,
> The moon and the stars, which thou hast ordained;
> What is man, that thou art mindful of him?

From earliest times people have responded to the beauty and wonder of the natural world. Like the psalmist David, they have questioned their relationship to the universe. They have sought answers to such questions as these: What responsibilities do human beings have to the natural world? How can they live in harmony with the earth and the different forms of life on it? In this unit you will find different expressions of the relationship between human beings and the earth, which is their home.

THE EARTH IS HOME

Noah's Ark (1846). Oil painting by Edward Hicks.
Philadelphia Museum of Art: Bequest of Lisa Norris Elkins (Mrs. William M. Elkins)

157

Father said that the boys would have to give up their pet fox, that no amount of love could tame him. But Colin knew that the fox loved them still, that the old bond was not broken.

Last Cover   *Paul Annixter*

I'm not sure I can tell you what you want to know about my brother; but everything about the pet fox is important, so I'll tell all that from the beginning.

It goes back to a winter afternoon after I'd hunted the woods all day for a sign of our lost pet. I remember the way my mother looked up as I came into the kitchen. Without my speaking, she knew what had happened. For six hours I had walked, reading signs, looking for a delicate print in the damp soil or even a hair that might have told of a red fox passing that way—but I had found nothing.

"Did you go up in the foothills?" Mom asked.

I nodded. My face was stiff from held-back tears. My brother, Colin, who was going on twelve, got it all from one look at me and went into a heartbroken, almost silent, crying.

Three weeks before, Bandit, the pet fox Colin and I had raised from a tiny kit, had disappeared, and not even a rumor had been heard of him since.

"He'd have had to go off soon anyway," Mom comforted. "A big, lolloping fellow like him, he's got to live his life same as us. But he may come back. That fox set a lot of store by you boys in spite of his wild ways."

"He set a lot of store by our food, anyway," Father said. He sat in a chair by the kitchen window mending a piece of harness. "We'll be seeing a lot more of that fellow, never fear. That fox learned to pine for table scraps and young chickens. He was getting to be an egg thief, too, and he's not likely to forget that."

"That was only pranking when he was little," Colin said desperately.

From the first, the tame fox had made tension in the family. It was Father who said we'd better name him Bandit, after he'd made away with his first young chicken.

"Maybe you know," Father said shortly. "But when an animal turns to egg sucking he's usually incurable. He'd better not come pranking around my chicken run again."

It was late February, and I remember the bleak, dead cold that had set in, cold that was a rare thing for our Carolina hills. Flocks of sparrows and snowbirds had appeared to peck hungrily at all that the pigs and chickens didn't eat.

"This one's a killer," Father would say of a morning, looking out at the whitened barn roof. "This one will make the shoats[1] squeal."

A fire snapped all day in our cookstove and

---

1. **shoats:** young hogs.

another in the stone fireplace in the living room, but still the farmhouse was never warm. The leafless woods were bleak and empty, and I spoke of that to Father when I came back from my search.

"It's always a sad time in the woods when the seven sleepers are under cover," he said.

"What sleepers are they?" I asked. Father was full of woods lore.

"Why, all the animals that have got sense enough to hole up and stay hid in weather like this. Let's see, how was it the old rhyme named them?

> Surly bear and sooty bat,
> Brown chuck and masked coon,
> Chippy-munk and sly skunk,
> And all the mouses
> 'Cept in men's houses.

"And man would have joined them and made it eight, Granther Yeary always said, if he'd had a little more sense."

"I was wondering if the red fox mightn't make it eight," Mom said.

Father shook his head. "Late winter's a high time for foxes. Time when they're out deviling, not sleeping."

My chest felt hollow. I wanted to cry like Colin over our lost fox, but at fourteen a boy doesn't cry. Colin had squatted down on the floor and got out his small hammer and nails to start another new frame for a new picture. Maybe then he'd make a drawing for the frame and be able to forget his misery. It had been that way with him since he was five.

I thought of the new dress Mom had brought home a few days before in a heavy cardboard box. That box cover would be fine for Colin to draw on. I spoke of it, and Mom's glance thanked me as she went to get it. She and I worried a lot about Colin. He was small

for his age, delicate and blond, his hair much lighter and softer than mine, his eyes deep and wide and blue. He was often sick, and I knew the fear Mom had that he might be predestined.[2] I'm just ordinary, like Father. I'm the sort of stuff that can take it—tough and strong—but Colin was always sort of special.

Mom lighted the lamp. Colin began cutting his white cardboard carefully, fitting it into his frame. Father's sharp glance turned on him now and again.

"There goes the boy making another frame before there's a picture for it," he said. "It's too much like cutting out a man's suit for a fellow that's, say, twelve years old. Who knows whether he'll grow into it?"

Mom was into him then, quick. "Not a single frame of Colin's has ever gone to waste. The boy has real talent, Sumter, and it's time you realized it."

"Of course he has," Father said. "All kids have 'em. But they get over 'em."

"It isn't the pox[3] we're talking of," Mom sniffed.

"In a way it is. Ever since you started talking up Colin's art, I've had an invalid for help around the place."

Father wasn't as hard as he made out, I knew, but he had to hold a balance against all Mom's frothing. For him the thing was the land and all that pertained to it. I was following in Father's footsteps, true to form, but Colin threatened to break the family tradition with his leaning toward art, with Mom "aiding and abetting him," as Father liked to put it. For the past two years she had had dreams of my brother becoming a real artist and going away to the city to study.

It wasn't that Father had no understanding of such things. I could remember, through the

---

2. **predestined** (prē-dĕs′tĭnd): here, fated to die young.
3. **the pox:** chicken pox.

years, Colin lying on his stomach in the front room making pencil sketches, and how a good drawing would catch Father's eyes halfway across the room, and how he would sometimes gather up two or three of them to study, frowning and muttering, one hand in his beard, while a great pride rose in Colin, and in me too. Most of Colin's drawings were of the woods and wild things, and there Father was a master critic. He made out to scorn what seemed to him a passive "white-livered" interpretation of nature through brush and pencil instead of rod and rifle.

At supper that night Colin could scarcely eat. Ever since he'd been able to walk, my brother had had a growing love of wild things, but Bandit had been like his very own, a gift of the woods. One afternoon a year and a half before, Father and Laban Small had been running a vixen through the hills with their dogs. With the last of her strength the she-fox had made for her den, not far from our house. The dogs had overtaken her and killed her just before she reached it. When Father and Laban came up, they'd found Colin crouched nearby holding her cub in his arms.

Father had been for killing the cub, which was still too young to shift for itself, but Colin's grief had brought Mom into it. We'd taken the young fox into the kitchen, all of us, except Father, gone a bit silly over the little thing. Colin had held it in his arms and fed it warm milk from a spoon.

"Watch out with all your soft ways," Father had warned, standing in the doorway. "You'll make too much of him. Remember, you can't make a dog out of a fox. Half of that little critter has to love, but the other half is a wild hunter. You boys will mean a whole lot to him while he's kit, but there'll come a day when you won't mean a thing to him and he'll leave you shorn."

For two weeks after that Colin had nursed the cub, weaning it from milk to bits of meat. For a year they were always together. The cub grew fast. It was soon following Colin and me about the barnyard. It turned out to be a patch fox, with a saddle of darker fur across its shoulders.

I haven't the words to tell you what the fox meant to us. It was far more wonderful owning him than owning any dog. There was something rare and secret like the spirit of the woods about him, and back of his calm, straw-gold eyes was the sense of a brain the equal to a man's. The fox became Colin's whole life.

Each day, going and coming from school, Colin and I took long side trips through the woods, looking for Bandit. Wild things' memories were short, we knew; we'd have to find him soon or the old bond would be broken.

Ever since I was ten I'd been allowed to hunt with Father, so I was good at reading signs. But, in a way, Colin knew more about the woods and wild things than Father or me. What came to me from long observation, Colin seemed to know by instinct.

It was Colin who felt out, like an Indian, the stretch of woods where Bandit had his den, who found the first slim, small fox-print in the damp earth. And then, on an afternoon in March, we saw him. I remember the day well, the racing clouds, the wind rattling the tops of the pine trees and swaying the Spanish moss. Bandit had just come out of a clump of laurel; in the maze of leaves behind him we caught a glimpse of a slim red vixen, so we knew he had found a mate. She melted from sight like a shadow, but Bandit turned to watch us, his mouth open, his tongue lolling as he smiled his old foxy smile. On his thin chops, I saw a telltale chicken feather.

Colin moved silently forward, his movements so quiet and casual he seemed to be

standing still. He called Bandit's name, and the fox held his ground, drawn to us with all his senses. For a few moments he let Colin actually put an arm about him. It was then I knew that he loved us still, for all of Father's warnings. He really loved us back, with a fierce, secret love no tame thing ever gave. But the urge of his life just then was toward his new mate. Suddenly, he whirled about and disappeared in the laurels.

Colin looked at me with glowing eyes. "We haven't really lost him, Stan. When he gets through with his spring sparking[4] he may come back. But we've got to show ourselves to him a lot, so he won't forget."

"It's a go," I said.

"Promise not to say a word to Father," Colin said, and I agreed. For I knew by the chicken feather that Bandit had been up to no good.

A week later the woods were budding and the thickets were rustling with all manner of wild things scurrying on the love scent. Colin managed to get a glimpse of Bandit every few days. He couldn't get close though, for the spring running was a lot more important to a fox than any human beings were.

Every now and then Colin got out his framed box cover and looked at it, but he never drew anything on it; he never even picked up his pencil. I remember wondering if what Father had said about framing a picture before you had one had spoiled something for him.

I was helping Father with the planting now, but Colin managed to be in the woods every day. By degrees he learned Bandit's range, where he drank and rested and where he was likely to be according to the time of day. One day he told me how he had petted Bandit again, and how they had walked together a

4. **sparking:** courting.

long way in the woods. All this time we had kept his secret from Father.

As summer came on, Bandit began to live up to the prediction Father had made. Accustomed to human beings he moved without fear about the scattered farms of the region, raiding barns and hen runs that other foxes wouldn't have dared go near. And he taught his wild mate to do the same. Almost every night they got into some poultry house, and by late June Bandit was not only killing chickens and ducks but feeding on eggs and young chicks whenever he got the chance.

Stories of his doings came to us from many sources, for he was still easily recognized by the dark patch on his shoulders. Many a farmer took a shot at him as he fled and some of them set out on his trail with dogs, but they always returned home without even sighting him. Bandit was familiar with all the dogs in the region, and he knew a hundred tricks to confound them. He got a reputation that year beyond that of any fox our hills had known. His confidence grew, and he gave up wild hunting altogether and lived entirely off the poultry farmers. By late September the hill farmers banded together to hunt him down.

It was Father who brought home that news one night. All time-honored rules of the fox chase were to be broken in this hunt; if the dogs couldn't bring Bandit down, he was to be shot on sight. I was stricken and furious. I remember the misery of Colin's face in the lamplight. Father, who took pride in all the ritual of the hunt, had refused to be a party to such an affair, though in justice he could do nothing but sanction any sort of hunt, for Bandit, as old Sam Wetherwax put it, had been "purely getting in the Lord's hair."

The hunt began next morning, and it was the biggest turnout our hills had known.

There were at least twenty mounted men in the party and as many dogs. Father and I were working in the lower field as they passed along the river road. Most of the hunters carried rifles, and they looked ugly.

Twice during the morning I went up to the house to find Colin, but he was nowhere around. As we worked, Father and I could follow the progress of the hunt by the distant hound music on the breeze. We could tell just where the hunters first caught sight of the fox and where Bandit was leading the dogs during the first hour. We knew as well as if we'd seen it how Bandit roused another fox along Turkey Branch and forced it to run for him, and how the dogs swept after it for twenty minutes before they sensed their mistake.

Noon came, and Colin had not come in to eat. After dinner Father didn't go back to the field. He moped about, listening to the hound talk. He didn't like what was on any more than I did, and now and again I caught his smile of satisfaction when we heard the broken, angry notes of the hunting horn, telling that the dogs had lost the trail or had run another fox.

I was restless, and I went up into the hills in midafternoon. I ranged the woods for miles, thinking all the time of Colin. Time lost all meaning for me, and the short day was nearing an end, when I heard the horn talking again, telling that the fox had put over another trick. All day he had deviled the dogs and mocked the hunters. This new trick and the coming night would work to save him. I was wildly glad, as I moved down toward Turkey Branch and stood listening for a time by the deep, shaded pool where for years we boys had gone swimming, sailed boats, and dreamed summer dreams.

Suddenly, out of the corner of my eye, I saw the sharp ears and thin, pointed mask of a fox — in the water almost beneath me. It was Bandit, craftily submerged there, all but his head, resting in the cool water of the pool and the shadow of the two big beeches that spread above it. He must have run forty miles or more since morning. And he must have hidden in this place before. His knowing, crafty mask blended perfectly with the shadows and a mass of drift and branches that had collected by the bank of the pool. He was so still that a pair of thrushes flew up from the spot as I came up, not knowing he was there.

Bandit's bright, harried eyes were looking right at me. But I did not look at him direct. Some woods instinct, swifter than thought, kept me from it. So he and I met as in another world, indirectly, with feeling but without sign or greeting.

Suddenly I saw that Colin was standing almost beside me. Silently as a water snake, he had come out of the bushes and stood there. Our eyes met, and a quick and secret smile passed between us. It was a rare moment in which I really "met" my brother, when something of his essence flowed into me and I knew all of him. I've never lost it since.

My eyes still turned from the fox, my heart pounding. I moved quietly away, and Colin moved with me. We whistled softly as we went, pretending to busy ourselves along the bank of the stream. There was magic in it, as if by will we wove a web of protection about the fox, a ring-pass-not that none might penetrate. It was so, too, we felt, in the brain of Bandit, and that doubled the charm. To us he was still our little pet that we had carried about in our arms on countless summer afternoons.

Two hundred yards upstream, we stopped beside slim, fresh tracks in the mud where Bandit had entered the branch. The tracks angled upstream. But in the water the wily creature had turned down.

We climbed the far bank to wait, and Colin told me how Bandit's secret had been his secret ever since an afternoon three months before, when he'd watched the fox swim downstream to hide in the deep pool. Today he'd waited on the bank, feeling that Bandit, hard pressed by the dogs, might again seek the pool for sanctuary.

We looked back once as we turned homeward. He still had not moved. We didn't know until later that he was killed that same night by a chance hunter, as he crept out from his hiding place.

That evening Colin worked a long time on his framed box cover that had lain about the house untouched all summer. He kept at it all the next day too. I had never seen him work so hard. I seemed to sense in the air the feel-ing he was putting into it, how he was *believing* his picture into being. It was evening before he finished it. Without a word he handed it to Father. Mom and I went and looked over his shoulder.

It was a delicate and intricate pencil draw-ing of the deep branch pool, and there was Bandit's head and watching, fear-filled eyes hiding there amid the leaves and shadows, woven craftily into the maze of twigs and branches, as if by nature's art itself. Hardly a fox there at all, but the place where he was—or should have been. I recognized it in-stantly, but Mom gave a sort of incredulous sniff.

"I'll declare," she said, "It's mazy as a puz-zle. It just looks like a lot of sticks and leaves to me."

Long minutes of study passed before Father's eye picked out the picture's secret, as few men's could have done. I laid that to Father's being a born hunter. That was a picture that might have been done especially for him. In fact, I guess it was.

Finally he turned to Colin with his deep, slow smile. "So that's how Bandit fooled them all," he said. He sat holding the picture with a sort of tenderness for a long time, while we glowed in the warmth of the shared secret. That was Colin's moment. Colin's art stopped being a pox[5] to Father right there. And later, when the time came for Colin to go to art school, it was Father who was his solid backer.

---

5. **pox:** here, an annoyance.

SEEKING MEANING

1. Both Colin and his father love the woods and wild things, but their responses to the pet fox are different. How is this difference shown when Colin finds the cub? When Bandit runs away?

2. Father refers to Colin's drawings as a "passive 'white-livered' interpretation of nature." What does he believe is a more appropriate response to nature?

3. You learn from Stan that Father is full of woods *lore,* or knowledge. How do Father's predictions about Bandit show that this statement is true?

4. How does Colin show that he knows even more about the woods and wild things than his father and his brother?

5. At the beginning of the story, Father does not take a serious interest in Colin's art. How does he come to respect and appreciate Colin's talent?

6. At first, the pet fox creates tension in the family. How does Bandit's secret finally bring the family closer together?

DEVELOPING SKILLS IN READING

Following the Order of Events

The events in this story cover a period of about six months, from late winter, after Bandit disappears, until September, when he is hunted down and killed. The storyteller carefully notes the passage of time for the reader:

. . . on an afternoon in March . . .
                    (page 161, column 2)
A week later . . .   (page 162, column 1)
As summer came on . . .
                    (page 162, column 2)
. . . by late June . . .   (page 162, column 2)
By September . . .   (page 162, column 2)

The storyteller also interrupts the action of his story twice to relate events that have already occurred. These interruptions, which are called *flashbacks*, fill in the background of the story. The first of these flashbacks, which begins on page 158, takes the action back about a year. Stan recalls, "From the first, the tame fox had made tension in the family." We learn how Bandit got his name. We also learn that Father had tried to warn the boys that Bandit would become a chicken thief.

Locate the second flashback, which tells how Bandit was found. How long was Bandit with the family before he ran away?

Reread the passages of the story that relate the events on the day of the hunt (pages 162–163). Identify the words and phrases that specify the time of each action.

DEVELOPING VOCABULARY

Identifying Animal Names
The word *vixen* is the name of a particular animal—a female fox. The words *cub* and *kit* have a more general meaning. The young of many mammals, such as wolves, whales, bears, tigers, lions, and foxes, are known as *cubs*. The word *kit* is short for *kitten*, but it may be used for any fur-bearing animal.

See if you can identify each of the animal names in the following list. Tell whether the name refers to the male or female, the adult or young of the species. Tell whether the name is used for one or more species of animals. Use a dictionary to check your answers.

boar	drake	mare
buck	ewe	pup
bull	gander	sow
cow	gosling	stag
doe	kid	tom

DEVELOPING SKILLS OF EXPRESSION

Using Examples to Develop a Topic
When he is pursued by the farmers and their dogs, Bandit takes cover in the branch pool, where he blends into the background. The color pattern of Bandit's "mask," or face, helps to camouflage him. His mask cannot be distinguished from the shadows and the driftwood around the branch pool.

Many animals conceal themselves from their enemies by *protective coloration,* which allows them to blend into their environment. Think about the natural coloration of animals that are familiar to you. How is a grasshopper protected by its color? A frog? What disguise does a sparrow have? A fawn?

Write a paragraph in which you use several examples to show that animals are protected by their coloration. If you wish, you may concentrate on a particular group—birds, fish, insects, reptiles, cats, and so on. Open your paragraph with a sentence that states the central idea. You may use this sentence if you like: Natural coloration helps animals conceal themselves from their enemies.

ABOUT THE AUTHOR

Paul Annixter (1894–   ), whose real name is Howard Sturtzel, was born in Minneapolis, Minnesota. He began writing stories when he was nineteen. At that time he lived alone in the woods of northern Minnesota, working on a timber claim. During the next thirty-seven years he published more than five hundred short stories. One of his best-known books, *Swiftwater,* is about a boy growing up in the Maine woods. In 1955 he and his wife, Jane Annixter, began collaborating on novels for young people. Among them are the adventure stories *Windigo* and *Horns of Plenty.*

Wol never seemed to realize that he was an owl. He enjoyed being with people so much that he insisted on being taken to school and dropping in on French class.

Owls in the Family *Farley Mowat*

Wol and Weeps were with us long enough to be well known in Saskatoon.[1] Particularly Wol. As my father said, Wol never quite realized he was an owl. Most of the time he seemed to think he was people. At any rate, he liked being with people and he wanted to be with us so much that we finally had to stop trying to keep him out of the house. If we locked him out he would come and bang his big beak against the window panes so hard we were afraid the glass would break. Screens were no good either, because he would tear

them open with one sweep of his big claws. So eventually he became a house owl. He was always very well mannered in the house, and he caused no trouble — except on one particular occasion.

One midsummer day we had a visit from the new minister of our church. He had just arrived in Saskatoon, so he didn't know about our owls. Mother took him into the living room, and he sat down on our sofa with a cup of tea balanced on his knee, and began to talk to Mother about me skipping Sunday school.

Wol had been off on an expedition down on the riverbank. When he got home he ambled across the lawn, jumped up to the ledge of one

1. **Saskatoon** (săs′kə-tōōn′): a city in the province of Saskatchewan (săs-kăch′ə-wän′), Canada.

of the living room windows and peered in. Spotting the stranger he gave another leap and landed heavily on the minister's shoulder.

Mother had seen him coming and had tried to warn the minister, but she was too late. By the time she had her mouth open, Wol was already hunched down on the man's shoulder, peering around into his face, making friendly owl noises.

"*Who-who?*" he asked politely.

Instead of answering, the minister let out a startled yelp and sprang to his feet. The tea spilled all over the rug, and the teacup shot into the fireplace and smashed into a million pieces.

It was all so sudden that Wol lost his balance; and when he lost his balance his talons just naturally tightened up to help him steady himself. When Wol tightened his grip the minister gave a wild yell, and made a dash for the door.

Wol had never been treated this way before. He didn't like it. Just as the minister reached the front porch, Wol spread his wings and took off. His wings were big, and they were strong too. One of them clipped the man a bang on the side of his head, making him yell even louder. But by then Wol was airborne. He flew up into his favorite poplar tree, and he was in such a huff at the way he had been treated that he wouldn't come down again till after supper.

Riding on people's shoulders was a favorite pastime with Wol. Usually he was so careful with his big claws that you couldn't even feel them. Sometimes when he was on your shoulder and feeling specially friendly, he would nibble your ear. His beak was sharp enough to have taken the ear right off your head at a single bite, but he would just catch the bottom of your ear in his beak and very gently nibble it a little. It didn't hurt at all,

though it used to make some people nervous. One of my father's friends was a man who worked for the railroad, and he had very big, red ears. Every time he came for a visit to our house he wore a cap—a cap with earflaps. He wore it even in summertime because, he said, with ears as big as his and an ear-nibbling owl around he just couldn't afford to take chances.

Wol was usually good-natured, but he *could* get mad. One morning Mother sent me to the store for some groceries. My bike had a flat tire so I had to walk, and Wol walked with me. We were only a little way from our house when we met the postman coming toward us. He had a big bundle of letters in his hand, and he was sorting them and not watching where he was going. Instead of stepping around Wol, he walked right into him.

Worse still, he didn't even look down to see what it was he had stumbled over. He just gave a kind of kick to get whatever it was out of his way.

Well, you could do a lot of things to Wol and get away with it—but kicking him was something different. Hissing like a giant tea-kettle, he spread his wings wide out and clomped the postman on the shins with them. A whack from one of his wings was like the kick of a mule. The postman dropped his handful of letters and went pelting down the street, yelling blue murder—with Wol right on his heels.

After I got hold of Wol and calmed him down, I apologized to the postman. But for a month after that he wouldn't come into our yard at all. He used to stand at the gate and whistle until one of us came out to get the mail.

Our owls were so used to going nearly everywhere with me now that when school started that fall I had a hard time keeping them at

home. I used to bicycle to school, which was about two miles away across the river. During the first week after school opened, I was late four times because of having to take the owls back home after they had followed me partway.

Finally Dad suggested that I lock them up in the big pen each morning just before I left. Wol and Weeps hadn't used that pen for a long time, and when I put them in they acted as if it was a jail. Wol was particularly furious, and

he began to tear at the chicken wire with his beak and claws. I sneaked off fast. I was almost late anyway, and I knew if I was late once more I'd be kept in after school.

I was about halfway over the river bridge when a man on the footpath gave a shout and pointed to something behind my back. At the same time a car, coming toward me, jammed on its brakes and nearly skidded into the cement railings. Not knowing what was going on, I put on my brakes too, and I just had time to stop when there was a wild rush of air on the back of my neck, a deep "HOOO-HOOO-HOO!" in my ear, and Wol landed on my shoulder.

He was out of breath—but he was so pleased with himself that I didn't have the heart to take him home. Anyway, there wasn't time. So he rode the handlebars the rest of the way to school.

I skidded into the yard just as the two-minute bell was ringing and all the other kids were going through the doors. I couldn't decide what on earth to do with Wol. Then I remembered that I had some twine in my pocket. I fished it out and used it to tie him by one leg to the handlebars.

The first class I had that morning was French. Well, between worrying about Wol and not having done my homework, I was soon in trouble with the teacher (whom we called Fifi behind her back). Fifi made me come up in front of the class so she could tell me how dumb I was. I was standing beside her desk, wishing the floor would open and swallow me up, when there was a whump-whump-whump at the window. I turned my head to look, and there sat Wol.

It hadn't taken him long to untie the twine.

I heard later that he had banged on the windows of two or three other classrooms before he found the right one. Having found the right room at last, he didn't waste any time. Unluckily Fifi had left one of our windows open. Wol ducked down, saw me, and flew right in.

He was probably aiming to land on my shoulder, but he missed and at the last second tried to land on Fifi's desk. It was a polished hardwood desk; he couldn't get a grip on it. His brakes just wouldn't hold; he skated straight across the desk scattering papers and books all over the floor. Fifi saw him coming and tried to get up out of her chair, but she wasn't fast enough. Wol skidded off the end of the desk and plumped right into her lap.

There were some ructions[2] after that. I was sent to the principal's office and Fifi went home for the rest of the day.

We finally figured out a way to keep the owls from following me to school. Each morning, just before I left, we would let Wol and Weeps into the kitchen. Mother would feed them the bacon rinds left over from breakfast, while I sneaked out the front door and rode away. It worked fine, but it was a little hard on Mother because the owls got so fond of the kitchen she usually couldn't get them out of it again. Once I heard her telling a friend that until a woman had tried to bake a cake with two horned owls looking over her shoulders, she hadn't really lived at all!

---

2. **ructions:** disturbances.

SEEKING MEANING

1. Wol tried to make friends with people by riding on their shoulders. In what other way did he express his affection?

2. According to the author, Wol's friendly intentions were misunderstood by strangers. How did Wol introduce himself to the minister? Why was he annoyed by the minister's reaction?

3. The author says that Wol was usually good-natured but that "he *could* get mad." On what occasions did Wol lose his temper? How did he behave when he was angry?

4. After Wol flew into the classroom, there were some *ructions,* or disturbances. How do you imagine the class reacted to Wol's dramatic entrance?

5. People often think of their pets as having human qualities. Why do you suppose this is so?

DEVELOPING SKILLS IN READING

Recognizing Unity

A piece of writing is unified when all its parts help to develop a single idea. Any sentence or paragraph that doesn't deal with this idea weakens the unity of the whole piece.

The selection about Wol is made up of a series of short, humorous incidents drawn from the author's personal experience. These brief, entertaining accounts are known as *anecdotes*. All the anecdotes in the selection are used to illustrate the idea that Wol seemed to think he was human. Where does the author first state this idea? Which anecdote do you think is the most convincing example of this idea?

DEVELOPING SKILLS IN LANGUAGE

Distinguishing Homophones

Words like *feet* and *feat* are called *homophones*. They sound the same, but they are different in meaning and in spelling. In order to decide which homophone to use, you must decide which meaning is intended in any given sentence. Which of the pair, *feet* or *feat*, would you use in this sentence?

News of Samson's heroic _____ spread quickly.

What words are homophones of these words taken from "Owls in the Family"?

pane, mail, brake, rode, too, right

Use each of the homophones in a sentence that makes its meaning clear.

DEVELOPING SKILLS IN EXPRESSION

Writing About a Pet

Wol was an owl who "seemed to think he was people." The author develops this idea partly through the words that are used to describe Wol's behavior. Words such as *friendly, well-mannered, politely, good-natured,* and *furious* are generally used in talking about people. Wol reminds us of a very sensitive person whose feelings are easily hurt.

Have you ever owned or known of a pet that seemed to possess human characteristics? Write a short narrative telling about an incident in which that pet seemed to think it was human. Use words that reveal its special personality.

ABOUT THE AUTHOR

Farley Mowat (1921–   ) is a Canadian writer whose real-life experiences have found their way into many of his short stories and novels. Wol and Weeps, the subjects of his book *Owls in the Family*, are two owls he actually had as pets. The main character of *The Dog Who Wouldn't Be* was his own dog, Mutt. Mowat has written more than twenty novels and has received many awards for books he has written for young people. *Lost in the Barrens* is a suspenseful novel of two boys lost in the Arctic, an area where Mowat has done scientific work. Among his many other books are *The Serpent's Coil, People of the Deer,* and *The Snow Walker.*

This song is from a long poem called Pippa Passes. *In the song Pippa expresses her joy in the beauty of a spring morning.*

Song   *Robert Browning*

The year's at the spring
And day's at the morn;
Morning's at seven;
The hillside's dew-pearled;
The lark's on the wing;
The snail's on the thorn:°   6. **thorn**: a tree or shrub having thorns.
God's in his heaven—
All's right with the world!

SEEKING MEANING

This poem expresses a belief in the harmony, or order, of the natural world. Which lines state this idea directly?

On the Grasshopper and the Cricket

John Keats

The poetry of earth is never dead:
  When all the birds are faint with the hot sun,
  And hide in cooling trees, a voice will run
From hedge to hedge about the new-mown mead;°   **4. mead** (mēd): meadow.
That is the Grasshopper's—he takes the lead   5
  In summer luxury—he has never done
  With his delights; for when tired out with fun
He rests at ease beneath some pleasant weed.
The poetry of earth is ceasing never:
  On a lone winter evening, when the frost   10
    Has wrought° a silence, from the stove there shrills   **11. wrought** (rôt): brought about.
The Cricket's song, in warmth increasing ever,
  And seems to one in drowsiness half lost,
    The Grasshopper's among some grassy hills.

SEEKING MEANING

1. The "poetry of earth" in line 1 refers to the sounds made by creatures of the natural world. Which is the poet of summer? Which is the poet of winter?

2. Contrast the times and places where the Grasshopper and the Cricket make their music. Refer to specific lines in the poem.

3. In lines 11–14 how does the Cricket's song remind the poet of summer? How do you think memory of the summer and "grassy hills" would make the poet feel on a "lone winter evening"?

4. How does Keats show that the "poetry of earth is never dead"? Consider your answers to the previous questions.

ABOUT THE AUTHORS

Robert Browning (1812–1889) and John Keats (1795–1821), two of the greatest poets of the nineteenth century, were both born in England. Their backgrounds were very different. Browning was born into a rich family and was educated by private tutors. He was an avid reader and traveled widely. At the time that he eloped with Elizabeth Barrett, her fame as a poet was greater than his. His reputation grew steadily, however, and during the latter part of his life, Browning achieved worldwide recognition.

John Keats came from a humble family. He lost both his parents when he was young. For a time he was apprenticed to a surgeon, but he gave up medicine to devote himself to poetry. During his brief life, he wrote some of the most beautiful poems in the English language.

Animals Go to School

Edwin Way Teale

Loons are calling in the late-summer dusk on this lonely Adirondack lake.[1] At night I hear the cry of the great horned owl. Swallows—cliff and tree—have moved down from the north at the start of their long migration. Each evening, in my cabin backed by dark forests that go up and up to the very top of a mountain, I light a kerosene lamp and in its yellow glow set down the events of the day. Sitting here, this evening, while the last light has flowed westward out of the sky, I have been remembering an occurrence of the afternoon,

a little adventure in Nature's summer school.

I was coming slowly down a trail so thick with moss that it deadened my footfalls like a plush rug. The only sound that I could hear was the thin shrilling of a distant cicada.[2] All the creatures of the woods seemed slumbering in the hushed heat of the afternoon. The trail crossed the dry bed of a brook and climbed a hillside. At the top, it turned sharply and entered a little open space floored with ferns and uneven with the moldering mounds of old logs. The hillside, to the right

---

1. **Adirondack** (ăd'ə-rŏn'dăk') **lake:** lake in the Adirondack Mountains, a branch of the Appalachian Mountains in northeast New York State.

2. **cicada** (sĭ-kā'də): an insect that makes a high-pitched sound.

of the path, fell away in a steep descent.

Just as I reached the edge of this clearing, a grayish form scuttled across the path and a shrill, high crying, like the squealing of a pig, broke the silence of the woods. The gray form dodged this way and that. It ran among the fern clumps to the left of the trail. It appeared and disappeared while the squealing continued. Then, to the right, there was a sudden windy roaring of wings. A whole brood of partly grown ruffed grouse[3] skimmed away down the slope and disappeared among the trees. The squealing ceased; the mother bird disappeared. She had attracted my attention while the young birds silently ran to the right and launched themselves into the air. The brood had received one of those lessons in caution and escape which, through the wisdom of instinct, mother birds teach their young during the summer months of their earliest growth.

It is during the summertime that most young wild creatures go to school. They are growing up during those long, warm days of plenty. They are learning lessons continually that will aid them in many ways in later life. In Nature's summer school, they acquire knowledge by example, by observation, and by experience.

Because the red fox is legendary for its cunning and resourcefulness, it is not surprising to find that the schooling that red-fox kits receive is almost human in its program of progressive training. The parents use an elaborate and careful system for educating their offspring in the art of making a living.

As soon as the kits are weaned, the mother fox begins bringing captured mice, birds and rabbits into the den. As the young foxes grow older, the food is dropped at the entrance instead of being brought inside. A little later, it is deposited a few feet outside the entrance. Then it is placed several yards away and, finally, the kits have to search over an area of several hundred square yards to find their dinners. During the last part of the training, the parent foxes begin hiding the captured birds or rabbits beneath leaves and rubbish, thus forcing the kits to use their sense of smell as well as their eyes in making their discoveries. In this practical, progressive manner, the school for foxes educates the young animals for the vital work of hunting.

The primary lesson taught to most wild creatures is who and what to fear. Over and over again, the need for eternal vigilance and caution is impressed upon them.

A friend of mine was walking down a village street lined with maple trees, one summer morning, when a baby gray squirrel scrambled fearlessly down a nearby trunk. It came directly toward him in a series of little loping hops, its tiny tail flipping at every jump. When it was six feet away, it came to a sudden stop. An ear-piercing chatter had reached it from the branches overhead. Rattling over the bark, the mother squirrel came racing down the tree. She scurried to the baby, scolding at the top of her lungs. She gave him a nip that made him jump. Then she grabbed him by the back of the neck and lugged him, kittenwise, to the foot of the tree trunk. The youngster had learned a lesson in caution, a lesson that might save its life on a later day.

A knowledge of the dangers of the world is far from instinctive in many creatures. When kittens and mice grow up together, the mice show no instinctive fear of the cats. That fear is learned. Young crows are far more fearless than their parents. Among the Indiana dunes, I once passed close to a dead tree in which two young crows perched, eyeing me without any

---

3. **ruffed grouse:** birds with a ring of neck feathers resembling a stiff collar.

sign of concern while their parents circled at a distance, cawing their alarm.

On this Adirondack lake, the other morning, I rounded a rocky headland in my canoe and came upon a family of merganser ducks.[4] At the mother's warning quack, the ducklings disappeared behind a jutting rock. Then, quacking continually, rushing about, skittering over the surface of the lake, the mother merganser sought to hold my attention. Her performance was so good it defeated its purpose. The baby ducks peered out from behind their rock, then paddled out in a string, bobbing up and down in the choppy water, to watch the show. Like backward pupils, they still had to learn the primary lesson of their wild classroom, how to act in the presence of possible danger.

In contrast with these too-trusting mergansers, some creatures go to the other extreme. They have to be taught self-confidence. A farmboy, coming down a lonely backwoods road, witnessed such a lesson being taught to young mink. Near an old bridge which spanned a brook, he saw a procession of a mother mink and five quarter-grown babies appear from the bushes at the side of the road. The mother trotted on across. Then she looked back. The youngsters were huddled together, fearfully, in the bushes. They were afraid to enter the open roadway. She ran back and tried to encourage them. Time after time, the procession would start on across the road. And each time, the little mink would lose their courage and scurry back into the protection of the bushes. This went on until the mother lost patience. One by one, she grabbed them by the back of the neck and carried them to the other side. There the procession formed once more and, single file, the animals disappeared in the bushes.

4. **merganser** (mər-găn′sər) **ducks:** fish-eating, diving ducks.

What not to fear as well as what to fear is one of the basic studies in the school of the out-of-doors. A few blocks from my home, a bluejay, that had tumbled out of the nest before it was able to fly, was raised in the protection of a greenhouse. As it gained the use of its wings, it would dart back and forth within its transparent world, investigating, with bright eyes and sharp bill, every hole and cranny. One August day, a tiger swallowtail butterfly was released in the greenhouse. As it bobbed about in the sunshine, the young bluejay screamed in terror and fled to the farthest corner of the building. It had never seen a butterfly before and, lacking the outdoor training its wild kindred had received, it viewed it as an unknown and mortal foe.

A sagacious scientist once remarked that our consciences are the sum total of our mothers' scoldings. Similarly, much of the wisdom of the wild that is not instinctive is the product of the reprimands of the parents. Obedience is essential to safety. From the dappled fawn, remaining immobile in the presence of danger, to the young opossums, clinging pickaback with their tails curled about the arching tail of their mother, baby animals have to learn the lesson of obedience in order to sidestep danger. Their very lives may depend upon it. Punishment for failure in Nature's school is often swift and fatal.

On all sides, in woods and fields, during the summer days and nights, young animals and birds are learning specialized skills as well as fundamental knowledge. Baby raccoons, ambling along like miniature bears, follow their parents through the darkness to brooks and ponds there to learn the art of catching frogs and crayfish. Young barn swallows dart out from perches to scoop insects from the air that have been dropped close to them by their hovering parents and thus learn to secure their food on the wing. Young otters, riding

on their mothers' backs, are carried out into the water and gradually taught to swim.

On the south shore of Long Island, a bayman once observed a marsh hawk schooling its offspring in catching prey. With its parent, the young bird was circling over a wide stretch of sea moor, tilting this way and that in the light breeze. Below the two hawks, a flicker[5] darted from the edge of a woods. Rising and falling, with quick, strong thrusts of its wings, it passed below. The parent bird swept downward and snatched the woodpecker from the air. Then it did a surprising thing. It flapped upward to a height of several hundred feet, closely followed by the young hawk. At the height of its climb, it suddenly released the woodpecker. The young hawk swooped after it, overtook it, and grasped it in its talons before it could reach the protection of the trees. It had learned a valuable lesson in overtaking prey aloft, learned it by observation and personal experience.

---

5. **flicker:** a woodpecker.

Learning by doing, of course, plays an important part in the education of most creatures of the wild. In an open field, just north of my Insect Garden, I once almost stepped on a baby cottontail rabbit crouching in the grass. It bolted away. Instinct told it to run. Instinct told it to dodge this way and that. But only experience could teach it that it couldn't make right-angled turns when going at top speed. Four times, as it shot in one direction and then in another in its panic, it turned so abruptly it lost its balance. With its feet running in the air so fast they became almost a blur, it lay kicking on its side. Then it would right itself only to bolt off and repeat the procedure. It was discovering what it couldn't do. It was learning, and experience was its teacher.

An old beaver trapper, who for half a century had followed a trapline through the Dead River region of northern Maine, once told me that far back in the woods young beavers sometimes make practice dams of mud and twigs across rivulets. The youngsters of the beaver colony were gaining, in a kind of play, experience that someday would prove of real importance.

Similarly, as summer nears its end, young woodchucks begin digging practice burrows which they never use. On one sandy hillside in northern Indiana, I recall a place where six such holes were excavated among the mullein[6] stalks and the sandburs[7] within the space of a hundred yards. Young woodchucks from a burrow under a pine stump nearby were trying out their skill in making practice tunnels. Before winter came, each of the animals had made a satisfactory burrow— thanks, at least in part, to the experience of warm, late-summer days and nights.

All animals, even the most humble, appear to have some ability to learn from experience. An earthworm can learn to turn to the right or the left when it is placed in a maze in which it receives an unpleasant electric shock when it makes a wrong turn. Its nervous system records the lesson thus learned and the earthworm will even continue to make the correct turn after its head has been cut off. Crayfish can be taught to come to a certain spot for feeding. Frogs can remember the correct path through a laboratory maze after a lapse of a month. In one experiment, a single tentacle of a sea anemone[8] learned, independently of all the other tentacles, to reject wads of paper when they were offered as food. Even one-celled protozoa[9] have individuals that are able to learn simple lessons such as avoiding over-acid water or dye particles among their food.

---

6. **mullein** (mŭl'ən): a tall plant with woolly leaves.
7. **sandburs:** shrubby weeds.
8. **sea anemone** (ə-něm'ə-nē): a flowerlike animal with colorful tentacles, or armlike parts, which attaches itself to underwater rocks.
9. **protozoa** (prō'tə-zō'ə): the simplest forms of animal life, visible only under a microscope.

Always, the things a creature learns are in line with its inherited capacities. A meadowlark, sailing out over a hayfield, will drop down near its nest amid a sea of waving grass. How does it recognize the place? How does it find landmarks where everything looks the same? Tiny differences are caught by its keen eyes, differences which its inherited ability and its training fit it to see.

In truth, that accomplishment—over which I never cease to marvel—is far less surprising than the performance of two work horses I once saw standing in the shade of a tree at the edge of a pasture. They remained side by side, facing in opposite directions. In this position, the swishing of their tails kept them both, front and back, free from flies. This scheme, hit upon by chance or by experience, was advantageous to them both. All larks possess the ability to find their nests amid acres of moving grass; but only a few horses ever make use of the rational stratagem that aided those two animals under the pasture tree.

SEEKING MEANING

1. Teale says that the primary lesson baby animals must learn is "who and what to fear." Give three examples from the selection that show how animals are taught caution.

2. Teale says that the schooling of red-fox kits is "almost human in its program of progressive training." The word *progressive* here means "step-by-step." What steps are used in training baby foxes to become hunters? In what way is the training almost human?

3. In addition to behavior that is instinctive, animals learn new behavior through firsthand experience. How are both kinds of behavior shown in the actions of the cottontail rabbit?

4. Teale marvels over the ability of the meadowlark to find its nest in a sea of waving grass. Why does he find the stratagem of the two work horses even more remarkable? What have the horses learned through chance or experience?

5. How would you describe Teale's feelings for the natural world?

DEVELOPING SKILLS IN READING

Finding the Main Idea of a Paragraph

The word *paragraph* comes from two Greek words: *para*, meaning "beside," and *graphein*, meaning "to write." Centuries ago, when books were copied by hand, scribes did not divide a manuscript into paragraphs as we do today. Instead they wrote a certain mark beside the place where a new idea began. This mark was called a paragraph.

Today, of course, we use the word *paragraph* to refer to a series of sentences that develop a single idea or topic. We indicate the beginning of a paragraph by indenting the first sentence in the series.

Sometimes a writer will state the main idea or topic of a paragraph in a sentence called the *topic sentence*. The topic sentence is usually placed at the beginning of the paragraph.

Look at this paragraph from "Animals Go to School." Which sentence states the main idea of the paragraph?

A knowledge of the dangers of the world is far from instinctive in many creatures. When kittens and mice grow up together, the mice show no instinctive fear of the cats. That fear is learned. Young crows are far more fearless than their parents. Among the Indiana dunes, I once passed close to a dead tree in which two young crows perched, eyeing me without any sign of concern while their parents circled at a distance, cawing their alarm.

What examples does Teale give in the paragraph? How do they support the main idea?

DEVELOPING VOCABULARY

Analyzing Words from a Latin Root

How are *education* and *duke* related? The answer is that they both come from the Latin verb *ducere*, meaning "to lead." Because it is the source of several English words, *ducere* is called a *root word*. It usually appears in the form -*duce* (as in pro*duce*) or in the form -*duct* (as in pro*duct*).

Many English words are related because they come from the same root word. Such related words are considered members of a *word family*. Here are some other members of the *ducere* family:

reduce	conduct	induct

Reduce comes from a Latin word meaning "to lead back." What happens when you *reduce* fractions to their lowest terms? Someone who *conducts* an orchestra leads or guides the individual musicians. What is the meaning of *induct*?

Look up the meanings of the following words in a dictionary. What does each word have to do with the Latin root word meaning "to lead"?

adduce	deduct	ductile
conducive	educe	traduce

Among the Pueblos, a group of Indians of the Southwest, "warrior priest" is a religious title. The warrior priest has special powers or special kinds of knowledge that are useful to the Pueblos in time of war or when the community is threatened in some way. The weapons of the warrior priest are mainly spiritual or psychological: he can cast or break spells, and initiate prayers or chants. In this story, Humaweepi recalls how he was prepared for his role as a warrior priest.

Humaweepi, the Warrior Priest   *Leslie Silko*

The old man didn't really teach him much; mostly they just lived. Occasionally Humaweepi would meet friends his own age who still lived with their families in the pueblo,[1] and they would ask him what he was doing; they seemed disappointed when he told them.

"That's nothing," they would say.

Once this had made Humaweepi sad and his uncle noticed. "Oh," he said when Humaweepi told him, "that shows you how little they know."

They returned to the pueblo for the ceremonials and special days. His uncle stayed in the kiva[2] with the other priests, and Humaweepi usually stayed with clan members because his mother and father had been very old when he was born and now they were gone. Some-times during these stays, when the pueblo was full of the activity and excitement of the dances or the fiesta when the Christians paraded out of the pueblo church carrying the saint, Humaweepi would wonder why he was living out in the hills with the old man. When he was twelve he thought he had it all figured out: the old man just wanted someone to live with him and help him with the goat and to chop wood and carry water. But it was peaceful in this place, and Humaweepi discovered that after all these years of sitting beside his uncle in the evenings, he knew the songs and chants for all the seasons, and he was beginning to learn the prayers for the trees and plants and animals. "Oh," Humaweepi said to himself, "I have been learning all this time and I didn't even know it."

Once the old man told Humaweepi to prepare for a long trip.

"Overnight?"

---

1. **pueblo** (pwĕb′lō): a village in which several families live together in dwellings built of stone or adobe.
2. **kiva** (kē′və): an underground room used for religious ceremonies or council meetings.

The old man nodded.

So Humaweepi got out a white cotton sack and started filling it with jerked venison,[3] piki bread,[4] and dried apples. But the old man shook his head sternly. It was late June then, so Humaweepi didn't bother to bring the blankets; he had learned to sleep on the ground like the old man did.

"Human beings are special," his uncle had told him once, "which means they can do anything. They can sleep on the ground like the doe and fawn."

And so Humaweepi had learned how to find the places in the scrub-oak thickets where the deer had slept, where the dry oak leaves were arranged into nests. This is where he and his uncle slept, even in the autumn when the nights were cold and Humaweepi could hear the leaves snap in the middle of the night and drift to the ground.

Sometimes they carried food from home, but often they went without food or blankets. When Humaweepi asked him what they would eat, the old man had waved his hand at the sky and earth around them. "I am a human being, Humaweepi," he said; "I eat anything." On these trips they had gathered grass roots and washed them in little sandstone basins made by the wind to catch rain water. The roots had a rich, mealy taste. Then they left the desert below and climbed into the mesa country, and the old man had led Humaweepi to green leafy vines hanging from crevasses in the face of the sandstone cliffs. "Wild grapes," he said as he dropped some tiny dark-purple berries into Humaweepi's open palms. And in the high mountains there were wild iris roots and the bulbs from wild tulips which grew among the lacy ferns and

---

3. **jerked venison:** sun-dried strips of deer meat.
4. **piki** (pē′kē) **bread:** thin sheets of corn bread.

green grass beside the mountain streams. They had gone out like this in each season. Summer and fall, and finally, spring and winter. "Winter isn't easy," the old man had said. "All the animals are hungry—not just you."

So this time, when his uncle shook his head at the food, Humaweepi left it behind as he had many times before. His uncle took the special leather pouch off the nail on the wall, and Humaweepi pulled his own buckskin bundle out from under his mattress. Inside he had a few objects of his own. A dried blossom. Fragile and yellow. A smooth pink quartz crystal in the shape of a star. Tiny turquoise beads the color of a summer sky. And a black obsidian[5] arrowhead, shiny and sharp. They each had special meaning to him, and the old man had instructed him to assemble these things with special meaning. "Someday maybe you will derive strength from these things." That's what the old man had said.

They walked west toward the distant blue images of the mountain peaks. The water in the Rio Grande was still cold. Humaweepi was aware of the dampness on his feet: when he got back from his journey he decided he would make sandals for himself because it took hours for his boots to dry out again. His uncle wore old sandals woven from twisted yucca[6] fiber and they dried out almost immediately. The old man didn't approve of boots and shoes—bad for you, he said. In the winter he wore buckskin moccasins and in the warm months, these yucca sandals.

They walked all day, steadily, stopping occasionally when the old man found a flower or herb or stone that he wanted Humaweepi to see. And it seemed to Humaweepi that he

had learned the names of everything, and he said so to his uncle.

The old man frowned and poked at a small blue flower with his walking stick. "That's what a priest must know," he said and walked rapidly then, pointing at stones and shrubs. "How old are you?" he demanded.

"Nineteen," Humaweepi answered.

"All your life," he said, "every day, I have been teaching you."

After that they walked along in silence, and Humaweepi began to feel anxious; all of a sudden he knew that something was going to happen on this journey. That night they reached the white sandstone cliffs at the foot of the mountain foothills. At the base of these cliffs were shallow overhangs with sandy floors. They slept in the sand under the rock overhang; in the night Humaweepi woke up to the call of a young owl; the sky was bright with stars and a half-moon. The smell of the night air made him shiver and he buried himself more deeply in the cliff sand.

In the morning they gathered tumbleweed sprouts that were succulent and tender. As they climbed the cliffs there were wild grapevines, and under the fallen leaves around the vine roots, the old man uncovered dried grapes shrunken into tiny sweet raisins. By noon they had reached the first of the mountain streams. There they washed and drank water and rested.

The old man frowned and pointed at Humaweepi's boots. "Take them off," he told Humaweepi; "leave them here until we come back."

So Humaweepi pulled off his cowboy boots and put them under a lichen-covered[7] boulder near a big oak tree where he could find them.

---

5. **obsidian** (əb-sĭd′ē-ən): a shiny glass produced by volcanoes.
6. **yucca:** a plant with stiff, sharp leaves and white flowers.

7. **lichen** (lī′kən) **-covered:** covered with a grayish-green, mosslike plant growth.

Then Humaweepi relaxed, feeling the coolness of air on his bare feet. He watched his uncle, dozing in the sun with his back against a big pine. The old man's hair had been white and long ever since Humaweepi could remember; but the old face was changing, and Humaweepi could see the weariness there—a weariness not from their little journey but from a much longer time in this world. Someday he will die, Humaweepi was thinking. He will be gone and I will be by myself. I will have to do the things he did. I will have to take care of things.

Humaweepi had never seen the lake before. It appeared suddenly as they reached the top of a hill covered with aspen trees. Humaweepi looked at his uncle and was going to ask him about the lake, but the old man was singing and feeding corn pollen from his leather pouch to the mountain winds. Humaweepi stared at the lake and listened to the songs. The songs were snowstorms with sounds as soft and cold as snowflakes; the songs were spring rain and wild ducks returning. Humaweepi could hear this; he could hear his uncle's voice become the night wind—high-pitched and whining in the trees. Time was lost and there was only the space, the depth, the distance of the lake surrounded by the mountain peaks.

When Humaweepi looked up from the lake he noticed that the sun had moved down into the western part of the sky. He looked around to find his uncle. The old man was below him, kneeling on the edge of the lake, touching a big gray boulder and singing softly. Humaweepi made his way down the narrow rocky trail to the edge of the lake. The water was crystal and clear like air; Humaweepi could see the golden rainbow colors of the trout that lived there. Finally the old man motioned for Humaweepi to come to him. He pointed at the gray boulder that lay half in the lake and half on the shore. It was then that Humaweepi saw what it was. The bear. Magic creature of the mountains, powerful ally to men. Humaweepi unrolled his buckskin bundle and picked up the tiny beads—sky-blue turquoise and coral that was dark red. He sang the bear song and stepped into the icy, clear water to lay the beads on bear's head, gray granite rock, resting above the lake, facing west.

"Bear
  resting in the mountains
  sleeping by the lake
Bear
  I come to you, a man,
  to ask you:
Stand beside us in our battles
  walk with us in peace.
Bear
  I ask you for your power
  I am the warrior priest,
  I ask you for your power
  I am the warrior priest."

It wasn't until he had finished singing the song that Humaweepi realized what the words said. He turned his head toward the old man. He smiled at Humaweepi and nodded his head. Humaweepi nodded back.

Humaweepi tells a friend of a trip he and his uncle took to the mountain in the winter.

Humaweepi and his friend were silent for a long time. Finally Humaweepi said, "I'll tell you what my uncle told me, one winter, before he left. We took a trip to the mountain. It was early January, but the sun was warm and down here the snow was gone. We left early in the morning when the sky in the east was dark gray and the brightest star was still shining low in the western sky. I remember he didn't wear his ceremonial moccasins; he wore his old yucca sandals. I asked him about that.

"He said, 'Oh, you know the badger and the squirrel. Same shoes summer and winter,' but I think he was making that up, because when we got to the sandstone cliffs he buried the sandals in the sandy bottom of the cave where we slept and after that he walked on bare feet —up the cliff and along the mountain trail.

"There was snow on the shady side of the trees and big rocks, but the path we followed was in the sun and it was dry. I could hear melting snow—the icy water trickling down into the little streams and the little streams flowing into the big stream in the canyon where yellow bee flowers grow all summer. The sun felt warm on my body, touching me, but my breath still made steam in the cold mountain air.

" 'Aren't your feet cold?' I asked him.

"He stopped and looked at me for a long time, then shook his head. 'Look at these old feet,' he said. 'Do you see any corns or bunions?'

"I shook my head.

" 'That's right,' he said, 'my feet are beautiful. No one has feet like these. Especially you people who wear shoes and boots.' He walked on ahead before he said anything else. 'You have seen babies, haven't you?' he asked.

"I nodded, but I was wondering what this had to do with the old man's feet.

" 'Well, then you've noticed their grandmothers and their mothers, always worried about keeping the feet warm. But have you watched the babies? Do they care? No!' the old man said triumphantly; 'they do not care. They play outside on a cold winter day, no shoes, no jacket, because they aren't cold.' He hiked on, moving rapidly, excited by his own words; then he stopped at the stream. 'But human beings are what they are. It's not long

before they are taught to be cold and they cry for their shoes.'

"The old man started digging around the edge of a stream, using a crooked, dry branch to poke through the melting snow. 'Here,' he said as he gave me a fat, round root, 'try this.'

"I squatted at the edge of the rushing, swirling water, full of mountain dirt, churning, swelling, and rolling—rich and brown and muddy with ice pieces flashing in the sun. I held the root motionless under the force of the stream water; the ice coldness of the water felt pure and clear as the ice that clung to the rocks in midstream. When I pulled my hand back it was stiff. I shook it and the root and lifted them high toward the sky.

"The old man laughed, and his mouth was full of the milky fibers of the root. He walked up the hill, away from the sound of the muddy stream surging through the snowbanks. At the top of the hill there was a grove of big aspens; it was colder, and the snow hadn't melted much.

" 'Your feet,' I said to him. 'They'll freeze.'

"The snow was up to my ankles now. He was sitting on a fallen aspen, with his feet stretched out in front of him and his eyes half closed, facing into the sun.

" 'Does the wolf freeze his feet?' the old man asked me.

"I shook my head.

" 'Well then,' he said.

" 'But you aren't a wolf,' I started to say.

"The old man's eyes opened wide and then looked at me narrowly, sharply, squinting and shining. He gave a long, wailing, wolf cry with his head raised toward the winter sky.

"It was all white—pale white—the sky, the aspens bare white, smooth and white as the snow frozen on the ground. The wolf cry echoed off the rocky mountain slopes around us; in the distance I thought I heard a wailing answer."

SEEKING MEANING

1. Each season Humaweepi and his uncle make trips into the desert and into the mountains, often without food or blankets. What does Humaweepi learn during these trips?

2. Humaweepi takes no food for the journey to the lake. What objects does he take? What special meaning do you think they might have for him?

3. Humaweepi's uncle feels close to nature. He feels that he is part of the natural world. What indication is there at the lake that Humaweepi is beginning to share his uncle's feelings for nature?

4. Humaweepi realizes that he will have to take his uncle's place someday. How does the bear song show that he is ready? What understanding occurs between him and his uncle?

5. On their trip to the mountain, Humaweepi's uncle takes off his sandals and walks barefoot in the snow. What lesson is he trying to teach Humaweepi? Why does he howl like a wolf?

ABOUT THE AUTHOR

Leslie Marmon Silko (1942–   ) was born in Albuquerque and attended the University of New Mexico. A Laguna Pueblo, she brings a direct knowledge of Indian lore and tradition to her writing. The events and characters in "Humaweepi, the Warrior Priest" are fictitious, but the details of Laguna Pueblo life are accurate.

Leslie Marmon Silko has published short stories, poetry, and a novel. She now lives in New Mexico with her family and teaches literature and creative writing at the University of New Mexico.

The Wreck of the *Hesperus*

Henry Wadsworth Longfellow

It was the schooner *Hesperus,*
   That sailed the wintry sea;
And the skipper had taken his little daughter
   To bear him company.

Blue were her eyes as the fairy flax,   5
   Her cheeks like the dawn of day,
And her bosom white as the hawthorn buds
   That ope° in the month of May.   8. **ope:** open.

The skipper he stood beside the helm,
   His pipe was in his mouth,   10
And he watched how the veering flaw° did blow   11. **flaw:** a sudden blast of wind.
   The smoke now west, now south.

Then up and spake an old sailor,
   Had sailed to the Spanish Main,°   14. **Spanish Main:** parts of the
"I pray thee, put into yonder port,   15   Caribbean Sea once traveled by
   For I fear a hurricane.   Spanish ships.

"Last night, the moon had a golden ring,
   And tonight no moon we see!"
The skipper, he blew a whiff from his pipe,
   And a scornful laugh laughed he.   20

Colder and louder blew the wind,
    A gale from the northeast,
The snow fell hissing in the brine,
    And the billows frothed like yeast.

Down came the storm, and smote amain°   25   25. **smote amain:** struck with
    The vessel in its strength;   great force.
She shuddered and paused, like a frightened steed,
    Then leaped her cable's length.

"Come hither! come hither! my little daughter,
    And do not tremble so;   30
For I can weather the roughest gale
    That ever wind did blow."

He wrapped her warm in his seaman's coat
    Against the stinging blast;
He cut a rope from a broken spar,   35
    And bound her to the mast.

"O Father! I hear the church bells ring;
    Oh, say, what may it be?"
" 'Tis a fog bell on a rock-bound coast!"
    And he steered for the open sea.   40

"O Father! I hear the sound of guns;
  Oh, say, what may it be?"
"Some ship in distress, that cannot live
  In such an angry sea!"

"O Father! I see a gleaming light;   45
  Oh, say, what may it be?"
But the father answered never a word,
  A frozen corpse was he.

Lashed to the helm, and stiff and stark,
  With his face turned to the skies,   50
The lantern gleamed through the gleaming snow
  On his fixed and glassy eyes.

Then the maiden clasped her hands and prayed
  That savèd she might be;
And she thought of Christ, who stilled the wave   55
  On the Lake of Galilee.°

55–56. **Christ . . . Galilee:** This story is told in Matthew 8: 23–27.

And fast through the midnight dark and drear,
  Through the whistling sleet and snow,
Like a sheeted ghost, the vessel swept
  Toward the reef of Norman's Woe.°   60

60. **Norman's Woe:** a chain of rocks near Gloucester, Massachusetts.

And ever the fitful gusts between,
  A sound came from the land;
It was the sound of the trampling surf
  On the rocks and the hard sea sand.

The breakers were right beneath her bows,   65
  She drifted a dreary wreck,
And a whooping billow swept the crew
  Like icicles from her deck.

She struck where the white and fleecy waves
  Looked soft as carded° wool,   70   70. **carded:** combed.
But the cruel rocks, they gored her side
  Like the horns of an angry bull.

Her rattling shrouds,° all sheathed in ice,   73. **shrouds:** ropes hanging from
  With the masts went by the board;   the mast.
Like a vessel of glass, she stove° and sank;   75   75. **stove:** smashed.
  Ho! ho! the breakers roared!

At daybreak, on the black sea beach,
  A fisherman stood aghast,
To see the form of a maiden fair,
  Lashed close to a drifting mast.   80

The salt sea was frozen on her breast,
  The salt tears in her eyes;
And he saw her hair, like the brown seaweed,
  On the billows fall and rise.

Such was the wreck of the *Hesperus*,   85
  In the midnight and the snow!
Christ save us all from a death like this,
  On the reef of Norman's Woe!

SEEKING MEANING

1. What signs are there of the approaching storm? Why is the skipper confident that he can ride out the storm?

2. Why does the skipper bind his daughter to the mast?

3. What is the first warning from the people on land? How does the skipper react to this warning?

4. Two other warnings are sent to the ship. What do you think is the meaning of the guns in line 41? The gleaming light in line 45?

5. What is the fate of the skipper and his crew? Of the skipper's daughter?

6. In which lines does Longfellow emphasize the strength and cruelty of the storm?

DEVELOPING SKILLS IN READING

Understanding Comparisons

Longfellow gives this description of the ship's movement when the storm strikes:

> She shuddered and paused, like a frightened steed,
>   Then leaped her cable's length.

The ship is compared here to a frightened horse that trembles, then springs from the ground. What can you picture happening to the ship?

In which lines does the poet compare the rocks to the horns of a bull? How does this comparison emphasize the violence of the storm?

How do the comparisons in lines 5–8 stress the girl's delicate beauty? Compare this picture with the one in lines 81–84.

Tell in your own words what the comparisons in the following lines suggest to you.

> And the billows frothed like yeast.
>   (line 24)
> Like a sheeted ghost, the vessel swept
>   Toward the reef of Norman's Woe.
>   (lines 59–60)
> And a whooping billow swept the crew
>   Like icicles from her deck. (lines 67–68)
> She struck where the white and fleecy waves
>   Looked soft as carded wool, (lines 69–70)
> Like a vessel of glass, she stove and sank;
>   (line 75)

Helen Keller lost her sight and hearing as a result of a childhood illness. With the help of a remarkable teacher, Anne Sullivan, she learned how to communicate with others. An extraordinary pupil, she learned to speak and to read Braille. She attended college and became a writer and a lecturer. Her achievements are legendary.

In this selection from her autobiography, Helen Keller recalls a childhood experience which taught her that nature could be frightening. Her sensitivity to the changing moods of nature almost makes us forget that she was totally blind and deaf.

The Two Faces of Nature

Helen Keller

I recall many incidents of the summer of 1887 that followed my soul's sudden awakening. I did nothing but explore with my hands and learn the name of every object that I touched; and the more I handled things and learned their names and uses, the more joyous and confident grew my sense of kinship with the rest of the world.

When the time of daisies and buttercups came Miss Sullivan took me by the hand across the fields, where men were preparing the earth for the seed, to the banks of the Tennessee River, and there, sitting on the warm grass, I had my first lessons in the beneficence[1] of nature. I learned how the sun and the rain make to grow out of the ground every tree that is pleasant to the sight and good for food, how birds build their nests and live and thrive from land to land, how the squirrel, the deer, the lion and every other creature finds food and shelter. As my knowledge of things grew I felt more and more the delight of the world I was in. Long before I learned to do a sum in arithmetic or describe the shape of the earth, Miss Sullivan had taught me to find beauty in the fragrant woods, in every blade of grass, and in the curves and dimples of my baby sister's hand. She linked my earliest thoughts with nature, and made me feel that "birds and flowers and I were happy peers."

But about this time I had an experience which taught me that nature is not always kind. One day my teacher and I were returning from a long ramble. The morning had been fine, but it was growing warm and sultry when at last we turned our faces homeward. Two or three times we stopped to rest under a tree by the wayside. Our last halt was under a wild cherry tree a short distance from the house. The shade was grateful, and the tree was so easy to climb that with my teacher's assistance I was able to scramble to a seat in the branches. It was so cool up in the tree that

---

1. **beneficence** (bə-něf′ə-səns): goodness.

Miss Sullivan proposed that we have our luncheon there. I promised to keep still while she went to the house to fetch it.

Suddenly a change passed over the tree. All the sun's warmth left the air. I knew the sky was black, because all the heat, which meant light to me, had died out of the atmosphere. A strange odor came up from the earth. I knew it, it was the odor that always precedes a thunderstorm, and a nameless fear clutched at my heart. I felt absolutely alone, cut off from my friends and the firm earth. The immense, the unknown, enfolded me. I remained still and expectant; a chilling terror crept over me. I longed for my teacher's return; but above all things I wanted to get down from that tree.

There was a moment of sinister silence, then a multitudinous stirring of the leaves.[2] A shiver ran through the tree, and the wind sent

---

2. **multitudinous** (mul′tə-tōod′n-əs) . . . **leaves:** stirring of a great number of leaves.

forth a blast that would have knocked me off had I not clung to the branch with might and main. The tree swayed and strained. The small twigs snapped and fell about me in showers. A wild impulse to jump seized me, but terror held me fast. I crouched down in the fork of the tree. The branches lashed about me. I felt the intermittent jarring that came now and then, as if something heavy had fallen and the shock had traveled up till it reached the limb I sat on. It worked my suspense up to the highest point, and just as I was thinking the tree and I should fall together, my teacher seized my hand and helped me down. I clung to her, trembling with joy to feel the earth under my feet once more. I had learned a new lesson — that nature "wages open war against her children, and under softest touch hides treacherous claws."

After this experience it was a long time before I climbed another tree. The mere thought filled me with terror. It was the sweet allurement of the mimosa tree in full bloom that finally overcame my fears. One beautiful spring morning when I was alone in the summerhouse, reading, I became aware of a wonderful subtle fragrance in the air. I started up and instinctively stretched out my hands. It seemed as if the spirit of spring had passed through the summerhouse. "What is it?" I asked, and the next minute I recognized the odor of the mimosa blossoms. I felt my way to the end of the garden, knowing that the mimosa tree was near the fence, at the turn of the path. Yes, there it was, all quivering in the warm sunshine, its blossom-laden branches almost touching the long grass. Was there ever anything so exquisitely beautiful in the world before! Its delicate blossoms shrank from the slightest earthly touch; it seemed as if a tree of paradise had been transplanted to earth. I made my way through a shower of petals to the great trunk and for one minute

stood irresolute; then, putting my foot in the broad space between the forked branches, I pulled myself up into the tree. I had some difficulty in holding on, for the branches were very large and the bark hurt my hands. But I had a delicious sense that I was doing something unusual and wonderful, so I kept on climbing higher and higher, until I reached a little seat which somebody had built there so long ago that it had grown part of the tree itself. I sat there for a long, long time, feeling like a fairy on a rosy cloud. After that I spent many happy hours in my tree of paradise, thinking fair thoughts and dreaming bright dreams.

SEEKING MEANING

1. Helen Keller could not see or hear the changes that passed over the tree. How did she respond to the approaching storm with her other senses?

2. The author compares nature to an animal that "under softest touch hides treacherous claws." How did her own experience convince her that nature could be treacherous?

3. What made Helen Keller climb a tree again? How did she feel when she did?

DEVELOPING VOCABULARY

Building Words with Prefixes and Suffixes

Some prefixes and suffixes occur so frequently in our language that knowing their meanings can help you work out the meanings of many new words. One of the most common prefixes in our language is *pre-*, which means "before." Find the sentence on page 193 in which *precedes* occurs. What does the word mean? Can you guess the meaning of the root *-cede*? Check your answers in a dictionary.

Add the prefix *pre-* to each of the following words. Work out the meanings of the new words. Then check your answers.

arrange	determine	mature
caution	judge	view

Another prefix that appears in many English words is *trans-*, which means "across" or "through." Find the sentence on page 194 in which the word *transplanted* occurs. Using context clues and structure clues, tell what the word means.

What is the meaning of *transatlantic*? Of *transform*? Of *transport*?

The suffix *-ous* means "full of." By adding *-ous* to a noun, you form an adjective. Form adjectives from the following nouns by adding the suffix *-ous*. What changes in spelling are necessary?

adventure	fame	outrage
envy	marvel	treachery

Another adjective-forming suffix is *-less*, which means "without." Form adjectives from these nouns by adding the suffix *-less*:

form	hope	shape
home	point	thought

"A rifle might be a symbol of power, but unless a man was also a hunter, a rifle did him no good."

The Tiger's Heart

Jim Kjelgaard

The approaching jungle night was, in itself, a threat. As it deepened, an eerie silence enveloped the thatched village. People were silent. Tethered cattle stood quietly. Roosting chickens did not stir and wise goats made no noise. Thus it had been for countless centuries and thus it would continue to be. The brown-skinned inhabitants of the village knew the jungle. They had trodden its dim paths, forded its sulky rivers, borne its streaming heat, and were intimately acquainted with its deer, tapir,[1] crocodiles, screaming green parrots and countless other creatures.

That was the daytime jungle they could see, feel and hear, but at night everything became different. When darkness came, the jungle was alive with strange and horrible things which no man had ever seen and no man could describe. They were shadows that had no substance and one was unaware of them until they struck and killed. Then, with morning, they changed themselves back into the shape of familiar things. Because it was a time of the unknown, night had to be a time of fear.

Except, Pepe Garcia[2] reflected, to the man who owned a rifle. As the night closed in, Pepe reached out to fondle his rifle and make sure that it was close beside him. As long as it was, he was king.

That was only just, for the rifle had cost

---

1. **tapir** (tā′pər): large jungle animals related to the rhinoceros.

2. **Pepe Garcia** (pā′pä gär-sē′ä).

him dearly. With eleven others from his village, Pepe had gone to help chop a right of way for the new road. They used machetes,[3] the indispensable long knife of all jungle dwellers, and they had worked hard. Unlike the rest, Pepe had saved every peso[4] he didn't have to spend for immediate living expenses. With his savings, and after some haggling, he had bought his muzzle-loading rifle, a supply of powder, lead, and a mold in which he could fashion bullets for his rifle.

Eighty pesos the rifle had cost him. But it was worth the price. Though the jungle at night was fear itself, no man with a rifle had to fear. The others, who had only machetes with which to guard themselves from the terrors that came in the darkness, were willing to pay well for protection. Pepe went peacefully to sleep.

He did not know what awakened him, only that something was about. He listened intently, but there was no change in the jungle's monotonous night sounds. Still, something was not as it should be.

Then he heard it. At the far end of the village, near Juan Aria's[5] hut, a goat bleated uneasily. Silence followed. The goat bleated again, louder and more fearful. There was a pattering rush of small hoofs, a frightened bleat cut short, again silence.

Pepe, who did not need to people the night with fantastic creatures because he owned a rifle, interpreted correctly what he had heard. A tiger, a jaguar,[6] had come in the night, leaped the thorn fence with which the village was surrounded, and made off with one of Juan Aria's goats.

Pepe went peacefully back to sleep. With morning, certainly, Juan Aria would come to him.

He did not awaken until the sun was up. Then he emerged from his hut, breakfasted on a papaya he had gathered the day before, and awaited his expected visitor. They must always come to him; it ill befitted a man with a rifle to seek out anyone at all.

Presently Pepe saw two men, Juan Aria and his brother, coming up one of the paths that wound through the village. Others stared curiously, but nobody else came because their flocks had not been raided. They had no wish to pay, or to help pay, a hunter.

---

3. **machetes** (mə-shĕt'ēz).
4. **peso** (pā'sō): a monetary unit in several Latin American countries.

5. **Juan Aria** (hwän ä-rē'ä).
6. **jaguar** (jăg'wär'): a large cat of tropical America, similar to the leopard. The word *tiger* is often used for several animals of the cat family; here, for the jaguar.

Pepe waited until the two were near, then said, "*Buenos días.*"[7]

"*Buenos días,*" They replied.

They sat down in the sun, looking at nothing in particular, not afraid any more, because the day was never a time of fear. By daylight, only now and again did a tiger come to raid a flock of goats, or kill a burro or a cow.

After a suitable lapse of time, Juan Aria said, "I brought my goats into the village last night, thinking they would be safe."

"And were they not?"

"They were not. Something came and killed one, a fine white-and-black nanny, my favorite. When the thing left, the goat went too. Never again shall I see her alive."

"What killed your goat?" Pepe inquired.

"A devil, but this morning I saw only the tracks of a tiger."

"Did you hear it come?"

"I heard it."

"Then why did you not defend your flock?"

Juan Aria gestured with eloquent hands. "To attack a devil, or a tiger, with nothing but a machete would be madness."

"That is true," Pepe agreed. "Let us hope that the next time it is hungry, this devil, or tiger, will not come back for another goat."

"But it will!"

Pepe relaxed, for Juan Aria's admission greatly improved Pepe's bargaining position. And it was true that, having had a taste of easy game, the tiger would come again. Only death would end his forays, and since he knew where to find Juan Aria's goats, he would continue to attack them.

Pepe said, "That is bad, for a man may lose many goats to a tiger."

"Unless a hunter kills him," Juan Aria said.

"Unless a hunter kills him," Pepe agreed.

"That is why I have come to you, Pepe," Juan Aria said. A troubled frown overspread his face. "I hope you will follow and kill this tiger, for you are the only man who can do so."

"It would give me pleasure to kill him, but I cannot work for nothing."

"Nor do I expect you to. Even a tiger will not eat an entire goat, and you are sure to find what is left of my favorite nanny. Whatever the tiger has not eaten, you may have for your pay."

Pepe bristled. "You are saying that I should put myself and my rifle to work for carrion left by a tiger?"

"No, no!" Juan Aria protested. "In addition I will give you one live goat!"

"Three goats."

"I am a poor man!" the other wailed. "You would bankrupt me!"

"No man with twenty-nine goats is poor, though he may be if a tiger raids his flock a sufficient number of times," Pepe said.

"I will give you one goat and two kids."

"Two goats and one kid."

"You drive a hard bargain," Juan Aria said, "but I cannot deny you now. Kill the tiger."

Affecting an air of nonchalance, as befitted the owner of a firearm, Pepe took his rifle from the fine blanket upon which it lay when he was not carrying it. He looked to his powder horn and bullet pouch, strapped his machete on, and sauntered toward Juan Aria's hut. A half-dozen worshipful children followed.

"Begone!" Pepe ordered.

They fell behind, but continued to follow until Pepe came to that place where Juan Aria's flock had passed the night. He glanced at the dust, and saw the tiger's great paw marks imprinted there. It was a huge cat, lame in the right front paw, or it might have been injured in battle with another tiger.

7. *Buenos días* (bwā'nōs dē'äs): Spanish for "Good day."

198   *The Earth Is Home*

Expertly, Pepe located the place where it had gone back over the thorn fence. Though the tiger had carried the sixty-pound goat in its jaws, only a couple of thorns were disturbed at the place where it had leaped.

Though he did not look around, Pepe was aware of the villagers watching him and he knew that their glances would be very respectful. Most of the men went into the jungle from time to time to work with their machetes, but none would work where tigers were known to be. Not one would dare take a tiger's trail. Only Pepe dared and, because he did, he must be revered.

Still affecting nonchalance, Pepe sauntered through the gate. Behind him, he heard the village's collective sigh of mingled relief and admiration. A raiding tiger was a very real and terrible threat, and goats and cattle were not easily come by. The man with a rifle, the man able to protect them, must necessarily be a hero.

Once in the jungle, and out of the villagers' sight, Pepe underwent a transformation.

He shed his air of indifference and became as alert as the little doe that showed him only her white tail. A rifle might be a symbol of power, but unless a man was also a hunter, a rifle did him no good. Impressing the villagers was one thing; hunting a tiger was quite another.

Pepe knew the great cats were dappled death incarnate. They could move with incredible swiftness and were strong enough to kill an ox. They feared nothing.

Jungle-born, Pepe slipped along as softly as

a jungle shadow. His machete slipped a little, and he shifted it to a place where his legs would not be bumped. From time to time he glanced at the ground before him.

To trained eyes, there was a distinct trail. It consisted of an occasional drop of blood from the dead goat, a bent or broken plant, a few hairs where the tiger had squeezed between trees, paw prints in soft places. Within the first quarter-mile Pepe knew many things about this tiger.

He was not an ordinary beast, or he would have gone only far enough from the village so his nostrils could not be assailed by its unwelcome scents and eaten what he wanted there, then covered the remainder of the goat with sticks and leaves. He was not old, for his was not the lagging gait of an old cat, and the ease with which he had leaped the thorn fence with a goat in his jaws was evidence of his strength.

Pepe stopped to look to the loading and priming of his rifle. There seemed to be nothing amiss, and there had better not be. When he saw the tiger, he must shoot straight and true. Warned by some super jungle sense, Pepe slowed his pace. A moment later he found his game.

He came upon it suddenly in a grove of scattered palms. Because he had not expected it there, Pepe did not see it until it was nearer than safety allowed.

The tiger crouched at the base of a palm whose fronds waved at least fifty feet above the roots. Both the beast's front paws were on what remained of the dead goat. It did not snarl or grimace, or even twitch its tail. But there was a lethal quality about the great cat and an extreme tension. The tiger was bursting with raw anger that seemed to swell and grow.

Pepe stopped in his tracks and cold fear crept up his spine. But he did not give way to fear. With deliberate, studied slowness he brought the rifle to his shoulder and took aim. He had only one bullet and there would be no time to reload, but even a tiger could not withstand the smash of that enormous leaden ball right between the eyes. Pepe steadied the rifle.

His finger tightened slowly on the trigger, for he must not let nervousness spoil his aim. When the hammer fell, Pepe's brain and body became momentarily numb.

There was no satisfying roar and no puff of black powder smoke wafting away from the muzzle. Instead there was only a sudden hiss, as though cold water had spilled on a hot stone, and the metallic click of the falling hammer. Pepe himself had loaded the rifle, but he could not have done so correctly. Only the powder in the priming pan flashed.

It was the spark needed to explode the anger in the tiger's lithe and deadly body. He emitted a coughing snarl and launched his charge. Lord of the jungle, he would crush this puny man who dared interfere with him.

Pepe jerked back to reality, but he took time to think of his rifle, leaning it lovingly against a tree and in the same motion jerking his machete from its sheath.

It was now a hopeless fight, to be decided in the tiger's favor, because not within the memory of the village's oldest inhabitant had any man ever killed a tiger with a machete. But it was as well to fight hopelessly, as to turn and run, for if he did that he would surely be killed. No tiger that attacked anything was ever known to turn aside.

Machete in hand, Pepe studied the onrushing cat. He had read the tracks correctly, for from pad to joint the tiger's right front foot was swollen to almost twice the size of the other. It must have stepped on a poisonous thorn or been bitten by a snake.

Even with such a handicap, a tiger was

more than a match for a man armed only with a machete—but Pepe watched the right front paw carefully. If he had any advantage, it lay there. Then the tiger, a terrible, pitiless engine of destruction, flung himself at Pepe. Pepe had known from the first that the tiger's initial strike would be exactly this one, and he was ready for it. He swerved, bending his body outward as the great cat brushed past him. With all the strength in his powerful right arm, he swung the machete. He stopped his downward stroke just short of the tiger's silken back, for he knew suddenly that there was just one way to end this fight.

The tiger whirled, and hot spittle from his mouth splashed on the back of Pepe's left hand. Holding the machete before him, like a sword, he took a swift backward step. The tiger sprang, launching himself from the ground as though his rear legs were made of powerful steel springs, and coming straight up. His flailing left paw flashed at Pepe. It hooked in his shirt, ripping it away from the arm as though it were paper, and burning talons sank into the flesh. Red blood welled out.

Pepe did not try again to slash with the machete, but thrust, as he would have thrust

with a knife or sword. The machete's point met the tiger's throat, and Pepe put all his strength and weight behind it. The blade explored its way into living flesh, and the tiger gasped. Blood bubbled over the machete.

With a convulsive effort, the tiger pulled himself away. But blood was rushing from his throat now and he shook his head, then stumbled and fell. He pulled himself erect, looked with glazing eyes at Pepe and dragged himself toward him. There was a throttled snarl. The tiger slumped to the ground. The tip of his tail twitched and was still.

Pepe stared, scarcely seeing the blood that flowed from his lacerated arm. He had done the impossible, he had killed a tiger with a machete. Pepe brushed a hand across his eyes and took a trembling forward step.

He picked up his rifle and looked again to the priming. There seemed to be nothing wrong. Repriming, Pepe clasped the rifle with his elbow and seized the machete's hilt. Bracing one foot against the tiger's head, he drew the machete out.

Then he held his rifle so close to the machete wound that the muzzle caressed silken fur. He pulled the trigger. The wound gaped wider and smoke-blackened fur fringed it. All traces of the machete wound were obliterated. Pepe knew a second's anguished regret, then steeled himself, for this was the way it must be.

Everybody had a machete. In his village, the man who owned a rifle must remain supreme.

SEEKING MEANING

1. The opening paragraphs of the story contrast daytime and nighttime in the jungle. How is the imagination of the villagers affected by the darkness?

2. How does Pepe earn a living? How does Pepe take advantage of the villagers' fears?

3. How does Pepe show that he is a shrewd businessman when Juan Aria comes to seek his help?

4. To the people of the village, Pepe acts like a man without fear or concern. How does Pepe's attitude change when he enters the jungle?

5. Pepe knows that unless a man is a hunter, a rifle does him no good. How does Pepe's experience as a hunter help him to follow the jaguar's trail? How does he show that he is a great hunter when his rifle proves to be useless?

6. You are told that no one in the village had ever killed a tiger with a machete. Instead of boasting about his amazing deed, Pepe chooses to keep the truth from the villagers. Why?

7. The word *heart* is sometimes used as a synonym for *courage*. To be *stouthearted* or *lionhearted* is to be very brave. What do you think the title of the story means?

DEVELOPING SKILLS IN READING

Focusing on Details of Background
A writer generally attempts to catch the reader's attention at the beginning of a story. Notice how Kjelgaard arouses interest with the opening sentence of "The Tiger's Heart":

The approaching jungle night was, in itself, a threat.

This sentence draws you into the world of the story—the jungle—and promises you excitement and danger. Notice how the first two paragraphs carry out both purposes of the opening sentence in developing the physical background of the story. What details in the first paragraph give you a vivid picture of the village life of jungle dwellers? Compare this description with the description in the second paragraph. Why does the author deliberately choose less specific details in the second paragraph? What characteristic of the jungle does he wish to emphasize there?

The writer of a short story seeks to create a world the reader can believe in. One way to get the reader to believe in the characters and events of a story is to present them against a lifelike background. Look back at the story and find additional details that give you a realistic picture of village life.

DEVELOPING VOCABULARY

Finding the Appropriate Meaning

A dictionary often gives more than one meaning for a word. To determine which of the definitions is appropriate for a particular word, you must decide how the word is being used. You must decide which meaning best fits the context. For example, the word *air* may be used as a noun, an adjective, or a verb. As a noun, it has several different meanings. It may mean the mixture of gases that surrounds the earth. It may also mean a song or tune. It may also mean a person's outward appearance or manner. Which meaning does *air* have in this sentence?

He shed his *air* of indifference and became as alert as the little doe that showed him only her white tail.

Use a dictionary to find the appropriate meaning of the italicized word in each of these sentences.

Pepe stopped to look at the loading and *priming* of his rifle.

Pepe had known from the first that the tiger's *initial* strike would be exactly this one, and he was ready for it.

Bracing one foot against the tiger's head, he drew the machete out.

ABOUT THE AUTHOR

Jim Kjelgaard (1910–1959) was born in New York City but grew up in the Pennsylvania mountains. He worked at several different jobs before turning to writing. His first book, *Forest Patrol,* which appeared in 1941, was based on his own experiences and those of his brother, a forest ranger. Kjelgaard is well known for his stories about dogs. Three of his books are about Irish setters: *Big Red, Irish Red,* and *Outlaw Red.* In addition to stories about dogs and other animals, Kjelgaard wrote two books about the American frontier— *Rebel Siege* and *Buckskin Brigade.*

The Runaway *Robert Frost*

Once when the snow of the year was beginning to fall,
We stopped by a mountain pasture to say, "Whose colt?"
A little Morgan had one forefoot on the wall,
The other curled at his breast. He dipped his head
And snorted at us. And then he had to bolt.   5
We heard the miniature thunder where he fled,
And we saw him, or thought we saw him, dim and gray,
Like a shadow against the curtain of falling flakes.
"I think the little fellow's afraid of the snow.
He isn't winter-broken. It isn't play   10
With the little fellow at all. He's running away.
I doubt if even his mother could tell him, 'Sakes,
It's only weather.' He'd think she didn't know!
Where is his mother? He can't be out alone."
And now he comes again with clatter of stone,   15
And mounts the wall again with whited eyes
And all his tail that isn't hair up straight.
He shudders his coat as if to throw off flies.
"Whoever it is that leaves him out so late,
When other creatures have gone to stall and bin,   20
Ought to be told to come and take him in."

SEEKING MEANING

1. In the poem we are told that some people stop by a mountain pasture to watch a colt. What does the colt do when he sees them? What is the "miniature thunder" in line 6?

2. One of the onlookers believes that the colt is afraid of the snow because he isn't "winter-broken." What does the speaker mean by this expression?

3. What details in lines 15–18 confirm the onlooker's belief that the colt is afraid?

4. Many readers think that Frost uses this incident of the colt to express his deep concern for nature's creatures. Other readers believe that the poem also touches on the issue of responsibility. What is your interpretation of the poem?

ABOUT THE AUTHOR

Although he was born in the West (San Francisco) and named after a Southerner (Robert E. Lee), Robert Frost (1874–1963) has become known as a New England poet. After his father died, his mother brought the family to Lawrence, Massachusetts. There Frost wrote poems while working as a mill hand, a school-teacher, a baseball coach, a newspaper reporter, and a cobbler.

From 1900 to 1912, while raising chickens on a small farm in Derry, New Hampshire, Frost wrote some of his best-known poems. However, magazine editors rejected them. He had no greater success at farming. In 1912 Frost decided to end his isolation and frustration. He sold the farm and sailed for England with his wife and four children. There he made friends with other struggling poets who were interested in his work. He put together two major collections, *A Boy's Will* (1913) and *North of Boston* (1914). These books brought Frost to the attention of influential critics, including Ezra Pound, who helped Frost build a reputation in America.

By the time he returned to this country in 1915, Frost was already a famous poet. He settled once again on a farm, this time on a hill near Franconia, New Hampshire. For the rest of his life, he was America's unofficial poet laureate. He received many honors, including four Pulitzer Prizes. In 1961 he was asked to participate in the inauguration of John F. Kennedy. At the ceremony, he recited one of his poems, "The Gift Outright."

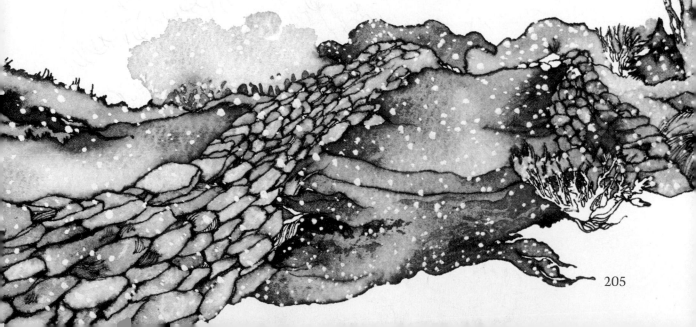

Colm learned that even
though he took delight in
nature, he could easily injure
or destroy the things he loved.

The Wild Duck's Nest

Michael McLaverty

The sun was setting, spilling gold light on the low western hills of Rathlin Island.[1] A small boy walked jauntily along a hoof-printed path that wriggled between the folds of these hills and opened out into a craterlike valley on the clifftop. Presently he stopped as if remembering something, then suddenly he left the path, and began running up one of the hills. When he reached the top he was out of breath and stood watching streaks of light radiating from golden-edged clouds, the scene reminding him of a picture he had seen of the Transfiguration.[2] A short distance below him was the cow standing at the edge of a reedy lake. Colm[3] ran down to meet her waving his stick in the air, and the wind rumbling in his ears made him give an exultant whoop which splashed upon the hills in a shower of echoed sound. A flock of gulls lying on the short grass near the lake rose up languidly, drifting like blown snowflakes over the rim of the cliff.

The lake faced west and was fed by a stream, the drainings of the semicircling hills. One side was open to the winds from the sea and in winter a little outlet trickled over the cliffs making a black vein in their gray sides. The boy lifted stones and began throwing them into the lake, weaving web after web on its calm surface. Then he skimmed the water with flat stones, some of them jumping the surface and coming to rest on the other side. He was delighted with himself and after listening to his echoing shouts of delight he ran to fetch his cow. Gently he tapped her on the side and reluctantly she went towards the brown-mudded path that led out of the valley.

---

1. **Rathlin Island:** an island a few miles off the northern coast of Ireland.
2. **the Transfiguration:** an event in the life of Jesus Christ, told in Matthew 17. 1–8. A painting of this event would probably show a mountaintop with a shining cloud overhead.
3. **Colm** (kŭl′əm).

The Wild Duck's Nest 207

The boy was about to throw a final stone into the lake when a bird flew low over his head, its neck astrain, and its orange-colored legs clear in the soft light. It was a wild duck. It circled the lake twice, thrice, coming lower each time and then with a nervous flapping of wings it skidded along the surface, its legs breaking the water into a series of silvery arcs. Its wings closed, it lit silently, gave a slight shiver, and began pecking indifferently at the water.

Colm with dilated eyes eagerly watched it making for the farther end of the lake. It meandered between tall bulrushes,[4] its body black and solid as stone against the graying water. Then as if it had sunk it was gone. The boy ran stealthily along the bank looking away from the lake, pretending indifference. When he came opposite to where he had last seen the bird he stopped and peered through the sighing reeds whose shadows streaked the water in a maze of black strokes. In front of him was a soddy islet guarded by the spears of sedge[5] and separated from the bank by a narrow channel of water. The water wasn't too deep—he could wade across with care.

Rolling up his short trousers he began to wade, his arms outstretched, and his legs brown and stunted in the mountain water. As he drew near the islet, his feet sank in the cold mud and bubbles winked up at him. He went more carefully and nervously. Then one trouser leg fell and dipped into the water; the boy dropped his hands to roll it up, he unbalanced, made a splashing sound, and the bird arose with a squawk and whirred away over the cliffs. For a moment the boy stood frightened. Then he clambered onto the wet-soaked sod of land, which was spattered with sea gulls' feathers and bits of wind-blown rushes.

Into each hummock[6] he looked, pulling back the long grass. At last he came on the nest, facing seawards. Two flat rocks dimpled the face of the water and between them was a neck of land matted with coarse grass containing the nest. It was untidily built of dried rushes, straw and feathers, and in it lay one solitary egg. Colm was delighted. He looked around and saw no one. The nest was his. He lifted the egg, smooth and green as the sky, with a faint tinge of yellow like the reflected light from a buttercup; and then he felt he had done wrong. He put it back. He knew he shouldn't have touched it and he wondered would the bird forsake the nest. A vague sadness stole over him and he felt in his heart he had sinned. Carefully smoothing out his footprints he hurriedly left the islet and ran after his cow. The sun had now set and the cold shiver of evening enveloped him, chilling his body and saddening his mind.

In the morning he was up and away to school. He took the grass rut that edged the road, for it was softer on the bare feet. His house was the last on the western headland and after a mile or so he was joined by Paddy McFall; both boys dressed in similar hand-knitted blue jerseys and gray trousers carried homemade schoolbags. Colm was full of the nest and as soon as he joined his companion he said eagerly: "Paddy, I've a nest—a wild duck's with one egg."

"And how do you know it's a wild duck's?" asked Paddy, slightly jealous.

"Sure I saw her with my own two eyes, her brown speckled back with a crow's patch on it, and her yellow legs——"

"Where is it?" interrupted Paddy in a challenging tone.

"I'm not going to tell you, for you'd rob it!"

---

4. **bulrushes** (bŏŏl′rŭsh′ĭz): grasslike plants.
5. **sedge**: a grasslike plant with pointed leaves.

6. **hummock** (hŭm′ək): a small mound of earth.

"Aach! I suppose it's a tame duck's you have or maybe an old gull's."

Colm put out his tongue at him. "A lot you know!" he said; "for a gull's egg has spots and this one is greenish-white, for I had it in my hand."

And then the words he didn't want to hear rushed from Paddy in a mocking chant. "You had it in your hand! . . . She'll forsake it! She'll forsake it! She'll forsake it!" he said, skipping along the road before him.

Colm felt as if he would choke or cry with vexation.

His mind told him that Paddy was right, but somehow he couldn't give in to it and he replied: "She'll not forsake it! She'll not! I know she'll not!"

But in school his faith wavered. Through the windows he could see moving sheets of rain—rain that dribbled down the panes filling his mind with thoughts of the lake creased and chilled by wind; the nest sodden and black with wetness; and the egg cold as a cave stone. He shivered from the thoughts and fidgeted with the inkwell cover, sliding it backwards and forwards mechanically. The mischievous look had gone from his eyes and the school day dragged on interminably. But at last they were out in the rain, Colm rushing home as fast as he could.

He was no time at all at his dinner of potatoes and salted fish until he was out in the valley now smoky with drifts of slanting rain. Opposite the islet he entered the water. The wind was blowing into his face, rustling noisily the rushes heavy with the dust of rain. A moss cheeper,[7] swaying on a reed like a mouse, filled the air with light cries of loneliness.

The boy reached the islet, his heart thumping with excitement, wondering did the bird

---

7. **moss cheeper:** a songbird.

forsake. He went slowly, quietly, onto the strip of land that led to the nest. He rose on his toes, looking over the ledge to see if he could see her. And then every muscle tautened. She was on, her shoulders hunched up, and her bill lying on her breast as if she were asleep. Colm's heart hammered wildly in his ears. She hadn't forsaken. He was about to turn stealthily away. Something happened. The bird moved, her neck straightened, twitching nervously from side to side. The boy's head swam with lightness. He stood transfixed. The wild duck with a panicky flapping, rose heavily, and flew off towards the sea. . . . A guilty silence enveloped the boy. . . . He turned to go away, hesitated, and glanced back at the bare nest; it'd be no harm to have a look. Timidly he approached it, standing straight, and gazing over the edge. There in the nest lay two eggs. He drew in his breath with delight, splashed quickly from the island, and ran off whistling in the rain.

SEEKING MEANING

1. At the opening of the story, you learn that Colm enjoys the beauty of the countryside. What details in the first paragraph show his delight in nature?

2. How do Colm's actions show that he suspects the wild duck has built a nest on the islet?

3. Colm does not wish to rob the nest. Why, then, does he lift the egg? Why does he feel that he has sinned?

4. What steps does Colm take to protect the nest from further harm?

5. Why does Colm return to the wild duck's nest? How is he relieved by what he finds?

6. When Colm first finds the nest, he feels that it is his. Do you think he still feels this way at the end of the story? Explain your answer.

7. Sometimes human beings destroy nature through thoughtlessness or carelessness. What do you think Colm learns from his experience with the wild duck's nest?

DEVELOPING VOCABULARY

Forming Adverbs from Adjectives

In "The Wild Duck's Nest," Michael McLaverty uses a great many adverbs as modifiers of verbs. In the first paragraph of the story, you are told that Colm "walked *jauntily.*" The gulls, disturbed by his shouting, "rose up *languidly.*"

Many adverbs in our language are formed by adding the suffix *-ly* to an adjective. When you add *-ly* to the adjective *languid,* you form the adverb *languidly.* The adverb *jauntily* is formed from the adjective *jaunty.* Notice that the *y* in *jaunty* changes to *i* when *-ily* is added. What happens when you change the adjective *gentle* to an adverb?

How many adverbs ending in *-ly* can you locate in the story? List them and give the adjectives from which they are formed.

DEVELOPING SKILLS OF EXPRESSION

Using Vivid Verbs

In the first paragraph of the story, the author says that a path "wriggled" between the hills. *Wriggled* is an effective verb because it makes the reader think of the path weaving in and out like a snake.

There are other good descriptive verbs in the story. Explain why each of the following italicized verbs is a good choice.

Then he *skimmed* the water with flat stones . . . .

. . . his feet sank in the cold mud and bubbles *winked* up at him.

And then, every muscle *tautened*.

Colin's heart *hammered* wildly in his ears.

Using vivid verbs will make your own writing more lively and interesting. Think of an effective verb to substitute for each of the italicized verbs in these sentences.

The stealthy cat *moved* across the lawn toward the unsuspecting birds.

The surprised winner of the contest *went* to the stage when her name was called.

The hungry lion *ate* its prey.

Explaining Differences

Paddy accuses Colm of mistaking a sea gull's egg for a wild duck's egg, but Colm indicates that he knows the difference.

"A lot you know!" he said; "for a gull's egg has spots and this one is greenish-white— for I had it in my hand."

Colm is a close observer of nature. One detail —color—is sufficient to tell him the difference between the two eggs.

Write a paragraph in which you explain the difference between two things that are sometimes confused. You might explain the difference between two animals: a frog and a toad, or a guinea pig and a hamster, for example. You might explain the difference between two musical instruments: a violin and a viola, or a flute and a piccolo. You might explain the difference between two sports: football and soccer, or tennis and badminton.

Before you write your paragraph, you may want to list your ideas, beginning with the most important or obvious difference. Open with a sentence that follows this pattern:

There are three (four, five) major differences between *x* and *y*.

In a story told by the ancient Greeks, Antaeus was a giant whose strength came from the earth. As long as he remained in contact with the earth, no one could defeat him in combat. This is a story about a modern Antaeus.

Antaeus°   *Borden Deal*

This was during the wartime, when lots of people were coming North for jobs in factories and war industries, when people moved around a lot more than they do now, and sometimes kids were thrown into new groups and new lives that were completely different from anything they had ever known before. I remember this one kid, T. J. his name was, from somewhere down South, whose family moved into our building during that time. They'd come North with everything they owned piled into the back seat of an old-model sedan that you wouldn't expect could make the trip, with T. J. and his three younger sisters riding shakily on top of the load of junk.

Our building was just like all the others there, with families crowded into a few rooms, and I guess there were twenty-five or thirty kids about my age in that one building. Of course, there were a few of us who formed a gang and ran together all the time after school, and I was the one who brought T. J. in and started the whole thing.

The building right next door to us was a factory where they made walking dolls. It was a low building with a flat, tarred roof that had a parapet[1] all around it about head-high, and we'd found out a long time before that no one, not even the watchman, paid any attention to the roof because it was higher than any of the other buildings around. So my gang used the roof as a headquarters. We could get up there by crossing over to the fire escape from our own roof on a plank and then going on up. It was a secret place for us, where nobody else could go without our permission.

I remember the day I first took T. J. up there to meet the gang. He was a stocky, robust kid with a shock of white hair, nothing sissy about him except his voice; he talked in this slow, gentle voice like you never heard before. He talked different from any of us and you noticed it right away. But I liked him anyway, so I told him to come on up.

We climbed up over the parapet and dropped down on the roof. The rest of the gang were already there.

"Hi," I said. I jerked my thumb at T. J. "He just moved into the building yesterday."

He just stood there, not scared or anything, just looking, like the first time you see somebody you're not sure you're going to like.

°**Antaeus** (ăn-tē′əs).

1. **parapet** (păr′ə-pĭt): a low protective wall.

"Hi," Blackie said. "Where are you from?"

"Marion County," T. J. said.

We laughed. "Marion County?" I said. "Where's that?"

He looked at me for a moment like I was a stranger, too. "It's in Alabama," he said, like I ought to know where it was.

"What's your name?" Charley said.

"T. J.," he said, looking back at him. He had pale blue eyes that looked washed-out, but he looked directly at Charley, waiting for his reaction. He'll be all right, I thought. No sissy in him, except that voice. Who ever talked like that?

"T. J.," Blackie said. "That's just initials. What's your real name? Nobody in the world has just initials."

"I do," he said. "And they're T. J. That's all the name I got."

His voice was resolute with the knowledge of his rightness, and for a moment no one had anything to say. T. J. looked around at the rooftop and down at the black tar under his feet. "Down yonder where I come from," he said, "we played out in the woods. Don't you-all have no woods around here?"

"Naw," Blackie said. "There's the park a few blocks over, but it's full of kids and cops and old women. You can't do a thing."

T. J. kept looking at the tar under his feet. "You mean you ain't got no fields to raise nothing in?—no watermelons or nothing?"

"Naw," I said scornfully. "What do you want to grow something for? The folks can buy everything they need at the store."

He looked at me again with that strange, unknowing look. "In Marion County," he said, "I had my own acre of cotton and my own acre of corn. It was mine to plant and make ever' year."

He sounded like it was something to be proud of, and in some obscure way it made the rest of us angry. Blackie said, "Who'd

want to have their own acre of cotton and corn? That's just work. What can you do with an acre of cotton and corn?"

T. J. looked at him. "Well, you get part of the bale offen your acre," he said seriously. "And I fed my acre of corn to my calf."

We didn't really know what he was talking about, so we were more puzzled than angry; otherwise, I guess, we'd have chased him off the roof and wouldn't let him be part of our gang. But he was strange and different, and we were all attracted by his stolid sense of rightness and belonging, maybe by the strange softness of his voice contrasting our own tones of speech into harshness.

He moved his foot against the black tar. "We could make our own field right here," he said softly, thoughtfully. "Come spring we could raise us what we want to—watermelons and garden truck[2] and no telling what all."

"You'd have to be a good farmer to make these tar roofs grow any watermelons," I said. We all laughed.

But T. J. looked serious. "We could haul us some dirt up here," he said. "And spread it out even and water it, and before you know it, we'd have us a crop in here." He looked at us intently. "Wouldn't that be fun?"

"They wouldn't let us," Blackie said quickly.

"I thought you said this was you-all's roof," T. J. said to me. "That you-all could do anything you wanted to up here."

"They've never bothered us," I said. I felt the idea beginning to catch fire in me. It was a big idea, and it took a while for it to sink in; but the more I thought about it, the better I liked it. "Say," I said to the gang. "He might have something there. Just make us a regular roof garden, with flowers and grass and trees

---

2. **truck:** here, vegetables grown to be sold.

and everything. And all ours, too," I said. "We wouldn't let anybody up here except the ones we wanted to."

"It'd take a while to grow trees," T. J. said quickly, but we weren't paying any attention to him. They were all talking about it suddenly, all excited with the idea after I'd put it in a way they could catch hold of it. Only rich people had roof gardens, we knew, and the idea of our own private domain excited them.

"We could bring it up in sacks and boxes," Blackie said. "We'd have to do it while the folks weren't paying any attention to us, for we'd have to come up the roof of our building and then cross over with it."

"Where could we get the dirt?" somebody said worriedly.

"Out of those vacant lots over close to school," Blackie said. "Nobody'd notice if we scraped it up."

I slapped T. J. on the shoulder. "Man, you had a wonderful idea," I said, and everybody grinned at him, remembering that he had started it. "Our own private roof garden."

He grinned back. "It'll be ourn," he said. "All ourn." Then he looked thoughtful again. "Maybe I can lay my hands on some cotton seed, too. You think we could raise us some cotton?"

We'd started big projects before at one time or another, like any gang of kids, but they'd always petered out for lack of organization and direction. But this one didn't; somehow or other T. J. kept it going all through the winter months. He kept talking about the watermelons and the cotton we'd raise, come spring, and when even that wouldn't work, he'd switch around to my idea of flowers and grass and trees, though he was always honest enough to add that it'd take a while to get any trees started. He always had it on his mind and he'd mention it in school, getting them lined up to carry dirt that afternoon, saying in a casual way that he reckoned a few more weeks ought to see the job through.

Our little area of private earth grew slowly. T. J. was smart enough to start in one corner of the building, heaping up the carried earth two or three feet thick so that we had an immediate result to look at, to contemplate with awe. Some of the evenings T. J. alone was carrying earth up to the building, the rest of the gang distracted by other enterprises or interests, but T. J. kept plugging along on his own, and eventually we'd all come back to him again and then our own little acre would grow more rapidly.

He was careful about the kind of dirt he'd let us carry up there, and more than once he dumped a sandy load over the parapet into the areaway below because it wasn't good enough. He found out the kinds of earth in all the vacant lots for blocks around. He'd pick it up and feel it and smell it, frozen though it was sometimes, and then he'd say it was good growing soil or it wasn't worth anything, and we'd have to go on somewhere else.

Thinking about it now, I don't see how he kept us at it. It was hard work, lugging paper sacks and boxes of dirt all the way up the stairs of our own building, keeping out of the way of the grown-ups so they wouldn't catch on to what we were doing. They probably wouldn't have cared, for they didn't pay much attention to us, but we wanted to keep it secret anyway. Then we had to go through the trapdoor to our roof, teeter over a plank to the fire escape, then climb two or three stories to the parapet and drop down onto the roof. All that for a small pile of earth that sometimes didn't seem worth the effort. But T. J. kept the vision bright within us, his words shrewd and

calculated toward the fulfillment of his dream; and he worked harder than any of us. He seemed driven toward a goal that we couldn't see, a particular point in time that would be definitely marked by signs and wonders that only he could see.

The laborious earth just lay there during the cold months, inert and lifeless, the clods lumpy and cold under our feet when we walked over it. But one day it rained, and afterward there was a softness in the air, and the earth was live and giving again with moisture and warmth.

That evening T. J. smelled the air, his nostrils dilating with the odor of the earth under his feet. "It's spring," he said, and there was a gladness rising in his voice that filled us all with the same feeling. "It's mighty late for it, but it's spring. I'd just about decided it wasn't never gonna get here at all."

We were all sniffing at the air, too, trying to smell it the way that T. J. did, and I can still remember the sweet odor of the earth under our feet. It was the first time in my life that spring and spring earth had meant anything to me. I looked at T. J. then, knowing in a faint way the hunger within him through the toilsome winter months, knowing the dream that lay behind his plan. He was a new Antaeus, preparing his own bed of strength.

"Planting time," he said. "We'll have to find us some seed."

"What do we do?" Blackie said. "How do we do it?"

"First we'll have to break up the clods," T. J. said. "That won't be hard to do. Then we plant the seeds, and after a while they come up. Then you got you a crop." He frowned. "But you ain't got it raised yet. You got to tend it and hoe it and take care of it, and all the time it's growing and growing, while you're awake and while you're asleep. Then you lay it by when it's growed and let it ripen, and then you got you a crop."

"There's those wholesale seed houses over on Sixth," I said. "We could probably swipe some grass seed over there."

T. J. looked at the earth. "You-all seem mighty set on raising some grass," he said. "I ain't never put no effort into that. I spent all my life trying not to raise grass."

"But it's pretty," Blackie said. "We could play on it and take sunbaths on it. Like having our own lawn. Lots of people got lawns."

"Well," T. J. said. He looked at the rest of us, hesitant for the first time. He kept on looking at us for a moment. "I did have it in mind to raise some corn and vegetables. But we'll plant grass."

He was smart. He knew where to give in. And I don't suppose it made any difference to him, really. He just wanted to grow something, even if it was grass.

"Of course," he said, "I do think we ought to plant a row of watermelons. They'd be mighty nice to eat while we was a-laying on that grass."

We all laughed. "All right," I said. "We'll plant us a row of watermelons."

Things went very quickly then. Perhaps half the roof was covered with the earth, the half that wasn't broken by ventilators, and we swiped pocketfuls of grass seed from the open bins in the wholesale seed house, mingling among the buyers on Saturdays and during the school lunch hour. T. J. showed us how to prepare the earth, breaking up the clods and smoothing it and sowing the grass seed. It looked rich and black now with moisture, receiving of the seed, and it seemed that the grass sprang up overnight, pale green in the early spring.

We couldn't keep from looking at it, unable to believe that we had created this delicate growth. We looked at T. J. with understanding now, knowing the fulfillment of the plan he had carried along within his mind. We had worked without full understanding of the task, but he had known all the time.

We found that we couldn't walk or play on the delicate blades, as we had expected to, but we didn't mind. It was enough just to look at it, to realize that it was the work of our own hands, and each evening the whole gang was there, trying to measure the growth that had been achieved that day.

One time a foot was placed on the plot of ground, one time only, Blackie stepping onto it with sudden bravado. Then he looked at the crushed blades and there was shame in his face. He did not do it again. This was his grass, too, and not to be desecrated.[3] No one said anything, for it was not necessary.

T. J. had reserved a small section for watermelons, and he was still trying to find some seed for it. The wholesale house didn't have any watermelon seeds, and we didn't know where we could lay our hands on them. T. J. shaped the earth into mounds, ready to receive them, three mounds lying in a straight line along the edge of the grass plot.

We had just about decided that we'd have to buy the seeds if we were to get them. It was a violation of our principles, but we were anxious to get the watermelons started. Somewhere or other, T. J. got his hands on a seed catalog and brought it one evening to our roof garden.

"We can order them now," he said, showing us the catalog. "Look!"

We all crowded around, looking at the fat, green watermelons pictured in full color on the pages. Some of them were split open, showing the red, tempting meat, making our mouths water.

---

3. **desecrated** (dĕs ə-krāt′ĭd): treated with disrespect.

"Now we got to scrape up some seed money." T. J. said, looking at us. "I got a quarter. How much you-all got?"

We made up a couple of dollars among us and T. J. nodded his head. "That'll be more than enough. Now we got to decide what kind to get. I think them Kleckley Sweets. What do you-all think?"

He was going into esoteric matters[4] beyond our reach. We hadn't even known there were different kinds of melons. So we just nodded our heads and agreed that yes, we thought the Kleckley Sweets too.

"I'll order them tonight," T. J. said. "We ought to have them in a few days."

"What are you boys doing up here?" an adult voice said behind us.

It startled us, for no one had ever come up here before in all the time we had been using the roof of the factory. We jerked around and saw three men standing near the trap door at the other end of the roof. They weren't policemen or night watchmen, but three men in plump business suits, looking at us. They walked toward us.

"What are you boys doing up here?" the one in the middle said again.

We stood still, guilt heavy among us, levied[5] by the tone of voice, and looked at the three strangers.

The men stared at the grass flourishing behind us. "What's this?" the man said. "How did this get up here?"

"Sure is growing good, ain't it?" T. J. said conversationally. "We planted it."

The men kept looking at the grass as if they didn't believe it. It was a thick carpet over the earth now, a patch of deep greenness startling in the sterile industrial surroundings.

"Yes, sir," T. J. said proudly. "We toted that earth up here and planted that grass." He fluttered the seed catalog. "And we're just fixing to plant us some watermelon."

The man looked at him then, his eyes strange and faraway. "What do you mean, putting this on the roof of my building?" he said. "Do you want to go to jail?"

T. J. looked shaken. The rest of us were silent, frightened by the authority of his voice. We had grown up aware of adult authority, of policemen and night watchmen and teachers, and this man sounded like all the others. But it was a new thing to T. J.

"Well, you wasn't using the roof," T. J. said. He paused a moment and added shrewdly, "So we just thought to pretty it up a little bit."

"And sag it so I'd have to rebuild it," the man said sharply. He started turning away, saying to another man beside him, "See that all that junk is shoveled off by tomorrow."

"Yes, sir," the man said.

T. J. started forward. "You can't do that," he said. "We toted it up here, and its our earth. We planted it and raised it and toted it up here."

The man stared at him coldly. "But it's my building," he said. "It's to be shoveled off tomorrow."

"It's our earth," T. J. said desperately. "You ain't got no right!"

The men walked on without listening and descended clumsily through the trapdoor. T. J. stood looking after them, his body tense with anger, until they had disappeared. They wouldn't even argue with him, wouldn't let him defend his earth-rights.

He turned to us. "We won't let 'em do it," he said fiercely. "We'll stay up here all day tomorrow and the day after that, and we won't let 'em do it."

We just looked at him. We knew there was no stopping it.

---

4. **esoteric** (ĕs'ə-tĕr'ĭk) **matters:** special knowledge not understood by most people.
5. **levied** (lĕv'ēd): imposed or placed upon. The man's tone of voice makes the boys feel guilty.

He saw it in our faces, and his face wavered for a moment before he gripped it into determination. "They ain't got no right," he said. "It's our earth. It's our land. Can't nobody touch a man's own land."

We kept looking at him, listening to the words but knowing that it was no use. The adult world had descended on us even in our richest dream, and we knew there was no calculating the adult world, no fighting it, no winning against it.

We started moving slowly toward the parapet and the fire escape, avoiding a last look at the green beauty of the earth that T. J. had planted for us, had planted deeply in our minds as well as in our experience. We filed slowly over the edge and down the steps to the plank, T. J. coming last, and all of us could feel the weight of his grief behind us.

"Wait a minute," he said suddenly, his voice harsh with the effort of calling.

We stopped and turned, held by the tone of his voice, and looked up at him standing above us on the fire escape.

"We can't stop them?" he said, looking down at us, his face strange in the dusky light. "There ain't no way to stop 'em?"

"No," Blackie said with finality. "They own the building."

We stood still for a moment, looking up at T. J., caught into inaction by the decision working in his face. He stared back at us, and his face was pale and mean in the poor light, with a bald nakedness in his skin like cripples have sometimes.

"They ain't gonna touch my earth," he said fiercely. "They ain't gonna lay a hand on it! Come on."

He turned around and started up the fire escape again, almost running against the effort of climbing. We followed more slowly, not knowing what he intended. By the time we reached him, he had seized a board and thrust it into the soil, scooping it up and flinging it over the parapet into the areaway below. He straightened and looked at us.

"They can't touch it." he said. "I won't let 'em lay a dirty hand on it!"

We saw it then. He stooped to his labor again and we followed, the gusts of his anger moving in frenzied labor among us as we scattered along the edge of earth, scooping it and throwing it over the parapet, destroying with anger the growth we had nurtured with such tender care. The soil carried so laboriously upward to the light and the sun cascaded swiftly into the dark areaway, the green blades of grass crumpled and twisted in the falling.

It took less time than you would think; the task of destruction is infinitely easier than that of creation. We stopped at the end, leaving only a scattering of loose soil, and when it was finally over, a stillness stood among the group and over the factory building. We looked down at the bare sterility of black tar, felt the harsh texture of it under the soles of our shoes, and the anger had gone out of us, leaving only a sore aching in our minds like overstretched muscles.

T. J. stood for a moment, his breathing slowing from anger and effort, caught into the same contemplation of destruction as all of us. He stooped slowly, finally, and picked up a lonely blade of grass left trampled under our feet and put it between his teeth, tasting it, sucking the greenness out of it into his mouth. Then he started walking toward the fire escape, moving before any of us were ready to move, and disappeared over the edge.

We followed him, but he was already halfway down to the ground, going on past the board where we crossed over, climbing down into the areaway. We saw the last section swing down with his weight, and then he stood on the concrete below us, looking at the small pile of anonymous earth scattered by our throwing. Then he walked across the place where we could see him and disappeared toward the street without glancing back, without looking up to see us watching him.

They did not find him for two weeks.

Then the Nashville police caught him just outside the Nashville freight yards. He was walking along the railroad track, still heading south, still heading home.

As for us, who had no remembered home to call us, none of us ever again climbed the escapeway to the roof.

SEEKING MEANING

1. The boys in the narrator's gang are city boys accustomed to living without trees or grass of their own. Why do they become so excited at the idea of a roof garden?

2. The boys work at the garden without fully understanding what it means to T. J. At what point do they begin to experience the wonder of making things grow? Find the passage that gives the answer.

3. In the ancient story, Antaeus' bond with the earth was broken when he was held in midair and strangled. How is T. J.'s bond with the earth broken? In what way is his return to the South an attempt to renew that bond?

4. The narrator says that he avoided "a last look at the green beauty of the earth that T. J. had planted for us, had planted deeply in our minds as well as in our experience." What gift has T. J. given the boys that will last even though the garden is gone?

5. Like the character Antaeus in the Greek story, T. J. seems to gain strength from contact with the earth. Antaeus' strength was physical. How would you describe the kind of strength T. J. draws from the earth?

DEVELOPING VOCABULARY

Using Context Clues

You can often get the meaning of an unfamiliar word by using clues supplied by the context.

The laborious earth just lay there during the cold months, *inert* and lifeless, the clods lumpy and cold under our feet when we walked over it.

The word *inert* means "not moving; inactive." What clues in the sentence help give you this meaning?

What context clues help you get the meaning of the word *cascaded* in this sentence?

The soil carried so laboriously upward to the light and the sun *cascaded* swiftly into the dark areaway, the green blades of grass crumpled and twisted in the falling.

The verb *cascade* means "to fall swiftly from a height, like a waterfall."

Write sentences of your own using the words *inert* and *cascade*.

Use context clues to determine the meaning of these words. Check your answers in the glossary.

domain   (page 214, column 1)
contemplate   (page 215, column 1)
distracted   (page 215, column 1)

DEVELOPING SKILLS OF EXPRESSION

Explaining a Procedure

T. J. shows the boys how to plant a garden on the factory roof. First he helps the boys find good growing soil in vacant lots. Then he shows them how to prepare the earth for planting by breaking up the clods, smoothing the soil, and sowing the grass seed.

When you explain how to do something, it is helpful to present your instructions as a series of separate steps. If you arrange the steps in order carefully, the reader will be able to follow your directions. You can make the order clear by using expressions such as *first, second, as soon as, next, in addition to, now, then,* and *finally.* These expressions are *transitional*—that is, they are used to connect the sentences in your writing and speaking.

Write a paragraph in which you explain, step by step, how to do something. Be sure to include all the materials that will be needed. If you must use any technical words, be sure to explain what they mean.

Here are some topics you might want to use:

How to repot a plant
How to bathe a dog
How to fix a flat tire on a bicycle
How to make a pizza
How to paint a room

ABOUT THE AUTHOR

Borden Deal (1922–   ) was born on a cotton farm in Mississippi. Before devoting himself full time to writing, he had a variety of jobs. He worked as a firefighter for the Civilian Conservation Corps, a roustabout for a circus and a showboat, an auditor, a finance collector, and a writer for a radio station. He is the author of several novels and more than one hundred short stories. His work has been adapted for the stage, the movies, and television, and has been translated into many languages.

After the Winter   *Claude McKay*

Some day, when trees have shed their leaves
   And against the morning's white
The shivering birds beneath the eaves
   Have sheltered for the night,
We'll turn our faces southward, love,   5
   Toward the summer isle
Where bamboos spire° the shafted grove   7. **spire:** shoot up.
   And wide-mouthed orchids smile.

And we will seek the quiet hill
   Where towers the cotton tree,   10
And leaps the laughing crystal rill,°   11. **rill:** a small stream.
   And works the droning bee.
And we will build a cottage there
   Beside an open glade,
With black-ribbed bluebells blowing near,   15
   And ferns that never fade.

SEEKING MEANING

1. What kind of place does the poet long for? What details in the poem tell you?

2. Where do you think the "summer isle" might be? Why is it called a "summer isle"?

Practice in Reading and Writing

EXPOSITION

The form of writing we use most frequently is *exposition*. Exposition is the kind of writing that explains something or gives information. Science and history books, reports, and even directions on how to assemble a piece of furniture all make use of exposition.

Reading Exposition

The following paragraph from "Animals Go to School" by Edwin Way Teale states and supports a certain idea about the learning abilities of animals.

> All animals, even the most humble, appear to have some ability to learn from experience. An earthworm can learn to turn to the right or the left when it is placed in a maze in which it receives an unpleasant electric shock when it makes a wrong turn. Its nervous system records the lesson thus learned and the earthworm will even continue to make the correct turn after its head has been cut off. Crayfish can be taught to come to a certain spot for feeding. Frogs can remember the correct path through a laboratory maze after a lapse of a month. In one experiment, a single tentacle of a sea anemone learned, independently of all the other tentacles, to reject wads of paper when they were offered as food. Even one-celled protozoa have individuals that are able to learn simple lessons such as avoiding over-acid water or dye particles among their food.

1. When you read an expository passage, look for a sentence that states or summarizes its topic, or main idea. This sentence is called the topic sentence.

What is the topic sentence in the model paragraph?

2. When you read exposition, look for the details, examples, or reasons that support the topic sentence.

List the specific examples that are used to support the topic sentence in the model paragraph.

In this paragraph Teale tells how young foxes learn to become hunters. Each step is presented in chronological order. Find words or groups of words that help to establish the time sequence.

As soon as the kits are weaned, the mother fox begins bringing captured mice, birds and rabbits into the den. As the young foxes grow older, the food is dropped at the entrance instead of being brought inside. A little later, it is deposited a few feet outside the entrance. Then it is placed several yards away and, finally, the kits have to search over an area of several hundred square yards to find their dinners. During the last part of the training, the parent foxes begin hiding the captured birds or rabbits beneath leaves and rubbish, thus forcing the kits to use their sense of smell as well as their eyes in making their discoveries. In this practical, progressive manner, the school for foxes educates the young animals for the vital work of hunting.

Where is the topic sentence in this paragraph?

Writing Exposition

Here are some points to remember when you write a paragraph of exposition:

1. *State the topic clearly in a sentence. Most writers place the topic sentence at the beginning of the paragraph. However, the topic sentence may appear anywhere in the paragraph.*
2. *Provide specific details, examples, or reasons to develop your topic.*
3. *Keep to the topic. Do not introduce unrelated details.*
4. *Arrange your sentences in a logical, effective manner.*
5. *Use transitional expressions (such as first, next, later) to connect your ideas.*

Write an expository paragraph developing one of these topics or a topic of your own:

An amateur photographer's equipment
A beginner's stamp collection
Tuning a guitar
Making yogurt
Reading a road map

For Further Reading

Adamson, Joy, *Born Free: A Lioness of Two Worlds* (Pantheon, 1960; paperback, Random House)
The author tells how she and her husband raised Elsa, a lion cub, as a pet and then trained her to survive in the jungle. *Living Free* (Harcourt Brace Jovanovich, 1961) is a sequel to this book.

Annixter, Paul, *Swiftwater* (Hill & Wang, 1950; paperback, Starline)
Young Buck Calloway and his father, trappers who love the endangered wilderness, try to establish a bird sanctuary in northern Maine.

Burgess, Robert F., *The Sharks* (Doubleday, 1971)
The author gives a factual account of shark habits and shark attacks. Black-and-white photographs accompany the text.

Burnford, Sheila, *The Incredible Journey* (Little, Brown, 1961; paperback, Bantam)
Three house pets—a young Labrador retriever, and old bull terrier, and a Siamese cat—travel two hundred miles across the Canadian wilderness to return to their home.

Cousteau, Jacques-Yves, and Frederic Dumas, *The Silent World* (Harper & Row, 1953; paperback, Harper)
The aqualung, developed during World War II, enables divers to explore far below the ocean surface, to search for ancient treasures, and to gain new knowledge of the inhabitants of the deep.

Darling, Louis, *The Gull's Way* (Morrow, 1965)
From his home on an island off the coast of Maine, the author observes and photographs the life cycle of a pair of herring gulls.

George, Jean Craighead, *Julie of the Wolves* (Harper & Row, 1972; paperback, Harper)
A thirteen-year-old Eskimo girl, lost in the Alaskan wilderness, survives by living with a pack of wolves.

Herriot, James, *All Creatures Great and Small* (St. Martin's, 1972; paperback, Bantam)
The author recounts his experiences as a veterinarian in Yorkshire, England.

London, Jack, *The Call of the Wild* (many editions)
The hero is a dog named Buck, stolen from his California home and sold as a sled dog during the Alaskan Gold Rush. Buck serves many masters but loves only one, and in the end yields to his primitive instincts by joining a wolf pack.

Maxwell, Gavin, *Ring of Bright Water* (Dutton, 1961; paperback, Ballantine Books)
Life in a lonely cottage on the northwest coast of Scotland is enlivened by Mijkel and Edal, the author's pet otters.

Mowat, Farley, *Owls in the Family* (Little, Brown, 1961)
Pet owls named Wol and Weeps take over the author's household and upset the town of Saskatoon in Saskatchewan, Canada. In *The Dog Who Wouldn't Be* (Atlantic Monthly Press, 1957; paperback, Pyramid), Mowat tells the story of Mutt, who was almost too smart to be a dog.

Murphy, Robert, *The Pond* (Dutton, 1964)
Fourteen-year-old Joey discovers a pond in the woods outside Richmond, Virginia, where he learns about dogs, fishing, hunting, and life.

North, Sterling, *Rascal: A Memoir of a Better Era* (Dutton, 1963; paperback, Avon)
The author tells about his adventures with a pet raccoon.

O'Dell, Scott, *Island of the Blue Dolphins* (Houghton Mifflin, 1960; paperback, Dell)
Karana, a young Indian girl, lives alone for eighteen years on a desolate island off the California coast. The novel is based on a true story.

O'Hara, Mary, *My Friend Flicka* (Lippincott, 1941; paperback, Dell)
Ken's dream comes true when his father gives him a colt of his own.

Ullman, James Ramsey, *Banner in the Sky* (Lippincott, 1954; paperback, Archway)
Rudi, the son of a Swiss mountain-climber, struggles to conquer the mountain where his father lost his life.

When you examine the stories in this unit closely, you will find that they are made up of similar elements. For example, each story has a main character. In "The Erne from the Coast," the main character is a boy of your own age. In "Rikki-tikki-tavi," the central character is an animal. You will find that each story has a *plot*, or sequence of events. "Zlateh the Goat" has a relatively simple plot. "A Christmas Carol," in which there are many threads to the action, has a more complicated plot. Each story has a location in place and time called the *setting*. One of the stories in this unit is set in nineteenth-century India. Another is set in the Catskill Mountains in New York State in the late 1700's. In addition to entertaining readers, a short story generally reveals some idea about life or interpretation of experience. This element is called the *theme* of the story. Sometimes the theme is stated directly. Sometimes it is not stated, but may be inferred from other elements in the story.

In this unit you will be introduced to these and other basic elements in short stories. An understanding of these elements will help you read and reread short stories with increased knowledge and pleasure.

SHORT STORIES

I and the Village (1911).
Oil painting by Marc Chagall.
Collection, the Museum of
Modern Art, New York
Mrs. Simon Guggenheim Fund

225

*" 'But my dear girl,' Mr. Willoughby exclaimed testily,
'you have a National Magic Insurance card, haven't you?
Good heavens — why don't you go to the Public
Magician?' "*

All You've Ever Wanted

Joan Aiken

Matilda, you will agree, was a most unfortunate child. Not only had she three names each worse than the others — Matilda, Eliza, and Agatha — but her father and mother died shortly after she was born, and she was brought up exclusively by her six aunts. These were all energetic women, and so on Monday Matilda was taught algebra and arithmetic by her Aunt Aggie, on Tuesday biology by her Aunt Beattie, on Wednesday classics by her Aunt Cissie, on Thursday dancing and deportment by her Aunt Dorrie, on Friday essentials by her Aunt Effie, and on Saturday French by her Aunt Florrie. Friday was the most alarming day, as Matilda never knew beforehand what Aunt Effie would decide on as the day's essentials — sometimes it was cooking, or revolver practice, or washing, or boilermaking ("For you never know what a girl may need nowadays," as Aunt Effie rightly observed).

So that by Sunday, Matilda was often worn out, and thanked her stars that her seventh aunt, Gertie, had left for foreign parts many years before, and never threatened to come back and teach her geology or grammar on the only day when she was able to do as she liked.

However, poor Matilda was not entirely free from her Aunt Gertie, for on her seventh birthday, and each one after it, she received a little poem wishing her well, written on pink paper, decorated with silver flowers, and signed "Gertrude Isabel Jones, to her niece, with much affection." And the terrible disadvantage of the poems, pretty though they were, was that the wishes in them invariably came true. For instance, the one on her eighth birthday read:

> Now you're eight Matilda dear
> May shining gifts your place adorn
> And each day through the coming year
> Awake you with a rosy morn.

The shining gifts were all very well — they consisted of a torch,[1] a luminous watch, pins, needles, a steel soapbox, and a useful little silver brooch which said "Matilda" in case she ever forgot her name — but the rosy morns were a great mistake. As you know, a red sky in the morning is the shepherd's warning, and the fatal results of Aunt Gertie's well-meaning verse were that it rained every day for the entire year.

---

1. **torch:** here, a flashlight.

Now you're eight Matilda dear
May shining gifts your place adorn
And each day
through the coming year
Awake you with a rosy morn.

Gertrude Isabel Jones,
to her niece,
with much affection

Another one read:

Each morning make another friend
Who'll be with you till light doth end.
Cheery and frolicsome and gay,
To pass the sunny hours away.

For the rest of her life Matilda was over-whelmed by the number of friends she made in the course of that year — three hundred and sixty-five of them. Every morning she found another of them, anxious to cheer her and frolic with her, and the aunts complained that her lessons were being constantly inter-rupted. The worst of it was that she did not really like all the friends — some of them were so *very* cheery and frolicsome, and insisted on pillow fights when she had a toothache, or sometimes twenty-one of them would get to-gether and make her play hockey, which she

hated. She was not even consoled by the fact that all her hours were sunny, because she was so busy in passing them away that she had no time to enjoy them.

Long miles and weary though you stray
Your friends are never far away,
And every day though you may roam,
Yet night will find you back at home

was another inconvenient wish. Matilda found herself forced to go for long, tiresome walks in all weathers, and it was no comfort to know that her friends were never far away, for although they often passed her on bicycles or in cars, they never gave her lifts.

However, as she grew older, the poems became less troublesome, and she began to enjoy bluebirds twittering in the garden, and endless vases of roses on her windowsill. No-body knew where Aunt Gertie lived, and she never put in an address with her birthday greetings. It was therefore impossible to write and thank her for her varied good wishes, or hint that they might have been more carefully worded. But Matilda looked forward to meet-ing her one day, and thought that she must be a most interesting person.

"You never knew what Gertrude would be up to next," said Aunt Cissie. "She was a thoughtless girl, and got into endless scrapes, but I will say for her, she was very good-hearted."

When Matilda was nineteen she took a job in the Ministry of Alarm and Despondency, a very cheerful place where, instead of type-writer ribbon, they used red tape, and there was a large laundry basket near the main en-trance labeled The Usual Channels, where all the letters were put which people did not want to answer themselves. Once every three months the letters were re-sorted and dealt out afresh to different people.

Matilda got on very well here and was perfectly happy. She went to see her six aunts on Sundays, and had almost forgotten the seventh by the time that her twentieth birthday had arrived. Her aunt, however, had not forgotten her.

On the morning of her birthday Matilda woke very late, and had to rush off to work, cramming her letters unopened into her pocket, to be read later on in the morning. She had no time to read them until ten minutes to eleven, but that, she told herself, was as it should be, since, as she had been born at eleven in the morning, her birthday did not really begin till then.

Most of the letters were from her three hundred and sixty-five friends, but the usual pink and silver envelope was there, and she opened it with the usual feeling of slight uncertainty.

May all your leisure hours be blest
Your work prove full of interest,
Your life hold many happy hours
And all your way be strewn with flowers,

said the pink and silver slip in her fingers. "From your affectionate Aunt Gertrude."

Matilda was still pondering this when a gong sounded in the passage outside. This was the signal for everyone to leave their work and dash down the passage to a trolley which sold them buns and coffee. Matilda left her letters and dashed with the rest. Sipping her coffee and gossiping with her friends, she had forgotten the poem, when the voice of the Minister of Alarm and Despondency himself came down the corridor.

"What is all this? What does this mean?" he was saying.

The group around the trolley turned to see what he was talking about. And then Matilda flushed scarlet and spilled some of her coffee

on the floor. For all along the respectable brown carpeting of the passage were growing flowers in the most riotous profusion — daisies, campanulas, crocuses, mimosas, foxgloves, tulips, and lotuses. In some places the passage looked more like a jungle than anything else. Out of this jungle the little red-faced figure of the Minister fought its way.

"Who did it?" he said. But nobody answered.

Matilda went quietly away from the chattering group and pushed through the vegetation to her room, leaving a trail of buttercups and rhododendrons across the floor to her desk.

"I can't keep this quiet," she thought desperately. And she was quite right. Mr. Willoughby, who presided over the General Gloom Division, noticed almost immediately that when his secretary came into his room, there was something unusual about her.

"Miss Jones," he said, "I don't like to be personal, but have you noticed that wherever you go, you leave a trail of mixed flowers?"

Poor Matilda burst into tears.

"I know, I don't know *what* I shall do about it," she sobbed.

Mr. Willoughby was not used to secretaries who burst into tears, let alone ones who left lobelias, primroses, and the rarer forms of cactus behind them when they entered the room.

"It's very pretty," he said, "but not very practical. Already it's almost impossible to get along the passage, and I shudder to think what this room will be like when these have grown a bit higher. I really don't think you can go on with it, Miss Jones."

"You don't think I do it on purpose, do you?" said Matilda, sniffing into her handkerchief. "I can't stop it. They just keep on coming."

"In that case, I am afraid," replied Mr. Willoughby, "that you will not be able to keep on coming. We really cannot have the Ministry overgrown in this way. I shall be very sorry to lose you, Miss Jones. You have been most efficient. What caused this unfortunate disability, may I ask?"

"It's a kind of spell," Matilda said, shaking the damp out of her handkerchief onto a fine polyanthus.

"But my dear girl," Mr. Willoughby exclaimed testily, "you have a National Magic Insurance card, haven't you? Good heavens—why don't you go to the Public Magician?"

"I never thought of that," she confessed. "I'll go at lunchtime."

Fortunately for Matilda the Public Magician's office lay just across the square from where she worked, so that she did not cause too much disturbance, though the Borough Council could never account for the rare and exotic flowers which suddenly sprang up in the middle of their dusty lawns.

The Public Magician received her briskly, examined her with an occultiscope, and asked her to state particulars of her trouble.

"It's a spell," said Matilda, looking down at a pink Christmas rose growing unseasonably beside her chair.

"In that case we can soon help you. Fill in that form, *if* you please." He pushed a printed slip at her across the table.

It said: "To be filled in by persons suffering from spells, incantations, philters, evil eye, etc."

Matilda filled in name and address of patient, nature of spell, and date, but when she came to name and address of person by whom spell was cast, she paused.

"I don't know her address," she said.

"Then I'm afraid you'll have to find it. Can't do anything without an address," the Public Magician replied.

Matilda went out into the street very disheartened. The Public Magician could do nothing better than advise her to put an advertisement into the *Times* and the *International Sorcerers' Bulletin*, which she accordingly did:

AUNT GERTRUDE please communicate Matilda much distressed by last poem.

While she was in the post office sending off her advertisements (and causing a good deal of confusion by the number of forget-me-nots she left about), she wrote and posted her resignation to Mr. Willoughby, and then went sadly to the nearest underground station.

"Ain'tcher left something behind?" a man said to her at the top of the escalator. She looked back at the trail of daffodils across the station entrance and hurried anxiously down the stairs. As she ran around a corner at the

bottom, angry shouts told her that blooming lilies had interfered with the works and the escalator had stopped.

She tried to hide in the gloom at the far end of the platform, but a furious station official found her.

"Wotcher mean by it?" he said, shaking her elbow. "It'll take three days to put the station right, and look at my platform!"

The stone slabs were split and pushed aside by vast peonies, which kept growing, and threatened to block the line.

"It isn't my fault—really it isn't," poor Matilda stammered.

"The company can sue you for this, you know," he began, when a train came in. Pushing past him, she squeezed into the nearest door.

She began to thank her stars for the escape, but it was too soon. A powerful and penetrating smell of onions rose around her feet where the white flowers of wild garlic had sprung.

When Aunt Gertie finally read the advertisement in a ten-months-old copy of the *International Sorcerers' Bulletin*, she packed her luggage and took the next airplane back to England. For she was still just as Aunt Cissie had described her—thoughtless, but very good-hearted.

"Where is the poor child?" she asked Aunt Aggie.

"I should say she was poor," her sister replied tartly. "It's a pity you didn't come home before, instead of making her life a misery for twelve years. You'll find her out in the summerhouse."

Matilda had been living out there ever since she left the Ministry of Alarm and Despondency, because her aunts kindly but firmly, and quite reasonably, said that they could not have the house filled with vegetation.

She had an ax, with which she cut down the worst growths every evening, and for the rest of the time she kept as still as she could, and earned some money by doing odd jobs of typing and sewing.

"My poor dear child," Aunt Gertie said breathlessly, "I had no idea that my little verses would have this sort of effect. Whatever shall we do?"

"Please do something," Matilda implored her, sniffing. This time it was not tears, but a cold she had caught from living in perpetual drafts.

"My dear, there isn't anything I can do. It's bound to last till the end of the year—that sort of spell is completely unalterable."

"Well, at least can you stop sending me the verses?" asked Matilda. "I don't want to sound ungrateful."

"Even that I can't do," her aunt said gloomily. "It's a banker's order at the Magician's Bank. One a year from seven to twenty-one. Oh dear, and I thought it would be such *fun* for you. At least you only have one more, though."

"Yes, but heaven knows what that'll be." Matilda sneezed despondently and put another sheet of paper into her typewriter. There seemed to be nothing to do but wait. However, they did decide that it might be a good thing to go and see the Public Magician on the morning of Matilda's twenty-first birthday.

Aunt Gertie paid the taxi driver and tipped him heavily not to grumble about the mass of delphiniums sprouting out of the mat of his cab.

"Good heavens, if it isn't Gertrude Jones!" the Public Magician exclaimed. "Haven't seen you since we were at college together. How are you? Same old irresponsible Gertie? Remember that hospital you endowed with endless beds and the trouble it caused? And the row with the cigarette manufacturers over the extra million boxes of cigarettes for the soldiers?"

When the situation was explained to him he laughed heartily.

"Just like you, Gertie. Well-meaning isn't the word."

At eleven promptly, Matilda opened her pink envelope.

> Matilda, now you're twenty-one,
> May you have every sort of fun;
> May you have all you've ever wanted,
> And every future wish be granted.

"Every future wish be granted—then I wish Aunt Gertie would lose her power of wishing," cried Matilda; and immediately Aunt Gertie did.

But as Aunt Gertie with her usual thoughtlessness had said, "May you have all you've *ever wanted*," Matilda had quite a lot of rather inconvenient things to dispose of, including a lion cub and a baby hippopotamus.

SEEKING MEANING

1. Much of the humor in Joan Aiken's story results from the contrast between what we expect and what actually happens. The reader is constantly being surprised by the results of Aunt Gertrude's birthday poems. For example, Aunt Gertrude's wishes for Matilda's eighth birthday include "shining gifts" (page 226). What "shining gifts" does Matilda receive? What unexpected results are produced by the rest of that birthday poem?

2. In the poem to Matilda on her twentieth birthday, Aunt Gertrude's wish is for her niece's way to be "strewn with flowers." How do you think most people would interpret that wish? In what way does the wish come true for Matilda?

3. On her twenty-first birthday, how does Matilda make sure that her Aunt Gertrude will cause no more trouble? Why does Matilda have a lion cub and a baby hippopotamus to dispose of? (What does the title tell you?)

DEVELOPING SKILLS IN READING

Distinguishing Literal from Figurative Language

There are many expressions in everyday speech that are not meant to be taken literally. When it is raining very hard, you may say that it is "raining cats and dogs." People understand that you are saying one thing but that you actually mean something else. The expression "raining cats and dogs" is an example of *figurative* language, or language that says one thing but that actually means something else. If you were to wish someone a "rosy future," you would be wishing that person success and happiness. The phrase "rosy future" is another example of figurative language.

In Joan Aiken's story, Aunt Gertrude's birthday wishes seem to be figurative expressions, but they come true literally. Select one example from the story and show how it supports this statement.

DEVELOPING VOCABULARY

Analyzing words with *-scope*

Many words in English have been formed by combining words or parts of words from other languages. The root *-scope* comes from Greek. It means "an instrument for observing something."

The word *telescope* is made up of two parts: *tele-*, a root meaning "far off," and *-scope*. A *telescope* is an instrument for observing distant objects, such as the stars. What is a *microscope*? A *periscope*? A *stethoscope*? Check your answers by consulting a dictionary.

Joan Aiken has made up the word *occultiscope* (page 230). If a doctor uses a stethoscope to examine a patient's heart and lungs, for what purpose would the Public Magician use an occultiscope? (Find the meaning of *occult* in a dictionary.)

ABOUT THE AUTHOR

Joan Aiken (1924–   ) says she began writing when she was five years old. She spent two shillings (a considerable sum then) for a thick notebook in which to write "poems, stories, and thoughts as they occurred." The work that introduced her to the public was a story she wrote when she was seventeen, which was read on a radio program for children. Along with children's fiction, she has written more than ten adult books, including several collections of horror and suspense tales.

" 'I'm so glad you appeared,'
she said, looking earnestly
into his face. 'I was beginning
to get worried.' "

The Landlady   *Roald Dahl*

Billy Weaver had traveled down from London on the slow afternoon train, with a change at Reading on the way, and by the time he got to Bath it was about nine o'clock in the evening and the moon was coming up out of a clear starry sky over the houses opposite the station entrance. But the air was deadly cold and the wind was like a flat blade of ice on his cheeks.

"Excuse me," he said, "but is there a fairly cheap hotel not too far away from here?"

"Try The Bell and Dragon," the porter answered, pointing down the road. "They might take you in. It's about a quarter of a mile along on the other side."

Billy thanked him and picked up his suitcase and set out to walk the quarter-mile to The Bell and Dragon. He had never been to Bath before. He didn't know anyone who lived there. But Mr. Greenslade at the Head Office in London had told him it was a splendid town. "Find your own lodgings," he had said, "and then go along and report to the Branch Manager as soon as you've got yourself settled."

Billy was seventeen years old. He was wearing a new navy-blue overcoat, a new brown trilby hat,[1] and a new brown suit, and he was feeling fine. He walked briskly down the street. He was trying to do everything briskly these days. Briskness, he had decided, was *the* one common characteristic of all successful businessmen. The big shots up at Head Office were absolutely fantastically brisk all the time. They were amazing.

There were no shops on this wide street that he was walking along, only a line of tall houses on each side, all of them identical. They had porches and pillars and four or five steps going up to their front doors, and it was obvious that once upon a time they had been very swanky residences. But now, even in the darkness, he could see that the paint was peeling from the woodwork on their doors and windows, and that the handsome white façades were cracked and blotchy from neglect.

Suddenly, in a downstairs window that was brilliantly illuminated by a streetlamp not six yards away, Billy caught sight of a printed notice propped up against the glass in one of

---

1. **trilby hat:** a soft felt hat.

the upper panes. It said BED AND BREAKFAST. There was a vase of yellow chrysanthemums, tall and beautiful, standing just underneath the notice.

He stopped walking. He moved a bit closer. Green curtains (some sort of velvety material) were hanging down on either side of the window. The chrysanthemums looked wonderful beside them. He went right up and peered through the glass into the room, and the first thing he saw was a bright fire burning in the hearth. On the carpet in front of the fire, a pretty little dachshund was curled up asleep with its nose tucked into its belly. The room itself, so far as he could see in the half-darkness, was filled with pleasant furniture. There

was a baby-grand piano and a big sofa and several plump armchairs; and in one corner he spotted a large parrot in a cage. Animals were usually a good sign in a place like this, Billy told himself; and all in all, it looked to him as though it would be a pretty decent house to stay in. Certainly it would be more comfortable than The Bell and Dragon.

On the other hand, a pub[2] would be more congenial than a boardinghouse. There would be beer and darts in the evenings, and lots of people to talk to, and it would probably be a good bit cheaper, too. He had stayed a couple of nights in a pub once before and he had liked

_____

2. **pub:** tavern or inn.

it. He had never stayed in any boarding-houses, and, to be perfectly honest, he was a tiny bit frightened of them. The name itself conjured up images of watery cabbage, rapacious[3] landladies, and a powerful smell of kippers[4] in the living room.

After dithering about[5] like this in the cold for two or three minutes, Billy decided that he would walk on and take a look at The Bell and Dragon before making up his mind. He turned to go.

And now a queer thing happened to him. He was in the act of stepping back and turning away from the window when all at once his eye was caught and held in the most peculiar manner by the small notice that was there. BED AND BREAKFAST, it said. BED AND BREAKFAST, BED AND BREAKFAST, BED AND BREAKFAST. Each word was like a large black eye staring at him through the glass, holding him, compelling him, forcing him to stay where he was and not to walk away from that house, and the next thing he knew, he was actually moving across from the window to the front door of the house, climbing the steps that led up to it, and reaching for the bell.

He pressed the bell. Far away in a back room he heard it ringing, and then *at once*—it must have been at once because he hadn't even had time to take his finger from the bell-button—the door swung open and a woman was standing there.

Normally you ring the bell and you have at least a half-minute's wait before the door opens. But this dame was like a jack-in-the-box. He pressed the bell—and out she popped! It made him jump.

She was about forty-five or fifty years old, and the moment she saw him, she gave him a warm welcoming smile.

"*Please* come in," she said pleasantly. She stepped aside, holding the door wide open, and Billy found himself automatically starting forward. The compulsion or, more accurately, the desire to follow after her into that house was extraordinarily strong.

"I saw the notice in the window," he said, holding himself back.

"Yes, I know."

"I was wondering about a room."

"It's *all* ready for you, my dear," she said. She had a round pink face and very gentle blue eyes.

"I was on my way to The Bell and Dragon," Billy told her. "But the notice in your window just happened to catch my eye."

"My dear boy," she said, "why don't you come in out of the cold?"

"How much do you charge?"

"Five and sixpence[6] a night, including breakfast."

It was fantastically cheap. It was less than half of what he had been willing to pay.

"If that is too much," she added, "then perhaps I can reduce it just a tiny bit. Do you desire an egg for breakfast? Eggs are expensive at the moment. It would be sixpence less without the egg."

"Five and sixpence is fine," he answered. "I should like very much to stay here."

"I knew you would. Do come in."

She seemed terribly nice. She looked exactly like the mother of one's best school friend welcoming one into the house to stay for the Christmas holidays. Billy took off his hat, and stepped over the threshold.

---

3. **rapacious** (rə-pā′shəs): greedy; also, living on prey.
4. **kippers:** dried or smoked fish, regularly eaten for breakfast in Great Britain.
5. **dithering about:** hesitating.

6. **Five and sixpence:** about seventy-five cents at the time of the story.

"Just hang it there," she said, "and let me help you with your coat."

There were no other hats or coats in the hall. There were no umbrellas, no walking sticks—nothing.

"We have it *all* to ourselves," she said, smiling at him over her shoulder as she led the way upstairs. "You see, it isn't very often I have the pleasure of taking a visitor into my little nest."

The old girl is slightly dotty, Billy told himself. But at five and sixpence a night, who gives a hang about that? "I should've thought you'd be simply swamped with applicants," he said politely.

"Oh, I am, my dear, I am, of course I am. But the trouble is that I'm inclined to be just a teeny-weeny bit choosy and particular—if you see what I mean."

"Ah, yes."

"But I'm always ready. Everything is always ready day and night in this house just on the off chance that an acceptable young gentleman will come along. And it is such a pleasure, my dear, such a very great pleasure when now and again I open the door and I see someone standing there who is just *exactly* right." She was halfway up the stairs, and she paused with one hand on the stair rail, turning her head and smiling down at him with pale lips. "Like you," she added, and her blue eyes traveled slowly all the way down the length of Bill's body, to his feet, and then up again.

On the second-floor landing she said to him, "This floor is mine."

They climbed up another flight. "And this one is *all* yours," she said. "Here's your room. I do hope you'll like it." She took him into a small but charming front bedroom, switching on the light as she went in.

"The morning sun comes right in the window, Mr. Perkins. It *is* Mr. Perkins, isn't it?"

"No," he said. "It's Weaver."

"Mr. Weaver. How nice. I've put a water bottle between the sheets to air them out, Mr. Weaver. It's such a comfort to have a hot water bottle in a strange bed with clean sheets, don't you agree? And you may light the gas fire at any time if you feel chilly."

"Thank you," Billy said. "Thank you ever so much." He noticed that the bedspread had been taken off the bed, and that the bedclothes had been neatly turned back on one side, all ready for someone to get in.

"I'm so glad you appeared," she said, looking earnestly into his face. "I was beginning to get worried."

"That's all right," Billy answered brightly. "You mustn't worry about me." He put his suitcase on the chair and started to open it.

"And what about supper, my dear? Did you manage to get anything to eat before you came here?"

"I'm not a bit hungry, thank you," he said. "I think I'll just go to bed as soon as possible because tomorrow I've got to get up rather early and report to the office."

"Very well, then. I'll leave you now so that you can unpack. But before you go to bed, would you be kind enough to pop into the sitting room on the ground floor and sign the book? Everyone has to do that because it's the law of the land, and we don't want to go breaking any laws at *this* stage in the proceedings, do we?" She gave him a little wave of the hand and went quickly out of the room and closed the door.

Now, the fact that his landlady appeared to be slightly off her rocker didn't worry Billy in the least. After all, she not only was harmless—there was no question about that—but she was also quite obviously a kind and generous soul. He guessed that she had probably lost a son in the war, or something like that, and had never gotten over it.

So a few minutes later, after unpacking his suitcase and washing his hands, he trotted downstairs to the ground floor and entered the living room. His landlady wasn't there, but the fire was glowing in the hearth, and the little dachshund was still sleeping soundly in front of it. The room was wonderfully warm and cozy. I'm a lucky fellow, he thought, rubbing his hands. This is a bit of all right.

He found the guest book lying open on the piano, so he took out his pen and wrote down his name and address. There were only two other entries above his on the page, and, as one always does with guest books, he started to read them. One was a Christopher Mulholland from Cardiff. The other was Gregory W. Temple from Bristol.

That's funny, he thought suddenly. Christopher Mulholland. It rings a bell.

Now where on earth had he heard that rather unusual name before?

Was it a boy at school? No. Was it one of his sister's numerous young men, perhaps, or a friend of his father's? No, no, it wasn't any of those. He glanced down again at the book.

Christopher Mulholland
       231 Cathedral Road, Cardiff
Gregory W. Temple
       27 Sycamore Drive, Bristol

As a matter of fact, now he came to think of it, he wasn't at all sure that the second name didn't have almost as much of a familiar ring about it as the first.

"Gregory Temple?" he said aloud, searching his memory. "Christopher Mulholland? . . ."

"Such charming boys," a voice behind him answered, and he turned and saw his landlady sailing into the room with a large silver tea tray in her hands. She was holding it well out in front of her, and rather high up, as though

the tray were a pair of reins on a frisky horse.

"They sound somehow familiar," he said.

"They do? How interesting."

"I'm almost positive I've heard those names before somewhere. Isn't that odd? Maybe it was in the newspapers. They weren't famous in any way, were they? I mean famous cricketers[7] or footballers or something like that?"

"Famous," she said, setting the tea tray down on the low table in front of the sofa. "Oh no, I don't think they were famous. But they were incredibly handsome, both of them, I can promise you that. They were tall and young and handsome, my dear, just exactly like you."

Once more, Billy glanced down at the book. "Look here," he said, noticing the dates. "This last entry is over two years old."

"It is?"

"Yes, indeed. And Christopher Mulholland's is nearly a year before that—more than *three years* ago."

"Dear me," she said, shaking her head and heaving a dainty little sigh. "I would never have thought it. How time does fly away from us all, doesn't it, Mr. Wilkins?"

"It's Weaver," Billy said. *"W-e-a-v-e-r."*

"Oh, of course it is!" she cried, sitting down on the sofa. "How silly of me. I do apologize. In one ear and out the other, that's me, Mr. Weaver."

"You know something?" Billy said. "Something that's really quite extraordinary about all this?"

"No, dear, I don't."

"Well, you see, both of these names—Mulholland and Temple—I not only seem to remember each one of them separately, so to

---

7. **cricketers:** Cricket is a popular national sport in Great Britain. It is played on a large field with bats, a ball, and wickets.

speak, but somehow or other, in some peculiar way, they both appear to be sort of connected together as well. As though they were both famous for the same sort of thing, if you see what I mean—like . . . well . . . like Dempsey and Tunney,[8] for example, or Churchill and Roosevelt."

"How amusing," she said. "But come over here now, dear, and sit down beside me on the sofa and I'll give you a nice cup of tea and a ginger biscuit before you go to bed."

"You really shouldn't bother," Billy said. "I didn't mean you to do anything like that." He stood by the piano, watching her as she fussed about with the cups and saucers. He noticed that she had small, white, quickly moving hands, and red fingernails.

"I'm almost positive it was in the newspapers I saw them," Billy said. "I'll think of it in a second. I'm sure I will."

There is nothing more tantalizing than a thing like this that lingers just outside the borders of one's memory. He hated to give up.

"Now wait a minute," he said. "Wait just a minute. Mulholland . . . Christopher Mulholland . . . wasn't *that* the name of the Eton schoolboy who was on a walking tour through the West Country, and then all of a sudden . . ."

"Milk?" she said. "And sugar?"

"Yes, please. And then all of a sudden . . ."

"Eton schoolboy?" she said. "Oh no, my dear, that can't possibly be right because *my* Mr. Mulholland was certainly not an Eton schoolboy when he came to me. He was a Cambridge undergraduate. Come over here now and sit next to me and warm yourself in front of this lovely fire. Come on. Your tea's all

ready for you." She patted the empty place beside her on the sofa, and she sat there smiling at Billy and waiting for him to come over.

He crossed the room slowly, and sat down on the edge of the sofa. She placed his teacup on the table in front of him.

"*There* we are," she said. "How nice and cozy this is, isn't it?"

Billy started sipping his tea. She did the same. For half a minute or so, neither of them spoke. But Billy knew that she was looking at him. Her body was half turned toward him, and he could feel her eyes resting on his face, watching him over the rim of her teacup. Now and again, he caught a whiff of a peculiar smell that seemed to emanate directly from her person. It was not in the least unpleasant, and it reminded him—well, he wasn't quite sure what it reminded him of. Pickled walnuts? New leather? Or was it the corridors of a hospital?

At length, she said, "Mr. Mulholland was a great one for his tea. Never in my life have I seen anyone drink as much tea as dear, sweet Mr. Mulholland."

"I suppose he left fairly recently," Billy said. He was still puzzling his head about the two names. He was positive now that he had seen them in the newspapers—in the headlines.

"Left?" she said, arching her brows. "But my dear boy, he never left. He's still here. Mr. Temple is also here. They're on the fourth floor, both of them together."

Billy set his cup down slowly on the table and stared at his landlady. She smiled back at him, and then she put out one of her white hands and patted him comfortingly on the knee. "How old are you, my dear?" she asked.

"Seventeen."

"Seventeen!" she cried. "Oh, it's the perfect age! Mr. Mulholland was also seventeen. But I

8. **Dempsey and Tunney:** Jack Dempsey and Gene Tunney, heavyweight boxing champions. Tunney defeated Dempsey in a fight for the world title in 1926, and again in 1927.

think he was a trifle shorter than you are; in fact I'm sure he was, and his teeth weren't *quite* so white. You have the most beautiful teeth, Mr. Weaver, did you know that?"

"They're not as good as they look," Billy said. "They've got simply masses of fillings in them at the back."

"Mr. Temple, of course, was a little older," she said, ignoring his remark. "He was actually twenty-eight. And yet I never would have guessed it if he hadn't told me, never in my whole life. There wasn't a *blemish* on his body."

"A what?" Billy said.

"His skin was *just* like a baby's."

There was a pause. Billy picked up his teacup and took another sip of his tea, then he set it down again gently in its saucer. He waited for her to say something else, but she seemed to have lapsed into another of her silences. He sat there staring straight ahead of him into the far corner of the room, biting his lower lip.

"That parrot," he said at last. "You know something? It had me completely fooled when I first saw it through the window. I could have sworn it was alive."

"Alas, no longer."

"It's most terribly clever the way it's been done," he said. "It doesn't look in the least bit dead. Who did it?"

"I did."

"*You* did?"

"Of course," she said. "And have you met my little Basil as well?" She nodded toward the dachshund curled up so comfortably in front of the fire. Billy looked at it. And suddenly, he realized that this animal had all the time been just as silent and motionless as the parrot. He put out a hand and touched it gently on the top of its back. The back was hard and cold, and when he pushed the hair to one side with his fingers, he could see the skin underneath, grayish-black and dry and perfectly perserved.

"Good gracious me," he said. "How absolutely fascinating." He turned away from the dog and stared with deep admiration at the little woman beside him on the sofa. "It must be most awfully difficult to do a thing like that."

"Not in the least," she said. "I stuff *all* my little pets myself when they pass away. Will you have another cup of tea?"

"No, thank you," Billy said. The tea tasted faintly of bitter almonds, and he didn't much care for it.

"You did sign the book, didn't you?"

"Oh, yes."

"That's good. Because later on, if I happen to forget what you were called, then I could always come down here and look it up. I still do that almost every day with Mr. Mulholland and Mr. . . . Mr. . . . ."

"Temple," Billy said. "Gregory Temple. Excuse my asking, but haven't there been *any* other guests here except them in the last two or three years?"

Holding her teacup high in one hand, inclining her head slightly to the left, she looked up at him out of the corners of her eyes and gave him another gentle little smile.

"No, my dear," she said. "Only you."

SEEKING MEANING

1. What you learn about Billy Weaver at the beginning of the story helps explain why he later chooses to stay at the landlady's house. When you first meet Billy, he is looking for a fairly cheap hotel. How does his desire for a bargain drive him into a trap?

2. Billy is impressed by appearances. What details of the landlady's house first attract him? Which of these details are not what they appear to be?

3. Billy overlooks dangers that are quite obvious to the reader. What he finds in the landlady's house does not arouse his suspicions. What clues does he ignore? What explanation does he give for the landlady's odd behavior?

4. The landlady tells Billy, "I was beginning to get worried." How does Billy interpret this remark? Considering the number of entries in her guest book, what do you think she was worried about?

5. Potassium cyanide, which is extremely poisonous, is known for its faint, bitter-almond taste. This is what Billy tastes in the landlady's tea. Find as many clues as you can that indicate what Billy's fate is to be.

6. Billy is shown to be quite observant throughout the story. Why does he fail to recognize the danger he is in?

DEVELOPING SKILLS IN READING

Understanding Suspense and Foreshadowing
When you read "The Landlady," you find yourself responding to danger signals that Billy Weaver fails to recognize. You can see clearly what is going to happen, but you have no way of warning Billy. You read on, eager to see whether he will connect the clues and act in time to save himself.

This uncertainty about what is going to happen next in a story is known as *suspense*.

Roald Dahl creates suspense by placing Billy in danger and keeping you uncertain about whether he will escape or not.

Early in the story, Dahl creates suspense by presenting you with a mystery. When Billy sees the sign in the landlady's window, something strange happens to him.

> Each word was like a large black eye staring at him through the glass, holding him, compelling him, forcing him to stay where he was and not to walk away from that house, and the next thing he knew, he was actually moving across from the window to the front door of the house, climbing the steps that led up to it, and reaching for the bell.

What is this magnetic force that attracts Billy? What will happen when Billy presses the doorbell? Who will be waiting there behind the door? These are the questions that the reader wants answered.

To build up suspense, a writer will drop hints about what is going to come later in the story. This practice is called *foreshadowing.* All the information about Billy's fate is supplied in hints. The author never tells what the landlady plans to do to Billy. But you, the reader, can guess.

DEVELOPING SKILLS OF EXPRESSION

Describing a Street Scene
As Billy walks toward The Bell and Dragon, he carefully observes the scene around him.

> There were no shops on this wide street that he was walking along, only a line of tall houses on each side, all of them identical. They had porches and pillars and four or five steps going up to their front doors,

and it was obvious that once upon a time they had been very swanky residences. But now, even in the darkness, he could see that the paint was peeling from the woodwork on their doors and windows, and that the handsome white facades were cracked and blotchy from neglect.

The impression you receive through Billy's eyes is one of faded elegance. In a few well-chosen details, the author lets you know that this neighborhood has begun to deteriorate.

Choose a street in your own neighborhood and decide what general impression that street makes on you, the observer. Give as many specific details as you can to support that impression.

ABOUT THE AUTHOR

Roald Dahl (1916–   ) grew up in the beautiful countryside surrounding Llandaff in Wales. At sixteen he left school to join an exploratory expedition to Newfoundland. When World War II broke out in 1939, he volunteered for the Royal Air Force as a fighter pilot. Although he was wounded while flying over the Libyan Desert and was hospitalized for four months, he continued to fly until 1942, when he was sent to Washington as an assistant to the British ambassador.

Dahl's writing career began when the novelist C. S. Forester asked him to write an account of his most exciting flying experience. The story he wrote was subsequently published in the *Saturday Evening Post.* Dahl has published several collections of short stories. One critic has noted his ability "to steer an unwavering course along the hairline where the gruesome and the comic meet and mingle." "The Landlady" is a good example of the bizarre element in Dahl's work.

"He prayed . . . that the eagle would come back next morning and attack the sheep again, and give him one more chance."

The Erne from the Coast

T. O. Beachcroft

I

"Where's Harry?" Mr. Thorburn came out of the back of the farmhouse. He stood in the middle of the well-kept farmyard. "Here, Harry!" he shouted. "Hi, Harry!"

He stood leaning on a stick and holding a letter in his hand as he looked round the farmyard.

Mr. Thorburn was a red-faced, powerful man; he wore knee breeches and black leather gaiters.[1] His face and well-fleshed body told you at a glance that Thorburn's Farm had not done too badly during the twenty years of his married life.

Harry, a fair-haired boy, came running across the yard.

"Harry," said the farmer to his son, "here's a letter come for old Michael. It will be about this visit he's to pay to his sick brother. Nice time of year for this to happen, I must say. You'd better take the letter to him at once."

"Where to?" said Harry.

"He's up on the hill, of course," said the farmer. "In his hut, or with the sheep somewhere. Your own brains could have told you that. Can't you ever use them? Go on, now."

"Right," said Harry. He turned to go.

"Don't take all day," said his father.

Mr. Thorburn stood looking after his son. He leaned heavily on the thorn stick which he always carried. Harry went through the gate in the low gray wall which ran round one side of the yard, where there were no buildings. Directly he left the farmyard, he began to climb. Thorburn's Farm was at the end of a valley. Green fields lay in front of it, and a wide road sloped gently down to the village a mile away; behind, the hill soared up, and high on the ridge of the hill was Michael's hut, three miles off, and climbing all the way.

Harry was thirteen, very yellow-haired and blue-eyed. He was a slip of a boy. It seemed unlikely that he could ever grow into such a stolid, heavy man as his father. Mr. Thorburn was every pound of fourteen stone,[2] as the

---

1. **gaiters:** coverings worn over shoes, and sometimes, as here, the calves of the legs.

2. **stone:** a unit of weight used in Great Britain, equal to 14 pounds (about 6 kilograms).

men on the farm could have told you the day he broke his leg and they had to carry him back to the farmhouse on a hurdle.[3]

Harry started off far too fast, taking the lower slopes almost at a run. His body was loose in its movements, and coltish, and by the time the real work began he was already tiring. However, the April day was fresh and rainy, and the cold of it kept him going. Gray gusts and showers swept over the hillside, and between them, with changing light, came faint gleams of sunshine, so that the shadows of the clouds raced along the hill beside him. Presently he cleared the gorse and heather[4] and came out on to the open hillside, which was bare except for short, tussocky grass.[5] His home began to look far-off beneath him. He could see his mother walking down towards the village with one of the dogs, and the baker's cart coming up from the village towards her. The fields were brown and green

round the farmhouse, and the buildings were gray, with low stone walls.

He stopped several times to look back on the small distant farm. It took him well over an hour to reach the small hut where Michael lived by day and slept during most nights throughout the lambing season. He was not in his hut, but after a few minutes' search Harry found him. Michael was sitting without movement, watching the sheep and talking to his gray-and-white dog. He had a sack across his shoulders, which made him look rather like a rock with gray lichen on it. He looked up at Harry without moving.

"It's a hildy wildy day," he said, "but there'll be a glent of sunsheen yet."

Harry handed Michael the letter. Michael looked at it, and opened it very slowly, and spread the crackling paper out on his knee with brown hands. Harry watched him for some minutes as he studied the letter in silence.

"Letter'll be aboot my brother," said Michael at length. "I'm to goa and see him." He handed the letter to Harry. "Read it, Harry," he said. Harry read the letter to him twice.

---

3. **hurdle:** here, a movable framework of twigs, used to enclose sheep.
4. **gorse and heather** (hĕ*th*'ər): low-growing shrubs found in the highlands of Great Britain.
5. **tussocky** (tŭs'ək-ē) **grass:** grass growing in clumps.

"Tell thy dad," said Michael, "I'll be doon at farm i' the morn. Happen[6] I'll be away three days. And tell him new lamb was born last neet, but it's sickly."

They looked at the small white bundle that lay on the grass beside its mother, hardly moving.

" 'T'll pick up," said Michael. He slowly stood and looked round at the distance.

Michael had rather long hair; it was between gray and white in color, and it blew in the wind. It was about the hue of an old sheep's skull that has lain out on the bare mountain. Michael's clothes and face and hair made Harry feel that he had slowly faded out on the hillside. He was all the color of rain on the stones and last year's bracken.[7]

"It'll make a change," said Michael, "going off and sleeping in a bed."

"Goodbye," said Harry. "You'll be down at the farm tomorrow, then?"

"Aw reet," said Michael.

"Aw reet," said Harry.

Harry went slowly back to the farm. The rain had cleared off, and the evening was sunny, with a watery light, by the time he was home. Michael had been right. Harry gave his father the message, and told him about the lamb.

"It's a funny thing," said Harry, "that old Michael can't even read."

"Don't you be so smart." said Mr. Thorburn. "Michael knows a thing or two you don't. You don't want to go muckering about with[8] an old fellow like Michael—best shepherd I've ever known."

Harry went away feeling somewhat abashed. Lately it seemed his father was always down on him, telling him he showed no sign of sense; telling him he ought to grow up a bit; telling him he was more like seven than thirteen.

He went to the kitchen. This was a big stone-floored room with a huge plain table, where the whole household and several of the farm hands could sit down to dinner or tea at the same time. His mother and his aunt from the village were still lingering over their teacups, but there was no one else in the room except a small tortoise-shell cat, which was pacing round them asking for milk in a loud voice. The yellow evening light filled the room. His mother gave him tea and ham and bread and butter, and he ate it in silence, playing with the cat as he did so.

II

Next morning at nine o'clock there was a loud rap with a stick at the kitchen door, and there by the pump, with the hens running round his legs, stood Michael.

"Good morning, Mrs. Thorburn," he said. "Is Measter about?"

"Come on in with you," said Mrs. Thorburn, "and have a good hot cup o' tea. Have you eaten this morning?"

Michael clanked into the kitchen, his hobnails striking the flags,[9] and he sat down at one end of the table.

"Aye," he said, "I've eaten, Missus. I had a good thoom-bit[10] when I rose up, but a cup of tea would be welcome."

As he drank the tea, Mr. Thorburn came in, bringing Harry with him. Michael, thought

---

6. **Happen:** perhaps.
7. **bracken:** coarse ferns. "Last year's bracken" would be dried out and therefore brownish in color.
8. **muckering about with:** getting in the way of; hindering.

9. **flags:** here, flagstones, which are used in paving.
10. **thoom-bit:** a piece of meat eaten on bread.

Harry, always looked rather strange when he was down in the village or in the farmhouse; rather as a pile of bracken or an armful of leaves would look if it were emptied out onto the parlor floor.

Michael talked to Mr. Thorburn about the sheep; about the new lamb; about young Bob, his nephew, who was coming over from another farm to look after the sheep while he was away.

"Tell en to watch new lamb." said Michael; "it's creachy.[11] I've put en in my little hut, and owd sheep is looking roun' t' doorway."

After his cup of tea Michael shook hands all round. Then he set off down to the village, where he was going to fall in with a lift.

Soon after he had gone, Bob arrived at the farm. He was a tall young man with a freckled face and red hair, big-boned and very gentle in his voice and movements. He listened to all Mr. Thorburn's instructions and then set out for the shepherd's hut.

However, it seemed that Mr. Thorburn's luck with his shepherds was dead out. For the next evening, just as it was turning dark, Bob walked into the farmhouse kitchen. His face was tense with pain, and he was nursing his left arm with his right hand. Harry saw the ugly distorted shape and swelling at the wrist. Bob had fallen and broken the wrist earlier in the day, and by evening the pain had driven him back.

"I'm sorry, Mr. Thorburn," he kept on saying. "I'm a big fule."

The sheep had to be left for that night. Next morning it was again a cold, windy day, and clouds the color of gunmetal raced over the hill. The sun broke through fitfully, filling the valley with a steel-blue light in which the green grass looked vivid. Mr. Thorburn decided to send Harry out to the shepherd's hut for the day and night.

"Happen old Michael will be back sometime tomorrow," he said. "You can look to the sheep, Harry, and see to that sick lamb for us. It's a good chance to make yourself useful."

Harry nodded.

"You can feed the lamb. Bob said it didn't seem to suck enough, and you can let me know if anything else happens. And you can keep an eye on the other lambs and see they don't get over the edges. There's no need to fold them at night; just let the dog round them up and see the flock is near the hut."

"There's blankets and everything in the hut, Harry," said Mrs. Thorburn, "and a spirit lamp to make tea. You can't come to harm."

Harry set off up the hill and began to climb. Out on the hilltop it was very lonely, and the wind was loud and gusty, with sudden snatches of rain. The sheep kept near the wooden hut most of the time; it was built in the lee[12] of the ridge, and the best shelter was to be found near it. Harry looked after the sick lamb and brewed himself tea. He had Tassie, the gray and white sheep dog, for company. Time did not hang heavy. When evening came he rounded up the sheep and counted them, and, true to advice that Michael had given him, he slept in his boots as a true shepherd does, warmly wrapped up in the rugs.

He was awakened as soon as it was light by the dog barking. He went out in the gray dawn light and found a rustle and agitation among the sheep. Tassie ran to him and back towards the sheep. The sheep were starting up alert, and showed a tendency to scatter. Harry looked round, wondering what the trouble was. Then he saw. A bird was hovering over

---

11. **creachy:** sick.

12. **in the lee:** on the protected side.

the flock, and it was this that had attracted the sheep's attention. But what bird was it? It hovered like a hawk, soaring on outstretched wings; yet it was much too big for a hawk. As the bird came nearer Harry was astonished at its size. Once or twice it approached and then went soaring and floating away again. It was larger than any bird he had ever seen before— brownish in color, with a gray head and a hawk's beak.

Suddenly the bird began to drop as a hawk drops. A knot of sheep dashed apart. Tassie rushed towards the bird, his head down and his tail streaming out behind him. Harry followed. This must be an eagle, he thought. He saw it, looking larger still now it was on the ground, standing with outstretched wings over a lamb.

Tassie attacked, snarling in rage. The eagle rose at him. It struck at him with its feet and a flurry of beating wings. The dog was thrown back. He retreated slowly, snarling savagely as he went, his tail between his legs. He was frightened now, and uncertain what to do.

The eagle turned back to the lamb, took it in its talons again, and began to rise. It could not move quickly near the ground, and Harry came up with it. At once the eagle put the lamb on a rock and turned on him. He saw its talons driving towards his face, claws and spurs of steel—a stroke could tear your eyes out. He put up his arms in fear, and he felt the rush of wings round his face. With his arm above his head he sank on one knee.

When he looked up again, the eagle was back on the lamb. It began to fly with long slow wingbeats. At first it scarcely rose, and flew with the lamb almost on the ground.

Harry ran, throwing a stone. He shouted. Tassie gave chase, snapping at the eagle as it went. But the eagle was working towards a chasm,[13] a sheer drop in the hillside where no one could follow it. In another moment it was floating in the air, clear and away. Then it rose higher, and headed towards the coast, which was a few miles away over the hill.

Harry stood and watched it till it was out of sight. When it was gone, he turned and walked slowly back to the hut. There was not a sound to be heard now except the sudden rushes of wind. The hillside was bare and coverless except for the scattered black rocks. Tassie walked beside him. The dog was very subdued and hardly glanced to right or left.

It took some time to round the sheep up, or to find, at least, where the various parts of the flock had scattered themselves. The sick lamb and its mother had been enclosed all this time in a fold near the hut. The ewe[14] was still terrified.

An hour later Harry set off down the mountainside to the farm. Tassie looked after him doubtfully. He ran several times after him, but Harry sent him back to the hut.

It was the middle of the morning when Harry came back to the farmyard again. His father was standing in the middle of the yard, leaning on his stick, and giving advice to one of his cowmen. He broke off when he saw Harry come in through the gate and walk towards him across the farmyard.

"Well," he said, "anything wrong, Harry? I thought you were going to stay till Michael came back."

"We've lost a lamb," said Harry, breathlessly. "It's been carried off by an eagle. It must have been an eagle."

"An eagle?" said Mr. Thorburn. He gave a laugh which mocked Harry. "Why didn't you stop it?"

"I tried," said Harry. "But I . . ."

Mr. Thorburn was in a bad mood. He had sold some heifers[15] the day before at a disappointing price. He had had that morning a letter from the builders about repairs to some of the farm buildings, and there was work to be done which he could hardly afford. He was worried about Michael's absence. He felt as if the world were bearing down on him and he had too many burdens to support.

He suddenly shouted at Harry, and his red face turned darker red.

"That's a lie!" he said. "There's been no eagle here in my lifetime. What's happened? Go on—tell me."

Harry stood before him. He looked at his father, but said nothing.

"You've lost that lamb," said Thorburn. "Let it fall down a hole or something. Any child from the village could have watched those sheep for a day. Then you're frightened and come back here and lie to me."

Harry still said nothing.

"Come here," said Thorburn suddenly. He caught him by the arm and turned him round. "I'll teach you not to lie to me," he said. He raised his stick and hit Harry as hard as he could; then again and again.

"It's true," began Harry, and then cried out with pain at the blows.

At the third or fourth blow he wrenched himself away. Thorburn let him go. Harry walked away as fast as he could, through the gate and out of the yard without looking round.

"Next time it will be a real beating," his father shouted after him. "Bring the eagle back, and then I'll believe you."

---

13. **chasm** (kăz'əm).
14. **ewe** (yo͞o): a female sheep.

15. **heifers** (hĕf'ərz): young cows.

III

As soon as Harry was through the gate, he turned behind one of the barns where he was out of sight from the yard. He stood trembling and clenching his fists. He found there were tears on his face, and he forced himself not to cry. The blows hurt, yet they did not hurt very seriously. He would never have cried for that. But it had been done in front of another man. The other man had looked on, and he and his father had been laughing as he had almost run away. Harry clenched his fists; even now they were still talking about him.

He began to walk and then run up the hillside toward the hut. When he reached it, he was exhausted. He flung himself on the mattress and punched it again and again and clenched his teeth.

The day passed and nobody came from the farm. He began to feel better, and presently a new idea struck him, and with it a new hope. He prayed now that old Michael would not return today; that he would be able to spend another night alone in the hut; and that the eagle would come back next morning and attack the sheep again, and give him one more chance.

Harry went out and scanned the gray sky, and then knelt down on the grass and prayed for the eagle to come. Tassie, the gray and white sheep dog, looked at him questioningly. Soon it was getting dark, and he walked about the hill and rounded up the sheep. He counted the flock, and all was well. Then he looked round for a weapon. There was no gun in the hut, but he found a thick stave[16] tipped with metal, part of some broken tool that had been thrown aside. He poised the stave in his hand and swung it; it was just a good weight to hit

---

16. **stave:** a stick of wood.

with. He would have to go straight at the eagle without hesitation and break its skull. After thinking about this for some time, he made himself tea, and ate some bread and butter and cold meat.

Down at the farm Mr. Thorburn in the evening told his wife what had happened. He was quite sure there had been no eagle. Mrs. Thorburn did not say much, but she said it was an extraordinary thing for Harry to have said. She told her husband that he ought not to have beaten the boy, but should have found out what the trouble really was.

"But I dare say there is no great harm done," she ended, philosophically.

Harry spent a restless night. He slept and lay awake by turns, but, sleeping or waking, he was tortured by the same old images. He saw all the events of the day before. He saw how the eagle had first appeared above him; how it had attacked; how it had driven off Tassie and then him. He remembered his fear, and he planned again just how he could attack the eagle when it came back. Then he thought of himself going down towards the farm, and he saw again the scene with his father.

All night long he saw these pictures and other scenes from his life. In every one of them he had made some mistake; he had made himself look ridiculous, and grown men had laughed at him. He had failed in strength or in common sense; he was always disappointing himself and his father. He was too young for his age. He was still a baby.

So the night passed. Early in the morning he heard Tassie barking.

He jumped up, fully clothed, and ran outside the hut. The cold air made him shiver; but he saw at once that his prayer had been answered. There was the eagle, above him, and already dropping down towards the sheep. It floated, poised on huge wings. The flock stood nervously huddled. Suddenly, as before, the attacker plunged towards them. They scattered, running in every direction. The eagle followed and swooped on one weakly running lamb. At once it tried to rise again, but its heavy wingbeats took it along the earth. Near the ground it seemed cumbersome and awkward. Tassie was after it like a flash; Harry seized his weapon, the stave tipped with iron, and followed. When Tassie caught up with the eagle it turned and faced him, standing over the lamb.

Harry, as he ran, could see blood staining the white wool of the lamb's body; the eagle's wings were half spread out over it and moving slowly. The huge bird was grayish-brown with a white head and tail. The beak was yellow and the legs yellow and scaly.

It lowered its head, and with a fierce movement threatened Tassie; then, as the dog approached, it began to rock and stamp from foot to foot in a menacing dance; then it opened its beak and gave its fierce, yelping cry. Tassie hung back, his ears flattened against his head, snarling, creeping by inches towards the eagle; he was frightened, but he was brave. Then he ran in to attack.

The eagle left the lamb. With a lunging spring it aimed heavily at Tassie. It just cleared the ground and beat about Tassie with its wings, hovering over him. Tassie flattened out his body to the earth and turned his head upwards with snapping jaws. But the eagle was over him and on him, its talons plunged into his side, and a piercing scream rang out. The eagle struck deliberately at the dog's skull three times; the beak's point hammered on his head, striking downwards and sideways. Tassie lay limp on the ground, and, where his head had been, a red mixture of blood and brains flowed on the grass. When Harry took his eyes away from the blood, the eagle was standing on the lamb again.

Harry approached the eagle slowly, step by

step. He gripped his stick firmly as he came. The eagle put its head down. It rocked on its feet as if preparing to leap. Behind the terrific beak, sharp as metal, was a shallow head, flat and broad as a snake's, glaring with light yellow un-animal eyes. The head and neck made weaving movements towards him.

At a pace or two from the eagle Harry stood still. In a second he would make a rush. He could break the eagle's skull, he told himself, with one good blow; then he could avenge Tassie and stand up to his father.

But he waited too long. The eagle tried to rise, and with its heavy sweeping beats was beginning to gain speed along the ground. Harry ran, stumbling over the uneven ground, among boulders and outcroppings of rock, trying to strike at the eagle as he went. But as soon as the eagle was in the air it was no longer heavy and clumsy. There was a sudden rush of wings and buffeting about his head as the eagle turned to drive him off. For a second he saw the talons sharp as metal, backed by the metal strength of the legs, striking at his face. He put up his arm. At once it was seared with a red-hot pain, and he could see the blood rush out.

He stepped back, and back again. The eagle, after this one fierce swoop at him, went round in a wide, low circle and returned to the lamb. Harry saw that his coat sleeve was in ribbons, and that blood was running off the ends of his fingers and falling to the ground.

He stood panting; the wind blew across the empty high ground. The sheep had vanished from sight. Tassie lay dead nearby, and he was utterly alone on the hills. There was nobody to watch what he did. The eagle might hurt him, but it could not jeer at him. He attacked it again, but already the eagle with its heavy wingbeats had cleared the ground; this time it took the lamb with it. Harry saw that it meant to fly, as it had flown yesterday, to an edge; and then out into the free air over the chasm, and over the valley far below.

Harry gave chase, stumbling over the broken ground and between the boulders – striking at the eagle as he went, trying to beat it down before it could escape. The eagle was hampered by his attack; and suddenly it swooped onto a projection of rock and turned again to drive him off. Harry was now in a bad position. The eagle stood on a rock at the height of his own shoulders, with the lamb beside it. It struck at his chest with its talons, beating its wings as it did so. Harry felt clothes and flesh being torn; buffeting blows began about his head, but he kept close to the eagle and struck at it again. He did not want simply to frighten it away, but to kill it. The eagle fought at first simply to drive Harry off; then, as he continued to attack, it became ferocious.

Harry saw his only chance was to keep close to the eagle and beat it down; but already it was at the height of his face. It struck at him from above, driving its steel claws at him, beating its wings about him. He was dazed by the buffeting which went on and on all round him; then with an agonizing stab he felt the claws seize and pierce his shoulder and neck. He struck upwards desperately and blindly. As the eagle drove its beak at his head, his stick just turned the blow aside. The beak struck a glancing blow off the stick and tore away his eyebrow.

Harry found that something was blinding him, and he felt a new sickening fear that already one of his eyes was gone. The outspread beating wings and weight of the eagle dragged him about, and he nearly lost his footing. He had forgotten, now, that he was proving anything to his father; he was fighting for his eyes. Three times he fended off the hammer stroke of the beak, and at these close quarters the blows of his club found their mark. He

caught the eagle's head each time, and the bird was half stunned.

Harry, reeling and staggering, felt the grip of the claws gradually loosen, and almost unbelievably the body of his enemy sagged, half fluttering to the ground. With a sudden spurt of new strength, Harry attacked and rained blows on the bird's skull. The eagle struggled, and he followed, beating it down among the rocks. At last the eagle's movements stopped. He saw its skull was broken and that it lay dead.

He stood for many minutes panting and unmoving, filled with a tremendous excitement; then he sat on a boulder. The fight had taken him near a steep edge a long way from the body of Tassie.

His wounds began to ache and burn. The sky and the horizon spun round him, but he forced himself to be firm and collected. After a while he stooped down and hoisted the eagle onto his shoulder. The wings dropped loosely down in front and behind. He set off towards the farm.

IV

When he reached his home, the low gray walls, the plowed fields, and the green pasture fields were swimming before his eyes in a dizzy pattern. It was still the early part of the morning, but there was plenty of life in the farmyard, as usual. Some cows were being driven out. One of the carthorses was standing harnessed to a heavy wagon. Harry's father was talking to the carter and looking at the horse's leg.

When they saw Harry come towards them, they waited, unmoving. They could hardly see at first who or what it was. Harry came up and dropped the bird at his father's feet. His coat was gone. His shirt hung in bloodstained rags about him; one arm was caked in blood;

his right eyebrow hung in a loose flap, with the blood still oozing stickily down his cheek.

"Harry!" said Thorburn, catching him by the arm as he reeled.

He led the boy into the kitchen. There they gave him a glass of brandy and sponged him with warm water. There was a deep long wound in his left forearm. His chest was criss-crossed with cuts. The flesh was torn away from his neck where the talons had sunk in.

Presently the doctor came. Harry's wounds began to hurt like fire, but he talked excitedly. He was happier than he had ever been in his life. Everybody on the farm came in to see him and to see the eagle's body.

All day his father hung about him, looking into the kitchen every half-hour. He said very little but asked Harry several times how he felt. "Are you aw reet?" he kept saying. Once he took a cup of tea from his wife and carried it across the kitchen in order to give it to Harry with his own hands.

Later in the day old Michael came back, and Harry told him the whole story. Michael turned the bird over. He said it was an erne, a white-tailed sea eagle from the coast. He measured the wingspan, and it was seven and a half feet. Michael had seen two or three when he was a boy — always near the coast — but this one, he said, was easily the largest.

Three days later Mr. Thorburn took Harry, still stiff and bandaged, down to the village inn. There he set him before a blazing fire all the evening, and in the presence of men from every cottage and farm Thorburn praised his son. He bought him a glass of beer and made Harry tell the story of his fight to everyone.

As he told it, Thorburn sat by him, hearing the story himself each time, making certain that Harry missed nothing about his struggle. Afterwards every man drank Harry's health, and clapped Thorburn on the back and told him he ought to be proud of his son.

Later, in the silent darkness, they walked back to the farm again, and neither of them could find anything to say. Harry wondered if his father might not refer to the beating and apologize. Thorburn moved round the house, raking out fires and locking up. Then he picked up the lamp and, holding it above his head, led the way upstairs.

"Good night, Harry," said his father at last, as he took him to his bedroom door. "Are you aw reet?"

His father held the lamp up and looked into Harry's face. As the lamplight fell on it, he nodded. He said nothing more.

"Aye," said Harry, as he turned into his bedroom door, "I'm aw reet."

SEEKING MEANING

1. Some characters are the same at the end of a story as they are at the beginning. Other characters change as a result of the experiences they undergo. At the beginning of this story, Harry has no confidence in himself. How do you know at the end of the story that he has changed?

2. Taking care of the sheep is not Harry's re-sponsibility. How does he come to assume that job?

3. From Harry's point of view, "his father was always down on him, telling him he showed no sign of sense; telling him he ought to grow up a bit; telling him he was more like seven than thirteen" (page 244). Find three incidents in the story that confirm Harry's judgment.

4. After Mr. Thorburn beats Harry, you learn that "the blows hurt, yet they did not hurt

very seriously. He would never have cried for that." Why, then, are there tears on Harry's face?

5. Why does Harry pray for the eagle to return? What does Harry find out about himself during the restless night he spends on the mountain?

6. When Harry and his father return from the village inn, Harry wonders if his father will apologize for beating him. Has Mr. Thorburn already apologized in some way? Explain your answer.

7. Harry wins two victories in this story. What are they?

DEVELOPING SKILLS IN READING

Understanding Conflict and Plot

Conflict. In most stories, the characters are involved in some sort of problem or struggle called a *conflict.* Sometimes the characters are involved in more than one conflict.

A conflict with a person, with an animal, or with some force of nature is known as an *external conflict.* What is Harry's conflict with his father? What other external conflict is there in "The Erne from the Coast"?

In addition to these external conflicts, Harry has to overcome his feelings of shame and inadequacy. He also has to struggle against panic when he fights the eagle. Struggles within a character are known as *internal conflicts.*

Plot. The sequence of incidents or actions that make up a story is known as the *plot.* Once the conflict or conflicts of a story have been established, the reader wants to know how things will turn out. The author chooses events that develop the conflict to a peak, or *climax,* and that provide an ending, or *resolution,* to the conflict.

One way to recognize the climax of a story

is to look for the moment of most intense, exciting action. Which event is the climax in "The Erne from the Coast"? How does it solve Harry's internal and external conflicts?

DEVELOPING SKILLS IN LANGUAGE

Understanding Dialect

Writers use regional expressions to make the backgrounds and characters of their stories seem authentic. A number of the expressions in Beachcroft's story belong to the *dialect*— the regional variety of English—spoken in the sheep country of Great Britain. The words *thoom-bit* and *creachy* have been defined for you in footnotes. What do you think *hildy-wildy, glent of sunsheen, fule,* and *aw reet* mean?

ABOUT THE AUTHOR

T. O. Beachcroft (1902–   ) was born in Clifton, England, and educated at Oxford University. In the 1920's, while he was working for the British Broadcasting Corporation in London, several of his short stories were accepted for publication by literary magazines. This success later prompted him to collect the stories in a book called *A Young Man in a Hurry, and Other Stories* (1934). Since then he has written ten more books, including two studies on the art of the short story.

In *The Modest Art: A Survey of the Short Story in English* (1968), Beachcroft says that a short story often takes very little time to read. "Yet in those few minutes it may enter into the reader's mind, in a way which will never be forgotten. Plainly it must go deep to do this. It is not a trick. It is an encounter between two people—a passage of truth from one mind to another."

" 'About what time do you
think I'm going to die?'
he asked."

A Day's Wait   *Ernest Hemingway*

He came into the room to shut the windows while we were still in bed, and I saw he looked ill. He was shivering, his face was white, and he walked slowly as though it ached to move.

"What's the matter, Schatz?"[1]

"I've got a headache."

"You better go back to bed."

"No, I'm all right."

"You go to bed. I'll see you when I'm dressed."

But when I came downstairs he was dressed, sitting by the fire, looking a very sick and miserable boy of nine years. When I put my hand on his forehead I knew he had a fever.

"You go up to bed," I said, "you're sick."

"I'm all right," he said.

When the doctor came he took the boy's temperature.

"What is it?" I asked him.

"One hundred and two."

Downstairs, the doctor left three different medicines in different colored capsules with instructions for giving them. One was to bring down the fever, another a purgative, the third to overcome an acid condition. The germs of influenza can only exist in an acid condition, he explained. He seemed to know all about influenza and said there was nothing to worry about if the fever did not go above one hundred and four degrees. This was a light epidemic of flu and there was no danger if you avoided pneumonia.

Back in the room I wrote the boy's temperature down and made a note of the time to give the various capsules.

"Do you want me to read to you?"

"All right. If you want to," said the boy. His face was very white and there were dark areas under his eyes. He lay still in the bed and seemed very detached from what was going on.

I read aloud from Howard Pyle's *Book of Pirates;* but I could see he was not following what I was reading.

"How do you feel, Schatz?" I asked him.

"Just the same, so far," he said.

I sat at the foot of the bed and read to myself while I waited for it to be time to give another capsule. It would have been natural for him to go to sleep, but when I looked up he was looking at the foot of the bed, looking very strangely.

"Why don't you try to go to sleep? I'll wake you up for the medicine."

"I'd rather stay awake."

---

1. **Schatz:** a nickname taken from a German term of affection.

After a while he said to me, "You don't have to stay in here with me, Papa, if it bothers you."

"It doesn't bother me."

"No, I mean you don't have to stay if it's going to bother you."

I thought perhaps he was a little light-headed and after giving him the prescribed capsules at eleven o'clock I went out for a while.

It was a bright, cold day, the ground covered with a sleet that had frozen so that it seemed as if all the bare trees, the bushes, the cut brush and all the grass and the bare ground had been varnished with ice. I took the young Irish setter for a little walk up the road and along a frozen creek, but it was difficult to stand or walk on the glassy surface, and the red dog slipped and slithered and I fell twice, hard, once dropping my gun and having it slide away over the ice.

We flushed a covey of quail under a high clay bank with overhanging brush and I killed two as they went out of sight over the top of the bank. Some of the covey lit in trees, but most of them scattered into brush piles and it was necessary to jump on the ice-coated mounds of brush several times before they would flush. Coming out while you were poised unsteadily on the icy, springy brush they made difficult shooting, and I killed two, missed five, and started back pleased to have found a covey close to the house and happy there were so many left to find on another day.

At the house they said the boy had refused to let anyone come into the room.

"You can't come in," he said. "You mustn't get what I have."

I went up to him and found him in exactly the position I had left him, white-faced, but with the tops of his cheeks flushed by the fever, staring still, as he had stared, at the foot of the bed.

I took his temperature.

"What is it?"

"Something like a hundred," I said. It was one hundred and two and four tenths.

"It was a hundred and two," he said.

"Who said so?"

"The doctor."

"Your temperature is all right," I said. "It's nothing to worry about."

"I don't worry," he said, "but I can't keep from thinking."

"Don't think," I said. "Just take it easy."

"I'm taking it easy," he said and looked straight ahead. He was evidently holding tight on to himself about something.

"Take this with water."

"Do you think it will do any good?"

"Of course it will."

I sat down and opened the *Pirate* book and commenced to read, but I could see he was not following, so I stopped.

"About what time do you think I'm going to die?" he asked.

"What?"

"About how long will it be before I die?"

"You aren't going to die. What's the matter with you?"

"Oh, yes, I am. I heard him say a hundred and two."

"People don't die with a fever of one hundred and two. That's a silly way to talk."

"I know they do. At school in France the boys told me you can't live with forty-four degrees. I've got a hundred and two."

He had been waiting to die all day, ever since nine o'clock in the morning.

"You poor Schatz," I said. "Poor old Schatz. It's like miles and kilometers. You aren't going to die. That's a different thermometer. On that thermometer thirty-seven is normal. On this kind it's ninety-eight."

"Are you sure?"

"Absolutely," I said. "It's like miles and kilometers. You know, like how many kilometers we make when we do seventy miles in the car?"

"Oh," he said.

But his gaze at the foot of the bed relaxed slowly. The hold over himself relaxed too, finally, and the next day it was very slack and he cried very easily at little things that were of no importance.

SEEKING MEANING

1. The boy in the story assumes that he is going to die before the day is over. What mistake leads him to this conclusion?

2. The father in the story doesn't realize what is going on in his son's mind. What does he assume is troubling the boy?

3. How does the boy show courage in facing what he believes to be his own death? How does he show concern for his father?

4. People often hold back their emotions when they face a crisis. How does the boy finally show the strain he has been under?

DEVELOPING SKILLS IN READING

Understanding the Narrator's Point of View
The person telling this story—the *narrator*—is a character in the story. You see the other characters and events from his point of view. Everything you learn in the story is what the narrator tells you—what he sees, what he hears, what he thinks. What you learn about the boy in the story is what the narrator reveals through direct observation. You have only his impressions of what is happening.

In real life you perceive events the way the narrator in this story does. You cannot read the minds of other people any more than the father in this story can read his son's thoughts.

What the author is able to show through this point of view is how the characters in the story fail to communicate. They talk without making themselves clear to each other. Here, for example, the father and son do not realize that they are talking about different things:

> After a while he said to me, "You don't have to stay here with me, Papa, if it bothers you."
>
> "It doesn't bother me."
>
> "No, I mean you don't have to stay if it's going to bother you."
>
> I thought perhaps he was a little light-headed and after giving him the prescribed capsules at eleven o'clock I went out for a while.

What does the boy think is going to bother his father? How does the father interpret the boy's words?

Find another passage in the story that shows a similar misunderstanding between father and son.

DEVELOPING VOCABULARY

Learning Prefixes Used in Measurement

The boy in the story confuses two systems of measurement. He assumes that the doctor is using the Celsius scale of temperature. On this scale, a normal temperature is 37 degrees. The boy doesn't realize that the doctor is using a Fahrenheit thermometer, on which the normal reading is 98.6 degrees.

In order to clear up the boy's confusion, the father uses the example of miles and kilometers, which are two different units of distance. As you probably know, a kilometer is a unit of

measurement in the metric system. The *meter* is the basic unit of measurement for length or distance. A kilometer is one thousand meters, which is equal to 0.6214 miles. The prefix *kilo-* comes from a Greek word meaning "a thousand." What is the word for a thousand grams? A thousand liters?

The prefix *milli-* comes from a Latin word meaning "thousand." When it is used in units of measurement, it means "one thousandth." What is the word for a thousandth of a meter? Of a gram? Of a liter?

Here are other prefixes used in the metric system and their meanings:

deca- (*or* deka-)	ten
deci-	one tenth
hecto-	one hundred
centi-	one hundredth

What is the meaning of *decameter?* Of *decagram?* Of *decigram?* Of *deciliter?* What is the difference between a *hectometer* and a *centimeter?*

ABOUT THE AUTHOR

Ernest Hemingway (1899–1961), who once defined courage as "grace under pressure," admired people who could face their own suffering bravely. The events in "A Day's Wait" are based on an actual incident in Hemingway's life when one of his sons was ill.

Hemingway perfected a simple, spare style that has influenced many other writers. He won the Pulitzer Prize in 1953 for his novel *The Old Man and the Sea,* which has become a favorite with young readers. In 1954 he was awarded the Nobel Prize for literature.

"Rikki-tikki listened. The house was still as still, but he thought he could just catch the faintest scratch-scratch *in the world—a noise as faint as that of a wasp walking on a windowpane—the dry scratch of a snake's scales on brickwork."*

Rikki-tikki-tavi

Rudyard Kipling

This is the story of the great war that Rikki-tikki-tavi fought single-handed, through the bathrooms of the big bungalow in Segowlee cantonment.[1] Darzee, the tailorbird, helped him, and Chuchundra,[2] the muskrat, who never comes out into the middle of the floor, but always creeps round by the wall, gave him advice; but Rikki-tikki did the real fighting.

He was a mongoose, rather like a little cat in his fur and his tail, but quite like a weasel in his head and his habits. His eyes and the end of his restless nose were pink; he could scratch himself anywhere he pleased, with any leg, front or back, that he chose to use; he could fluff up his tail till it looked like a bottle brush, and his war cry, as he scuttled through the long grass, was *"Rikk-tikk-tikki-tikki-tchk!"*

One day, a high summer flood washed him out of the burrow where he lived with his father and mother, and carried him, kicking and clucking, down a roadside ditch. He found a little wisp of grass floating there, and clung to it till he lost his senses. When he revived, he was lying in the hot sun on the middle of a garden path, very draggled indeed, and a small boy was saying: "Here's a dead mongoose. Let's have a funeral."

---

1. **Segowlee** (sē-gou′lē) **cantonment:** a British army post in Segowlee, India.
2. **Chuchundra** (chōō-chŭn′drə).

"No," said his mother; "let's take him in and dry him. Perhaps he isn't really dead."

They took him into the house, and a big man picked him up between his finger and thumb and said he was not dead but half choked; so they wrapped him in cotton wool and warmed him, and he opened his eyes and sneezed.

"Now," said the big man (he was an Englishman who had just moved into the bungalow), "don't frighten him, and we'll see what he'll do."

It is the hardest thing in the world to frighten a mongoose, because he is eaten up from nose to tail with curiosity. The motto of all the mongoose family is "Run and find out"; and Rikki-tikki was a true mongoose. He looked at the cotton wool, decided that it was not good to eat, ran all round the table, sat up and put his fur in order, scratched himself, and jumped on the small boy's shoulder.

"Don't be frightened, Teddy," said his father. "That's his way of making friends."

"Ouch! He's tickling under my chin," said Teddy.

Rikki-tikki looked down between the boy's collar and neck, snuffed at his ear, and climbed down to the floor, where he sat rubbing his nose.

"Good gracious," said Teddy's mother, "and that's a wild creature! I suppose he's so tame because we've been kind to him."

"All mongooses are like that," said her husband. "If Teddy doesn't pick him up by the tail, or try to put him in a cage, he'll run in and out of the house all day long. Let's give him something to eat."

They gave him a little piece of raw meat. Rikki-tikki liked it immensely, and when it was finished he went out into the veranda and sat in the sunshine and fluffed up his fur to make it dry to the roots. Then he felt better.

"There are more things to find out about in this house," he said to himself, "than all my family could find out in all their lives. I shall certainly stay and find out."

He spent all that day roaming over the house. He nearly drowned himself in the bathtubs, put his nose into the ink on a writing table, and burned it on the end of the big man's cigar, for he climbed up in the big man's lap to see how writing was done. At nightfall he ran into Teddy's nursery to watch how kerosene lamps were lighted, and when Teddy went to bed Rikki-tikki climbed up too; but he was a restless companion, because he had to get up and attend to every noise all through the night and find out what made it. Teddy's mother and father came in, the last thing, to look at their boy, and Rikki-tikki was awake on the pillow. "I don't like that," said Teddy's mother; "he may bite the child."

"He'll do no such thing," said the father. "Teddy's safer with that little beast than if he had a bloodhound to watch him. If a snake came into the nursery now——"

But Teddy's mother wouldn't think of anything so awful.

Early in the morning Rikki-tikki came to early breakfast in the veranda, riding on Teddy's shoulder, and they gave him banana and some boiled egg; and he sat on all their laps one after the other, because every well-brought-up mongoose always hopes to be a house mongoose someday and have rooms to run about in, and Rikki-tikki's mother (she used to live in the general's house at Segowlee) had carefully told Rikki what to do if ever he came across Englishmen.

Then Rikki-tikki went out into the garden to see what was to be seen. It was a large garden, only half cultivated, with bushes as big as summer houses of roses, lime and orange trees, clumps of bamboos, and thickets of high grass. Rikki-tikki licked his lips. "This is a splendid hunting ground," he said, and his tail grew bottle-brushy at the thought of it, and he scuttled up and down the garden, snuffling here and there till he heard very sorrowful voices in a thornbush.

It was Darzee, the tailorbird, and his wife. They had made a beautiful nest by pulling two big leaves together and stitching them up the edges with fibers, and had filled the hollow with cotton and downy fluff. The nest swayed to and fro, as they sat on the brim and cried.

"What is the matter?" asked Rikki-tikki.

"We are very miserable," said Darzee. "One of our babies fell out of the nest yesterday, and Nag[3] ate him."

"H'm!" said Rikki-tikki; "that is very sad—but I am a stranger here. Who is Nag?"

Darzee and his wife only cowered down in the nest without answering, for from the thick grass at the foot of the bush came a low hiss—a horrid cold sound that made Rikki-tikki jump back two clear feet. Then inch by inch out of the grass rose up the head and spread hood of Nag, the big black cobra, and he was five feet long from tongue to tail. When he had lifted one third of himself clear of the ground, he stayed balancing to and fro exactly as a dandelion tuft balances in the wind, and he looked at Rikki-tikki with the wicked snake's eyes that never change their expression, whatever the snake may be thinking of.

"Who is Nag?" he said. "*I* am Nag. The great god Brahm[4] put his mark upon all our people when the first cobra spread his hood to keep the sun off Brahm as he slept. Look, and be afraid!"

He spread out his hood more than ever, and Rikki-tikki saw the spectacle mark on the back of it that looks exactly like the eye part of a hook-and-eye fastening. He was afraid for the minute; but it is impossible for a mongoose to stay frightened for any length of time, and though Rikki-tikki had never met a live cobra before, his mother had fed him on dead ones, and he knew that all a grown mongoose's business in life was to fight and eat snakes. Nag knew that too, and at the bottom of his cold heart he was afraid.

"Well," said Rikki-tikki, and his tail began to fluff up again, "marks or no marks, do you think it is right for you to eat fledglings out of a nest?"

Nag was thinking to himself, and watching the least little movement in the grass behind Rikki-tikki. He knew that mongooses in the garden meant death sooner or later for him and his family, but he wanted to get Rikki-tikki off his guard. So he dropped his head a little and put it on one side.

"Let us talk," he said. "You eat eggs. Why should not I eat birds?"

"Behind you! Look behind you!" sang Darzee.

3. **Nag** (näg).

4. **Brahm** (bräm): in the Hindu religion, the creator of the universe; usually known as *Brahma*.

Rikki-tikki knew better than to waste time in staring. He jumped up in the air as high as he could go, and just under him whizzed by the head of Nagaina,[5] Nag's wicked wife. She had crept up behind him as he was talking, to make an end of him; and he heard her savage hiss as the stroke missed. He came down almost across her back, and if he had been an old mongoose, he would have known that then was the time to break her back with one bite; but he was afraid of the terrible lashing return stroke of the cobra. He bit, indeed, but did not bite long enough, and he jumped clear of the whisking tail, leaving Nagaina torn and angry.

"Wicked, wicked Darzee!" said Nag, lashing up as high as he could reach toward the nest in the thornbush; but Darzee had built it out of the reach of snakes, and it only swayed to and fro.

Rikki-tikki felt his eyes growing red and hot (when a mongoose's eyes grow red, he is angry), and he sat back on his tail and hind legs like a little kangaroo, and looked all around him, and chattered with rage. But Nag and Nagaina had disappeared into the grass. When a snake misses its stroke, it never says anything or gives any sign of what it means to do next. Rikki-tikki did not care to follow them, for he did not feel sure that he could manage two snakes at once. So he trotted off to the gravel path near the house, and sat down to think. It was a serious matter for him.

If you read the old books of natural history, you will find they say that when the mongoose fights the snake and happens to get bitten, he runs off and eats some herb that cures him. That is not true. The victory is only a matter of quickness of eye and quickness of foot—snake's blow against mongoose's jump—and as no eye can follow the motion of a snake's head when it strikes, that makes things much more wonderful than any magic herb. Rikki-tikki knew he was a young mongoose, and it made him all the more pleased to think that he had managed to escape a blow from behind. It gave him confidence in himself, and when Teddy came running down the path, Rikki-tikki was ready to be petted.

But just as Teddy was stooping, something flinched a little in the dust, and a tiny voice said: "Be careful. I am death!" It was Karait,[6] the dusty brown snakeling that lies for choice on the dusty earth; and his bite is as dangerous as the cobra's . But he is so small that nobody thinks of him, and so he does the more harm to people.

Rikki-tikki's eyes grew red again, and he danced up to Karait with the peculiar rocking, swaying motion that he had inherited from his family. It looks very funny, but it is so perfectly balanced a gait that you can fly off from it at any angle you please; and in dealing with snakes this is an advantage. If Rikki-tikki had only known, he was doing a much more dangerous thing than fighting Nag, for Karait is so small, and can turn so quickly, that unless Rikki bit him close to the back of the head, he would get the return stroke in his eye or lip. But Rikki did not know: his eyes were all red, and he rocked back and forth, looking for a good place to hold. Karait struck out. Rikki jumped sideways and tried to run in, but the wicked little dusty gray head lashed within a fraction of his shoulder, and he had to jump over the body, and the head followed his heels close.

Teddy shouted to the house: "Oh, look

---

5. **Nagaina** (nə-gī'nə).

6. **Karait** (kə-rīt').

here! Our mongoose is killing a snake''; and Rikki-tikki heard a scream from Teddy's mother. His father ran out with a stick, but by the time he came up, Karait had lunged out once too far, and Rikki-tikki had sprung, jumped on the snake's back, dropped his head far between his forelegs, bitten as high up the back as he could get hold, and rolled away. That bite paralyzed Karait, and Rikki-tikki was just going to eat him up from the tail, after the custom of his family at dinner, when he remembered that a full meal makes a slow mongoose, and if he wanted all his strength and quickness ready, he must keep himself thin.

He went away for a dust bath under the castor-oil bushes, while Teddy's father beat the dead Karait. "What is the use of that?" thought Rikki-tikki. "I have settled it all"; and then Teddy's mother picked him up from the dust and hugged him, crying that he had saved Teddy from death, and Teddy's father said that he was a providence, and Teddy looked on with big scared eyes. Rikki-tikki was rather amused at all the fuss, which, of course, he did not understand. Teddy's mother might just as well have petted Teddy for playing in the dust. Rikki was thoroughly enjoying himself.

That night, at dinner, walking to and fro among the wineglasses on the table, he could have stuffed himself three times over with nice things; but he remembered Nag and Nagaina, and though it was very pleasant to be patted and petted by Teddy's mother, and to sit on Teddy's shoulder, his eyes would get red from time to time, and he would go off into his long war cry of "Rikk-tikk-tikki-tikki-tchk!"

Teddy carried him off to bed and insisted on Rikki-tikki sleeping under his chin. Rikki-tikki was too well bred to bite or scratch, but as soon as Teddy was asleep he went off for his nightly walk round the house, and in the dark he ran up against Chuchundra, the muskrat, creeping round by the wall. Chuchundra is a brokenhearted little beast. He whimpers and cheeps all the night, trying to make up his mind to run into the middle of the room, but he never gets there.

"Don't kill me," said Chuchundra, almost weeping. "Rikki-tikki, don't kill me."

"Do you think a snake-killer kills muskrats?" said Rikki-tikki scornfully.

"Those who kill snakes get killed by snakes," said Chuchundra, more sorrowfully than ever. "And how am I to be sure that Nag won't mistake me for you some dark night?"

"There's not the least danger," said Rikki-tikki; "but Nag is in the garden, and I know you don't go there."

"My cousin Chua, the rat, told me——" said Chuchundra, and then he stopped.

"Told you what?"

"H'sh! Nag is everywhere, Rikki-tikki. You should have talked to Chua in the garden."

"I didn't—so you must tell me. Quick, Chuchundra, or I'll bite you!"

Chuchundra sat down and cried till the tears rolled off his whiskers. "I am a very poor man," he sobbed. "I never had spirit enough to run out into the middle of the room. H'sh! I mustn't tell you anything. Can't you *hear*, Rikki-tikki?"

Rikki-tikki listened. The house was as still as still, but he thought he could just catch the faintest *scratch-scratch* in the world—a noise as faint as that of a wasp walking on a windowpane—the dry scratch of a snake's scales on brickwork.

"That's Nag or Nagaina," he said to himself; "and he is crawling into the bathroom sluice. You're right, Chuchundra; I should have talked to Chua."

He stole off to Teddy's bathroom, but there was nothing there, and then to Teddy's mother's bathroom. At the bottom of the smooth plaster wall there was a brick pulled out to make a sluice for the bath water, and as Rikki-tikki stole in by the masonry curb where the bath is put, he heard Nag and Nagaina whispering together outside in the moonlight.

"When the house is emptied of people," said Nagaina to her husband, "*he* will have to go away, and then the garden will be our own again. Go in quietly, and remember that the big man who killed Karait is the first one to bite. Then come out and tell me, and we will hunt for Rikki-tikki together."

"But are you sure that there is anything to be gained by killing the people?" said Nag.

"Everything. When there were no people in the bungalow, did we have any mongoose in the garden? So long as the bungalow is empty, we are king and queen of the garden; and remember that as soon as our eggs in the melon bed hatch (as they may tomorrow), our children will need room and quiet."

"I had not thought of that," said Nag. "I will go, but there is no need that we should hunt for Rikki-tikki afterward. I will kill the big man and his wife, and the child if I can, and come away quietly. Then the bungalow will be empty, and Rikki-tikki will go."

Rikki-tikki tingled all over with rage and hatred at this, and then Nag's head came through the sluice, and his five feet of cold body followed it. Angry as he was, Rikki-tikki was very frightened as he saw the size of the big cobra. Nag coiled himself up, raised his head, and looked into the bathroom in the dark, and Rikki could see his eyes glitter.

"Now, if I kill him there, Nagaina will know; and if I fight him on the open floor, the odds are in his favor. What am I to do?" said Rikki-tikki-tavi.

Nag waved to and fro, and then Rikki-tikki heard him drinking from the biggest water jar

that was used to fill the bath. "That is good," said the snake. "Now, when Karait was killed, the big man had a stick. He may have that stick still, but when he comes in to bathe in the morning he will not have a stick. I shall wait here till he comes. Nagaina—do you hear me? I shall wait here in the cool till daytime."

There was no answer from outside, so Rikki-tikki knew Nagaina had gone away. Nag coiled himself down, coil by coil, round the bulge at the bottom of the water jar, and Rikki-tikki stayed still as death. After an hour he began to move, muscle by muscle, toward the jar. Nag was asleep, and Rikki-tikki looked at his big back, wondering which would be the best place for a good hold. "If I don't break his back at the first jump," said Rikki, "he can still fight; and if he fights—O Rikki!" He looked at the thickness of the neck below the hood, but that was too much for him; and a bite near the tail would only make Nag savage.

"It must be the head," he said at last; "the

head above the hood; and when I am once there, I must not let go."

Then he jumped. The head was lying a little clear of the water jar, under the curve of it; and, as his teeth met, Rikki braced his back against the bulge of the red earthenware to hold down the head. This gave him just one second's purchase,[7] and he made the most of it. Then he was battered to and fro as a rat is shaken by a dog—to and fro on the floor, up and down, and round in great circles; but his eyes were red, and he held on as the body cartwhipped over the floor, upsetting the tin dipper and the soap dish and the fleshbrush, and banged against the tin side of the bath. As he held, he closed his jaws tighter and tighter, for he made sure[8] he would be banged to death, and, for the honor of his family, he preferred to be found with his teeth locked.

7. **purchase:** here, advantage.
8. **made sure:** here, felt sure.

He was dizzy, aching, and felt shaken to pieces when something went off like a thunderclap just behind him; a hot wind knocked him senseless, and red fire singed his fur. The big man had been wakened by the noise, and had fired both barrels of a shotgun into Nag just behind the hood.

Rikki-tikki held on with his eyes shut, for now he was quite sure he was dead; but the head did not move, and the big man picked him up and said: "It's the mongoose again, Alice; the little chap has saved *our* lives now." Then Teddy's mother came in with a very white face, and saw what was left of Nag, and Rikki-tikki dragged himself to Teddy's bedroom and spent half the rest of the night shaking himself tenderly to find out whether he really was broken into forty pieces, as he fancied.

When morning came he was very stiff, but well pleased with his doings. "Now I have Nagaina to settle with, and she will be worse than five Nags, and there's no knowing when the eggs she spoke of will hatch. Goodness! I must go and see Darzee," he said.

Without waiting for breakfast, Rikki-tikki ran to the thornbush where Darzee was singing a song of triumph at the top of his voice. The news of Nag's death was all over the garden, for the sweeper had thrown the body on the rubbish heap.

"Oh, you stupid tuft of feathers!" said Rikki-tikki angrily. "Is this the time to sing?"

"Nag is dead—is dead—is dead!" sang Darzee. "The valiant Rikki-tikki caught him by the head and held fast. The big man brought the bang-stick, and Nag fell in two pieces! He will never eat my babies again."

"All that's true enough; but where's Nagaina?" said Rikki-tikki, looking carefully round him.

"Nagaina came to the bathroom sluice and called for Nag," Darzee went on; "and Nag came out on the end of a stick—the sweeper picked him up on the end of a stick and threw him upon the rubbish heap. Let us sing about the great, the red-eyed Rikki-tikki!" And Darzee filled his throat and sang.

"If I could get up to your nest, I'd roll all your babies out!" said Rikki-tikki. "You don't know when to do the right thing at the right time. You're safe enough in your nest there, but it's war for me down here. Stop singing a minute, Darzee."

"For the great, the beautiful Rikki-tikki's sake I will stop," said Darzee. "What is it, O Killer of the terrible Nag?"

"Where is Nagaina, for the third time?"

"On the rubbish heap by the stables, mourning for Nag. Great is Rikki-tikki with the white teeth."

"Bother[9] my white teeth! Have you ever heard where she keeps her eggs?"

---

9. **Bother:** here, never mind.

"In the melon bed, on the end nearest the wall, where the sun strikes nearly all day. She hid them there weeks ago."

"And you never thought it worthwhile to tell me? The end nearest the wall, you said?"

"Rikki-tikki, you are not going to eat her eggs?"

"Not eat exactly; no. Darzee, if you have a grain of sense you will fly off to the stables and pretend that your wing is broken, and let Nagaina chase you away to this bush! I must get to the melon bed, and if I went there now she'd see me."

Darzee was a featherbrained little fellow who could never hold more than one idea at a time in his head; and just because he knew that Nagaina's children were born in eggs like his own, he didn't think at first that it was fair to kill them. But his wife was a sensible bird, and she knew that cobras' eggs meant young cobras later on; so she flew off from the nest, and left Darzee to keep the babies warm, and continue his song about the death of Nag. Darzee was very like a man in some ways.

She fluttered in front of Nagaina by the rubbish heap and cried out, "Oh, my wing is broken! The boy in the house threw a stone at me and broke it." Then she fluttered more desperately than ever.

Nagaina lifted up her head and hissed, "You warned Rikki-tikki when I would have killed him. Indeed and truly, you've chosen a bad place to be lame in." And she moved toward Darzee's wife, slipping along over the dust.

"The boy broke it with a stone!" shrieked Darzee's wife.

"Well! It may be some consolation to you when you're dead to know that I shall settle accounts with the boy. My husband lies on the rubbish heap this morning, but before night the boy in the house will lie very still. What is the use of running away? I am sure to catch you. Little fool, look at me!"

Darzee's wife knew better than to do *that*, for a bird who looks at a snake's eyes gets so frightened that she cannot move. Darzee's wife fluttered on, piping sorrowfully, and never leaving the ground, and Nagaina quickened her pace.

Rikki-tikki heard them going up the path from the stables, and he raced for the end of the melon patch near the wall. There, in the warm litter about the melons, very cunningly hidden, he found twenty-five eggs, about the size of a bantam's eggs,[10] but with whitish skin instead of shell.

"I was not a day too soon," he said; for he could see the baby cobras curled up inside the skin, and he knew that the minute they were hatched they could each kill a man or a mongoose. He bit off the tops of the eggs as fast as he could, taking care to crush the

young cobras, and turned over the litter from time to time to see whether he had missed any. At last there were only three eggs left, and Rikki-tikki began to chuckle to himself, when he heard Darzee's wife screaming:

"Rikki-tikki, I led Nagaina toward the house, and she has gone into the veranda, and—oh, come quickly—she means killing!"

Rikki-tikki smashed two eggs, and tumbled backward down the melon bed with the third egg in his mouth, and scuttled to the veranda as hard as he could put foot to the ground. Teddy and his mother and father were there at early breakfast; but Rikki-tikki saw that they were not eating anything. They sat stone-still, and their faces were white. Nagaina was coiled up on the matting by Teddy's chair, within easy striking distance of Teddy's bare leg, and she was swaying to and fro singing a song of triumph.

"Son of the big man that killed Nag," she hissed, "stay still. I am not ready yet. Wait a little. Keep very still, all you three. If you

---

10. **bantam's eggs:** small eggs. A bantam is a small chicken.

move I strike, and if you do not move I strike. Oh, foolish people, who killed my Nag!"

Teddy's eyes were fixed on his father, and all his father could do was to whisper, "Sit still, Teddy. You mustn't move. Teddy, keep still."

Then Rikki-tikki came up and cried: "Turn round, Nagaina; turn and fight!"

"All in good time," said she, without moving her eyes. "I will settle my account with *you* presently. Look at your friends, Rikki-tikki. They are still and white; they are afraid. They dare not move, and if you come a step nearer I strike."

"Look at your eggs," said Rikki-tikki, "in the melon bed near the wall. Go and look, Nagaina."

The big snake turned half round and saw the egg on the veranda. "Ah-h! Give it to me," she said.

Rikki-tikki put his paws one on each side of the egg, and his eyes were blood-red. "What price for a snake's egg? For a young cobra? For a young king cobra? For the last—the very last of the brood? The ants are eating all the others down by the melon bed."

Nagaina spun clear round, forgetting everything for the sake of the one egg; and Rikki-tikki saw Teddy's father shoot out a big hand, catch Teddy by the shoulder, and drag him across the little table with the teacups, safe and out of reach of Nagaina.

"Tricked! Tricked! Tricked! *Rikk-tck-tck!*" chuckled Rikki-tikki. "The boy is safe, and it was I—I—I that caught Nag by the hood last night in the bathroom." Then he began to jump up and down, all four feet together, his head close to the floor. "He threw me to and fro, but he could not shake me off. He was dead before the big man blew him in two. I did it. *Rikki-tikki-tck-tck!* Come then, Nagaina. Come and fight with me. You shall not be a widow long."

Nagaina saw that she had lost her chance of killing Teddy, and the egg lay between Rikki-tikki's paws. "Give me the egg, Rikki-tikki. Give me the last of my eggs, and I will go away and never come back," she said, lowering her hood.

"Yes, you will go away, and you will never come back; for you will go to the rubbish heap with Nag. Fight, widow! The big man has gone for his gun! Fight!"

Rikki-tikki was bounding all round Nagaina, keeping just out of reach of her stroke, his little eyes like hot coals. Nagaina gathered herself together and flung out at him. Rikki-tikki jumped up and backward. Again and again and again she struck, and each time her head came with a whack on the matting of the veranda, and she gathered herself together like a watchspring. Then Rikki-tikki danced in a circle to get behind her, and Nagaina spun round to keep her head to his head, so that the rustle of her tail on the matting sounded like dry leaves blown along by the wind.

He had forgotten the egg. It still lay on the veranda, and Nagaina came nearer and nearer to it, till at last, while Rikki-tikki was drawing breath, she caught it in her mouth, turned to the veranda steps, and flew like an arrow down the path, with Rikki-tikki behind her. When the cobra runs for her life, she goes like a whiplash flicked across a horse's neck.

Rikki-tikki knew that he must catch her, or all the touble would begin again. She headed straight for the long grass by the thornbush, and as he was running Rikki-tikki heard Darzee singing his foolish little song of triumph. But Darzee's wife was wiser. She flew off her nest as Nagaina came along, and flapped her wings about Nagaina's head. If Darzee had helped they might have turned her; but Nagaina only lowered her hood and went on. Still, the instant's delay brought Rikki-tikki up to her, and as she plunged into the rathole

where she and Nag used to live, his little
white teeth were clenched on her tail, and he
went down with her—and very few mongooses, however wise and old they may be,
care to follow a cobra into its hole. It was dark
in the hole; and Rikki-tikki never knew when
it might open out and give Nagaina room to
turn and strike at him. He held on savagely
and struck out his feet to act as brakes on the
dark slope of the hot, moist earth.

Then the grass by the mouth of the hole
stopped waving, and Darzee said: "It is all
over with Rikki-tikki! We must sing his death
song. Valiant Rikki-tikki is dead. For Nagaina
will surely kill him underground."

So he sang a very mournful song that he
made up all on the spur of the minute, and
just as he got to the most touching part the
grass quivered again, and Rikki-tikki, covered
with dirt, dragged himself out of the hole leg

by leg, licking his whiskers. Darzee stopped
with a little shout. Rikki-tikki shook some of
the dust out of his fur and sneezed. "It is all
over," he said. "The widow will never come
out again." And the red ants that live between
the grass stems heard him, and began to troop
down one after another to see if he had spoken
the truth.

Rikki-tikki curled himself up in the grass
and slept where he was—slept and slept till it
was late in the afternoon, for he had done a
hard day's work.

"Now," he said, when he awoke, "I will go
back to the house. Tell the coppersmith, Darzee, and he will tell the garden that Nagaina is
dead."

The coppersmith is a bird who makes a
noise exactly like the beating of a little hammer on a copper pot; and the reason he is
always making it is because he is the town

crier to every Indian garden, and tells all the news to everybody who cares to listen. As Rikki-tikki went up the path, he heard his "attention" notes like a tiny dinner gong; and then the steady *"Ding-dong-tock!* Nag is dead —*dong!* Nagaina is dead! *Ding-dong-tock!"* That set all the birds in the garden singing, and the frogs croaking, for Nag and Nagaina used to eat frogs as well as little birds.

When Rikki got to the house, Teddy and Teddy's mother (she still looked very white, for she had been fainting) and Teddy's father came out and almost cried over him; and that night he ate all that was given him till he could eat no more, and went to bed on Teddy's shoulder, where Teddy's mother saw him when she came to look late at night.

"He saved our lives and Teddy's life," she said to her husband. "Just think, he saved all our lives!"

Rikki-tikki woke up with a jump, for all mongooses are light sleepers.

"Oh, it's you," said he. "What are you bothering for? All the cobras are dead; and if they weren't, I'm here."

Rikki-tikki had a right to be proud of himself; but he did not grow too proud, and he kept that garden as a mongoose should keep it, with tooth and jump and spring and bite, till never a cobra dared show its head inside the walls.

SEEKING MEANING

1. The major characters in the story are animals that have been given human motives. Identify the major characters in the story that represent the forces of good and those that represent the forces of evil.

2. What conflict, or struggle, does Rikki-tikki face?

3. Kipling says that his story is about "the great war that Rikki-tikki-tavi fought single-handed . . . ." Identify at least five "battles" in this war. At what points in the war does Darzee's wife assist Rikki-tikki?

4. Match each character in the left-hand column with one or more of the adjectives in the right-hand column. You may use each adjective as often as you like, but be sure to use each adjective at least once. Support your answers with passages from the story.

Darzee	cold
	cunning
	curious
	featherbrained
Darzee's wife	intelligent
	proud
	quick-witted
	resourceful
Rikki-tikki	sensible
	stupid
	valiant
	wicked
Nagaina	wise

5. Writers frequently treat animals in stories as if they could think, talk, and feel as people do. Why do you suppose they write about animals in this way? What other selections have you read in which animals have been given human characteristics?

DEVELOPING SKILLS IN READING

Understanding Methods of Characterization

The way in which writers let you know what the individuals in a story are like is called *characterization*. When writers *tell* you what characters are like through description, they are using *direct characterization*. For instance, Kipling tells us: "Chuchundra is a brokenhearted little beast. He whimpers and cheeps all the night, trying to make up his mind to run into the middle of the room, but he never gets there."

Writers may also *show* you what characters are like through their thoughts, their speech, their actions, and the reactions of other characters to them. This kind of characterization is called *indirect characterization*. What does Chuchundra say and do (page 261) that confirms Kipling's description of him? What is Rikki-tikki's opinion of Chuchundra? Does his opinion add anything to Kipling's statement?

Show how Kipling develops Rikki-tikki's character through direct and indirect characterization. Be sure to answer the following questions:

Direct Characterization
   What does the author tell you about the character?
Indirect Characterization
   What does the character think, say, and do?
   What do others think and say about the character? How do they treat the character?

DEVELOPING SKILLS OF EXPRESSION

Writing About Characters in Action

Rikki-tikki's last fight with Nagaina occurs "offstage," so to speak. Kipling does not describe the battle. He leaves it to the reader's imagination.

Using your knowledge of the characters of Rikki-tikki and Nagaina, write your version of the missing battle. Remember that Nagaina is almost a match for Rikki-tikki and that she is fighting to save her very last egg.

You might open with these sentences taken from the story:

It was dark in the hole, and Rikki-tikki never knew when it might open out and give Nagaina room to turn and strike at him. He held on savagely and struck out his feet to act as brakes on the dark slope of the hot, moist earth.

ABOUT THE AUTHOR

When Rudyard Kipling (1865–1936) wrote "Rikki-tikki-tavi," he drew on his memories of India, where he was born. Kipling was six when his parents sent him to school in England. He returned to India in 1882 and became a journalist. He soon began to write sketches, short stories, and light verse.

In 1886 his first book, a collection of poems called *Departmental Ditties*, appeared. Between 1887 and 1889 he produced six volumes of short stories. When he returned to England in 1889, he was already considered one of the great writers of his day.

Kipling's short stories, novels, and poems have delighted readers of all ages. Some of his best-known works of fiction are *The Light That Failed, The Jungle Books, Captains Courageous*, and *Kim*. Among his most popular poems are "If," "The Ballad of East and West," and "Danny Deever." Several of Kipling's works have been made into movies. In 1907 he became the first Englishman to win the Nobel Prize for literature.

" '. . . I was myself last night, but I fell asleep on the mountain, and they've changed my gun, and everything's changed, and I'm changed, and I can't tell what's my name, or who I am!' "

Rip Van Winkle   *Washington Irving*

Whoever has made a voyage up the Hudson must remember the Catskill Mountains. They are a branch of the great Appalachian family,[1] and are seen away to the west of the river, swelling up to a noble height, and lording it over the surrounding country. Every change of season, every change of weather, indeed, every hour of the day, produces some change in the magical hues and shapes of these mountains, and they are regarded by all the good wives, far and near, as perfect barometers. When the weather is fair and settled, they are clothed in blue and purple, and print their bold outlines on the clear evening sky; but, sometimes, when the rest of the landscape is cloudless, they will gather a hood of gray vapors about their summits, which, in the last rays of the setting sun, will glow and light up like a crown of glory.

At the foot of these fairy mountains, the voyager may have seen the light smoke curling up from a village, whose shingle roofs gleam among the trees, just where the blue tints of the upland melt away into the fresh green of the nearer landscape. It is a little village, of great antiquity, having been founded by some of the Dutch colonists, in the early times of the province. There were some of the houses of the original settlers standing within a few years,[2] built of small yellow bricks brought from Holland, having latticed windows and gable fronts, surmounted with weathercocks.

In that same village, and in one of these very houses, which was sadly timeworn and weather-beaten, there lived many years since, while the country was yet a province of Great Britain, a simple, good-natured fellow, of the

---

1. **Appalachian** (ăp′ə-lā′chē-ən) **family:** a chain of mountains that extends from Quebec in eastern Canada to northern Alabama.

2. **within a few years:** until a few years ago. This story was written around 1820.

ing the virtues of patience and long-suffering. A quarrelsome wife may, therefore, in some respects, be considered a tolerable blessing; and if so, Rip Van Winkle was thrice blessed.

Certain it is, that he was a great favorite among all the good wives of the village, who took his part in all family squabbles, and never failed, whenever they talked those matters over in their evening gossipings, to lay all the blame on Dame Van Winkle. The children of the village, too, would shout with joy whenever he approached. He assisted at their sports, made their playthings, taught them to fly kites and shoot marbles, and told them long stories of ghosts, witches, and Indians. Whenever he went dodging about the village, he was surrounded by a troop of them, hanging on his coat skirts, clambering on his back, and playing a thousand tricks on him with impunity;[5] and not a dog would bark at him throughout the neighborhood.

The great error in Rip's character was an insuperable dislike of all kinds of profitable labor. It could not be from the want of perseverance; for he would sit on a wet rock, with a rod as long and heavy as a Tartar's lance,[6] and fish all day without a murmur, even though he should not be encouraged by a single nibble. He would carry a fowling piece[7] on his shoulder for hours together, trudging through woods and swamps, and up hill and down dale, to shoot a few squirrels or wild pigeons. He would never refuse to assist a neighbor even in the roughest toil, and was a foremost man at all country frolics for husking Indian corn, or building stone fences. The women of

name of Rip Van Winkle. He was a descendant of the Van Winkles who figured so gallantly in the chivalrous days of Peter Stuyvesant.[3] He inherited, however, but little of the martial character of his ancestors. I have observed that he was a simple, good-natured man; he was, moreover, a kind neighbor, and an obedient, henpecked husband. Indeed, to the latter circumstance might be owing that meekness of spirit which gained him such universal popularity; for those men are most apt to be conciliating[4] abroad who are under the discipline of shrews at home. Their tempers, doubtless, are rendered pliant in the fiery furnace of domestic trouble, which is worth all the sermons in the world for teach-

---

3. **Peter Stuyvesant** (stī'və-sənt): the last governor (1646-1664) of the Dutch colony of New Netherland, which was renamed New York after the British took control of it in 1664.
4. **conciliating:** friendly; easygoing.

5. **with impunity** (ĭm-pyōō'nə-tē): without fear of punishment.
6. **Tartar's** (tär'tərz) **lance:** The Tartars were Mongolian tribes that invaded Europe in the thirteenth century. The Tartar warriors used lances, or long, heavy spears.
7. **fowling piece:** a light gun, used most often for shooting birds.

the village, too, used to employ him to run their errands, and to do such little odd jobs as their less obliging husbands would not do for them. In a word, Rip was ready to attend to anybody's business but his own; but as to doing family duty, and keeping his farm in order, he found it impossible.

In fact, he declared it was of no use to work on his farm; it was the most pestilent[8] little piece of ground in the whole country; everything about it went wrong, and would go wrong, in spite of him. His fences were continually falling to pieces; his cow would either go astray or get among the cabbages; weeds were sure to grow quicker in his fields than anywhere else; the rain always made a point of setting in just as he had some outdoor work to do; so that his estate had dwindled away under his management, acre by acre, until there was little more left than a mere patch of Indian corn and potatoes, and was the worst-conditioned farm in the neighborhood.

His children, too, were as ragged and wild as if they belonged to nobody. His son Rip promised to inherit the habits, with the old clothes, of his father. He was generally seen trooping like a colt at his mother's heels, equipped in a pair of his father's castoff galligaskins,[9] which he had to hold up with one hand, as a fine lady does her train in bad weather.

Rip Van Winkle, however, was one of those happy mortals, of foolish, well-oiled dispositions, who take the world easy, eat white bread or brown, whichever can be got with least thought or trouble, and would rather starve on a penny than work for a pound.[10] If left to himself, he would have whistled life away in perfect contentment; but his wife kept continually dinning in his ears about his idleness, his carelessness, and the ruin he was bringing on his family. Morning, noon, and night, her tongue was incessantly going, and everything he said or did was sure to produce a torrent of household eloquence. Rip had but one way of replying to all lectures of the kind, and that, by frequent use, had grown into a habit. He shrugged his shoulders, shook his head, cast up his eyes, but said nothing. This, however, always provoked a fresh volley from his wife; so that he would take to the outside of the house—the only side which, in truth, belongs to a henpecked husband.

Rip's sole domestic adherent[11] was his dog Wolf, who was as much henpecked as his master; for Dame Van Winkle regarded them as companions in idleness, and even looked upon Wolf with an evil eye, as the cause of his master's going so often astray. True it is, in all points of spirit befitting an honorable dog, he was as courageous an animal as ever scoured the woods—but what courage can withstand the terrors of a woman's tongue? The moment Wolf entered the house his crest fell, his tail drooped to the ground, or curled between his legs, he sneaked about with a gallows air, casting many a sidelong glance at Dame Van Winkle, and at the least flourish of a broomstick or ladle, he would fly to the door, yelping.

Times grew worse and worse with Rip Van Winkle as years of matrimony rolled on; a tart temper never mellows with age, and a sharp tongue is the only edged tool that grows keener with constant use. For a long while he

---

8. **pestilent:** here, troublesome.
9. **galligaskins** (gǎl′ĭ-gǎs′kĭnz): loose, wide breeches.
10. **pound:** the basic unit of British money, used in the colonies.

11. **adherent** (ăd-hîr′ənt): follower or supporter.

used to console himself, when driven from home, by frequenting a kind of perpetual club of the sages, philosophers, and other idle personages of the village, which held its sessions on a bench before a small inn, designated by a portrait of His Majesty George the Third. Here they used to sit in the shade through a long, lazy summer's day, talking listlessly over village gossip, or telling endless sleepy stories about nothing. But it would have been worth any statesman's money to have heard the profound discussions that sometimes took place, when by chance an old newspaper fell into their hands from some passing traveler. How solemnly they would listen to the contents, as drawled out by Derrick Van Bummel, the schoolmaster, a dapper, learned little man, who was not to be daunted by the most gigantic word in the dictionary; and how sagely they would deliberate upon public events some months after they had taken place.

The opinions of this club were completely controlled by Nicholas Vedder, a patriarch[12] of the village, and landlord of the inn, at the door of which he took his seat from morning till night, just moving sufficiently to avoid the sun and keep in the shade of a large tree; so that the neighbors could tell the hour by his movements as accurately as by a sundial. It is true he was rarely heard to speak, but smoked his pipe incessantly. His adherents, however, perfectly understood him, and knew how to gather his opinions. When anything that was read or related displeased him, he was observed to smoke his pipe vehemently, and to send forth short, frequent, and angry puffs; but when pleased, he would inhale the smoke slowly and tranquilly, and emit it in light and placid clouds; and sometimes, taking the pipe from his mouth, and letting the fragrant vapor curl about his nose, would gravely nod his head in token of perfect approbation.

From even this stronghold the unlucky Rip was at length routed by his wife, who would suddenly break in upon the tranquillity of the assemblage and call the members all to naught; nor was that august[13] personage, Nicholas Vedder himself, sacred from the daring tongue of this terrible shrew, who charged him outright with encouraging her husband in habits of idleness.

Poor Rip was at last reduced almost to despair; and his only alternative, to escape from the labor of the farm and clamor of his wife, was to take gun in hand and stroll away into the woods. Here he would sometimes seat himself at the foot of a tree, and share the contents of his wallet[14] with Wolf, with whom he sympathized as a fellow sufferer in persecution. "Poor Wolf," he would say, "thy mistress leads thee a dog's life of it; but never mind, my lad, whilst I live thou shalt never want a friend to stand by thee!" Wolf would wag his tail, look wistfully in his master's face, and if dogs can feel pity, I believe he returned the sentiment with all his heart.

In a long ramble of the kind on a fine autumnal day, Rip had unconsciously scrambled to one of the highest parts of the Catskill Mountains. He was after his favorite sport of squirrel shooting, and the still solitudes[15] had echoed and reechoed with the reports of his gun. Panting and fatigued, he threw himself, late in the afternoon, on a green knoll, covered with mountain herbage, that crowned the brow of a precipice. From an opening be-

---

12. **patriarch** (pā'trē-ärk'): a man who is head of a family or a tribe; here, an old man of great dignity and authority.

13. **august** (ô-gŭst'): deserving respect.
14. **wallet:** here, a bag for carrying provisions.
15. **solitudes:** deserted places.

tween the trees he could overlook all the lower country for many a mile of rich woodland. He saw at a distance the lordly Hudson, far, far below him, moving on its silent but majestic course, with the reflection of a purple cloud, or the sail of a lagging bark,[16] here and there sleeping on its glassy bosom, and at last losing itself in the blue highlands.

On the other side he looked down into a deep mountain glen, wild, lonely, and shagged, the bottom filled with fragments from the overhanging cliffs, and scarcely lighted by the reflected rays of the setting sun. For some time Rip lay musing on this scene. Evening was gradually advancing. The mountains began to throw their long blue shadows over the valleys. He saw that it would be dark before he could reach the village, and he heaved a heavy sigh when he thought of encountering the terrors of Dame Van Winkle.

As he was about to descend, he heard a voice from a distance, hallooing, "Rip Van Winkle! Rip Van Winkle!" He looked round, but could see nothing but a crow winging its solitary flight across the mountain. He thought his fancy[17] must have deceived him, and turned again to descend, when he heard the same cry ring through the still evening air: "Rip Van Winkle! Rip Van Winkle!" At the same time Wolf bristled up his back, and giving a low growl, skulked to his master's side, looking fearfully down into the glen. Rip now felt a vague apprehension[18] stealing over him; he looked anxiously in the same direction, and perceived a strange figure slowly toiling up the rocks, and bending under the weight of something he carried on his back. He was surprised to see any human being in this lonely and unfrequented place, but sup-

posing it to be someone of the neighborhood in need of his assistance, he hastened down to yield it.

On nearer approach he was still more surprised at the singularity of the stranger's appearance. He was a short, square-built old fellow, with thick, bushy hair and a grizzled beard. His dress was of the antique Dutch fashion—a cloth jerkin[19] strapped round the waist—several pairs of breeches, the outer one of ample volume, decorated with rows of buttons down the sides, and bunches at the knees. He bore on his shoulder a stout keg, that seemed full of liquor, and made signs for Rip to approach and assist him with the load. Though rather shy and distrustful of this new acquaintance, Rip complied with his usual readiness; and mutually relieving one another, they clambered up a narrow gully, apparently the dry bed of a mountain torrent. As they ascended, Rip every now and then heard long rolling peals, like distant thunder, that seemed to issue out of a deep ravine, or rather cleft, between lofty rocks, toward which their rugged path conducted. He paused for an instant, but supposing it to be the muttering of one of those transient thundershowers which often take place in mountain heights, he proceeded. Passing through the ravine, they came to a hollow, like a small amphitheater,[20] surrounded by perpendicular precipices, over the brinks of which trees shot their branches, so that you only caught glimpses of the azure sky and the bright evening cloud. During the whole time Rip and his companion had labored on in silence; for though Rip marveled greatly what could be the object of carrying a keg of liquor up this wild mountain, yet there was something strange and incomprehensible

---

16. **bark:** boat.
17. **fancy:** imagination.
18. **apprehension** (ăp′rĭ-hĕn′shən): fear.

19. **jerkin:** a short, fitted jacket.
20. **amphitheater** (ăm′fə-thē′ə-tər): here, a level area surrounded by mountain slopes.

about the unknown, that inspired awe and checked familiarity.

On entering the amphitheater, new objects of wonder presented themselves. On a level spot in the center was a company of odd-looking personages playing at ninepins. They were dressed in a quaint, outlandish fashion; some wore short doublets,[21] others jerkins, with long knives in their belts, and most of them had enormous breeches, of style similar to that of the guide's. Their visages,[22] too, were peculiar. One had a large beard, broad face, and small, piggish eyes. The face of another seemed to consist entirely of nose, and was

surmounted by a white sugar-loaf hat,[23] set off with a little red cock's tail. They all had beards, of various shapes and colors. There was one who seemed to be the commander. He was a stout old gentleman, with a weather-beaten countenance; he wore a laced doublet, broad belt and hanger,[24] high-crowned hat and feather, red stockings, and high-heeled shoes, with roses in them. The whole group reminded Rip of the figures in an old Flemish[25] painting, in the parlor of the village parson, which had been brought over from Holland at the time of the settlement.

What seemed particularly odd to Rip was

---

21. **doublets:** close-fitting, elaborate jackets.
22. **visages** (vĭz'ĭj-əz): faces.

23. **sugar-loaf hat:** a cone-shaped hat.
24. **hanger:** here, a short sword.
25. **Flemish:** referring to Flanders, a former country in northwest Europe that included part of modern-day France, all of Belgium, and the southern portion of the Netherlands, or Holland.

that, though these folks were evidently amusing themselves, yet they maintained the gravest faces, the most mysterious silence, and were the most melancholy party of pleasure he had ever witnessed. Nothing interrupted the stillness of the scene but the noise of the balls, which, whenever they were rolled, echoed along the mountains like rumbling peals of thunder.

As Rip and his companion approached them, they suddenly stopped their play, and stared at him with such fixed, statuelike gaze, and such strange, lackluster countenances, that his heart turned within him, and his knees smote together. His companion now emptied the contents of the keg into large flagons,[26] and made signs to him to wait upon the company. He obeyed with fear and trembling; they quaffed[27] the liquor in profound silence, and then returned to their game.

By degrees Rip's awe and apprehension subsided. He even ventured, when no eye was fixed upon him, to taste the beverage, which he found had much of the flavor of excellent Holland gin. He was naturally a thirsty soul, and was soon tempted to repeat the draft.[28] One taste provoked another; and he repeated his visits to the flagon so often that at length his senses were overpowered, his eyes swam in his head, his head gradually declined, and he fell into a deep sleep.

On waking, he found himself on the green knoll whence he had first seen the old man of the glen. He rubbed his eyes—it was a bright sunny morning. The birds were hopping and twittering among the bushes, and the eagle was wheeling aloft, and breasting the pure mountain breeze. "Surely," thought Rip, "I have not slept here all night." He recalled the occurrences before he fell asleep. The strange man with a keg of liquor—the mountain ravine—the wild retreat among the rocks—the woebegone party at ninepins—the flagon—"Oh! that flagon! that wicked flagon!" thought Rip—"what excuse shall I make to Dame Van Winkle?"

He looked round for his gun, but in place of the clean, well-oiled fowling piece, he found an old firelock lying by him, the barrel incrusted with rust, the lock falling off, and the stock worm-eaten. He now suspected that the grave roisters[29] of the mountain had put a trick upon him, and, having dosed him with liquor, had robbed him of his gun. Wolf, too, had disappeared, but he might have strayed away after a squirrel or partridge. He whistled after him and shouted his name, but all in vain; the echoes repeated his whistle and

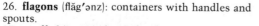

26. **flagons** (flăg'ənz): containers with handles and spouts.
27. **quaffed** (kwäft): drank deeply.
28. **draft:** here, a drink.

29. **roisters:** merrymakers; also called *roisterers.*

shout, but no dog was to be seen.

He determined to revisit the scene of the last evening's gambol,[30] and if he met with any of the party, to demand his dog and gun. As he rose to walk, he found himself stiff in the joints. "These mountain beds do not agree with me," thought Rip, "and if this frolic should lay me up with a fit of the rheumatism, I shall have a blessed time with Dame Van Winkle." With some difficulty he got down into the glen. He found the gully up which he and his companion had ascended the preceding evening; but to his astonishment a mountain stream was now foaming down it, leaping from rock to rock, and filling the glen with babbling murmurs. He, however, made shift to scramble up its sides, working his toilsome way through thickets of birch, sassafras, and witch hazel, and sometimes tripped up or entangled by the wild grapevines that twisted their coils or tendrils from tree to tree, and spread a kind of network in his path.

30. **gambol:** frolic.

At length he reached to where the ravine had opened through the cliffs to the amphitheater; but no traces of such opening remained. The rocks presented a high wall over which the torrent came tumbling in a sheet of feathery foam, and fell into a broad, deep basin, black from the shadows of the surrounding forest. Here, then, poor Rip was brought to a stand. He again called and whistled after his dog; he was only answered by the cawing of a flock of idle crows, who seemed to look down and scoff at the poor man's perplexities. What was to be done? The morning was passing away, and Rip felt famished for want of his breakfast. He grieved to give up his dog and gun; he dreaded to meet his wife; but it would not do to starve among the mountains. He shook his head, shouldered the rusty firelock, and, with a heart full of trouble and anxiety, turned his steps homeward.

As he approached the village, he met a number of people, but none whom he knew, which somewhat surprised him, for he had thought himself acquainted with everyone in the country round. Their dress, too, was of a different fashion from that to which he was accustomed. They all stared at him with equal marks of surprise, and whenever they cast their eyes upon him, invariably stroked their chins. The recurrence of this gesture induced Rip to do the same, when, to his astonishment, he found his beard had grown a foot long!

He had now entered the outskirts of the village. A troop of strange children ran at his heels, hooting after him, and pointing at his gray beard. The dogs, too, not one of which he recognized for an old acquaintance, barked at him as he passed. The very village was altered; it was larger and more populous. There were rows of houses which he had never seen before, and those which had been his familiar haunts had disappeared. Strange names were over the doors—strange faces at the windows—everything was strange. His mind now misgave him; he began to doubt whether both he and the world around him were not bewitched. Surely this was his native village, which he had left but the day before. There stood the Catskill Mountains—there ran the silver Hudson at a distance—there was every hill and dale precisely as it had always been—Rip was sorely perplexed. "That flagon last night," thought he, "has addled[31] my poor head sadly!"

It was with some difficulty that he found the way to his own house, which he approached with silent awe, expecting every moment to hear the shrill voice of Dame Van Winkle. He found the house gone to decay—the roof fallen in, the windows shattered, and the doors off the hinges. A half-starved dog that looked like Wolf was skulking about it. Rip called him by name, but the cur snarled,

showed his teeth, and passed on. This was an unkind cut indeed. "My very dog," sighed poor Rip, "has forgotten me!"

He entered the house, which, to tell the truth, Dame Van Winkle had always kept in neat order. It was empty, forlorn, and apparently abandoned. This desolateness overcame all his fears—he called loudly for his wife and children—the lonely chambers rang for a moment with his voice, and then all again was silence.

He now hurried forth, and hastened to his old resort, the village inn—but it too was gone. A large, rickety wooden building stood in its place, with great gaping windows, some of them broken and mended with old hats and petticoats, and over the door was painted, "The Union Hotel, by Jonathan Doolittle." Instead of the great tree that used to shelter the quiet little Dutch inn of yore, there now was reared a tall naked pole, with something on the top that looked like a red nightcap,[32] and from it was fluttering a flag, on which was a singular assemblage of stars and stripes—all this was strange and incomprehensible. He recognized on the sign, however, the ruby face of King George, under which he had smoked so many a peaceful pipe; but even this was singularly changed. The red coat was changed for one of blue and buff, a sword was held in the hand instead of a scepter, the head was decorated with a cocked hat, and underneath was painted in large characters, GENERAL WASHINGTON.

There was, as usual, a crowd of folk about the door, but none that Rip recollected. The very character of the people seemed changed. There was a busy, bustling tone about it, instead of the accustomed tranquillity. He looked in vain for the sage Nicholas Vedder,

---

31. **addled:** confused.

32. **red nightcap:** Rip's interpretation of the liberty cap, a symbol of freedom.

with his broad face, double chin, and fair long pipe, uttering clouds of tobacco smoke instead of idle speeches; or Van Bummel, the schoolmaster, doling forth the contents of an ancient newspaper. In place of these, a lean, bilious-looking[33] fellow, with his pockets full of handbills, was talking vehemently about rights of citizens—elections—members of Congress—liberty—Bunker's Hill—heroes of seventy-six—and other words, which were a perfect Babylonish jargon[34] to the bewildered Van Winkle.

The appearance of Rip, with his long, grizzled beard, his rusty fowling piece, his uncouth dress, and an army of women and children at his heels, soon attracted the attention of the tavern politicians. They crowded round him, eyeing him from head to foot with great curiosity. The orator bustled up to him, and drawing him partly aside, inquired "on which side he voted?" Rip stared in vacant stupidity. Another short but busy little fellow pulled him by the arm, and, rising on tiptoe, inquired in his ear, "whether he was Federal or Democrat?"[35] Rip was equally at a loss to comprehend the question, when a knowing, self-important old gentleman, in a sharp cocked hat, made his way through the crowd, putting them to the right and left with his elbows as he passed, and planting himself before Van Winkle, with one arm akimbo,[36] the other resting on his cane, his keen eyes and sharp

hat penetrating, as it were, into his very soul, demanded in an austere tone, "what brought him to the election with a gun on his shoulder, and a mob at his heels; and whether he meant to breed a riot in the village?"

"Alas! gentlemen," cried Rip, somewhat dismayed, "I am a poor quiet man, a native of the place, and a loyal subject of the King, God bless him!"

---

33. **bilious** (bĭl′yəs) **-looking:** having a bad-tempered look.
34. **Babylonish** (băb′ə-lon′ĭsh) **jargon:** unintelligible language. According to Genesis 11:1–9, the people of Babel, or Babylon, tried to build a tower that would reach to heaven. They were forced to stop their work when God caused them to speak different languages.
35. **Federal or Democrat:** a member of the Federalist Party or the Democratic-Republican Party. These were the two political parties in the early years of United States history.
36. **akimbo:** holding the hand on the hip with the elbow outward.

Here a general shout burst from the bystanders—"A Tory![37] a Tory! a spy! a refugee! hustle him! away with him!" It was with great difficulty that the self-important man in the cocked hat restored order; and demanded again of the unknown culprit, what he came there for, and whom he was seeking. The poor man humbly assured him that he meant no harm, but merely came there in search of some of his neighbors, who used to keep about the tavern.

"Well—who are they?—name them."

Rip bethought himself a moment, and inquired, "Where's Nicholas Vedder?"

There was a silence for a little while, when an old man replied, in a thin, piping voice, "Nicholas Vedder! why, he is dead and gone these eighteen years! There was a wooden tombstone in the churchyard that used to tell all about him, but that's rotten and gone too."

"Where's Brom Dutcher?"

"Oh, he went off to the army in the beginning of the war; some say he was killed at the storming of Stony Point[38]—others say he was drowned in a squall at the foot of Antony's Nose.[39] I don't know—he never came back again."

"Where's Van Bummel, the schoolmaster?"

"He went off to the wars too, was a great militia general, and is now in Congress."

Rip's heart died away at hearing of these sad changes in his home and friends, and finding himself thus alone in the world. Every answer puzzled him, too, by treating of such enormous lapses of time, and of matters which he could not understand: war—Congress—Stony Point; he had no courage to ask after any more friends, but cried out in despair, "Does nobody here know Rip Van Winkle?"

"Oh, Rip Van Winkle!" exclaimed two or three; "oh, to be sure! that's Rip Van Winkle yonder, leaning against the tree."

Rip looked, and beheld a precise copy of himself, as he went up the mountain; apparently as lazy, and certainly as ragged. The poor fellow was now completely bewildered. He doubted his own identity, and whether he was himself or another man. In the midst of his bewilderment, the man in the cocked hat demanded who he was, and what was his name.

"God knows," exclaimed he, at his wit's end; "I'm not myself—I'm somebody else—that's me yonder—no—that's somebody else got into my shoes—I was myself last night, but I fell asleep on the mountain, and they've changed my gun, and everything's changed, and I'm changed, and I can't tell what's my name, or who I am!"

The bystanders began now to look at each other, nod, wink significantly, and tap their fingers against their foreheads. There was a whisper, also, about securing the gun, and keeping the old fellow from doing mischief, at the very suggestion of which the self-important man in the cocked hat retired quickly. At this critical moment a fresh, comely[40] woman pressed through the throng to get a peep at the gray-bearded man. She had a chubby child in her arms, which, frightened at his looks,

---

37. **Tory:** someone who sided with the British cause during the American Revolution.
38. **Stony Point:** a town on the Hudson River where American Revolutionary troops under General Anthony Wayne won an important battle against the British in July 1779.
39. **Antony's Nose:** a mountain on the Hudson River. It was called *Antonies Neus* by the Dutch, and changed to *Anthony's Nose* by the British.

40. **comely** (kŭm'lē): beautiful.

began to cry. "Hush, Rip," cried she, "hush, you little fool; the old man won't hurt you." The name of the child, the air of the mother, the tone of her voice, all awakened a train of recollections in his mind. "What is your name, my good woman?" asked he.

"Judith Gardenier."

"And your father's name?"

"Ah, poor man, Rip Van Winkle was his name, but it's twenty years since he went away from home with his gun, and never has been heard of since—his dog came home without him; but whether he shot himself, or was carried away by the Indians, nobody can tell. I was then but a little girl."

Rip had but one question more to ask; but he put it with a faltering voice: "Where's your mother?"

"Oh, she too had died but a short time since; she broke a blood vessel in a fit of passion at a New England peddler."

There was a drop of comfort, at least, in this intelligence.[41] The honest man could contain himself no longer. He caught his daughter and her child in his arms. "I am your father!" cried he—"Young Rip Van Winkle once—old Rip Van Winkle now!—Does nobody know poor Rip Van Winkle?"

All stood amazed, until an old woman, tottering out from among the crowd, put her hand to her brow, and peering under it in his face for a moment, exclaimed, "Sure enough! it is Rip Van Winkle—it is himself! Welcome home again, old neighbor. Why, where have you been these twenty long years?"

Rip's story was soon told, for the whole twenty years had been to him as but one night. The neighbors stared when they heard it; some were seen to wink at each other, and put their tongues in their cheeks; and the self-important man in the cocked hat, who, when the alarm was over, had returned to the field, screwed down the corners of his mouth, and shook his head—upon which there was a general shaking of the head throughout the assemblage.

It was determined, however, to take the opinion of old Peter Vanderdonk, who was seen slowly advancing up the road. He was a descendant of the historian of that name, who wrote one of the earliest accounts of the province. Peter was the most ancient inhabitant of the village, and well versed in all the wonderful events and traditions of the neighborhood. He recollected Rip at once, and corroborated his story in the most satisfactory manner. He assured the company that it was a fact, handed down from his ancestor the historian, that the Catskill Mountains had always been haunted by strange beings. That it was affirmed that the great Henry Hudson, the first discoverer of the river and country,[42] kept a kind of vigil there every twenty years, with his crew of the *Half-Moon*; being permitted in this way to revisit the scenes of his enterprise and keep a guardian eye upon the river and the great city called by his name. That his father had once seen them in their old Dutch dresses playing at ninepins in a hollow of the mountain; and that he himself had heard, one summer afternoon, the sound of their balls, like distant peals of thunder.

To make a long story short, the company broke up, and returned to the more important concerns of the election. Rip's daughter took him home to live with her; she had a snug, well-furnished house, and a stout, cheery farmer for a husband, whom Rip recollected for one of the urchins that used to climb upon his back. As to Rip's son and heir, who was

---

41. **intelligence:** here, a piece of news.

42. **country:** here, the Catskill area.

the ditto of himself, seen leaning against the tree, he was employed to work on the farm; but showed an hereditary disposition to attend to anything else but his business.

Rip now resumed his old walks and habits; he soon found many of his former cronies, though all rather the worse for the wear and tear of time; and preferred making friends among the rising generation, with whom he soon grew into great favor.

Having nothing to do at home, and being arrived at that happy age when a man can be idle with impunity, he took his place once more on the bench at the inn door, and was reverenced as one of the patriarchs of the village, and a chronicle of the old times "before the war." It was some time before he

could get into the regular track of gossip, or could be made to comprehend the strange events that had taken place during his sleep. How that there had been a Revolutionary War — that the country had thrown off the yoke of old England — and that, instead of being a subject of His Majesty George the Third, he was now a free citizen of the United States. Rip, in fact, was no politician; the changes of states and empires made but little impression on him; but there was one species of despotism under which he had long groaned, and that was — petticoat government. Happily that was at an end; he had got his neck out of the yoke of matrimony, and could go in and out whenever he pleased, without dreading the tyranny of Dame Van Winkle. Whenever her name was mentioned, however, he shook his head, shrugged his shoulders, and cast up his eyes; which might pass either for an expression of resignation to his fate, or joy at his deliverance.

He used to tell his story to every stranger that arrived at Mr. Doolittle's hotel. He was observed, at first, to vary on some points every time he told it, which was, doubtless, owing to his having so recently awaked. It at last settled down precisely to the tale I have related, and not a man, woman, or child in the neighborhood but knew it by heart. Some always pretended to doubt the reality of it, and insisted that Rip had been out of his head, and that this was one point on which he always remained flighty. The old Dutch inhabitants, however, almost universally gave it full credit. Even to this day they never hear a thunderstorm of a summer afternoon about the Catskills but they say Henry Hudson and his crew are at their game of ninepins; and it is a common wish of all henpecked husbands in the neighborhood, when life hangs heavy on their hands, that they might have a quieting draft out of Rip Van Winkle's flagon.

SEEKING MEANING

1. Although this story is about Rip Van Winkle, Washington Irving doesn't introduce Rip until the third paragraph of the story. In the first two paragraphs, Irving describes the *setting* of the story—the place and the time of the action. How do the phrases "magical hues and shapes" and "fairy mountains" prepare you for the strange events to come?

2. Rip is described as having a "dislike of all kinds of profitable labor." What kinds of "unprofitable labor" does he enjoy? What "unprofitable labor" does he find in the mountains?

3. What contrast is there between Rip's temperament and that of Dame Van Winkle? How would you describe Rip's conflict? How is this conflict related to the two places where the action occurs, the village and the mountains?

4. "Rip Van Winkle" opens during the colonial period of American history. By the end of the story, you learn that the colonies have "thrown off the yoke of old England" and become free. What changes does Rip find in the village when he returns? In what way is Rip's "history" like the history of his country?

5. The story "Rip Van Winkle" has appealed to generations of readers who have recognized in Rip's experience the fulfillment of their own wishes. Why do you think readers can put themselves in Rip's place so easily?

DEVELOPING SKILLS IN READING

Focusing on Setting

Some readers become impatient with descriptions of setting. They are eager to get on with the action and may wonder why the writer interrupts the story with passages describing the physical surroundings.

The setting of "Rip Van Winkle" brings Rip's conflict into sharp focus for the reader. The world of Rip's everyday existence is drawn in realistic detail. Irving describes the houses "built of small yellow bricks brought from Holland," which have "latticed windows and gable fronts, surmounted with weathercocks." He also gives you a detailed and comic picture of Rip's domestic troubles. In this passage he tells you how everything on Rip's farm would go wrong: "His fences were continually falling to pieces; his cow would either go astray or get among the cabbages; weeds were sure to grow quicker in his fields than anywhere else . . . ."

Find the passage that shows you why Rip was a great favorite with the children in the village. What kinds of "unprofitable labor" did Rip perform for the children?

When Irving describes the Catskill Mountains, he dwells on their unreal, magical quality:

Every change of season, every change of weather, indeed, every hour of the day, produces some change in the magical hues and shapes of these mountains . . . . When the weather is fair and settled, they are clothed in blue and purple, and print their bold outlines on the clear evening sky; but, sometimes, when the rest of the landscape is cloudless, they will gather a hood of gray vapors about their summits, which, in the last rays of the setting sun, will glow and light up like a crown of glory.

The description suggests what the mountains represent for Rip—an escape from the real world and all its problems.

Find the passage on page 274 in which Irving describes evening falling on the mountains. Which words give you an eerie feeling about the mountains?

Understanding Character Types

Dame Van Winkle's situation is hardly comical. She has a shiftless husband who allows his farm to fall to pieces, who spends more time away from his family than with them, and who leaves his children ill-fed and ill-clothed. Yet Irving treats Dame Van Winkle as a comic character who provides a great deal of humor in the story.

You can laugh at Dame Van Winkle because Irving shows her in only one light. Whenever you see Dame Van Winkle in the story, she is scolding or nagging Rip, his dog Wolf, or his cronies in the village. If you were allowed to see Dame Van Winkle laughing with her children or crying in despair over her hardships, your reaction to her would probably be very different. However, Irving does not show these other qualities in Dame Van Winkle. She is represented only as a *shrew*, a bad-tempered, quarrelsome woman.

You have seen that a writer can use the element of surprise—the contrast between the expected and the unexpected—to produce humor. A writer can also use *exaggeration* for humorous effects. Irving makes Dame Van Winkle laughable by exaggerating one side of her character.

> Morning, noon, and night, her tongue was incessantly going, and everything he said or did was sure to produce a torrent of household eloquence.

The word *torrent* generally refers to a heavy rain. What does Irving mean by the phrase "a torrent of household eloquence"? Find other examples in the story where Dame Van Winkle's bad temper is humorously exaggerated.

Irving also enjoys treating the conflict between Rip and his wife as a series of battles. By shrugging his shoulders, Rip "always provoked a fresh *volley* from his wife." What is a *volley*?

Dame Van Winkle is described as invading the "club of the sages": "From even this stronghold the unlucky Rip was at length *routed* by his wife" (page 273). The word *routed* calls up the image of an army being driven from a fortress in complete disorder and bewilderment. When you realize that this invader uses no weapon but her tongue, the comparison becomes laughable. Rip has as great a fear of his wife's harsh words as a soldier might have of his enemy's firearms.

Irving, of course, is not suggesting that all wives are shrewish any more than he is saying that all husbands are lazy. Irving is showing the reader that there are some qualities in people that provoke laughter if they are carried to excess.

Dame Van Winkle is not presented as a fully rounded individual. She is a *character type*—someone who fits a pattern and who can be recognized by certain typical characteristics. In the case of a shrew, the typical characteristics are nagging and scolding.

ABOUT THE AUTHOR

Washington Irving (1783–1859) said, "When I first wrote the legend of Rip Van Winkle, my thoughts had been for some time turned toward giving a color of romance and tradition to interesting points of our national scenery." Irving borrowed the idea for his story from an Old German folk tale, but he set it in the Hudson River country of New York. In this way, he glorified an American place as no writer before him had done. Today he is remembered as America's first major literary figure.

As a boy, Irving was adventurous and restless. When he was fourteen, he planned to run away to sea. He prepared for this adventure by eating salt pork and sleeping on the hard floor of his room. He liked to spend his time wandering around New York. "I knew every spot," he said, "where a murder or robbery had been committed, or a ghost seen." He had a lively imagination, and although he studied law, he was quickly drawn to a literary career.

From 1807 to 1808, he contributed humorous essays to *Salmagundi*, a periodical he had helped to create. In 1809 he published the first of his two great books, a comic history of New York with a long title, now known simply as *Knickerbocker's History of New York*. Irving's masterpiece, *The Sketch Book*, appeared ten years later. It was a collection of over thirty pieces, including his two most famous stories, "Rip Van Winkle" and "The Legend of Sleepy Hollow." In his later years, Irving spent a great deal of time in Europe searching for more old tales and anecdotes. After he returned to America, he built himself a remarkable house in Tarrytown, New York, which he called "Sunnyside." There he spent his remaining days writing a five-volume biography of George Washington.

*"Zlateh's bleating began to
sound like crying. Those
humans in whom she had
so much confidence had
dragged her into a trap."*

Zlateh the Goat

Isaac Bashevis Singer

At Hanukkah[1] time the road from the village to the town is usually covered with snow, but this year the winter had been a mild one. Hanukkah had almost come, yet little snow had fallen. The sun shone most of the time. The peasants complained that because of the dry weather there would be a poor harvest of winter grain. New grass sprouted, and the peasants sent their cattle out to pasture.

For Reuven the furrier it was a bad year, and after long hesitation he decided to sell Zlateh the goat. She was old and gave little milk. Feyvel the town butcher had offered eight gulden[2] for her. Such a sum would buy Hanukkah candles, potatoes and oil for pancakes, gifts for the children, and other holiday necessaries for the house. Reuven told his oldest boy, Aaron, to take the goat to town.

Aaron understood what taking the goat to Feyvel meant, but he had to obey his father. Leah, his mother, wiped the tears from her eyes when she heard the news. Aaron's younger sisters, Anna and Miriam, cried loudly. Aaron put on his quilted jacket and a cap with earmuffs, bound a rope around Zlateh's neck, and took along two slices of bread with cheese to eat on the road. Aaron was supposed to deliver the goat by evening, spend the night at the butcher's, and return the next day with the money.

While the family said goodbye to the goat, and Aaron placed the rope around her neck, Zlateh stood as patiently and good-naturedly as ever. She licked Reuven's hand. She shook her small white beard. Zlateh trusted human beings. She knew that they always fed her and never did her any harm.

When Aaron brought her out on the road to town, she seemed somewhat astonished. She'd never been led in that direction before. She looked back at him questioningly, as if to say, "Where are you taking me?" But after a while she seemed to come to the conclusion that a goat shouldn't ask questions. Still, the road was different. They passed new fields, pastures, and huts with thatched roofs. Here and there a dog barked and came running after them, but Aaron chased it away with his stick.

The sun was shining when Aaron left the village. Suddenly the weather changed. A

---

1. **Hanukkah** (KHä′nōō-kə): a Jewish holiday, usually in December, celebrated for eight days.
2. **gulden** (gōōl′dən): coins used in several European countries; also called *guilders*.

large black cloud with a bluish center appeared in the east and spread itself rapidly over the sky. A cold wind blew in with it. The crows flew low, croaking. At first it looked as if it would rain, but instead it began to hail as in summer. It was early in the day, but it became dark as dusk. After a while the hail turned to snow.

In his twelve years Aaron had seen all kinds of weather, but he had never experienced a snow like this one. It was so dense it shut out the light of the day. In a short time their path was completely covered. The wind became as cold as ice. The road to town was narrow and winding. Aaron no longer knew where he was. He could not see through the snow. The cold soon penetrated his quilted jacket.

At first Zlateh didn't seem to mind the change in weather. She too was twelve years old and knew what winter meant. But when her legs sank deeper and deeper into the snow, she began to turn her head and look at Aaron in wonderment. Her mild eyes seemed to ask, "Why are we out in such a storm?" Aaron hoped that a peasant would come along with his cart, but no one passed by.

The snow grew thicker, falling to the ground in large, whirling flakes. Beneath it Aaron's boots touched the softness of a plowed field. He realized that he was no longer on the road. He had gone astray. He could no longer figure out which was east or west, which way was the village, the town. The wind whistled, howled, whirled the snow about in eddies. It looked as if white imps were playing tag on the fields. A white dust rose above the ground. Zlateh stopped. She could walk no longer. Stubbornly she anchored her cleft hooves in the earth and bleated as if pleading to be taken home. Icicles hung from her white beard, and her horns were glazed with frost.

Aaron did not want to admit the danger, but

Man with Goat (1922-23).
Lithograph by Marc Chagall.
Jane Kahan Gallery.

he knew just the same that if they did not find shelter they would freeze to death. This was no ordinary storm. It was a mighty blizzard. The snowfall had reached his knees. His hands were numb, and he could no longer feel his toes. He choked when he breathed. His nose felt like wood, and he rubbed it with snow. Zlateh's bleating began to sound like crying. Those humans in whom she had so much confidence had dragged her into a trap. Aaron began to pray to God for himself and for the innocent animal.

Suddenly he made out the shape of a hill.

Zlateh the Goat 287

He wondered what it could be. Who had piled snow into such a huge heap? He moved toward it, dragging Zlateh after him. When he came near it, he realized that it was a large haystack which the snow had blanketed.

Aaron realized immediately that they were saved. With great effort he dug his way through the snow. He was a village boy and knew what to do. When he reached the hay, he hollowed out a nest for himself and the goat. No matter how cold it may be outside, in the hay it is always warm. And hay was food for Zlateh. The moment she smelled it she became contented and began to eat. Outside the snow continued to fall. It quickly covered the passageway Aaron had dug. But a boy and an animal need to breathe, and there was hardly any air in their hideout. Aaron bored a kind of a window through the hay and snow and carefully kept the passage clear.

Zlateh, having eaten her fill, sat down on her hind legs and seemed to have regained her confidence in man. Aaron ate his two slices of bread and cheese, but after the difficult journey he was still hungry. He looked at Zlateh and noticed her udders were full. He lay down next to her, placing himself so that when he milked her he could squirt the milk into his mouth. It was rich and sweet. Zlateh was not accustomed to being milked that way, but she did not resist. On the contrary, she seemed eager to reward Aaron for bringing her to a shelter whose very walls, floor, and ceiling were made of food.

Through the window Aaron could catch a glimpse of the chaos outside. The wind carried before it whole drifts of snow. It was completely dark, and he did not know whether night had already come or whether it was the darkness of the storm. Thank God that in the hay it was not cold. The dried hay, grass, and field flowers exuded the warmth of the summer sun. Zlateh ate frequently; she

nibbled from above, below, from the left and right. Her body gave forth an animal warmth, and Aaron cuddled up to her. He had always loved Zlateh, but now she was like a sister. He was alone, cut off from his family, and wanted to talk. He began to talk to Zlateh. "Zlateh, what do you think about what has happened to us?" he asked.

"Maaaa," Zlateh answered.

"If we hadn't found this stack of hay, we would both be frozen stiff by now," Aaron said.

"Maaaa," was the goat's reply.

"If the snow keeps on falling like this, we may have to stay here for days," Aaron explained.

"Maaaa," Zlateh bleated.

"What does 'Maaaa' mean?" Aaron asked. "You'd better speak up clearly."

"Maaaa. Maaaa," Zlateh tried.

"Well, let it be 'Maaaa' then," Aaron said patiently. "You can't speak, but I know you understand. I need you and you need me. Isn't that right?"

"Maaaa."

Aaron became sleepy. He made a pillow out of some hay, leaned his head on it, and dozed off. Zlateh too fell asleep.

When Aaron opened his eyes, he didn't know whether it was morning or night. The snow had blocked up his window. He tried to clear it, but when he had bored through to the length of his arm, he still hadn't reached the outside. Luckily he had his stick with him and was able to break through to the open air. It was still dark outside. The snow continued to fall and the wind wailed, first with one voice and then with many. Sometimes it had the sound of devilish laughter. Zlateh too awoke, and when Aaron greeted her, she answered, "Maaaa." Yes, Zlateh's language consisted of only one word, but it meant many things. Now she was saying, "We must accept all that God gives us—heat, cold, hunger, satisfaction, light, and darkness."

Aaron had awakened hungry. He had eaten up his food, but Zlateh had plenty of milk.

For three days Aaron and Zlateh stayed in the haystack. Aaron had always loved Zlateh, but in these three days he loved her more and more. She fed him with her milk and helped him keep warm. She comforted him with her patience. He told her many stories, and she always cocked her ears and listened. When he patted her, she licked his hand and his face. Then she said, "Maaaa," and he knew it meant, I love you too.

The snow fell for three days, though after the first day it was not as thick and the wind quieted down. Sometimes Aaron felt that there could never have been a summer, that the snow had always fallen, ever since he could remember. He, Aaron, never had a father or mother or sisters. He was a snow child, born of the snow, and so was Zlateh. It was so quiet in the hay that his ears rang in the stillness. Aaron and Zlateh slept all night and a good part of the day. As for Aaron's dreams, they were all about warm weather. He dreamed of green fields, trees covered with blossoms, clear brooks, and singing birds. By the third night the snow had stopped, but Aaron did not dare to find his way home in the darkness. The sky became clear and the moon shone, casting silvery nets on the snow. Aaron dug his way out and looked at the world. It was all white, quiet, dreaming dreams of heavenly splendor. The stars were large and close. The moon swam in the sky as in a sea.

On the morning of the fourth day Aaron heard the ringing of sleigh bells. The haystack was not far from the road. The peasant who drove the sleigh pointed out the way to him— not to the town and Feyvel the butcher, but home to the village. Aaron had decided in the haystack that he would never part with Zlateh.

Aaron's family and their neighbors had searched for the boy and the goat but had found no trace of them during the storm. They feared they were lost. Aaron's mother and sisters cried for him; his father remained silent and gloomy. Suddenly one of the neighbors came running to their house with the news that Aaron and Zlateh were coming up the road.

There was great joy in the family. Aaron told them how he had found the stack of hay and how Zlateh had fed him with her milk. Aaron's sisters kissed and hugged Zlateh and gave her a special treat of chopped carrots and potato peels, which Zlateh gobbled up hungrily.

Nobody ever again thought of selling Zlateh, and now that the cold weather had finally set in, the villagers needed the services of Reuven the furrier once more. When Hanukkah came, Aaron's mother was able to fry pancakes every evening, and Zlateh got her portion too. Even though Zlateh had her own pen, she often came to the kitchen, knocking on the door with her horns to indicate that she was ready to visit, and she was always admitted. In the evening Aaron, Miriam, and Anna played dreidel.[3] Zlateh sat near the stove watching the children and the flickering of the Hanukkah candles.

Once in a while Aaron would ask her, "Zlateh, do you remember the three days we spent together?"

And Zlateh would scratch her neck with a horn, shake her white bearded head and come out with the single sound which expressed all her thoughts, and all her love.

---

3. **dreidel** (drā′dəl): a game played with a four-sided top; also, the top itself.

SEEKING MEANING

1. Nature plays an important role in this story. How does nature bring misery and then happiness to Reuven's family?
2. Why does Reuven decide to sell Zlateh?
3. Just when it seems that Aaron and Zlateh will perish in the storm, Aaron finds the haystack. How does the storm, which threatens their lives, become the means of saving Zlateh?
4. During the three days that Aaron and Zlateh spend in the haystack, they become completely dependent upon each other. What decision does Aaron come to?
5. When Aaron is alone with Zlateh, he begins to acquire wisdom about the meaning of his experience. What do you think he learns? What evidence in the story supports your opinion?

DEVELOPING SKILLS IN READING

Interpreting Theme

You have seen that a short story is made up of several basic elements. Often, the elements in a short story work together to express a central meaning or idea called the *theme*. Sometimes the theme of a story is stated directly. Sometimes the theme must be inferred from the other elements in a story.

The theme of "Zlateh the Goat" might be stated in this way: The hardships of life often serve to bind us more closely to those we love. Let us see how this statement grows out of the specific events in the story.

The characters in the story are faced with circumstances they cannot control. Reuven is forced through necessity to sell Zlateh. Both Zlateh and Aaron seem headed for tragedy through no fault of their own. They are saved quite unexpectedly when Aaron comes across a haystack. The storm turns out to be a godsend, for the family's circumstances are reversed by the change in weather. The events of the story suggest that the fate of all living creatures is beyond their understanding or control.

However, while the characters have no power to control their circumstances, they are not helpless, for they are sustained by love and trust. This idea becomes clear in the central episode of the story. When Aaron and Zlateh are cut off from the rest of the world, Aaron grows to love Zlateh more and more, and he determines that he will never part with her. When he returns to the village, there is no more talk of selling Zlateh, for the family has learned how much Zlateh means to all of them. We see that the bonds of this family have been strengthened by their ordeal.

Have you a different interpretation of the story? How would you express the theme?

ABOUT THE AUTHOR

Isaac Bashevis Singer (1904–   ), who writes in Yiddish, is well known for his stories of Jewish family life in eastern Europe. Singer was born in Radzymin, Poland. He received his formal education in Warsaw, the nation's capital, where he worked as a proofreader and editor for several literary magazines. In 1935 he moved to New York City. In 1950 he published *The Family Moskat*, the first of his books to appear in English. Singer says he loves his profession: "When I began to write, I was fifteen . . . I very often met situations which baffled me, and from the moment I knew that there was such a thing as literature, I thought how wonderful it would be to be able to describe such things." He received the Nobel Prize for literature in 1978.

"Oh! But he was a tightfisted hand at the grindstone, was Scrooge! A squeezing, wrenching, grasping, scraping, clutching, covetous old sinner!"

A Christmas Carol *Charles Dickens*

Stave[1] One: Marley's Ghost

Marley was dead, to begin with. There is no doubt whatever about that. The register of his burial was signed by the clergyman, the clerk, the undertaker, and the chief mourner. Scrooge signed it. And Scrooge's name was good upon 'Change[2] for anything he chose to put his hand to.

Old Marley was as dead as a doornail.

Scrooge knew he was dead? Of course he did. How could it be otherwise? Scrooge and he were partners for I don't know how many years. Scrooge was his sole executor, his sole administrator, his sole assign, his sole residuary legatee,[3] his sole friend, his sole mourner.

Scrooge never painted out old Marley's name, however. There it yet stood, years afterward, above the door — SCROOGE AND MARLEY. The firm was known as SCROOGE AND MARLEY. Sometimes people new to the business called Scrooge "Scrooge," and sometimes "Marley." He answered to both names. It was all the same to him.

Oh! But he was a tightfisted hand at the grindstone, was Scrooge! A squeezing, wrenching, grasping, scraping, clutching, covetous old sinner! External heat and cold had little influence on him. No warmth could warm, no cold could chill him. No wind that blew was bitterer than he, no falling snow was more intent upon its purpose, no pelting rain less open to entreaty. Foul weather didn't know where to have him. The heaviest rain and snow and hail and sleet could boast of the advantage over him in only one respect — they often "came down"[4] handsomely, and Scrooge never did.

Nobody ever stopped him in the street to say, with gladsome looks, "My dear Scrooge, how are you? When will you come to see me?" No beggars implored him to bestow a

---

1. **Stave:** a stanza of a poem or song; here, a section of Dickens' "carol."
2. **'Change:** the Exchange, the place where merchants, brokers, and bankers conduct their business.
3. **executor** (ĕg-zĕk′yə-tər); **administrator; assign; residuary legatee** (rĭ-zĭj′oo-ĕr′ē lĕg′ə-tē′): legal terms used in a will. Marley had left everything he owned to Scrooge, who handled all the business arrangements after Marley's death.
4. **"came down":** slang for "made a gift or donation."

trifle, no children asked him what it was o'clock, no man or woman ever once in all his life inquired the way to such and such a place of Scrooge. Even the blind men's dogs appeared to know him, and when they saw him coming on, would tug their owners into doorways and up courts, and then would wag their tails as though they said, "No eyes at all is better than an evil eye, dark master!"

But what did Scrooge care! It was the very thing he liked. To edge his way along the crowded paths of life, warning all human sympathy to keep its distance, was what the knowing ones call "nuts" to Scrooge.

Once upon a time—of all the good days in the year, upon a Christmas Eve—old Scrooge sat busy in his countinghouse. It was cold, bleak, biting, foggy weather; and the city clocks had only just gone three, but it was quite dark already.

The door of Scrooge's countinghouse was open, that he might keep his eye upon his clerk, who, in a dismal little cell beyond, a sort of tank, was copying letters. Scrooge had a very small fire, but the clerk's fire was so very much smaller that it looked like one coal. But he couldn't replenish it, for Scrooge kept the coalbox in his own room, and so surely as the clerk came in with the shovel, the master predicted that it would be necessary for them to part. Wherefore the clerk put on his white comforter[5] and tried to warm himself at the candle; in which effort, not being a man of a strong imagination, he failed.

"A Merry Christmas, Uncle! God save you!" cried a cheerful voice. It was the voice of Scrooge's nephew, who came upon him so quickly that this was the first intimation Scrooge had of his approach.

"Bah!" said Scrooge. "Humbug!"

---

5. **comforter:** a long scarf.

"Christmas a humbug, Uncle! You don't mean that, I am sure?"

"I do. Out upon merry Christmas! What's Christmastime to you but a time for paying bills without money; a time for finding yourself a year older, and not an hour richer; a time for balancing your books and having every item in 'em through a round dozen of months presented dead against you? If I had my will, every idiot who goes about with 'Merry Christmas' on his lips should be boiled with his own pudding and buried with a stake of holly through his heart. He should!"

"Uncle!"

"Nephew, keep Christmas in your own way, and let me keep it in mine."

"Keep it! But you don't keep it."

"Let me leave it alone, then. Much good may it do you! Much good it has ever done you!"

"There are many things from which I might have derived good, by which I have not profited, I dare say, Christmas among the rest. But I am sure I have always thought of Christmastime, when it has come round—apart from the veneration due to its sacred origin, if anything belonging to it *can* be apart from that—as a good time; a kind, forgiving, charitable, pleasant time; the only time I know of, in the long calendar of the year, when men and women seem by one consent to open their shut-up hearts freely and to think of people below them as if they really were fellow travelers to the grave, and not another race of creatures bound on other journeys. And therefore, Uncle, though it has never put a scrap of gold or silver in my pocket, I believe that it *has* done me good, and *will* do me good; and I say, God bless it!"

The clerk in the tank involuntarily applauded.

"Let me hear another sound from *you*," said Scrooge, "and you'll keep your Christmas by losing your situation! You're quite a powerful speaker, sir," he added, turning to his nephew. "I wonder you don't go into Parliament."

"Don't be angry, Uncle. Come! Dine with us tomorrow."

"Good afternoon."

"I want nothing from you; I ask nothing of you; why cannot we be friends?"

"Good afternoon."

"I am sorry, with all my heart, to find you so resolute. We have never had any quarrel to which I have been a party. But I have made the trial in homage to Christmas, and I'll keep my Christmas humor to the last. So a Merry Christmas, Uncle!"

"Good afternoon!"

"And a Happy New Year!"

"Good afternoon!"

His nephew left the room without an angry word, notwithstanding. The clerk, in letting Scrooge's nephew out, had let two other people in. They were portly gentlemen, pleasant to behold, and now stood, with their hats off, in Scrooge's office. They had books and papers in their hands, and bowed to him.

"Scrooge and Marley's, I believe," said one of the gentlemen, referring to his list. "Have I the pleasure of addressing Mr. Scrooge or Mr. Marley?"

"Mr. Marley has been dead these seven years. He died seven years ago this very night."

"At this festive season of the year, Mr. Scrooge," said the gentleman, taking up a pen, "it is more than usually desirable that we should make some slight provision for the poor and destitute, who suffer greatly at the present time. Many thousands are in want of common necessaries; hundreds of thousands are in want of common comforts, sir."

"Are there no prisons?"

"Plenty of prisons. But under the impression that they scarcely furnish Christian cheer of mind or body to the unoffending multitude, a few of us are endeavoring to raise a fund to buy the poor some meat and drink, and means of warmth. We choose this time, because it is a time, of all others, when want is keenly felt, and abundance rejoices. What shall I put you down for?"

"Nothing!"

"You wish to be anonymous?"

"I wish to be left alone. Since you ask me what I wish, gentlemen, that is my answer. I don't make merry myself at Christmas, and I can't afford to make idle people merry. I help to support the prisons and workhouses — they cost enough — and those who are badly off must go there."

"Many can't go there; and many would rather die."

"If they would rather die, they had better do it, and decrease the surplus population."

At length the hour of shutting up the countinghouse arrived. With an ill will Scrooge, dismounting from his stool, tacitly[6] admitted the fact to the expectant clerk in the tank, who instantly snuffed his candle out and put on his hat.

"You want all day tomorrow, I suppose?"

"If quite convenient, sir."

"It's not convenient, and it's not fair. If I was to stop half a crown for it, you'd think yourself mightily ill-used, I'll be bound?"

"Yes, sir."

"And yet you don't think *me* ill-used when I pay a day's wages for no work."

"It's only once a year, sir."

"A poor excuse for picking a man's pocket every twenty-fifth of December! But I suppose you must have the whole day. Be here all the earlier *next* morning."

---

6. **tacitly** (tăs′ĭt-lē): without speaking.

The clerk promised that he would, and Scrooge walked out with a growl. The office was closed in a twinkling, and the clerk, with the long ends of his white comforter dangling below his waist (for he boasted no greatcoat), went down a slide, at the end of a lane of boys, twenty times, in honor of its being Christmas Eve, and then ran home as hard as he could pelt, to play at blindman's buff.

Scrooge took his melancholy dinner in his usual melancholy tavern; and having read all the newspapers and beguiled[7] the rest of the evening with his banker's book, went home to bed. He lived in chambers which had once belonged to his deceased partner. They were a gloomy suite of rooms in a lowering[8] pile of a building up a yard. The building was old enough now, and dreary enough, for nobody lived in it but Scrooge, the other rooms being all let out as offices.

Now it is a fact that there was nothing at all particular about the knocker on the door of his house, except that it was very large; also, that Scrooge had seen it, night and morning, during his whole residence in that place; also, that Scrooge had as little of what is called fancy[9] about him as any man in the city of London. And yet Scrooge, having his key in the lock of the door, saw in the knocker, without its undergoing any intermediate process of change, not a knocker, but Marley's face.

Marley's face, with a dismal light about it, like a bad lobster in a dark cellar. It was not angry or ferocious, but it looked at Scrooge as Marley used to look—ghostly spectacles turned up upon its ghostly forehead.

As Scrooge looked fixedly at this phenomenon, it was a knocker again. He said, "Pooh,

pooh!" and closed the door with a bang.

The sound resounded through the house like thunder. Every room above, and every cask in the wine merchant's cellars below, appeared to have a separate peal of echoes of its own. Scrooge was not a man to be frightened by echoes. He fastened the door and walked across the hall and up the stairs. Slowly, too, trimming his candle as he went.

Up Scrooge went, not caring a button for its being very dark. Darkness is cheap, and Scrooge liked it. But before he shut his heavy door, he walked through his rooms to see that all was right. He had just enough recollection of the face to desire to do that.

Sitting room, bedroom, lumber room,[10] all as they should be. Nobody under the table,

---

7. **beguiled** (bĭ-gīld'): spent or whiled away.
8. **lowering** (lou'ər-ĭng): dark and threatening.
9. **fancy:** imagination.

10. **lumber room:** storeroom.

nobody under the sofa; a small fire in the grate; spoon and basin ready; and the little saucepan of gruel (Scrooge had a cold in his head) upon the hob.[11] Nobody under the bed; nobody in the closet; nobody in his dressing gown, which was hanging up in a suspicious attitude against the wall. Lumber room as usual. Old fireguards, old shoes, two fish baskets, washing stand on three legs, and a poker.

Quite satisfied, he closed his door and locked himself in; double-locked himself in, which was not his custom. Thus secured against surprise, he took off his cravat,[12] put on his dressing gown and slippers and his nightcap, and sat down before the very low fire to take his gruel.

As he threw his head back in the chair, his glance happened to rest upon a bell, a disused bell, that hung in the room and communicated, for some purpose now forgotten, with a chamber in the highest story of the building. It was with great astonishment, and with a strange inexplicable dread, that, as he looked, he saw this bell begin to swing. Soon it rang out loudly, and so did every bell in the house.

This was succeeded by a clanking noise, deep down below, as if some person were dragging a heavy chain over the casks in the wine merchant's cellar.

Then he heard the noise much louder on the floors below; then coming up the stairs; then coming straight toward his door.

It came on through the heavy door, and a specter passed into the room before his eyes. And upon its coming in, the dying flame leaped up, as though it cried, "I know him! Marley's ghost!"

The same face, the very same. Marley in his pigtail, usual waistcoat, tights, and boots. His

body was transparent; so that Scrooge, observing him, and looking through his waistcoat, could see the two buttons on his coat behind.

Scrooge had often heard it said that Marley had no bowels,[13] but he had never believed it until now.

No, nor did he believe it even now. Though he looked the phantom through and through and saw it standing before him — though he felt the chilling influence of its death-cold eyes and noticed the very texture of the folded kerchief bound about its head and chin — he was still incredulous.

"How now!" said Scrooge, caustic and cold as ever. "What do you want with me?"

---

11. **hob:** a small shelf at the back or side of a fireplace, used to keep a kettle or a saucepan warm.
12. **cravat** (krə-văt'): a necktie, or a scarf resembling a necktie.

13. **bowels:** the intestines, which used to be regarded as the source of pity and mercy. When people said Marley had no bowels, they meant that he was cruel.

"Much!"—Marley's voice, no doubt about it.

"Who are you?"

"Ask me who I *was.*"

"Who *were* you then?"

"In life I was your partner, Jacob Marley."

"Can you—can you sit down?"

"I can."

"Do it, then."

Scrooge asked the question because he didn't know whether a ghost so transparent might find himself in a condition to take a chair, and felt that, in the event of its being impossible, it might involve the necessity of an embarrassing explanation. But the ghost sat down on the opposite side of the fireplace, as if he were quite used to it.

"You don't believe in me."

"I don't."

"What evidence would you have of my reality beyond that of your senses?"

"I don't know."

"Why do you doubt your senses?"

"Because a little thing affects them. A slight disorder of the stomach makes them cheats. You may be an undigested bit of beef, a blot of mustard, a crumb of cheese, a fragment of an underdone potato. There's more of gravy than of grave about you, whatever you are!"

Scrooge was not much in the habit of cracking jokes, nor did he feel in his heart by any means waggish then. The truth is that he tried to be smart, as a means of distracting his own attention and keeping down his horror.

But how much greater was his horror when, the phantom taking off the bandage round its head, as if it were too warm to wear indoors, its lower jaw dropped down upon its breast!

"Mercy! Dreadful apparition, why do you trouble me? Why do spirits walk the earth, and why do they come to me?"

"It is required of every man that the spirit within him should walk abroad among his fellowmen and travel far and wide; and if that spirit goes not forth in life, it is condemned to do so after death. I cannot tell you all I would. A very little more is permitted to me. I cannot rest, I cannot stay, I cannot linger anywhere. My spirit never walked beyond our counting-house—mark me!—in life my spirit never roved beyond the narrow limits of our money-changing hole; and weary journeys lie before me!"

"Seven years dead. And traveling all the time? You travel fast?"

"On the wings of the wind."

"You might have got over a great quantity of ground in seven years."

"O blind man, blind man! not to know that ages of incessant labor by immortal creatures for this earth must pass into eternity before the good of which it is susceptible is all developed.[14] Not to know that any Christian spirit working kindly in its little sphere, whatever it may be, will find its mortal life too short for its vast means of usefulness. Not to know that no space of regret can make amends for one life's opportunities misused! Yet I was like this man; I once was like this man!"

"But you were always a good man of business, Jacob," faltered Scrooge, who now began to apply this to himself.

"Business!" cried the ghost, wringing its hands again. "Mankind was my business. The common welfare was my business; charity, mercy, forbearance, benevolence, were all my business. The dealings of my trade were but a drop of water in the comprehensive ocean of my business!"

Scrooge was very much dismayed to hear

---

14. **ages . . . developed:** In other words, heavenly spirits must work for countless years before the goodness that is possible in the world can come into being.

the specter going on at this rate, and began to quake exceedingly.

"Hear me! My time is nearly gone."

"I will. But don't be hard upon me! Don't be flowery, Jacob! Pray!"

"I am here tonight to warn you that you have yet a chance and hope of escaping my fate. A chance and hope of my procuring,[15] Ebenezer."

"You were always a good friend to me Thankee!"

"You will be haunted by three spirits."

"Is that the chance and hope you mentioned, Jacob? I—I think I'd rather not."

"Without their visits, you cannot hope to shun the path I tread. Expect the first tomorrow night, when the bell tolls one. Expect the second on the next night at the same hour. The third, upon the next night, when the last stroke of twelve has ceased to vibrate. Look to see me no more; and look that, for your own sake, you remember what has passed between us!"

It walked backward from him; and at every step it took, the window raised itself a little, so that, when the apparition reached it, it was wide open.

Scrooge closed the window, and examined the door by which the ghost had entered. It was double-locked, as he had locked it with his own hands, and the bolts were undisturbed. Scrooge tried to say, "Humbug!" but stopped at the first syllable. And being, from the emotion he had undergone, or the fatigues of the day, or his glimpse of the invisible world, or the dull[16] conversation of the ghost, or the lateness of the hour, much in need of repose, he went straight to bed, without undressing, and fell asleep on the instant.

---

15. **of my procuring:** that I got for you.
16. **dull:** here, gloomy.

Stave Two: The First of the Three Spirits

When Scrooge awoke, it was so dark that, looking out of bed, he could scarcely distinguish the transparent window from the opaque walls of his chamber, until suddenly the church clock tolled a deep, dull, hollow, melancholy ONE.

Light flashed up in the room upon the instant, and the curtains of his bed were drawn aside by a strange figure—like a child; yet not so like a child as like an old man, viewed through some supernatural medium, which gave him the appearance of having receded from the view and being diminished to a child's proportions. Its hair, which hung about its neck and down its back, was white as if with age; and yet the face had not a wrinkle in it, and the tenderest bloom was on the skin. It held a branch of fresh green holly in its hand; and, in singular contradiction of that wintry emblem, had its dress trimmed with summer flowers. But the strangest thing about it was that from the crown of its head there sprang a bright, clear jet of light by which all this was visible; and which was doubtless the occasion of its using, in its duller moments, a great extinguisher for a cap, which it now held under its arm.

"Are you the spirit, sir, whose coming was foretold to me?"

"I am!"

"Who and what are you?"

"I am the Ghost of Christmas Past."

"Long past?"

"No. Your past. The things that you will see with me are shadows of the things that have been; they will have no consciousness of us."

Scrooge then made bold to inquire what business brought him there.

"Your welfare. Rise and walk with me!"

It would have been in vain for Scrooge to plead that the weather and the hour were not adapted to pedestrian purposes; that bed was warm, and the thermometer a long way below freezing; that he was clad but lightly in his slippers, dressing gown, and nightcap; and that he had a cold upon him at that time. The grasp, though gentle as a woman's hand, was not to be resisted. He rose; but finding that the spirit made toward the window, clasped its robe in supplication.

"I am a mortal, and liable to fall."

"Bear but a touch of my hand *there*," said the spirit, laying it upon his heart, "and you shall be upheld in more than this!"

As the words were spoken, they passed through the wall and stood in the busy thoroughfares of a city. It was made plain enough by the dressing of the shops that here, too, it was Christmastime. The ghost stopped at a certain warehouse door and asked Scrooge if he knew it.

"Know it! I was apprenticed here!"

They went in. At sight of an old gentleman in a Welsh wig, sitting behind such a high desk that, if he had been two inches taller, he must have knocked his head against the ceiling, Scrooge cried in great excitement: "Why, it's old Fezziwig! Bless his heart, it's Fezziwig, alive again!"

Old Fezziwig laid down his pen and looked up at the clock, which pointed to the hour of seven. He rubbed his hands; adjusted his capacious waistcoat; laughed all over himself, from his shoes to his organ of benevolence;[17] and called out in a comfortable, oily, rich, fat, jovial voice: "Yo ho, there! Ebenezer! Dick!"

A living and moving picture of Scrooge's former self, a young man, came briskly in, accompanied by his fellow apprentice.

---

17. **organ of benevolence** (bə-nĕv'ə-ləns): the part of the head where the forehead meets the crown.

"Dick Wilkins, to be sure!" said Scrooge to the ghost. "My old fellow 'prentice, bless me, yes. There he is. He was very much attached to me, was Dick. Poor Dick! Dear, dear!"

"Yo ho, my boys!" said Fezziwig. "No more work tonight. Christmas Eve, Dick. Christmas, Ebenezer! Let's have the shutters up, before a man can say 'Jack Robinson'! Clear away, my lads, and let's have lots of room here!"

Clear away! There was nothing they wouldn't have cleared away, or couldn't have cleared away, with old Fezziwig looking on. It was done in a minute. Every movable was packed off, as if it were dismissed from public life forevermore; the floor was swept and watered, the lamps were trimmed, fuel was heaped upon the fire; and the warehouse was as snug and warm and dry and bright a ballroom as you would desire to see on a winter night.

In came a fiddler with a music book, and went up to the lofty desk, and made an orchestra of it, and tuned like fifty stomachaches. In came Mrs. Fezziwig, one vast substantial smile. In came the three Miss Fezziwigs, beaming and lovable. In came the six young followers whose hearts they broke. In came all the young men and women employed in the business. In came the housemaid, with her cousin, the baker. In came the cook, with her brother's particular friend, the milkman. In they all came one after another; some shyly, some boldly, some gracefully, some awkwardly, some pushing, some pulling; in they all came, anyhow and everyhow. Away they all went, twenty couples at once; hands half round and back again the other way; down the middle and up again; round and round in various stages of affectionate grouping; old top couple always turning up in the wrong place; new top couple starting off again, as soon as they got there; all top couples at last, and not a bottom one to help them. When this result was brought about, old Fezziwig, clapping his hands to stop the dance, cried out, "Well done"; and the fiddler plunged his hot face into a pot of porter[18] especially provided for that purpose.

There were more dances, and there were forfeits[19] and more dances, and there was cake, and there was negus,[20] and there was a great piece of cold roast, and there was a great piece of cold boiled,[21] and there were mince pies, and plenty of beer. But the great effect of the evening came after the roast and boiled,

---

18. **porter:** dark brown beer.
19. **forfeits** (fôr′fĭts): a game in which the players must forfeit, or give up, something if they lose.
20. **negus** (nē′gəs): punch.
21. **boiled:** boiled beef.

when the fiddler struck up "Sir Roger de Coverley."[22] Then old Fezziwig stood out to dance with Mrs. Fezziwig. Top couple, too; with a good stiff piece of work cut out for them; three- or four-and-twenty pairs of partners; people who were not to be trifled with; people who *would* dance, and had no notion of walking.

But if they had been twice as many—four times—old Fezziwig would have been a match for them, and so would Mrs. Fezziwig. As to *her*, she was worthy to be his partner in every sense of the term. A positive light appeared to issue from Fezziwig's calves. They shone in every part of the dance. You couldn't have predicted, at any given time, what would become of 'em next. And when old Fezziwig and Mrs. Fezziwig had gone all through the dance—advance and retire, turn your partner, bow and curtsy, corkscrew, thread the needle, and back again to your place—Fezziwig "cut"—cut so deftly, that he appeared to wink with his legs.

When the clock struck eleven this domestic ball broke up. Mr. and Mrs. Fezziwig took their stations, one on either side of the door, and, shaking hands with every person individually as he or she went out, wished him or her a Merry Christmas. When everybody had retired but the two 'prentices, they did the same to them; and thus the cheerful voices died away, and the lads were left to their beds, which were under a counter in the back shop.

"A small matter," said the ghost, "to make these silly folks so full of gratitude. He has spent but a few pounds of your mortal money—three or four perhaps. Is that so much that he deserves this praise?"

"It isn't that," said Scrooge, heated by the remark, and speaking unconsciously like his former, not his latter, self—"it isn't that,

---

22. **"Sir Roger de Coverley":** a square-dance tune.

Spirit. He has the power to render us happy or unhappy; to make our service light or burdensome; a pleasure or a toil. Say that his power lies in words and looks; in things so slight and insignificant that it is impossible to add and count 'em up: what then? The happiness he gives is quite as great as if it cost a fortune."

He felt the spirit's glance, and stopped.

"What is the matter?"

"Nothing particular."

"Something, I think?"

"No, no. I should like to be able to say a word or two to my clerk just now. That's all."

"My time grows short," observed the spirit. "Quick!"

This was not addressed to Scrooge, or to anyone whom he could see, but it produced an immediate effect. For again he saw himself. He was older now; a man in the prime of life.

He was not alone, but sat by the side of a fair young girl in a black dress, in whose eyes there were tears.

"It matters little," she said softly to Scrooge's former self. "To you very little. Another idol has displaced me; and if it can comfort you in time to come, as I would have tried to do, I have no just cause to grieve."

"What idol has displaced you?"

"A golden one. You fear the world too much. I have seen your nobler aspirations fall off one by one, until the master passion, gain, engrosses you. Have I not?"

"What then? Even if I have grown so much wiser, what then? I am not changed toward you. Have I ever sought release from our engagement?"

"In words, no. Never."

"In what, then?"

"In a changed nature; in an altered spirit; in another atmosphere of life; another hope as its great end. If you were free today, tomorrow, yesterday, can even I believe that you would choose a dowerless[23] girl; or, choosing her, do I not know that your repentance and regret would surely follow? I do; and I release you. With a full heart, for the love of him you once were."

"Spirit! remove me from this place."

"I told you these were shadows of the things that have been," said the ghost. "That they are what they are, do not blame me!"

"Remove me!" Scrooge exclaimed. "I cannot bear it! Leave me! Take me back! Haunt me no longer!"

As he struggled with the spirit, he was conscious of being exhausted and overcome by an irresistible drowsiness; and, further, of being in his own bedroom. He had barely time to reel to bed before he sank into a heavy sleep.

Stave Three:
The Second of the Three Spirits

Scrooge awoke in his own bedroom. There was no doubt about that. But it and his own adjoining sitting room, into which he shuffled in his slippers, attracted by a great light there, had undergone a surprising transformation. The walls and ceiling were so hung with living green that it looked a perfect grove. The leaves of holly, mistletoe, and ivy reflected back the light, as if so many little mirrors had been scattered there; and such a mighty blaze went roaring up the chimney, as that petrifaction[24] of a hearth had never known in Scrooge's time, or Marley's, or for many and many a winter season gone. Heaped upon the

---

23. **dowerless** (dou′ər-lĭs): without a dowry, the money and property that a woman formerly brought to her husband at marriage.

24. **petrifaction** (pĕt′rə-făk′shən): something petrified, or turning to stone. The hearth, or fireplace, is cold and hard because it has never known a generous fire.

floor, to form a kind of throne, were turkeys, geese, game, brawn,[25] great joints of meat, suckling pigs, long wreaths of sausages, mince pies, plum puddings, barrels of oysters, red-hot chestnuts, cherry-cheeked apples, juicy oranges, luscious pears, immense twelfth-cakes,[26] and great bowls of punch. In easy state upon this couch there sat a giant glorious to see, who bore a glowing torch, in shape not unlike Plenty's horn, and who raised it high to shed its light on Scrooge, as he came peeping round the door.

"Come in—come in! and know me better, man! I am the Ghost of Christmas Present. Look upon me! You have never seen the like of me before?"

"Never."

"Have never walked forth with the younger members of my family; meaning (for I am very young) my elder brothers born in these later years?" pursued the phantom.

"I don't think I have; I am afraid I have not. Have you had many brothers, Spirit?"

"More than eighteen hundred."[27]

"A tremendous family to provide for! Spirit, conduct me where you will. I went forth last night on compulsion, and I learned a lesson which is working now. Tonight, if you have aught to teach me, let me profit by it."

"Touch my robe!"

Scrooge did as he was told, and held it fast.

The room and its contents all vanished instantly, and they stood in the city streets upon a snowy Christmas morning.

Scrooge and the ghost passed on, invisible, straight to Scrooge's clerk's; and on the threshold of the door the spirit smiled, and stopped to bless Bob Cratchit's dwelling with the sprinklings of his torch. Think of that! Bob had but fifteen "bob"[28] a week himself; he pocketed on Saturdays but fifteen copies of his Christian name; and yet the Ghost of Christmas Present blessed his four-roomed house!

Then up rose Mrs. Cratchit, Cratchit's wife, dressed out but poorly in a twice-turned[29] gown, but brave in ribbons, which are cheap and make a goodly show for sixpence; and she laid the cloth, assisted by Belinda Cratchit, second of her daughters, also brave in ribbons; while Master Peter Cratchit plunged a fork into the saucepan of potatoes, and, getting the corners of his monstrous shirt collar (Bob's private property, conferred upon his son and heir in honor of the day) into his mouth, rejoiced to find himself so gallantly attired, and yearned to show his linen in the fashionable parks. And now two smaller Cratchits, boy and girl, came tearing in, screaming that outside the baker's[30] they had smelled the goose and known it for their own; and basking in luxurious thoughts of sage and onion, these young Cratchits danced about the table, and exalted Master Peter Cratchit to the skies, while he (not proud, although his collar nearly choked him) blew the fire until the slow potatoes, bubbling up, knocked loudly at the saucepan lid to be let out and peeled.

"What has ever got your precious father then?" said Mrs. Cratchit. "And your brother Tiny Tim! And Martha warn't as late last Christmas Day by half an hour!"

---

25. **brawn:** boar meat.
26. **twelfth-cakes:** fruitcakes made for Epiphany, or Twelfth Day, a holiday that occurs on January 6, twelve days after Christmas.
27. **More . . . hundred:** Since this story was written in 1843, the Ghost of Christmas Present would have more than eighteen hundred brothers.

28. **"bob":** slang for "shilling" (or "shillings"), a former British coin worth one twentieth of a pound.
29. **twice-turned:** remade twice so that worn parts would not show.
30. **the baker's:** In the days when people of small means had fireplaces but no ovens, they would rent space in the local baker's oven to roast poultry or large pieces of meat.

"Here's Martha, Mother!" said a girl, appearing as she spoke.

"Here's Martha, Mother!" cried the two young Cratchits. "Hurrah! There's *such* a goose, Martha!"

"Why, bless your heart alive, my dear, how late you are!" said Mrs. Cratchit, kissing her a dozen times, and taking off her shawl and bonnet for her.

"We'd a deal of work to finish up last night," replied the girl, "and had to clear away this morning, Mother!"

"Well! Never mind so long as you are come," said Mrs. Cratchit. "Sit ye down before the fire, my dear, and have a warm, Lord bless ye!"

"No, no! There's Father coming," cried the two young Cratchits, who were everywhere at once. "Hide, Martha, hide!"

So Martha hid herself, and in came little Bob, the father, with at least three feet of comforter, exclusive of the fringe, hanging down before him; and his threadbare clothes darned up and brushed, to look seasonable; and Tiny Tim upon his shoulder. Alas for Tiny Tim, he bore a little crutch and had his limbs supported by an iron frame!

"Why, where's our Martha?" cried Bob Cratchit, looking round.

"Not coming," said Mrs. Cratchit.

"Not coming!" said Bob, with a sudden declension[31] in his high spirits; for he had been Tim's blood horse all the way from church, and had come home rampant[32] — "not coming upon Christmas Day!"

Martha didn't like to see him disappointed, if it were only in joke; so she came out prematurely from behind the closet door, and ran into his arms, while the two young Cratchits hustled Tiny Tim, and bore him off into the washhouse, that he might hear the pudding singing in the copper.

"And how did little Tim behave?" asked Mrs. Cratchit, when she had rallied Bob on his credulity,[33] and Bob had hugged his daughter to his heart's content.

"As good as gold," said Bob, "and better. Somehow he gets thoughtful, sitting by himself so much, and thinks the strangest things you ever heard. He told me, coming home, that he hoped the people saw him in the church because he was a cripple, and it might be pleasant to them to remember, upon Christmas Day, who made lame beggars walk and blind men see."

Bob's voice was tremulous when he told them this, and trembled more when he said that Tiny Tim was growing strong and hearty.

His active little crutch was heard upon the floor, and back came Tiny Tim before another word was spoken, escorted by his brother and sister to his stool beside the fire; and while Bob, turning up his cuffs — as if, poor fellow, they were capable of being made more shabby — compounded some hot mixture in a jug with gin and lemons, and stirred it round and round, and put it on the hob to simmer, Master Peter and the two ubiquitous[34] young Cratchits went to fetch the goose, with which they soon returned in high procession.

Mrs. Cratchit made the gravy (ready beforehand in a little saucepan) hissing hot; Master Peter mashed the potatoes with incredible vigor; Miss Belinda sweetened up the applesauce; Martha dusted the hot plates; Bob took Tiny Tim beside him in a tiny corner at the table; the two young Cratchits set chairs for everybody, not forgetting themselves, and, mounting guard upon their posts, crammed spoons into their mouths, lest they should shriek for goose before their turn came to be helped. At last the dishes were set on, and grace was said. It was succeeded by a breathless pause, as Mrs. Cratchit, looking slowly all along the carving knife, prepared to plunge it in the breast; but when she did, and when the long-expected gush of stuffing issued forth, one murmur of delight arose all around the board, and even Tiny Tim, excited by the two young Cratchits, beat on the table with the handle of his knife, and feebly cried; "Hurrah!"

There never was such a goose. Bob said he didn't believe there ever was such a goose cooked. Its tenderness and flavor, size and cheapness, were the themes of universal admiration. Eked out by applesauce and mashed potatoes, it was a sufficient dinner for the

---

31. **declension:** sinking or falling off.
32. **rampant:** rearing up like a horse; here, high-spirited.
33. **rallied Bob on his credulity** (krə-dōō′lə-tē): teased Bob for being so easily fooled by their joke.

34. **ubiquitous** (yōō-bik′wə-təs): being everywhere at the same time.

whole family; indeed, as Mrs. Cratchit said with great delight (surveying one small atom of a bone upon the dish), they hadn't ate[35] it all at last! Yet everyone had had enough, and the youngest Cratchits in particular were steeped in sage and onion to the eyebrows! But now, the plates being changed by Miss Belinda, Mrs. Cratchit left the room alone—too nervous to bear witnesses—to take the pudding up and bring it in.

Suppose it should not be done enough! Suppose it should break in turning out! Suppose somebody should have got over the wall of the backyard and stolen it while they were merry with the goose—a supposition at which the two young Cratchits became livid![36] All sorts of horrors were supposed.

Hallo! A great deal of steam! The pudding was out of the copper. A smell like a washing day! That was the cloth.[37] A smell like an eating house and a pastry cook's next door to each other, with a laundress' next door to that! That was the pudding! In half a minute Mrs. Cratchit entered—flushed but smiling proudly—with the pudding, like a speckled cannonball, so hard and firm, blazing in half of half a quartern[38] of ignited brandy and bedight[39] with Christmas holly stuck into the top.

Oh, a wonderful pudding! Bob Cratchit said, and calmly too, that he regarded it as the greatest success achieved by Mrs. Cratchit since their marriage. Mrs. Cratchit said that now the weight was off her mind, she would confess she had had her doubts about the quantity of flour. Everybody had something to

say about it, but nobody said or thought it was at all a small pudding for a large family. Any Cratchit would have blushed to hint at such a thing.

At last the dinner was all done, the cloth was cleared, the hearth swept, and the fire made up. The compound in the jug being tasted, and considered perfect, apples and oranges were put upon the table, and a shovelful of chestnuts on the fire.

Then all the Cratchit family drew round the hearth, in what Bob Cratchit called a circle, and at Bob Cratchit's elbow stood the family display of glass—two tumblers, and a custard cup without a handle.

These held the hot stuff from the jug, however, as well as golden goblets would have done; and Bob served it out with beaming looks, while the chestnuts on the fire spluttered and crackled noisily. Then Bob proposed:

"A Merry Christmas to us all, my dears. God bless us!"

Which all the family reechoed.

"God bless us every one!" said Tiny Tim, the last of all.

He sat very close to his father's side, upon his little stool. Bob held his withered little hand in his, as if he loved the child and wished to keep him by his side, and dreaded that he might be taken from him.

Scrooge raised his head speedily, on hearing his own name.

"Mr. Scrooge!" said Bob; "I'll give you Mr. Scrooge, the Founder of the Feast!"

"The Founder of the Feast indeed!" cried Mrs. Cratchit, reddening. "I wish I had him here. I'd give him a piece of my mind to feast upon, and I hope he'd have a good appetite for it."

"My dear," said Bob, "the children! Christmas Day."

"It should be Christmas Day, I am sure,"

---

35. **ate** (ĕt): an alternate form of *eaten*, used in Great Britain.
36. **livid:** pale.
37. **cloth:** The pudding was wrapped in cloth and then boiled.
38. **quartern:** one fourth of a pint.
39. **bedight** (bĭ-dīt'): decorated.

said she, "on which one drinks the health of such an odious, stingy, hard, unfeeling man as Mr. Scrooge. You know he is, Robert! Nobody knows it better than you do, poor fellow!"

"My dear," was Bob's mild answer, "Christmas Day."

"I'll drink his health for your sake and the day's," said Mrs. Cratchit, "not for his. Long life to him! A Merry Christmas and a Happy New Year! He'll be very merry and very happy, I have no doubt!"

The children drank the toast after her. It was the first of their proceedings which had no heartiness in it. Tiny Tim drank it last of all, but he didn't care twopence for it. Scrooge was the ogre of the family. The mention of his name cast a dark shadow on the party, which was not dispelled for full five minutes.

After it had passed away, they were ten times merrier than before from the mere relief of Scrooge the Baleful[40] being done with. Bob Cratchit told them how he had a situation in his eye for Master Peter, which would bring him, if obtained, full five and sixpence weekly. The two young Cratchits laughed tremendously at the idea of Peter's being a man of business; and Peter himself looked thoughtfully at the fire from between his collars, as if he were deliberating what particular investments he should favor when he came into the receipt of that bewildering income. Martha, who was a poor apprentice at a milliner's, then told them what kind of work she had to do, and how many hours she worked at a stretch, and how she meant to lie abed tomorrow morning for a good long rest — tomorrow being a holiday she passed at home. Also how she had seen a countess and a lord some days before, and how the lord "was much about as tall as Peter"; at which Peter pulled up his collars so high that you couldn't

40. **Baleful:** wretched.

have seen his head if you had been there. All this time the chestnuts and the jug went round and round; and by and by they had a song about a lost child traveling in the snow from Tiny Tim, who had a plaintive little voice, and sang it very well indeed.

There was nothing of high mark in this. They were not a handsome family; they were not well dressed; their shoes were far from being waterproof; their clothes were scanty; and Peter might have known, and very likely did, the inside of a pawnbroker's. But they were happy, grateful, pleased with one another, and contented with the time; and when they faded, and looked happier yet in the bright sprinklings of the spirit's torch at parting, Scrooge had his eye upon them, and especially on Tiny Tim, until the last.

It was a great surprise to Scrooge, as this scene vanished, to hear a hearty laugh. It was a much greater surprise to Scrooge to recognize it as his own nephew's, and to find himself in a bright, dry, gleaming room, with the spirit standing smiling by his side and looking at that same nephew.

It is a fair, even-handed, noble adjustment of things, that while there is infection in disease and sorrow, there is nothing in the world so irresistibly contagious as laughter and good humor. When Scrooge's nephew laughed, Scrooge's niece by marriage laughed as heartily as he. And their assembled friends, being not a bit behindhand, laughed out lustily.

"He said that Christmas was a humbug, as I live!" cried Scrooge's nephew. "He believed it, too!"

"More shame for him, Fred!" said Scrooge's niece, indignantly. Bless those women! they never do anything by halves. They are always in earnest.

She was very pretty; exceedingly pretty. With a dimpled, surprised-looking, capital face; a ripe little mouth that seemed made to be kissed—as no doubt it was; all kinds of good little dots about her chin that melted into one another when she laughed; and the sunniest pair of eyes you ever saw in any little creature's head. Altogether she was what you would have called provoking, but satisfactory, too. Oh, perfectly satisfactory.

"He's a comical old fellow," said Scrooge's nephew, "that's the truth, and not so pleasant as he might be. However, his offenses carry their own punishment, and I have nothing to say against him. Who suffers by his ill whims? Himself, always. Here he takes it into his head to dislike us, and he won't come and dine with us. What's the consequence? He don't lose much of a dinner."

"Indeed, I think he loses a very good dinner," interrupted Scrooge's niece. Everybody else said the same, and they must be allowed to have been competent judges, because they had just had dinner; and, with the dessert upon the table, were clustered round the fire, by lamplight.

"Well, I am very glad to hear it," said Scrooge's nephew, "because I haven't any great faith in these young housekeepers. What do *you* say, Topper?"

Topper clearly had his eye on one of Scrooge's niece's sisters, for he answered that a bachelor was a wretched outcast, who had no right to express an opinion on the subject. Whereat Scrooge's niece's sister—the plump one with the lace tucker,[41] not the one with the roses—blushed.

After tea they had some music. For they were a musical family and knew what they were about when they sang a glee or catch,[42] I can assure you—especially Topper, who could growl away in the bass like a good one, and

never swell the large veins in his forehead, or get red in the face over it.

But they didn't devote the whole evening to music. After a while they played at forfeits; for it is good to be children sometimes, and never better than at Christmas, when its mighty Founder was a child himself. There was first a game at blindman's buff though. And I no more believe Topper was really blinded than I believe he had eyes in his boots. Because the way in which he went after that plump sister in the lace tucker was an outrage on the credulity of human nature. Knocking down the fire irons, tumbling over

---

41. **tucker:** a covering for the neck and shoulders, something like a large collar.
42. **glee; catch:** songs for three or more voices, unaccompanied by instruments.

the chairs, bumping up against the piano, smothering himself among the curtains; wherever she went, there went he! He always knew where the plump sister was. He wouldn't catch anybody else. If you had fallen up against him, as some of them did, and stood there, he would have made a feint[43] of endeavoring to seize you, which would have been an affront to your understanding, and would instantly have sidled off in the direction of the plump sister.

"Here is a new game," said Scrooge. "One half-hour, Spirit, only one!"

It was a game called Yes and No, where Scrooge's nephew had to think of something, and the rest must find out what; he only answering to their questions Yes or No, as the case was. The fire of questioning to which he was exposed elicited from him that he was thinking of an animal, a live animal, rather a disagreeable animal, a savage animal, an animal that growled and grunted sometimes, and talked sometimes, and lived in London, and walked about the streets, and wasn't made a show of, and wasn't led by anybody, and didn't live in a menagerie, and was never killed in a market, and was not a horse, or an ass, or a cow, or a bull, or a tiger, or a dog, or a pig, or a cat, or a bear. At every new question put to him, this nephew burst into a fresh roar of laughter, and was so inexpressibly tickled, that he was obliged to get up off the sofa and stamp. At last the plump sister cried out: "I have found it out! I know what it is, Fred! I know what it is!"

"What is it?" cried Fred.

"It's your Uncle Scro-o-o-oge!"

Which it certainly was. Admiration was the universal sentiment, though some objected that the reply to "Is it a bear?" ought to have been "Yes."

Uncle Scrooge had imperceptibly become so gay and light of heart, that he would have drunk to the unconscious company in an inaudible speech. But the whole scene passed off in the breath of the last word spoken by his nephew; and he and the spirit were again upon their travels.

Much they saw, and far they went, and many homes they visited, but always with a happy end. The spirit stood beside sickbeds, and they were cheerful; on foreign lands, and they were close at home; by struggling men, and they were patient in their greater hope; by poverty, and it was rich. In almshouse, hospital, and jail, in misery's every refuge, where vain man in his little brief authority had not made fast the door and barred the spirit out, he left his blessing, and taught Scrooge his precepts.[44] Suddenly, as they stood together in an open place, the bell struck twelve.

Scrooge looked about him for the ghost, and saw it no more. As the last stroke ceased to vibrate, he remembered the prediction of old Jacob Marley, and, lifting up his eyes, beheld a solemn phantom, draped and hooded, coming like a mist along the ground toward him.

Stave Four:
The Last of the Spirits

The phantom slowly, gravely, silently approached. When it came near him, Scrooge bent down upon his knee; for in the air through which this spirit moved it seemed to scatter gloom and mystery.

It was shrouded in a deep black garment, which concealed its head, its face, its form, and left nothing of it visible save one outstretched hand. He knew no more, for the spirit neither spoke nor moved.

"I am in the presence of the Ghost of

---

43. **feint** (fānt): pretense.

44. **precepts** (prē′sĕpts′): rules of living.

Christmas Yet to Come? Ghost of the Future! I fear you more than any specter I have seen. But as I know your purpose is to do me good, and as I hope to live to be another man from what I was, I am prepared to bear you company, and do it with a thankful heart. Will you not speak to me?''

It gave him no reply. The hand was pointed straight before them.

"Lead on! Lead on! The night is waning fast, and it is precious time to me, I know. Lead on, Spirit!''

They scarcely seemed to enter the city; for the city rather seemed to spring up about them. But there they were in the heart of it; on 'Change, among the merchants.

The spirit stopped beside one little knot of businessmen. Observing that the hand was pointed to them, Scrooge advanced to listen to their talk.

"No," said a great fat man with a monstrous chin. "I don't know much about it either way. I only know he's dead.''

"When did he die?" inquired another.

"Last night, I believe.''

"Why, what was the matter with him? I thought he'd never die.''

"Goodness knows," said the first, with a yawn.

"What has he done with his money?" asked a red-faced gentleman.

"I haven't heard," said the man with the large chin. "Company, perhaps. He hasn't left it to me. That's all I know. Bye-bye.''

Scrooge was at first inclined to be surprised that the spirit should attach importance to conversation apparently so trivial, but feeling assured that it must have some hidden purpose, he set himself to consider what it was likely to be. It could scarcely be supposed to have any bearing on the death of Jacob, his old partner, for that was past, and this ghost's province was the future.

He looked about in that very place for his own image; but another man stood in his accustomed corner, and though the clock pointed to his usual time of day for being there, he saw no likeness of himself among the multitudes that poured in through the porch. It gave him little surprise, however; for he had been revolving in his mind a change of life, and he thought and hoped he saw his newborn resolutions carried out in this.

They left this busy scene and went into an obscure part of the town to a low shop where iron, old rags, bottles, bones, and greasy offal[45] were bought. A gray-haired rascal, of great age, sat smoking his pipe. Scrooge and the phantom came into the presence of this man just as a woman with a heavy bundle slunk into the shop. But she had scarcely entered, when another woman, similarly laden, came in too; and she was closely followed by a man in faded black. After a short period of blank astonishment, in which the old man with the pipe had joined them, they all three burst into a laugh.

"Let the charwoman[46] alone to be the first!" cried she who had entered first. "Let the laundress alone to be the second; and let the undertaker's man alone to be the third. Look here, old Joe, here's a chance! If we haven't all three met here without meaning it!''

"You couldn't have met in a better place. You were made free of it long ago, you know; and the other two ain't strangers. What have you got to sell? What have you got to sell?''

"Half a minute's patience, Joe, and you shall see.''

"What odds then! What odds, Mrs. Dilber?" said the woman. "Every person has a right to

---

45. **offal** (ôf′əl): the waste parts of an animal that has been butchered for meat.
46. **charwoman:** a woman employed to clean a house or an office.

take care of themselves. *He* always did! Who's the worse for the loss of a few things like these? Not a dead man, I suppose."

Mrs. Dilber, whose manner was remarkable for general propitiation,[47] said, "No, indeed, ma'am."

"If he wanted to keep 'em after he was dead, a wicked old screw, why wasn't he natural in his lifetime? If he had been, he'd have had somebody to look after him when he was struck with death, instead of lying gasping out his last there, alone by himself."

"It's the truest word that ever was spoke, it's a judgment on him."

"I wish it was a little heavier judgment, and it should have been, you may depend upon it, if I could have laid my hands on anything else. Open that bundle, old Joe, and let me know the value of it. Speak out plain. I'm not afraid to be the first, nor afraid for them to see it."

Joe went down on his knees for the greater convenience of opening the bundle, and dragged out a large and heavy roll of some dark stuff.

"What do you call this? Bed curtains!"

"Ah! Bed curtains! Don't drop that oil upon the blankets, now."

"*His* blankets?"

"Whose else's do you think? He isn't likely to take cold without 'em, I dare say. Ah! You may look through that shirt till your eyes ache; but you won't find a hole in it, nor a threadbare place. It's the best he had, and a fine one too. They'd have wasted it by dressing him up in it, if it hadn't been for me."

Scrooge listened to this dialogue in horror.

"Spirit! I see, I see. The case of this unhappy man might be my own. My life tends that way, now. Merciful Heaven, what is this?"

The scene had changed, and now he almost touched a bare, uncurtained bed. A pale light, rising in the outer air, fell straight upon this bed; and on it, unwatched, unwept, uncared for, was the body of this plundered unknown man.

"Spirit, let me see some tenderness connected with a death, or this dark chamber, Spirit, will be forever present to me."

The ghost conducted him to poor Bob Cratchit's house—the dwelling he had visited before—and found the mother and the children seated round the fire.

Quiet. Very quiet. The noisy little Cratchits were as still as statues in one corner and sat looking up at Peter, who had a book before him. The mother and her daughters were engaged in needlework. But surely they were very quiet!

" 'And he took a child, and set him in the midst of them.' "[48]

Where had Scrooge heard those words? He had not dreamed them. The boy must have read them out, as he and the spirit crossed the threshold. Why did he not go on?

The mother laid her work upon the table and put her hand up to her face. "The color hurts my eyes," she said.

The color? Ah, poor Tiny Tim!

"They're better now again. It makes them weak by candlelight; and I wouldn't show weak eyes to your father when he comes home, for the world. It must be near his time."

"Past it rather," Peter answered, shutting up his book. "But I think he has walked a little slower than he used, these few last evenings, Mother."

"I have known him walk with—I have known him walk with Tiny Tim upon his shoulder, very fast indeed."

---

47. **propitiation** (prō-pĭsh′ē-ā′shən): ability to keep the peace.

48. **"And he . . . them"**: a quotation from Mark 9:36.

"And so have I," cried Peter. "Often."

"And so have I," exclaimed another. So had all.

"But he was very light to carry, and his father loved him so, that it was no trouble—no trouble. And there is your father at the door!"

She hurried out to meet him; and little Bob in his comforter—he had need of it, poor fellow—came in. His tea was ready for him on the hob, and they all tried who should help him to it most. Then the two young Cratchits got upon his knees and laid, each child, a little cheek against his face, as if they said, "Don't mind it, Father. Don't be grieved!"

Bob was very cheerful with them, and spoke pleasantly to all the family. He looked at the work upon the table, and praised the industry and speed of Mrs. Cratchit and the girls. They would be done long before Sunday, he said.

"Sunday! You went today, then, Robert?"

"Yes, my dear," returned Bob. "I wish you could have gone. It would have done you good to see how green a place it is. But you'll see it often. I promised him that I would walk there on a Sunday. My little, little child! My little child!"

He broke down all at once. He couldn't help it. If he could have helped it, he and his child would have been farther apart, perhaps, than they were.

"Specter," said Scrooge, "something informs me that our parting moment is at hand. I know it, but I know not how. Tell me what man that was, with the covered face, whom we saw lying dead?"

The Ghost of Christmas Yet to Come conveyed him to a dismal, wretched, ruinous churchyard.

The spirit stood among the graves, and pointed down to one.

"Before I draw nearer to that stone to which

you point, answer me one question. Are these the shadows of the things that will be, or are they shadows of the things that may be only?"

Still the ghost pointed downward to the grave by which it stood.

"Men's courses will foreshadow certain ends, to which, if persevered in, they must lead. But if the courses be departed from, the ends will change. Say it is thus with what you show me!"

The spirit was immovable as ever.

Scrooge crept toward it, trembling as he went; and following the finger, read upon the stone of the neglected grave his own name— EBENEZER SCROOGE.

"Am *I* that man who lay upon the bed? No, Spirit! Oh no, no! Spirit! hear me! I am not the man I was. I will not be the man I must have been but for this intercourse. Why show me this, if I am past all hope? Assure me that I yet may change these shadows you have shown me by an altered life."

For the first time the kind hand faltered.

"I will honor Christmas in my heart, and try to keep it all the year. I will live in the Past, the Present, and the Future. The spirits of all three shall strive within me. I will not shut out the lessons that they teach. Oh, tell me I may sponge away the writing on this stone!"

Holding up his hands in one last prayer to have his fate reversed, he saw an alteration in the phantom's hood and dress. It shrunk, collapsed, and dwindled down into a bedpost.

Stave Five: The End of It

Yes! and the bedpost was his own. The bed was his own, the room was his own. Best and happiest of all, the time before him was his own, to make amends in!

"I will live in the Past, the Present, and the Future!" Scrooge repeated, as he scrambled out of bed. "The spirits of all three shall strive within me. Oh, Jacob Marley! Heaven and the Christmastime be praised for this! I say it on my knees, old Jacob, on my knees!"

He was so fluttered and so glowing with his good intentions that his broken voice would scarcely answer to his call. He had been sobbing violently in his conflict with the spirit, and his face was wet with tears.

"They are not torn down," cried Scrooge, folding one of his bed curtains in his arms; "they are not torn down, rings and all. They are here; I am here; the shadows of the things that would have been may be dispelled. They will be. I know they will!"

His hands were busy with his garments all this time; turning them inside out, putting them on upside down, tearing them, mislaying them, making them parties to every kind of extravagance.

"I don't know what to do!" cried Scrooge, laughing and crying in the same breath, and making a perfect Laocoon[49] of himself with his stockings. "I am as light as a feather; I am as happy as an angel; I am as merry as a schoolboy; I am as giddy as a drunken man. A Merry Christmas to everybody! A Happy New Year to all the world. Hallo here! Whoop! Hallo!"

He had frisked into the sitting room, and was now standing there perfectly winded.

"There's the saucepan that the gruel was in!" cried Scrooge, starting off again and frisking round the fireplace. "There's the door by which the ghost of Jacob Marley entered! There's the corner where the Ghost of Christmas Present sat! There's the window

---

49. **Laocoon** (lā-ŏk′ō-ŏn′): a character in a Greek myth who was strangled by sea serpents.

where I saw the wandering spirits! It's all right; it's all true; it all happened. Ha, ha, ha!"

Really, for a man who had been out of practice for so many years, it was a splendid laugh, a most illustrious laugh. The father of a long, long line of brilliant laughs!

"I don't know what day of the month it is!" said Scrooge. "I don't know how long I've been among the spirits. I don't know anything. I'm quite a baby. Never mind. I don't care. I'd rather be a baby. Hallo! Whoop! Hallo here!"

He was checked in his transports,[50] by the churches' ringing out the lustiest peals he had ever heard. Clash, clang, hammer, ding, dong, bell. Bell, dong, ding, hammer, clang, clash! Oh, glorious, glorious!

Running to the window, he opened it and put out his head. No fog, no mist; clear, bright, jovial, stirring cold; cold, piping for the blood to dance to; golden sunlight; heavenly sky; sweet fresh air; merry bells. Oh, glorious. Glorious!

"What's today?" cried Scrooge, calling downward to a boy in Sunday clothes, who perhaps had loitered in to look about him.

"Eh?" returned the boy, with all his might of wonder.

"What's today, my fine fellow?" said Scrooge.

"Today!" replied the boy. "Why, CHRISTMAS DAY."

"It's Christmas Day!" said Scrooge to himself. "I haven't missed it. The spirits have done it all in one night. They can do anything they like. Of course they can. Of course they can. Hallo, my fine fellow?"

"Hallo!" returned the boy.

"Do you know the poulterer's,[51] in the next street but one, at the corner?" Scrooge inquired.

"I should hope I did," replied the lad.

"An intelligent boy!" said Scrooge. "A remarkable boy! Do you know whether they've sold the prize turkey that was hanging up there? Not the little prize turkey; the big one?"

"What, the one as big as me?" returned the boy.

"What a delightful boy!" said Scrooge. "It's a pleasure to talk to him. Yes, my buck!"

"It's hanging there now," replied the boy.

"Is it?" said Scrooge. "Go buy it."

"Walk-ER!"[52] exclaimed the boy.

"No, no," said Scrooge, "I am in earnest. Go and buy it, and tell 'em to bring it here, that I may give them the direction where to take it. Come back with the man, and I'll give you a shilling. Come back with him in less than five minutes, and I'll give you half a crown!"[53]

The boy was off like a shot. He must have had a steady hand at a trigger who could have got a shot off half so fast.

"I'll send it to Bob Cratchit's!" whispered Scrooge, rubbing his hands, and splitting with a laugh. "He shan't know who sends it. It's twice the size of Tiny Tim. No one ever made such a joke as sending it to Bob's will be!"

The hand in which he wrote the address was not a steady one, but write it he did, somehow, and went downstairs to open the street door, ready for the coming of the poulterer's man. As he stood there, waiting his arrival, the knocker caught his eye.

"I shall love it as long as I live!" cried Scrooge, patting it with his hand. "I scarcely ever looked at it before. What an honest expression it has in its face! It's a wonderful

---

50. **transports:** feelings of great joy.
51. **poulterer's:** shop where poultry is sold.

52. **Walk-ER!:** a slang word used to express disbelief. equivalent to "You're kidding!"
53. **half a crown:** a coin equal to one eighth of a pound.

knocker! Here's the turkey. Hallo! Whoop! How are you? Merry Christmas!"

It *was* a turkey! He could never have stood upon his legs, that bird. He would have snapped 'em off short in a minute, like sticks of sealing wax.

"Why, it's impossible to carry that to Camden Town," said Scrooge. "You must have a cab."

The chuckle with which he said this, and the chuckle with which he paid for the turkey, and the chuckle with which he paid for the cab, and the chuckle with which he recompensed the boy were only to be exceeded by the chuckle with which he sat down, breathless, in his chair again, and chuckled till he cried.

Shaving was not an easy task, for his hand continued to shake very much; and shaving requires attention, even when you don't dance while you are at it. But if he had cut the end of his nose off, he would have put a piece of sticking plaster over it, and been quite satisfied.

He dressed himself "all in his best," and at last got out into the streets. The people were by this time pouring forth, as he had seen them with the Ghost of Christmas Present; and walking with his hands behind him, Scrooge regarded everyone with a delighted smile. He looked so irresistibly pleasant, in a word, that three or four good-humored fellows said, "Good morning, sir! A Merry Christmas to you!" And Scrooge said often, afterward, that of all the blithe[54] sounds he had ever heard, those were the blithest in his ears.

He had not gone far, when coming on toward him he beheld the portly gentleman who had walked into his countinghouse the day before and said, "Scrooge and Marley's, I believe?" It sent a pang across his heart to think how this old gentleman would look upon him when they met; but he knew what path lay straight before him, and he took it.

"My dear sir," said Scrooge, quickening his pace, and taking the old gentleman by both his hands. "How do you do? I hope you succeeded yesterday. It was very kind of you. A Merry Christmas to you, sir!"

"Mr. Scrooge?"

"Yes," said Scrooge. "That is my name, and I fear it may not be pleasant to you. Allow me to ask your pardon. And will you have the goodness——" Here Scrooge whispered in his ear.

"Lord bless me!" cried the gentleman, as if his breath were gone. "My dear Mr. Scrooge, are you serious?"

"If you please," said Mr. Scrooge. "Not a farthing[55] less. A great many back payments are included in it, I assure you. Will you do me that favor?"

"My dear sir," said the other, shaking hands with him, "I don't know what to say to such munifi——"[56]

"Don't say anything, please," retorted Scrooge. "Come and see me. Will you come and see me?"

"I will!" cried the old gentleman. And it was clear he meant to do it.

"Thankee," said Scrooge. "I am much obliged to you. I thank you fifty times. Bless you!"

He went to church, and walked about the streets, and watched the people hurrying to

---

54. **blithe** (blīth): cheerful.

55. **farthing** (fär′thĭng): a former British coin worth one quarter of a penny.
56. **munificence** (myōō-nĭf′ə-səns): great generosity. Scrooge prevents the gentleman from finishing the word.

and fro, and patted children on the head, and questioned beggars, and looked down into the kitchens of houses, and up to the windows; and found that everything could yield him pleasure. He had never dreamed that any walk—that anything—could give him so much happiness. In the afternoon, he turned his steps toward his nephew's house.

He passed the door a dozen times before he had the courage to go up and knock. But he made a dash, and did it.

"Is your master at home, my dear?" said Scrooge to the girl. Nice girl! Very.

"Yes, sir."

"Where is he, my love?" said Scrooge.

"He's in the dining room, sir, along with mistress. I'll show you upstairs, if you please."

"Thankee. He knows me," said Scrooge, with his hand already on the dining-room lock. "I'll go in here, my dear."

He turned it gently, and sidled his face in round the door. They were looking at the table (which was spread out in great array); for these young housekeepers are always nervous on such points, and like to see that everything is right.

"Fred!" said Scrooge.

Dear heart alive, how his niece by marriage started! Scrooge had forgotten, for the moment, about her sitting in the corner with the footstool, or he wouldn't have done it, on any account.

"Why, bless my soul!" cried Fred. "Who's that?"

"It is I. Your Uncle Scrooge. I have come to dinner. Will you let me in, Fred?"

Let him in! It is a mercy he didn't shake his arm off. He was at home in five minutes. Nothing could be heartier. His niece looked just the same. So did Topper when *he* came. So did the plump sister when *she* came. So did everyone when *they* came. Wonderful party,

wonderful games, wonderful unanimity,[57] wonderful happiness!

But he was early at the office next morning. Oh, he was early there. If he could only be there first, and catch Bob Cratchit coming late! That was the thing he had set his heart upon.

And he did it; yes, he did! The clock struck nine. No Bob. A quarter past. No Bob. He was full eighteen minutes and a half behind his time. Scrooge sat with his door wide open, that he might see him come into the tank.

His hat was off before he opened the door; his comforter too. He was on his stool in a jiffy, driving away with his pen as if he were trying to overtake nine o'clock.

"Hallo!" growled Scrooge, in his accustomed voice as near as he could feign it. "What do you mean by coming here at this time of day?"

"I am very sorry, sir," said Bob. "I *am* behind my time."

"You are?" repeated Scrooge. "Yes, I think you are. Step this way, sir, if you please."

"It's only once a year, sir," pleaded Bob, appearing from the tank. "It shall not be repeated. I was making rather merry yesterday, sir."

"Now, I'll tell you what, my friend," said Scrooge, "I am not going to stand this sort of thing any longer. And therefore," he continued, leaping from his stool, and giving Bob such a dig in the waistcoat that he staggered back into the tank again, "and therefore I am about to raise your salary!"

Bob trembled, and got a little nearer to the ruler. He had a momentary idea of knocking Scrooge down with it, holding him, and calling to the people in the court for help and a strait waistcoat.[58]

---

57. **unanimity** (yo͞o'-nə-nĭ'mĭ-tē): agreement.
58. **strait waistcoat:** a straitjacket.

"A Merry Christmas, Bob!" said Scrooge, with an earnestness that could not be mistaken, as he clapped him on the back. "A merrier Christmas, Bob, my good fellow, than I have given you for many a year! I'll raise your salary, and endeavor to assist your struggling family, and we will discuss your affairs this very afternoon, over a Christmas bowl of smoking bishop,[59] Bob! Make up the fires, and buy another coal scuttle before you dot another *i*, Bob Cratchit!"

Scrooge was better than his word. He did it all, and infinitely more; and to Tiny Tim, who did *not* die, he was a second father. He became as good a friend, as good a master, and as good a man, as the good old city knew, or any other good old city, town, or borough, in the good old world. Some people laughed to see the alteration in him, but he let them laugh, and little heeded them; for he was wise enough to know that nothing ever happened on this globe, for good, at which some people did not have their fill of laughter in the outset; and knowing that such as these would be blind anyway, he thought it quite as well that they should wrinkle up their eyes in grins, as have the malady in less attractive forms. His own heart laughed, and that was quite enough for him.

He had no further intercourse with spirits, but lived upon the total-abstinence principle,[60] ever afterward; and it was always said of him that he knew how to keep Christmas well, if any man alive possessed the knowledge. May that be truly said of us, and all of us! And so, as Tiny Tim observed, God Bless Us, Every One!

---

59. **bishop:** a hot drink made of spiced port wine.
60. **total-abstinence** (ăb'stə·nəns) **principle:** the giving up of "spirits" completely, usually alcoholic "spirits," but here ghostly "spirits."

SEEKING MEANING

Character

1. "A Christmas Carol" contains many sequences with supernatural characters and events. Yet it is Ebenezer Scrooge, the human being, who is the center of attention. It is his transformation, or change, that forms the central action of the story. How is Scrooge different at the end of the story?

2. At the beginning of the story, the author must convince you that Scrooge is a hard-hearted miser. He does this through direct and indirect characterization. He *tells* you that Scrooge is a "tightfisted hand at the grindstone"—in other words, a stingy person. Locate other passages that *tell* you how miserly Scrooge is. You learn that in his countinghouse, Scrooge keeps the coalbox in his own room, and that his clerk tries to warm himself at his candle. This scene *shows* you how stingy Scrooge is. Point out other passages that *show* Scrooge's miserliness. (For a review of direct and indirect characterization, see page 269.)

3. During the visit of each Christmas spirit, Scrooge learns something about himself that helps him to change. At the end of Stave Two, for example, Scrooge realizes that he lost his fiancée through his own greed and stupidity. What does Scrooge learn about himself by the end of Stave Three? By the end of Stave Four?

4. At the beginning of the story, Scrooge is described as a "squeezing, wrenching, grasping, scraping, clutching, covetous old sinner!" What words would you use to describe him at the end of the story?

Plot

5. The plot of a story turns upon a conflict, or struggle, of some kind. What is the conflict in this story? (For a review of conflict, see page 252.)

6. The first thing the author tells you is that Marley is dead. What later events are being foreshadowed? You are also told that Scrooge is a man of no "fancy," or imagination (page 294). Why is it important to emphasize this fact about Scrooge?

7. Which scene in the story forms the climax, the point at which Scrooge makes a decision to change?

Setting

8. An important part of the action of the story is set in Scrooge's rooms. In what way are the rooms a reflection of Scrooge's character? How is this setting transformed, or changed, by the appearance of the Ghost of Christmas Present? How is the spirit of Christmas reflected in Fezziwig's warehouse? In the homes of Bob Cratchit and of Scrooge's nephew?

Theme

9. Marley's ghost tells Scrooge, "Mankind was my business . . . charity, mercy, forbearance, benevolence, were all my business" (page 296). What does the word *business* mean in Marley's statement? How do you know by the end of the story that Scrooge has made mankind *his* business? What does the story suggest is everyone's business?

10. Scrooge asks the Ghost of Christmas Yet to Come if the visions he has seen are shadows of what will be or what may be (page 311). What does the conclusion of "A Christmas Carol" imply about the ability of people to determine their own futures?

DEVELOPING SKILLS IN READING

Recognizing Words That Echo Sounds

Many words in English imitate sounds. For example, when you say the word *buzz*, you hear the sound of buzzing at the end of the word. When you say *plop*, you hear the sound that is made by an object when it strikes water.

In "A Christmas Carol" there is a "clanking" of chains before Marley's ghost enters; Mrs. Cratchit makes the gravy "hissing" hot; and you are told that the chestnuts "crackled" in the fire. The words *clank, hiss*, and *crackle* imitate the sounds made by dragging chains, steaming gravy, and roasting chestnuts, respectively. When Dickens uses these words, he helps you experience vividly what he is describing.

Writers may also use the sounds of words to suggest something about character. Read aloud these lines describing Scrooge:

Oh! But he was a tightfisted hand at the grindstone, was Scrooge! A squeezing, wrenching, grasping, scraping, clutching, covetous old sinner!

Many sounds in the passage are harsh sounds. The sound **s** suggests hissing. How often is the sound **s** repeated? Where do you hear the harsh sound **k?** The repetition of these harsh sounds reinforces what the reader already knows about Scrooge—that he is a hardhearted and unfeeling man.

ABOUT THE AUTHOR

Charles Dickens (1812–1870) spent the happiest years of his childhood in Chatham, a dockyard town near London. He was a keen observer of the city life around him. He roamed the area, observing the great black prisons that jutted out over the Medway River and the gray, square ruins of Rochester Castle. He saw the inhumane conditions existing in the local hospitals, prisons, and poorhouses.

Dickens was an avid reader. He spent many free hours reading the works of Shakespeare and *The Arabian Nights*, and rummaging through old novels piled up in the attic of his home. Dickens' schooling was cut short when his father fell deeply into debt. At the age of twelve, he was forced to take a job in a warehouse, where he worked twelve hours a day, pasting labels on bottles. This experience was shattering, and it aroused in Dickens a fierce determination to fight poverty and social injustice—an ideal he expressed passionately in many of his books.

Dickens' literary career began in 1836, when he published *Sketches by Boz*, a collection of short, fictional pieces based on his observations of London life. Shortly afterward, he was asked to write a comic narrative to accompany a set of engravings by a well-known artist. The result was *The Pickwick Papers*, which brought him instant fame. In such classics as *Oliver Twist* (1837–1838), *David Copperfield* (1850), and *Great Expectations* (1861), he created some of the most vivid characters and memorable situations in English literature.

Dickens also acted in amateur plays and gave readings from his works in England and in America. The version of "A Christmas Carol" that appears in this book was prepared by Dickens for his public readings.

Practice in Reading and Writing

STORIES

Point of view is the standpoint from which a writer tells a story. This important narrative technique helps to shape your impression of the characters and events in a story.

The Omniscient Point of View

A writer may choose to tell a story from the point of view of an observer who does not play an active role in the events but who knows what each character does and thinks. Read the following passage from "Rikki-tikki-tavi." Find details that tell what Rikki-tikki thinks and feels about Nag. What is Nag thinking about Rikki-tikki?

> He spread out his hood more than ever, and Rikki-tikki saw the spectacle mark on the back of it that looks exactly like the eye part of a hook-and-eye fastening. He was afraid for the minute; but it is impossible for a mongoose to stay frightened for any length of time, and though Rikki-tikki had never met a live cobra before, his mother had fed him on dead ones, and he knew that all a grown mongoose's business in life was to fight and eat snakes. Nag knew that too, and at the bottom of his cold heart he was afraid.

This story is written from the point of view of an observer who can see what is going on in the minds of the characters. When a writer tells what all the different characters in a story see, hear, think, and feel, we say that the story has been written from an *omniscient*, or all-knowing, point of view. As readers, we are allowed to know as much about each character as the writer. Stories with the omniscient point of view are always written in the third person.

Limited Third-Person Point of View

Sometimes a writer using the third person will purposely limit the point of view to what one particular character sees, hears, and thinks. "The Landlady" is written in the third person, but the author has chosen to reveal only what Billy knows and feels.

"*There* we are," she said. "How nice and cozy this is, isn't it?"

Billy started sipping his tea. She did the same. For half a minute or so, neither of them spoke. But Billy knew that she was looking at him. Her body was half turned toward him, and he could feel her eyes resting on his face, watching him over the rim of her teacup. Now and again, he caught a whiff of a peculiar smell that seemed to emanate directly from her person. It was not in the least unpleasant, and it reminded him—well, he wasn't quite sure what it reminded him of. Pickled walnuts? New leather? Or was it the corridors of a hospital?

Find those parts in the passage that tell you what Billy is thinking as he sips his tea. Do you know what the landlady is thinking in this passage? If the author had revealed the landlady's thoughts during this scene, would the end of the story have been a surprise?

First-Person Point of View

In some stories, the author decides to have one of the characters narrate the story in the first person (using "I"). Then everything the reader learns about the events in the story is influenced by the narrator's feelings and opinions. "A Day's Wait" is an example of a story written from a first-person point of view. The narrator is the father. If the story were narrated by the son, it would be a very different story. At what point in the story would you probably learn that the boy believes he is fatally ill?

Writing a Story

Write a brief story about a contest or disagreement in which you were involved. Write the story in the first person from your own point of view, including what you thought and felt at the time. Then rewrite part of the story, still using the first person, from your opponent's point of view.

For Further Reading

Aiken, Joan, *The Green Flash and Other Tales of Horror, Suspense, and Fantasy* (Holt, Rinehart & Winston, 1971; paperback, Dell)
   The fourteen stories in this collection deal with revenge, ghosts, fantasy, and humor.

Alexander, Lloyd, *The Foundling and Other Tales of Prydain* (Holt, Rinehart & Winston, 1973; paperback, Holt)
   These six fantasies introduce characters and events in the mythical kingdom of Prydain.

Asimov, Isaac, editor, *Tomorrow's Children* (Doubleday, 1966)
   Here are eighteen stories about the future written by masters of science fiction.

Avery, Gillian, editor, *Authors' Choice* (Thomas Y. Crowell, 1970)
   Here are seventeen stories chosen by writers as their favorites. *Authors' Choice 2*, edited by Joan Aiken (Crowell, 1973), is a second volume in this series.

Bennett, George, editor, *Great Tales of Action and Adventure* (paperback, Dell, 1959)
   The classic tales of suspense in this collection include "The Most Dangerous Game" by Richard Connell, "The Pit and the Pendulum" by Edgar Allan Poe, and "To Build a Fire" by Jack London.

Boles, Paul Darcy, *A Million Guitars and Other Stories* (Little, Brown, 1968)
   This anthology contains thirteen stories, all told from the viewpoint of adolescent boys.

Bradbury, Ray, *S Is for Space* (Doubleday, 1966; paperback, Bantam)
   An accomplished science-fiction writer presents sixteen of his best stories.

Christie, Agatha, *13 Clues for Miss Marple*, edited by R. T. Bond (Dodd, Mead, 1966)
   Here is a collection of detective stories about Miss Marple, one of Agatha Christie's memorable sleuths.

Doyle, Sir Arthur Conan, *Adventures of Sherlock Holmes* (Harper & Row, 1930)
   Readers who like mysteries will enjoy this collection of stories about the most famous and brilliant detective in literature.

Henry, O., *The Gift of the Magi and Five Other Stories* (Franklin Watts, 1967)
   Here are six exciting short stories by the writer who perfected surprise endings.

Irving, Washington, *Rip Van Winkle, The Legend of Sleepy Hollow, and Other Tales* (Grossett & Dunlap)
   Two other strange tales—"The Specter Bridegroom" and "The Moor's Legacy"—are included in this collection.

Kipling, Rudyard, *The Jungle Book* and *The Second Jungle Book* (many editions)
   Kipling's tales about the jungles of India include the story of Mowgli, a boy who was raised by animals.

Manley, Seon, and Gogo Lewis, editors, *Baleful Beasts* (Lothrop, Lee & Shepard, 1974)
   In this anthology the characters are humans as well as animals, and the stories are strange, sinister, and bizarre.

Nash, Ogden, editor, *I Couldn't Help Laughing* (Lippincott, 1957)
   Here are sixteen humorous stories by English and American writers.

Sechrist, Elizabeth, editor, *Thirteen Ghostly Yarns* (Macrae Smith, 1963)
   A beautiful maiden in a great bell, a murdered father who cries for revenge, a water ghost, and a mysterious traveler are some of the ghosts you will meet in these tales by Twain, Dickens, Shakespeare, Kipling, and others.

Silverberg, Barbara, editor, *Phoenix Feathers* (Dutton, 1973)
   Here are eight stories about such mythical monsters as griffins and dragons.

There is a great difference between seeing a play performed in a theater or on a screen and reading that play in class or at home. When you watch a performance, you are seeing the results of other people's imaginative efforts. For many weeks or months before a play is produced, there is careful planning. Sets must be created; costumes must be designed and fitted; actors and actresses must study and rehearse their parts. When you read a play, you must rely on your own imagination to create the performance. You must visualize the setting and costumes; you must imagine the shifting tones of voice in which the performers would deliver their lines. You must interpret the different roles as they would be interpreted for you by the players.

The plays in this unit were written for different media. *The Mazarin Stone,* a stage play, deals with a crime that is solved by the great detective Sherlock Holmes. *The Pussycat and the Expert Plumber Who Was a Man,* a radio play, is a fantasy about a talking cat with political ambitions. *The Big Wave,* a television play, portrays the struggle of human beings against the hostile forces of nature.

At the end of the unit, you will find suggestions for creating and performing plays of your own.

DRAMA

Poster for a production of *H.M.S. Pinafore.*
Harvard Theatre Collection

Puppet show in Liverpool,
England.
© Farrell Grehan 1972/Photo
Researchers, Inc.

Performance of *Meiboku Sendai
Hagi*, a Kabuki play, in Tokyo,
Japan, in 1968.
Jacques Jangoux/Photo Researchers, Inc.

Performance of the musical *Oklahoma* at New Canaan High School, New Canaan, Connecticut.
Philip Greenberg 1976/Photo Researchers, Inc.

Performance of *Ti-Jean and His Brothers*, a fable with music by Derek Walcott, at the Delacorte Theater, Central Park, New York City.
Margot Granitsas/Photo Researchers, Inc.

A scene from the *Oresteia*, a group of three plays by the Greek dramatist Aeschylus, performed by the Touring National Players at Catholic University, Washington, D.C. The first performance of these plays was in 458 B.C.
Fred J. Maroon/Photo Researchers, Inc.

The great yellow Mazarin Stone, worth a fortune, has been stolen. The police and government officials are baffled, but Sherlock Holmes has a plan for catching the thieves and recovering the diamond.

The Mazarin Stone

Michael and Molly Hardwick
adapted from a story by Sir Arthur Conan Doyle

Characters

Sherlock Holmes
Dr. Watson, Holmes's friend and associate
Billy, Holmes's attendant
Count Negretto Sylvius, a big-game hunter
   and adventurer
Sam Merton, a boxer

Lord Cantlemere, a nobleman of high
   standing and political influence
Police Sergeant
Constables[1]

The play takes place in London around the beginning of the twentieth century.

Setting: *The parlor of 221B Baker Street. For this play, whose entire action takes place here, a curtain at the back of the stage must be capable of being drawn aside to reveal an alcove, backed by a window with blinds drawn. Seated beside this window, in profile to it and to the audience, is a dummy representing* Sherlock Holmes. *It is wearing an old dressing gown, and sits in a large, high-backed chair. If the window blind were not down, it would appear to occupants of the houses opposite that* Holmes *himself is seated there. When the play begins, the chair and its occupant are concealed from the audience by the alcove curtain.*

Two doorways are necessary: one for characters arriving and departing—"parlor door"—and one leading off into Holmes's *bedroom —"bedroom door." As the course of the action will reveal, an offstage route is necessary between the "bedroom" and the alcove.*

The lamp is lit. A parasol stands against a chair. Billy, *the page boy, is holding up* Holmes's *ulster,[2] brushing it vigorously.*

There is a tap at the parlor door. It opens, and Watson's *head peers round.*

---

1. **Constables** (kŏn′stə-bəlz): in England, policemen.
2. **ulster:** a long, loose overcoat made of heavy material, usually worn with a belt.

Billy. Dr. Watson, sir! Come in, sir!

[Watson *enters, closing the door.*]

Watson. Well, Billy, my boy! Keeping the moths at bay?
Billy. That's it, sir.

[*He folds the coat and puts it down on a chair, as* Watson *lays aside his hat and stick.* Watson *glances round the room.*]

Watson. It doesn't seem to have changed much, Billy.
Billy. Not much, sir.
Watson. You don't change, either. I hope the same can be said of *him?*
Billy. I think he's in bed and asleep.
Watson (*laughs*). At seven o'clock of a lovely summer's evening. He *hasn't* changed, then! I suppose it means a case?
Billy. Yes, sir. He's very hard at it just now. Fair frightens me.
Watson. What does?
Billy. His health, Dr. Watson. He gets paler, and thinner, and he never eats nothing. I heard Mrs. Hudson asking him when he would take his dinner. "Seven thirty," he told her—"*the day after tomorrow!*"
Watson (*sighs*). Yes, Billy, I know how it is.
Billy (*confidentially*). I can tell you one thing, sir—he's following somebody.

[Watson, *amused, copies* Billy's *manner and leans towards him conspiratorially.*]

Watson. Really?
Billy. One disguise after another. Yesterday he was a workman, looking for a job. Today he was an old woman. Fairly took me in, he did—and I ought to know his ways by now. (*He picks up the parasol briefly.*) Part of the old girl's outfit.
Watson (*laughs*). What's it all about, Billy?
Billy (*glancing round cautiously*). I don't mind telling *you*, sir—but it shouldn't go no farther. . . . (Watson *gives his head a meaningful shake and places a finger to his lips.*) It's this case of the Crown diamond.[3]

---

3. **Crown diamond:** a diamond belonging to the monarchy.

Watson. What — the hundred-thousand-pound burglary?

Billy. Yes, sir. They must get it back. Why, we've had the Prime Minister and Home Secretary[4] both sat in this very room!

Watson. You don't say!

Billy. Mr. Holmes was very nice to them. Promised he would do all he could. Then there's Lord Cantlemere.

Watson *(dismally).* Oh!

Billy. Ah, you know what that means, Dr. Watson! He's a stiff 'un, and no mistake. Now, I can get along with the Prime Minister — and I've nothing against the Home Secretary. . . . But I can't *stand* His Lordship! (Watson *laughs heartily.)* Mr. Holmes can't, neither, sir! You can tell, Lord Cantlemere don't believe in Mr. Holmes. He was against employing him, and he'd rather he failed.

Watson. And Mr. Holmes knows it?

Billy. Mr. Holmes *always* knows what there is to know.

Watson *(hastily).* Oh, quite, quite! Well, Billy, we'll just hope that he won't fail, and then Lord Cantlemere will be confounded. But I'd better be getting home to my wife. *(He moves towards his hat and stick, but catches sight of the curtain.)* I say, Billy! Bit early to have the curtains drawn and the lamp lit, isn't it?

Billy. Well — there's something funny behind there.

Watson. Something *funny?*

Billy. You can see it, sir. (Billy *draws the curtain, revealing the dummy.)*

Watson. Bless my soul!

Billy. Yes, sir.

Watson *(examining the figure).* A perfect replica of Sherlock Holmes! Dressing gown and all!

---

4. **Home Secretary:** a British Cabinet minister in charge of keeping internal law and order, with authority over the London police.

[Billy *turns the chair so that the dummy chances to finish up with its back to the parlor door.*]

Billy. We put it at different angles every now and then, like this, so's it'll look more life-like. Mind, I wouldn't dare touch it if the blind wasn't drawn. When it's up you can see this from right across the way.

Watson. We used something of the sort once before, you know.

Billy. Before my time, sir.

Watson. Er — yes.

[*Unseen by either of them the bedroom door opens and* Holmes *appears in his dressing gown.*]

Billy. There's folk who watch us from over yonder, sir. You may catch a peep of them now. *(He is about to pull back a corner of the blind to enable* Watson *to look out.)*

Holmes *(sharply).* That will do, Billy!

[Billy *and* Watson *spin round.*]

Watson. Holmes!

Holmes *(severely).* You were in danger of your life, then, my boy. I can't do without you just yet.

Billy. *(humbly).* Yes, sir.

Holmes. That will be all for now.

Billy. Very good, sir. *(He exits by the parlor door.)*

Holmes. That boy is a problem, Watson. How far am I justified in letting him be in danger?

Watson. Danger of what, Holmes?

Holmes. Of sudden death.

Watson. Holmes!

Holmes. But it's good to see you in your old quarters once again, my dear Watson!

Watson *(concerned).* Holmes — this talk of sudden death. What are you expecting?

Holmes (*simply*). To be murdered.

Watson. Oh, come now! You're joking!

Holmes. Even my limited sense of humor could evolve a better joke than that, Watson. (*Brightening*) But we may be comfortable in the meantime, mayn't we? Let me see you once more in the customary chair.

Watson. Pleasure, Holmes! But why not eat?

Holmes. Because the faculties[5] become refined when you starve them. Surely, as a doctor, you must admit that what your digestion gains in the way of blood supply is so much lost to the brain? *I* am a brain, Watson. The rest of me is mere appendix. Therefore, it's the brain I must consider.

Watson. But—this danger . . . ?

Holmes. Ah, yes. Just in case it should come off, it would be as well for you to know the name of the murderer. You can give it to Scotland Yard, with my love and a parting blessing.

Watson. Holmes!

Holmes. His name is Sylvius—Count Negretto Sylvius, No. 136 Moorside Gardens, London N.W. Got it?

Watson. Yes. (*Hesitantly*) Er—Holmes . . . I've got nothing to do for a day or two. Count me in.

Holmes. (*sadly shaking his head*). Your morals don't improve, Watson.

Watson. My *morals*?

Holmes. You've added fibbing to your other vices. You bear every sign of the busy medical man, with calls on him every hour.

Watson. Not such important ones. But—can't you have this fellow arrested?

Holmes. Yes, Watson, I could. That's what worries him so.

Watson. Then why don't you?

Holmes. Because I don't know where the diamond is.

Watson. Ah! Billy was telling me—the missing Crown jewel!

Holmes. The great yellow Mazarin Stone. I've cast my net and I have my fish. But I have *not* got the stone. Yes, I could make the world a better place by laying *them* by the heels; but it's the stone I want.

Watson. And is Count Sylvius one of your fish?

Holmes. Yes—and he's a *shark*. He bites. The other is Sam Merton, the boxer. Not a bad fellow, Sam, but the Count has used him. Sam's just a great, big, silly, bull-headed gudgeon;[6] but he's flopping about in my net, all the same.

Watson. Where is Count Sylvius now?

Holmes. I've been at his elbow all morning. (*He gets up.*) You've seen me as an old lady, Watson?

Watson (*chuckling*). Oh, yes indeed!

[Holmes *assumes the posture and walk of an old lady.*]

Holmes (*in a cracked old voice*). I was never more convincing, Doctor. Never! (Watson *laughs as* Holmes *straightens up. Normal voice*) He actually picked up my parasol for me once. (Holmes *picks up the parasol and gesticulates with it.*)

Watson. He didn't!

[Holmes *makes an elaborate bow, holding out the parasol in both hands.*]

Holmes (*mimicking* Sylvius). By your leave, madam. (Holmes *resumes his normal voice*

---

5. **faculties** (făk'əl-tēz): natural abilities.

6. **gudgeon** (gŭj'ən): a small fish that is easily caught and used for bait; here, a person who is easily tricked or used.

and manner and lays the parasol aside.) He's half Italian, you know. Full of the Southern[7] graces when he's in the mood. But he's a devil incarnate[8] in the other mood. Life is full of whimsical happenings, Watson.

Watson (with a snort). Whimsical! It might have been tragedy!

Holmes. Well, perhaps it might. Anyway, I followed him to old Straubenzee's workshop in the Minories.[9] Straubenzee made the air gun—a very pretty bit of work, as I understand. I fancy it's in the opposite window at present, ready to put a bullet through this dummy's beautiful head whenever I choose to raise that blind.

[*Knock at parlor door, which opens. Billy enters, carrying a salver.*[10]]

Billy. Mr. Holmes, sir . . .
Holmes. What is it, Billy?
Billy. There's a gentleman to see you, sir.

[Holmes *takes the visiting card from the salver and looks at it.*]

Holmes. Thank you. (He replaces the card.) The man himself, Watson!
Watson. Sylvius!
Holmes (nods). I'd hardly expected this. Grasp the nettle,[11] eh! A man of nerve, Watson. But possibly you've heard of his reputation as a big-game shooter? It'd be a triumphant ending to his excellent sporting record if he added me to his bag.

Watson. Send for the police, Holmes!
Holmes. I probably shall—but not just yet. Would you just glance carefully out of the window and see if anyone is hanging about in the street?
Watson. Certainly. (He goes to the window and peeps cautiously round the corner of the blind.) Yes—there's a rough-looking fellow near the door.
Holmes. That will be Sam Merton—the faithful but rather fatuous[12] Sam. Billy, where is Count Sylvius?
Billy. In the waiting room, sir.
Holmes. Show him up when I ring.
Billy. Yes, sir.
Holmes. If I'm not in the room, show him in all the same.
Billy. Very good, Mr. Holmes. (He leaves by the parlor door.)
Watson. Look here, Holmes, this is simply ridiculous. This is a desperate man who sticks at nothing, you'd have me believe. He may have *come* to murder you.
Holmes. I shouldn't be surprised.
Watson. Then I insist on staying with you!
Holmes. You'd be horribly in the way.
Watson. In *his* way!
Holmes. No, my dear fellow—in mine.

[Watson *sits down stubbornly.*]

Watson. Be that as it may, I can't possibly leave you.

---

7. **Southern:** The reference is to southern Europe. The Count is from Italy.
8. **devil incarnate** (ĭn-kär′nĭt): a devil in human form.
9. **Minories:** a street in London, once famous for its gun makers.
10. **salver:** a small tray.
11. **Grasp the nettle:** a proverbial expression meaning "Act boldly to gain an advantage over someone." A nettle is a plant with delicate thorns. If the plant is touched gently, the thorns sting. If it is grasped firmly, they feel soft.

---

12. **fatuous** (făch′ōō-əs): foolish.

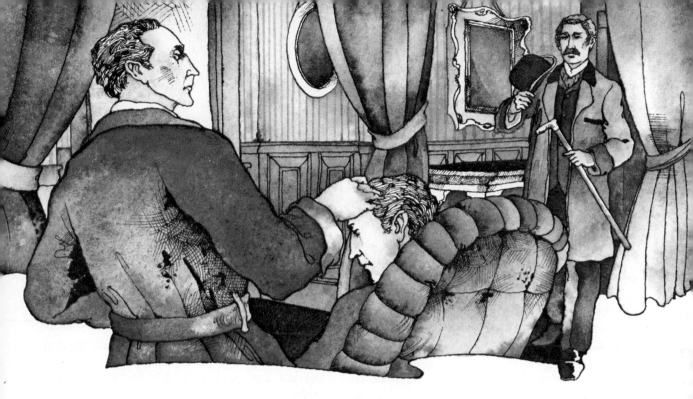

Holmes. Yes you can, Watson. And you will — for you've never failed to play the game. I'm sure you'll play it to the end. *(He crosses to his desk and begins to scribble a note.)* This man has come for his own purpose, but he may stay for mine. I want you to take a cab to Scotland Yard and give this note to Youghal, of the C.I.D.[13] Come back with the police.

Watson *(rising).* I'll do that with joy!

Holmes *(handing* Watson *the note).* Before you get back I may just have time to find out where the stone is. Now, I'll just ring for Billy to show him up, and I think we'll go out through the bedroom. (Holmes *presses a bell, while Watson gathers his things. Holmes ushers him toward the bedroom door.)* This second exit is exceedingly useful, you know. I rather want to see my shark without his seeing me.

---

13. **C.I.D.:** Criminal Investigation Department, a division of the London Police.

[Watson *halts.*]

Watson. The dummy! Shouldn't the curtain be drawn over it again?

Holmes. No, no. We'll leave it as it is. (He *moves swiftly to the dummy.)* Perhaps just a touch to this noble head . . . *(He adjusts the head to bow upon the breast)* as though somewhere in the middle of forty winks. *(He ensures that the dummy has its back to the parlor door.)* There! Now, come along.

Watson. I hope you know what you're doing, that's all!

[*They exit by the bedroom door, closing it behind them. A slight pause, then the parlor door opens.* Billy *enters and* Count Sylvius *walks in past him.*]

Billy. If you'll just wait, sir.

[Sylvius *ignores him.* Billy *withdraws, closing the door behind him.* Sylvius *looks round the room for a moment, then notices the dummy. He grips his stick more firmly and creeps a cautious pace or two towards it. Satisfied that the figure is dozing, he steps forward and raises his stick to strike.* Holmes *enters silently from the bedroom.*]

Holmes. Don't break it, Count Sylvius!

[Sylvius *whirls round, his stick still upraised, a look of disbelief on his face.*]

Sylvius. What!
Holmes. It's a pretty little thing. (Sylvius *lowers the stick and walks round to look at the dummy in astonishment.*) Tavernier, the French modeler, made it. He's as good at waxworks as your friend Straubenzee is at air guns. (Holmes *turns the chair to face the window. The dummy is now completely hidden from the audience.*)
Sylvius. Air guns? What do you mean, sir?
Holmes. Put your stick on the side table, before you're tempted to do any other form of damage.

[*There is a momentary hesitation, in which we think* Sylvius *might spring at* Holmes. *But* Holmes *stands still, looking at him hard, one hand in his pocket, in which we sense him to have a revolver.* Sylvius *relaxes and obeys.*]

Sylvius. Very well.
Holmes. Thank you. Would you care to put your revolver out, also? (*At the mention of "revolver"* Sylvius' *hand flies to his hip pocket. He does not draw, but stands poised defiantly. Blandly*) Oh, very well, if you prefer to sit on it. (Holmes *moves to a chair and sits.*) Your visit is really most opportune, Count Sylvius. I wanted badly to have a few minutes' chat with you.

[Sylvius *stumps over to a chair opposite* Holmes.]

Sylvius. I, too, wished to have some words with you, Holmes! That is why I am here. Because you have gone out of your way to annoy me. Because you have put your creatures on my track!
Holmes. Oh, I assure you no!
Sylvius. I have had them followed! Two can play at that game, Holmes!
Holmes. It's a small point, Count Sylvius, but perhaps you would kindly give me my prefix[14] when you address me? You can understand that, with my routine of work, I should find myself on familiar terms with half the rogues' gallery,[15] and you'll agree that exceptions are invidious.[16]
Sylvius (*sneering*). Well, *Mr.* Holmes, then.
Holmes. That's better. But I assure you that you're mistaken about my alleged agents.
Sylvius (*laughs contemptuously*). Other people can observe as well as you! Yesterday there was an old sporting man. Today it was an elderly woman. They kept me in view all day.
Holmes. Really, sir, you compliment me! Old Baron Dowson said the night before he was hanged that in my case what the law had gained the stage had lost.
Sylvius. It . . . It was you?
Holmes. You can see in the corner the parasol which you so politely handed to me in the Minories before you began to suspect.
Sylvius. If I had known that, you might never have . . .

---

14. **prefix:** here, a title, such as *Dr., Mr.,* or *Mrs.,* before a person's name.
15. **rogues' gallery:** photographs of criminals kept in police files for purposes of identification.
16. **invidious** (ĭn-vĭd′ē-əs): unfair; offensive. Holmes isn't on familiar terms with criminals and says (jokingly) that it wouldn't be fair to make an exception in the Count's case.

Holmes. . . . have seen this humble abode again? I was well aware of that. But, as it happens, you did *not* know, so here we are!

Sylvius. So it was not your agents, but your play-acting, busybodying self! You admit that you dogged me. Why?

Holmes. Come now, Count: you used to shoot lions in Algeria.

Sylvius. What about it?

Holmes. Why did you?

Sylvius. The sport — the excitement — the danger.

Holmes. And, no doubt, to free the country from a pest?

Sylvius. Exactly.

Holmes. My reasons in a nutshell!

[Sylvius *springs to his feet in fury and reaches instinctively towards his revolver pocket.*]

Sylvius. For that, I will . . . !

Holmes. Sit down, sir, sit down! *(He gives* Sylvius *a steely stare.* Sylvius *hesitates for a moment, then obeys.)* I had another, more practical reason for following your movements. I want that yellow diamond.

[Sylvius *begins to relax and chuckle. He stretches his legs and makes himself comfortable.*]

Sylvius. Upon my word — *Mr*. Holmes!

Holmes. You know that I was after you for that. The real reason why you're here tonight is to find out how much I know and how far my removal is absolutely essential. Well, I should say that from *your* point of view it *is* absolutely essential. You see, I know all about the diamond — save only one thing, which you are about to tell me.

Sylvius. Indeed? Pray, what is this missing fact?

Holmes. Where the Crown diamond now is.

Sylvius. And how should I be able to tell you that?

Holmes. You can, and you will.

Sylvius. You astonish me!

Holmes. You can't bluff me, Count Sylvius. You are absolute plate glass. I can see to the very back of your mind.

Sylvius. Oh! Then, of course, you can see where the diamond is.

Holmes *(delighted).* Then you *do* know!

Sylvius. No!

Holmes. You've admitted it.

Sylvius. I admit nothing!

[Holmes *gets up and goes to a drawer, which he opens.*]

Holmes. Now, Count, if you'll be reasonable we can do business.

Sylvius. And *you* talk about bluff!

[Holmes *takes a notebook from the drawer.*]

Holmes. Do you know what I keep in this book?

Sylvius. No, sir. I do not.

Holmes. I keep *you* in it.

Sylvius. Me?

Holmes. You are all here — every action of your vile and dangerous life.

Sylvius. There are limits to my patience, Holmes!

Holmes *(waving the book at* Sylvius). Yes, it's all here: the real facts about the death of old Mrs. Harold, who left you the Blymer estate to gamble away. (Holmes *taunts* Sylvius *with the book,* Sylvius *making a grab for it whenever it approaches, but always missing.)*

Sylvius. You're dreaming!

Holmes. And the complete life history of Miss Minnie Warrender.

Sylvius. You'll make nothing of that!

Holmes. There's plenty more, Count: the robbery in the train-de-luxe to the Riviera[17] on February 13, 1892; the forged check in the same year on the Credit Lyonnais.[18]

Sylvius. No! There you *are* mistaken!

Holmes. Then I *am* right on the others! *(He throws the book into the drawer, which he closes, resuming his seat.)* Now, Count, you're a card player. You know that when the other fellow has all the trumps it saves time to throw in your hand.

Sylvius. Just what has all this talk to do with the jewel?

Holmes. Gently, Count! Restrain that eager mind! Let me get to the points in my own humdrum fashion. *(Gesturing towards the closed drawer)* I have all that against you. But, above all, I have a clear case against you and your fighting bully in the theft of the Crown diamond.

Sylvius. Indeed?

Holmes *(enumerating the points on his fingers).* I have the cabman who took you to Whitehall,[19] and the cabman who brought you away. I have the commissionaire[20] who saw you near the case. I have Ikey Sanders, who refused to cut the stone up for you. Ikey has talked, Count, and the game is up!

Sylvius. I don't believe you!

Holmes. That's the hand I play from. I put it all on the table. Only one card is missing. It's the King of Diamonds. I don't know where the stone is. *(He presses the bell.)*

Sylvius. And you never will! Why are you ringing that bell? *(He gets to his feet suspiciously.)*

Holmes. Be reasonable, Count! Consider the situation. You are going to be locked up for twenty years. So is Sam Merton. What good are you going to get out of your diamond? None in the world. But if you hand it over—well, I'm prepared to compound a felony.[21] We don't want you or Sam. We want the stone. Give that up, Count Sylvius, and so far as I'm concerned you can go free. But if you make another slip in the future . . . ! Well, it'll be the last.

Sylvius. And if I refuse?

Holmes *(sighs).* Then I'm afraid it must be you, and not the stone.

[*Knock at parlor door.* Billy *enters.*]

Billy. Did you ring, sir?

Holmes. Yes, Billy. You will see a large and ugly gentleman outside the front door. Ask him to come up.

Billy. Yes, sir. *(He is about to go, but hesitates.)* What if he won't, sir?

Holmes. Oh, no violence, Billy! Don't be rough with him! If you tell him that Count Sylvius wants him he will come.

Billy. Very good, sir. *(He exits with a grin, closing the door.)*

Holmes. I think it would be as well to have your friend Sam at this conference. After all, his interests should be represented.

[Sylvius *resumes his seat.*]

Sylvius. Just what do you intend to do now?

Holmes. I was remarking to my friend, Dr.

---

17. **Riviera** (rĭv′ē-âr′ə): a resort area along the Mediterranean Sea.
18. **Credit Lyonnais** (krĕ′dē lē′ō-nā′): a French bank.
19. **Whitehall:** a London street where many government departments are located.
20. **commissionaire** (kə-mĭsh′ə-nâr′): in England, a doorman.

21. **compound a felony:** to add to a crime by not telling the police.

Watson, a short while ago that I had a shark and a gudgeon in my net. Now I'm drawing in the net, and up they come together.

Sylvius. You won't die in your bed, Holmes!

Holmes. I've often had that same idea. But does it matter very much? After all, Count, your own exit is more likely to be perpendicular than horizontal. (Sylvius' *hand jerks towards his gun pocket.* Holmes *waves an admonishing finger.*) It's no use, my friend. Even if I gave you time to draw it, you know perfectly well you daren't use it. Nasty, noisy things, revolvers. Better stick to air guns. *(Knock at parlor door.* Billy *shows in* Sam Merton *coldly and withdraws without speaking.* Merton *glares about him, tensed for action.*) Good day, Mr. Merton. Rather dull in the street, isn't it?

Merton. What's up, Count?

Holmes. If I may put it in a nutshell, Mr. Merton, I should say the *game* was up.

Merton. 'Ere! Is this cove[22] trying to be funny? I'm not in the funny mood meself.

Holmes. I think I can promise you'll feel even less humorous as the evening advances.

[Merton *lumbers aggressively towards* Holmes, *but is halted by a gesture from* Sylvius.]

Sylvius. That will do, Sam!

Holmes. Thank you, Count. (Holmes *gets to his feet.*) Now, look here—I'm a busy man and I can't waste time. I'm going into that bedroom to try over the *Hoffmann* "Barcarolle"[23] on my violin. You can explain to your friend how the matter lies, without the

---

22. **cove:** slang for "fellow."
23. **"Barcarolle"** (bär′kə-rōl′): a famous piece of music in *The Tales of Hoffmann,* an opera by Jacques Offenbach.

restraint of my presence. (Holmes *goes to the bedroom door.*) In five minutes I shall return for your final answer. You quite grasp the alternative, don't you? Shall we take you, or shall we have the stone?

[Holmes *exits, closing the bedroom door behind him.* Sylvius *jumps up and paces about thoughtfully.*]

Merton. 'Offmann who? What's the chap on about?

Sylvius. Shut up, Sam! Let me think!

[*Sounds of violin strings being plucked and tuned in the bedroom.*]

Merton. If it's trouble, why didn't you plug 'im?

Sylvius. You're a fool, Sam! Anyone but you could have seen he was holding a revolver in his dressing-gown pocket.

Merton. Aw! (*The violin begins to play the "Barcarolle" from* The Tales of Hoffmann. *It is expertly played. Having established it, diminish somewhat under following dialogue. Disgustedly*) Cor!

Sylvius. Ikey Sanders has split[24] on us.

Merton. Split, 'as 'e? I'll do 'im a thick 'un for that, if I swing for it!

Sylvius. How do you think that will help us? We've got to make up our minds what to do.

Merton. (*lowering his voice*). 'Arf a mo',[25] Count! That's a leary cove[26] in there. D'you suppose 'e's listening?

Sylvius. How can he listen and play that thing?

Merton. Aw, that's right!

Sylvius. Now *you* listen! He can lag[27] us over this stone, but he's offered to let us slip if we only tell him where it is.

Merton. Wot! Give up a 'undred thousand quid![28]

Sylvius. It's one or the other. He knows too much.

Merton. Well . . . listen! 'E's alone in there. Let's do 'im! Then we've nothing to fear of.

Sylvius. He's armed and ready. If we shot him we could hardly get away in a place like this. Besides, it's likely enough the police know he's on to something. Listen! (*They listen. The violin plays steadily on.*) It was just a noise in the street, I think.

Merton. Look, guv'nor — you've got the brains. If slugging's no use, then it's up to you.

Sylvius. I've fooled better men than Holmes. The stone's here, in my secret pocket. I take no chances leaving it about. It can be out of England tonight and cut into four pieces in Amsterdam before Sunday. One of us must slip round to Lime Street with the stone and tell Van Seddar to get off by the next boat.

Merton. But the false bottom ain't ready yet. Van Seddar don't expect to go till next week!

Sylvius. He must go now, and chance it. As to Holmes, we can fool him. We'll promise him the stone, then put him on the wrong track; and by the time he finds out we'll be in Holland, too.

Merton. Now you're talking, Count!

Sylvius. You go now and see the Dutchman, Sam. Here . . . (Sylvius *pulls* Sam *aside.*) Just in case, come out of line with that keyhole.

[Sylvius *reaches into his secret pocket and produces a large yellow gem. The "dummy"*

---

24. **split:** slang for "informed on one's partners."
25. **'Arf a mo':** Merton's pronunciation of "Half a mo'," an expression meaning "Wait a moment."
26. **leary cove:** slang for "clever fellow."

27. **lag:** slang for "arrest."
28. **quid** (kwĭd): slang for "pound" (or "pounds"), the basic unit of British money.

in the chair near the window begins to move cautiously, and we see that during the preceding dialogue Holmes has contrived to seat himself in its place. Unobserved by Sylvius or Merton he sidles towards them. He has a revolver in his hand.]

Merton. I don't know 'ow you dare carry it about!

Sylvius. Where could I keep it safer? If we could take it out of Whitehall, someone else could easily take it from my lodgings.

[Holmes sneaks quickly forward and plucks the stone from Sylvius' hand.]

Holmes. Or out of your hand! (Sylvius and Merton are too flabbergasted to react. They stare speechlessly at Holmes, and then at the chair.) Thank you, Count. It will be safe with me.

Merton. There was a blooming waxworks in that chair!

[He jerks the chair round; it is empty. Holmes moves carefully back to a position from where he can cover them both.]

Holmes. Your surprise is very natural, Mr. Merton. You are not aware, of course, that a second door from my bedroom leads behind that curtain. I fancied you must have heard me, Count, as I slipped into the dummy's chair, but luck and a passing cab were on my side. They enabled me to listen to your racy conversation, which would have been painfully constrained had you been aware of my presence.

[Sylvius lurches towards Holmes, who raises the revolver slightly.]

Sylvius. Deuce take you, Holmes!

Holmes. No violence, gentlemen! Consider the furniture! (They stand still.) It must be very clear to you that the position is an impossible one. The police are waiting below.

Merton. Guv'nor? Shall I . . .?

Sylvius (resignedly). No, Sam. I give you best, Holmes. I believe you are the devil himself.

Holmes. Not far from him, at any rate.

[Merton suddenly points to the bedroom door.]

Merton. 'Ere! That blooming fiddle! It's playing itself!

Holmes. Oh, let it play. These modern gramophones[29] are a remarkable invention!

Merton. Aw!

[Men's voices approaching the parlor door. It opens suddenly. Watson hastens in.]

Watson. This way, officers!

[A Police Sergeant and two Constables hurry after him and seize Sylvius and Merton.]

Sergeant. Come on, Sam! We've been waiting to get hold of you!

Merton. Gar!

Sylvius. Take your hands off me, my man!

Constable. Not blooming likely![30]

[They are led away, struggling. At the door, Merton stops, looks back into the room, then at Holmes.]

Merton. Waxworks! Grammerphones! Garrr! (He is led off as Billy enters.)

Billy (with distaste). Lord Cantlemere is here, sir.

---

29. **gramophones:** phonographs.
30. **Not blooming likely:** slang for "not very likely."

[Holmes *goes to the bedroom door.*]

Holmes. Show His Lordship up, Billy, while I turn off the — er — "grammerphone."
Billy. Very good, sir.

[Holmes *and* Billy *exit by the bedroom and parlor doors respectively, leaving both of them open.* Watson *lays down his hat and stick. The music ceases abruptly and* Holmes *returns, shutting the bedroom door.* Billy *reenters the parlor door.*]

Billy. Lord Cantlemere, sir. *(He steps aside to let* Cantlemere *enter, then goes out, closing the door.)*
Cantlemere. What on earth's going on here, Holmes? Constables and fellahs all over the place!
Holmes. How do you do, Lord Cantlemere? May I introduce my friend and colleague, Dr. Watson?
Watson. How d'you do, my lord?
Cantlemere *(brusquely).* D'yer do?
Holmes. Watson, pray help me with His Lordship's overcoat. (Holmes *takes hold of the coat, preparing to take it off.)*
Cantlemere. No, thank you. I will not take it off.

[Holmes *pawing the coat.*]

Holmes. Oh, but my friend Dr. Watson would assure you that it is most unhealthy to retain a coat indoors, even at this time of the year.
Cantlemere *(releasing himself).* I am quite comfortable as I am, sir! I have no need to stay. I have simply looked in to know how your self-appointed task is progressing.

[Holmes *assumes a troubled air.*]

Holmes. It's difficult — very difficult.

Cantlemere *(with gleeful malice).* Ha! I feared you'd find it so! Every man finds his limitations, Holmes — but at least it cures us of the weakness of self-satisfaction.
Holmes. Yes, sir. I admit I have been much perplexed.
Cantlemere. No doubt!
Holmes. Especially upon one point. Perhaps you could help me?

[Cantlemere *takes a chair.* Holmes *sits opposite him,* Watson *standing behind his chair.*]

Cantlemere. You apply for my advice rather late in the day. I thought you had your own self-sufficient methods. Still, I am ready to help you.
Holmes. Your Lordship is most obliging. You see, we can no doubt frame a case against the actual thieves.
Cantlemere. *When* you've caught them.
Holmes. Exactly. But the question is, how shall we proceed against the receiver?
Cantlemere. Receiver? Isn't this rather premature?
Holmes. It's as well to have our plans ready. Now, what would you regard as final evidence against the receiver?
Cantlemere. The actual possession of the stone, of course.
Holmes. You'd arrest him on that?
Cantlemere. Undoubtedly.
Holmes *(slyly).* In that case, my dear sir, I shall be under the painful necessity of advising your arrest!

[Cantlemere *leaps to his feet.*]

Cantlemere. Holmes! In fifty years of official life I cannot recall such a liberty being taken! I am a busy man, engaged upon important affairs, and I have neither time nor taste for foolish jokes. (Holmes *slowly rises*.) I may tell you frankly, sir, that I have never been a believer in your powers. I have always been of the opinion that the matter was far safer in the hands of the regular police force. Your conduct confirms all my conclusions. *(He moves stiffly towards the parlor door.)* I have the honor, sir, to wish you good evening!

Holmes. One moment, sir! (Cantlemere *turns to face him inquiringly.)* Actually to go off with the Mazarin Stone would be an even more serious offense than to be found in temporary possession of it!

Cantlemere. Sir, this is intolerable!

Holmes. Put your hand in the right-hand pocket of your overcoat.

Cantlemere. What? What do you mean?

Holmes. Come, come! Do what I ask!

[Cantlemere *splutters with fury, but feels in his pocket.*]

Cantlemere. I'll make an end to this charade,[31] and you'll wish you'd never begun it! I . . . I . . . *(His fury suddenly abates, giving way to surprise, then astonishment, as he slowly withdraws from his pocket the Mazarin Stone and holds it up.)*

Watson. Great heavens!

Holmes. Too bad of me, Lord Cantlemere. My old friend here will tell you that I have an impish habit of practical joking. Also that I can never resist a dramatic situation. I took the liberty — the very great liberty, I confess — of putting the stone into your pocket at the beginning of our interview.

Cantlemere. I . . . I'm bewildered! This *is* the Mazarin Stone! (Holmes *bows slightly.*) Hol . . . Mr. Holmes, we are greatly your debtors. Your sense of humor may, as you admit, be somewhat perverted, and its exhibition untimely — remarkably untimely! (Watson *stifles a grin.*) But at least I withdraw any reflection I have made upon your professional powers.

Holmes. Thank you, Lord Cantlemere. I hope your pleasure in reporting this successful result in the exalted circle to which you return will be some small atonement for my joke. I will supply the full particulars in a written report.

[Cantlemere *bows and goes to the parlor door.* Watson *hastens to open it for him.*]

Cantlemere. Once more, good evening. *(He nods to* Watson.*)* And to you, sir, good evening.

Watson.
Holmes. } Good evening.

[Cantlemere *exits.* Watson *gives him a rigid military salute behind his retreating back, then closes the door.*]

Watson. *Well,* Holmes.

Holmes. He's an excellent and loyal person, but rather of the old regime.[32] *(He goes to* Watson *and claps him on the shoulder.)* And now, my dear Watson, pray touch the bell, and Mrs. Hudson shall lay dinner for two — as of old!

[*Final curtain.*]

---

31. **charade** (shə-rād′): game; pretense.

32. **old regime** (rə-zhēm′): the old order of things, now out of date.

SEEKING MEANING

Holmes says that he is a "brain," a person of great intelligence. In the play we see how Holmes uses intelligence to outwit his opponents.

1. One of Holmes's well-known talents is "play-acting." How does he show that he is skillful at disguise?

2. Holmes is expert at tricking criminals into telling him what he wants to know. How does he trick the Count into admitting that he knows where the diamond is?

3. Holmes is sure that the Count has stolen the diamond. What evidence has he used in building his case?

4. Describe Holmes's plan for recovering the diamond. What part do the dummy and the gramophone play in this plan?

5. The Count claims that he has fooled better men than Holmes. How does he plan to get away with the diamond? How does Holmes prevent his escape?

6. Why does Holmes play a practical joke on Lord Cantlemere? How does Lord Cantlemere become convinced that Holmes is a "brain"?

DEVELOPING SKILLS IN READING

Imagining a Play in Performance

In reading a play, you let your imagination do the work that would be done for you in a theater by actors, costumes, scenery, lighting, and sound effects. You imagine how the characters would be dressed, how they would speak their lines, what facial expressions they would use, and what movements they would make.

A playwright often gives players instructions for acting. These are called *stage directions*. Stage directions appear in italics within parentheses or brackets. A stage direction may tell the actor how a line should be spoken.

Watson *(dismally)*. Oh!
Holmes *(sharply)*. That will do, Billy!
Billy *(humbly)*. Yes, sir.

A stage direction may call for a specific action or movement.

Holmes *(sadly shaking his head)*. Your morals don't improve, Watson.

[Holmes *makes an elaborate bow, holding out the parasol in both hands.*]

Stage directions may tell an actor what kind of facial expression to use.

[Sylvius *whirls round, his stick still upraised, a look of disbelief on his face.*]

Most of the time, directions for acting are built into the dialogue of the play. As you read the speeches of the characters, you must imagine what they feel and think as well as what they do with their voices, their expressions, and their gestures.

Here is some dialogue from the play. Decide how the actors would speak these lines. How would they move? What facial expressions would they use?

Watson. Look here, Holmes, this is simply ridiculous. This is a desperate man who sticks at nothing, you'd have me believe. He may have *come* to murder you.

(page 328)

Sylvius. I, too, wished to have some words with you, Holmes! That is why I am here. Because you have gone out of your way to annoy me. Because you have put your creatures on my track! (page 330)

Holmes. Oh, no violence, Billy! Don't be rough with him! If you tell him that Count Sylvius wants him he will come.

(page 332)

Cantlemere. I'll make an end to this charade, and you'll wish you'd never begun it! I . . . I . . .

(page 337)

Understanding Plot

In a play, as in a short story, the plot, or sequence of events, follows a certain pattern. The action generally develops out of one or more conflicts or problems. At the opening of *The Mazarin Stone*, we learn that a diamond has been stolen and that Holmes has been called in on the case. Holmes's problem is to get the criminals to assist him in recovering the stone. The central conflict of the play is not physical—it is a battle of wits between Sherlock Holmes and the thieves. That battle is won and the conflict resolved when Holmes takes the diamond from the thieves and has them arrested.

What is Holmes's conflict with Lord Cantlemere? How is it resolved?

DEVELOPING SKILLS OF EXPRESSION

Improvising a Scene

A good way to learn about writing and performing plays is to improvise. When you improvise, you act without a script. You do not plan what you will say or do. You make up the words and actions as you go along, responding to what the other actors say and do.

Try improvising one of the following situations with one or more partners. Notice that each situation contains a conflict. Before you begin, make sure that you know who you are, where you are, and what you want. Pay no attention to the audience, but speak loudly enough for them to hear you. All will go well if you relax and use your imagination.

You have not practiced your music. You try to distract the teacher so that your hour will be up before you have to play.

You would like to go to the beach. Your friends would like to go to the mountains. You try to persuade them to go to the beach.

You are trying to persuade your parents to give you some money. They think you should earn it.

You are at a sale counter. Two other people wish to buy the article you have selected.

Several people are trapped in an elevator with you. You do not agree with them about what is to be done.

ABOUT THE AUTHOR

Sir Arthur Conan Doyle (1859–1930) began writing detective fiction while he was practicing medicine. His greatest creation was the brilliant detective Sherlock Holmes, one of the most famous characters in all English fiction. Holmes first appeared in *A Study in Scarlet*, published in 1887. He became a great success with readers. The demand for new books about Holmes meant that Doyle had to spend more and more time creating new adventures for his popular hero. Tiring of his creation or perhaps running out of ideas, Doyle had Holmes killed off in *The Memoirs of Sherlock Holmes*. However, Sherlock Holmes's fans had become so numerous and their appetite for new stories so strong that Doyle was persuaded to bring him back. He explained that Holmes had merely disappeared, not died.

Radio is ideally suited to plays of fantasy. Actions that might be difficult or impossible to perform on a stage can be suggested effectively through dialogue, music, and sound effects. Here is a humorous fantasy that shows how imaginatively the techniques of radio drama can be put to use.

The Pussycat and the Expert Plumber Who Was a Man
Arthur Miller

Characters

George Beeker
Adele, his wife
Mr. Tom Thomas, a cat
Mayor Johnson
John, his assistant
A Woman in a beauty shop
Sally, a beauty operator
Dan Billings, an important citizen

Mr. Fairchild
Mr. Peters
A Railroad Conductor
Sam, a plumber
Joey, his young assistant
Manager of the Victoria Hotel
Convention Speaker
Convention Delegates
A Woman who screams
Several Voices

[Sound: *Clock being wound.*]

George *(timid voice).* Shouldn't have stayed up so late, Adele.
Adele *(sleepily).* Did you lock the door?
George. Oh, leave it open tonight. It's stuffy.
Adele. Turn out the light.

[Sound: *Light switch — bed creaking as man gets in.*]

Voice *(trifle high-pitched — peculiar — small).* George. *(Pause; breathing)* Mr. Beeker . . .
George *(softly).* Adele . . . Del!
Adele. What's the matter now?

George. Did you hear someone calling my name?

Adele. Oh, go to sleep.

George. But really, I . . .

Voice. It's me, Mr. Beeker.

Adele *(frightened).* Who's in the room?

Voice. It's only me, Mr. Thomas.

George. Thomas? Who . . .

Adele. Turn on the light.

[Sound: *Light switch. Pause.*]

George. Why, nobody's here.

Adele. Push the cat off the bed.

Voice. Please don't.

George. There, again.

Adele. Go down and call the police.

Voice. You'd better not.

Adele *(loud).* There's someone in the room and we can't see him.

Voice. But you're looking straight at me, Adele.

George. Del . . . don't talk. Close your eyes.

Adele. Why?

George. Close them. All right?

Adele. Yes . . .

George. Mr. Thomas, ah . . . would you walk toward me, just come this way?

Voice. Certainly.

[*Pause.*]

George. Del! Del! . . . It's the cat . . . the cat can talk.

[Adele *screams.*]

George *(as* Adele *sobs in a terrified scream).* Oh, Father in Heaven, forgive our sins, we didn't mean anything, we'll be good, whatever we did wrong we'll do right.

Tom. Oh, come on. Really, it's not that bad.

George. Who . . . Who are you? I mean . . .

Tom. I'm Mr. Thomas

George. But we don't know any Mr. Thomas, I never . . .

Tom. All right then. My name is Tom. Tom, Tom the cat. Now are you satisfied?

George. But whose spirit is in you?

Tom. What spirit? Don't you give me credit for learning how to talk?

George (frightened). Yeh, sure . . . but after all . . .

Tom. Now, look, calm yourselves, and let's talk sense.

George (softly). Look how his whiskers move.

Tom. One doesn't whisper in company, Mr. Beeker.

George. Oh, pardon me.

Tom. It's hard enough for me, so let's not make it any harder.

Adele. But how did you learn?

Tom. I'll explain everything. Will you shade that bulb, please? It's hard seeing you. Thanks. It's like this. You took me in, I was a kitten. Well, it wasn't long before I discovered that I was pretty smart. Follow me?

George. Ah . . . Yeh, yeh, I follow.

Tom. Now will you stop watching my whiskers, George, you make me nervous. Well, as I was saying, I discovered I was smarter than most cats. At the age of nine months I began setting traps for mice.

George. Where did you get the traps?

Tom. Made 'em.

George. Oh.

Tom. Anyhow, last year, I began watching you people talk and I got a feeling it might be worth my while to pick up the lingo,[1] so to speak. So I did.

Adele. But how?

Tom. What do you mean, how? What do you think a cat is, an idiot?

Adele. I'm sorry.

Tom. Just keep it in mind, please. But being able to talk English wasn't much good because . . . well, there was nobody to talk to.

People ran like mad when I addressed them, and the cats, of course, only understand cat language.

George. You don't mean cats talk to each other.

Tom. Cats, Mr. Beeker, speak much more beautifully than men do. You'll never find a cat walking down a street saying to everyone he meets, "Hot enough for you?" or "It ain't the heat, it's the humidity." No, a cat only talks when he's got something important to say, and he says it in one word. Things like: "Love me, darling?" . . . meow? Or, "I'm hungry." . . . meow. Or, "I'm hurt." . . . yow! Or, "Gosh, I feel good." . . . purr. Important things, get it?

George. Yeh, I get it. I get it. Tell me, what do you want with us?

Tom. I want your help. To carry out my plan I must have human aid.

George. What do you mean?

Tom. This. I am the only cat in America who can speak and understand and read the English language.

Adele. You read.

Tom. I love to read—except the funnies. They frighten me.

George. What's this plan you mentioned?

Tom. It's the most daring idea in the history of the world.

George. You don't say.

Tom. Mr. Beeker, I am going to be the mayor of this town.

George. You? A cat?

Tom. I, Mr. Tom Thomas. Everything is ready. All I need is a man who can write. I can't hold a pencil.

George. Now look here, Tom, that's going a little too far. I think . . .

Tom. I don't care what you think. You'll do as I say.

George. I won't stand for a cat ordering me around, Tom.

---

1. **lingo:** a humorous term for an unfamiliar language.

Tom. Mrs. Beeker, would you like to know what was going on in this house while you were away in Chicago last summer?

George. Say now, Tom, you can't . . .

Adele. What's this? What?

George. You keep your mouth shut, Tom.

Tom. That's better. Now here's my proposition. Practically every one of the finest families in town keeps a cat. I've taught those cats to read and understand English. But only I can speak because I'm so clever. Now they've been reporting to me for the past five months. I have enough on every big man in this town to make him do whatever I command.

George. That's blackmail!

Tom. I've been around, George. That's politics. So what you will do is buy a big ledger and enter the private scandal of every person I give you.

George. But some people have no scandal to be ashamed of.

Tom. Then I make one up and spread it in the papers.

George. No editor would do such a thing!

Tom. The editor of the *Gazette* has two wives.

Adele. Mr. Stevens, George!

Tom. Right. He'll be in the palm of my hand.

George. Oh . . .

Tom. Don't interrupt. Election for mayor is two weeks off. I've got the goods on both candidates so they'll campaign for me. . . .

George. But will people vote for a cat, Tom?

Tom. Leave that strictly to me, George. Are you with me? Will you keep my books?

George. Well I—I don't know, I . . .

Tom. I can ruin your business in ten days. You take opium.

George. I take . . .

Adele. But it's not so!

Tom. What do you say, George? I'm not kidding.

Adele *(sobs)*. Oh, George . . .

George. All right, I'll buy a ledger tomorrow.

Tom. Put it there, George old boy.

George. Where?

Tom. Shake hands, I won't scratch. There! And now I must be off. I'm going to dictate a speech to the Mayor in which he will explain to the voters why he recommends me for office. The Mayor, you see, has evaded his income tax three years hand running and I have all the documents socked away in a milk bottle. Good night.

George. Good night. See you in the morning.

Tom. And George, please don't water my milk from now on. I'm going to need all my strength. Bye-bye!

[Music: *Jaunty—cattish—gay, which lowers and fades into . . .*]

John. Now pull out of it, Your Honor. You're falling to pieces.

Mayor. Take him away! A talking cat!

John. But Your Honor . . .

Mayor. No, no, I won't believe it! Get him off my desk!

Tom. Your Honor, if you won't hear me I'll just have to tell the authorities! I did not come here to be . . .

Mayor. Authorities! But I'm the Mayor, young man, I mean ca . . . that is . . .

Tom. Thomas is the name. Tom Thomas. And I was referring to the federal authorities, the Income Tax Bureau.

Mayor. What's this. What's this?

Tom. I have the papers to prove you've evaded taxes, cashed in on city construction, shielded murderers . . .

Mayor. How do you know all this?

Tom. Mayor, I know more about you than you do. I've read every letter you've written or received in the past four months, gotten reports on every phone call. I have enough on you to send you up for six hundred years, and if you don't believe me look in your safe for your bankbook. (*The* Mayor *is silent.*) Go on, look.

Mayor. It's been missing for a week. What do you want?

Tom. I am going to be the mayor of this city.

Mayor. You . . . that is . . . mayor.

Tom. You swing your machine behind me and withdraw your support from Wilcox. I've taken care of the opposition candidate. He has insanity in his family and he's decided not to run.

Mayor. Well . . . so you have . . . mhm . . . well . . . grab him, John!

John. Ha! Got him!

Tom. Yowww!

Mayor. Now you little devil, you Beelzebub,[2] we'll see who'll be mayor! Drown him!

Tom. Let me go, you fool. Yowwww!

Mayor. Take him to the river, John, and hold him under till he busts!

Tom. Wait. (*Coughs*) Hey, you're choking me! Mayor, for your own sake let me talk!

Mayor. For my sake!

Tom. You can drown me, but the minute I'm dead all your private papers will be dragged along Main Street by every cat in Billington! My organization stands ready for revenge!

Mayor. What organization?

Tom. I have a full-grown cat in every third house in this city. Your chief of police alone keeps three of my operatives[3] in his office.

Mayor. You mean?

Tom. I mean that if I'm killed you're up the creek and that goes for every politician in town!

Mayor. Unloose him, John.

Tom. And let go of my tail. Well, Your Honor? Who's the new mayor of Billington?

Mayor. Thomas, my honest opinion is that the people of Billington will not vote for a cat.

Tom. But they won't vote for a cat, they'll vote for a name . . . Tom Thomas, and with the papers on my side, by the time the people go to the polls they won't know what they're voting for. No photographs, no personal appearances, just the name and anything you want to say about it. I'll be the publicity-hating crusader, the unseen marvel. I say it can be done and you'd better see that it is done!

Mayor. I've gotta have time to think. . . .

Tom. Fine, then it's settled!

[Music: *Crash of music—victorious but still cattish—blending into the sound of a hair dryer-blower.*]

Woman. Say, Sally, you've got that dryer on too hot! It's burning my scalp!

Sally. There, how's that?

Woman. Oh, that's fine. Look at the *Gazette,* will you? That Thomas is certainly a wonderful man.

Sally. He'd get my vote even if there was another man running.

Woman. You know, they say he's got a lovely tenor voice.

Sally. Where'd you hear that?

Woman. Why, read your papers, dear. That man will put this town on the map, I bet. Anyway, he must be wonderful to look at— blond and tall and all that.

Sally. Wonder why he doesn't let anybody see him though?

Woman. But he does. The Mayor's seen him, and besides, why shouldn't he stay at home? I think he's very modest, and besides, people will vote for him just to see what he looks like, and besides, a man has a right to his privacy, and besides . . . (*Fade*)

[Music: *Up—then lower—then telephone bell.*]

---

2. **Beelzebub** (bē-ĕl′zĭ-bŭb): a devil.
3. **operatives** (ŏp′ə-rə-tĭvz): here, spies.

George. George Beeker speaking.

Mayor *(through telephone)*. This is the Mayor. Give me the cat. Hurry.

George. Tom. Want to jump up here and take it? The Mayor.

[Sound: *Thump of cat landing on table.*]

Tom. Hold that receiver a little higher, George. Hello?

Mayor. Thomas?

Tom. Yes?

Mayor. The votes, Thomas.

Tom. What about the votes?

Mayor. They have just finished counting them, Thomas.

Tom. Well? So?

Mayor. You have just been elected mayor of Billington.

Tom. That's very nice, Johnson. But why is your voice shaking?

Mayor. Because, Tom, old boy, there happens to be five hundred people surging outside my door demanding to see the new mayor. Now what do I do, tell them he's out chasing mice?

Tom. Don't be so sassy. I'll be right over.

Mayor. Yeh? And how'll you get in? They've packed the hallways!

Tom. There's a tree next to your window, isn't there?

Mayor. So what?

Tom. So I'll be right up.

Mayor. But you're mayor now, Tom, a mayor doesn't come into City Hall by a tree! And anyway they'll hang me if they see you! Enough is enough, Tom! Hello . . . Hello! Tom! Tom! Hello! . . . *(Fade)*

[Music: *Bridge.*[4]]

4. **Bridge:** music used to connect two scenes.

John. They're still pouring into the hallway, Your Honor.

Mayor. Come down from that transom and get me an aspirin, John.

John. I guess I shouldn't call you "Your Honor" any more, sir.

Mayor. No, John, from now on address me as mud.

[Sound: *Scratching of nails on wood.*]

Mayor. What's that?

[Sound: *Same.*]

John. Scratching outside the door, sir.

Mayor. It's the Mayor. Open the door a wee bit.

[Sound: *Burst of crowd noise—shut out by closing door.*]

Mayor. Ah, don't leap up at me so, Tom. I thought you were going to climb the tree.

Tom. Wanted to get a look at the crowd.

Mayor. Well, I guess the joke's over, eh, feller?

Tom. Yes. We've got to be more serious from now on. There's a man named Billings out there. Seems to be the leader.

Mayor. Sure, Dan Billings; been on the City Board fourteen years, vice president of the bank, president of . . .

Tom. I want to see him.

Mayor. What . . . But he'll see you're a cat, Tom!

Tom. Every so often certain people will be informed that I am a cat. This is one of those people. Bring me Billings, John.

John. Uh . . . yes, sir.

Mayor. But Tom, Billings is one of our first citizens; he'll have my head for this, he'll . . .

Tom. Open the door, John, and don't stare so.

[Sound: *Door opening, admitting babble of crowd as . . .*]

Tom. Get off that chair, Mayor—or Mr. Johnson, I'm sitting down.

John (*shouting over crowd*). His Honor wants to see Dan Billings!

Tom. Keep away from that window, Johnson, I don't want you falling out.

John. Mr. Billings is coming through the crowd, Your Honor.

Mayor (*hushed*). If you talk to Billings I'll die!

Tom. Let him in, John.

[Sound: *Crowd noise is shut out by slamming door.*]

Billings (*well-fed voice*). Well! It's about time a citizen got a look at his mayor. But where is Thomas? I thought he was in here.

Tom. How do you do, sir?

Billings. How do you—who said that?

Mayor. You see, Billings, I ah . . .

Tom. Won't you sit down, sir?

Billings. Why, certain . . . Who's talking in here?

Mayor. Ah . . . the cat, Billings. The one in the chair.

Billings. The cat!

Mayor. Yes, Billings, this cat is Tom. Tom Thomas . . . ah . . . the Mayor.

[Sound: *A body hitting the floor.*]

Mayor. There, you see, Tom? He's fainted. Throw some water at him, John, the poor man has fainted.

[Music: *Comes up quickly and dies.*]

Tom. So you see, Mr. Billings, I know all about your youthful career on the chain gang.

Billings (*pleading*). But I was so young, I . . .

Tom. Oh, I understand, old boy, we all make mistakes, but I'm sure you wouldn't care to have the public or perhaps your wife know that you . . .

Billings. Oh, no, no . . . What do you want? What?

Tom. The people—they respect you, don't they?

Billings. This town was named for my great-great-great-grandfather. I've been vice president of . . .

Tom. That's fine. Now go right out to that crowd and tell them that you've met Tom Thomas, that he's a fine fellow, etc., but that he's so darned shy he'd rather keep to himself for a while longer. Tell them I'm already up to my ears in official work and that I'm going to be the best mayor Billington ever had. Got it?

Billings. Couldn't I just go home?

Tom. And when you're through, come back here and maybe we can arrange to get your father admitted to the fife-and-drum corps of the fire department.

Billings. How did you know he wanted to get on?

Tom. Oh, you'll find I know a lot of things, Daniel.

Billings. You don't know what that would mean to Dad. He's . . .

Tom. Well, you just do your part and I'll do mine.

Billings. I'll appreciate it, Tom . . . er . . . Your Honor.

Tom. Tom's good enough. 'Bye.

Billings. Well . . . here goes.

[Sound: *Footsteps—door opening, admitting crowd babble.*]

Billings (*over the crowd*). Citizens!

[Sound: *Crowd hushes.*]

Billings. I have just seen Tom Thomas, and let me tell you that there is an individual Billington will be famous for.

Tom. Close the door, John.

Billings. Why, do you know what he told me? He said, Dan, what this town needs is . . .

[Sound: *Door closing.*]

Mayor. I would never have believed that in ten million years.

Tom. Johnson, we are going to talk. Heart to heart.

Mayor. What about?

Tom. Take the inkwell and those books off the desk. I want room to walk around. Now listen. How would you like to be lieutenant governor of this state?

Mayor. Now Tom, Tom, you're starting something again, and I'm not quite up to it, I . . .

Tom. Johnson, I am going to be governor.

Mayor. Now, Tom, no pussycat ever has been or ever will be governor of this state! It simply isn't done!

Tom. But you would like to be lieutenant governor?

Mayor. Yes, I would, I would, but I don't see how you're going to . . .

Tom. Listen. Why am I mayor of Billington?

Mayor. You got me there, Tom, I . . .

Tom. Because practically every important man in town has something in his past of which he is so ashamed that he'd sell his soul to keep it covered.

Mayor. What I can't figure out is why nobody ever thought of this stunt before.

Tom. Because no prospective blackmailer has a clean enough record himself to dare do what I've done. And the only reason I succeeded is because I'm a cat with nothing to hide. Johnson, what I've done in Billington can be done in every city in this state.

Mayor. How?

Tom. There are housecats in every city.

Mayor. You mean?

Tom. I mean that you are going to buy two animal suitcases and meet me at the railroad station in half an hour. I'll bring two cats, my lieutenants. You'll carry one to Hillsboro, and the other to Brycetown. They will contact the housecats of the big shots in those towns, or the neighbors of the big shots. Then in ten days you pick them up and they'll bring me the goods. We'll keep sending out cats to every important town until we've got something on every politician and newspaper owner in the state. In six months I'll be ready, and with publicity going full blast I'll have the votes in my pocket.

Mayor. But will those out-of-town cats become spies for nothing, Tom?

Tom. Silly man. There is one thing cats and people will gladly do free of charge—and that's snoop. What do you say, ex-Mayor Johnson?

Mayor. Tom, the world is yours.

[Music: *Becoming the hissing of a locomotive standing at station.*]

Conductor *(off mike).* Board! All aboard!

Mayor *(whisper).* Just drop them off in those towns, eh, Tom?

Tom *(whisper).* That's all. They know the rest. Hurry!

Mayor. 'Bye!

Conductor *(off mike).* Board for Hillsboro, Brycetown, Makersville, Rostentown, Saul, and Lantzbury!

[Sound: *Train starts — goes for a moment — then . . .*]

Tom *(over train noise).* Good work, Johnson! Now take two more to Greenville and Bentley!

[Sound: *Up on train — hold a moment — then lower again.*]

Tom *(over train noise).* Fine, Johnson, now one to Greer, one to Bolton, one to Strongsville, and then one to Price!

[Sound: *Up on train — hold — then lower again.*]

Tom. Excellent, Johnson, now take them to Cardsbury, Melton, Burnandale, Monroe, Henley, Elsworth . . .

[Sound: *Up on train, which drowns him out and continues a moment, then fades into the distance.*]

Tom. . . . so you see, gentlemen, I've got it on every one of you, so that's that. In short, I have called you here tonight because you run this state and it is you who will make me governor. Now what's the answer?

Fairchild. Thomas, I . . . do you mind if I call you Tom?

Tom. Please do.

Fairchild. It's true, Tom, that we run the state machine, true you've got every one of us cornered, but here's the hitch: the voters will simply not elect a governor they've never laid their eyes on!

Tom. The voters . . . !

Voices. Right . . . never work . . . not a chance . . . *etc.*

Tom. But, gentlemen, that's exactly why I will run away with the elections! What's the weakest plate in any candidate's armor? His record, right? If he's been too pro-labor the employers are afraid, if he's too pro-farmer the workers wonder, and so on down the line. But me, why I've got the ideal record, the perfect political past—none whatsoever. No actions to be sorry for, no foolish statements to regret; in fact, gentlemen, it is just because I am nothing to any man that I will be everything to all men. Make me what you like in the papers, I will be that, and why? . . . Because all I am is a piece of fur with some vital information and a future. Now what's the verdict? *(Pause)*

[Voices: *talking among themselves—deliberating—ad lib.*]

Peters. Fellush! I don't care what he shays, hic! That man on the table is a pussycat!

Voices. That's all right, Peters, just sit down, that's better.

Peters. But he ish! He said so himself!

Voices. Sssh! Quiet, old boy. . . . *etc.*

Fairchild. Tom, we'll admit you're right.

Tom. I'm happy to hear that, Mr. Fairchild.

Fairchild. For the sake of argument, let's assume a pussycat could become governor. But what then? If one man discovers you, if one man finds out the Governor is a cat . . .

Tom. Now you've hit it, Fairchild, the secret of my success. I am a housecat not only by birth but by profession. All my friends are housecats, so I speak from experience. Gentlemen, I have seen life. Life in the bathtub, life in dark cellars, and I've seen it from the bottom up and I tell you that under the threat of slander, of being publicly defamed, no man will dare tell a soul that Tom Thomas, Governor Thomas, is a pussycat, should he make the discovery.

Voice. But why not?

Tom. Because the one thing a man fears most next to death is the loss of his good name. Man is evil in his own eyes, my friends, worthless, and the only way he can find respect for himself is by getting other people to say he's a nice fellow. So be sure of it, the only man who'd expose me is one who really believes he's upright and clean, really in his secret heart, and such a man does not exist in this world.

Voice. Boys, that cat has got a head on him.

Voice. Say, Tom, couldn't we settle for $50,000? I'm getting dizzy.

Tom. I will be governor, Mr. Wynne.

Voice. Well, Fairchild, it's up to you. If his cats start dragging our skeletons into the streets we're in the soup.

Voice. What'll it be, Fairchild?

Fairchild. Don't be so sad, boys. We are going to nominate him at the convention next week, we are going to elect him in November, and it's my guess that Tom Thomas is going to be the smartest governor this state ever had!

[Music: *"There'll Be a Hot Time in the Old Town Tonight"—played by the usual convention brass band accompanied by shouting of the crowd, etc.—then whole thing is lowered and over it is heard the sound of a hammer hitting on a lead pipe—the music now comes as though from a few floors below.*]

Sam. They sure are whoopin' it up for Tom Thomas in the auditorium downstairs.

[*The hammering continues.*]

Joey (*boyish*). Yeh, he better show his face tonight. . . .

[Sound: *Door pushed open.*]

Manager. Hey! Hey! Cut that noise. The guests in the next room're complaining!
Sam. You want the sink fixed, I gotta make noise. Tell the guests to go for a walk.
Manager. Now you lay off. That's Tom Thomas in there with the state big shots. I don't want any more of it.

[Sound: *Door closing.*]

Sam. Tom Thomas . . . in the next room!
Joey. What do we do now, Sam?
Sam. Tom . . . heh? Here's a dime. Go get yourself a soda.
Joey. Oh, swell.

[Sound: *Door opening.*]

Sam. And don't hurry back.

[Sound: *Door shutting.*]

Sam (*to himself*). The next room! Gosh, I wonder what he really looks like. . . . Boy, I bet he's a big guy with . . . this window . . . I bet I could walk right along that ledge and . . . and look right in on him . . . let's see . . .

[Sound: *Window sliding up.*]

Sam. What a snap . . . why not!

[Sound: *He climbs the sill.*]

Sam. Now if I can innnnnch aloooong . . . gee, it's high . . . just to that window . . .

[*Undistinguishable voices of several men in conference coming through the window.*]

Sam. There . . . sit . . . the biggest shots in the state, and what a view! (*On mike—to himself*) I wonder which one is Tom Thomas. . . . That fat one . . . No, he's too fat. The one walking around, I bet . . . funny, that cat sitting right on the table . . .
First Voice (*off mike*). Nominate tonight, eh, Fairchild?
Fairchild. That depends on the southern counties.
Second Voice. We got all but three.
Third Voice. Let Fairchild settle this.
Fourth Voice. Now don't be too sure about those southern counties. . . .
Fifth Voice. Well, I think Tom ought to settle it.
Sam (*to himself*). Now!
Sixth Voice. Yes, Mr. Thomas, what's your opinion?
Sam. Gosh, they don't seem to be looking at anybody!
Fairchild. Well, Tom? What will it be? Nominate tomorrow morning?
Tom. You see, Mr. Fairchild, my only objection to tomorrow is that I'm afraid a lot of the delegates won't be rounded up and then we'll have to wait another day. So I'd prefer tonight.
Sam. That cat . . . I'm going nuts. . . . That cat is talking! They're shaking his paw! (*Loud*) Holy smoke!
Voices in the Room. Who's that . . . hey . . . (*Ad-lib shock*) . . . Grab him! Get him in here. . . . (*Ad lib*) Stand up, you! What were you doing out there?
Sam. That cat . . .

Voice. That cat is none of your business!

Sam. That cat is Tom Thomas! He can talk words!

Fairchild. You're crazy! I'll have you . . .

Sam. Now don't tell me! I heard him talk and you called him Tom Thomas!

Fairchild (amid hubbub). You say that again and I'll have you put . . .

Tom. Gentlemen!

Sam. There, he talked!

Fairchild. But Tom . . .

Tom. I'll handle him, Fairchild. Young man, what do you want?

Sam. Want?

Tom. Yes, everybody wants something, what do you want?

Sam. Well, right now I want everybody to know Tom Thomas is a cat, that's what!

Tom. Why must anyone know?

Sam. Why? You're a cat, mister! . . . As sure as my name is Sam!

Tom. But that's fairly obvious.

Sam. But . . . well, the governor is not supposed to be a cat!

Tom. As far as the people know, I'm a man, and if I can govern well, what difference will a few hairs make?

Sam. Listen, there's a little more between you and being a man than a few hairs.

Tom. Is there? What? I can do everything you can except write, and if my nails grow a little longer maybe I'll do that, too. Anyway, lots of men can't write.

Sam. But a man is different.

Tom. Just how?

Sam. Well, a man is got . . . he's got ideals. Has a cat got ideals?

Tom. Certainly. My ideal, for instance, is to become the most powerful individual in this state. You're all wet, Sam, there's no difference between a cat and a man. So why expose me? I'll give you $25,000 to keep your mouth shut.

Sam. But there is a difference, there must be!

Tom. You'll have to get rid of your superior attitude, Sam. You can do nothing that I can't do.

Sam. Yeh? Can you fix a leaky pipe?

Tom. No, but can you catch a mouse with your teeth—no hands?

Sam. All right, can you build a house?

Tom. All right, can your wife bear eight children at once without batting an eye? Drop it, Sam, we'll come out tied. Now look here, you won't be bribed, but if you open your mouth about this to a soul, your reputation isn't worth a thin dime. I'll smear you like mud and I can do it!

Sam. Look. What would a cat do in my place?

Tom. Same as a man. He'd take the money and buy a house in the country.

Sam. And you're the same as me, right?

Tom. Right.

Sam. You really believe that?

Tom. I am what I am because men are like cats.

Sam. OK, do you believe it enough to come into the convention hall under my arm?

Tom. Certainly.

Voices. What? Tom, you can't do that. . . . etc.

Tom. But don't forget, Sam, you won't ever again be able to walk out of your house in daylight. You'll be ashamed to show your face. . . .

Sam. That's OK. I'll carry you.

Voices. Now, Tom, you're not going with him! . . . etc.

Tom. People will despise you, Sam, I'll see to it. You'll be alone in the world with your evil heart!

Sam. I don't think so.

Voices. Don't go, Tom! . . . etc.

Tom. Sam, I offer you $40,000 to keep shut!

Sam. Listen, Tom Thomas, and the rest of you, too. A pussycat might think he's a man because he got to be mayor; he might think he's a man because he's almost governor. But there's one thing that shows he ain't a man, and that's the same thing that'll keep my head up if nobody in the world'll say a civil word to me till the day I die—no pussycat could ever become an expert plumber, and that's the difference between you and me! Let's go!

Fairchild. Oh, no, you don't.

Tom. Out of the way, Fairchild, I want to test my theory once and for all.

Fairchild. But if he tells the convention!

Tom. Then that's the end of my career. But he won't, and then, gentlemen, on to the presidency!

Fairchild. But what about us? If he tells, we're finished!

Tom. Well, Fairchild, if one cat is discovered in public office you can't expect the others to go off scot-free. Let us through, and don't worry; Sam, the plumber, will regret the night he climbed out the window of the Victoria Hotel!

[Music: *"Hot Time in the Old Town Tonight"*—out short.]

Speaker (off mike in a hall). Ladies and gentlemen! We will now start the first ballot for governor! The delegate from the county of Atcheson!

Delegate. County Atcheson casts three votes for Tom Thomas!

[Crowd cheers.]

Sam (on mike). Let me through there!

Voice. You got your nerve!

Speaker. County Barton!

Sam. Let me pass, thanks.

Delegate. County Barton casts four votes for Tom Thomas!

Tom (hushed). I'll make it $50,000. Sam, fifty thousand!

Sam. Pardon me, I'm going up on the platform, thank you.

Speaker. The delegate from Carroway County!

Sam. Say, Mister Speaker.

Delegate. Carroway County votes for Jack Halsey!

Speaker. What do you want? Who are you?

Sam. I got something to tell the delegates about Tom Thomas. It's something terrific.

Speaker. Are you for or against?

Sam. Oh, I'm for, all right.

Speaker. Go ahead, but keep that cat out of the microphones.

Sam. Ladies and gentlemen, I . . . I am a plumber. . . .

[Crowd cheers.]

Sam. The great Tom Thomas, the tall, blond

publicity-hating crusader, the unseen mystery marvel, is none other than this cat in my hands!

[*Crowd: uproar of laughter.*]

Sam. I tell you he can talk. He's got you all buffaloed![5]

[*Crowd roars laughing.*]

Sam. OK! Tom, stand on this table. Now—confess! Talk!

[*Pause.*]

Tom. Meow!

[*Crowd roars.*]

---

5. **buffaloed:** slang for "fooled."

Sam. Just a few words, Tom, for the audience, the delegates!
Tom. Meeeooooww!

[*Crowd: bigger laughing.*]

Sam. OK, you fourflusher, now!

[*Tom screeches.*]

Speaker. *Hey! Don't twist his tail!*
Voices. He's crazy! Stop him! . . . *etc.*
Sam. Talk, Tom, or I'll . . .
Tom. Oww . . . All right—!
Sam. There!

[*A Woman screams.*]

Voice. Help that woman, she's fainted!

Sam. Talk into the microphone, Tom, I got your tail!

Tom. Ladies and gentlemen. I am Tom Thomas. *(Hush in the hall)* I am a talking cat. Now I beg you not to let this unfortunate incident alter your votes. Because I have not changed. I am still as much Tom Thomas as I was before. And although I may not be good enough to govern expert plumbers, I assure you that as for the rest of the population you couldn't make a wiser choice. For, after all . . .

Voice. How dare you! Grab him!

[*Crowd roars.*]

Voice. He's under the table!
Voice. No, that way!
Voice. There he is, heading for the window!
Voice. What a leap! He's out!
Voice. After him!
Voice. Come on, get that cat!

[Sound: *Complete uproar taken up by music — hold — then fade into the panting of* Tom.]

George. Take it easy, Tom, you're home now.
Tom. My thoughts are still racing, George.
George. You think too much, Tom. A cat must be . . . calm.
Tom. You know what, George? I found the difference between a man and a cat.
George. Since you started talking English, that's worried me.
Tom. The difference, George, if you want to know, is that a cat will do anything, the worst things, to fill his stomach, but a man . . . a man will actually prefer to stay poor because of an ideal. That's why I could never be President: because some men are not like cats. Because some men, some useful men, like expert plumbers, are so proud of their usefulness that they don't need the respect of their neighbors and so they aren't afraid to speak the truth.

George. Maybe you're right. But what are you going to do now?
Tom. I hate to get back into the rut, George.
George. I know, Tom, but the house is running with mice since you left.
Tom. Ahh, mice. What kind of a life is that for me? So I catch a mouse. So what? That's a rut, George. And anyway, I'm too sad to put my mind to it now. What've you got for me to read? Something tragic — as tragic as I am.
George. Well, look on the shelf. There's *Puss in Boots.* . . .
Tom. That's kid stuff. Here . . . here it is . . . *Paradise Lost.* And here's another . . . *The Decline and Fall of the Roman Empire.*[6]
George. Tom, you've got to get used to being a cat again. You've got to stop talking.
Tom. Yeh, George, there's no use pretending, I guess.
George. Come now, let's hear you meow! Come on!
Tom *(uninterestedly).* Oh . . . meow.
George. What kind of a meow is that? Give it!
Tom *(a little more energy).* Meoww. Oh, I can't, George.
George. But try, put your heart into it! Come on!
Tom *(better).* Meeoow!
George. Attaboy! Now like the old days, Tom . . . a good one . . . Like on the back fence, you remember? . . . With that light tan babe?
Tom. Meeeeoooowwwwwwww!!!!! . . . *(To a fade)*

---

6. *Paradise Lost . . . Roman Empire:* Tom refers to two great masterpieces of English literature. *Paradise Lost* was written by the poet John Milton, and *The Decline and Fall of the Roman Empire* by the historian Edward Gibbon.

1. A fantasy often depends upon some far-fetched or incredible idea, such as the idea of a talking cat. The playwright makes Tom convincing by treating him in all other respects like an ordinary cat. For example, Tom can use his paws to shake hands, but he cannot hold a pencil. What other realistic details persuade the characters in the play and the audience that Tom is really a cat?

2. When George calls Tom's plan blackmail (page 343), Tom replies, "I've been around, George. That's politics." Tom's attitude is *cynical.* Tom does not believe that people have ideals. He believes the worst of people and expects their actions to be selfish. What are some other cynical remarks Tom makes in the play?

3. Tom's ideas about people are put to a test when he meets Sam, the plumber. Tom says that there is no difference between a cat and a man (page 351). What does he learn is the difference between them?

4. A writer can sometimes make a point more effectively by treating a serious subject with humor. Although Tom's rise to power is comical, the playwright shows us that it is made possible by the illegal and corrupt behavior of human beings. When Tom is building his political machine, he says he has no fear of being discovered. The only man who would expose him is "one who really believes he's upright and clean, really in his secret heart, and such a man does not exist in this world" (page 349). How does the playwright show that such people do exist and that they aren't afraid to speak the truth?

DEVELOPING SKILLS IN READING

Reading a Radio Play

In radio drama, sound effects are as important as dialogue. A dramatist can establish setting and mood through sound effects. The sound of wind can suggest a lonely road; the sound of rain, a dismal swamp. Bird and insect noises can suggest a jungle. Sound effects also allow for quick shifts of scene. In Miller's play the action of several months is presented in only a few minutes by the Railroad Conductor's voice and the background noises of a train (page 348). What sound effects does Miller use for the convention? What purpose does music have in the play?

ABOUT THE AUTHOR

Arthur Miller (1915–   ) was born in New York City. He began writing plays while he was a student at the University of Michigan. After graduation he returned to New York and wrote for radio. The first of his plays to achieve popular success was *All My Sons,* which was performed on Broadway in 1947. His most famous play, *Death of a Salesman,* won the Pulitzer Prize and the New York Drama Critics' Circle Award in 1949. *The Crucible,* another of his well-known plays, deals with the Salem witch trials of the seventeenth century.

Many times the big wave had come rushing out of the sea, swallowing the shore and sweeping over the village. Perhaps the big wave would never come back. But if it did, Jiya would be ready.

The Big Wave

Pearl Buck
Dramatized for Television

Shore at Shingawa, Edo. Painting by Shiba Kokan.
Museum of Fine Arts. Boston

Fenollosa-Weld Collection

Characters

Narrator
Kino Uchiyama (kē′nō ōō′chē-yä′mä),
  a farmer's son
Mother
Father, the farmer
Setsu (set′sōō), Kino's sister
Jiya (jē′yä), a fisherman's son

Jiya's Father, the fisherman
Old Gentleman, a wealthy
  landowner
Two Menservants
Gardener
First Man
Second Man
Woman
Child

Act One

Open on: *A scene in Japan, sea and mountainside, and in the distance Fuji.[1]*

Dissolve to:[2] *A small farmhouse, built on top of terraces.*

This, as the Narrator *speaks, dissolves to: The inside of the house, a room with the simplest of Japanese furniture.*

Narrator. Kino lives on a farm. The farm lies on the side of a mountain in Japan. The fields are terraced by walls of stone, each one of them like a broad step up the mountain. Centuries ago, Kino's ancestors built the stone walls that hold up the fields. Above the fields stands this farmhouse, which is Kino's home. Sometimes he feels the climb is hard, especially when he has been working in the lowest field and he is hungry.

[*Dissolve to:* Kino *comes into the room. He is a sturdy boy of about thirteen, dressed in shorts and a Japanese jacket, open on his bare chest.*]

Kino. Mother!

[Mother *hurries in. She is a small, serious-looking woman dressed in an everyday cotton kimono,[3] sleeves tucked up. She is carrying a jar of water.*]

Mother. Dinner is ready. Where's your father?

Kino. Coming. I ran up the terraces. I'm starving.

---

1. **Fuji** (fŏŏ′jē): the highest peak in Japan, a volcano extinct since 1707.
2. **Dissolve to:** Fade from one picture into another.
3. **kimono** (kə-mō′nə): a loose robe with wide sleeves and a sash, worn as an outer garment by Japanese men and women.

Mother. Call Setsu. She is playing outside.

Kino (*turning his head*). Setsu!

Father. Here she is. (*He comes in, holding by the hand a small roguish girl.*) Getting so big! I can't lift her any more. (*But he does lift her so high that she touches the low rafters.*)

Setsu. Don't put me down. I want to eat my supper up here.

Father. And fall into the soup?

Kino. How that would taste!

Setsu (*willfully*). It would taste nice.

Mother. Come, come . . .

[*They sit on the floor around the little table. The* Mother *serves swiftly from a small bucket of rice, a bowl of soup, a bowl of fish. She serves the* Father *first, then* Kino, *then* Setsu, *and herself.*]

Father. Kino, don't eat so fast.

Kino. I have promised Jiya to swim in the sea with him.

Mother. Obey your father.

Father (*smiling*). Let him eat fast. (*He puts a bit of fish in* Setsu's *bowl.*) There — that's a good bit.

Kino. Father, why is it that Jiya's father's house has no window to the sea?

Father. No fisherman wants windows to the sea.

Mother. The sea is their enemy.

Kino. Mother, how can you say so? Jiya's father catches fish from the sea and that is how their family lives.

Father. Do not argue with your mother. Ask Jiya your question. See what he says.

Kino. Then may I go?

Father. Go.

[*Dissolve to: A sandy strip of seashore at the foot of the mountain. A few cottages stand there.*]

Dissolve to: *A tall slender boy, Jiya. He stands at the edge of the sea, looking up the mountain.*]

Jiya *(calling through his hands)*. Kino!
Kino. Coming!

[*He is running and catches Jiya's out-stretched hand, so that they nearly fall down. They laugh and throw off their jackets.*]

Kino. Wait—I am out of breath. I ate too much.
Jiya *(looking up the mountain)*. There's Old Gentleman standing at the gate of his castle.
Kino. He is watching to see whether we are going into the sea.
Jiya. He's always looking at the sea—at dawn, at sunset.

[Dissolve to: Old Gentleman, *standing on a rock, in front of his castle, halfway up the mountain. The wind is blowing his beard. He wears the garments of an aristocrat. With-draw the cameras to the beach again.*]

Jiya. He is afraid of the sea—always watching!
Kino. Have you ever been in his castle?
Jiya. Only once. Such beautiful gardens—like a dream in a fairy tale. The old pines are bent with the wind, and under them the moss is deep and green and so smooth. Every day men sweep the moss with brooms.
Kino. Why does he keep looking at the sea?
Jiya. He is afraid of it, I tell you.
Kino. Why?
Jiya. The sea is our enemy. We all know it.
Kino. Oh, how can you say it? When we have so much fun——
Jiya. It is our enemy. . . .
Kino. Not mine—let's swim to the island!
Jiya. No. I must find clams for my mother.

Kino. Then let's swim to the sand bar. There are millions of clams there!
Jiya. But the tide is ready to turn. . . .
Kino. It's slow—we'll have time.

[*They plunge into the sea and swim to the sand bar. Jiya has a small, short-handled hoe hanging from his girdle. He digs into the sand. Kino kneels to help him. But Jiya digs only for a moment; then he pauses to look out over the sea.*]

Kino. What are you looking for?
Jiya. To see if the sea is angry with us.
Kino *(laughing)*. Silly—the sea can't be angry with people!
Jiya. Down there, a mile down, the old sea god lives alone. When he is angry he heaves and rolls, and the waves rush back and forth. Then he gets up and he stamps his feet, and earth shakes at the bottom of the sea. . . . I wish I were a farmer's son, like you. . . .
Kino. And I wish I were a fisherman's son. It is stupid to plow and plant and cut sheaves, when I could just sit in a boat and reap fish from the sea!
Jiya. The earth is safe.
Kino. When the volcano is angry the earth shakes, too.
Jiya. The angry earth helps the angry sea.
Kino. They work together.
Jiya. But fire comes out of the volcano.

[*Meanwhile, the tide is coming in and swirls about their feet.*]

Jiya *(noticing)*. Oh—we have not half-enough clams. . . .

[*They fall to digging frantically.*
Dissolve to: *The empty seashore and the tide rushing in. A man paces the sand at the water's edge. He wears shorts and a fisher-*

man's jacket, open over his bare breast. It is Jiya's Father. *He calls, his hands cupped at his mouth.*]

Jiya's Father. Ji—ya!

[*There is only the sound of the surf. He wades into the water, still calling. Suddenly he sees the boys, their heads out of water, swimming, and he beckons fiercely. They come in, and he gives a hand to each and pulls them out of the surf.*]

Jiya's Father. Jiya! You have never been so late before!

Jiya. Father, we were on the sand bar, digging clams. We had to leave them.

Jiya's Father (*shaking his shoulder*). Never be so late!

Kino (*wondering*). You are afraid of the sea, too.

Jiya's Father. Go home, farmer's son! Your mother is calling you.

[*In the distance a woman's voice is calling Kino's name. He hears and runs toward the mountain.*]

Jiya. Father, I have made you angry.

Jiya's Father. I am not angry.

Jiya. Then why do you seem angry?

Jiya's Father. Old Gentleman sent down word that a storm is rising behind the horizon. He sees the cloud through his great telescope.

Jiya. Father, why do you let Old Gentleman make you afraid? Just because he is rich and lives in a castle, everybody listens to him.

Jiya's Father. Not because he is rich—not because he lives in the castle, but because he is old and wise and he knows the sea. He doesn't want anybody to die. (*He looks over the sea, and his arm tightens about his son,*

and he mutters as though to himself.*) Though all must die . . .

Jiya. Why must all die, Father?

Jiya's Father. Who knows? Simply, it is so.

[*They stand, looking over the sea.*]

Act Two

Open on: *The Japanese scene of sea and mountainside, with Fuji in the distance, as in Act One.*

Narrator. Yet there was much in life to enjoy. Kino had a good time every day. In the winter he went to school in the fishing village, and he and Jiya shared a bench and a writing table. They studied reading and arithmetic and learned what all children must learn in school. But in summer Kino had to work hard on the farm. Even Setsu and the mother had to help when the rice seedlings were planted in the watery terraced fields. On those days Kino could not run down the mountainside to find Jiya. When the day was ended he was so tired he fell asleep over his supper.

There were days when Jiya, too, could not play. Schools of fish came into the channel between the shore and the island, and early in the morning Jiya and his father sailed their boats out to sea to cast their nets at dawn. If they were lucky, their nets came up so heavy with fish that it took all their strength to haul them in, and soon the bottom of the boat was flashing and sparkling with wriggling fish.

Sometimes, if it were not seedtime or harvest, Kino went with Jiya and his father. It was exciting to get up in the night and put on his warm padded jacket; for even in summer the wind was cool over the sea at dawn. However early he got up, his mother was up even earlier to give him a bowl of hot rice soup and some bean curd[1] and tea before he went. She packed for him a lunch in a clean little wooden box—cold rice and fish and a radish pickle. Down the stone steps of the mountain path, Kino ran straight to the narrow dock where the fishing boats bobbed up and down with the tide. Jiya and his father were already there, and in a few minutes their boat was nosing its way past the sand bar toward the open sea. Sails set and filling with wind, they sped straight into the dawnlit horizon. Kino crouched down in the bow, and his heart rose with joy and excitement. It was like flying into the sky. The winds were so mild, the sea lay so calm and blue, that it was hard to believe it could be cruel and angry. Actually it was the earth that brought the big wave.

One day, as Kino helped his father plant turnips, a cloud came over the sun.

[Dissolve to: *A field, and* Kino *and his* Father. *The volcano is in the background.*]

Kino. Look, Father, the volcano is burning again!
Father *(straightens and gazes anxiously at the sky).* It looks very angry. I shall not sleep tonight. We must hurry home.
Kino. Why should the volcano be angry, Father?
Father. Who knows? Simply, the inner fire burns. Come—make haste.

[*They gather their tools.*

Dissolve to: *Night. The threshing floor outside the farmhouse.* Kino's Father *sits on a bench outside the door. He gets up and walks to and fro and gazes at the red sky above the volcano. The* Mother *comes to the door.*]

Red Fuji from *Thirty-Six Views of Fuji.*

Mother. Can you put out the volcano fire by not sleeping?
Father. Look at the fishing village! Every house is lit. And the lamps are lit in the castle. Shall I sleep like a fool?
Mother *(silent, troubled, watching him).* I have taken the dishes from the shelves and put away our good clothes in boxes.
Father *(gazing down at the village).* If only I knew whether it would be earth or sea! Both work evil together. The fires rage under the sea, the rocks boil. The volcano is the vent unless the sea bottom breaks.
Kino *(coming to the door).* Shall we have an earthquake, Father?
Father. I cannot tell.
Mother. How still it is! There's no wind. The sea is purple.

---

1. **bean curd:** a soft cheese made from soybeans.

Print by Katsushika Hokusai.

Kino. Why is the sea such a color?
Father. Sea mirrors sky. Sea and earth and sky — if they work against man, who can live?
Kino *(coming to his Father's side).* Where are the gods? Do they forget us?
Father. There are times when the gods leave men alone. They test us to see how able we are to save ourselves.
Kino. What if we are not able?
Father. We must be able. Fear makes us weak. If you are afraid, your hands tremble, your feet falter. Brain cannot tell hands what to do.
Setsu *(her voice calling from inside the house).* Mother, I'm afraid!
Mother. I am coming! *(She goes away.)*
Father. The sky is growing black. Go into the house, Kino.

Kino. Let me stay with you.
Father. The red flag is flying over the castle. Twice I've seen that red flag go up, both times before you were born. Old Gentleman wants everybody to be ready.
Kino *(frightened).* Ready for what?
Father. For whatever must be.

[*A deep-toned bell tolls over the mountain-side.*]

Kino. What is that bell? I've never heard it before.
Father. It rang twice before you were born. It is the bell inside Old Gentleman's temple. He is calling to the people to come up out of the village and shelter within his walls.
Kino. Will they come?
Father. Not all of them. Parents will try to make their children go, but the children will not want to leave their parents. Mothers will not want to leave fathers, and the fathers will stay by the boats. But some will want to be sure of life.

[*The bell continues to ring urgently. Soon from the village comes a straggling line of people, nearly all of them children.*]

Kino *(gazing at them).* I wish Jiya would come. *(He takes off his white cloth girdle and waves it.)*

[Dissolve to: Jiya *and his* Father *by their house. Sea in the background, roaring.*]

Jiya's Father. Jiya, you must go to the castle.
Jiya. I won't leave you . . . and Mother.
Jiya's Father. We must divide ourselves. If we die, you must live after us.
Jiya. I don't want to live alone.
Jiya's Father. It's your duty to obey me, as a good Japanese son.

The Big Wave 361

Jiya. Let me go to Kino's House.
Jiya's Father. Only go . . . go quickly.

[Jiya *and his* Father *embrace fiercely, and* Jiya *runs away, crying, to leap up the mountain-side.*

  Dissolve to: Terrace *and farmhouse, and center on* Kino *and his* Father, *who put out their hands to help* Jiya *up the last terrace. Suddenly* Kino *screams.*]

Kino. Look . . . look at the sea!
Father. May the gods save us.

[*The bell begins to toll, deep, pleading, incessant.*]

Jiya (*shrieking*). I must go back. . . . I must tell my father. . . .
Father (*holding him*). It is too late. . . .

[*Dissolve to:* The sea rushes up in a terrible wave and swallows the shore. The water roars about the foot of the mountain. Jiya, held by Kino *and his* Father, *stares transfixed, and then sinks unconscious to the ground. The bell tolls on.*]

Act Three

Narrator. So the big wave came, swelling out of the sea. It lifted the horizon while the people watched. The air was filled with its roar

The Big Wave from *Thirty-Six Views of Fuji.* Print by Katsushika Hokusai.

and shout. It rushed over the flat, still waters of the sea; it reached the village and covered it fathoms deep in swirling, wild water — green, laced with fierce white foam. The wave ran up the mountainside until the knoll upon which the castle stood was an island. All who were still climbing the path were swept away, mere tossing scraps in the wicked waters. Then with a great sucking sigh, the wave ebbed into the sea, dragging everything with it — trees, rocks, houses, people. Once again it swept over the village, and once again returned to the sea, subsiding, sinking into great stillness.

Upon the beach, where the village had stood, not a house remained, no wreckage of wood or fallen stone wall, no street of little shops, no docks, not a single boat. The beach was as clean of houses as if no human beings had ever lived there. All that had been was now no more.

[Dissolve to: *Inside the farmhouse. The farm family is gathered about the mattress on which* Jiya *lies.*]

Mother. This is not sleep. . . . Is it death?
Father. Jiya is not dead. His soul has withdrawn for a time. He is unconscious. Let him remain so until his own will wakes him.
Mother (*rubbing* Jiya's *hands and feet*). Kino, do not cry.

[Kino *cannot stop crying, though silently.*]

Father. Let him cry. Tears comfort the heart. (*He feels* Kino's *hands and cheeks.*) He is cold. Heat a little rice soup for him and put some ginger in it. I will stay with Jiya.

[Mother *goes out.* Setsu *comes in, rubbing her eyes and yawning.*]

Father. Sleepy eyes! You have slept all through the storm. Wise one!
Setsu (*coming to stare at* Jiya). Is Jiya dead?
Father. No, Jiya is living.
Setsu. Why doesn't he open his eyes?
Father. Soon he will open his eyes.
Setsu. If Jiya is not dead, why does Kino stand there crying?
Father. As usual, you are asking too many questions. Go back to the kitchen and help your mother.

[Setsu *goes out, staring and sucking her finger.* Father *puts his arm around* Kino.]

Father. The first sorrow is always the hardest to bear.
Kino. What will we say to Jiya when he wakes? How can we tell him?
Father. We will not talk. We will give him warm food and let him rest. We will help him to feel he still has a home.
Kino. Here?
Father. Here. I have always wanted another son, and Jiya will be that son. As soon as he knows this is his home, we must help him to understand what has happened. Ah, here is Mother, with your hot rice soup. Eat it, my son—food for the body is food, too, for the heart, sometimes.

[Kino *takes the bowl from his* Mother *with both hands and drinks. The parents look at each other and at him, sorrowfully and tenderly.* Setsu *comes in and leans her head against her* Mother.]

Dissolve to: *Evening. The same room, the same scene except that* Mother *and* Setsu *are not there.* Father *sits beside* Jiya's *bed.* Kino *is at the open door.*]

Kino. The sky is golden, Father, and the sea is smooth. How cruel—
Father. No, it is wonderful that after the storm the sea grows calm again, and the sky is clear. It was not the sea or the sky that made the evil storm.
Kino (*not turning his head*). Who made it?
Father. Ah, no one knows who makes evil storms. (*He takes* Jiya's *hand and rubs it gently.*) We only know that they come. When they come we must live through them as bravely as we can, and after they are gone we must feel again how wonderful is life. Every day of life is more valuable now than it was before the storm.
Kino. But Jiya's father and mother . . . and the other fisherfolk . . . so good and kind . . . all of them . . . lost. (*He cannot go on.*)
Father. We must think of Jiya—who lives. (*He stops.* Jiya *has begun to sob softly in his unconsciousness.*) Quick, Kino—call your mother and Setsu. He will open his eyes at any moment, and we must all be here—you to be his brother, I his father, and the mother, the sister. . . .

[Kino *runs out.* Father *kneels beside* Jiya, *who stirs, still sobbing.* Kino *comes back with* Mother *and* Setsu. *They kneel on the floor beside the bed.* Jiya's *eyelids flutter. He opens his eyes and looks from one face to the other. He stares at the beams of the roof, the walls of the room, the bed, his own hands. All are quiet except* Setsu, *who cannot keep from laughing. She claps her hands.*]

Setsu. Oh, Jiya has come back. Jiya, did you have a good dream?

Jiya (faintly). My father, my mother . . .
Mother (taking his hand in both hers). I will be your mother now, dear Jiya.
Father. I will be your father.
Kino. I am your brother now, Jiya. (He falters.)
Setsu (joyfully). Oh, Jiya, you will live with us.

[Jiya gets up slowly. He walks to the door, goes out, and looks down the hillside.

Dissolve to: The peaceful empty beach. Then back to the farmhouse and Jiya, standing outside and looking at the sea. Setsu comes to him.]

Setsu. I will give you my pet duck. He'll follow you—he'll make you laugh.
Mother (leaving the room). We ought all to eat something, I have a fine chicken for dinner.
Kino (coming to Jiya). Mother makes such good chicken soup.
Setsu. I'm hungry, I tell you.
Father. Come, Jiya, my son.

[Jiya still stands dazed.]

Kino. Eat with us, Jiya.
Jiya. I am tired . . . very tired.
Kino. You have been sleeping so long.
Jiya (slowly). I shall never see them again. (He puts his hands over his eyes.) I shall keep thinking about them . . . floating in the sea.
Mother (coming in). Drink this bowl of soup at least, Jiya, my son.

[Jiya drinks and lets the bowl fall. It is wooden and does not break.]

Jiya, I want to sleep.
Father. Sleep, my son. Sleep is good for you.

(He leads Jiya to the bed and covers him with the quilt. To them all) Jiya is not yet ready to live. We must wait.
Kino. Will he die?
Father. Life is stronger than death. He will live.

Act Four

Narrator. The body heals first, and the body heals the mind and the soul. Jiya ate food, he got out of bed sometimes, but he was still tired. He did not want to think or remember. He only wanted to sleep. He woke to eat, and then he went to sleep again. In the quiet, clean room Jiya slept, and the mother spread the quilt over him and closed the door and went away.

All through these days Kino did not play about as once he had. He was no longer a child. He worked hard beside his father in the fields. They did not talk much, and neither of them wanted to look at the sea. It was enough to look at the earth, dark and rich beneath their feet.

One evening Kino climbed the mountain behind the house and looked up at the volcano. The heavy cloud of smoke had gone away, and the sky was clear. He was glad that the volcano was no longer angry, and he went down again to the house. On the threshold his father was smoking his usual evening pipe. In the house his mother was giving Setsu her evening bath.

Kino (dropping down on the bench beside his Father). Is Jiya asleep again?
Father. Yes, and it is a good thing for him. When he sleeps enough, he will wake and remember.
Kino. But should he remember?
Father. Only when he dares to remember his parents will he be happy again.

[*A silence.*]

Kino. Father, are we not very unfortunate people to live in Japan?

Father. Why do you think so?

Kino. The volcano is behind our house, and the sea is in front. When they work together to make earthquake and big wave, we are helpless. Always, many of us are lost.

Father. To live in the presence of death makes us brave and strong. That is why our people never fear death. We see it too often, and we do not fear it. To die a little sooner or a little later does not matter. But to live bravely, to love life, to see how beautiful the trees are and the mountains — yes, and even the sea — to enjoy work because it produces food — in these we are fortunate people. We love life because we live in danger. We do not fear death, for we understand that death and life are necessary to each other.

Kino. What is death?

Father. Death is the great gateway.

Kino. The gateway . . . where?

Father. Can you remember when you were born?

Kino. I was too small.

Father (*smiling*). I remember very well. Oh, how hard you thought it was to be born. You cried and you screamed.

Kino (*much interested*). Didn't I want to be born?

Father. You did not. You wanted to stay just where you were, in the warm dark house of the unborn. But the time came to be born, and the gate of life opened.

Kino. Did I know it was the gate of life?

Father. You did not know anything about it, and so you were afraid. But see how foolish you were! Here we were waiting for you, your parents, already loving you and eager to welcome you. And you have been very happy, haven't you?

Kino. Until the big wave came. Now I am afraid again because of the death the big wave brought.

Father. You are only afraid because you don't know anything about death. But someday you will wonder why you were afraid, even as today you wonder why you once feared to be born.

Kino. I think I understand. . . . I begin to understand. . . .

Father. Do not hurry yourself. You have plenty of time. (*He rises to his feet.*) Now what do I see? A lantern coming up the hill.

Kino (*running to the edge of the threshold*). Who can be coming now? It is almost night.

Father. A visitor . . . ah, why, it's Old Gentleman!

[Old Gentleman *indeed is climbing the hill. He is somewhat breathless in spite of his long staff. His* Manservant *carries the lantern and, when they arrive, steps to one side.*]

Old Gentleman (*to* Manservant). Is this the house of Uchiyama, the farmer?

Manservant. It is — and this is the farmer himself and his son.

Father (*bowing deeply*). Please, Honored Sir, what can I do for you?

Old Gentleman. Do you have a lad here by the name of Jiya?

Father. He lies sleeping in my house.

Old Gentleman. I wish to see him.

Father. Sir, he suffered the loss of his parents when the big wave came. Now sleep heals him.

Old Gentleman. I will not wake him. I only wish to look at him.

Father. Please come in.

[Dissolve to: Jiya *asleep. The* Manservant *holds the lantern so that the light does not fall on* Jiya's *face directly.* Old Gentleman *looks at him carefully.*]

Old Gentleman. Tall and strong for his age—intelligent—handsome. Hmm . . . yes. *(He motions to the* Manservant *to lead him away, and the scene returns to the dooryard. To* Father*)* It is my habit, when the big wave comes, to care for those who are orphaned by it. Thrice in my lifetime I have searched out the orphans, and I have fed them and sheltered them. But I have heard of this boy Jiya and wish to do more for him. If he is as good as he is handsome, I will take him for my own son.

Kino. But Jiya is ours!

Father *(sternly).* Hush. We are only poor people. If Old Gentleman wants Jiya, we cannot say we will not give him up.

Old Gentleman. Exactly. I will give him fine clothes and send him to a school, and he may become a great man and an honor to our whole province and even to the nation.

Kino. But if he lives in the castle we can't be brothers!

Father. We must think of Jiya's good. *(He turns to* Old Gentleman.*)* Sir, it is very kind of you to propose this for Jiya. I had planned to take him for my own son, now that he has lost his birth parents; but I am only a poor farmer, and I cannot pretend that my house is as good as yours or that I can afford to send Jiya to a fine school. Tomorrow when he wakes I will tell him of your kind offer. He will decide.

Old Gentleman. Very well. But let him come and tell me himself.

Father *(proudly).* Certainly. Jiya must speak for himself.

[Old Gentleman *bows slightly and prepares to depart.* Father *bows deeply and taps* Kino *on the head to make him bow.* Old Gentleman *and his* Manservant *return down the mountain.*]

Kino. If Jiya goes away, I shall never have a brother.

Father. Kino, don't be selfish. You must allow Jiya to make his own choice. It would be wrong to persuade him. I forbid you to speak to him of this matter. When he wakes, I will tell him myself.

Kino *(pleading).* Don't tell him today, Father.

Father. I must tell him as soon as he wakes. It would not be fair to Jiya to let him grow used to thinking of this house as his home. He must make the choice today, before he has time to put down his new roots. Go now, Kino, and weed the lower terrace.

[Dissolve to: Kino *working in the terrace, weeding. It is evident that he has worked for some time. He looks hot and dusty, and he has quite a pile of weeds. He stops to look up at the farmhouse, but he sees no one and re signs himself again to his task. Suddenly his name is called.*]

Father. Kino!

Kino. Shall I come?

Father. No, I am coming—with Jiya.

[Kino *stands, waiting.* Father *and* Jiya *come down the terraces.* Jiya *is very sad. When he sees* Kino, *he tries not to cry.*]

Father *(putting his arm about* Jiya's *shoulder).* Jiya, you must not mind that you cry easily. Until now you couldn't cry because you weren't fully alive. You had been hurt too much. But today you are beginning to live, and so your tears flow. It is good for you. Let your tears come—don't stop them. *(He turns to* Kino.*)* I have told Jiya that he must not decide where he will live until he has seen the inside of the castle. He must see all that Old Gentleman can give him. Jiya, you know how our house is—four small rooms, and the kitchen, this farm, upon which we have to work hard for our food. We have only what our hands earn for us. (He holds out his two workworn hands.) If you live in the castle, you need never have hands like these.

Jiya. I don't want to live in the castle.

Father. You don't know whether you do or not; you have never seen the castle inside. (He turns to Kino.) Kino, you are to go with Jiya, and when you reach the castle you must persuade him to stay there for his own sake.

Kino. I will go and wash myself—and put on my good clothes.

Father. No—go as you are. You are a farmer's son.

[Kino and Jiya go, reluctantly, and Father stands looking after them.

Dissolve to: The mountainside and the two boys nearing the gate of the castle. The gate is open, and inside an old Gardener is sweeping moss under pine trees. He sees them.]

Gardener. What do you want, boys?

Kino. My father sent us to see the honored Old Gentleman.

Gardener. Are you the Uchiyama boy?

Kino. Yes, please, and this is Jiya, whom Old Gentleman wishes to come and live here.

Gardener (bowing to Jiya). Follow me, young sir.

[They follow over a pebbled path under the leaning pine trees. In the distance the sun falls upon a flowering garden and a pool with a waterfall.]

Kino (sadly). How beautiful it is—of course you will want to live here. Who could blame you?

[Jiya does not answer. He walks with his head held high. They come to a great door, where a Manservant bids them take off their shoes. The Gardener leaves them.]

Manservant. Follow me.

[They follow through passageways into a great room decorated in the finest Japanese fashion. In the distance at the end of the room, they see Old Gentleman sitting beside a small table. Behind him the open panels reveal the garden. Old Gentleman is writing. He holds his brush upright in his hand, and he is carefully painting letters on a scroll, his silver-rimmed glasses sliding down his nose. When the two boys approach, the Manservant announces them.]

Manservant. Master, the two boys are here.

Old Gentleman (to boys). Would you two like to know what I have been writing?

[Jiya looks at Kino, who is too awed to speak.]

Jiya. Yes, Honored Sir, if you please.

Old Gentleman (taking up the scroll). It is not my own poem. It is the saying of a wise man of India, but I like it so much that I have painted it on this scroll to hang there in the alcove where I can see it every day. (He reads clearly and slowly.)

"The children of God are very dear,
But very queer—
Very nice, but very narrow."

(He looks up over his spectacles.) What do you think of it?

Jiya (looking at Kino, who is too shy to speak). We do not understand it, sir.

Old Gentleman (shaking his head and laughing softly). Ah, we are all children of God!

(He takes off his spectacles and looks hard at Jiya.) Well? Will you be my son?

[Jiya, *too embarrassed to speak, bites his lip, looks away, etc.*]

Old Gentleman. Say yes or no. Either word is not hard to speak.

Jiya. I will say . . . no. *(He feels this is too harsh, and he smiles apologetically.)* I thank you, sir, but I have a home . . . on a farm.

Kino *(trying to repress his joy and speaking very solemnly as a consequence).* Jiya, remember how poor we are.

Old Gentleman *(smiling, half sad).* They are certainly very poor and here, you know, you would have everything. You can even invite this farm boy to come and play, sometimes, if you like. And I am quite willing for you to give the family some money. It would be suitable as my son for you to help the poor.

Jiya *(suddenly, as though he had not heard).* Where are the others who were saved from the big wave?

Old Gentleman. Some wanted to go away, and the ones who wanted to stay are out in the backyard with my servants.

Jiya. Why do you not invite them to come into this castle and be your sons and daughters.

Old Gentleman *(somewhat outraged by this).* Because I don't want them for my sons and daughters. You are a bright, handsome boy. They told me you were the best boy in the village.

Jiya. I am not better than the others. My father was a fisherman.

Old Gentleman *(taking up his spectacles and his brush).* Very well—I will do without a son.

[*The* Manservant *motions to the boys to come away, and they follow.*]

Manservant *(to* Jiya*).* How foolish you are! Our Old Gentleman is very kind. You would have everything here.

Jiya. Not everything . . .

Kino. Let's hurry home—let's hurry—hurry . . .

[*They run down the mountain and up the hill to the farmhouse. Setsu sees them and comes flying to meet them, the sleeves of her bright kimono like wings, and her feet clattering in their wooden sandals.*]

Setsu. Jiya has come home—Jiya, Jiya . . .

[Jiya *sees her happy face and opens his arms and gives her a great hug.*]

Act Five

Narrator. Now happiness began to live in Jiya, though secretly and hidden inside him, in ways he did not understand. The good food warmed him, and his body welcomed it. Around him the love of the four people who received him for their own glowed like a warm and welcoming fire upon his heart.

Time passed. Eight years. Jiya grew up in the farmhouse to be a tall young man, and Kino grew at his side, solid and strong, but never as tall as Jiya. Setsu grew, too, from a mischievous laughing child into a gay, willful, pretty girl. But time, however long, was split in two parts, the time before and the time after the big wave. The big wave had changed everybody's life.

In all these years no one returned to live on the empty beach. The tides rose and fell, sweeping the sands clear every day. Storms came and went, but there was never such a wave as the big one. At last people began to

Fuji on a Clear Day from the Sea off Tsukuda (c. 1837–1843). Print by Utagawa Kuniyoshi. Museum of Fine Arts, Springfield, Massachusetts

think that never again would there be such a big wave. The few fishermen who had listened to the tolling bell from the castle, and were saved with their wives and children, went to other shores to fish, and they made new fishing boats. Then, as time passed, they told themselves that no beach was quite as good as the old one. There, they said, the water was deep and great fish came close to the shore. They did not need to go far out to sea to find the booty.

Jiya and Kino had not often gone to the beach, either. At first they had walked along the empty sands where once the street had been, and Jiya searched for some keepsake from his home that the sea might have washed back to the shore. But nothing was ever found. So the two boys, as they grew to

be young men, did not visit the deserted beach. When they went to swim in the sea, they walked across the farm and over another fold of the mountains to the shore.

Yet Jiya had never forgotten his father and mother. He thought of them every day, their faces, their voices, the way his father talked, his mother's smile. The big wave had changed him forever. He did not laugh easily or speak carelessly. In school he had earnestly learned all he could, and now he worked hard on the farm. Now, as a man, he valued deeply everything that was good. Since the big wave had been so cruel, he was never cruel, and he grew kind and gentle. Jiya never spoke of his loneliness. He did not want others to be sad because of his sadness. When he laughed at some mischief of Setsu's, when she teased him, his laughter was wonderful to hear because it was whole and real. And sometimes, in the morning, he went to the door of the farmhouse and looked at the empty beach below, searching with his eyes as though something might one day come back. One day he did see something. . . .

Jiya. Kino, come here! *(Kino comes out, his shoes in his hand.)* Look—is someone building a house on the beach?

Kino. Two men—pounding posts into the sand—

Jiya. And a woman . . . yes, and even a child.

Kino. They can't be building a house.

Jiya. Let's go and see.

[*Dissolve to: The beach. The two* Men, Jiya *and* Kino, Woman *and* Child.]

Jiya *(out of breath)*. Are you building a house?

First Man *(wiping sweat from his face)*. Our father used to live here, and we with him. We are two brothers. During these years we have lived in the houses of the castle, and we have fished from other shores. Now we are tired of having no homes of our own. Besides, this is still the best beach for fishing.

Kino. What if the big wave comes again?

Second Man *(shrugging his shoulders)*. There was a big wave, too, in our great-grandfather's time. All the houses were swept away. But our grandfather came back. In our father's time there was again the big wave. Now we return.

Kino *(soberly)*. What of your children?

First Man. The big wave may never come back.

[*The* Men *begin to dig again. The* Woman *takes the* Child *into her arms and gazes out to sea. Suddenly there is a sound of a voice calling. All look up the mountain.*]

First Man. Here comes our Old Gentleman.

Second Man. He's very angry or he wouldn't have left the castle.

[*Both throw down their shovels and stand waiting. The* Woman *sinks to a kneeling position on the sand, still holding the* Child. Old Gentleman *shouts as he comes near, his voice high and thin. He is very old now, and is supported by two* Menservants. *His beard flies in the wind.*]

Old Gentleman. You foolish children! You leave the safety of my walls and come back to this dangerous shore, as your father did before you! The big wave will return and sweep you into the sea.

First Man. It may not, Ancient Sir.

Old Gentleman. It will come. I have spent my whole life trying to save foolish people from the big wave. But you will not be saved.

Jiya *(stepping forward)*. Sir, here is our home. Dangerous as it is, threatened by the volcano and by the sea, it is here we were born.

Old Gentleman *(looking at him)*. Don't I know you?

Jiya. Sir, I was once in your castle.

Old Gentleman *(nodding)*. I remember you. I wanted you for my son. Ah, you made a great mistake, young man. You could have lived safely in my castle all your life, and your children would have been safe there. The big wave never reaches me.

Kino. Sir, your castle is not safe, either. If the earth shakes hard enough, even your castle will crumble. There is no refuge for us who live on these islands. We are brave because we must be.

Second Man. Ha—you are right.

[*The two* Men *return to their building.*]

Old Gentleman *(rolling his eyes and wagging his beard)*. Don't ask me to save you the next time the big wave comes!

Jiya *(gently)*. But you will save us, because you are so good.

Old Gentleman *(looking at him and then smiling sadly)*. What a pity you would not be my son! *(He turns and, leaning on his* Men-servants, *climbs the mountain.)*

[Dissolve to: *His arrival at the castle gate. He enters, and the gates clang shut.*

Dissolve to: *The field, where* Father *and* Jiya *and* Kino *are working.*]

Father *(to* Jiya*)*. Did you soak the seeds for the rice?

Jiya *(aghast)*. I forgot.

Kino. I did it.

Jiya *(throwing down his hoe)*. I forget everything these days.

Father. I know you are too good a son to be forgetful on purpose. Tell me what is on your mind.

Jiya. I want a boat. I want to go back to fishing.

[Father *does not pause in his hoeing; but* Kino *flings down his hoe.*]

Kino. You, too, are foolish!

Jiya *(stubbornly)*. When I have a boat, I shall build my house on the beach.

Kino. Oh, fool, fool!

Father. Be quiet! Jiya is a man. You are both men. I shall pay you wages from this day.

Jiya. Wages! *(He falls to hoeing vigorously.)*

[Dissolve to: *The beach, where* Kino *and* Jiya *are inspecting a boat.*]

Jiya. I knew all the time that I had to come back to the sea.

Kino. With this boat, you'll soon earn enough to build a house. But I'm glad I live on the mountain.

[*They continue inspecting the boat, fitting the oars, etc., as they talk.*]

Jiya *(abruptly)*. Do you think Setsu would be afraid to live on the beach?

Kino *(surprised)*. Why would Setsu live on the beach?

Jiya *(embarrassed but determined)*. Because when I have my house built, I want Setsu to be my wife.

Kino *(astonished)*. Setsu? You would be foolish to marry her.

Jiya *(smiling)*. I don't agree with you.

Kino *(seriously)*. But why . . . why do you want her?

Jiya. Because she makes me laugh. It is she who made me forget the big wave. For me, she is life.

Kino. But she is not a good cook. Think how she burns the rice when she runs outside to look at something.

Jiya. I don't mind burned rice, and I will run out with her to see what she sees.

Kino *(with all the gestures of astonishment and disbelief)*. I can't understand. . . .

[Dissolve to: *The farmhouse, and* Father, *who is looking over his seeds.*]

Kino *(coming in stealthily)*. Do you know that Jiya wants to marry Setsu?

Father. I have seen some looks pass between them.

Kino. But Jiya is too good for Setsu.

Father. Setsu is very pretty.

Kino. With that silly nose?

Father *(calmly)*. I believe that Jiya admires her nose.

Kino. Besides, she is such a tease.

Father. What makes you miserable will make him happy.

Kino. I don't understand that, either.

Father *(laughing).* Someday you will understand.

[Dissolve to: Narrator.]

Narrator. One day, one early summer, Jiya and Setsu were married. Kino still did not understand, for up to the last, Setsu was naughty and mischievous. Indeed on the very day of her wedding she hid Kino's hairbrush under his bed. "You are too silly to be married," Kino said, when he had found it. "I feel sorry for Jiya," he said. Setsu's big brown eyes laughed at him, and she stuck out her red tongue. "I shall always be nice to Jiya," she said.

But when the wedding was over and the family had taken the newly married pair down the hill to the new house on the beach, Kino felt sad. The farmhouse was very quiet without Setsu. Already he missed her. Every day he could go to see Jiya, and many times he would go fishing with him. But Setsu would not be in the farmhouse kitchen, in the rooms, in the garden. He would miss even her teasing. And then he grew very grave indeed. What if the big wave came again?

[Dissolve to: *The new house.* Kino, Jiya, Father, Mother, *and* Setsu *are standing outside.* Kino *turns to* Jiya.]

Kino. Jiya, it is all very pretty—very nice. But, Setsu—what if the big wave comes again?

Jiya. I have prepared for that. Come—all of you. *(He calls the family in.)* This is where we will sleep at night, and where we will live by day. But look——

[*The family stands watching, and* Jiya *pushes back a long panel in the wall. Before their eyes is the sea, swelling and stirring under the evening wind. The sun is sinking into the water.*]

Jiya. I have opened my house to the sea. If ever the big wave comes back, I shall be ready. I face it, night and day. I am not afraid.

Kino. Tomorrow I'll go fishing with you, Jiya—shall I?

Jiya *(laughing).* Not tomorrow, brother!

Father. Come—come! *(*Setsu *comes to his side and leans against him, and he puts his arm about her.)* Yes, life is stronger than death. *(He turns to his family.)* Come, let us go home.

[Father *and* Mother *and* Kino *bow and leave.* Jiya *and* Setsu *stand looking out to sea.*]

Jiya. Life is stronger than death—do you hear that, Setsu?

Setsu. Yes, I hear.

SEEKING MEANING

1. The characters in this play depend upon the land and the sea for their livelihood. How are they threatened by these natural elements?
2. Before the tidal wave strikes, what warnings are there of the coming disaster?
3. Old Gentleman wants to adopt Jiya as his son. Why does Jiya choose to live with Kino and his family?
4. The statement "Life is stronger than death" occurs several times in the play. How does Jiya's decision to return to the beach prove his faith in this statement?
5. In Act One, Jiya says, "The sea is our enemy." Why, then, does Jiya open his house to the sea at the end of the play?
6. In a play, as in a short story, there is conflict. How would you describe Jiya's conflict? How does he resolve this conflict?
7. How is the Narrator in this play like the narrator in a short story or novel?

DEVELOPING SKILLS IN READING

Understanding Types of Dialogue

In everyday speech, we don't always use complete sentences. We may give one-word answers to questions. Someone may interrupt us before we finish a sentence. Sometimes we start one sentence, change our minds, and go on to another. The dialogue of Arthur Miller's *The Pussycat and the Expert Plumber Who Was a Man* is a good example of this kind of everyday speech.

> **Mayor.** Ah, don't leap up at me so, Tom. I thought you were going to climb the tree.
> **Tom.** Wanted to get a look at the crowd.
> **Mayor.** Well, I guess the joke's over, eh, feller?

> **Tom.** Yes. We've got be more serious from now on. There's a man named Billings out here. Seems to be the leader.

Good dialogue can be natural; that is, it can sound like everyday speech. Good dialogue can also be formal. Pearl Buck uses formal speech for the characters in *The Big Wave*. The dialogue contains almost no contractions, no slang, and few broken thoughts.

> **Kino.** Father, are we not very unfortunate people to live in Japan?
> **Father.** Why do you think so?
> **Kino.** The volcano is behind our house, and the sea is in front. When they work together to make earthquake and big wave, we are helpless. Always, many of us are lost.
> **Father.** To live in the presence of death makes us brave and strong. That is why our people never fear death. We see it too often, and we do not fear it. To die a little sooner or a little later does not matter. But to live bravely, to love life, to see how beautiful the trees are and the mountains—yes, and even the sea—to enjoy work because it produces food—in these we are a fortunate people. We love life because we live in danger. We do not fear death, for we understand that death and life are necessary to each other.
> **Kino.** What is death?
> **Father.** Death is the great gateway.

This language has the effect of making the action of the play seem distant, timeless, and foreign. Father and Old Gentleman make thoughtful statements about the meaning of life. Formal speech is more appropriate for these statements than everyday speech would be. The language helps us understand and appreciate the deeper meanings of the characters' experiences.

DEVELOPING SKILLS OF EXPRESSION

Assembling a Director's Notebook

Suppose you were asked to direct *The Big Wave*. You would have to make many decisions about how to film the play for a television audience. Read through the play again, scene by scene, and jot down what you might need under the following headings:

Sets. How many separate sets would you need? Could you use a travel poster for the opening view of Japan, with Mount Fuji in the background? How realistic would you want your sets to be? If you were working on a low budget, could any of the sets be combined? What furniture would you need?

Costumes. Some costumes are specified in the stage directions: kimonos, fishermen's jackets, shorts. Other costumes are not specified and might need to be researched. What would the aristocratic garments of Old Gentleman look like?

Props. Some props are mentioned: Jiya's clamming hoe, a lantern, Old Gentleman's scroll and brush, soup bowls, and water jars. List others. How would you provide weeds and rice plants if you were filming in a studio?

Lighting. Would lights of different colors help set the mood from moment to moment? How would you light the approach of the storm?

Sound. Would you use a real bell or sounds that have been recorded? How would you create the sounds of the sea?

Staging. Should the Narrator appear on screen? What would you show on camera during the long narrations?

ABOUT THE AUTHOR

Pearl Buck (1892–1973) was born in Hillsboro, West Virginia, but spent most of her first sixteen years in Chinkiang, a city on the Yangtse River in China. Her parents, who were missionaries, took her there when she was only three months old. Since she grew up among the Chinese, she learned to speak Chinese before she learned English. Encouraged by her mother, who taught her "the beauty that lies in words and in what words will say," she began writing at an early age.

Her novel *The Good Earth* (1931) brought her international fame. One of the most popular novels of this century, it was adapted for stage and screen and was translated into more than thirty languages. In 1938 she received the Nobel Prize for literature. Before her death at the age of eighty, she filled more than eighty-five novels and collections of short stories with a unique richness.

The Big Wave is based on a book of the same title, which she wrote after a trip to Japan.

Practice in Reading and Writing

PLAYS

Reading a Play

The following dialogue appears in Pearl Buck's play *The Big Wave*. As you read it, put your imagination to work. How should the lines be spoken to show the moods of the characters?

> **Father** *(to* Jiya*)*. Did you soak the seeds for the rice?
> **Jiya** *(aghast).* I forgot.
> **Kino**. I did it.
> **Jiya** *(throwing down his hoe).* I forget everything these days.
> **Father**. I know you are too good a son to be forgetful on purpose. Tell me what is on your mind.
> **Jiya**. I want a boat. I want to go back to fishing.
>
> [Father *does not pause in his hoeing;* but Kino *flings down his hoe.*]
>
> **Kino**. You, too, are foolish!

What do the stage directions in this brief scene tell you about the characters' feelings and actions?

Stage directions can't tell everything, of course. What other actions do you picture the characters carrying out in this scene?

Writing a Play

In order to write a play, you must begin with a dramatic situation. A dramatic situation is built around a conflict or problem. You must then create characters who are involved in the conflict. You must also have a clear idea of where and when the action of your play takes place.

Choose one of the stories you have read and adapt it or a portion of it as a play for the stage, for radio, or for television. Turn passages of description and narration into scenes of action with dialogue. You may need to create additional dialogue to make clear what the characters are thinking or feeling.

Choose an episode from history in which the character or characters must deal with a conflict.

Columbus faces the threat of mutiny from his crew.
A colonial family resists the Quartering Act.
Elizabeth Blackwell defies the prejudice of the community against women physicians.
A pioneer family crossing the prairie in a covered wagon becomes separated from their wagon train.

Write a sequel to one of the plays you have read in this unit, inventing additional characters and new situations.

Write a play celebrating a holiday. Remember to provide:

a title
a cast of characters
a description of the setting
stage directions for the actors

For Further Reading

Aiken, Joan, *The Mooncusser's Daughter* (Viking, 1974)

A mooncusser is a person who deliberately wrecks ships. In this humorous play, a lighthouse keeper, his blind wife, and a ghost try to prevent a gang of thieves from gaining a treasure. *Winterthing* (Holt, Rinehart & Winston, 1972), another play by the same author, is a fantasy (with music and lyrics) about four children and their aunt, who live on Winter Island off the coast of Scotland.

Henshaw, James Ene, *The Jewels of the Shrine*, in *Voices from the Black Experience: African and Afro-American Literature*, edited by Darwin T. Turner, Jean M. Bright, and Richard Wright (Ginn, 1972)

In this folk play from Nigeria, Okorie, a shrewd old man, manages to outwit his selfish grandsons.

Hughes, Ted, *The Tiger's Bones and Other Plays for Children* (Viking, 1974)

Hughes, who is one of the greatest living English poets, has written several plays based on folklore and myth. Included in this collection are *Beauty and the Beast* and *Orpheus*.

Kamerman, Sylvia, E., editor, *Dramatized Folk Tales of the World* (Plays, Inc., 1971)

This is a useful collection for student actors because it contains very short plays based on folk tales from all over the world.

L'Engle, Madeline, *The Journey with Jonah* (Farrar, Straus & Giroux, 1967)

This is a dramatization of the story of Jonah from the Bible.

Lerner, Alan Jay, *My Fair Lady* (Coward McCann, 1956; paperback, New American Library)

An English professor transforms a flower girl into a genteel lady in this musical comedy based on George Bernard Shaw's *Pygmalion*.

Lipton, Betty Jean, editor, *Contemporary Children's Theater* (Avon, 1974)

The eight plays in this collection represent a variety of forms and approaches: plays based on legend and folk tales, science-fiction plays, and plays in which the audience participates.

Simon, Neil, *A Defenseless Creature*, in *The Good Doctor* (Random House, 1974)

In this comedy, adapted from a story by Anton Chekhov, a woman proves that she is not a "defenseless creature."

Stein, Joseph, *Fiddler on the Roof* (Crown, 1965; paperback, Pocket Books)

Sholom Aleichem's stories of Jewish life in a Russian village in 1905 are the basis of this lively musical drama about Tevye, the milkman, and his family.

Swortzell, Lowell, editor, *All the World's a Stage: Modern Plays for Young People* (Delacorte, 1972)

This collection of twenty-one plays includes *The Genie of Sutton Place*, a TV comedy by Kenneth Heuer and George Selden; *The Man with the Heart in the Highlands* by William Saroyan; *The Post Office* by the Hindu poet Rabindranath Tagore; and *Poem-Plays*, experimental dramas by Ruth Krauss.

Valency, Maurice, *Feathertop*, in *Fifteen American One-Act Plays*, edited by Paul Kozelka (paperback, Washington Square Press, 1961)

In this fantasy, adapted from a story by Nathaniel Hawthorne, a scarecrow is brought to life and then falls in love.

Wilder, Thornton, *The Long Christmas Dinner*, in *The Long Christmas Dinner and Other Plays in One Act* (Harper & Row, 1963)

This play traces the lives of several generations of an American family. *The Happy Journey to Trenton and Camden*, another play about family life, is also in this collection.

NONFICTION

Nonfiction deals with facts, but, like other forms of literature, it appeals to the imagination. The rich world of nonfiction includes exciting adventures, great discoveries, and stimulating ideas. In nonfiction, real people are the characters, and real life is the setting.

There are many kinds of nonfiction. Newspaper and magazine articles, biographies and autobiographies, serious and humorous essays, interviews, memoirs, diaries, speeches, letters, and scientific articles all fall into this broad category of literature.

In this unit you will find an eyewitness account of the San Francisco earthquake of 1906; an expert's view of marathon swimming, one of the world's most difficult sports; a humorous inventory of dogs with peculiar habits; the story of a rattlesnake hunt in the Everglades; a writer's account of the peak experience of his life; and an artist's recollections of her struggle to achieve mastery of her art.

As you will see, nonfiction can be both informative and enjoyable.

More than seventy years have passed since much of San Francisco was destroyed by an awesome earthquake and fire, but Jack London's vivid account makes us feel as though we have witnessed the disaster.

The Story of an Eyewitness

Jack London

The San Francisco Earthquake
April 18, 1906

The earthquake shook down in San Francisco hundreds of thousands of dollars' worth of walls and chimneys. But the conflagration[1] that followed burned up hundreds of millions of dollars' worth of property. There is no estimating within hundreds of millions the actual damage wrought. Not in history has a modern imperial city been so completely destroyed. San Francisco is gone. Nothing remains of it but memories and a fringe of dwelling houses on its outskirts. Its industrial section is wiped out. Its business section is wiped out. Its social and residential section is wiped out. The factories and warehouses, the great stores and newspaper buildings, the hotels and the palaces of the nabobs,[2] are all gone. Remains only the fringe of dwelling houses on the outskirts of what was once San Francisco.

Within an hour after the earthquake shock, the smoke of San Francisco's burning was a lurid tower visible a hundred miles away. And for three days and nights this lurid tower swayed in the sky, reddening the sun, darkening the day, and filling the land with smoke.

On Wednesday morning at a quarter past five came the earthquake. A minute later the flames were leaping upward. In a dozen different quarters south of Market Street, in the working-class ghetto, and in the factories, fires started. There was no opposing the flames. There was no organization, no communication. All the cunning adjustments of a twentieth-century city had been smashed by the earthquake. The streets were humped into ridges and depressions, and piled with the debris of fallen walls. The steel rails were twisted into perpendicular and horizontal angles. The telephone and telegraph systems were disrupted. And the great water mains had burst. All the shrewd contrivances and safeguards of man had been thrown out of

---

1. **conflagration** (kon'flə-grā'shən): a big, destructive fire.
2. **nabobs** (nā'bŏbz'): very rich and important people.

gear by thirty seconds' twitching of the earth-crust.

By Wednesday afternoon, inside of twelve hours, half the heart of the city was gone. At that time, I watched the vast conflagration from out on the bay. It was dead calm. Not a flicker of wind stirred. Yet from every side wind was pouring in upon the city. East, west, north, and south, strong winds were blowing upon the doomed city. The heated air rising made an enormous suck. Thus did the fire of itself build its own colossal chimney through the atmosphere. Day and night this dead calm continued, and yet, near to the flames, the wind was often half a gale, so mighty was the suck.

Wednesday night saw the destruction of the very heart of the city. Dynamite was lavishly used, and many of San Francisco's proudest structures were crumbled by man himself into ruins, but there was no withstanding the onrush of the flames. Time and again successful stands were made by the firefighters, and every time the flames flanked around on either side, or came up from the rear, and turned to defeat the hard-won victory.

An enumeration of the buildings destroyed would be a directory of San Francisco. An enumeration of the buildings undestroyed would be a line and several addresses. An enumeration of the deeds of heroism would stock a library and bankrupt the Carnegie Medal Fund.[3] An enumeration of the dead—will never be made. All vestiges of them were destroyed by the flames. The number of the victims of the earthquake will never be known. South of Market Street, where the loss of life was particularly heavy, was the first to catch fire.

Remarkable as it may seem, Wednesday night, while the whole city crashed and roared into ruin, was a quiet night. There

---

3. **Carnegie Medal Fund:** an organization established by Andrew Carnegie, which awards medals and money to persons who perform heroic acts.

were no crowds. There was no shouting and yelling. There was no hysteria, no disorder. I passed Wednesday night in the path of the advancing flames, and in all those terrible hours I saw not one woman who wept, not one man who was excited, not one person who was in the slightest degree panic-stricken.

Before the flames, throughout the night, fled tens of thousands of homeless ones. Some were wrapped in blankets. Others carried bundles of bedding and dear household treasures. Sometimes a whole family was harnessed to a carriage or delivery wagon that was weighted down with their possessions. Baby buggies, toy wagons, and go-carts were used as trucks, while every other person was dragging a trunk. Yet everybody was gracious. The most perfect courtesy obtained.[4] Never, in all San Francisco's history, were her people so kind and courteous as on this night of terror.

4. **obtained:** here, was in effect.

All night these tens of thousands fled before the flames. Many of them, the poor people from the labor ghetto, had fled all day as well. They had left their homes burdened with possessions. Now and again they lightened up, flinging out upon the street clothing and treasures they had dragged for miles.

They held on longest to their trunks, and over these trunks many a strong man broke his heart that night. The hills of San Francisco are steep, and up these hills, mile after mile, were the trunks dragged. Everywhere were trunks, with across them lying their exhausted owners, men and women. Before the march of the flames were flung picket lines of soldiers. And a block at a time, as the flames advanced, these pickets retreated. One of their tasks was to keep the trunk pullers moving. The exhausted creatures, stirred on by the menace of bayonets, would arise and struggle up the steep pavements, pausing from weakness every five or ten feet.

Often, after surmounting a heartbreaking hill, they would find another wall of flame advancing upon them at right angles and be compelled to change anew the line of their retreat. In the end, completely played out, after toiling for a dozen hours like giants, thousands of them were compelled to abandon their trunks. Here the shopkeepers and soft members of the middle class were at a disadvantage. But the workingmen dug holes in vacant lots and backyards and buried their trunks.

At nine o'clock Wednesday evening I walked down through the very heart of the city. I walked through miles and miles of magnificent buildings and towering skyscrapers. Here was no fire. All was in perfect order The police patrolled the streets. Every building had its watchman at the door. And yet it was doomed, all of it. There was no water. The dynamite was giving out. And at right angles two different conflagrations were sweeping down upon it.

At one o'clock in the morning I walked down through the same section. Everything still stood intact. There was no fire. And yet there was a change. A rain of ashes was falling. The watchmen at the doors were gone. The police had been withdrawn. There were no firemen, no fire engines, no men fighting with dynamite. The district had been absolutely abandoned. I stood at the corner of Kearney and Market, in the very innermost heart of San Francisco. Kearney Street was deserted. Half a dozen blocks away it was burning on both sides. The street was a wall of flame. And against this wall of flame, silhouetted sharply, were two United States cavalrymen sitting their horses, calmly watching. That was all. Not another person was in sight. In the intact heart of the city two troopers sat their horses and watched.

Surrender was complete. There was no water. The sewers had long since been pumped dry. There was no dynamite. Another fire had broken out further uptown, and now from three sides conflagrations were sweeping down. The fourth side had been burned earlier in the day. In that direction stood the tottering walls of the Examiner building, the burned-out Call building, the smoldering ruins of the Grand Hotel, and the gutted, devastated, dynamited Palace Hotel.

The following will illustrate the sweep of the flames and the inability of men to calculate their spread. At eight o'clock Wednesday evening I passed through Union Square. It was packed with refugees. Thousands of them had gone to bed on the grass. Government tents had been set up, supper was being cooked, and the refugees were lined up for free meals.

At half past one in the morning three sides of Union Square were in flames. The fourth side, where stood the great St. Francis Hotel, was still holding out. An hour later, ignited

from top and sides, the St. Francis was flaming heavenward. Union Square, heaped high with mountains of trunks, was deserted. Troops, refugees, and all had retreated.

It was at Union Square that I saw a man offering a thousand dollars for a team of horses. He was in charge of a truck piled high with trunks from some hotel. It had been hauled here into what was considered safety, and the horses had been taken out. The flames were on three sides of the Square, and there were no horses.

Also, at this time, standing beside the truck, I urged a man to seek safety in flight. He was all but hemmed in by several conflagrations. He was an old man and he was on crutches. Said he, "Today is my birthday. Last night I was worth thirty thousand dollars. I bought five bottles of wine, some delicate fish, and other things for my birthday dinner. I have had no dinner, and all I own are these crutches."

I convinced him of his danger and started him limping on his way. An hour later, from a distance, I saw the truckload of trunks burning merrily in the middle of the street.

On Thursday morning, at a quarter past five, just twenty-four hours after the earthquake, I sat on the steps of a small residence on Nob Hill. With me sat Japanese, Italians, Chinese, and Negroes—a bit of the cosmopolitan flotsam[5] of the wreck of the city. All about were the palaces of the nabob pioneers of Forty-nine.[6] To the east and south, at right angles, were advancing two mighty walls of flame.

I went inside with the owner of the house on the steps of which I sat. He was cool and cheerful and hospitable. "Yesterday morning," he said, "I was worth six hundred thousand dollars. This morning this house is all I have left. It will go in fifteen minutes." He pointed to a large cabinet. "That is my wife's collection of china. This rug upon which we stand is a present. It cost fifteen hundred dollars. Try that piano. Listen to its tone. There are few like it. There are no horses. The flames will be here in fifteen minutes."

Outside, the old Mark Hopkins residence, a palace, was just catching fire. The troops were falling back and driving the refugees before them. From every side came the roaring of flames, the crashing of walls, and the detonations of dynamite.

I passed out of the house. Day was trying to dawn through the smoke-pall.[7] A sickly light was creeping over the face of things. Once only the sun broke through the smoke-pall, blood-red, and showing a quarter its usual size. The smoke-pall itself, viewed from beneath, was a rose color that pulsed and fluttered with lavender shades. Then it turned to mauve[8] and yellow and dun.[9] There was no sun. And so dawned the second day on stricken San Francisco.

An hour later I was creeping past the shattered dome of the City Hall. Than it, there was no better exhibit of the destructive forces of the earthquake. Most of the stone had been shaken from the great dome, leaving standing the naked framework of steel. Market Street was piled high with the wreckage, and across

---

5. **cosmopolitan flotsam** (kŏz′mə-pŏl′ə-tən flŏt′səm): *Cosmopolitan* means "from all parts of the world." *Flotsam* is debris left floating on the sea after a shipwreck. London uses this phrase to describe the mixture of people who have been made homeless by the earthquake.
6. **Forty-nine:** 1849, the year of the great gold rush to California.

7. **smoke-pall:** a dark, gloomy covering of smoke.
8. **mauve** (mōv): a shade of purple.
9. **dun:** grayish-brown.

the wreckage lay the overthrown pillars of the City Hall shattered into short crosswise sections.

This section of the city, with the exception of the Mint and the Post Office, was already a waste of smoking ruins. Here and there through the smoke, creeping warily under the shadows of tottering walls, emerged occasional men and women. It was like the meeting of the handful of survivors after the day of the end of the world.

On Mission Street lay a dozen steers, in a neat row stretching across the street, just as they had been struck down by the flying ruins of the earthquake. The fire had passed through afterward and roasted them. The human dead had been carried away before the fire came. At another place on Mission Street I saw a milk wagon. A steel telegraph pole had smashed down sheer through the driver's seat and crushed the front wheels. The milk cans lay scattered around.

All day Thursday and all Thursday night, all day Friday and Friday night, the flames still raged.

Friday night saw the flames finally conquered, though not until Russian Hill and Telegraph Hill had been swept and three quarters of a mile of wharves and docks had been licked up.

The great stand of the firefighters was made Thursday night on Van Ness Avenue. Had they failed here, the comparatively few remaining houses of the city would have been swept. Here were the magnificent residences of the second generation of San Francisco nabobs, and these, in a solid zone, were dynamited down across the path of the fire. Here and there the flames leaped the zone, but these fires were beaten out, principally by the

use of wet blankets and rugs.

San Francisco, at the present time, is like the crater of a volcano, around which are camped tens of thousands of refugees. At the Presidio[10] alone are at least twenty thousand. All the surrounding cities and towns are jammed with the homeless ones, where they are being cared for by relief committees. The refugees were carried free by the railroads to any point they wished to go, and it is estimated that over one hundred thousand people have left the peninsula on which San Francisco stood. The government has the situation in hand, and, thanks to the immediate relief given by the whole United States, there is not the slightest possibility of a famine. The bankers and businessmen have already set about making preparations to rebuild San Francisco.

10. **Presidio** (prĭ-sĭ′dē-ō′): a military post in San Francisco.

SEEKING MEANING

1. Jack London describes the earthquake as "thirty seconds' twitching of the earth-crust" (page 381). In less than a minute, buildings crumbled, streets buckled, and lines of communication snapped. Which details in the third paragraph convey the destructive force of the earthquake?

2. The worst damage was done not by the earthquake itself, but by the great fire that followed. How does London depict the vast extent of the fire in the second paragraph?

3. As the fire burned into the night, "the whole city crashed and roared into ruin," and many lives were lost. Yet London describes it as "a quiet night." What did he find most remarkable about the behavior of people on "this night of terror"?

4. As London walked through the city, he met and talked with several victims of the disaster. Summarize what the old man on crutches and the owner of the house said to him. Why do you think London includes incidents of this kind in an account of a natural disaster?

5. London describes the dawn of the second day as a "sickly light . . . creeping over the face of things." The sun was "blood-red, and showing a quarter its usual size" (page 384). What other colors does London use in describing the dawn? How does his description, particularly his choice of colors, create an atmosphere of destruction?

DEVELOPING SKILLS IN READING

Understanding Inverted Word Order

The usual order of words in an English sentence is subject-and-predicate. Here is a sentence written in that order:

Two mighty walls of flame, at right angles, were advancing to the east and south.

Compare it with this sentence from "The Story of an Eyewitness":

To the east and south, at right angles, were advancing two mighty walls of flame.

What difference is there in the word order of the two sentences?

A skillful writer may deliberately change the normal word order in a sentence in order to make the sentence more exciting or dramatic. Here are some other examples of unusual word order from London's article:

From every side came the roaring of flames, the crashing of walls, and the detonation of dynamite.
The hills of San Francisco are steep, and up these hills, mile after mile, were the trunks dragged.

Notice the word order in the first sentence, which builds up to a climax of sound. As you read it, you "hear" first the roar of flames, then the crashing of walls, and finally the explosion of dynamite. The second sentence describes the slow and torturous process of dragging trunks up steep hills. How does the word order suggest an exhausted, strained movement?

Find other sentences in the selection that have unusual word order. Explain the effects London achieves by inverting word order.

ABOUT THE AUTHOR

Jack London (1876–1916), who became one of the most successful and popular writers in the world, was born in grim poverty in San Francisco. He never received much formal education. He educated himself by studying for hours at a time in public libraries.

In his teens he was a longshoreman, an oyster pirate, a seaman, and a hobo. When he was nineteen, he decided to finish high school. He condensed a four-year course into one year and was able to pass the entrance examination at the University of California in the following year. In 1897 he left college to seek gold in the Klondike. He found no gold and returned to San Francisco, sailing 1,900 miles (about 3,060 kilometers) in an open boat. His experiences in the Arctic gave him the material for many short stories and for his famous novels *The Call of the Wild* and *White Fang*.

London worked hard at being a writer. In seventeen years he produced fifty books. His popularity grew until he became the highest-paid writer in the United States. When he died at the age of forty, he had either spent or given away all his money. London's tale of rough adventure are widely read today. His books and short stories have been translated into many languages.

In the fifth century B.C., the Greeks defeated the Persians in a battle on the plain near Marathon in Greece. According to legend, a Greek messenger ran from Marathon to Athens— a distance of about 25 miles or roughly 40 kilometers— to report the victory.

Today the word marathon *refers to any contest of endurance. One of the events in the Olympic Games is a marathon footrace, in which the contestants run more than 26 miles. Perhaps the most difficult of all marathon sports is marathon swimming. In this article, a champion marathon swimmer tells about this extraordinary sport.*

Mind over Water *Diana Nyad*

I have been working on swimming since I was ten, four hours a day or more, every day, skipping the greater part of my social life, not a huge sacrifice, but something. I have put more grueling hours into it than someone like Jimmy Connors[1] will ever know in a lifetime. I don't begrudge him his talent in that particular sport. There is simply no way he could comprehend the *work* that goes into marathon swimming.

What I do is analogous to other long-distance competitions: running, cycling, rowing, those sports where training time far exceeds actual competition time. But swimming burns more calories[2] per minute than anything else. The lungs, heart and muscles must all be working at peak efficiency for this sport, which doesn't require brute strength

---

1. **Jimmy Connors:** a champion tennis player.
2. **calories** (kăl′ər-ēz): units of heat energy used to measure the amount of energy that food gives the body.

but rather the strength of endurance. I can do a thousand sit-ups in the wink of an eye — and I never do sit-ups on a regular basis. I've run the mile in 5:15, not exactly Olympic caliber, but better than most women can do. My lung capacity is 6.1 liters, greater than a lot of football players. My heartbeat is forty-seven or forty-eight when I am at rest; this is compared to the normal seventy-two for other people.[3] A conditioned athlete usually has a heartbeat of sixty plus. These characteristics are not due to genetics[4] — I attained them by swimming hour after hour, year after year.

My first marathon, the ten-miler at Hamilton, Ontario, scared me to death. Judith De Nijs, the best in the world throughout the sixties, was there, saying that if a woman ever beat her she would retire from the sport. She came over to me and said, ''Well, I hear you're a very good swimmer. Well, you are not going to beat me.'' She put on her cap and walked away. I thought, whew. I swam the race and beat her by about fifteen minutes, which is a lot for a ten-miler. Judith De Nijs never swam again.

Greta Andersen was the same way. She swam the Channel[5] I don't know how many times, as well as the Juan de Fuca Strait,[6] and sixty miles across Lake Michigan. She beat every man she swam against at least once. She could have gone on forever. But she said that if another woman ever beat her, she'd quit. When Marty Sinn beat her, Andersen kept her word.

I'm not like that. Sandra Bucha has beaten me a couple of times in individual swims. I've been beaten by Corrie Dixon. They were better than I was on those days.

Because I'm interested in people who are involved in exploring their potential, there is no one group I can respect more than marathon swimmers. When I'm in a hospital bed in La Tuque,[7] for instance, after swimming in a twenty-four-hour team race, weak from exposure and nearly having frozen to death, and next to me is the guy I passed at three in the morning, we look at each other as if we're kings of the mountain. We have a love for each other, a close camaraderie.

There is considerable anxiety before a swim. I don't know until the day of the race whether the wind will be whipping up fifteen-foot waves or whether the surface will be glass. On the morning of a swim, our trainers wake us around three A.M. for breakfast. We see the press, we eat. Nobody talks. The tension in the room is amazing. I never look at the swimmers; I look out at the lake and wonder what it will do to me, whether I'll be able to cross it. The race is more than me versus my competition. There is always the risk that I may not conquer the water.

At breakfast I have five or six raw eggs, a lot of cereal, toast and jam, juice. For my feedings during the race from the boat, I drink a hot powdered liquid that provides me with thirteen hundred calories and more protein per tablespoon than a four-ounce steak. It gets my blood sugar[8] back up. In a race my blood sugar

---

3. **My heartbeat . . . people:** The slower a person's heart beats, the greater that person's endurance is.
4. **genetics** (jə-nĕt′ĭks): inherited characteristics.
5. **the Channel:** the English Channel, a body of water between England and France, 21 miles (about 34 kilometers) wide at its narrowest point.
6. **Juan de Fuca** (hwän′ də foo′kə) **Strait:** a body of water between Vancouver Island, Canada, and the state of Washington, 15–20 miles (24–32 kilometers) wide.

7. **La Tuque** (lə tyük′): a river port town in Quebec, Canada.
8. **blood sugar:** The body must keep a certain amount of sugar in the blood. Without it, a person feels tired and depressed.

drops below metabolism level in three minutes. A cup of this stuff every hour barely helps. Before the hour's up my sugar is way down. I can feel it. I feel depressed. But if my protein level stays high, I'm not really in trouble.

I would say that eighty percent of success in

isolation in long-distance swimming is more extreme. I'm cut off physically from communication. The water sloshing over my cap leaves me virtually deaf. I wear tiny goggles that fit just over my eyes—they're always foggy, so I can't see very well. I turn my head to breathe on every stroke, sixty times a min-

a race is due to mind. Before starting, all natural reserves are working for me, my adrenalin,[9] everything. Once out there, it's a matter of mental guts. After twelve hours in cold water, my blood sugar down, I'm seventeen pounds lighter, exhausted, it takes more than knowing I've trained hard for this. I have to dig down deep.

I've done some marathon running, but the

ute, six hundred strokes every mile for hours and hours. As I turn my head I see the blur of the boat and some people on it.

These countless rhythmic hours make marathon swimming unique. John Lilly, the dolphin experimenter, has found that a subject floating in a tank with eyes and ears covered becomes disoriented,[10] slipping into a near-dream state. During a long swim I'm left with

---

9. **adrenalin** (ə-drĕn′əl-ĭn): a chemical produced by the body that increases muscular strength and endurance.

10. **disoriented** (dĭs-ôr′ē-ĕnt′ĭd): confused about time and place.

my own thoughts. My mind drifts in a mesmerized[11] world. It's hypnotic. My subconscious[12] comes to the fore. I have fantasies and sometimes flashbacks to my childhood. It's dreaming hours on end. All I hear is the water slapping and my arms whishing through water. All I see is fog. It is extremely lonely.

I'm strong at the beginning of a swim, then I have low points. I know the pain in my shoulders will be bad all the way. I've rolled over on my back, thinking this body will not do another stroke. Sometimes at a low point a swimmer will get out. In ten minutes he's saying to himself, "Why didn't I stick it out? I could have made it. I could have come back around." That's happened to me, too, when I couldn't get back into it.

In rough ocean, I have thrown up from beginning to end of a thirteen-hour swim, swishing around like a cork, violently sick to my stomach. I would do anything to stop this feeling—and the only thing that will is to be on dry land. But I can put up with it—I have to. In my first year of marathon swimming, I got out because of seasickness. Now I get just as seasick and stick it.

Fatigue, pain, and huge waves are manageable. The toughest condition is cold water. Cliff Lumsdon, my trainer since 1972, swam in the Canadian Nationals in 1955. Lake Ontario was 45 degrees. The life expectancy[13] for a normal-weight person in 45-degree water is something like forty minutes. A marathon swimmer has only a film of grease for insulation, which wears off after a little while. After one hour, everyone was out of the water but Lumsdon. The temperature simply couldn't be handled. But Cliff stayed in for the entire fifteen miles, finishing in nineteen hours, eighteen minutes. He went through a substantial recovery period but was never hospitalized.

My coldest time was training on Ontario for the Capri-to-Naples race[14] in 1974. I was supposed to leave later that day for Europe, but thought, why waste the time? Why not swim for an hour, just to loosen up? I did a thousand strokes out, then stopped to turn around, empty my goggles, get a sighting onshore. But I realized I hadn't been feeling my legs. I couldn't bring them to the surface. My skin was lobster-red. My breath stuck in my throat. I tried to scream to some boys onshore, but nothing came out. I started to swim a slow breaststroke. My hands were so cold I couldn't close my fingers. People onshore finally saw I was in trouble. By now I was onto shallow rocks. A man waded out and grabbed me under my arms to lift me out of the water. His hands, his 98.6-degree hands, burned my skin. They took me to the hospital and put me in a warmer. I had severe burns all the way through the Capri–Naples race.

The temperature that day in Ontario was 40. I'd been in the water an hour. It freaks me out when I think Cliff lasted nineteen hours in 45-degree water. I just couldn't do it. My body weight is less than his, but still . . . I really have to psych myself up for cold water.

There are still a few bodies of water I want to conquer. I'm considering all of the five Great

---

11. **mesmerized** (mĕz'mə-rīzd'): spellbound.
12. **subconscious** (sŭb'kŏn'shəs): the part of a person's mind that stores thoughts, memories, and wishes of which the person is normally not aware.
13. **life expectancy:** the amount of time a person can be expected to live.

14. **Capri-to-Naples race:** a 25-mile (40-kilometer) race from the island of Capri, off the southwest coast of Italy, to Naples.

Lakes in the summer of '76. Each lake is a different challenge.

The lakes are pretty cold. Superior is so cold I'd have to cross it at the shortest point. A legal marathon may be undertaken only in a regular racing suit, cap, goggles, and grease—no flotation devices,[15] no insulating suit. Even at the shortest crossing, Superior may be impossible, given these requirements.

I've found suitable start and finish options for each lake. I could swim from Michigan City to Chicago, for instance, which is thirty miles; or from Benton Harbor to Chicago, which is sixty. My route will depend on how cold the water is. Distance doesn't mean anything to me; it's the condition of the water that counts.

Marathon swimming will never be as popular as other sports for obvious reasons. Spectators can only watch the finish, not the whole process. It's like the Tour de France—the most popular cycling race in the country and you can't see anything. But there is empathy[16] among the spectators when the contestants stop for the night. You see their huge legs, muscular bodies dust-covered and sweaty, their power exhausted.

There is the same empathy at the end of a marathon swim. People have spent the whole day waiting. From a mile out I can hear clapping and screaming. The people realize I swam from a place they couldn't see on the clearest day. They know I may faint when I arrive. They share with me the most extreme moment of all—for after the pain, the cold, the hours, the distance, after the fatigue and the loneliness, after all this comes my emergence. And my emergence is what it's all about.

---

15. **flotation** (flō-tā'shən) **devices:** equipment that helps a person float.
16. **empathy** (ĕm'pə-thē): the sharing of another person's thoughts or feelings.

SEEKING MEANING

1. At the beginning of this selection, Diana Nyad tells about the work that goes into becoming a marathon swimmer. What does she do to keep fit? How does her physical condition compare with that of athletes in other sports?

2. According to the author, in what way is a marathon swimmer isolated?

3. Marathon swimmers must endure seasickness, fatigue, and often severe pain. According to the author, the hardest condition of all is cold water. What happened when she tried to swim in 40-degree water? How much protection does a swimmer have against the temperature of the water?

4. The author says that marathon swimmers need more than physical strength. What does she mean by the phrase "mental guts" (page 390)? What do you think the title of this selection means?

5. Marathon swimming is a lonely and painful sport. How does the author feel she is repaid for her efforts?

Have you ever had a pet that simply refused to behave the way it was supposed to? In this humorous essay Jean Kerr tells about the curious and comic habits of her pet dogs.

Dogs That Have Known Me

Jean Kerr

I never meant to say anything about this, but the fact is that I have never met a dog that didn't have it in for me. You take Kelly, for instance. He's a wire-haired fox terrier and he's had us for three years now. I wouldn't say that he was terribly handsome but he does have a very nice smile. What he *doesn't* have is any sense of fitness.[1] All the other dogs in the neighborhood spend their afternoons yapping at each other's heels or chasing cats. Kelly spends his whole day, every day, chasing swans on the millpond. I don't actually worry because he will never catch one. For

one thing, he can't swim. Instead of settling for a simple dogpaddle like everybody else, he has to show off and try some complicated overhand stroke, with the result that he always sinks and has to be fished out. Naturally, people talk, and I never take him for a walk that somebody doesn't point him out and say, "There's that crazy dog that chases swans."

Another thing about that dog is that he absolutely refuses to put himself in the other fellow's position. We have a pencil sharpener in the kitchen and Kelly used to enjoy having an occasional munch on the plastic cover. As long as it was just a nip now and then, I didn't mind. But one day he simply lost his head and

---

1. **fitness:** here, the proper way to behave.

ate the whole thing. Then I had to buy a new one and of course I put it up high out of Kelly's reach. Well, the scenes we were treated to—and the sulking! In fact, ever since he has been eating things I know he doesn't like just to get even. I don't mean things like socks and mittens and paper napkins, which of course are delicious. Lately he's been eating plastic airplanes, suede brushes, and light bulbs. Well, if he wants to sit under the piano and make low and loving growls over a suede brush just to show me, okay. But frankly I think he's lowering himself.

Time and again I have pointed out to Kelly that with discriminating dogs, dogs who are looking for a finer, lighter chew—it's bedroom slippers two to one. I have even dropped old, dilapidated bedroom slippers here and there behind the furniture, hoping to tempt him. But the fact is, that dog wouldn't touch a bedroom slipper if he was starving.

Although we knew that, as a gourmet,[2] he was a washout, we did keep saying one thing about Kelly. We kept saying, "He's a good little old watchdog." Heaven knows why we thought so, except that he barks at the drop of a soufflé.[3] In fact, when he's in the basement a stiff toothbrush on the third floor is enough to set him off into a concerto of deep, murderous growls followed by loud hysterical yappings. I used to take real pleasure in imagining the chagrin of some poor intruder who'd bring that cacophony[4] upon himself. Last month we had an intruder. He got in the porch window and took twenty-two dollars and my wristwatch while Kelly, that good little old watchdog, was as silent as a cathedral. But that's the way it's been.

The first dog I remember well was a large black and white mutt that was part German shepherd, part English sheepdog, and part collie—the wrong part in each case. With what strikes me now as unforgivable whimsy, we called him Ladadog from the title by Albert Payson Terhune.[5] He was a splendid dog in many respects but, in the last analysis, I'm afraid he was a bit of a social climber. He used to pretend that he was just crazy about us. I mean, if you just left the room to comb your hair he would greet you on your return with passionate lickings, pawings, and convulsive tail-waggings. And a longer separation—let's say you had to go out on the front porch to pick up the mail—would send Ladadog off into such a demonstration of rapture and thanksgiving that we used to worry for his heart.

However, all this mawkish, slobbering sentiment disappeared the moment he stepped over the threshhold. I remember we kids used to spot him on our way home from school, chasing around the Parkers' lawn with a cocker friend of his, and we'd rush over to him with happy squeals of "Laddy, oleboy, oleboy, oleboy," and Ladadog would just stand there looking slightly pained and distinctly cool. It wasn't that he cut us dead. He nodded, but it was with the remote air of a celebrity at a cocktail party saying, "Of *course* I remember you, and how's Ed?"

We kept making excuses for him and even worked out an elaborate explanation for his behavior. We decided that Ladadog didn't see very well, that he could only recognize us by smell and that he couldn't smell very well in the open air. However, the day came when

---

2. **gourmet** (gŏor-mā′): someone who enjoys and is a good judge of fine foods.
3. **soufflé** (sōō-flā′): baked dish with a light, puffy crust.
4. **cacophony** (kă-kŏf′ə-nē): harsh, jarring sounds.

5. **Albert Payson Terhune:** an author of popular stories about dogs, including *Lad: A Dog.*

my mother met Ladadog in front of the A & P. She was wearing her new brown coat with the beaver collar, and, lo and behold, Ladadog greeted her with joy and rapture. After that we just had to face the truth—that dog was a snob.

He also had other peculiarities. For instance, he saved lettuce. He used to beg for lettuce and then he would store it away in the cellar behind the coalbin. I don't know whether he was saving up to make a salad or what, but every so often we'd have to clean away a small, soggy lump of decayed vegetation.

And every time the phone rang he would run from wherever he was and sit there beside the phone chair, his tail thumping and his ears bristling, until you'd make some sort of an announcement like "It's just the Hoover man" or "Eileen, it's for you." Then he would immediately disappear. Clearly, this dog had put a call in to someone, but we never did figure out who.

Come to think of it, the dog that gave us the most trouble was a beagle named Murphy. As far as I'm concerned, the first thing he did wrong was to turn into a beagle. I had seen him bouncing around in the excelsior[6] of a pet-shop window, and I went in and asked the man, "How much is that adorable fox terrier in the window?" Did he say, "That adorable fox terrier is a beagle"? No, he said, "Ten dollars, lady." Now, I don't mean to say one word against beagles. They have rights just like other people. But it is a bit of a shock when you bring home a small ball of fluff in a shoebox, and three weeks later it's as long as the sofa.

Murphy had a habit that used to leave us open to a certain amount of criticism from our friends, who were not dogophiles.[7] He never climbed up on beds or chairs or sofas. But he always sat on top of the piano. In the beginning we used to try to pull him off of

6. **excelsior** (ĕk-sĕl′sē-ər): wood shavings.
7. **dogophiles:** a made-up word meaning "dog lovers."

there. But after a few noisy scuffles in which he knocked a picture off the wall, scratched the piano, and smashed a lamp, we just gave in—only to discover that, left to his own devices, he hopped up and down as delicately as a ballet dancer. We became quite accustomed to it, but at parties at our house it was not unusual to hear a guest remark, "I don't know what I'm drinking but I think I see a big dog on the piano."

It's not just our own dogs that bother me. The dogs I meet at parties are even worse. I don't know what I've got that attracts them; it just doesn't bear thought. My husband swears I rub chopped meat on my ankles. But at every party it's the same thing. I am sitting in happy conviviality with a group in front of the fire when all of a sudden the large mutt of mine host appears in the archway. Then, without a single bark of warning, he hurls himself upon me. It always makes me think of that line from *A Streetcar Named Desire*[8]

—"Baby, we've had this date right from the beginning." My martini flies into space and my stockings are torn before he finally settles down peacefully in the lap of my new black faille.[9] I blow out such quantities of hair as I haven't swallowed and glance at my host, expecting to be rescued. He murmurs, "Isn't that wonderful? You know, Brucie is usually so distant with strangers."

At a dinner party in Long Island last week, after I had been mugged by a large sheepdog, I announced quite piteously, "Oh dear, he seems to have swallowed one of my earrings." The hostess looked really distressed for a moment, until she examined the remaining earring. Then she said, "Oh, I think it will be all right. It's small and it's round."

Nowadays if I go anywhere I just ask if they have a dog. If they do, I say, "Maybe I'd better keep away from him—I have this bad allergy." This does not tend to endear me to my hostess. But it is safer. It really is.

---

8. *A Streetcar Named Desire:* a play by Tennessee Williams.

9. **faille** (fāl): a dress made of a soft, slighty ribbed fabric.

SEEKING MEANING

1. Kelly is described as a dog with no "sense of fitness." How is his behavior different from that of other dogs?

2. What led the family to believe that Kelly would make a good watchdog? How did he surprise them?

3. Snobbishness is ordinarily associated with human beings, not with animals. Yet the author refers to another of her dogs, Ladadog, as "a snob" (page 395). Why? What other peculiarities does the author recall about Ladadog?

4. In describing Murphy, the author says she has nothing against beagles: "They have rights just like other people" (page 395). Find other examples in the essay where she refers to dogs as if they were people.

DEVELOPING SKILLS IN READING

Finding Humor in the Unexpected

Laughter is often a reaction to something unexpected or surprising. For example, we expect lions to roar and birds to chirp. But imagine a chirping lion or a roaring bird.

In Jean Kerr's essay, dogs behave in odd and unexpected ways. Their actions surprise us. Consider this description of Murphy:

> He never climbed up on beds or chairs or sofas. But he always sat on top of the piano. In the beginning we used to try to pull him off of there. But after a few noisy scuffles in which he knocked a picture off the wall, scratched the piano, and smashed a lamp, we just gave in — only to discover that, left to his own devices, he hopped up and down as delicately as a ballet dancer.

Most pet dogs enjoy resting quietly on soft furniture, such as beds, chairs, and sofas.

What is unusual about Murphy's behavior? Which of his actions do you find the most humorous?

Find another example of odd or unexpected behavior in the essay and tell why it is humorous.

ABOUT THE AUTHOR

When she was eight years old, Jean Kerr (1923–   ) decided that all she wanted when she grew up was to be able to sleep until noon every day. She concluded that the fastest way to arrive at this goal was to become a professional writer. Thus began her career as a writer of stories. However, her interests took a sudden turn. She says: "I decided to write plays, spurred on by a chance compliment my father had paid me years earlier. 'Look,' he exploded one evening over the dinner table, 'the only thing in this world you're good for is *talk.*' By talk I assumed he meant dialogue — and I was off." Jean Kerr has since added another goal — "to make people laugh." She has been called one of the funniest writers of her generation.

She is the author of several successful plays, including *Song of Bernadette,* which she adapted with her husband, critic Walter Kerr. She has also contributed many autobiographical essays to magazines. Her first collection of these essays resulted in her most famous book, *Please Don't Eat the Daisies,* from which the selection "Dogs That Have Known Me" is taken.

Each of us has felt nervous or afraid at the beginning of some new, exciting experience. In this selection, the narrator begins as a terrified observer, but gradually learns to overcome her fears.

Rattlesnake Hunt

Marjorie Kinnan Rawlings

Ross Allen, a young Florida herpetologist,[1] invited me to join him on a hunt in the upper Everglades[2]—for rattlesnakes.

The hunting ground was Big Prairie, south of Arcadia and west of the northern tip of Lake Okeechobee. Big Prairie is a desolate cattle country, half marsh, half pasture, with islands of palm trees and cypresses and oaks. At that time of year the cattlemen and Indians were burning the country, on the theory that the young fresh wire grass that springs up

---

1. **herpetologist** (hûr′pə-tŏl′ə-jĭst): a person who studies reptiles and amphibians.
2. **Everglades:** a large area of swampland in southern Florida.

from the roots after a fire is the best cattle forage. Ross planned to hunt his rattlers in the forefront of the fires. They lived in winter, he said, in gopher holes, coming out in the midday warmth to forage, and would move ahead of the flames and be easily taken. We joined forces with a big fellow named Will, his snake-hunting companion of the territory, and set out in early morning, after a long rough drive over deep-rutted roads into the open wilds.

I hope never in my life to be so frightened as I was in those first few hours. I kept on Ross's footsteps, I moved when he moved, sometimes jolting into him when I thought he might leave me behind. He does not use the forked stick of conventional snake hunting, but a steel prong, shaped like an L, at the end of a long stout stick. He hunted casually, calling my attention to the varying vegetation, to hawks overhead, to a pair of the rare whooping cranes that flapped over us. In midmorning he stopped short, dropped his stick, and brought up a five-foot rattlesnake draped limply over the steel L. It seemed to me that I should drop in my tracks.

"They're not active at this season," he said quietly. "A snake takes on the temperature of its surroundings. They can't stand too much heat for that reason, and when the weather is cool, as now, they're sluggish."

The sun was bright overhead, the sky a translucent blue, and it seemed to me that it was warm enough for any snake to do as it willed. The sweat poured down my back. Ross dropped the rattler in a crocus sack[3] and Will carried it. By noon, he had caught four. I felt faint and ill. We stopped by a pond and went swimming. The region was flat, the horizon limitless, and as I came out of the cool

blue water I expected to find myself surrounded by a ring of rattlers. There were only Ross and Will, opening the lunch basket. I could not eat. Ross never touches liquor and it seemed to me that I would give my hope of salvation for a dram of whiskey. Will went back and drove his truck closer, for Ross expected the hunting to be better in the afternoon. The hunting was much better. When we went back to the truck to deposit two more rattlers in the wire cage, there was a rattlesnake lying under the truck.

Ross said, "Whenever I leave my car or truck with snakes already in it, other rattlers always appear. I don't know whether this is because they scent or sense the presence of other snakes, or whether in this arid area they come to the car for shade in the heat of the day."

---

3. **crocus sack:** a sack made of coarse material, such as burlap.

The problem was scientific, but I had no interest.

That night Ross and Will and I camped out in the vast spaces of the Everglades prairies. We got water from an abandoned well and cooked supper under buttonwood bushes by a flowing stream. The campfire blazed cheerfully under the stars and a new moon lifted in the sky. Will told tall tales of the cattlemen and the Indians and we were at peace.

Ross said, "We couldn't have a better night for catching water snakes."

After the rattlers, water snakes seemed innocuous[4] enough. We worked along the edge of the stream and here Ross did not use his L-shaped steel. He reached under rocks and along the edge of the water and brought out harmless reptiles with his hands. I had said nothing to him of my fears, but he understood them. He brought a small dark snake from under a willow root.

"Wouldn't you like to hold it?" he asked. "People think snakes are cold and clammy, but they aren't. Take it in your hands. You'll see that it is warm."

Again, because I was ashamed, I took the snake in my hands. It was not cold, it was not clammy, and it lay trustingly in my hands, a thing that lived and breathed and had mortality[5] like the rest of us. I felt an upsurgence of spirit.

The next day was magnificent. The air was crystal, the sky was aquamarine, and the far horizon of palms and oaks lay against the sky. I felt a new boldness and followed Ross bravely. He was making the rounds of the gopher holes. The rattlers came out in the midmorning warmth and were never far away. He could tell by their trails whether one had come out or was still in the hole. Sometimes the two men dug the snake out. At times it was down so long and winding a tunnel that the digging was hopeless. Then they blocked the entrance and went on to other holes. In an hour or so they made the original rounds, unblocking the holes. The rattler in every case came out hurriedly, as though anything was preferable to being shut in. All the time Ross talked to me, telling me the scientific facts he had discovered about the habits of the rattlers.

"They pay no attention to a man standing perfectly still," he said, and proved it by letting Will unblock a hole while he stood at the entrance as the snake came out. It was exciting to watch the snake crawl slowly beside and past the man's legs. When it was at a safe distance he walked within its range of vision, which he had proved to be no higher than a man's knee, and the snake whirled and drew back in an attitude[6] of fighting defense. The rattler strikes only for paralyzing and killing its food, and for defense.

"It is a slow and heavy snake," Ross said. "It lies in wait on a small game trail and strikes the rat or rabbit passing by. It waits a few minutes, then follows along the trail, coming to the small animal, now dead or dying. It noses it from all sides, making sure that it is its own kill, and that it is dead and ready for swallowing."

A rattler will lie quietly without revealing itself if a man passes by and it thinks it is not seen. It slips away without fighting if given the chance. Only Ross's sharp eyes sometimes picked out the gray and yellow diamond pattern, camouflaged among the grasses. In the cool of the morning, chilled by

---

4. **innocuous** (ĭ-nŏk′yo͞o-əs): harmless.
5. **had mortality** (môr-tăl′ĭ-tē): like all living things, would someday die.

6. **attitude:** here, a position of the body.

the January air, the snakes showed no fight. They could be looped up limply over the steel L and dropped in a sack or up into the wire cage on the back of Will's truck. As the sun mounted in the sky and warmed the moist Everglades earth, the snakes were warmed too, and Ross warned that it was time to go more cautiously. Yet having learned that it was we who were the aggressors;[7] that immobility meant complete safety; that the snakes, for all their lightning flash in striking, were inaccurate in their aim, with limited vision; having watched again and again the liquid grace of movement, the beauty of pattern, suddenly I understood that I was drinking in freely the magnificent sweep of the horizon, with no fear of what might be at the moment under my feet. I went off hunting by

myself, and though I found no snakes, I should have known what to do.

The sun was dropping low in the west. Masses of white cloud hung above the flat marshy plain and seemed to be tangled in the tops of distant palms and cypresses. The sky turned orange, then saffron. I walked leisurely back toward the truck. In the distance I could see Ross and Will making their way in too. The season was more advanced than at the Creek, two hundred miles to the north, and I noticed that spring flowers were blooming among the lumpy hummocks. I leaned over to pick a white violet. There was a rattlesnake under the violet.

If this had happened the week before, if it had happened the day before, I think I should have lain down and died on top of the rattlesnake, with no need of being struck and poisoned. The snake did not coil, but lifted its head and whirred its rattles lightly. I stepped

---

7. **aggressors** (ə-grĕs′ərz): those who attack first.

back slowly and put the violet in a buttonhole. I reached forward and laid the steel L across the snake's neck, just back of the blunt head. I called to Ross: "I've got one."

He strolled toward me.

"Well, pick it up," he said.

I released it and slipped the L under the middle of the thick body.

"Go put it in the box."

He went ahead of me and lifted the top of the wire cage. I made the truck with the rattler, but when I reached up the six feet to drop it in the cage, it slipped off the stick and dropped on Ross's feet. It made no effort to strike.

"Pick it up again," he said. "If you'll pin it down lightly and reach just back of its head with your hand, as you've seen me do, you can drop it in more easily."

I pinned it and leaned over.

"I'm awfully sorry," I said, "but you're pushing me a little too fast."

He grinned. I lifted it on the stick and again as I had it at head height, it slipped off, down

Ross's boots and on top of his feet. He stood as still as a stump. I dropped the snake on his feet for the third time. It seemed to me that the most patient of rattlers might in time resent being hauled up and down, and for all the man's quiet certainty that in standing motionless there was no danger, would strike at whatever was nearest, and that would be Ross.

I said, "I'm just not man enough to keep this up any longer," and he laughed and reached down with his smooth quickness and lifted the snake back of the head and dropped it in the cage. It slid in among its mates and settled in a corner. The hunt was over and we drove back over the uneven trail to Will's village and left him and went on to Arcadia and home. Our catch for the two days was thirty-two rattlers.

I said to Ross, "I believe that tomorrow I could have picked up that snake."

Back at the Creek, I felt a new lightness. I had done battle with a great fear, and the victory was mine.

SEEKING MEANING

1. During the first day of the rattlesnake hunt, how does the author show her terror?

2. Ross Allen is a herpetologist—an expert on reptiles and amphibians. At the start of the hunt, he calmly picks up a five-foot rattlesnake with a steel prong. Why is he able to hunt so "casually"?

3. At first, the author thinks snakes are cold and clammy. What does she discover when she holds a small, dark snake in her own hands? How does this new knowledge affect her?

4. Why is she less frightened on the second day of the hunt?

5. The author's new-found courage is put to a test when she encounters a rattlesnake on her own. What small gesture indicates that she is no longer afraid (see pages 401–402)? How successful is she in catching the snake?

6. At the end of the selection, the author indicates that she has gained control over her fear. How does she now feel?

DEVELOPING VOCABULARY

Forming Words with *-logy*

In "Rattlesnake Hunt," Ross Allen is described as a *herpetologist*, someone who specializes in *herpetology*. The word *herpetology* has two parts. The first part, *herpeto-*, comes from a Greek word meaning "reptile." The second part, *-logy*, also comes from Greek and means "the science or study of something." *Herpetology* is the science or study of reptiles.

Geo- is a root meaning "of the earth." What is *geology? Biology? Zoology?* Check your answers in a dictionary.

Look up the following roots in a dictionary. What does each one mean?

anthropo-   ethno-   theo-

What word is formed by adding *-logy* to each root? Tell what each word means.

DEVELOPING SKILLS OF EXPRESSION

Writing About a Personal Experience
The narrator's attitude toward snakes begins to change after she holds a water snake in her hands.

> Again, because I was ashamed, I took the snake in my hands. It was not cold, it was not clammy, and it lay trustingly in my hands, a thing that lived and breathed and had mortality like the rest of us. I felt an upsurgence of spirit.

Up to this moment, the narrator has been terrified of snakes. After she touches the water snake, her fears begin to diminish. She feels "an upsurgence of spirit."

Think about the first time you tried to do something that took courage—performing in a school play, singing in a chorus, diving from a board, getting on a roller coaster, going to a dance. Describe the experience in a short paragraph, telling as specifically as you can what your reactions were. Use words that convey your feelings.

ABOUT THE AUTHOR

Marjorie Kinnan Rawlings (1896–1953) grew up on a farm in Maryland. She attended the University of Wisconsin, where she was active in theater productions and literary magazines. In 1919 she married Charles Rawlings, a newspaperman. The next ten years involved a great deal of moving and traveling, and during that time; she worked as a newspaper reporter. She disliked this kind of work, however, and began to devote time to writing fiction.

In 1938 she published her most famous novel, *The Yearling,* a story about a boy's love for his pet fawn. This book, which won the Pulitzer Prize, is now considered an American classic. In 1942 she published a collection of remembrances, *Cross Creek,* from which the selection "Rattlesnake Hunt" is taken.

When Alex Haley was growing up in his grandmother's home in Tennessee, he heard a story about an African ancestor named "Kin-tay," who had been kidnapped and sold into slavery. In the story that Haley came to know, there were fragments of his ancestor's language: "Kin-tay" had called a guitar a "ko," and a river in Virginia "Kamby Bolongo."

Years later, after Haley had become a journalist, he began extensive research to learn more about his African heritage. The search for his roots took him to a small village in The Gambia, a country in West Africa. In this excerpt from his book Roots, *Haley describes his meeting with the people of the village.*

Roots   *Alex Haley*

There is an expression called "the peak experience"—that which, emotionally, nothing in your life ever transcends. I've had mine, that first day in the back country of black West Africa.

When we got within sight of Juffure,[1] the children who were playing outside gave the alert, and the people came flocking from their huts. It's a village of only about seventy people. Like most back-country villages, it was still very much as it was two hundred years ago, with its circular mud houses and their conical thatched roofs. Among the people as they gathered was a small man wearing an off-white robe, a pillbox hat over an aquiline-featured black face, and about him was an aura of "somebodiness" until I knew he was the man we had come to see and hear.

As the three interpreters left our party to converge upon him, the seventy-odd other villagers gathered closely around me, in a kind of horseshoe pattern, three or four deep all around; had I stuck out my arms, my fingers would have touched the nearest ones on either side. They were all staring at me. The eyes just raked me. Their foreheads were furrowed with their very intensity of staring. A kind of visceral surging or a churning sensation started up deep inside me; bewildered, I was wondering what on earth was this . . . then in a little while it was rather as if some full-gale force of realization rolled in on me: many times in my life I had been among crowds of people, but never where *every one was jet-black!*

Rocked emotionally, my eyes dropped downward as we tend to do when we're uncertain, insecure, and my glance fell upon my own hands' brown complexion. This time

---

1. **Juffure** (jōō′fōō-rā′).

Alex Haley shown with interpreters and villagers. Haley is the
third figure from the left.

more quickly than before, and even harder,
another gale-force emotion hit me: I felt myself some variety of a hybrid . . . I felt somehow impure among the pure; it was a terribly
shaming feeling. About then, abruptly the old
man left the interpreters. The people immediately also left me now to go crowding about
him.

One of my interpreters came up quickly
and whispered in my ears, ''They stare at you
so much because they have never here seen a
black American.'' When I grasped the significance, I believe that hit me harder than what
had already happened. They hadn't been looking at me as an individual, but I represented in
their eyes a symbol of the twenty-five millions of us black people whom they had never
seen, who lived beyond an ocean.

The people were clustered thickly about
the old man, all of them intermittently flick-
ing glances toward me as they talked anima-

tedly in the Mandinka[2] tongue. After a while,
the old man turned, walked briskly through
the people, past my three interpreters, and
right up to me. His eyes piercing into mine,
seeming to feel I should understand his Mandinka, he expressed what they had all decided
they *felt* concerning those unseen millions of
us who lived in those places that had been
slave ships' destinations—and the translation
came: ''We have been told by the forefathers
that there are many of us from this place who
are in exile in that place called America—
and in other places.''

The old man sat down, facing me, as the
people hurriedly gathered behind him. Then
he began to recite for me the ancestral history
of the Kinte clan, as it had been passed along
orally down across centuries from the forefa-

___

2. **Mandinka** (măn-dĭng′kə): a language spoken in West
Africa.

thers' time. It was not merely conversational, but more as if a scroll were being read; for the still, silent villagers, it was clearly a formal occasion. The *griot*[3] would speak, bending forward from the waist, his body rigid, his neck cords standing out, his words seeming almost physical objects. After a sentence or two, seeming to go limp, he would lean back, listening to an interpreter's translation. Spilling from the *griot*'s head came an incredibly complex Kinte clan lineage that reached back across many generations: who married whom; who had what children; what children then married whom; then their offspring. It was all just unbelievable. I was struck not only by the profusion of details, but also by the narrative's Biblical style, something like: "— and so-and-so took as a wife so-and-so, and begat . . . and begat . . . and begat . . ." He would next name each begat's eventual spouse, or spouses, and their averagely numerous offspring, and so on. To date things the *griot* linked them to events, such as " — in the year of the big water" — a flood — "he slew a water buffalo." To determine the calendar date, you'd have to find out when that particular flood occurred.

Simplifying to its essence the encyclopedic saga[4] that I was told, the *griot* said that the Kinte clan had begun in the country called Old Mali. Then the Kinte men traditionally were blacksmiths, "who had conquered fire," and the women mostly were potters and weavers. In time, one branch of the clan moved into the country called Mauretania; and it was from Mauretania that one son of this clan, whose name was Kairaba Kunta Kinte — a *marabout*,[5] or holy man of the Mos-

lem faith — journeyed down into the country called The Gambia. He went first to a village called Pakali N'Ding, stayed there for a while, then went to a village called Jiffarong, and then to the village of Juffure.

The griot *continued the history of the Kinte clan. At last he came to Omoro Kinte.*

Omoro Kinte begat four sons, whose names were, in the order of their birth, Kunta, Lamin, Suwadu, and Madi.

The old *griot* had talked for nearly two hours up to then, and perhaps fifty times the narrative had included some detail about someone whom he had named. Now after he had just named those four sons, again he appended a detail, and the interpreter translated:

"About the time the King's soldiers came" — another of the *griot*'s time-fixing references — "the eldest of these four sons, Kunta, went away from his village to chop wood . . . and he was never seen again. . . ." And the *griot* went on with his narrative.

I sat as if I were carved of stone. My blood seemed to have congealed. This man whose lifetime had been in this back-country African village had no way in the world to know that he had just echoed what I had heard all through my boyhood years on my grandma's front porch in Henning, Tennessee . . . of an African who always had insisted that his name was "Kin-tay"; who had called a guitar a "ko,"[6] and a river within the state of Virginia, "Kamby Bolongo";[7] and who had been kidnapped into slavery while not far from his

---

3. *griot* (grē'ō): the elderly man who serves as oral historian of the village. On special occasions he recites the histories of famous heroes and of families.
4. **saga** (sä'gə): a long historical or legendary story.
5. *marabout* (măr'ə-boō').

6. **"ko"**: In Mandinka, *kora* is the name of a musical instrument similar to the banjo.
7. **"Kamby Bolongo"**: Mandinka for "Gambia River."

village, chopping wood, to make himself a drum.

I managed to fumble from my dufflebag my basic notebook, whose first pages containing Grandma's story I showed to an interpreter. After briefly reading, clearly astounded, he spoke rapidly while showing it to the old *griot*, who became agitated; he got up, exclaiming to the people, gesturing at my notebook in the interpreter's hands, and *they* all got agitated.

I don't remember hearing anyone giving an order, I only recall becoming aware that those seventy-odd people had formed a wide human ring around me, moving counterclockwise, chanting softly, loudly, softly; their bodies close together, they were lifting their knees high, stamping up reddish puffs of the dust. . . .

The woman who broke from the moving circle was one of about a dozen whose infant children were within cloth slings across their backs. Her jet-black face deeply contorting,

the woman came charging toward me, her bare feet slapping the earth, and snatching her baby free, she thrust it at me almost roughly, the gesture saying "Take it!" . . . and I did, clasping the baby to me. Then she snatched away her baby; and another woman was thrusting her baby, then another, and another . . . until I had embraced probably a dozen babies. I wouldn't learn until maybe a year later, from a Harvard University professor, Dr. Jerome Bruner, a scholar of such matters, "You didn't know you were participating in one of the oldest ceremonies of humankind, called 'the laying on of hands'! In their way,

they were telling you 'Through this flesh, which is us, we are you, and you are us!' "

Later the men of Juffure took me into their mosque[8] built of bamboo and thatch, and they prayed around me in Arabic. I remember thinking, down on my knees, "After I've found out where I came from, I can't understand a word they're saying." Later the crux of their prayer was translated for me: "Praise be to Allah for one long lost from us whom Allah has returned."

---

8. **mosque** (mŏsk): a Moslem house of worship.

SEEKING MEANING

1. Alex Haley went to Juffure with only a few fragments of information about his ancestor, who called himself "Kin-tay." At what point in the *griot*'s narrative did Haley become certain that Kunta, a member of the Kinte clan, was the ancestor for whom he was searching?

2. When the villagers learned that Haley was a descendant of Kunta Kinte, they formed a moving circle around him. Then several women placed their infant children in his arms. What was the meaning behind this ceremony? What ceremony did Haley participate in with the men of the village?

3. Haley describes his visit to Juffure as "the peak experience" of his life. In what way was his appearance in the village an important experience for the people of Juffure?

ABOUT THE AUTHOR

Alex Haley (1921–   ) spent twelve years researching and writing *Roots,* which tells the story of seven generations of his family. The idea for this work came to him when he was on a magazine assignment in London. During a visit to the British Museum, he became fascinated by the Rosetta Stone, a tablet discovered in Egypt that contained the same passage in three different kinds of writing. Once scholars cracked its code, they were able to decipher hieroglyphics, an ancient Egyptian form of writing. Haley felt that the oral history he had heard during his boyhood might be a key that could unlock the door to his family's past. With only a few fragments of information, Haley began the search that finally brought him to the village of Juffure in The Gambia.

In this excerpt from **No Chinese Stranger**, *Jade Snow Wong tells about her struggle to become a ceramic artist. Because she had no money to rent a studio, Jade Snow Wong persuaded one of the merchants in the community to let her use part of his shop for her work. She set up her potter's wheel in a store window.*

Although this story is an autobiography, the author writes about her experiences in the third person.

A Time of Beginnings

Jade Snow Wong

After Jade Snow began working in Mr. Fong's window, which confined her clay spatters, her activity revealed for the first time to Chinatown residents an art which had distinguished Chinese culture. Ironically, it was not until she was at college that she became fascinated with Tang and Sung Dynasty[1] achievements in clay, a thousand years ago.

Her ability to master pottery made her father happy, for Grandfather Wong believed that a person who could work with his hands would never starve. When Father Wong was young, Grandfather made him learn how to hand-pierce and stitch slipper soles, and how to knot Chinese button heads, both indispensable in clothing. But to Mother Wong, the merits of making pottery escaped her — to see her college-educated daughter up to her elbows in clay, and more clay flying around as she worked in public view, was strangely unladylike. As for Chinatown merchants, they laughed openly at her, "Here comes the girl who plays with mud. How many bowls could you sell today?" Probably they thought: Here is a college graduate foolish enough to dirty her hands.

It has been the traditional belief from Asia to the Middle East, with Japan the exception, that scholars do not soil their hands and that a person studies literature in order to escape hard work. This attitude is still prevalent in most Asian countries outside of the People's Republic of China and Japan.

From the first, the local Chinese were not Jade Snow's patrons. The thinness and whiteness of porcelains imported from China and ornate decorations which came into vogue during the late Ching Dynasty[2] satisfied their tastes. They could not understand why "silly Americans" paid dollars for a hand-thrown

---

1. **Tang and Sung Dynasty:** The Tang Dynasty lasted from 618 to 906; the Sung Dynasty, from 960 to 1279.

2. **Ching Dynasty:** the period from 1644 to 1912.

bowl utilizing crude California colored clays, not much different from the inexpensive peasant ware of China. That the Jade Snow Wong bowl went back to an older tradition of understated beauty was not apparent. They could see only that she wouldn't apply a dragon or a hundred flowers.

Many years later when Jade Snow met another atypical artist, a scholar and calligrapher[3] born and educated in China, he was to say to her, "I shudder if the majority of people look at my brush work and say it is pretty, for then I know it is ordinary and I have failed. If they say they do not understand it, or even that it is ugly, I am happy, for I have succeeded."

However, there were enough numbers of the American public who bought Jade Snow's pottery to support her modestly. The store window was a temporary experiment which proved what she needed to know. In the meantime, her aging father, who was fearful that their home and factory might be in a redevelopment area, made a down payment with lifetime savings to purchase a small white wooden building with six rentable apartments at the perimeter of Chinatown. Jade Snow agreed to rent the two tiny empty ground-floor storefronts which he did not yet need, one for a display room, with supplies and packing center at its rear, the other for the potter's wheel, kiln, glazing booth, compressor, and other equipment. Now, instead of paying Mr. Fong a commission on gross sales, she had bills to pay. Instead of sitting in a window, she worked with doors thrown open to the street.

Creativeness was 90 percent hard work and 10 percent inspiration. It was learning from errors, either from her lack of foresight or because of the errors of others. The first firing in an unfamiliar new gas kiln brought crushing disappointment when the wares blew up into tiny pieces. In another firing, glaze results were uneven black and dark green, for the chemical supply house had mistakenly labeled five pounds of black copper oxide as black iron oxide. One morning there was a personal catastrophe. Unaware of a slow leak all night from the partially opened gas cock, she lit a match at the kiln. An explosion injured both hands, which took weeks to heal.

The day-to-day work of pottery making tested her deepest discipline. A "wedged" ball of clay (prepared by kneading) would be "thrown" (shaped) on the potter's wheel, then dried overnight and trimmed, sometimes decorated with Chinese brush or bamboo tools. It took about a hundred thoroughly dried pieces to fill a kiln for the first firing that transformed fragile mud walls into hard bisque[4] ware. Glazes, like clays the results of countless experiments, were then applied to each piece. A second twelve-hour firing followed, with the temperatures raised hour by hour up to the final maturing point of somewhere around 2,000 degrees Fahrenheit. Then the kiln was turned off for twenty-four hours of cooling. Breakage was a potential hazard at every stage; each step might measure short in technical and artistic accomplishment. A piece she worked on diligently could disappoint. Another made casually had been enhanced successively until it delighted. One piece in ten might be of exhibition quality, half might be salable, and the others would be flawed "seconds" she would discard.

Yet Jade Snow never wavered from her belief that if moments in time could result in a thing of beauty that others could share,

---

3. **calligrapher** (kə-lĭg′rə-fər): an expert in the art of beautiful and decorative handwriting.

4. **bisque** (bĭsk) **ware**: pottery that is left unglazed.

"Throwing a pot" on a kick wheel. The wheel is worked by a foot pedal or by kicking a disk at the base of the structure.

those moments were immeasurably satisfying. She owned two perfect Sung tea bowls. Without copying, she tried to make her pottery "stand up" in strength and grace to that standard.

It became routine to work past midnight without days off. Handwork could not be rushed; failures had to be replaced, and a host of other unanticipated business chores suddenly manifested themselves. She had kept comparable hours when she worked all through college to meet her expenses. Again, the hope of reaching valued goals was her spur. If she should fail, then she could accept what tradition dictated for most Chinese daughters—to be a wife, daughter-in-law, and mother. But unlike her college, the American business world was not dedicated to helping her. Because she was pioneering in a new venture, her identity was a liability. Her brains and hands were her only assets. How could she convert that liability? How could she differ from other struggling potters?

To enlarge her production base, she experimented with enamels on copper forms conceived in the fluid shapes of her pottery, layering jewel tones for brilliant effects. They differed from the earth tints of clay and attracted a new clientele. With another kiln and new equipment, she made functional forms, believing that fine things should become part of the user's everyday life. The best results were submitted to exhibitions. Some juries rejected them, some accepted, and others awarded prizes.

To reach a market larger than San Francisco, she wrote to store buyers around the country, and, encouraged, she called on them. Traveling to strange cities far across the United States, as a rare Oriental woman alone in hotel dining rooms, she developed strong nerves against curious stares. That trip produced orders. Stipulated delivery and cancellation dates made it necessary to hire first one and then more helpers who had to be trained, checked, kept busy and happy.

The strains increased. So did the bills, and she borrowed in small amounts from her sympathetic father, who said, "A hundred dollars is easy to come by, but the first thousand is very, very tricky. Look at the ideograph[5] for hundred—solidly square. Look at it for thousand—pointed, slippery. The ancients knew

(hundred)   (thousand)

this long ago." When hundreds were not enough, tactful Western friends offered help. Oldest Brother, noticing her worries and struggles, sniffed scornfully, "You'll be out of business in a year."

She had learned to accept family criticism in silence, but she was too deeply involved to give up. Money was a worry, but creating was exciting and satisfying. These were lonely years. Jade Snow's single-minded pursuit did not allow her pleasant interludes with friends. To start a kiln at dawn, then watch till its critical maturing moment, which could happen any time between early evening and midnight or later (when gas pressure was low, it took until the next dawn), kept her from social engagements.

Then, gradually, signs indicated that she was working in the right direction. The first was a letter from the Metropolitan Museum of Art in New York, where the Eleventh Ceramic National Syracuse Show had been sent. The curator wrote, "We think the green, gold, and ivory enamel bowl a skillful piece of workmanship and are anxious to add it to our collections." They referred to a ten-inch shallow bowl which Jade Snow had made.

A reviewer in *Art Digest* wrote, "In plain enamels without applied design, Jade Snow Wong of San Francisco seemed to this critic to top the list."

Recognition brought further recognition. National decorating magazines featured her enamels, and in the same year, 1947, the Museum of Modern Art installed an exhibit by Mies van der Rohe[6] which displayed 100 objects of fine design costing less than $100. A note introducing this exhibit read, "Every so often the Museum of Modern Art selects and exhibits soundly designed objects available to American purchasers in the belief that this will encourage more people to use beautiful things in their everyday life. . . ." Two of Jade Snow's enamels, a dinner plate in Chinese red and a dessert plate in grayish-gold, were included in the exhibition, which subsequently went to Europe.

So it did not seem unusual to receive an interviewer from *Mademoiselle*, but it was indeed unexpected to receive one of the magazine's ten awards for 1948 to women outstanding in ten different fields. They invited Jade Snow to fly to New York to claim her silver medal.

The more deeply one delves into a field, the more one realizes limitations. When Bernard Leach, the famous English potter, accepted an invitation from Mills College to teach a special course, Jade Snow attended. Another summer, Charles Merritt came from Alfred University's staff to give a course in precise glaze chemistry. Again, she commuted to Oakland. She became friends with these two unusual teachers. Both agreed that in potterymaking, one never found a final answer. A mass-produced bathtub may be a technical

5. **ideograph** (ĭd′ē-ə-grăf′): a written symbol that represents an idea or a thing in the form of a picture.

6. **Mies van der Rohe** (mēs′ vän dər rō′ə): Ludwig Mies van der Rohe (1886–1969), a famous American architect and industrial designer, born in Germany.

triumph; yet a chemically balanced glaze on a pot can be aesthetically dull. Some of the most pleasing glaze effects could never be duplicated, for they were the combination of scrapings from the glaze booth. Like the waves of the sea, no two pieces of pottery art can be identical.

After three years of downs, then ups, the business promised to survive. Debts had been cleared. A small staff could handle routine duties. A steady clientele of San Franciscans came to her out-of-the-way shop. A beginning had been made.

SEEKING MEANING

1. In striving to become an artist, Jade Snow Wong had her father's support. However, she had to overcome the prejudices of other people in her family and in her community. Why was her behavior considered unladylike and foolish?

2. In the work that she had chosen for herself, Jade Snow Wong felt that "her identity was a liability. Her brains and hands were her only assets" (page 411). How was her identity a disadvantage to her?

3. What steps did Jade Snow Wong take to build up her business? What sacrifices did she have to make in order to devote herself to her art? How was she encouraged to continue with her work?

4. In order to achieve her goal, Jade Snow Wong had to overcome many obstacles. What qualities of character enabled her to do this?

DEVELOPING VOCABULARY

Tracing Word Histories

You can learn a good deal about the history of a word by consulting a dictionary. Most dictionaries use abbreviations to indicate the origin and development of words. Some of these abbreviations are *L.* (for Latin), *F.* or *Fr.* (for French), *Sp.* (for Spanish), and *Gk.* (for Greek). You will generally find information about the origin of a word given in parentheses or brackets.

The word *ceramic* comes from Greek. A dictionary will show you the history of the word in this way:

[< Gk. *keramikos* < *keramos,* potter's clay]

The symbol < means "derived from." The word *ceramic* comes from the Greek word *keramikos,* which in turn comes from another Greek word, *keramos,* meaning "potter's clay."

Use a dictionary to find the history of each of the following words from the selection:

hazard   interlude   kiln   vogue

ABOUT THE AUTHOR

Jade Snow Wong (1922–   ) wrote about her upbringing in San Francisco's Chinatown in *Fifth Chinese Daughter. No Chinese Stranger,* written more than twenty-five years later, is a sequel to that story. In this second of her memoirs, Jade Snow Wong describes the changes that have taken place in Chinese-American life as old customs have weakened and new problems have arisen. "A Time of Beginnings," which tells of her career as a ceramist, is part of the first chapter of this book.

Practice in Reading and Writing

NONFICTION

Writers of nonfiction, like writers of fiction, often combine exposition, description, and narration. In a single passage a writer might use exposition to explain, instruct, or express an opinion; description to communicate an impression of people or places; and narration to relate events.

The following passage is from "Rattlesnake Hunt." See if you can find examples of all three kinds of writing.

A rattler will lie quietly without revealing itself if a man passes by and it thinks it is not seen. It slips away without fighting if given the chance. Only Ross's sharp eyes sometimes picked out the gray and yellow diamond pattern, camouflaged among the grasses. In the cool of the morning, chilled by the January air, the snakes showed no fight. They could be looped up limply over the steel L and dropped in a sack or up into the wire cage on the back of Will's truck. As the sun mounted in the sky and warmed the moist Everglades earth, the snakes were warmed too, and Ross warned that it was time to go more cautiously. Yet having learned that it was we who were the aggressors; that immobility meant complete safety; that the snakes, for all their lightning flash in striking, were inaccurate in their aim, with limited vision; having watched again and again the liquid grace of movement, the beauty of pattern, suddenly I understood that I was drinking in freely the magnificent sweep of the horizon, with no fear of what might be at the moment under my feet. I went off hunting by myself, and though I found no snakes, I should have known what to do.

The sun was dropping low in the west. Masses of white cloud hung above the flat marshy plain and seemed to be tangled in the tops of distant palms and cypresses. The sky turned orange, then saffron. I walked leisurely back toward the truck. In the distance I could see Ross and Will making their way in too. The season was more advanced than at the

Creek, two hundred miles to the north, and I noticed that spring flowers were blooming among the lumpy hummocks. I leaned over to pick a white violet. There was a rattlesnake under the violet.

1. *The events in a narrative are related to one central action.*

What is the main action in this passage? Over what period of time does the action occur?

2. *Exposition is used to inform, to explain, or to persuade.*

Find the sentences that explain the habits of rattlesnakes.

3. *Description creates an impression of people, places, or things, by using details that appeal to the senses.*

The many descriptive details in the model passage add clarity and interest to the narrative. Which details help you picture the rattlesnakes? Which sentences help you see the surrounding countryside?

Writing About an Experience

Write a composition about an experience you have had. You may write about a "first" experience, such as the time that you learned to swim or to ride a bicycle. You may write about a vacation or a visit away from home. Here are some guidelines:

1. *Focus on one episode, and tell the important events in the order in which they occurred.*

2. *Help your reader imagine the action by describing the place and the people involved.*

Include specific details and choose words that appeal to the senses.

3. *Explain any facts or references that your reader might need to know.*

4. *Tell your reader how you felt.*

For Further Reading

Bradley, Bill, *Life on the Run* (Quadrangle, 1976)
Basketball star Bill Bradley describes the exciting but often lonely life of a professional basketball player.

Franchere, Ruth, *Jack London: The Pursuit of a Dream* (Thomas Y. Crowell, 1962)
This biography tells of London's efforts to educate himself, his cross-country wanderings, and his many jobs, including prospecting for gold in the Yukon.

Frank, Anne, *The Diary of a Young Girl*, translated by B. M. Mooyart (Doubleday, 1952; paperback, Pocket Books)
Anne Frank kept this diary while she and seven other people lived in hiding in Amsterdam during the Nazi occupation.

Hautzig, Esther, *The Endless Steppe: Growing Up in Siberia* (Thomas Y. Crowell, 1968; paperback, Starline)
The author and her family were forced to spend five years in Siberia when the Soviet Union invaded Poland in 1951. The loving spirit and humor of the family help to make "a young girl's heart . . . indestructible."

Heyerdahl, Thor, *Kon-Tiki: Across the Pacific by Raft* (Rand McNally, 1950; paperback, Ballantine)
This is an exciting account of how the author, four other men, and a parrot spent almost one hundred days traveling across the Pacific on a raft in order to test a theory.

Keller, Helen, *The Story of My Life* (Doubleday, 1954; paperback, Dell)
Although she was deprived of her sight and hearing by a childhood illness, Helen Keller triumphed over her handicaps and became a legend in her own time.

Kroeber, Theodora, *Ishi, Last of His Tribe* (Parnassus, 1964; paperback, Bantam)
This is the story of the last survivor of the Yahi tribe, an Indian people of California.

Latham, Jean Lee, *Carry On, Mr. Bowditch* (Houghton Mifflin, 1955; paperback, Houghton)
Here is a lively, fast-moving biography of Nathaniel Bowditch, skilled navigator and author of the classic guide *The American Practical Navigator*. The story begins in 1779, when Nathaniel is twelve, and follows him through many adventures.

Lord, Walter, *A Night to Remember* (Holt, Rinehart & Winston, 1955; paperback, Bantam)
The author gives a minute-by-minute account of the night of April 14, 1912, when the "unsinkable" ocean liner *Titanic* struck an iceberg and sank.

National Geographic Society, *Wondrous World of Fishes* (National Geographic Society, 1969)
This beautifully illustrated anthology about underwater life and exploration includes articles on fishing through ice and catfish that walk.

Petry, Ann, *Harriet Tubman: Conductor on the Underground Railroad* (Thomas Y. Crowell, 1955; paperback, Archway)
This is the biography of a daring and devoted woman who risked her life countless times to help more than three hundred slaves escape to freedom.

Scott, Robert Falcon, *Scott's Last Expedition* (Dodd, Mead, 1941)
This is the journal of Scott's tragic expedition to the Antarctic in 1910.

Singer, Isaac, Bashevis, *A Day of Pleasure: Stories of a Boy Growing Up in Warsaw* (Farrar, Straus & Giroux, 1969)
The author describes his boyhood in a Jewish ghetto from 1908 to 1918.

Stuart, Jesse, *The Thread That Runs So True* (Scribner, 1968; paperback, Scribner)
The novelist and poet tells of his experiences as a young teacher in a one-room Kentucky schoolhouse.

You may be surprised to learn that poetry is older than any other kind of literature. Poetry developed long before prose; as a matter of fact, there was poetry long before there was a written language of any kind. In early times, poems were committed to memory and passed down from generation to generation by word of mouth. We know that poems were often sung. Ancient Greek poets sang to the accompaniment of a lyre, a stringed instrument something like a small harp. Our word *lyric* shows this connection between poetry and music.

In this unit you will find poems of many kinds. Some of the poems tell stories, some describe scenes, some capture a mood, and some are humorous. All of them are meant to be read aloud.

POETRY

Before reading a poem aloud, you may find it helpful to read the poem through silently until you become familiar with its language. Use the questions that follow each selection to explore the meaning of the poem. Then practice reading the poem aloud, paying close attention to its meaning. You may find that you discover something new with each reading.

Unfolding a Poem

Unfolding Bud

Naoshi Koriyama

One is amazed
By a water-lily bud
Unfolding
With each passing day,
Taking on a richer color   5
And new dimensions.

One is not amazed,
At a first glance,
By a poem,
Which is as tight-closed   10
As a tiny bud.

Yet one is surprised
To see the poem
Gradually unfolding,
Revealing its rich inner self,   15
As one reads it
Again
And over again.

As you read the poems in this section, discover how a poem
unfolds to reveal "its rich inner self."

The 1st   *Lucille Clifton*

What I remember about that day
is boxes stacked across the walk
and couch springs curling through the air
and drawers and tables balanced on the curb
and us, hollering,
leaping up and around
happy to have a playground;

nothing about the emptied rooms
nothing about the emptied family

SEEKING MEANING

1. The first of the month is generally the day
when rent is due. What details in the poem
tell you what is happening to the family?
2. What do you think the phrase "emptied
family" means?

DEVELOPING SKILLS IN READING

Understanding the Purpose of Imagery
Imagery is language that appeals to the
senses. Imagery in poetry is most often *visual.*
For example, line 2 of the poem gives you a
specific picture of boxes stacked, or set one
above the other, across the walk, or path to
the house. Imagery can also appeal to any of
the other senses—hearing, smell, taste, and
touch.

Imagery is one of the elements through
which a poet reveals meaning. Lucille Clifton

doesn't attempt to describe everything that is
happening; instead, she uses a few images to
tell you what a particular day means to this
family. What images show that the children
are not aware of what is happening to the family? What image gives you a sense of the family's hardships?

ABOUT THE AUTHOR

Lucille Clifton (1936–   ) was born in
Depew, New York, and attended Howard
University. She has written two books of poetry, *Good Times* and *Good News About the
Earth,* a memoir of her family called *Generations,* and several books for children. Her
work has been published in a number of periodicals, including *The Massachusetts Review, Black World,* and *Negro Digest.* She
now lives in Baltimore with her husband,
who is also a writer, and their six children.

Living Tenderly   *May Swenson*

My body a rounded stone
with a pattern of smooth seams.
My head a short snake,
retractive,° projective.°
My legs come out of their sleeves   5
or shrink within,
and so does my chin.
My eyelids are quick clamps.

My back is my roof.
I am always at home.   10
I travel where my house walks.
It is a smooth stone.
It floats within the lake,
or rests in the dust.
My flesh lives tenderly   15
inside its bone.

4. **retractive** (rĭ-trăk′tĭv): capable of drawing back. **projective** (prə-jĕk′tĭv): capable of moving forward.

SEEKING MEANING

1. What does the poem describe? What details in the poem give you the answer?
2. What does the "pattern of smooth seams" refer to? What are the "sleeves" referred to in line 5?
3. Describe the way a clamp works. Why do you think the eyelids are called "quick clamps"?
4. State in your own words what the last two lines of the poem mean.

DEVELOPING SKILLS IN READING

Understanding Figurative Language
Look again at the opening lines of the poem:

My body a rounded stone
with a pattern of smooth seams.

In these lines a body is identified with a stone. In reality, that is not possible: a body cannot be a stone. But the poet is not speaking *literally*—that is, in terms of reality. She is speaking *figuratively* — that is, in terms of poetic imagination. The poet means to suggest that there is some similarity between two different things. To speak of a body as if it were a stone suggests something about the shape and feel of that body. What do the lines suggest to you?

In the opening lines the poet is using a kind of figurative language called *metaphor*. A metaphor draws a comparison between two things that are basically different. Explain the metaphors in line 3 and in line 8.

In addition to metaphor, poets use a figurative device called *simile*. Like metaphor, a simile draws a comparison between two unlike things. However, a simile uses a word such as *like, as,* or *than* to express the comparison. Explain the simile in these lines:

And green and blue his sharp eyes twinkled
Like a candle flame where salt is sprinkled.

What two things are compared in this simile?

My heart is like an apple tree
  Whose boughs are bent with thickset
  fruit.

Identify the metaphors and similes in the following lines. Explain each comparison.

Deep in the sun-scorched growths the dragonfly
Hangs like a blue thread, loosened from the sky.

The lightning is a yellow fork
From tables in the sky . . .

The day is done, and the darkness
  Falls from the wings of night,
As a feather is wafted downward
  From an eagle in his flight.

ABOUT THE AUTHOR

May Swenson (1919–   ) was born in Logan, Utah, and attended Utah State University. She worked as a reporter on the Salt Lake City *Deseret News* before moving to New York. A winner of many fellowships and awards, she has taught poetry seminars at a number of major universities. Her poems are notable for their close observation of nature.

A Riddle

Richard Wilbur

Where far in forest I am laid,
In a place ringed around by stones,
Look for no melancholy shade,
And have no thoughts of buried bones;
For I am bodiless and bright,
And fill this glade with sudden glow;
The leaves are washed in under-light;
Shade lies upon the boughs like snow.

DEVELOPING SKILLS OF EXPRESSION

Writing a Puzzle Poem

Choose some animal or object, and describe it in a poem without identifying it by name. See if other members of the class can guess its identity from your description.

ABOUT THE AUTHOR

Richard Wilbur (1921–   ) grew up on a secluded country estate in New Jersey. He began writing poems at an early age, but it was not until World War II took him to the battlefields that he started to write in earnest. In 1947 he published his first volume of poems, *The Beautiful Changes.* Since then he has become one of America's leading poets. He was awarded the Pulitzer Prize in 1950 for *Ceremony and Other Poems,* and again in 1957 for *Things of This World.* Wilbur has also written short stories and verse translations of plays by the classic French dramatist Molière. He collaborated with Leonard Bernstein and Lillian Hellman on the comic opera *Candide,* adapted from the book by the French writer Voltaire.

Some poems can be interpreted in more than one way. What meaning does each of the following poems have for you?

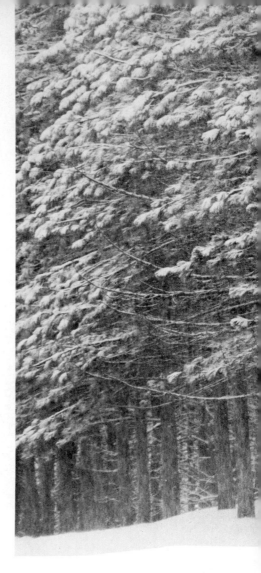

Stopping by Woods on a Snowy Evening

Robert Frost

Whose woods these are I think I know.
His house is in the village, though;
He will not see me stopping here
To watch his woods fill up with snow.

My little horse must think it queer   5
To stop without a farmhouse near
Between the woods and frozen lake
The darkest evening of the year.

He gives his harness bells a shake
To ask if there is some mistake.   10
The only other sound's the sweep
Of easy wind and downy flake.

The woods are lovely, dark, and deep,
But I have promises to keep,
And miles to go before I sleep,   15
And miles to go before I sleep.

SEEKING MEANING

In "Stopping by Woods on a Snowy Evening,"
Frost tells a story of a man who stops to watch
snow falling in the woods. Most readers of the
poem think that Frost is using a simple,
everyday experience to reveal some deep
truth or understanding about life.

1. Why has the speaker stopped? How do you
know that it is unusual for the speaker to stop
in these woods?
2. Describe the scene that you see in the
poem. What does the phrase "the darkest evening of the year" tell you?
3. Why can't the speaker linger to look at the
woods? What do you think his "promises"
are?
4. This poem has been interpreted in a number of ways. Some readers believe that the
woods in Frost's poem represent an escape
from the world and its pressures. Others believe that the poem is about the obligations
that keep people from enjoying the beauty of
the world. Still others suggest that the word
sleep in the last two lines of the poem is a reference to death. Do you agree with any of
these interpretations? Give reasons for your
answer.

The Listeners   *Walter de la Mare*

"Is there anybody there?" said the Traveler,
  Knocking on the moonlit door;
And his horse in the silence champed the grasses
  Of the forest's ferny floor:
And a bird flew up out of the turret,   5
  Above the Traveler's head:
And he smote upon the door again a second time;
  "Is there anybody there?" he said.
But no one descended to the Traveler;
  No head from the leaf-fringed sill   10
Leaned over and looked into his gray eyes,
  Where he stood perplexed and still.
But only a host of phantom listeners
  That dwelt in the lone house then
Stood listening in the quiet of the moonlight   15
  To that voice from the world of men:
Stood thronging the faint moonbeams on the dark stair
  That goes down to the empty hall,
Hearkening in an air stirred and shaken
  By the lonely Traveler's call.   20
And he felt in his heart their strangeness,
  Their stillness answering his cry,
While his horse moved, cropping the dark turf,
  'Neath the starred and leafy sky;
For he suddenly smote on the door, even   25
  Louder, and lifted his head—
"Tell them I came, and no one answered,
  That I kept my word," he said.
Never the least stir made the listeners,
  Though every word he spake   30
Fell echoing through the shadowiness of the still house
  From the one man left awake:
Aye, they heard his foot upon the stirrup,
  And the sound of iron on stone,
And how the silence surged softly backward,   35
  When the plunging hoofs were gone.

SEEKING MEANING

1. "The Listeners" tells of a man who knocks three times at the door of a house in a forest and, receiving no answer, mounts his horse and gallops away. Who do you think the Traveler is? Who do you think the listeners are?

2. Words like *phantom* in line 13 and *shadowiness* in line 31 add mystery to the poem. What other words can you find that contribute to the poem's eerie effect?

3. Why do you think the Traveler has come to the house? (What meaning do you see in lines 27–28?)

4. The Traveler is the central figure in the poem. Yet the poem is called "The Listeners." Why do you think the poet chose this title?

ABOUT THE AUTHOR

Walter de la Mare (1873–1956), who created magical worlds in his poems and stories, spent nearly twenty years as a bookkeeper in the London office of an oil company. In 1908 he received a grant that enabled him to become a full-time writer. Over a period of forty years he published many collections of enchanting poems and tales. "The Listeners" is famous for its beautiful music and its eerie mystery. According to one account, de la Mare got the idea for the poem from a class reunion. On the day that he and his former classmates were to meet at a school, no one but de la Mare appeared. The empty rooms and corridors of the building inspired him to write the poem.

Every Word Counts

In a Station of the Metro *Ezra Pound*

The apparition of these faces in the crowd;
Petals on a wet, black bough.

The poet identifies the faces he sees in a crowd at a Paris
subway station with petals in the rain. Here is the poet's account of how he came to write this two-line poem:

Three years ago in Paris I got out of a
"metro" train at La Concorde, and saw suddenly a beautiful face, and then another and
another, and then a beautiful child's face,
and then another beautiful woman, and I
tried all that day to find words for what this
had meant to me, and I could not find any
words that seemed to me worthy, or as
lovely as that sudden emotion. . . . I wrote a
thirty-line poem, and destroyed it. . . . Six
months later I made a poem half that
length; a year later I made the following . . .
sentence:

The apparition of these faces in the crowd;
Petals on a wet, black bough.

Park Pigeons   *Melville Cane*

Still blue stones,
Dull gray rocks,
Sunk in grass.
A child flings a peanut.
Stones flutter,
Rocks circle in the sun.

SEEKING MEANING

1. What metaphors does Cane use for pigeons in this poem? Explain the comparisons in your own words.
2. What image do you see in the first three lines?
3. What contrast is there between the first three lines and the last three lines of the poem?

DEVELOPING SKILLS OF EXPRESSION

Paraphrasing a Poem

Skillful poets never waste words. They choose words for their precise meanings and arrange them in the most effective order. Poets do not always use complete sentences or complete thoughts. A word or phrase may serve to communicate meaning. By using a few effective words, Melville Cane helps you to see the pigeons in a vivid way:

Still blue stones,
Dull gray rocks,
Sunk in grass.

As you read the lines, you supply your own connections in thought. Perhaps your ideas come together in this way:

The pigeons, half hidden in the grass, are so motionless, they might be mistaken for blue stones and gray rocks.

This sentence *paraphrases*, or restates in different words, the first three lines of the poem. By paraphrasing, you explain in your own words what a poem is saying.

Paraphrase the last three lines of "Park Pigeons."

Fog   *Carl Sandburg*

The fog comes
on little cat feet.

It sits looking
over harbor and city
on silent haunches
and then moves on.

SEEKING MEANING

1. The fog is compared to a cat. What phrases develop the metaphor?
2. How does fog settle on a city? Why is the poet's metaphor a good one?
3. Paraphrase the poem. Try to use as few words as you can to express its meaning.

ABOUT THE AUTHOR

Carl Sandburg (1878–1967) was born in Galesburg, Illinois. He left school at thirteen and helped support his family by working at odd jobs. After serving in the Spanish-American War, he decided to enroll in college. In 1914 his poem "Chicago," a vibrant picture of this Midwestern city, was published in *Poetry* magazine and won the Levinson Prize. His volume *Chicago Poems*, which came out in 1916, received wide acclaim. Five more volumes of poetry followed. Sandburg spent fifteen years writing a six-volume biography of Abraham Lincoln, his boyhood hero. He also wrote tales and lyrics for children and edited a collection of folk songs called *The American Songbag*. Sandburg was awarded the Pulitzer Prize for both poetry and history.

The Chipmunk's Day

Randall Jarrell

In and out the bushes, up the ivy,
Into the hole
By the old oak stump, the chipmunk flashes.
Up the pole

To the feeder full of seeds he dashes,   5
Stuffs his cheeks,
The chickadee and titmouse scold him.
Down he streaks.

Red as the leaves the wind blows off the maple,
Red as a fox,   10
Striped like a skunk, the chipmunk whistles
Past the love seat, past the mailbox,

Down the path,
Home to his warm hole stuffed with sweet
Things to eat.   15
Neat and slight and shining, his front feet

Curled at his breast, he sits there while the sun
Stripes the red west
With its last light: the chipmunk
Dives to his rest.   20

SEEKING MEANING

1. List the verbs that describe the chipmunk's movements. What kind of movement is emphasized?

2. The first sentence of the poem is interrupted three times by commas. Read these lines aloud. How do the lines suggest the chipmunk's movements?

DEVELOPING SKILLS IN READING

Understanding the Purpose of Inversion

Most sentences in the English language follow a pattern in which the subject comes before the predicate. Consider the effect of varying this pattern in a line from a familiar nursery rhyme.

> Jack and Jill went up the hill
> Up the hill went Jack and Jill

What change in emphasis occurs when the order of words is shifted?

A reversal of the normal arrangement of words in a sentence is called *inversion.* Inverting word order calls attention to the word or phrase that has been shifted. A poet can give a word or phrase special importance by placing it at the beginning or at the end of a line.

What would be the normal order of the words in the following lines?

> In and out the bushes, up the ivy,
> Into the hole
> By the old oak stump, the chipmunk
>   flashes.

What does the poet emphasize by inversion in these lines?

Locate another example of inversion in the poem and tell what its purpose is.

ABOUT THE AUTHOR

Randall Jarrell (1914–1965) was born in Nashville, Tennessee. He enjoyed a distinguished career as a poet, teacher, and literary critic. He served as Consultant in Poetry at the Library of Congress. In 1961 he won the National Book Award for poetry. In addition to poetry, he wrote a novel and two volumes of essays. "The Chipmunk's Day" is from *The Bat Poet,* a story about a bat that writes poems.

A haiku (hī'kōō) is a three-line poem, of Japanese origin, containing seventeen syllables. There are five syllables in the first line, seven syllables in the second line, and five syllables in the third line. Such a poem must communicate meaning through very few words. The subject matter of a haiku is usually drawn from nature.

Haiku

The lightning flashes!
And slashing through the darkness,
A night-heron's screech.

Matsuo Bashō

Autumn Moon. Woodblock print by Ando Hiroshige (1797-1858).
Crown Copyright, Victoria and Albert Museum

Broken and broken
again on the sea, the moon
so easily mends.

Chosu

I must go begging
for water . . . morning glories
have captured my well.

Chiyo

Morning Glories by Katsushika Hokusai (1760–1849).
Museum of Fine Arts, Boston   Bigelow Collection

SEEKING MEANING

1. What images do you see and hear in the first haiku? What words suggest pain or violence?

2. The second haiku uses the word *broken* in an unusual way. We speak of breaking an object such as a dish. In what way is the moon "broken" repeatedly on the sea?

3. What image is suggested by the word *captured* in the third haiku?

DEVELOPING SKILLS IN READING

Understanding Haiku

Harry Behn, who has translated Japanese haiku, believes that the best haiku are as "natural as breathing." He writes that a haiku "is made by speaking of something natural and simple suggesting spring, summer, autumn, or winter. There is no rhyme. Everything mentioned is just what it is, wonderful, here, but still beyond."

Haiku often use contrasts that catch the reader by surprise. What examples of this kind of contrast can you find in the poems on pages 434–435?

DEVELOPING SKILLS OF EXPRESSION

Writing Haiku

In the following poem the author begins with a general description: it is a bitter morning. The next two lines develop this idea with a specific image: the sparrows are so cold they have tucked their necks in.

> A bitter morning:
> Sparrows sitting together
> Without any necks.
>
> *J. W. Hackett*

Compose one or two haiku of your own. Follow the pattern of five syllables in line 1, seven syllables in line 2, and five syllables in line 3.

A quatrain *is a poem or stanza of four lines. Different rhyme patterns are used in quatrains.*

Fly Away, Fly Away *Christina Rossetti*

Fly away, fly away over the sea,
 Sun-loving swallow, for summer is done;
Come again, come again, come back to me,
 Bringing the summer and bringing the sun.

The Pedigree of Honey *Emily Dickinson*

The pedigree of honey
Does not concern the bee;
A clover, any time, to him,
Is aristocracy.

The Sea-Gull *Ogden Nash*

Hark to the whimper of the sea-gull;
He weeps because he's not an ea-gull.
Suppose you were, you silly sea-gull,
Could you explain it to your she-gull?

A limerick is a humorous poem of five lines with a characteristic rhythm and rhyme pattern.

The Bearded Man

Edward Lear

There was an old man with a beard,
Who said, "It is just as I feared!
  Two owls and a hen,
  Four larks and a wren
Have *all* built their nests in my beard!"

Anonymous Limericks

There was a young lady of Lynn,
Who was so uncommonly thin
  That when she essayed°
  To drink lemonade,
She slipped through the straw and fell in.

3. **essayed** (ĕ-sād´): tried.

There was an old man of Peru
Who dreamt he was eating a shoe.
  He awoke in the night
  With a terrible fright
And found it was perfectly true!

These limericks are tongue twisters. Try to read them rapidly.

A flea and a fly in a flue°
Were imprisoned, so what could they do?
  Said the fly, "Let us flee."
  Said the flea, "Let us fly."
So they flew through a flaw° in the flue.

1. **flue:** an air shaft in a chimney.

5. **flaw:** a crack.

A Tutor   *Carolyn Wells*

A tutor who tooted the flute
Tried to tutor two tooters to toot.
  Said the two to the tutor,
  "Is it harder to toot, or
To tutor two tooters to toot?"

DEVELOPING SKILLS OF EXPRESSION

Writing a Limerick

Limericks have a definite form. Which lines rhyme? Which lines are shorter than the others? The rhymes are often funny and unexpected. What comic rhymes can you find in the limericks on these pages? Limericks often begin in the same way. What similarities can you find in the opening lines of the poems on page 438?

Write a limerick of your own. Here are two lines you might use to begin:

There once was a student named Wayne,
Whose homework was lost on a train. . . .

Sound and Meaning

*Many people believe that Edgar Allan Poe wrote the poem
"Annabel Lee" about his wife, Virginia, who died of
tuberculosis in her twenties. This poem has become
famous for its beautiful and haunting music.*

Annabel Lee   *Edgar Allan Poe*

It was many and many a year ago,
  In a kingdom by the sea,
That a maiden there lived whom you may know
  By the name of Annabel Lee;
And this maiden she lived with no other thought   5
  Than to love and be loved by me.

I was a child and *she* was a child,
  In this kingdom by the sea,
But we loved with a love that was more than love—
  I and my Annabel Lee—   10
With a love that the wingèd seraphs° of Heaven
  Coveted° her and me.

> 11. **seraphs** (sĕr′əfs): angels.
> 12. **Coveted** (kŭv′ĭ-tĭd): envied.

And this was the reason that, long ago,
  In this kingdom by the sea,
A wind blew out of a cloud, chilling   15
  My beautiful Annabel Lee;
So that her highborn kinsmen came
  And bore her away from me,
To shut her up in a sepulcher°
  In this kingdom by the sea.   20

> 19. **sepulcher** (sĕp′əl-kər): a tomb
> or burial place.

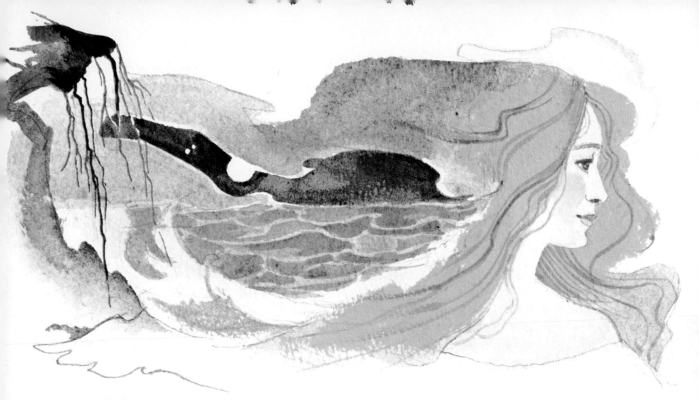

The angels, not half so happy in Heaven,
  Went envying her and me:
Yes!—that was the reason (as all men know,
  In this kingdom by the sea)
That the wind came out of the cloud by night,   25
  Chilling and killing my Annabel Lee.

But our love it was stronger by far than the love
  Of those who were older than we—
  Of many far wiser than we—
And neither the angels in Heaven above,   30
  Nor the demons down under the sea,
Can ever dissever° my soul from the soul   **32. dissever** (dĭ-sĕv′ər): separate.
  Of the beautiful Annabel Lee:

For the moon never beams, without bringing me dreams
  Of the beautiful Annabel Lee;   35
And the stars never rise, but I feel the bright eyes
  Of the beautiful Annabel Lee:
And so, all the nighttide,° I lie down by the side   **38. nighttide:** nighttime.
Of my darling—my darling—my life and my bride,
  In the sepulcher there by the sea—   40
  In her tomb by the sounding sea.

SEEKING MEANING

1. What do you learn about Annabel Lee in the first three stanzas of the poem?
2. Whom does the speaker blame for Annabel Lee's death? What reason does he give in lines 11–12 and lines 21–22?
3. Why does the speaker believe that his soul and the soul of Annabel Lee cannot be separated? How is he continually reminded of her?

DEVELOPING SKILLS IN READING

Understanding Repetition in Poetry

In "Annabel Lee" Poe repeats certain words, sounds, and phrases. The name Annabel Lee appears at least once in every stanza. What other words and phrases are repeated several times? What ideas and feelings are emphasized by these repetitions?

Rhyme is a form of repetition. What words are repeatedly linked together through rhyme?

Sometimes words within a single line are rhymed. This kind of rhyme is called *internal rhyme*. Look at line 26:

Chilling and *killing* my Annabel Lee.

How many times does Poe use internal rhyme in the last stanza?

DEVELOPING SKILLS OF EXPRESSION

Avoiding Singsong

In reading poetry aloud, people sometimes enjoy the sounds so much that they ignore the meaning of individual lines. In order to stress the rhyme of a poem, they may read in a monotonous pattern called *singsong*.

One way to avoid singsong is to read a poem naturally. Do not stress rhyme words by raising your voice or pausing mechanically at the end of each line. Follow the punctuation and meaning of the poem.

In "Annabel Lee," how would you read lines 3–4 in the first stanza? Lines 9–10 in the second stanza? Lines 23–25 in the fourth stanza? Practice reading the poem aloud, paying close attention to meaning as well as sound.

ABOUT THE AUTHOR

Edgar Allan Poe (1809–1849) was born in Boston to a family of traveling actors. After his mother died, he was taken into the home of a wealthy Virginia merchant named John Allan. Although Poe took Allan as his middle name, his relations with his guardian were always strained. In 1826 he entered the University of Virginia but had to leave within a year because of his heavy gambling debts. He then enlisted in the army and served two years. John Allan helped him secure an appointment to West Point, but Poe got himself dismissed for misconduct. At this point he turned to writing and editing in order to earn a living. In 1836 he married his young cousin Virginia, but this marriage ended tragically in 1847, when Virginia died of tuberculosis. Poe died in poverty at the age of forty.

Despite his personal difficulties, Poe produced a remarkable body of short stories, poems, and essays. His short-story masterpieces include "The Tell-Tale Heart," "The Cask of Amontillado," "The Pit and the Pendulum," and "The Fall of the House of Usher" —strange tales of terror and fantasy. Among his most beautiful and melodic poems are "Eldorado," "The Raven," and "The Bells."

Ring Out, Wild Bells   *Alfred, Lord Tennyson*

Ring out, wild bells, to the wild sky,
  The flying cloud, the frosty light;
  The year is dying in the night;
Ring out, wild bells, and let him die.

Ring out the old, ring in the new,   5
  Ring, happy bells, across the snow:
  The year is going, let him go;
Ring out the false, ring in the true.

Ring out the grief that saps the mind,
  For those that here we see no more;   10
  Ring out the feud of rich and poor,
Ring in redress° to all mankind.

12. **redress** (rĭ-drĕs′): the righting of all wrongs.

Ring out false pride in place and blood,
  The civic slander and the spite;
  Ring in the love of truth and right,   15
Ring in the common love of good.

Ring out old shapes of foul disease;
  Ring out the narrowing lust of gold;
  Ring out the thousand wars of old,
Ring in the thousand years of peace.   20

SEEKING MEANING

1. What occasion does this poem celebrate?
2. List the things that the poet wishes the bells to ring out. List those he wishes the bells to ring in. What title or heading would you give to each list?
3. Tennyson repeats the phrases "ring out" and "ring in" to emphasize a contrast. State in your own words what you think that contrast is.

ABOUT THE AUTHOR

Alfred, Lord Tennyson (1809–1892) was poet laureate of England for more more than forty years. "Ring Out, Wild Bells" is an excerpt from a long work called *In Memoriam*, which was inspired by the death of a close friend. Many readers consider this work to be Tennyson's masterpiece. Another well-known work is *Idylls of the King*, a collection of poems about King Arthur and his knights.

Season at the Shore   *Phyllis McGinley*

Oh, not by sun and not by cloud
And not by whippoorwill, crying loud,
And not by the pricking of my thumbs,
Do I know the way that the summer comes.
Yet here on this seagull-haunted strand,   5
Here is an omen I understand—
Sand:

Sand on the beaches,
   Sand at the door,
Sand that screeches   10
   On the new-swept floor;
In the shower, sand for the foot to crunch on;
Sand in the sandwiches spread for luncheon;
Sand adhesive to son and sibling,°   **14. sibling:** brother or sister.
From wallet sifting, from pockets dribbling;   15
Sand by the beaker
   Nightly shed
From odious° sneaker;   **18. odious** (ō′dē-əs): here, smelly.
   Sand in bed;
Sahara always in my seaside shanty   20
Like the sand in the voice
Of J. Durante.°   **22. J. Durante** (dŏo-răn′tē): Jimmy
                                                   Durante, a comedian known for
                                                   his hoarse, gravelly voice.

Winter is mittens, winter is gaiters°
Steaming on various radiators.
Autumn is leaves that bog the broom.   25
Spring is mud in the living room
Or skates in places one scarcely planned.
But what is summer, her seal and hand?
Sand:

Sand in the closets,   30
  Sand on the stair;
Desert deposits
  In the parlor chair;
Sand in the halls like the halls of ocean;
Sand in the soap and the sun-tan lotion;   35
Stirred in the porridge, tossed in the greens,
Poured from the bottoms of rolled-up jeans;
  In the elmy street,
    On the lawny acre;
  Glued to the seat   40
    Of the Studebaker;°
Wrapped in the folds of the *Wall Street Journal*;
Damp sand, dry sand,
Sand eternal.

When I shake my garments at the Lord's command, 45
What will I scatter in the Promised Land?
Sand.

23. **gaiters** (gā′tərz): overshoes.

41. **Studebaker:** an automobile, no longer manufactured.

SEEKING MEANING

1. What details in the poem make it apparent that the speaker is a homemaker and a mother?

2. A word or phrase may be repeated for comic exaggeration. Count the number of times that *sand* appears in the poem. In how many ways is the speaker's life affected by sand?

3. The Sahara is the world's largest desert. What does the use of *Sahara* in line 20 suggest? What other exaggerated statements can you find in the poem?

4. The speaker tells us that the sign of summer's arrival is sand. What are the signs of the other seasons?

5. Look at the verbs *sifting* and *dribbling* in line 15. What images do these verbs give you? What other verbs give precise images?

6. In this poem rhyme is often used in clever and amusing ways. What does the poet rhyme with *luncheon* in line 13? Find other examples of humorous rhymes in the poem.

DEVELOPING SKILLS OF EXPRESSION

Writing a Humorous Poem

Anyone who has spent a day at the beach can appreciate what the speaker is complaining about in "Season at the Shore." Think about some ordinary thing that frequently annoys you: a mosquito that won't let you get to sleep, commercials that interrupt your favorite television program, and so on. Write a poem in which you exaggerate your complaint.

ABOUT THE AUTHOR

Phyllis McGinley (1905–1978) was born in Ontario, Oregon, and educated at the University of Utah. She received the Pulitzer Prize in 1961 for a collection of her poems called *Times Three,* in which "Season at the Shore" appears. Although she is best known for her light, amusing poems, she has also written books for children, essays, lyrics for a Broadway revue, and film scripts.

Lincoln Monument: Washington
Langston Hughes

Let's go see old Abe
Sitting in the marble and the moonlight,
Sitting lonely in the marble and the moonlight,
Quiet for ten thousand centuries, old Abe.
Quiet for a million, million years.   5

Quiet—

And yet a voice forever
Against the
Timeless walls
Of time—   10
Old Abe.

SEEKING MEANING

1. What phrase in the poem tells you that the speaker thinks of Lincoln as an old friend?

2. Line 3 repeats line 2 with the addition of the word *lonely*. How does the word *lonely* enrich, or add to, the meaning of the line?

3. What ideas are emphasized through repetition in the first six lines of the poem?

4. A monument is built to last through time. According to the last five lines of the poem, what will outlast this marble monument? Can you quote some of Lincoln's famous lines that the speaker might have in mind?

ABOUT THE AUTHOR

Langston Hughes (1902–1967) was born in Joplin, Missouri. He went to sea in 1922 and worked at a variety of odd jobs around the world before returning to the United States. While he was working in a hotel in Washington, D. C., he came to the attention of the well-known poet Vachel Lindsay. Lindsay read some of Hughes's work at a poetry recital he was giving in the hotel auditorium. The next day newspapers acclaimed Lindsay's discovery of the young poet. *The Weary Blues*, Hughes's first volume of poems, appeared in 1926. Although Hughes is remembered chiefly as a poet, he also wrote short stories, plays, movie scripts, and children's books. In addition, he edited several anthologies of prose and poetry by black writers.

The Broncho That Would Not Be Broken

Vachel Lindsay

A little colt—broncho, loaned to the farm
To be broken in time without fury or harm,
Yet black crows flew past you, shouting alarm,
Calling "Beware," with lugubrious° singing. . . .
The butterflies there in the bush were romancing,   5
The smell of the grass caught your soul in a trance,
So why be a-fearing the spurs and the traces,
O broncho that would not be broken of dancing?

4. **lugubrious** (loo-goo'brē-əs): sad.

You were born with the pride of the lords great and olden
Who dance, through the ages, in corridors golden.   10
In all the wide farmplace the person most human.
You spoke out so plainly with squealing and capering,
With whinnying, snorting, contorting, and prancing,
As you dodged your pursuers, looking askance,
With Greek-footed figures, and Parthenon° paces,   15
O broncho that would not be broken of dancing.

15. **Parthenon** (pär'thə-nän'): an ancient Greek temple decorated with sculptures of lively horses.

The grasshoppers cheered. "Keep whirling," they said.
The insolent sparrows called from the shed,
"If men will not laugh, make them wish they were dead."
But arch° were your thoughts, all malice displacing.   20
Though the horse-killers came, with snakewhips advancing.
You bantered and cantered away your last chance.
And they scourged you, with hell in their speech and their faces,
O broncho that would not be broken of dancing.

20. **arch:** sly.

"Nobody cares for you," rattled the crows,   25
As you dragged the whole reaper, next day, down the
    rows.
The three mules held back, yet you danced on your toes.
You pulled like a racer, and kept the mules chasing.
You tangled the harness with bright eyes side-glancing,
While the drunk driver bled you—a pole for a lance—   30
And the giant mules bit at you—keeping their places.
O broncho that would not be broken of dancing.

In that last afternoon your boyish heart broke.
The hot wind came down like a sledge-hammer stroke.
The blood-sucking flies to a rare feast awoke.   35
And they searched out your wounds, your death warrant
    tracing.
And the merciful men, their religion enhancing,
Stopped the red reaper to give you a chance.
Then you died on the prairie, and scorned all disgraces,
O broncho that would not be broken of dancing.   40

SEEKING MEANING

1. What does the word *dancing* tell you about the broncho's natural grace and spirit?

2. What words in the poem describe the broncho's playfulness?

3. How do the men try to subdue the colt and break its spirit?

4. Other animals witness what is happening to the broncho. Which of them are in sympathy with the colt? In what way are the "broken" creatures cruel to the colt?

5. By dying, the broncho "scorned all disgraces." What disgraces would he have endured had he continued to live?

6. Explain in your own words what this poem is saying about "breaking," or destroying, nature's creatures.

DEVELOPING SKILLS IN READING

Understanding the Refrain

A phrase or line that is repeated regularly in a poem is called a *refrain*. A refrain usually occurs at the end of a stanza. A line that is repeated often in a poem can be easily learned and remembered. In folk songs and ballads, you will often find refrains at the end of each stanza, where an audience is expected to join in the singing.

What is the refrain in Lindsay's poem? How does it foreshadow the broncho's fate?

This song is from The Tempest, *one of William Shakespeare's plays. Prince Ferdinand believes that his father has been drowned in a shipwreck. The song tells him of a magical transformation that has taken place.*

Full Fathom Five   *William Shakespeare*

Full fathom° five thy father lies:
   Of his bones are coral made;
Those are pearls that were his eyes;
   Nothing of him that doth fade
But doth suffer° a sea-change
Into something rich and strange.
Sea nymphs° hourly ring his knell:°
            Ding-dong.
Hark! now I hear them—ding-dong, bell.

1. **fathom** (făth'əm): a depth of 6 feet (about 2 meters).

5. **suffer:** undergo.

7. **sea nymphs** (nĭmfs): goddesses once thought to inhabit the sea. **knell** (nĕl): the tolling of a death bell.

SEEKING MEANING

According to the song, what change has the sea made in Ferdinand's father? Why is this change "rich and strange"?

DEVELOPING SKILLS IN READING

Understanding How Sounds Convey Feeling
You have seen that a poet makes music by repeating key words and lines and by using rhyme. A poet also makes music by repeating the sounds of certain consonants and vowels.

Look again at the opening line of Shakespeare's poem: "*F*ull *f*athom *f*ive thy *f*ather lies." Shakespeare uses several words that begin with the same consonant sound: **f.** He also repeats sounds in the middle of words. The sound **th** is repeated in *fathom, thy,* and *father.* This technique is known as *alliteration* (ə-lit'ə-rā'shən).

The sounds **f** and **th** are gentle sounds. They do not explode the way the sound **p** does in this line: "Peter Piper picked a peck of pickled peppers." The long vowel sound in *five, thy,* and *lies* helps slow up the movement of the line and thereby contributes to the mood of the poem.

What sounds are repeated in lines 3–5? Can you find another example of alliteration in the poem?

Leaflight

Dorothy Donnelly

The trees turn:
flower-yellow
on the willow,
red of the rose
on maple boughs;   5
the sumacs burn.

The leaves fall:
walnut, alder,
poplar, elder,
and elms unveil,   10
dropping gold foil
on field and wall.

Detail from *Carnival of Autumn* (1908). Oil by Marsden Hartley.
Museum of Fine Arts, Boston   Charles Henry Hayden Fund

SEEKING MEANING

1. What season does the poem describe? How do you know?
2. What is the color of the leaves on the sumac tree? Which word tells you?
3. What does *unveil* mean in line 10?
4. *Foil* is a shiny wrapping, which crumples easily. In what way are the leaves of the elm like gold foil?

DEVELOPING SKILLS IN READING

Discovering Other Musical Effects
Many subtle and beautiful musical effects are discovered when "Leaflight" is read aloud. One technique the poet uses is alliteration:

> The *t*rees *t*urn
> *r*ed of the *r*ose

Note that alliteration is also used within or at the end of words:

> and e*l*ms unvei*l*,
> dropping go*l*d foi*l*

The consonant sound **l** dominates the poem. Find all the words in which the sound occurs. The sound **l** is a *liquid* consonant sound—that is, it makes the lines of a poem flow smoothly.

You may have discovered that several words in the poem seem to rhyme but do not match perfectly:

> yellow   alder
> willow   elder

This kind of rhyme is called *partial* (or *imperfect*) *rhyme*. What word would be a perfect rhyme for *yellow?* For *alder?*

Historically, the highwayman was an outlaw who held up travelers on public roads. In literature, he often appears as a handsome, bold, and romantic figure.

The Highwayman   *Alfred Noyes*

Part 1

The wind was a torrent of darkness among the gusty
    trees,
The moon was a ghostly galleon° tossed upon cloudy seas,
The road was a ribbon of moonlight over the purple moor,
And the highwayman came riding—
    Riding—riding—   5
The highwayman came riding, up to the old inn door.

He'd a French cocked hat on his forehead, a bunch of lace
    at his chin,
A coat of the claret° velvet, and breeches of brown doe-
    skin;
They fitted with never a wrinkle: his boots were up to the
    thigh!
And he rode with a jeweled twinkle,   10
    His pistol butts a-twinkle,
His rapier hilt° a-twinkle, under the jeweled sky.

Over the cobbles he clattered and clashed in the dark
    innyard
And he tapped with his whip on the shutters, but all was
    locked and barred;
He whistled a tune to the window, and who should be
    waiting there   15
But the landlord's black-eyed daughter,
    Bess, the landlord's daughter,
Plaiting ° a dark red love knot into her long black hair.

2. **galleon** (găl′ē-ən): a large sailing ship.

8. **claret** (klăr′ət): deep red, like claret wine.

12. **rapier** (rā′pē-ər) **hilt:** the handle of a light sword.

18. **Plaiting:** braiding.

And dark in the dark old innyard a stable wicket creaked
Where Tim the ostler° listened; his face was white and
    peaked;   20
His eyes were hollows of madness, his hair like moldy
    hay,
But he loved the landlord's daughter,
  The landlord's red-lipped daughter,
Dumb as a dog he listened, and he heard the robber say—

"One kiss, my bonny sweetheart, I'm after a prize to-
    night,   25
But I shall be back with the yellow gold before the morn-
    ing light;
Yet, if they press me sharply, and harry° me through the
    day,
Then look for me by moonlight,
  Watch for me by moonlight,
I'll come to thee by moonlight, though hell should bar the
    way."   30

20. **ostler** (ŏs′lər): stableman; also
called *hostler* (hŏs′lər).

27. **harry:** attack repeatedly.

He rose upright in the stirrups; he scarce could reach her hand,

But she loosened her hair i' the casement!° His face burned like a brand

As the black cascade of perfume came tumbling over his breast;

And he kissed its waves in the moonlight,

   (Oh, sweet black waves in the moonlight!)   35

Then he tugged at his rein in the moonlight, and galloped away to the west.

32. **casement:** a window that opens outward on hinges.

Part 2

He did not come in the dawning; he did not come at noon;

And out o' the tawny sunset, before the rise o' the moon,

When the road was a gypsy's ribbon, looping the purple moor,

A redcoat troop came marching—   40

   Marching—marching—

King George's men came marching, up to the old inn door.

They said no word to the landlord, they drank his ale instead,

But they gagged his daughter and bound her to the foot of her narrow bed;

Two of them knelt at her casement, with muskets at their side!   45

There was death at every window;

   And hell at one dark window;

For Bess could see, through her casement, the road that *he* would ride.

They had tied her up to attention, with many a sniggering jest;

They had bound a musket beside her, with the barrel beneath her breast!   50

"Now keep good watch!" and they kissed her. She heard the dead man say—

Look for me by moonlight;

   Watch for me by moonlight;

I'll come to thee by moonlight, though hell should bar the way!

She twisted her hands behind her; but all the knots held
  good!   55
She writhed her hands till her fingers were wet with
  sweat or blood!
They stretched and strained in the darkness, and the
  hours crawled by like years,
Till, now, on the stroke of midnight,
  Cold, on the stroke of midnight,
The tip of one finger touched it! The trigger at least was
  hers!   60

The tip of one finger touched it; she strove no more for
  the rest!
Up, she stood to attention, with the barrel beneath her
  breast,
She would not risk their hearing: she would not strive
  again;
For the road lay bare in the moonlight;
  Blank and bare in the moonlight;   65
And the blood in her veins in the moonlight throbbed to
  her love's refrain.

Tlot-tlot; tlot-tlot! Had they heard it? The horse hoofs
  ringing clear;
Tlot-tlot, tlot-tlot, in the distance? Were they deaf that
  they did not hear?
Down the ribbon of moonlight, over the brow of the hill,
The highwayman came riding,   70
  Riding, riding!
The redcoats looked to their priming! She stood up,
  straight and still!

Tlot-tlot, in the frosty silence! Tlot-tlot, in the echoing
  night!
Nearer he came and nearer! Her face was like a light!
Her eyes grew wide for a moment; she drew one last deep
  breath,   75
Then her finger moved in the moonlight,
  Her musket shattered the moonlight,
Shattered her breast in the moonlight and warned him—
  with her death.

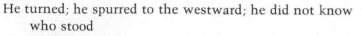

He turned; he spurred to the westward; he did not know
who stood
Bowed, with her head o'er the musket, drenched with her
own red blood!   80
Not till the dawn he heard it, his face grew gray to hear
How Bess, the landlord's daughter,
  The landlord's black-eyed daughter,
Had watched for her love in the moonlight, and died in
the darkness there.

Back, he spurred like a madman, shrieking a curse to the
sky,   85
With the white road smoking behind him, and his rapier
brandished high!
Blood-red were his spurs i' the golden noon; wine-red his
velvet coat,
When they shot him down on the highway,
  Down like a dog on the highway,
And he lay in his blood on the highway, with a bunch of
lace at his throat.   90

*And still of a winter's night, they say, when the wind is
in the trees,*
*When the moon is a ghostly galleon tossed upon cloudy
seas,*
*When the road is a ribbon of moonlight over the purple
moor,*
A highwayman comes riding—
  Riding—riding—   95
A highwayman comes riding, up to the old inn door.

*Over the cobbles he clatters and clangs in the dark
innyard;*
*And he taps with his whip on the shutters, but all is
locked and barred;*
*He whistles a tune to the window, and who should be
waiting there*
But the landlord's black-eyed daughter,   100
  Bess, the landlord's daughter,
Plaiting a dark red love knot into her long black hair.

SEEKING MEANING

1. This poem tells a story. Where and when does the story take place? Find details in the poem that help you to establish the time and place. (What do lines 40–42 tell you?)
2. Who are the major characters in the story? What details in the poem tell you what they look like? What role does Tim the ostler play in the story?
3. There are many references to moonlight in the poem. The meeting of lovers by moonlight is traditional in stories of romance. Why is moonlight also important to the action of the story?
4. Which lines in the fifth stanza are echoed in the second part of the poem? Why do you think the poet wants you to recall these lines?
5. How do the last two stanzas add to the mystery and romance of the poem?

DEVELOPING SKILLS OF EXPRESSION

Presenting a Choral Reading

"The Highwayman" lends itself well to choral presentation. In the choral reading of a poem, speaking voices are used much as singing voices are used in a chorus. Some lines are assigned to individuals as solo parts; some lines are assigned to small groups of voices; some are assigned to all voices.

Choral reading takes a good deal of preparation and practice. You must decide which lines are best for solo voices and which are best for many voices. You must interpret how lines are to be read. You must determine when the voices should be raised or lowered and when the pace of reading should be stepped up or slowed down.

When you have decided how you wish to read the poem, choose a chorus leader. The chorus leader acts as a conductor who signals when different members of the chorus are to speak. If there is a tape recorder available, record your practice sessions. Listen to the tapes and suggest ways to improve the performance of the group.

ABOUT THE AUTHOR

Alfred Noyes (1880–1958) drew material for some of his best-known poems from England's real and legendary past. He wrote "The Highwayman" at night while he was visiting Bagshot Heath, a lonely moor in England that outlaws had roamed two centuries before. Besides poetry, Noyes wrote plays, literary criticism, and an autobiography called *Two Worlds from Memory*. The first of his worlds was England, and the second was America. Noyes taught English literature at Princeton University from 1914 to 1923.

Dialect is a form of speech belonging to a particular region or to a particular group of people. A dialect may be distinguished by characteristics of vocabulary, grammar, and pronunciation.

This poem is written in a dialect that was spoken in rural Indiana many years ago. If you read the poem out loud, you will have no problem understanding words like russel *and* medder.

When the Frost Is on the Punkin

James Whitcomb Riley

When the frost is on the punkin and the fodder's in the
    shock,°
And you hear the kyouck and gobble of the struttin'
    turkey cock,
And the clackin' of the guineys,° and the cluckin' of the
    hens,
And the rooster's hallylooer as he tiptoes on the fence;
O, it's then's the time a feller is a-feelin' at his best,   5
With the risin' sun to greet him from a night of peaceful
    rest,
As he leaves the house, bareheaded, and goes out to feed
    the stock,
When the frost is on the punkin and the fodder's in the
    shock.

1. **shock:** a pile of stalks and leaves set in a field to dry.

3. **guineys** (gĭn′ēz): guinea fowls.

They's something kindo' harty-like about the atmusfere
When the heat of summer's over and the coolin' fall is
    here—   10
Of course we miss the flowers, and the blossums on the
    trees,
And the mumble of the hummin'birds and buzzin' of the
    bees;
But the air's so appetizin'; and the landscape through the
    haze
Of a crisp and sunny morning of the airly autumn days
Is a pictur' that no painter has the colorin' to mock—   15
When the frost is on the punkin and the fodder's in the
    shock.

The husky, rusty russel of the tossels of the corn,
And the raspin' of the tangled leaves, as golden as the
    morn;
The stubble in the furries—kindo' lonesome-like, but still
A-preachin' sermuns to us of the barns they growed to fill;   20
The strawstack in the medder, and the reaper in the shed;
The hosses in theyr stalls below—the clover overhead!—
O, it sets my hart a-clickin' like the tickin' of a clock,
When the frost is on the punkin and the fodder's in the
    shock!

Then your apples all is gethered, and the ones a feller
    keeps   25
Is poured around the celler floor in red and yeller heaps;
And your cider makin's over, and your wimmern folks is
    through
With theyr mince and apple butter, and theyr souse and
    sausage, too!
I don't know how to tell it—but ef sich a thing could be
As the Angels wantin' boardin', and they'd call around on
    me—   30
I'd want to 'commodate 'em—all the whole indurin'
    flock—
When the frost is on the punkin and the fodder's in the
    shock!

SEEKING MEANING

1. This poem tells what life was like on an Indiana farm during early autumn many years ago. In the first stanza the speaker notes the sounds he hears early in the morning. Which words imitate the sounds of farm animals?

2. In the second stanza the speaker describes the "atmusfere" of early fall. What characteristics of the morning does he enjoy?

3. Autumn is the time when crops are harvested. What details in the third stanza tell you that the harvesting is over? What are the "tossels" in line 17? The "furries" in line 19?

4. What tasks of the autumn season are described in the last stanza?

5. Why do you think autumn fills this farmer with such a sense of well-being?

ABOUT THE AUTHOR

James Whitcomb Riley (1849–1916), known as "the Hoosier poet," worked for some years as a sign painter, an actor, and a small-town journalist. Then he went to work for the *Indianapolis Daily Journal*, which regularly published his poems. Riley had a keen eye for the local scene and characters, and sometimes made use of the Hoosier (Indiana country) dialect. One of his best-known poems is "Little Orphant Annie."

Have you ever tapped your feet to the sound of a marching band or clapped your hands to a song? Have you ever been rocked to sleep by the movement of a bus or train? If you have, it is because your body responds to rhythm.

The rhythm of a poem grows out of its subject. The following poem tells about three men setting off on horseback to bring a message from Ghent in Belgium to Aix (āks) in Germany. As you read the poem aloud, see if you can hear the rhythmic, heavy beat of horses' hoofs.

How They Brought the Good News from Ghent to Aix
(16—) *Robert Browning*

I sprang to the stirrup, and Joris, and he;
I galloped, Dirck galloped, we galloped all three;
"Good speed!" cried the watch, as the gate bolts undrew;
"Speed!" echoed the wall to us galloping through;
Behind shut the postern,° the lights sank to rest,
And into the midnight we galloped abreast.

5. **postern** (pōs′tərn): city gate.

Not a word to each other; we kept the great pace
Neck by neck, stride by stride, never changing our place;
I turned in my saddle and made its girths tight,
Then shortened each stirrup, and set the pique° right,
Rebuckled the cheek strap, chained slacker the bit,
Nor galloped less steadily Roland a whit.

10   10. **pique** (pēk): probably the spur.

'Twas moonset at starting; but while we drew near
Lokeren,° the cocks crew° and twilight dawned clear;
At Boom,° a great yellow star came out to see;
At Düffeld,° 'twas morning as plain as could be;
And from Mecheln° church steeple we heard the half-
    chime,
So Joris broke silence with, "Yet there is time!"

14. **Lokeren** (lō′kə-rən). **crew**: crowed.
15   15. **Boom** (bōm).
16. **Düffeld** (dōōf′əlt).
17. **Mecheln** (měk′əln): usually spelled *Mechelen.*

At Aershot,° up leaped of a sudden the sun,
And against him the cattle stood black every one, 20
To stare through the mist at us galloping past,
And I saw my stout galloper Roland at last,
With resolute shoulders, each butting away
The haze, as some bluff river headland its spray;

And his low head and crest, just one sharp ear bent back 25
For my voice, and the other pricked out on his track;
And one eye's black intelligence—ever that glance
O'er its white edge at me, his own master, askance!
And the thick heavy spume-flakes which aye and anon°
His fierce lips shook upward in galloping on. 30

By Hasselt,° Dirck groaned; and cried Joris, "Stay spur!
Your Roos° galloped bravely, the fault's not in her,
We'll remember at Aix"—for one heard the quick wheeze
Of her chest, saw the stretched neck and staggering
    knees,
And sunk tail, and horrible heave of the flank, 35
As down on her haunches she shuddered and sank.

So we were left galloping, Joris and I,
Past Looz° and past Tongres,° no cloud in the sky;
The broad sun above laughed a pitiless laugh,
'Neath our feet broke the brittle bright stubble like chaff; 40
Till over by Dalhem° a dome spire sprang white,
And "Gallop," gasped Joris, "for Aix is in sight!

19. **Aershot** (ăr'shôt): usually
spelled *Aerschot.*

29. **aye** (ā) **and anon:** again and
again.

31. **Hasselt** (häs'əlt).
32. **Roos** (rōs).

38. **Looz** (lōz). **Tongres** (tôn'gr).

41. **Dalhem** (däl'əm).

"How they'll greet us!"—and all in a moment his roan°
Rolled neck and croup° over, lay dead as a stone;
And there was my Roland to bear the whole weight   45
Of the news which alone could save Aix from her fate,
With his nostrils like pits full of blood to the brim,
And with circles of red for his eye sockets' rim.

Then I cast loose my buffcoat, each holster let fall,
Shook off my jack boots, let go belt and all,   50
Stood up in the stirrup, leaned, patted his ear,
Called my Roland his pet name, my horse without peer;
Clapped my hands, laughed and sang, any noise, bad or
    good,
Till at length into Aix Roland galloped and stood.

And all I remember is—friends flocking round   55
As I sat with his head 'twixt my knees on the ground;
And no voice but was praising this Roland of mine,
As I poured down his throat our last measure of wine,
Which (the burgesses° voted by common consent)
Was no more than his due who brought good news from
    Ghent.   60

43. **roan:** reddish-brown horse.

44. **croup** (krōōp): the back part of the horse; rump.

59. **burgesses:** officers of the city.

SEEKING MEANING

1. A great deal of action is compressed into the first stanza. What happens in these six lines? What do you think the "watch" refers to? Explain the meaning of line 4. What are the "lights" mentioned in line 5?

2. When do the riders set out? What references in the poem help you keep track of the passing of time? How do these references to the passing of time build up excitement?

3. Roland is called a "stout galloper" in line 22. What evidence in the poem shows that this is an accurate description? What lines show the strain that Roland is under?

4. Which lines tell that the first horse, Roos, has collapsed? At what point does the second horse collapse?

5. How does the rider help Roland reach Aix? What reward does the horse receive?

DEVELOPING SKILLS IN READING

Responding to Rhythm

This poem is famous for the way it imitates a horse's gallop. Reread the first two lines of the poem and listen to the way your voice rises and falls on the syllables of the words:

> I **sprang** to the **stir**rup, and **Jor**is, and **he**;
> I **gal**loped, Dirck **gal**loped, we **gal**loped all **three**;

The syllables in boldface are those that are stressed when the lines are read aloud. The other syllables are unstressed.

Using your fingers, tap out the sound of a galloping horse on a desk or table. What pattern do you hear in the rhythm?

Below are lines 7–8 of the poem. The stressed syllables are marked ('); the unstressed syllables (˘). What pattern do you see?

> Not a word to each other; we kept the great
> pace
> Neck by neck, stride by stride, never chang-
> ing our place;

Is this the pattern you tapped out?

Reread the seventh stanza aloud. Do you hear the rhythm of horses' hoofs?

Reread "Annabel Lee" and "The Highwayman," listening carefully to the rhythms of these poems.

The Shape of a Poem

You have seen that the meaning of a poem is expressed through different elements—ideas, images, sounds, rhythm. Meaning can also be expressed through the arrangement of words on a page.

In a concrete poem, *words are arranged to look like the subject of the poem.*

Concrete Cat   *Dorthi Charles*

```
        A          A
      e  ɪ       e  ɪ

   e Y e   e Y e   stripestripestripestripe
 whisker        whisker  stripestripestripe        t
                        stripestripestripestripes  a  i  l  t  a  i  l
 whisker  m   h whisker  stripestripestripe
          o  t          stripestripestripe
          U             stripestripestripestripe

      paw paw      paw paw              ǝsnoɯ

   dishdish                      litterbox
                                 litterbox
```

SEEKING MEANING

1. Identify the different parts of the cat's body. What can you tell about this cat's fur?
2. What do you think the poet intends the capital letters to stand for? How does the poet indicate the length and position of the cat's tail?
3. Why do you think the word *mouse* is upside-down?

The lines in this poem have an unusual arrangement. As you read the poem, your eyes have to hop across spaces between words, or skip down the page, or jump from line to line.

in Just- *E. E. Cummings*

in Just-
spring   when the world is mud-
luscious the little
lame balloonman

whistles   far   and wee   5

and eddieandbill come
running from marbles and
piracies and it's
spring

when the world is puddle-wonderful   10

the queer
old balloonman whistles
far   and   wee
and bettyandisbel come dancing

from hop-scotch and jump-rope and   15

it's
spring
and
    the

        goat-footed°   20

balloonMan   whistles
far
and
wee

20. **goat-footed:** Pan, a god of woods and fields in Greek mythology, was represented with the legs of a goat.

SEEKING MEANING

1. When is "Just-spring"? From the point of view of a young child, why might the world be "mud-luscious" and "puddle-wonderful" at this time? What games do the children in the poem play?

2. Why do you think the words *eddieandbill* and *bettyandisbel* are run together? How would you read these lines aloud?

3. The word *wee*, meaning "very small or little," is often used in children's stories. It also sounds like *whee*, a word used by children when they are excited or happy. What other word might be intended?

4. The sound of the balloonman's whistle is first heard in line 5. Notice the space between the words *whistle, far, and*, and *wee*. What happens to the space between these words in lines 12–13? In lines 21–24? What do you think is happening to the sound of the whistle?

5. The balloonman is described as "goat-footed." As explained in the note to line 20, Pan was believed to have the legs of a goat. He was fond of music and dancing, and was thought to be the inventor of the shepherd's pipes. Why do you think the balloonman is associated with Pan?

6. How is the movement of the lines across the page like the movement of the children in the poem?

ABOUT THE AUTHOR

E. E. Cummings (1894–1962), whose full name was Edward Estlin Cummings, was born in Cambridge, Massachusetts, and educated at Harvard University. He went to France during World War I to serve as an ambulance driver, but because of a censor's mistake, he spent three months in a French detention camp. He later wrote about this experience in *The Enormous Room*.

Cummings is known for his highly individual poetic technique, particularly his unusual arrangement of words on the page and his minimal use of capital letters and punctuation. However, the subject matter of his poems is often traditional. Many of his poems are about the beauty and joy of nature.

Practice in Reading and Writing

Reading Poetry

A poem generally gains in meaning the more closely you study it. Read the following poem slowly and carefully. After you have read it, pause and think about it, and then read it again. The steps outlined below will guide you in analyzing the poem.

Lost

Desolate and lone
All night long on the lake
Where fog trails and mist creeps,
The whistle of a boat
Calls and cries unendingly,
Like some lost child
In tears and trouble
Hunting the harbor's breast
And the harbor's eyes.

Carl Sandburg

---

1. *Look for complete thoughts instead of reading line by line.*

How many sentences are there in Sandburg's poem? In reading the poem aloud, where should you pause?

2. *Note the effects of specific words and images.*

What feelings are suggested by the title of the poem? What associations do you have with the word *desolate*? What feelings are suggested by the image of a foggy lake at night?

3. *Note the comparisons chosen by the poet.*

Sandburg compares the whistle of a boat at night to the crying of a lost child. What feelings are suggested by this simile? How does the metaphor in the last two lines add to the overall effect of the poem?

4. *Listen for the sound effects.*

Notice that the **1** sound in the title is repeated in the first two lines of the poem. What emphasis or connection does Sandburg achieve by repetition of this sound? Find other examples of alliteration in the poem.

5. *Express the meaning of the poem in your own words.*

What experience do you think the poet wishes to share with the reader? What do you think he may have felt or thought?

Writing Poetry

Choose one of the images suggested below or think of another image that appeals to you. Write a brief poem that communicates a feeling or an idea about the image. Your poem may or may not use rhyme, and it may be serious or humorous. You might try comparing the subject of your poem with something else, as Sandburg has done in "Lost."

A worn-out pair of shoes
A siren in the night
The buzzing of a fly in a quiet room
Bare feet on a hot pavement or on cool grass
City streets on a rainy night

For Further Reading

Adoff, Arnold, editor, *I Am the Darker Brother: An Anthology of Modern Poems by Negro Americans* (Macmillan, 1968; paperback, Macmillan)

Twenty-eight black poets—including Gwendolyn Brooks, Paul Laurence Dunbar, and Langston Hughes—write about the past and future of black Americans, their feelings, hopes, and dreams.

Allen, Terry, editor, *The Whispering Wind: Poetry by Young American Indians* (Doubleday, 1972; paperback, Doubleday)

Here is a collection of poetry about nature, family, and identity, written by high school students who attended the Institute of American Indian Arts in Santa Fe, New Mexico.

Atwood, Ann, *Haiku, the Mood of Earth* (Scribner, 1971)

The book presents twenty-five haiku, each illustrated with two full-color photographs.

Bogan, Louise, and William Jay Smith, editors, *The Golden Journey: Poems for Young People* (Regnery, 1965)

The poems in this collection are grouped under these categories: rhymes, country poems, love poems, nonsense verses, war poems, and poems of dreams and fancies.

Brewton, Sara, and John E. Brewton, editors, *Laughable Limericks* (Thomas Y. Crowell, 1965)

"Crawlers, Croakers, and Creepers" is one of the chapter titles in this collection of old and new limericks.

Cole, William, editor, *The Poet's Tales: A New Book of Story Poems* (World Publishing, 1971)

Included in this anthology are old and new story poems. Another collection by Cole is *A Book of Nature Poems* (Viking, 1969).

De la Mare, Walter, *Collected Rhymes and Verses* (Faber & Faber, 1944)

This collection includes poems of humor, mystery, and magic.

Dickinson, Emily, *Poems for Youth*, edited by Alfred Leete Hampson (Little, Brown, 1934)

Emily Dickinson wrote many of these poems for her nieces and nephews.

Lewis, Richard, editor, *Miracles: Poems by Children of the English-Speaking World* (Simon and Schuster, 1966)

Here are more than two hundred poems written by children about their thoughts, feelings, and experiences. Another collection by Richard Lewis, *Out of the Earth I Sing: Poetry and Songs of Primitive Peoples of the World* (Norton, 1968), contains traditional songs and chants from many different countries.

Lindsay, Vachel, *Johnny Appleseed and Other Poems* (Macmillan, 1928)

This anthology includes Lindsay's nonsense rhymes, lyrics, and historical poems.

Read, Herbert, editor, *This Way Delight* (Pantheon, 1956)

The editor believes that "poetry should be a deep delight, which you should enjoy as you enjoy a day in spring . . . ." He has selected poems on such subjects as "Charms," "Enchantments," "Escapes," and "Stories."

Sandburg, Carl, *Wind Song* (Harcourt Brace Jovanovich, 1960; paperback, Harcourt)

Sandburg selected these poems especially for young people and grouped them into such chapters as "Blossom Themes," "Night," and "Wind, Sea, and Sky."

Untermeyer, Louis, editor, *Magic Circle: Stories and People in Poetry* (Harcourt Brace Jovanovich, 1952)

Here are more than one hundred story poems, both traditional and modern. Other collections by Untermeyer are *Stars to Steer By* (Harcourt Brace Jovanovich, 1941), which contains more than one hundred fifty poems with introductions; and *This Singing World* (Harcourt Brace Jovanovich, 1951).

A boy who drives a chariot across the sky, a goddess who returns from the land of the dead, a hero who slays a nine-headed serpent — these are some of the fantastic and exciting things that happen in the myths you are about to read.

Myths are stories that have come down to us from the distant past. They have survived for many centuries because they are good stories that appeal to old and young alike. The main characters in myths are generally gods and goddesses, but if you read closely, you will find that myths have much to say about human nature.

Every people has its own body of myths, or *mythology*. Classical myths, the name given to the myths of the ancient Greeks and Romans, are the best-known myths in Western culture. These stories were first told by the ancient Greeks more than twenty-five hundred years ago. Later the stories were retold by the Romans, who substituted the names of their own gods and goddesses for those of the Greeks.

The first selection in this unit will introduce you to the most important figures in Greek mythology — Zeus and his family.

MYTHS OF THE GREEKS AND ROMANS

The Mission of Athene. Cameo. Shown from left to right: Athene, Hermes, Zeus, Hera. Bibliothèque Nationale, Paris

471

The Gods and Goddesses of Mount Olympus

Olivia Coolidge

Greek legends have been favorite stories for many centuries. They are mentioned so often by famous writers that it has become impossible to read widely in English, or in many other literatures, without knowing what the best of these tales are about. Even though we no longer believe in the Greek gods, we enjoy hearing of them because they appeal to our imagination.

The Greeks thought all the forces of nature were spirits, so that the whole earth was filled with gods. Each river, each woodland, even each great tree had its own god or nymph.[1] In the woods lived the satyrs,[2] who had pointed ears and the shaggy legs of goats. In the sea

danced more than three thousand green-haired, white-limbed maidens. In the air rode wind gods, cloud nymphs, and the golden chariot of the sun. All these spirits, like the forces of nature, were beautiful and strong, but sometimes unreliable and unfair. Above all, however, the Greeks felt that they were tremendously interested in mankind.

From very early times the Greeks began to invent stories to account for the things that went on—the change of seasons, the sudden storms, the good and bad fortune of the farmer's year. These tales were spread by travelers from one valley to another. They were put together and altered by poets and musicians, until at last a great body of legends arose from the whole of Greece. These did not agree with one another in details, but, on the whole, gave a clear picture of who the chief gods were, how men should behave to please them, and

---

1. **nymph** (nĭmf): a goddess who inhabited a part of nature, such as a river, a mountain, or a tree.
2. **satyrs** (sā'tərz): woodland creatures who were part man and part goat.

Procession of twelve gods and goddesses. Marble relief. From left: Persephone, Hermes, Aphrodite, Ares, Demeter, Hephaestus, Hera, Poseidon, Athena, Zeus, Artemis, Apollo. The Walters Art Gallery, Baltimore.

what their relationships had been with heroes of the past.

The ruler of all the gods was Zeus, the sky god, titled by courtesy "Father of gods and men." He lived in the clouds with most of the great gods in a palace on the top of Mount Olympus, the tallest mountain in Greece. Lightning was the weapon of Zeus, thunder was the rolling of his chariot, and when he nodded his head, the whole earth shook.

Zeus, though the ruler of the world, was not the eldest of the gods. First had come a race of monsters with fifty heads and a hundred arms each. Next followed elder gods called Titans, the leader of whom, Cronus, had reigned before Zeus. Then arose mighty Giants, and finally Zeus and the Olympians. Zeus in a series of wars succeeded in banishing the Titans and imprisoning the Giants in various ways. One huge monster, Typhon, lay impris-

oned under the volcano of Aetna, which spouted fire when he struggled. Atlas, one of the Titans, was forced to stand holding the heavens on his shoulders so that they should not fall upon the earth.

Almost as powerful as Zeus were his two brothers, who did not live on Olympus: Poseidon,[3] ruler of the sea, and Hades,[4] gloomy king of the underworld, where the spirits of the dead belong. Queen of the gods was blue-eyed, majestic Hera. Aphrodite,[5] the laughing, sea-born goddess, was queen of love and most beautiful of all.

Apollo and Artemis were twins, god of the sun and goddess of the moon. Apollo was the more important. Every day he rode the heav-

---

3. **Poseidon** (pō-sī'dən).
4. **Hades** (hā'dēz).
5. **Aphrodite** (ăf'rə-dī'tē).

Apollo.
National Museum, Athens, Greece

stand. Nevertheless, the Greeks believed that if a man could interpret the words of the oracle, he would find the answer to his problem.

Artemis, the silver moon goddess, was goddess of unmarried girls and a huntress of wild beasts in the mountains. She also could send deadly arrows from her silver bow.

Gray-eyed Athene,[6] the goddess of wisdom, was patron of Athens. She was queen of the domestic arts, particularly spinning and weaving. Athene was warlike too; she wore helmet and breastplate, and carried a spear. Ares, however, was the real god of war, and the maker of weapons was Hephaestus,[7] the lame smith and metalworker.

One more god who lived on Olympus was Hermes, the messenger. He wore golden, winged sandals which carried him dry-shod over sea and land. He darted down from the peaks of Olympus like a kingfisher dropping to catch a fish, or came running down the sloping sunbeams bearing messages from Zeus to men. Mortal eyes were too weak to behold the dazzling beauty of the immortals; consequently the messages of Zeus usually came in dreams. Hermes was therefore also a god of sleep, and of thieves because they prowl by night. Healing was another of his powers. His rod, a staff entwined by two snakes, is commonly used as a symbol of medicine.

The Greeks have left us so many stories about their gods that it hardly would be possible for everyone to know them all. We can still enjoy them because they are good stories. In spite of their great age we can still understand them because they are about nature and about people. We still need them to enrich our knowledge of our own language and of the great masterpieces of literature.

ens in a golden chariot from dawn to sunset. The sun's rays could be gentle and healing, or they could be terrible. Apollo, therefore, was a great healer and the father of the god of medicine. At the same time he was a famous archer, and the arrows from his golden bow were arrows of infection and death. Apollo was also god of poetry and song; his instrument was a golden lyre, and the nine Muses, goddesses of music and the arts, were his attendants. He was the ideal of young manhood and the patron of athletes.

Apollo was also god of prophecy. There were temples of Apollo, known as oracles, at which a man could ask questions about the future. The priestesses of Apollo, inspired by the god, gave him an answer, often in the form of a riddle which was hard to under-

---

6. **Athene** (ə-thē′-nē): also called *Athena* (ə-thē′nə).
7. **Hephaestus** (hǐ-fēs′təs).

SEEKING MEANING

1. The ancient Greeks believed that all of nature was ruled by divine beings. How did they explain lightning and thunder? What did they believe happened when Zeus nodded his head?

2. The ancient Greeks believed that each of the gods and goddesses had control over a special area of life. For example, Hephaestus was the god of fire and metalworking. Blacksmiths would have prayed to him to help them in their craft. To which god or goddess would the following persons have prayed for special help?

athletes	robbers	soldiers
hunters	sailors	weavers

3. Why do people still read stories about the ancient Greek gods and goddesses? Give two reasons stated by the author.

DEVELOPING SKILLS IN READING

Recognizing Gods and Goddesses by Their Titles

The gods and goddesses in classical mythology are often identified by their titles rather than by their names. Zeus is known by several titles: "the sky god," "father of gods and men," "king of the gods." Writers frequently refer to Apollo by one of his titles: "god of the sun," "god of poetry and song," "god of prophecy."

The gods and goddesses are also identified by certain of their physical characteristics. For example, Hera is often described as "the ox-eyed goddess." She is also described as "the goddess of the white arms." Athena is described as "gray-eyed" or "bright-eyed." Aphrodite is called "the pale-gold goddess."

"Broad-browed" and "dark-misted" are often used to describe Zeus.

Sometimes the gods and goddesses are identified by their special powers. Zeus, for example, is referred to as "the summoner of clouds." Artemis is known as "goddess of wild things."

Which of the gods do you think is known as "the thunderer"?

Why would Poseidon be called the "blue-maned" god?

Why would Hephaestus be described as "strong-handed"?

CLASSICAL GODS AND GODDESSES

The Romans identified many of their gods and goddesses with those of the Greeks. The Roman god Jupiter was identified with the Greek god Zeus, the Roman goddess Juno with the Greek goddess Hera, and so on. For this reason, many gods and goddesses in classical mythology are known by both Greek and Roman names.

As you read the myths that follow, you may want to refer to this chart. For help with the pronunciation of these names and other names that appear in this unit, see the Index of Names on pages 523–525.

GREEK	ROMAN	DESCRIPTION
Zeus	Jupiter, Jove	king of the gods; god of the sky and the weather
Hera	Juno	queen of the gods; goddess of marriage and childbirth
Poseidon	Neptune	god of the sea
Hades, Pluto	Pluto	god of the underworld
Demeter	Ceres	goddess of grain, plants, and fruit
Athena, Athene, or Pallas Athena	Minerva	goddess of wisdom, arts, crafts, and war; protector of Athens
Hephaestus	Vulcan	god of fire and metalworking
Aphrodite	Venus	goddess of love and beauty
Ares	Mars	god of war

GREEK	ROMAN	DESCRIPTION
Apollo, Phoebus Apollo	Apollo, Phoebus Apollo	god of youth, music, prophecy, archery, healing, and the sun
Artemis	Diana	goddess of hunting, childbirth, wild animals, and the moon
Hermes	Mercury	messenger of the gods; god of travelers, merchants, and thieves
Persephone	Proserpina	goddess of spring and the underworld; Demeter's daughter
Dionysus, Bacchus	Bacchus	god of wine, fertility, and drama
Eros	Cupid	god of love; Aphrodite's son
Iris	Iris	goddess of the rainbow; messenger of the gods
Muses	Muses	nine goddesses who inspired artists
Fates	Fates	three goddesses who determined human destiny

For people of early times, mythology was part of religion. The myths of gods, goddesses, and heroes were sacred stories. But mythology also served another function. Through myths these early people provided explanations for natural events that puzzled them.

The ancient Greeks believed that the secret of making fire once belonged only to the gods. As you read the following myth, you will find out why the Greeks came to regard one of the Titans as their friend.

Prometheus° the Fire-Bringer

Retold by Jeremy Ingalls

Fire itself, and the civilized life which fire makes possible—these were the gifts of Prometheus to the men of ancient times. Prometheus himself was not of the oldest race of men. He was not alive in the first age of mankind.

Ancient writers tell us there were three ages of men on earth before the fourth age, in which we are now living. Each of the previous ages ended in terrible disasters which destroyed a large part of the human race. A raging fire ended the first age of the world. At the end of the second age, vast floods engulfed plains and mountains. According to the oldest poets, these misfortunes were punishments the gods visited upon men for their wickedness and wrongdoing.

The story of Prometheus, remembered by the Greeks and set down in their books, tells of the days when Zeus was king of the world

and Prometheus was his chief councilor. From their ancestors they and their companions upon Mount Olympus had inherited the secrets of fire, of rain, of farming and metalworking. This knowledge gave them a power so great that they appeared as gods to the men who served them.

After the flood which destroyed many of the men of the second age, Zeus, with the help of Prometheus, had bred a new race of men in Arcadia.[1] But Zeus did not find life on earth so simple for men and gods as it had been in earlier times.

When Cronus, the father of Zeus, had ruled the earth, summer had been the only season. Great land masses toward the north had barred all the icy winds. The age of Cronus was an age of contentment. No man had needed to work for food or clothes or a house to shelter him.

° **Prometheus** (prə-mē′thē-əs).

[1] **Arcadia** (är-kā′dē-ə): a pleasant, mountainous district in Greece.

After the first flood, the land masses were broken. Winter winds blew upon countries which before had known only summer.

The race of gods did not suffer. They warmed their houses, having the secret of fire. And the women of the race were weavers of cloth, so that the gods were clothed and defended from the north wind.

But winter was a harsh season for the men and women who did not live on the gods' mountain. Without defense from the cold, they huddled with the animals. They complained against the gods, whom they must serve for what little comfort they might find of food and warmth. They scarcely believed the stories which their ancestors had handed down to them of a time when men had lived in endless summer weather, when men were friends and favorites of the gods.

Men became rebels and grumblers. For this reason Zeus, seeing winter coming on again, determined to destroy the people of Arcadia. Then Prometheus, his chief councilor, sought to save this third race of man from destruction.

"They quarrel among themselves," said Zeus angrily. "They start trouble in the fields. We must train up a new race of men who will learn more quickly what it means to serve the gods."

Zeus was walking across the bronze floor of his mountain palace. A tremendous, tall figure of a man he was, the king god Zeus. But he who stood beside him, Prometheus of the family of Titans, was even taller.

"Worthless," Zeus was saying as if to himself. "Worthless," he repeated again, "the whole race. They complain of the winters. They are too weak a race for the climate of these times. Why should we continue to struggle with them? Better to be rid of them, every man and woman of the troublesome tribe."

"And then?" inquired Prometheus. "What if you create a new race to provide manpower for the farms and the bigger buildings? That race, too, will rebel while they can see and envy our knowledge and our power."

"Even so, I will destroy these Arcadians," insisted Zeus stubbornly. "Men are our creatures. Let them learn to serve us, to do our will."

"Up here on your mountain," observed Prometheus thoughtfully, "you make men and destroy them. But what about the men themselves? How can they learn wisdom when, time after time, you visit them with destruction?"

"You have too much sympathy for them," answered Zeus in a sharp voice. "I believe you love these huddling, sheepish men."

"They have minds and hearts," replied Prometheus warmly, "and a courage that is worth admiring. They wish to live even as the gods wish to live. Don't we feed ourselves on nectar and ambrosia[2] every day to preserve our lives?"

Prometheus was speaking rapidly. His voice was deep. "This is your way," he went on. "You won't look ahead. You won't be patient. You won't give men a chance to learn how to live. Over and over again, with floods or with cracking red thunderbolts, you destroy them."

"I have let you live, Prometheus," said Zeus in an ominous tone, "to advise me when you can. You are my cousin. But I am not your child to be scolded." Zeus was smiling, but there was thunder behind the smile.

Silently Prometheus turned away. Leaving the marble-columned hall, he went out among the gardens of Olympus, the gods' mountain. The last roses were fading before

---

2. **nectar and ambrosia** (ăm-brō′zhə): the drink and food of the Olympian gods.

the time of winter winds and rain.

This was not the first time Prometheus had heard thunder in the voice of Zeus. Prometheus knew that someday Zeus would turn against him, betray him, and punish him. Prometheus the Titan had the gift of reading the future. He could foresee the fate hidden and waiting for him and for others and even for Zeus himself.

Climbing among the upper gardens, Prometheus stopped at last beside an ancient, twisted ash tree. Leaning against its trunk, he looked toward the south. Beyond the last canal, the last steep sea wall, he could see the ocean. He looked far out toward that last shining circle of water. Then, with his head bent, he sat down on the tree roots bulging in thick knots above the ground.

It would be hard to tell you all the thoughts in the mind of the Titan — thoughts that coiled and twined like a nest of dragons. In his

mighty brain were long memories of the past and far-reaching prophecies of what was to come.

He thought most often of the future, but the talk with Zeus just now had brought the past before him once again. He remembered once more the terrible war in which Zeus had seized the kingship of the gods. He thought of the exile and imprisonment of Cronus, the father of Zeus. He remembered the Titans, his people, now chained in the black pit of Tartarus.[3]

The great god Cronus himself, who had given peace to gods and men, where was he now? And the mighty-headed Titans, the magnificent engineers, builders of bridges and temples, where were they? All of them fallen, helpless, as good as dead.

---

3. **Tartarus** (tär′tər-əs): a dark place below the underworld.

Zeus had triumphed. Of the Titans, only two now walked the upper earth—he, Prometheus, and Epimetheus, his brother.

And now, even now, Zeus was not content. It was not enough for his glory, it seemed, to have dethroned his own father, not enough to have driven the race of Titans from the houses of the gods. Now Zeus was plotting to kill the race of men.

Prometheus had endured the war against the Titans, his own people. He had even given help to Zeus. Having seen what was to come, he had thought, "Since Zeus must win, I'll guide him. I'll control his fierce anger and his greed for power."

But Prometheus could not submit to this latest plot of Zeus. He would use all his wits to save the men of Arcadia from destruction.

Why were they to be destroyed? Because they were cold and full of fears, huddled together in caves like animals. It was well enough in the warm months. They worked willingly in the fields of the gods and reared the horses and bulls and guarded the sheep. But when the cold days came, they grumbled against Olympus. They grumbled because they must eat and hunt like the animals and had no hoof nor claw nor heavy fur for protection.

What did they need? What protection would be better than hoof or claw? Prometheus knew. It was fire they needed—fire to cook with, to warm them, to harden metal for weapons. With fire they could frighten the wolf and the bear and the mountain lion.

Why did they lack the gift of fire? Prometheus knew that too. He knew how jealously the gods sat guard about their flame.

More than once he had told Zeus the need men had of fire. He knew why Zeus would not consent to teach men this secret of the gods. The gift of fire to men would be a gift of power. Hardened in the fire, the spears which men might make to chase the mountain lion might also, in time, be hurled against the gods. With fire would come comfort and time to think while the flames leaped up the walls of hidden caves. Men who had time to think would have time to question the laws of the gods. Among men who asked questions disorder might breed, and rebellion stronger than any mere squabble in the fields.

"But men are worth the gift of fire," thought Prometheus, sitting against the roots of his favorite ash tree. He could see ahead dimly into that time to come when gods would lose their power. And he, Prometheus, through his love for men, must help to bring on that time.

Prometheus did not hesitate. By the fall of night his plans were accomplished. As the sun went down, his tall figure appeared upon a sea beach. Above the sands a hundred caves, long ago deserted by the waters of the ocean, sheltered families of Arcadians. To them the Titan was bringing this very night the secret of the gods.

He came along the pebble line of high water. In his hand he carried a yellow reed.

This curious yellow stalk was made of metal, the most precious of the metals of the gods. From it the metalworkers molded rare and delicate shapes. From it they made the reedlike and hollow stalks which carried, in wisps of fennel[4] straw, coals from the gods' ever-burning fire. The gods who knew the sources of flame never built new fires in the sight of men. Going abroad on journeys, they took from their central hearth a smoldering coal.

Prometheus had left Olympus as one upon a journey. He alone knew he was not going to visit the home of Poseidon, Zeus's brother,

---

4. **fennel:** an herb.

lord of the sea — nor going into India, nor into the cold north. He was going only as far as the nearest sea beach.

He knew that, though he was going only to the sea beach, he was in truth starting upon a journey. He knew the hatred of Zeus would follow him. He knew that now he, Prometheus, could never return to the house of the gods. From this night he must live his life among the men he wished to save.

While the stars came out, bright as they are on nights when winter will soon come on, Prometheus gathered together a heap of driftwood. Opening the metal stalk, he set the flame of the gods in the waiting fuel.

Eating into the wood, the fire leaped up, fanned in the night breeze. Prometheus sat down beside the fire he had made. He was not long alone.

Shadowy figures appeared at the mouths of caves. One by one, men, women, and children crept toward the blaze. The night was cold. North winds had blown that day. The winds had blown on the lands of men, even as they had blown on the head of Zeus in his palace above them. Now in the night they came, the people of men, to the warmth of the beckoning fire.

Hundreds there were of them now. Those nearest the tall fire-bringer, the Titan, were talking with him. They knew him well. It was not the first time Prometheus had come to talk with them. But never before had he come late, alone, and lighted a fire against the dark.

It was not the first time men had seen a fire or felt its warmth. More than once a god, walking the earth, had set a fire, lit from the coals he carried secretly. Men reverenced the slender magic wands with which, it seemed, the gods could call up flame. But never before had they stood so near a fire nor seen the fire-wand.

Now men might hold in their own hands the mysterious yellow rod. They said, "Look" and "See" and, fingering the metal, "How wonderfully the gods can mold what is hard in the hands."

For a while Prometheus let them talk. He watched with pleasure the gleam of firelight in their shining eyes. Then quietly he took the metal stalk from the man who held it. With a swift gesture he threw it into the heap of burning wood.

The people groaned. The fire-wrought metal crumpled against the heat. The metal which carried well a single coal melted in the blazing fire.

The people murmured among themselves, "Hasn't he taken away the secret now? Hasn't he destroyed before our eyes the source of fire?"

Patiently, silently they waited. A few asked questions but got no answers. The cold wind cut them as the last of the burning driftwood grayed and blackened in the sand.

While the embers crumbled away, Prometheus rose, calling with him a few of the men who had asked him questions. Watching, they saw him scrape a hollow pit. Wondering, they followed his every movement, his hands holding a bronze knife, shaving chips of wood, taking from the fold of his cloak handfuls of bark and straw.

Next he set in his pit a chunk of ashwood, flat and firm, notched cleanly on one side. Beneath and around this notch he laid in bark and straw. Into the notch he set a pointed branch, slender, hard-tipped, and firm. Then slowly he swung the branch in his palms, twirled it in a steady rhythm, boring, drilling more and more rapidly with his skilled and powerful hands.

The wood grew warm. The dust ground from the ash block heated to smoldering. The straw caught. Light sputtered from the pit. Small sparks glowed, flew up, went out.

Tugged by the night wind, smoke curled from the dry straw, from the bark, from the wood shavings fed gently from the heap Prometheus had made ready to his hand. At last, more suddenly than the eye could follow, out of the pit in the sand rose the living flame.

Deftly Prometheus removed the ash block, added heavier kindling. Last of all, the driftwood yielded to the strengthening fire. He knelt beside it awhile, breathing upon it, guarding, urging the blaze. At last he rose, stood back, folded his arms. As if considering a thought, half sorrow, half pleasure, he looked up at the glare of fire invading the night sky.

Whispers and murmuring first, then cries, then shouting. Men ran to scoop new hollows in the sand. They begged Prometheus' knife. The children, running from the beach to the caves and fields, hurried back with fists crammed full of straw and withered leaves.

The people of the caves were breathless with excitement. Here was no secret. The fire-wand did not breed the fire as they had thought. No nameless power of the gods bred the flame.

The hard, pale ashwood passed from hand to hand as men struggled to light their own fires. They despaired at first. New sparks flew up and died. Or the hands were weak, too

weak to drill the flame. But at last came triumph. A dozen fires sprang up. Women and children ran with laden arms to feed each growing blaze.

The gods, from their distant houses, saw the glow. There to the south it shone, fighting against the starlight, the glare in the sky. Was it the end of the world? Would the terrible fire consume the earth again?

Hermes, the messenger, came at last with an answer to all their questions.

"Great Zeus," said Hermes gravely in the assembly of the gods, "Prometheus, your cousin, stands in the midst of those rising fires. He took coals from the central hearth as for a journey."

"So?" asked Zeus, nodding his head. Then, as if he were holding an argument with himself, he continued, saying, "But then? What then? The fire will die. It is not a crime for a god or for a Titan to light a fire for himself on a cold evening."

"But that fire will not die," interrupted Hermes. "That fire is not the fire of gods and Titans. Prometheus has taught men the source of fire. Those fires are their own, the fires of men. They've drilled flame out of hardwood with their own hands."

Then the gods knew the end of the world was not yet come upon them. But they knew, and Zeus most of all, that it might be their own great power that was burning away in the fires of men.

SEEKING MEANING

1. The reign of Cronus was known in Greek mythology as the Golden Age. How was life in that age different from life in later times? Why did this "age of contentment" end?
2. Why did Zeus want to destroy the third race of humans? What objections did Prometheus raise? Summarize Prometheus' arguments in your own words.
3. Why was Zeus unwilling to give mortals the gift of fire? Why did Prometheus deliberately disobey Zeus's wishes? Would you call Prometheus a hero? Why or why not?
4. What human characteristics are shown by Zeus and Prometheus in this myth?

DEVELOPING SKILLS IN RESEARCH

Locating Information
The myth of Pandora is part of the Prometheus story. Find the answers to these questions: How did Pandora get her name? What does the myth of Pandora explain?

An encyclopedia is a useful place to start looking for information. If there is no entry under "Pandora," what should you look under?

Whenever you need more information than an encyclopedia provides, find out if there is a special reference book on the subject you are investigating. There are dictionaries and encyclopedias of classical mythology. Your library may have a copy of the *Larousse Encyclopedia of Mythology* or *The Meridian Handbook of Classical Mythology.* Check the entry "Mythology" or "Greek Mythology" or "Classical Mythology" in the card catalog.

You can also find retellings of the myths in special collections of mythology, such as *Mythology* by Edith Hamilton and *Gods, Heroes and Men of Ancient Greece* by W. H. D. Rouse. Use the indexes at the back of these books to locate the Pandora story.

The Origin of the Seasons

Retold by Olivia Coolidge

Demeter,[1] the great earth mother, was goddess of the harvest. Tall and majestic was her appearance, and her hair was the color of ripe wheat. It was she who filled the ears with grain. In her honor white-robed women brought golden garlands of wheat as first fruits to the altar. Reaping, threshing, winnowing, and the long tables set in the shade for the harvesters' refreshment—all these were hers. Songs and feasting did her honor as the hard-working farmer gathered his abundant fruit. All the laws which the farmer knew came from her: the time for plowing, what land would best bear crops, which was fit for grapes, and which to leave for pasture. She was a goddess whom men called "the great mother" because of her generosity in giving. Her own special daughter in the family of the gods was named Persephone.[2]

Persephone was the spring maiden, young and full of joy. Sicily was her home, for it is a land where the spring is long and lovely, and where spring flowers are abundant. Here Persephone played with her maidens from day to day till the rocks and valleys rang with the sound of laughter, and gloomy Hades heard it as he sat on his throne in the dark land of the dead. Even his heart of stone was touched by her gay young beauty, so that he arose in his awful majesty and came up to Olympus to ask Zeus if he might have Persephone to wife.

1. **Demeter** (dĭ-mē′tər).
2. **Persephone** (pər-sĕf′ə-nē).

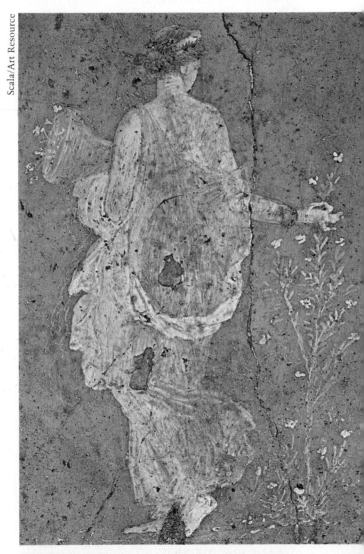

Girl picking flowers. Roman wall painting from house in Stabiae, Italy, 1st century.
National Museum, Naples

Zeus bowed his head in agreement, and mighty Olympus thundered as he promised.

Thus it came about that as Persephone was gathering flowers with her maidens in the vale of Enna, a marvelous thing happened. Enna was a beautiful valley in whose meadows all the most lovely flowers of the year grew at the same season. There were wild roses, purple crocuses, sweet-scented violets, tall irises, rich narcissus, and white lilies. All these the girl was gathering, yet fair as they were, Persephone herself was fairer far.

As the maidens went picking and calling to one another across the blossoming meadow, it happened that Persephone strayed apart from the rest. Then, as she looked a little ahead in the meadow, she suddenly beheld the marvelous thing. It was a flower so beautiful that none like it had ever been known. It seemed a kind of narcissus, purple and white, but from a single root there sprang a hundred blossoms, and at the sweet scent of it the very heavens and earth appeared to smile for joy. Without calling to the others, Persephone sprang forward to be the first to pick the precious bloom. As she stretched out her hand, the earth opened in front of her, and she found herself caught in a stranger's arms. Persephone shrieked aloud and struggled, while the armful of flowers cascaded down to earth. However, the dark-eyed Hades was far stronger than she. He swept her into his golden chariot, took the reins of his coal-black horses, and was gone amid the rumbling sound of the closing earth before the other girls in the valley could even come in sight of the spot. When they did get there, nobody was visible. Only the roses and lilies of Persephone lay scattered in wild confusion over the grassy turf.

Bitter was the grief of Demeter when she heard the news of her daughter's mysterious fate. Veiling herself with a dark cloud she sped, swift as a wild bird, over land and ocean for nine days, searching everywhere and asking all she met if they had seen her daughter. Neither gods nor men had seen her. Even the birds could give no tidings, and Demeter in despair turned to Phoebus Apollo,[3] who sees all things from his chariot in the heavens.

"Yes, I have seen your daughter," said the god at last. "Hades has taken her with the consent of Zeus, that she may dwell in the land of mist and gloom as his queen. The girl struggled and was unwilling, but Hades is far stronger than she."

When she heard this, Demeter fell into deep despair, for she knew she could never rescue Persephone if Zeus and Hades had agreed. She did not care any more to enter the palace of Olympus, where the gods live in joy and feasting and where Apollo plays the lyre while the Muses sing. She took on her the form of an old woman, worn but stately, and wandered about the earth, where there is much sorrow to be seen. At first she kept away from the homes of people, since the sight of little children and happy mothers gave her pain. One day, however, as she sat by the side of a well to rest her weary feet, four girls came down to draw water. They were kindhearted and charming as they talked with her and concerned themselves about the fate of the homeless stranger-woman who was sitting at their gates. To account for herself, Demeter told them that she was a woman of good family from Crete across the sea, who had been captured by pirates and was to have been sold for a slave. She had escaped as they landed once to cook a meal on shore, and now she was wandering to find work.

The four girls listened to this story, much impressed by the stately manner of the

---

3. **Phoebus** (fē′bəs) **Apollo:** Apollo, god of the sun, was sometimes called *Phoebus*, which means "shining."

The Seasons. From an illuminated manuscript,
the Codex Latinum.
State Library, Lucca, Italy

strange woman. At last they said that their mother, Metaneira,[4] was looking for a nurse for their newborn brother, Demophoon.[5] Perhaps the stranger would come and talk with her. Demeter agreed, feeling a great longing to hold a baby once more, even if it were not her own. She went therefore to Metaneira, who was much struck with the quiet dignity of the goddess and glad to give her charge of her little son. For a while thereafter Demeter was nurse to Demophoon, and his smiles and babble consoled her in some part for her own darling daughter. She began to make plans for Demophoon: he should be a great hero; he should become an immortal, so that when he grew up she could keep him with her.

Presently the whole household was amazed at how beautiful Demophoon was growing, the more so as they never saw the nurse feed him anything. Secretly Demeter would anoint him with ambrosia, like the gods, and from her breath as he lay in her lap, he would draw his nourishment. When the night came, she would linger by the great fireside in the hall, rocking the child in her arms while the embers burned low and the people went off to sleep. Then when all was still, she would stoop quickly down and put the baby into the fire itself. All night long the child would sleep in the red-hot ashes, while his earthly flesh and blood changed slowly into the substance of the immortals. In the morning when people came, the ashes were cold and dead, and by the hearth sat the stranger-woman, gently rocking and singing to the child.

Presently Metaneira became suspicious of the strangeness of it all. What did she know of this nurse but the story she had heard from her daughters? Perhaps the woman was a witch of some sort who wished to steal or transform the boy. In any case it was wise to be careful. One night, therefore, when she went up to her chamber, she set the door ajar and stood there in the crack silently watching the nurse at the fireside crooning over the child. The hall was very dark, so that it was hard to see clearly, but in a little while the mother beheld the dim figure bend forward. A log broke in the fireplace, a little flame shot up, and there clear in the light lay the baby on top of the fire.

Metaneira screamed loudly and lost no time in rushing forward, but it was Demeter who snatched up the baby. "Fool that you are," she said indignantly to Metaneira, "I would have made your son immortal, but that is now impossible. He shall be a great hero, but in the end he will have to die. I, the goddess Demeter, promise it." With that, old age fell from her and she grew in stature. Golden hair spread down over her shoulders, so that the great hall was filled with light. She turned and went out of the doorway, leaving the baby on the ground and Metaneira too amazed and frightened even to take him up.

All the while that Demeter had been wandering, she had given no thought to her duties as the harvest goddess. Instead she was almost glad that others should suffer because she was suffering. In vain the oxen spent their strength in dragging the heavy plowshare through the soil. In vain did the sower with his bag of grain throw out the even handfuls of white barley in a wide arc as he strode. The greedy birds had a feast off the seed corn that season, or if it started to sprout, sun baked it and rains washed it away. Nothing would grow. As the gods looked down, they saw threatening the earth a famine such as never had been known. Even the offerings to the gods were neglected by despairing men who could no longer spare anything from their dwindling stores.

---

4. **Metaneira** (mĕt'ə-nī'rə).
5. **Demophoon** (dī-mŏ'fō-ŏn').

At last Zeus sent Iris, the Rainbow, to seek out Demeter and appeal to her to save mankind. Dazzling Iris swept down from Olympus swift as a ray of light and found Demeter sitting in her temple, the dark cloak still around her and her head bowed on her hand. Though Iris urged her with the messages of Zeus and offered beautiful gifts or whatever powers among the gods she chose, Demeter would not lift her head or listen. All she said was that she would neither set foot on Olympus nor let fruit grow on the earth until Persephone was restored to her from the kingdom of the dead.

At last Zeus saw that he must send Hermes of the golden sandals to bring back Persephone to the light. The messenger found dark-haired Hades sitting upon his throne with Persephone beside him, pale and sad. She had neither eaten nor drunk since she had been in the land of the dead. She sprang up with joy at the message of Hermes, while the dark king looked gloomier than ever, for he really loved his queen. Though he could not disobey the command of Zeus, he was crafty, and he pressed Persephone to eat or drink with him as they parted. Now, with joy in her heart, she should not refuse all food. Persephone was eager to be gone; but since the king entreated her, she took a pomegranate[6] from him to avoid argument and delay. Giving in to his pleading, she ate seven of the seeds. Then Hermes took her with him, and she came out into the upper air.

When Demeter saw Hermes with her daughter, she started up, and Persephone too rushed forward with a glad cry and flung her arms about her mother's neck. For a long time the two caressed each other, but at last Demeter began to question the girl. "Did you eat

Hades and Persephone.
National Archaeological Museum, Rome

or drink anything with Hades?'' she asked her daughter anxiously, and the girl replied: "Nothing until Hermes released me. Then in my joy I took a pomegranate and ate seven of its seeds.''

"Alas,'' said the goddess in dismay, "my daughter, what have you done? The Fates have said that if you ate anything in the land of shadow, you must return to Hades and rule with him as his queen. However, you ate not the whole pomegranate, but only seven of the

---

6. **pomegranate** (pŏm'grăn'ĭt): a reddish fruit containing many seeds.

seeds. For seven months of the year, therefore, you must dwell in the underworld, and the remaining five you may live with me."

Thus the Fates had decreed, and even Zeus could not alter their law. For seven months of every year Persephone is lost to Demeter and rules pale and sad over the dead. At this time Demeter mourns, trees shed their leaves, cold comes, and the earth lies still and dead. But when in the eighth month Persephone returns, her mother is glad and the earth rejoices. The wheat springs up, bright, fresh, and green in the plowland. Flowers unfold, birds sing, and young animals are born. Everywhere the heavens smile for joy or weep sudden showers of gladness upon the springing earth.

SEEKING MEANING

1. Although the gods and goddesses had special powers denied to mortals, they often behaved like human beings. How was Demeter, goddess of the harvest, affected by her daughter's disappearance?

2. How was life on earth affected by Demeter's suffering? Why were the gods worried?

3. Tell why Persephone was allowed to return to the earth. Why couldn't she remain all year round?

4. What explanation of the cycle of the seasons is given in this myth?

5. Use the chart on page 476 to find the name of the Roman goddess associated with grains, plants, and fruit. What word do you know that comes from this goddess' name?

DEVELOPING SKILLS OF EXPRESSION

Dramatizing Scenes Based on a Myth

Write a sequel to the story of Demeter, Persephone, and Hades in the form of a play. Begin the action of your play where the action of the myth ends. You might try writing some of the following scenes:

Demeter and Persephone say goodbye as winter approaches and it is time for Persephone to leave.

Hades welcomes Persephone as she arrives in the underworld.

Demeter complains to the other gods and goddesses on Mount Olympus that she does not like her son-in-law.

Persephone returns to the earth in spring.

Through the power of a god or goddess, a human being could be changed into a plant, an animal, or a constellation. There are many stories of such transformations in classical mythology. The Greek word for "transformation" is metamorphosis, *a word scientists now use to describe the changes during the life cycles of such creatures as the butterfly and the frog.*

In mythology, metamorphosis is sudden and magical. Here are two stories about metamorphosis. In each case, the metamorphosis explains how something in nature came to be.

Arachne°
Retold by Rex Warner

Arachne was famous not for her birth or for her city, but only for her skill. Her father was a dyer of wool; her mother also was of no great family. She lived in a small village whose name is scarcely known. Yet her skill in weaving made her famous through all the great cities of Lydia. To see her wonderful work the nymphs of Tmolus would leave their vineyards, the nymphs of Pactolus would leave the golden waters of their river. It was a delight not only to see the cloth that she had woven, but to watch her at work, there was such beauty in the way she did it, whether she was winding the rough skeins into balls of wool, or smoothing it with her fingers, or drawing out the fleecy shiny wool into threads, or giving a twist to the spindle with her quick thumb, or putting in embroidery with her needle. You would think that she had learned the art from Minerva herself, the goddess of weaving.

Arachne, however, when people said this, would be offended at the idea of having had even so great a teacher as Minerva. "Let her come," she used to say, "and weave against me. If she won, she could do what she liked with me."

Minerva heard her words and put on the form of an old woman. She put false gray hair on her head, made her steps weak and tottering, and took a staff in her hand. Then she said to Arachne: "There are some advantages in old age. Long years bring experience. Do not, then, refuse my advice. Seek all the fame you like among men for your skill, but allow the goddess to take first place, and ask her forgiveness, you foolish girl, for the words which you have spoken. She will forgive you if you ask her."

Arachne dropped the threads from her hand and looked angrily at the old woman. She hardly kept her hands off her, and her face showed the anger that she felt. Then she spoke to the goddess in disguise: "Stupid old thing, what is wrong with you is that you

---

°**Arachne** (ə-răk′nē).

Detail from *The Month of March: The Triumph of Minerva*. Fresco by
Francesco del Cossa (1436–1478). Minerva was the patron of
household arts such as weaving and embroidery.
Palazzo Schiffanoia, Ferrara, Italy

have lived too long. Go and give advice to
your daughters, if you have any. I am quite
able to look after myself. As for what you say,
why does not the goddess come here herself?
Why does she avoid a contest with me?"

"She has come," Minerva replied, and she
put off the old woman's disguise, revealing
herself in her true form. The nymphs bowed
down to worship her, and the women also

who were there. Arachne alone showed no
fear. Nevertheless she started,[1] and a sudden
blush came to her unwilling face and then
faded away again, as the sky grows crimson at
the moment of sunrise and then again grows
pale. She persisted in what she had said al-

---

1. **started:** here, made a sudden movement from fear or
surprise.

ready, and stupidly longing for the desired victory, rushed headlong to her fate.

Minerva no longer refused the contest and gave no further advice. At once they both set up their looms and stretched out on them the delicate warp. The web was fastened to the beam; reeds separated the threads and through the threads went the sharp shuttles which their quick fingers sped. Quickly they worked, with their clothes tucked up round their breasts, their skilled hands moving backward and forward like lightning, not feeling the work since they were both so good at it. In their weaving they used all the colors that are made by the merchants of Tyre — purple of the oyster and every other dye, each shading into each, so that the eye could scarcely tell the difference between the finer shades, though the extreme colors were clear enough. So, after a storm of rain, when a rainbow spans the sky, between each color there is a great difference, but still between each an insensible shading. And in their work they wove in stiff threads of gold, telling ancient stories by pictures.

Minerva, in her weaving, showed the ancient citadel of Athens and the story of the old quarrel between her and Neptune, god of the sea, over the naming of this famous land.[2] There you could see the twelve gods as witnesses, and there Neptune striking with his huge trident[3] the barren rock from which leaped a stream of sea water. And there was Minerva herself, with shield and spear and helmet. As she struck the rock there sprang up a green olive tree, and the victory was hers. Athens was her city, named from her other name, Athene.

As for Arachne, the pictures which she wove were of the deceitful loves of the gods. There was Europa, carried away by a bull over the sea. You would have thought it a real bull and real waves of water. Then she wove Jupiter coming to Danae in a golden shower, to Aegina as a flame, to Mnemosyne,[4] mother of the Muses, in the disguise of a shepherd. There was Neptune too, disguised as a dolphin, a horse, or a ram. Every scene was different, and each scene had the surroundings that it ought to have. Round the edge of the web ran a narrow border filled with designs of flowers and sprays of ivy intertwined.

Neither Minerva nor Envy itself could find any fault with Arachne's work. Furious at the success of the mortal girl, Minerva tore to pieces the gorgeous web with its stories of the crimes of the gods. With the hard boxwood spindle that she held, she struck Arachne on the head over and over again.

Arachne could not bear such treatment. In her injured pride she put a noose round her neck and hanged herself. As she hung from the rope, Minerva, in pity, lifted her body and said: "You may keep your life, you rude and arrogant girl, but you and all your descendants will still hang."

Then, as she went out, she sprinkled over her some magic juices, and immediately her hair felt the poison it fell off; so did her nose and ears; her head became minute and all her body shrunk; her slender fingers were joined onto her body as legs; everything else was stomach and now, turned into a spider, she still spins threads out of her own stomach and everywhere still exercises her old craft of weaving.

---

2. **the naming . . . land:** a reference to a contest that was held to see which god could give the better gift to the city and thus become its protector.
3. **trident** (trīd′ənt): a spear with three prongs.

4. **Europa** (yōō-rō′pə); **Danae** (dăn′ə-ē′); **Aegina** (ē-jī′nə); **Mnemosyne** (nĭ-mŏs′ə-nē): women loved by Jupiter. Danae was the mother of the hero Perseus.

The Reward of Baucis and Philemon°

Retold by Sally Benson

Once upon a time, Jupiter assumed human shape and taking his son Mercury journeyed to Phrygia.[1] Mercury had left his wings behind so that no one would know he was a god, and the two presented themselves from door to door as weary travelers, seeking rest and shelter. They found all doors closed to them as it was late, and the inhospitable inhabitants would not bother to let them in. At last, they came to a small thatched cottage where Baucis, a feeble old woman, and her husband, Philemon, lived. They were a kindly couple, not ashamed of their poverty, and when the two strangers knocked at their door, they bade them enter. The old man placed a seat, on which Baucis, bustling and attentive, spread a cloth, and begged his guests to sit down. Then Baucis raked out the coals from the ashes and kindled up a fire, fed it with leaves and dry bark, and with her scanty breath blew it into flames. She brought split sticks and dry branches out of a corner, broke them up, and placed them under a small kettle. Philemon collected some potherbs in the garden, and she shred them from the stalks and prepared them for the pot. He reached down with a forked stick a flitch of bacon hanging in the chimney, cut a small piece, and put it in the pot to boil with the herbs. A beechen bowl was filled with warm water, that their guests might wash. Host and visitors talked amicably together.

On the bench designed for the guests, a cushion stuffed with seaweed was laid; and a cloth, only produced on great occasions, was spread over that. The old lady, with her apron on, set the table with trembling hands. When the table was fixed, she rubbed it down with sweet-smelling herbs, and upon it she set some of chaste Minerva's olives, some cornel berries preserved in vinegar, and added radishes and cheese, with eggs lightly cooked in the ashes. Everything was served in earthenware dishes, and an earthenware pitcher with wooden cups stood beside them. When all was ready, the stew, smoking hot, was set on the table. Some wine, mild and sweet, was served, and for desert they offered wild apples and honey. Over and above all, there were the friendly faces and simple, hearty welcome of the old couple.

As the visitors ate and drank, Baucis and Philemon were astonished to see that the wine, as fast as it was poured out, renewed itself in the pitcher. Struck with terror, they recognized their heavenly guests and, falling to their knees, implored forgiveness for the poor entertainment. They had an old goose which they kept as the guardian of their humble cottage and they decided to sacrifice him in honor of their illustrious visitors. But the goose was too nimble and eluded the elderly

---

°**Baucis** (bô′sĭs); **Philemon** (fĭ-lē′mən).
1. **Phrygia** (frĭj′ē-ə): an ancient country in western Asia, now part of Turkey.

Detail from *Philemon and Baucis.* Oil painting by Rembrandt van Rijn (1606–1669).
National Gallery of Art, Washington, D. C.   Widener Collection

couple, and at last he took shelter between the gods themselves.

Jupiter and Mercury forbade it to be slain, and spoke in these words: "We are gods. This inhospitable village shall pay the penalty of its impiety. You alone shall go free from the chastisement. Quit your house and come with us to the top of yonder hill."

Baucis and Philemon hastened to obey and labored up the steep ascent. They had reached up to an arrow's flight of the top, when they beheld all the country they had left sunk into a lake, only their own house left standing. While they gazed with wonder at the sight, their house was changed into a temple. Columns took the place of the corner posts, the thatch grew yellow and turned to gold, the floors became marble, the doors were enriched with exquisite carvings and ornaments of gold.

Then Jupiter spoke to them kindly. "Excellent old man, and woman worthy of such a husband," he said, "speak! Tell us your wishes. What favor have you to ask us?"

Philemon whispered to his wife for a few minutes, and then declared to the gods their united wish. "We ask to be priests and guardians of this your temple. And since we have passed our lives in love and concord, we wish that one and the same hour may take us both from life, that I may not live to see her grave nor be laid in my own by her."

Their prayers were granted. They were keepers of the temple as long as they lived. When they were very old, as they stood one day before the steps of the sacred temple and were telling the story of the place to some visitors, Baucis saw Philemon begin to put forth leaves, and old Philemon saw Baucis changing in a like manner. And now a leafy crown had grown over their heads. As long as they could speak they exchanged parting words. "Farewell, dear spouse," they said together, as the bark closed over their mouths.

Still on a certain hill in Phrygia, stand a linden tree and an oak enclosed by a low wall. Not far from the spot is a marsh, formerly good habitable land, but now dotted with pools, the haunt of fen birds and cormorants.[2] They are all that is left of the town and of Baucis and Philemon.

---

2. **fen birds and cormorants** (kôr′mər-ənts): birds that inhabit watery land.

SEEKING MEANING

"Arachne"

1. The ancient Greeks connected many things in nature with the actions of gods and mortals. How does the myth of Arachne explain the characteristics of the spider?

2. The myth of Arachne reveals that human beings could choose to please or offend the gods. What sin did Arachne commit?

3. What lesson do you think the ancient Greeks drew from the myth of Arachne?

"The Reward of Baucis and Philemon"

4. Why did Jupiter and Mercury punish the inhabitants of Phrygia? How was the metamorphosis of Baucis and Philemon a reward?

5. What lesson do you think was drawn from the myth of Baucis and Philemon?

DEVELOPING SKILLS IN RESEARCH

Using Reference Books

Here are the names of some other figures in Greek mythology who were transformed by the gods:

Adonis	Daphne	Narcissus
Alcyone	Echo	Orion
Clytie	Hyacinthus	Scylla

Choose one of these characters and find out: 1) why the person was transformed, 2) what the person was transformed into, and 3) which god or goddess was involved in the story. Then tell the story to the class in your own words.

You might begin your research by consulting a dictionary or an encyclopedia. If there is no entry in the encyclopedia under the character's name, see if the character is mentioned in the general article on "Mythology." Perhaps the encyclopedia will have a special entry on "Greek Mythology" or "Classical Mythology." Consult the special reference books listed on page 484.

DEVELOPING SKILLS OF EXPRESSION

Writing a Story About Metamorphosis

Choose some natural object, and write an original story explaining how and why someone was transformed into the object. Here are some suggestions:

a butterfly	an octopus
a diamond	a violet
a giraffe	a water lily
a lobster	a weeping willow
a mosquito	a whale

Decide which classical gods and goddesses might play a part in your story.

Classical Mythology in Today's World

The *zodiac* is an imaginary belt in the sky, divided into twelve parts called *signs* of the zodiac. Each of the signs is named for a different constellation. On its path through the sky, the sun passes through this imaginary circle, spending one month in each of the twelve parts.

The signs of the zodiac are shown on these pages. The first sign of the zodiac is *Aries,* "the ram." The second sign of the zodiac is *Taurus,* "the bull." The other signs, in order, are *Gemini,* "the twins"; *Cancer,* "the crab"; *Leo,* "the lion"; *Virgo,* "the maiden"; *Libra,* "the balance"; *Scorpio,* "the scorpion"; *Sagittarius,* "the archer"; *Capricorn,* "the horned goat"; *Aquarius,* "the water-bearer"; and *Pisces,* "the fish."

Each person has a sign determined by his or her date of birth. Find out what your sign is by looking up the entry for *zodiac* in a dictionary or an encyclopedia.

Find out how each of these signs is connected with classical mythology. (Consult the reference books listed on page 484.)

Aries	Leo	Capricorn
Cancer	Sagittarius	Pisces

Zodiac. From a 14th-century manuscript, Liber Astrologiae. Bibliothèque Nationale, Paris

Many of the constellations are named for figures in classical mythology. Locate, read, and summarize a myth associated with one of these constellations:

Andromeda   Perseus
Cassiopeia   Pleiades
Cepheus   Ursa Major (Big Dipper)
Cygnus   Ursa Minor (Little Dipper)

In this detail from a decorative cup, Zeus is shown holding a *cornucopia*. With what American holiday is this symbol associated? Find out why the cornucopia is associated with Zeus.

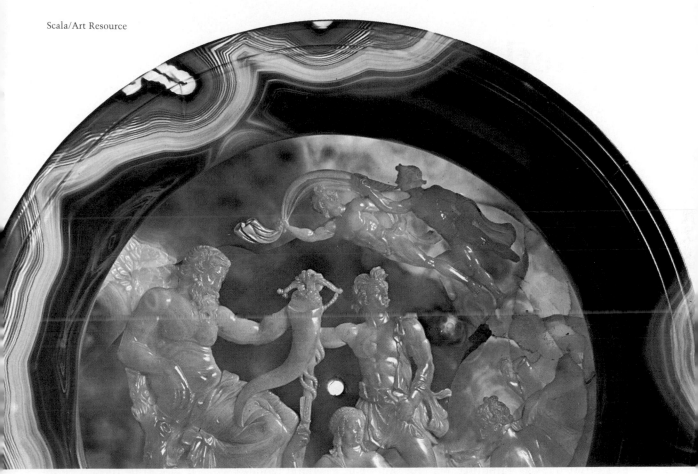

Farnese Cup, 2nd century B.C.
National Museum, Naples

Seven of the chemical elements in this list are named for figures in classical mythology. Identify the seven elements and the figures for whom they are named.

antimony	helium	plutonium
californium	krypton	selenium
cerium	mercury	uranium
einsteinium	neptunium	yttrium

Classical Mythology in Today's World   501

In classical mythology there are many stories of mortals who attempt too much, who try to rival the powers of the gods and goddesses. This is the story of a boy who for a few moments "felt himself the lord of the sky."

Phaethon°

Retold by Edith Hamilton

The palace of the Sun was a radiant place. It shone with gold and gleamed with ivory and sparkled with jewels. Everything without and within flashed and glowed and glittered. It was always high noon there. Shadowy twilight never dimmed the brightness. Darkness and night were unknown. Few among mortals could have long endured that unchanging brilliancy of light, but few had ever found their way thither.

Nevertheless, one day a youth, mortal on his mother's side, dared to approach. Often he had to pause and clear his dazzled eyes, but the errand which had brought him was so urgent that his purpose held fast and he pressed on, up to the palace, through the burnished doors, and into the throne room where surrounded by a blinding, blazing splendor the sun god sat. There the lad was forced to halt. He could bear no more.

Nothing escapes the eyes of the Sun. He saw the boy instantly and he looked at him very kindly. "What brought you here?" he asked.

"I have come," the other answered boldly, "to find out if you are my father or not. My mother said you were, but the boys at school laugh when I tell them I am your son. They will not believe me. I told my mother and she said I had better go and ask you."

Smiling, the Sun took off his crown of burning light so that the lad could look at him without distress. "Come here, Phaethon," he said. "You are my son. Clymene[1] told you the truth. I expect you will not doubt my word too? But I will give you a proof. Ask anything you want of me and you shall have it. I call the Styx[2] to be witness to my promise, the river of the oath of the gods."

No doubt Phaethon had often watched the Sun riding through the heavens and had told himself with a feeling, half awe, half excitement, "It is my father up there." And then he would wonder what it would be like to be in that chariot, guiding the steeds along that dizzy course, giving light to the world. Now at his father's words this wild dream had become possible. Instantly he cried, "I choose to take your place, Father. That is the only thing I want. Just for a day, a single day, let me have your car to drive."

The Sun realized his own folly. Why had he

°**Phaethon** (fā′ə-thən).

1. **Clymene** (klĭm′ə-nē).
2. **Styx** (stĭks): one of the rivers in the underworld.

Ship of the Line: A View of the Stern Between Two Galleys. An interpretation of
the Phaethon myth by Pieter Brueghel the Elder (1522–1569).
The Metropolitan Museum of Art, New York

Rogers Fund, 1921

taken that fatal oath and bound himself to
give in to anything that happened to enter a
boy's rash young head? "Dear lad," he said,
"this is the only thing I would have refused
you. I know I cannot refuse. I have sworn by
the Styx. I must yield if you persist. But I do

not believe you will. Listen while I tell you
what this is you want. You are Clymene's son
as well as mine. You are mortal and no mortal
could drive my chariot. Indeed, no god except
myself can do that. The ruler of the gods cannot. Consider the road. It rises up from the sea

so steeply that the horses can hardly climb it, fresh though they are in the early morning. In midheaven it is so high that even I do not like to look down. Worst of all is the descent, so precipitous that the sea gods waiting to receive me wonder how I can avoid falling headlong. To guide the horses, too, is a perpetual struggle. Their fiery spirits grow hotter as they climb and they scarcely suffer[3] my control. What would they do with you?

"Are you fancying that there are all sorts of wonders up there, cities of the gods full of beautiful things? Nothing of the kind. You will have to pass beasts, fierce beasts of prey, and they are all that you will see. The Bull, the Lion, the Scorpion, the great Crab, each will try to harm you. Be persuaded. Look around you. See all the goods the rich world holds. Choose from them your heart's desire and it shall be yours. If what you want is to be proved my son, my fears for you are proof enough that I am your father."

But none of all this wise talk meant anything to the boy. A glorious prospect opened before him. He saw himself proudly standing in that wondrous car, his hands triumphantly guiding those steeds which Jove himself could not master. He did not give a thought to the dangers his father detailed. He felt not a quiver of fear, not a doubt of his own powers. At last the Sun gave up trying to dissuade him. It was hopeless, as he saw. Besides, there was no time. The moment for starting was at hand. Already the gates of the east glowed purple, and Dawn had opened her courts full of rosy light. The stars were leaving the sky; even the lingering morning star was dim.

There was need for haste, but all was ready. The Seasons, the gatekeepers of Olympus, stood waiting to fling the doors wide. The

horses had been bridled and yoked to the car. Proudly and joyously Phaethon mounted it and they were off. He had made his choice. Whatever came of it he could not change now. Not that he wanted to in that first exhilarating rush through the air, so swift that the East Wind was outstripped and left far behind. The horses' flying feet went through the low-banked clouds near the ocean as through a thin sea mist and then up and up in the clear air, climbing the height of heaven. For a few ecstatic moments Phaethon felt himself the lord of the sky. But suddenly there was a change. The chariot was swinging wildly to and fro; the pace was faster; he had lost control. Not he, but the horses were directing the course. That light weight in the car, those feeble hands clutching the reins, had told them their own driver was not there. They were the masters then. No one else could command them. They left the road and rushed where they chose, up, down, to the right, to the left. They nearly wrecked the chariot against the Scorpion; they brought up short and almost ran into the Crab. By this time the poor charioteer was half fainting with terror, and he let the reins fall.

That was the signal for still more mad and reckless running. The horses soared up to the very top of the sky and then, plunging headlong down, they set the world on fire. The highest mountains were the first to burn, Ida and Helicon, where the Muses dwell, Parnassus, and heaven-piercing Olympus. Down their slopes the flame ran to the low-lying valleys and the dark forest lands, until all things everywhere were ablaze. The springs turned into steam; the rivers shrank. It is said that it was then the Nile fled and hid his head, which still is hidden.

In the car Phaethon, hardly keeping his place there, was wrapped in thick smoke and heat as if from a fiery furnace. He wanted

---

3. **suffer:** here, bear.

nothing except to have this torment and terror ended. He would have welcomed death. Mother Earth, too, could bear no more. She uttered a great cry which reached up to the gods. Looking down from Olympus they saw that they must act quickly if the world was to be saved. Jove seized his thunderbolt and hurled it at the rash, repentant driver. It struck him dead, shattered the chariot, and made the maddened horses rush down into the sea.

Phaethon all on fire fell from the car through the air to the earth. The mysterious river Eridanus, which no mortal eyes have ever seen, received him and put out the flames and cooled the body. The naiads,[4] in pity for him, so bold and so young to die, buried him and carved upon the tomb:

Here Phaethon lies who drove the sun god's
  car.
Greatly he failed, but he had greatly dared.

His sisters, the Heliades, the daughters of Helios,[5] the Sun, came to his grave to mourn for him. There they were turned into poplar trees, on the bank of the Eridanus,

Where sorrowing they weep into the stream
  forever.
And each tear as it falls shines in the water
A glistening drop of amber.

---

4. **naiads** (nā′ădz): nymphs who lived in rivers, springs, and lakes.

5. **Helios** (hē′lē-ŏs′): an early Greek sun god, later identified with Apollo.

SEEKING MEANING

1. According to this myth, what explanation did the ancient Greeks have for the rising and setting of the sun?
2. Why did Phaethon want to drive his father's chariot?
3. Why was Helios forced to keep his promise to Phaethon? What arguments did he use in an attempt to change his son's mind? Why was he unsuccessful?
4. What happened to the earth when Phaethon lost control of the chariot?
5. The inscription carved on Phaethon's tomb read: "Greatly he failed, but he had greatly dared." Was Phaethon's adventure an act of great daring or great folly? Explain your answer.

ABOUT THE AUTHOR

Edith Hamilton (1867–1963) became interested in the ancient Greek and Roman civilizations when she was very young. However, she did not begin writing about these ancient civilizations until she was sixty-three and had already had a career as the headmistress of a girls' school. One of her best-known works, *The Greek Way*, is a study of the life and thought of ancient Greece. She followed this book with *The Roman Way*, a study of ancient Roman civilization. *Mythology*, from which "Phaethon" is taken, contains retellings of Greek, Roman, and Norse myths. For her contributions to the study of ancient Greece, she was made an honorary citizen of Athens.

*In this poem, the sun god
is identified as Apollo.*

Phaethon   *Morris Bishop*

Apollo through the heavens rode
   In glinting gold attire;
His car was bright with chrysolite,°
   His horses snorted fire.
He held them to their frantic course   5
   Across the blazing sky.
His darling son was Phaethon,
   Who begged to have a try.

"The chargers are ambrosia-fed,
   They barely brook control;   10
On high beware the Crab, the Bear,
   The Serpent round the Pole;
Against the Archer and the Bull
   Thy form is all unsteeled!"°
But Phaethon could lay it on;   15
   Apollo had to yield.

Out of the purple doors of dawn
   Phaethon drove the horses;
They felt his hand could not command.
   They left their wonted° courses.   20
And from the chariot Phaethon
   Plunged like a falling star—
And so, my boy, no, no, my boy,
   You cannot take the car.

3. **chrysolite** (krĭs′ə-līt′): a greenish, transparent gem.

14. **unsteeled:** unprotected.

20. **wonted** (wôn′tĭd): habitual.

Study: *Falling Man* (1966). Silicon bronze by Ernest Trova.
Collection of Whitney Museum of American Art, New York

SEEKING MEANING

1. To whom is the speaker in this poem talking? Why does he tell this person the story of Phaethon?

2. The Serpent in line 12 is the constellation Draco, which is also called the Dragon. Identify the Crab, Bear, Archer, and Bull mentioned in lines 11 and 13.

3. Morris Bishop's story differs from Edith Hamilton's retelling of the myth in certain details. What differences can you find?

DEVELOPING VOCABULARY

Learning Words from the Myths

Helios, the early sun god, has given his name to a number of English words. Whenever you see a word that begins with *helio-*, you can be sure that it has something to do with the sun.

Find the meanings of these words and use each one in a sentence:

heliocentric   heliotherapy
heliograph   heliotropic

DEVELOPING SKILLS OF EXPRESSION

Using Specific Words in Description

Compare the italicized verbs in these two descriptions of the Sun's palace:

> It *was covered* with gold and ivory and jewels. Everything inside and outside *was* very bright and shiny.

> It *shone* with gold and *gleamed* with ivory and *sparkled* with jewels. Everything within and without *flashed* and *glowed* and *glittered*.

In the second description, all six verbs specify different ways of sending out light.

Selene, Helios' sister, was an early moon goddess, later identified with Artemis. The ancient Greeks believed that Selene drove the chariot of the moon across the sky. Imagine what Selene, her palace, and her chariot looked like. Write a description, using specific verbs to describe the colors, sights, and sounds of the moon goddess' palace, or of her chariot.

Phaethon 507

Icarus and Daedalus

Retold by Josephine Preston Peabody

Among all those mortals who grew so wise that they learned the secrets of the gods, none was more cunning than Daedalus.

He once built, for King Minos of Crete,[1] a wonderful Labyrinth[2] of winding ways so cunningly tangled up and twisted around that, once inside, you could never find your way out again without a magic clue.[3] But the King's favor veered with the wind, and one day he had his master architect imprisoned in a tower. Daedalus managed to escape from his cell; but it seemed impossible to leave the island, since every ship that came or went was well guarded by order of the King.

At length, watching the sea gulls in the air —the only creatures that were sure of liberty —he thought of a plan for himself and his young son Icarus, who was captive with him.

Little by little, he gathered a store of feathers great and small. He fastened these together with thread, molded them in with wax, and so fashioned two great wings like those of a bird. When they were done, Daedalus fitted them to his own shoulders, and after one or two efforts, he found that by waving his arms

The Fall of Icarus. An 18th-century etching by Bernard Picart.
Museum of Fine Arts, Boston
Harvey D. Parker collection

°**Daedalus** (dĕd′l-əs).
1. **King Minos** (mī′nŏs′) **of Crete:** Minos was a son of Zeus. Crete is a large island southeast of the Greek mainland.
2. **Labyrinth** (lăb′ə-rĭnth).
3. **clue:** here, a ball of thread. Theseus, an Athenian hero, was able to escape by tying one end of the thread to the entrance, unwinding the ball as he went in, and rewinding it as he came out.

he could winnow[4] the air and cleave it, as a swimmer does the sea. He held himself aloft, wavered this way and that with the wind, and at last, like a great fledgling, he learned to fly.

Without delay, he fell to work on a pair of wings for the boy Icarus and taught him carefully how to use them, bidding him beware of rash adventures among the stars. "Remember," said the father, "never to fly very low or very high, for the fogs about the earth would weigh you down, but the blaze of the sun will surely melt your feathers apart if you go too near."

For Icarus, these cautions went in at one ear and out by the other. Who could remember to be careful when he was to fly for the first time? Are birds careful? Not they! And not an idea remained in the boy's head but the one joy of escape.

The day came, and the fair wind that was to set them free. The father-bird put on his wings, and, while the light urged them to be gone, he waited to see that all was well with Icarus, for the two could not fly hand in hand. Up they rose, the boy after his father. The hateful ground of Crete sank beneath them; and the country folk, who caught a glimpse of them when they were high above the tree-tops, took it for a vision of the gods — Apollo, perhaps, with Cupid after him.

At first there was a terror in the joy. The wide vacancy of the air dazed them — a glance downward made their brains reel. But when a great wind filled their wings, and Icarus felt himself sustained, like a halcyon bird[5] in the hollow of a wave, like a child uplifted by his mother, he forgot everything in the world but joy. He forgot Crete and the other islands that he had passed over: he saw but vaguely that

winged thing in the distance before him that was his father Daedalus. He longed for one draft of flight to quench the thirst of his captivity: he stretched out his arms to the sky and made toward the highest heavens.

Alas for him! Warmer and warmer grew the air. Those arms, that had seemed to uphold him, relaxed. His wings wavered, dropped. He fluttered his young hands vainly — he was falling — and in that terror he remembered. The heat of the sun had melted the wax from his wings; the feathers were falling, one by one, like snowflakes; and there was none to help.

He fell like a leaf tossed down by the wind, down, down, with one cry that overtook Daedalus far away. When he returned and sought high and low for the poor boy, he saw nothing but the birdlike feathers afloat on the water, and he knew that Icarus was drowned.

The nearest island he named Icaria, in memory of the child; but he, in heavy grief, went to the temple of Apollo in Sicily and there hung up his wings as an offering. Never again did he attempt to fly.

SEEKING MEANING

1. At the opening of the myth, you are told that Daedalus was so cunning that he learned the secrets of the gods. Do you think he was punished for his knowledge? Explain your answer.

2. Both Icarus and Phaethon fell from the sky to their deaths. Compare them. How are they alike, and how are they different?

3. Myths often show what attitudes and behavior were expected of human beings. What lesson might have been drawn from the myth of Icarus and Daedalus about obedience to the laws of nature? About obedience of young people to their elders?

---

4. **winnow:** beat.
5. **halcyon** (hăl′sē-ən) **bird:** a legendary bird, identified with the kingfisher, which supposedly had the power of calming the winter seas.

To a Friend Whose Work Has Come to Triumph

Anne Sexton

Consider Icarus, pasting those sticky wings on,
testing that strange little tug at his shoulder blade,
and think of that first flawless moment over the lawn
of the labyrinth. Think of the difference it made!
There below are the trees, as awkward as camels;   5
and here are the shocked starlings pumping past
and think of innocent Icarus who is doing quite well:
larger than a sail, over the fog and the blast
of the plushy ocean, he goes. Admire his wings!
Feel the fire at his neck and see how casually   10
he glances up and is caught, wondrously tunneling
into that hot eye. Who cares that he fell back to the sea?
See him acclaiming the sun and come plunging down
while his sensible daddy goes straight into town.

SEEKING MEANING

This poem is addressed to someone whose work has been successful. According to the poem, was Icarus' death a defeat or a victory? Which lines support your answer?

DEVELOPING VOCABULARY

Learning Words from the Myths

Have you ever solved a puzzle like this one? It's called a *labyrinth* or a *maze*. Daedalus built the original Labyrinth in Crete to house the Minotaur, a monster that was half man and half bull. King Minos ordered young men and women to be fed to the Minotaur. The Labyrinth kept them from escaping.

We now use the word *labyrinth* to mean any complicated system of passageways and dead ends. The word *labyrinth* may also be used for anything that is intricate or confusing. The poet Tennyson has referred to "the *labyrinth* of the mind." What do you think the word means in this phrase?

DEVELOPING SKILLS IN RESEARCH

Tracking Down an Allusion

The authors of the poems that appear on pages 506 and 510 expect their readers to recognize the characters and events in certain classical myths. Readers who know these myths can better understand and appreciate the poems.

Writers often use references to characters and events from classical mythology. In these lines from *Childe Harold's Pilgrimage*, Byron, an English poet, compares the Rome of his day to Niobe, a character in mythology:

> The Niobe of nations! there she stands,
> Childless and crownless, in her voiceless
>   woe.

Such a reference as this is known as an *allusion*. What does modern Rome, fallen from its past grandeur as a great empire, have in common with Niobe? In order to understand what Byron means, you need to find out Niobe's story.

You might begin tracking down this allusion by looking in a dictionary:

Ni·o·be (nī′ō bē), *n. Class. Myth.* the daughter of Tantalus and wife of Amphion of Thebes; her children were slain and Zeus turned her into stone, in which state she continued to weep over her loss.

This entry tells why Niobe was childless and why she was voiceless—she was turned to stone. But the entry does not tell why her children were slain or why Zeus turned her to stone. A different dictionary may give more information. An encyclopedia may also tell more of Niobe's story. Your best source, however, is a book of myths or an encyclopedia of mythology. Consult one of the sources suggested on page 484.

The expression "Achilles' heel" is used to refer to a person's special weakness. Locate the story of Achilles and find out how that expression came into being.

Classical Mythology in Today's World

Gymnast.

The Fight in the Amphitheater. Roman fresco.
National Museum, Naples

Scala/Art Resource

The symbol of interlocking rings carved in the stone marker (shown above right) is the symbol of the Olympic Games. In classical times the Olympic Games were a festival held every four years at Olympia, a plain in the southern part of Greece, to honor Zeus. The festival was first celebrated in 776 B.C. and was discontinued in A.D. 394. It consisted of contests not only in sports but also in poetry and music. The events included foot races, chariot racing, the discus throw, the javelin throw, the broad jump, boxing, wrestling, and the pentathlon (a contest of five events). Greek women did not participate in the Olympic Games, but held games of their own called *Heraea*, in honor of the goddess Hera. The modern international revival of the Olympic Games began at Athens in 1896.

Discus thrower.

Discus Thrower. After a statue by Myron, 5th century B.C. Museo Nazionale delle Terme, Rome

Soccer game at the 1972 Olympics in Munich, Germany.

Gymnasts. Mosaic.
Piazza Amerina

Classical Mythology in Today's World   513

Throughout this unit you have been learning about English words that come from the myths. Many more words and phrases can be traced to classical mythology. What words can you think of that come from the names of these figures?

Hygeia, a Greek goddess of health
Hypnos, a Greek god of sleep
Oceanus, a Titan who was the father of the river gods and
    sea nymphs

Which planets are named for gods and goddesses of classical mythology? Use a dictionary to check your answers.

Several of our months get their names from figures in classical mythology. Which months are they and for what figures are they named?

Use a dictionary to find the origin of these words:

giant	psychology
lethargic	tantalize
music	titanic
panic	volcano

A book of maps is called an *atlas.* The word comes from the name of a figure in classical mythology. Find out who Atlas was and explain his connection with maps.

Many towns and cities in the United States have been named for characters or places in classical mythology. Here are some of them:

Atlas (Illinois, Michigan)
Hercules (California)
Juno Beach (Florida)
Jupiter (North Carolina)
Mercury (Nevada, Texas)
Mount Olympus (Utah, Washington)
Olympia (California, Kentucky, Washington)
Venus (Florida, Nebraska, Pennsylvania, Texas)

Are the names of any towns or cities in your state derived from classical mythology? Consult an almanac or an atlas.

The city of *Carthage* figures in the story of Aeneas and Dido. Aeneas was a Trojan. When Troy fell to the Greeks at the end of the Trojan War, Aeneas and many of his people escaped and began searching for a new homeland. Find out how Aeneas came to Carthage and what happened to Dido after he left.

Rome is named for Romulus. Look up the myth of Romulus and Remus. Find out how Rome, the City of the Seven Hills, was founded.

Sparta is associated in mythology with King Menelaus, who was married to Helen, the most beautiful woman in the world. Find out how Helen is connected with the Trojan War.

The island of *Ithaca* was the home of Odysseus, or Ulysses, one of the Greek heroes who fought in the Trojan War. Find out how Odysseus was responsible for the fall of Troy and why he was forced to wander for ten years before he reached his home.

What relationship is there between these place names and the characters and events in classical mythology?

Atlantic Ocean
Europe
Hellespont
Icarian Sea

The greatest hero in ancient Greece was Heracles, whose Roman name was Hercules. He was the strongest man on earth. Like many other heroes in classical mythology, he was the son of a god (Zeus) and a mortal (Alcmene). Throughout his life he suffered from fits of madness that the goddess Hera sent to plague him. In one of his fits, he killed his wife and children. In order to be purified of his crime, he sought the help of a priestess of Apollo, who brought him the message of the god: For twelve long years he was to serve as a slave, carrying out all-but-impossible labors.

The Adventures of Hercules

Retold by Edith Hamilton

Eurystheus[1] was by no means stupid, but of a very ingenious turn of mind, and when the strongest man on earth came to him humbly prepared to be his slave, he devised a series of penances which from the point of view of difficulty and danger could not have been improved upon. It must be said, however, that he was helped and urged on by Hera. To the end of Hercules' life she never forgave him for being Zeus's son. The tasks Eurystheus gave him to do are called "the labors of Hercules." There were twelve of them and each one was all but impossible.

The first was to kill the lion of Nemea, a beast no weapons could wound. That difficulty Hercules solved by choking the life out of him. Then he heaved the huge carcass up on his back and carried it into Mycenae.[2]

After that, Eurystheus, a cautious man, would not let him inside the city. He gave him his orders from afar.

The second labor was to go to Lerna and kill a creature with nine heads called the Hydra, which lived in a swamp there. This was exceedingly hard to do, because one of the heads was immortal and the others almost as bad, inasmuch as when Hercules chopped off one, two grew up instead. However, he was helped by his nephew Iolaus,[3] who brought him a burning brand with which he seared the neck as he cut each head off so that it could not sprout again. When all had been chopped off he disposed of the one that was immortal by burying it securely under a great rock.

The third labor was to bring back alive a stag with horns of gold, sacred to Artemis,

---

1. **Eurystheus** (yŏŏ-rĭs′thē-əs).
2. **Mycenae** (mī-sē′nē).

3. **Iolaus** (ī′ə-lā′əs).

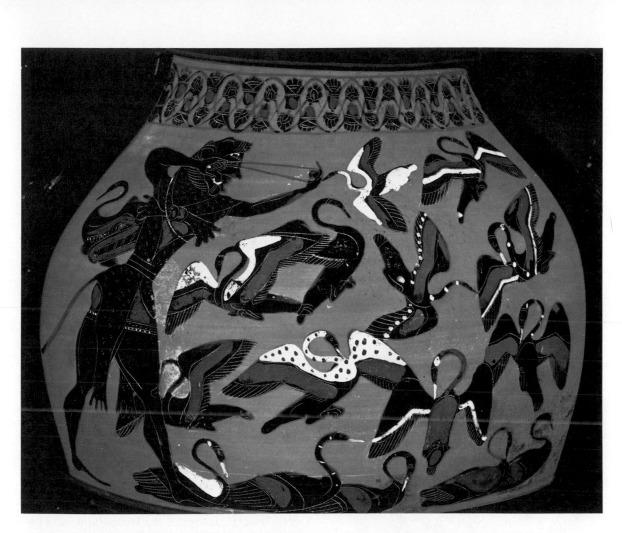

Heracles and the Stymphalian birds. Vase painting, from Vulci
(Etruria), mid 6th century B.C.
Courtesy Trustees, British Museum, London

which lived in the forests of Cerynitia. He
could have killed it easily, but to take it alive
was another matter and he hunted it a whole
year before he succeeded.

The fourth labor was to capture a great boar
which had its lair on Mount Erymanthus. He
chased the beast from one place to another
until it was exhausted; then he drove it into
deep snow and trapped it.

The fifth labor was to clean the Augean stables in a single day. Augeas had thousands of
cattle and their stalls had not been cleared out
for years. Hercules diverted the courses of two
rivers and made them flow through the stables in a great flood that washed out the filth
in no time at all.

The sixth labor was to drive away the Stymphalian birds, which were a plague to the people of Stymphalus because of their enormous
numbers. He was helped by Athena to drive
them out of their coverts, and as they flew up
he shot them.

The seventh labor was to go to Crete and fetch from there the beautiful savage bull that Poseidon had given Minos. Hercules mastered him, put him in a boat and brought him to Eurystheus.

The eighth labor was to get the man-eating mares of King Diomedes of Thrace. Hercules slew Diomedes first and then drove off the mares unopposed.

Heracles roping the Cretan bull. Vase painting, late 6th century B.C.
Metropolitan Museum of Art, New York

The ninth labor was to bring back the girdle[4] of Hippolyta, the Queen of the Amazons. When Hercules arrived she met him kindly and told him she would give him the girdle, but Hera stirred up trouble. She made the Amazons think that Hercules was going to carry off their queen, and they charged down on his ship. Hercules, without a thought of how kind Hippolyta had been, without any thought at all, instantly killed her, taking it for granted that she was responsible for the attack. He was able to fight off the others and get away with the girdle.

The tenth labor was to bring back the cattle of Geryon, who was a monster with three bodies living on Erythia, a western island. On his way there Hercules reached the land at the end of the Mediterranean and he set up as a memorial of his journey two great rocks, called the Pillars of Hercules (now Gibraltar and Ceuta). Then he got the oxen and took them to Mycenae.

The eleventh labor was the most difficult of all so far. It was to bring back the golden apples of the Hesperides,[5] and he did not know where they were to be found. Atlas, who bore the vault of heaven upon his shoulders, was the father of the Hesperides, so Hercules went to him and asked him to get the apples for him. He offered to take upon himself the burden of the sky while Atlas was away. Atlas, seeing a chance of being relieved forever from his heavy task, gladly agreed. He came back with the apples, but he did not give them to Hercules. He told Hercules he could keep on holding up the sky, for Atlas himself would take the apples to Eurystheus. On this

4. **girdle:** here, a belt.
5. **Hesperides** (hĕs-pĕr′ə-dēz′): sisters who guarded the golden apples belonging to Hera. These apples had been given to her as a wedding present by Gaea (jē′ə), an earth goddess.

occasion Hercules had only his wits to trust to; he had to give all his strength to supporting that mighty load. He was successful, but because of Atlas' stupidity rather than his own cleverness. He agreed to Atlas' plan, but asked him to take the sky back for just a moment so that Hercules could put a pad on his shoulders to ease the pressure. Atlas did so, and Hercules picked up the apples and went off.

The twelfth labor was the worst of all. It took him down to the lower world; and it was then that he freed Theseus from the Chair of Forgetfulness.[6] His task was to bring Cerberus, the three-headed dog, up from Hades. Pluto gave him permission provided Hercules used no weapons to overcome him. He could use his hands only. Even so, he forced the terrible monster to submit to him. He lifted him and carried him all the way up to the earth and on to Mycenae. Eurystheus very sensibly did not want to keep him and made Hercules carry him back. This was his last labor.

When all were completed and full expiation made for the death of his wife and children, he would seem to have earned ease and tranquillity for the rest of his life. But it was not so. He was never tranquil and at ease. An exploit quite as difficult as most of the labors was the conquest of Antaeus,[7] a Giant and a mighty wrestler who forced strangers to wrestle with him on condition that if he was victor he should kill them. He was roofing a temple with the skulls of his victims. As long as he could touch the earth he was invincible. If thrown to the ground he sprang up with renewed strength from the contact. Hercules lifted him up and holding him in the air strangled him.

Story after story is told of his adventures. He fought the river god Achelous[8] because Achelous was in love with the girl Hercules now wanted to marry. Like everyone else by this time, Achelous had no desire to fight him and he tried to reason with him. But that never worked with Hercules. It only made him more angry. He said, "My hand is better than my tongue. Let me win fighting and you may win talking." Achelous took the form of a bull and attacked him fiercely, but Hercules was used to subduing bulls. He conquered him and broke off one of his horns. The cause of the contest, a young princess named Deianira,[9] became his wife.

He traveled to many lands and did many other great deeds. At Troy he rescued a maiden who was in the same plight as Andromeda,[10] waiting on the shore to be devoured by a sea monster which could be appeased in no other way. She was the daughter of King Laomedon, who had cheated Apollo and Poseidon of their wages after at Zeus's command they had built for the King the walls of Troy. In return Apollo sent a pestilence, and Poseidon the sea serpent. Hercules agreed to rescue the girl if her father would give him the horses Zeus had given his grandfather. Laomedon promised, but when Hercules had slain the monster the King refused to pay. Hercules captured the city, killed the King, and gave the maiden to his friend, Telamon of Salamis, who had helped him.

On his way to Atlas to ask him about the Golden Apples, Hercules came to the Cauca-

---

6. **Chair of Forgetfulness:** Theseus, an Athenian hero and a cousin of Hercules, had been trapped in this chair when he accompanied a friend to Hades in order to kidnap Persephone.
7. **Antaeus** (ăn-tē′əs).

8. **Achelous** (ə-kĕl′ō-əs).
9. **Deianira** (dē′yə-nī′rə).
10. **Andromeda** (ăn-drŏm′ə-də): a princess rescued from a sea monster by Perseus, whom she later married.

sus, where he freed Prometheus,[11] slaying the eagle that preyed on him.

Along with these glorious deeds there were others not glorious. He killed with a careless thrust of his arm a lad who was serving him by pouring water on his hands before a feast. It was an accident and the boy's father forgave Hercules, but Hercules could not forgive himself and he went into exile for a time. Far worse was his deliberately slaying a good friend in order to avenge an insult offered him by the young man's father, King Eurytus.[12] For this base action Zeus himself punished him: he sent him to Lydia to be a slave to the Queen, Omphale,[13] some say for a year, some for three years. She amused herself with him, making him at times dress up as a woman and do woman's work, weave or spin. He submitted patiently, as always, but he felt himself degraded by this servitude and with complete unreason blamed Eurytus for it and swore he would punish him to the utmost when he was freed.

As Hercules had sworn to do while he was Omphale's slave, no sooner was he free than he started to punish King Eurytus because he himself had been punished by Zeus for killing Eurytus' son. He collected an army, captured the King's city and put him to death. But Eurytus, too, was avenged, for indirectly this victory was the cause of Hercules' own death.

Before he had quite completed the destruction of the city, he sent home—where Deianira, his devoted wife, was waiting for him to come back from Omphale in Lydia—a band of captive maidens, one of them especially beautiful, Iole, the King's daughter. The man who brought them to Deianira told her that Hercules was madly in love with this Princess. This news was not so hard for Deianira as might be expected, because she believed she had a powerful love-charm which she had kept for years against just such an evil, a woman in her own house preferred before her. Directly after her marriage, when Hercules was taking her home, they had reached a river where the centaur[14] Nessus acted as ferryman, carrying travelers over the water. He took Deianira on his back and in midstream insulted her. She shrieked and Hercules shot the beast as he reached the other bank. Before he died he told Deianira to take some of his blood and use it as a charm for Hercules if ever he loved another woman more than her. When she heard about Iole, it seemed to her the time had come, and she anointed a splendid robe with the blood and sent it to Hercules by the messenger.

As the hero put it on, the effect was the same as that of the robe Medea had sent her rival whom Jason was about to marry.[15] A fearful pain seized him, as though he were in a burning fire. In his first agony he turned on Deianira's messenger, who was, of course, completely innocent, seized him and hurled him down into the sea. He could still slay others, but it seemed that he himself could not die. The anguish he felt hardly weakened him. What had instantly killed the young Princess of Corinth could not kill Hercules. He was in torture, but he lived and they brought him home. Long before, Deianira had

---

11. **Prometheus:** See "Prometheus the Fire-Bringer," page 478. Zeus had punished Prometheus for his defiance by having him chained to a mountaintop and sending an eagle each day to devour his liver, which grew back each night.
12. **Eurytus** (yŏŏr'ĭ-təs).
13. **Omphale** (ŏm'fə-lē).

14. **centaur** (sĕn'tôr'): one of a group of mountain creatures who were part man and part horse.
15. **the robe . . . marry:** Jason's intended bride, the Princess of Corinth, died in agony when she tried on the robe, which Medea had anointed with poison.

heard what her gift had done to him and had killed herself. In the end he did the same. Since death would not come to him, he would go to death. He ordered those around him to build a great pyre on Mount Oeta and carry him to it. When at last he reached it he knew that now he could die and he was glad. "This is rest," he said. "This is the end." And as they lifted him to the pyre he lay down on it as one who at a banquet table lies down upon his couch.

He asked his youthful follower, Philoctetes, to hold the torch to set the wood on fire; and he gave him his bow and arrows, which were to be far-famed in the young man's hands, too, at Troy. Then the flames rushed up and Hercules was seen no more on earth. He was taken to heaven, where he was reconciled to Hera and married her daughter Hebe, and where

> After his mighty labors he has rest.
> His choicest prize eternal peace
> Within the homes of blessedness.

But it is not easy to imagine him contentedly enjoying rest and peace, or allowing the blessed gods to do so, either.

Heracles carrying the vault of heaven. From the Temple of Zeus, Olympia.
Museum of Olympia, Greece

SEEKING MEANING

1. All twelve labors required great strength, courage, and perseverance. Which labors required that Hercules also use his wits?
2. Which labors were useful tasks that benefited humanity? Which were simply tests of strength and patience? Explain your answer.
3. Since Hercules had superhuman strength, he could not be killed by poison. How did he die?

DEVELOPING VOCABULARY

Learning Words from the Myths
The Hydra was the nine-headed monster that Hercules killed in the second of his labors. The name *Hydra* comes from a Greek word meaning "water serpent." In English the root *hydro-* (or *hydr-*) means "water." Find the meaning of these words:

hydrant	hydroelectric
hydraulic	hydrophobia

DEVELOPING SKILLS IN RESEARCH

Using Reference Books
Hercules fought and killed the Nemean lion, the nine-headed Hydra, and other fearsome monsters. Here are some additional monsters from classical mythology:

Chimera	Gorgons	Python
Cyclopes	Harpies	Sphinx
Furies	Minotaur	Typhon

Choose four of these monsters. Consult one of the reference books listed on page 484, and identify each one in a sentence. If you like to draw, try drawing four of the monsters instead of writing about them.

DEVELOPING SKILLS OF EXPRESSION

Writing a Television Script
Imagine that you are the creator of a new television series based on the adventures of Hercules. Choose one of the episodes in his life — one of the labors or one of his other feats — and plan a script for a half-hour show. You may want to work with three or four other students in planning and writing the script.

Before you begin to write, consider these questions:

How many characters will appear in the play?
What will be the main events in the plot?
Where will the action take place?
How many different scenes will there be?
What details will have to be invented?
What dialogue will have to be written?

Index of Names

Where a character is known by more than one name, a separate entry has been provided for each name. For example, you will find Zeus also listed under his Roman names, Jove and Jupiter.

Aphrodite (ăf′rə-dī′tē): Greek goddess of love and beauty. She was identified with the Roman goddess **Venus.**   473

Apollo (ə-pŏl′ō): Greek and Roman god of youth, music, prophecy, archery, healing, and the sun. He was also called **Phoebus** (fē′bəs) **Apollo,** from the Greek word for "shining."   473, 486, 506

Arachne (ə-răk′nē): an arrogant young woman who boasted of her skill in weaving to Minerva and challenged the goddess to a contest. She was transformed into a spider by Minerva.   491

Ares (âr′ēz): Greek god of war. He was identified with the Roman god **Mars.**   474

Artemis (är′tə-mĭs): Greek goddess of wild animals, hunting, childbirth, and the moon. She was identified with the Roman goddess **Diana.**   473, 474

Athena (ə-thē′nə): Greek goddess of wisdom, arts, crafts, and war, and protector of the city of Athens. She was also called **Athene** (ə-thē′nē) and **Pallas** (păl′əs) **Athena,** and was identified with the Roman goddess **Minerva.**   474

Atlas (ăt′ləs): the Titan whom Zeus punished by making him hold up the sky on his shoulders.   473, 518

Bacchus. See **Dionysus.**

Baucis (bô′sĭs): a poor Phrygian peasant. She and her husband, **Philemon** (fĭ-lē′mən), gave shelter to Jupiter and Mercury when they visited Phyrgia in disguise.   494

Centaurs (sĕn′tôrz′): a race of mountain creatures, part man and part horse.   520

Ceres (sîr′ēz): Roman goddess of agriculture. She was identified with the Greek goddess **Demeter.**

Cronus (krō′nəs): the Titan who ruled the universe until he was overthrown by his son Zeus. The reign of Cronus was known as the Golden Age. He was identified with the Roman god **Saturn.**   473, 478

Cupid (kyōō′pĭd): Roman god of love, He was identified with the Greek god **Eros.**   509

Daedalus (dĕd′l-əs): an Athenian inventor and architect who built the Labyrinth for King Minos of Crete. He fashioned wings for himself and his son **Icarus** (ĭk′ə-rəs), who fell to his death when he flew too close to the sun.   508, 510

Demeter (dĭ-mē′tər): Greek goddess of agriculture and fertility. She was identified with the Roman goddess **Ceres.**   485

Diana (dī-ă′nə): Roman goddess of the moon and hunting. She was identified with the Greek goddess **Artemis.**

Dionysus (dī′ə-nī′səs): Greek god of wine, fertility, and drama. He was also called **Bacchus** (băk′əs) by the Greeks and the Romans.

Eros (îr′ŏs′): Greek god of love, Aphrodite's son. He was identified with the Roman god **Cupid**.

Fates: three goddesses who controlled human destiny and life. **Clotho** (klō′thō) spun the thread of each person's life, **Lachesis** (lăk′ə-sĭs) determined the length of each thread, and **Atropos** (ăt′rə-pŏs′) cut each thread.   490

Hades (hā′dēz): Greek god of the underworld, and husband of **Persephone**. He was also called **Pluto** (plōō′tō) by the Greeks and the Romans.   473, 485

Helios (hē′lē-ŏs′): early Greek god of the sun. He was later identified with **Apollo**.   502

Hephaestus (hĭ-fĕs′təs): Greek god of fire and metalworking. He was identified with the Roman god **Vulcan**.   474

Hera (hîr′ə): Greek goddess of marriage and childbirth, Zeus's wife, and queen of the gods of Olympus. She was identified with the Roman goddess **Juno**.   473, 516

Heracles (hĕr′ə-klēz′): a Greek hero, the son of Zeus and **Alcmene** (ălk-mē′nē). He was known as **Hercules** to the Romans.   516

Hercules. See **Heracles**.

Hermes (hûr′mēz): Greek god of travelers, merchants, and thieves, and messenger of the gods. He was identified with the Roman god **Mercury**.   474, 489

Icarus. See **Daedalus**.

Iris (ī′rĭs): goddess of the rainbow and messenger of the gods.   489

Jove. See **Jupiter**.

Juno (jōō′nō): Roman goddess of marriage and childbirth, Jupiter's wife, and the queen of the gods. She was identified with the Greek goddess **Hera**.

Jupiter (jōō′pə-tər): Roman god of the sky and the weather, and king of the gods. He was also called **Jove**, and was identified with the Greek god **Zeus**.   494

Mars (märz): Roman god of war. He was identified with the Greek god **Ares**.

Mercury (mûr′kyə-rē): Roman god of business, science, and thieves, and messenger of the gods. He was identified with the Greek god **Hermes**.   494

Minerva (mĭ-nûr-və): Roman goddess of the arts and wisdom. She was identified with the Greek goddess **Athena**.   491

Muses (myōō′zəz): nine sisters, daughters of Zeus and **Mnemosyne** (nĭ-mŏs′ə-nē), who were patronesses of the arts. Each Muse was associated with a different art: **Calliope** (kə-lī′ə-pē′), epic poetry; **Clio** (klī′ō), history; **Erato** (ĕr′ə-tō′), lyric poetry; **Euterpe** (yōō-tûr′pē), music; **Melpomene** (mĕl-pŏm′ə-nē), tragedy; **Polyhymnia** (pŏl′ē-hĭm′nē-ə), religious poetry; **Terpsichore** (tûrp-sĭk′ə-rē), dance; **Thalia** (thə-lī′ə), comedy; and **Urania** (yōō-rā′nē-ə), astronomy.   474, 504

Neptune (nĕp′tōōn′): Roman god of the sea. He was identified with the Greek god **Poseidon**.   493

Nymphs (nĭmfs): goddesses who inhabited parts of nature, such as rivers, mountains, and trees.   472, 491

Pan: Greek god of woodlands, shepherds, and goatherds. He was often represented as having the head, chest, and arms of a man, and the legs, horns, and ears of a goat.

Persephone (pər-sĕf'ə-nē): Greek goddess of spring and the underworld, Demeter's daughter. The Romans called her **Proserpina** (prō-sûr'pə-nə).   485

Phaethon (fā'ə-thən): Helios' son. He was killed when he tried to drive the chariot of the Sun.   502, 506

Philemon. See **Baucis**.

Pluto. See **Hades**.

Poseidon (pō-sī'dən): Greek god of the sea. He was identified with the Roman god **Neptune**.   473

Prometheus (prə-me'the-əs): the Titan who gave fire to mortals against the wishes of Zeus.   478

Proserpina. See **Persephone**.

Saturn (săt'ərn): Roman god of agriculture and fertility. He was identified with the Greek god **Cronus**.

Satyrs (sā'tərz): woodland creatures who were part human and part goat. They were followers of Dionysus.   472

Selene (sə-lē'nē): early Greek goddess of the moon. She was later identified with **Artemis**.   507

Titans (tīt'nz): a family of gods who ruled the universe before the Olympians.   473

Venus (vē'nəs): Roman goddess of gardens, spring, love, and beauty. She was identified with the Greek goddess **Aphrodite**.

Vulcan (vûl'kən): Roman god of fire and metalworking. He was identified with the Greek god **Hephaestus**.

Zeus (zōos): Greek god of the sky and the weather, and king of the gods of Olympus. He was identified with the Roman god **Jupiter**, also called **Jove**.   473, 478, 485

EXTENDING YOUR STUDY

1. In your notebook, keep a record of references to classical mythology that you find in your reading, in movies, and on television. Post some of these on a bulletin board as you find them.

2. Look in newspapers and magazines at home for advertisements that use names or symbols drawn from classical mythology. What association is the consumer expected to make? Post these advertisements on a bulletin board or paste them in your notebook.

3. Make a collection of myths that come from different cultures and share a common subject. For example, look for myths that explain the origin of the seasons. You can also look for myths in which people are transformed into animals or plants.

4. The following questions might inspire stories that are like myths:

Why does it rain?
Why are there thunder and lightning?
Why do rivers run toward the sea?
Why has the sky so many different colors at sunrise and at sunset?
Why is the moon sometimes visible during the day?
Why are there eclipses of the sun?
Why does the moon change its shape?
Why are there mountains?

Make up a story explaining one of these phenomena, to be told to the class. You will have to do some planning before you can tell your story. What characters are necessary? What happens to the characters to cause the phenomenon you are explaining?

5. Work with a group of students to retell one of the classical myths in the form of a drama. Write dialogue for the characters, and present the play to the class.

6. What do you imagine Hercules looked like? Illustrate one of the characters in a myth you have read, or show one or more scenes from a myth in the form of a collage, a poster, or a drawing.

Fables are brief tales that combine common sense with entertainment. The stories are fun to read. At the same time, they teach useful lessons about human behavior. The characters in fables are usually animals who speak and act like human beings. The meaning of a fable is often summed up in its *moral*, a statement of the lesson to be learned, such as *Do not trust flatterers.*

No one knows when fables were first told. Some say that the credit for creating the fable form belongs to Aesop, a Greek who probably lived around the sixth century B.C. Not much is known about Aesop, but his fables have remained popular for centuries. You will find several examples of his work in this unit.

In addition to the fables by Aesop, you will find modern retellings of well-known fables. Two examples, in verse, will show you how poets have adapted the fable form to their own needs. In the fables by James Thurber, one of America's most humorous writers, you will see that the old form has been given a new twist.

FABLES

The Hare and the Tortoise. Wood engraving after J. J. Grandville. From *Fables de la Fontaine,* Paris, 1838

Fables by Aesop

Retold by Joseph Jacobs

Belling the Cat

Long ago, the mice had a general council to consider what measures they could take to outwit their common enemy, the Cat. Some said this, and some said that; but at last a Young Mouse got up and said he had a proposal to make which he thought would meet the case. "You will all agree," said he, "that our chief danger consists in the sly and treacherous manner in which the enemy approaches us. Now, if we could receive some signal of her approach, we could easily escape from her. I venture, therefore, to propose that a small bell be procured and attached by a ribbon round the neck of the Cat. By this means we should always know when she was about and could easily retire while she was in the neighborhood."

This proposal met with general applause, until an Old Mouse got up and said, "That is all very well, but who is to bell the Cat?" The mice looked at one another and nobody spoke. Then the Old Mouse said:

"It is easy to propose impossible remedies."

The Town Mouse and the Country Mouse

Now you must know that a Town Mouse once upon a time went on a visit to his cousin in the country. He was rough and ready, this cousin, but he loved his town friend and made him heartily welcome. Beans and bacon, cheese and bread, were all he had to offer, but he offered them freely.

The Town Mouse rather turned up his long nose at this country fare, and said: "I cannot understand, Cousin, how you can put up with such poor food as this, but of course you cannot expect anything better in the country; come you with me and I will show you how to live. When you have been in town a week you will wonder how you could ever have stood a country life."

No sooner said than done: the two mice set off for the town and arrived at the Town Mouse's residence late at night. "You will want some refreshment after our long journey," said the polite Town Mouse, and took his friend into the grand dining room. There they found the remains of a fine feast, and soon the two mice were eating up jellies and cakes and all that was nice. Suddenly they heard growling and barking.

"What is that?" said the Country Mouse.

"It is only the dogs of the house," answered the other.

"Only!" said the Country Mouse. "I do not like that music at my dinner."

Just at that moment the door flew open, in came two huge mastiffs,[1] and the two mice had to scamper down and run off. "Goodbye, Cousin," said the Country Mouse.

"What! going so soon?" said the other.

"Yes," he replied:

"Better beans and bacon in peace than cakes and ale in fear."

---

1. **mastiffs:** a breed of dogs used for hunting and as watchdogs.

The Ant and the Grasshopper

In a field one summer's day a Grasshopper was hopping about, chirping and singing to its heart's content. An Ant passed by, bearing along with great toil an ear of corn he was taking to the nest.

"Why not come and chat with me," said the Grasshopper, "instead of toiling and moiling in that way?"

"I am helping to lay up food for the winter," said the Ant, "and recommend you to do the same."

"Why bother about winter?" said the Grasshopper; "we have got plenty of food at present."

But the Ant went on its way and continued its toil. When the winter came the Grasshopper had no food, and found itself dying of hunger, while it saw the ants distributing every day corn and grain from the stores they had collected in the summer. Then the Grasshopper knew:

It is best to prepare for the days of necessity.

The Fox and the Crow

A Fox once saw a Crow fly off with a piece of cheese in its beak and settle on a branch of a tree. "That's for me, as I am a Fox," said Master Reynard, and he walked up to the foot of the tree.

"Good day, Mistress Crow," he cried. "How well you are looking today: how glossy your feathers; how bright your eye. I feel sure your voice must surpass that of other birds, just as your figure does. Let me hear but one song from you, that I may greet you as the Queen of Birds."

The Crow lifted up her head and began to caw her best, but the moment she opened her mouth, the piece of cheese fell to the ground, only to be snapped up by Master Fox.

"That will do," said he. "That was all I wanted. In exchange for your cheese I will give you a piece of advice for the future:

"Do not trust flatterers."

SEEKING MEANING

1. The animals in a fable often show contrasting traits of character. For example, in "Belling the Cat," the Young Mouse is inexperienced and foolish; the Old Mouse is experienced and wise. What contrasts in character do you find in the other fables?

2. It is possible to state the moral of a fable in different ways. The moral of "The Town Mouse and the Country Mouse" might be stated in this way: *It is better to live humbly in peace than to live luxuriously in fear.* Restate the moral of "Belling the Cat" in your own words.

3. A fable expresses a general truth or gives practical advice about life and behavior. To what modern-day situations could you apply the moral of "The Ant and the Grasshopper"?

4. What kinds of behavior do these fables support or praise? What kinds of behavior do they ridicule or condemn?

5. Aesop's fables were first told more than two thousand years ago, yet we continue to enjoy them today. Why do you think these fables still appeal to readers?

DEVELOPING SKILLS IN READING

Recognizing Allusions

In one of Aesop's fables, there is a race between a tortoise and a hare. The hare, certain of an easy victory, becomes overconfident. Midway through the race, he decides to take a rest. As a result, he loses the race to the tortoise, who slowly but surely overtakes him. The fable makes this point: *Slow and steady wins the race.*

A number of expressions that we use in speaking and writing are *allusions,* or references, to Aesop's fables. People often use the moral *Slow and steady wins the race* when they wish to point out the rewards of perseverance and effort. In the following sentence, what kind of "race" has been run?

Everyone was surprised when Danny won the scholarship, but Danny has always believed that *slow and steady wins the race.*

Each italicized expression in the sentences below refers to a fable by Aesop. Which of these expressions have you read or heard before?

Whenever it comes to dividing a cake, Sylvia always takes the *lion's share.*
Reynaldo says that he wouldn't have attended the party even if he had been invited, but I think it's a case of *sour grapes.*

To find the meanings of the italicized expressions, look them up in a dictionary. If your library has a collection of Aesop's fables, locate "The Lion's Share" and "The Fox and the Grapes," and tell the fables to the class.

Fables in Verse

The following poems, which contain human characters, are retellings of well-known fables. The first fable, "The Blind Men and the Elephant," comes from India. Can you infer the moral of the fable from its story?

The Blind Men and the Elephant

John Godfrey Saxe

It was six men of Indostan°
  To learning much inclined,
Who went to see the Elephant
  (Though all of them were blind),
That each by observation   5
  Might satisfy his mind.

The *First* approached the Elephant,
  And happening to fall
Against his broad and sturdy side,
  At once began to bawl: 10
"God bless me! but the Elephant
  Is very like a wall!"

The *Second*, feeling of the tusk,
  Cried, "Ho! what have we here
So very round and smooth and sharp?   15
  To me 'tis mighty clear
This wonder of an Elephant
  Is very like a spear!"

The *Third* approached the animal,
  And happening to take   20
The squirming trunk within his hands,
  Thus boldly up and spake:
"I see," quoth he, "the Elephant
  Is very like a snake!"

1. **Indostan** (ĭn'dō-stăn'): Hindustan, an old name for India.

532 *Fables*

The *Fourth* reached out an eager hand,   25
  And felt about the knee.
"What most this wondrous beast is like
  Is mighty plain," quoth he;
"'Tis clear enough the Elephant
  Is very like a tree!"   30

The *Fifth*, who chanced to touch the ear,
  Said: "E'en the blindest man
Can tell what this resembles most;
  Deny the fact who can,
This marvel of an Elephant   35
  Is very like a fan!"

The *Sixth* no sooner had begun
  About the beast to grope,
Than, seizing on the swinging tail
  That fell within his scope,   40
"I see," quoth he, "the Elephant
  Is very like a rope!"

And so these men of Indostan
  Disputed loud and long,
Each in his own opinion   45
  Exceeding stiff and strong,
Though each was partly in the right,
  And all were in the wrong!

The Boy and the Wolf

*A Fable of Aesop adapted by
Louis Untermeyer*

A boy employed to guard the sheep
Despised his work. He liked to sleep.
And when a lamb was lost, he'd shout,
"Wolf! Wolf! The wolves are all about!"

The neighbors searched from noon till nine,   5
But of the beast there was no sign,
Yet "Wolf!" he cried next morning when
The villagers came out again.

One evening around six o'clock
A real wolf fell upon the flock.   10
"Wolf!" yelled the boy. "A wolf indeed!"
But no one paid him any heed.

Although he screamed to wake the dead,
"He's fooled us every time," they said,
And let the hungry wolf enjoy   15
His feast of mutton, lamb—and boy.

The moral's this: The man who's wise
Does not defend himself with lies.
Liars are not believed, forsooth,°   19. **forsooth:** indeed.
Even when liars tell the truth.   20

SEEKING MEANING

"The Blind Men and the Elephant"

1. Each blind man makes the same mistake in deciding what the Elephant is like. What is the mistake?

2. How would you state the moral of "The Blind Men and the Elephant"?

"The Boy and the Wolf"

3. Why did the boy cry "Wolf" every time a lamb was lost? "To cry wolf" has become a common expression in our language. What does it mean?

4. To what modern-day situations could you apply the moral of this fable?

DEVELOPING SKILLS IN READING

Understanding Proverbs

The moral of a fable generally gives some practical advice or warning that is intended to guide our behavior. A similar kind of common sense is contained in the sayings known as *proverbs*.

Proverbs are brief and to the point. They are often expressed in a catchy way that makes them easy to remember:

A fool and his money are soon parted.
Haste makes waste.
He who laughs last laughs best.
Better late than never.
Where there's a will, there's a way.

Some proverbs are metaphors. "A stitch in time saves nine" tells us that we can prevent a tear or a hole from growing by catching it early with a single stitch. By extension, the proverb means that we can avoid some future difficulty or problem by acting early enough to prevent it.

Explain these proverbs in your own words.

The early bird catches the worm.
A rolling stone gathers no moss.

Collect some proverbs that you like. Ask the older members of your family if they remember sayings or proverbs they heard when they were children.

The Boy and the Wolf 535

Fables by James Thurber

The following fables by James Thurber, the American humorist, show the traditional elements of the fable being used in new and distinctive ways. Thurber's fables, like those of Aesop, shed light on human nature. However, Thurber's fables are full of surprises, as you will see. The accompanying drawings are by the author.

The Fairly Intelligent Fly

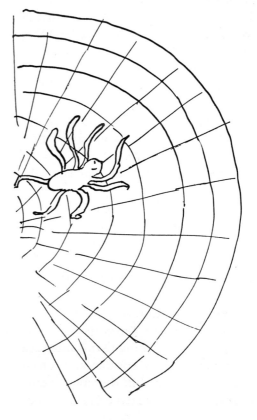

A large spider in an old house built a beautiful web in which to catch flies. Every time a fly landed on the web and was entangled in it the spider devoured him, so that when another fly came along he would think the web was a safe and quiet place in which to rest. One day a fairly intelligent fly buzzed around above the web so long without lighting that the spider appeared and said, "Come on down." But the fly was too clever for him and said, "I never light where I don't see other flies and I don't see any other flies in your house." So he flew away until he came to a place where there were a great many other flies. He was about to settle down among them when a bee buzzed up and said, "Hold it, stupid, that's flypaper. All those flies are trapped." "Don't be silly," said the fly, "they're dancing." So he settled down and became stuck to the flypaper with all the other flies.

Moral: There is no safety in numbers, or in anything else.

What Happened to Charles

A farm horse named Charles was led to town one day by his owner, to be shod. He would have been shod and brought back home without incident if it hadn't been for Eva, a duck, who was always hanging about the kitchen door of the farmhouse, eavesdropping, and never got anything quite right. Her farm-mates said of her that she had two mouths but only one ear.

On the day that Charles was led away to the smithy, Eva went quacking about the farm, excitedly telling the other animals that Charles had been taken to town to be shot.

"They're executing an innocent horse!" cried Eva. "He's a hero! He's a martyr! He died to make us free!"

"He was the greatest horse in the world," sobbed a sentimental hen.

"He just seemed like old Charley to me," said a realistic cow. "Let's not get into a moony mood."

"He was wonderful!" cried a gullible goose.

"What did he ever do?" asked a goat.

Eva, who was as inventive as she was inac-

curate, turned on her lively imagination. "It was butchers who led him off to be shot!" she shrieked. "They would have cut our throats while we slept if it hadn't been for Charles!"

"I didn't see any butchers, and I can see a burnt-out firefly on a moonless night," said a barn owl. "I didn't hear any butchers, and I can hear a mouse walk across moss."

"We must build a memorial to Charles the Great, who saved our lives," quacked Eva. And all the birds and beasts in the barnyard except the wise owl, the skeptical goat, and the realistic cow set about building a memorial.

Just then the farmer appeared in the lane, leading Charles, whose new shoes glinted in the sunlight.

It was lucky that Charles was not alone, for the memorial-builders might have set upon him with clubs and stones for replacing their hero with just plain old Charley. It was lucky, too, that they could not reach the barn owl, who quickly perched upon the weather vane of the barn, for none is so exasperating as he who is right. The sentimental hen and the gullible goose were the ones who finally called attention to the true culprit—Eva, the one-eared duck with two mouths. The others set upon her and tarred and unfeathered her, for none is more unpopular than the bearer of sad tidings that turn out to be false.

Moral: Get it right or let it alone. The conclusion you jump to may be your own.

The Fox and the Crow

A crow, perched in a tree with a piece of cheese in his beak, attracted the eye and nose of a fox. "If you can sing as prettily as you sit," said the fox, "then you are the prettiest singer within my scent and sight." The fox had read somewhere, and somewhere, and somewhere else, that praising the voice of a crow with a cheese in his beak would make him drop the cheese and sing. But this is not what happened to this particular crow in this particular case.

"They say you are sly and they say you are crazy," said the crow, having carefully removed the cheese from his beak with the claws of one foot, "but you must be nearsighted as well. Warblers wear gay hats and colored jackets and bright vests, and they are a dollar a hundred. I wear black and I am unique." He began nibbling the cheese, dropping not a single crumb.

"I am sure you are," said the fox, who was neither crazy nor nearsighted, but sly, "I recognize you, now that I look more closely, as the most famed and talented of all birds, and I fain would hear you tell about yourself, but I am hungry and must go."

"Tarry awhile," said the crow quickly, "and share my lunch with me." Whereupon he tossed the cunning fox the lion's share of the cheese and began to tell about himself. "A ship that sails without a crow's-nest sails to doom," he said. "Bars may come and bars may go, but crowbars last forever. I am the pioneer of flight, I am the map maker. Last, but never least, my flight is known to scientists and engineers, geometrists and scholars, as the shortest distance between two points.[1] Any two points," he concluded arrogantly.

"Oh, every two points, I am sure," said the fox. "And thank you for the lion's share of what I know you could not spare." And with this he trotted away into the woods, his appetite appeased, leaving the hungry crow perched forlornly in the tree.

Moral: 'Twas true in Aesop's time, and La Fontaine's,[2] and now, no one else can praise thee quite so well as thou.

---

1. **my flight . . . two points:** A crow is said to fly in a straight line, which is the shortest distance between two points.
2. **La Fontaine** (lə fŏn-tān'): Jean de la Fontaine, a seventeenth-century French poet who wrote verse fables that criticized the French court.

SEEKING MEANING

"The Fairly Intelligent Fly"

1. The familiar moral Thurber alludes to in this fable is *There is safety in numbers*. What happens to the fly when he puts his faith in this old moral? Explain Thurber's new moral in your own words.

2. Why do you think the fly is described as "fairly intelligent"? How might the fly have behaved if he had been "very intelligent"?

"What Happened to Charles"

3. What mistake does Eva, the duck, make after hearing the word *shod?*

4. In Aesop's fables the animals often reveal contrasting traits of character. Which characters in Thurber's fable are shown to be foolish or hasty? Which are shown to be wise or cautious?

5. The moral is not the only message in this fable. Find two statements that are direct comments on human behavior. What kinds of behavior is Thurber criticizing in this fable?

"The Fox and the Crow"

6. You have read two versions of "The Fox and the Crow," Aesop's version on page 530 and Thurber's version on page 539. Both fables have a clever fox and a vain crow. How is Thurber's crow different in character from Aesop's?

7. In Aesop's fable the fox uses flattery and succeeds in outwitting the crow. Thurber's fox also uses flattery to trick the crow. What difference is there in his approach?

8. Thurber's crow attaches a great deal of importance to words that carry his name. How do you think *crow's-nest* got its name? What does a crow have to do with a *crowbar?*

9. Compare the morals in the fables by Aesop and Thurber. What new advice does Thurber offer on the subject of flattery?

EXTENDING YOUR STUDY

1. What moral can you think of for this Eskimo fable?

The Owl and the Two Rabbits

An Owl spotted two Rabbits playing close together and seized them, one clutched in each foot. But they were too strong for him and ran away, sliding the Owl along the ice. The Owl's wife shouted to him, "Let one of them go and kill the other!"

But he replied, "The moon will soon disappear, and then we shall be hungry. We need both of them."

The Rabbits ran on; and when they came to a boulder, one ran to the right side of it, the other to the left. The Owl did not let go quick enough, and was torn in two.

2. A fable, as you have seen, has certain characteristics. It is brief, it has a few characters, and it teaches some lesson about human behavior. It generally ends with a moral.

Here are some common situations in fables:

A person or animal is the cause of his or her own misfortune.

A clever person or animal outwits a foolish one.

A strong person or animal preys upon a weaker one.

Write a fable of your own in prose or verse based on one of these situations. Use a moral that appears in this unit, some common saying, or an original moral of your own.

3. Choose a moral from one of the fables in this unit and write an entirely different story to illustrate that moral.

4. Collect cartoons or comic strips in which animals behave like people. What characteristics do these drawings share with fables?

The Enchanted Owl (1960).
Stone cut by Kenojuak.
Cape Dorset, Baffin Island
Courtesy of the West Baffin
Eskimo Co-operative Limited

Practice in Reading and Writing

BOOK REPORTS

During your school career you will often be asked to report on books read outside of class. A book report generally has two purposes: to summarize the overall content of the book and to give your opinion of the book. A good book report does not have to be long, but it should have a clear focus and organization.

Here are some rules to remember when you write a book report:

1. *Include the title of the book and the name of the author. Underline the title.*
2. *Identify the kind of book it is.*

If fiction, is the book a mystery, a romance, an adventure story? If nonfiction, is the book biography or autobiography? Or is it about science, sports, history, travel?

3. *Summarize the content of the book briefly.*

Do not tell everything that happens in the book. If the book is fiction, identify the setting, the central action of the story, and the main characters. If the book is nonfiction, tell what its subject is. Note the most interesting or important incidents.

4. *State your opinion of the book, and support your opinion with specific reasons.*
Are the people believable? Why or why not? Does the author describe action and events vividly? Is the subject interesting or enjoyable? Would you want to read other books by the same author or about the same subject?

Here is a sample book report:

The Call of the Wild, a novel by Jack London, takes place in Alaska during the time of the Gold Rush, when the only form of transportation across the frozen North was by sled. The central character is a dog named Buck, who is part Saint Bernard and part Scottish shepherd. Buck is stolen from his California home and shipped to Alaska to be trained as a sled dog. He is treated cruelly by several masters, and under this harsh treatment he comes to understand "the law of club and fang." Finally, he finds a kind master in John Thornton, whom he comes to worship. The most exciting incident in the book occurs when Buck wins a bet for Thornton by pulling a thousand-pound load. Although Buck loves Thornton, he is torn between devotion to his master and the "call of the wild." At the end of the story, Buck becomes the leader of a pack of wolves.

This is one of the best dog stories I have ever read. Buck seems more human than animal. Because London tells the story from Buck's point of view, the reader is able to see into Buck's mind, to feel as Buck feels about his enemies and his friends, and to understand why his primitive instincts are aroused by the savage experiences he undergoes. I also learned a great deal about what life was like in the Alaskan wilderness at the close of the nineteenth century.

Choose a book from one of the recommended lists in this book or from a list suggested by your teacher. Write a book report of two paragraphs. In the first paragraph, summarize what the book is about. In the second paragraph, give your opinion of the book, supported by reasons.

For Further Reading

Aesop, *The Fables of Aesop*, retold by Joseph Jacobs (Macmillan, 1964)
Here are more than eighty of Aesop's best fables.

Asimov, Isaac, *Words from the Myths* (Houghton Mifflin, 1961; paperback, New American Library)
Many words and phrases in English come from classical myths. The author explains the fascinating origins of scores of words and retells the myths associated with them.

Benson, Sally, *Stories of the Gods and Heroes* (Dial Press, 1940)
This book includes simple retellings of the major classical myths.

Colum, Padraic, *The Golden Fleece* (Macmillan, 1962)
One of the greatest hero tales in Greek mythology is the story of Jason and the Argonauts and their search for the Golden Fleece.

Coolidge, Olivia, *The Trojan War* (Houghton Mifflin, 1952)
According to legend, the Greeks fought the Trojan War in order to recover Helen, the most beautiful woman in the world.

Gaer, Joseph, *Fables of India* (Little, Brown, 1955)
Aesop may have based many of his fables on the fables of India. Here is a rich and varied sample of these ancient stories.

Graves, Robert, *Greek Gods and Heroes* (Doubleday, 1960)
The author retells some of the most famous myths in an informal, witty style. The opening chapter, "The Palace of the Gods," includes interesting information about the Olympian gods and goddesses, their temperaments, their special powers, and their emblems.

Green, Roger Lancelyn, *Heroes of Greece and Troy* (Walck, 1961)

This is a vivid narrative of the lives and deeds of the classical gods, goddesses, and heroes.

Hamilton, Edith, *Mythology* (Little, Brown, 1942; paperback, New American Library)
These retellings of the myths are based on a variety of classical sources, and there is a useful introduction. Norse myths are also included.

Hawthorne, Nathaniel, *A Wonder-Book and Tanglewood Tales* (many editions)
Hawthorne expands the classical myths with richness of detail, characterization, and dialogue. See especially his dramatic versions of "The Golden Fleece" and "The Golden Touch."

Picard, Barbara L., *The Odyssey of Homer* (Walck, 1952)
Here is a retelling of the exciting adventures of Odysseus: his outwitting of the Cyclops, his journey to the underworld, his narrow escape from the monsters Scylla and Charybdis, and many more.

Rouse, W. H. D., *Gods, Heroes and Men of Ancient Greece* (New American Library, 1971)
The author tells the myths "as parts of a connected whole, as the Greeks felt them to be."

Sabin, Frances Ellis, *Classical Myths That Live Today* (Silver Burdett, 1958)
This recounting of Greek and Roman myths includes examples of the way these famous stories have influenced our language, our art, and our literature.

Serraillier, Ian, *The Gorgon's Head: the Story of Perseus* (Walck, 1962)
Among the most famous heroes in mythology is Perseus, who killed Medusa, one of the Gorgons. The Gorgons were three sisters who had snakes for hair. They were so repulsive and terrifying that whoever looked at them was turned to stone.

Reading and Writing About Literature

INTRODUCTION

Many of the compositions you will be asked to write in English class will be about the literature you read. The writing may be in response to an examination question, a homework assignment, or a research project. At times you may be given a topic to work on; at other times you may have to choose your own subject for a paper.

In writing about literature, you generally focus on some aspect of a work. For example, you may give your impression of a character in a short story; you may discuss the suspense that is developed in a play; you may explain the main idea of a poem. Such writing assignments are an important part of literary study, which aims at greater understanding and appreciation of the works you read.

Writing about a literary work is a way of getting to know it better. Before you write a composition about a story, a poem, or a play, you must study the selection carefully. You must sort out your thoughts and reach conclusions. In putting your thoughts down on paper, you become more fully involved with the work.

Throughout your studies you will become familiar with a great many elements that are useful in analyzing literary works. When you refer to the sequence of events in a short story or play, for instance, you may use such terms as *plot, climax,* and *resolution* in describing the action. You may concern yourself with the *conflict,* or struggle, that a *character* faces. In discussing the meaning of a poem, you may refer to its *imagery* or *figurative language.* These words are part of a common vocabulary used in writing about literature. You can assume that your readers will understand what you mean when you write about such elements. (See the *Guide to Literary Terms and Techniques,* page 593.)

The material on the following pages offers help in planning and writing papers about literature. Here you will find suggestions for reading and analyzing literature, answering examination questions, choosing topics, gathering evidence, organizing essays, and writing and revising papers. Also included are model essays and several new selections for analysis along with suggested writing topics.

READING LITERATURE

When you read a chapter in a social studies or science textbook, you read primarily to get the facts. Your purpose may be to find out how a bill proposed in Congress becomes a law or to understand how bats capture their prey by using sonar. You read chiefly to gather information that is stated *directly* on the page.

Reading literature calls for more than understanding what all the words mean and getting the facts straight. Much of the meaning of a literary work may be stated *indirectly*. For example, a writer may not *tell* you directly that a character has courage. However, by having that character face up to some difficult or dangerous situation the writer may *show* you that the character is brave. In other words, when you read literature, you depend a good deal on *inference*, drawing conclusions from different kinds of evidence. To read literature critically and grasp its meaning, you have to be an active reader, aware of *what* the author is doing, *how* the author is doing it, and *why*.

When you are asked to write about a literary work, be sure to read it carefully before you begin writing. Read actively, asking yourself questions as you work through the selection.

Close Reading of a Short Story

A short story is made up of certain basic elements: plot (the sequence of related events); characters (persons, animals, or things presented as persons); point of view (the standpoint from which the writer tells the story); setting (the time and place of the action); and theme (the underlying idea about human life). The better you, the individual reader, understand how these elements work together, the better you will understand and appreciate the author's intent and meaning.

Here is a brief story that has been read carefully by an experienced reader. The notes in the margin show how this reader thinks in working through a story. Read the story at least twice before proceeding to the commentary on page 548. You may wish to make notes of your own on a separate sheet of paper as you read.

The Dinner Party   *Mona Gardner*

The country is India. A colonial official[1] and his wife are giving a large dinner party. They are seated with their guests — army officers and government attachés[2] and their wives, and a visiting American naturalist[3] — in their spacious dining room, which has a bare marble floor, open rafters and wide glass doors opening onto a veranda.

A spirited discussion springs up between a young girl who insists that women have outgrown the jumping-on-a-chair-at-the-sight-of-a-mouse era and a colonel who says that they haven't.

"A woman's unfailing reaction in any crisis," the colonel says, "is to scream. And while a man may feel like it, he has that ounce more of nerve control than a woman has. And that last ounce is what counts."

The American does not join in the argument but watches the other guests. As he looks, he sees a strange expression come over the face of the hostess. She is staring straight ahead, her muscles contracting slightly. With a slight gesture she summons the native boy standing behind her chair and whispers to him. The boy's eyes widen: he quickly leaves the room.

Of the guests, none except the American notices this or sees the boy place a bowl of milk on the veranda just outside the open doors.

The American comes to with a start. In India, milk in a bowl means only one thing — bait for a snake. He realizes there must be a cobra in the room. He looks up at the rafters — the likeliest place — but they are bare. Three corners of the room are empty, and in the fourth the servants are waiting to serve the next course. There is only one place left — under the table.

His first impulse is to jump back and warn the others, but he knows the commotion would frighten the cobra into striking. He speaks quickly, the tone of his voice so arresting that it sobers everyone.

"I want to know just what control everyone at this table has. I will count to three hundred — that's five minutes — and not one of you is

---

1. **colonial official:** When this story was published, in 1942, India was still a British colony.
2. **attachés** (ăt'ə shāz', ă-tă'shāz'): individuals on the diplomatic staff of an ambassador or a minister to another country.
3. **naturalist:** someone who is a trained observer of animals and plants.

to move a muscle. Those who move will forfeit[4] fifty rupees.[5] Ready!"

The twenty people sit like stone images while he counts. He is saying, ". . . two hundred and eighty . . ." when, out of the corner of his eye, he sees the cobra emerge and make for the bowl of milk. Screams ring out as he jumps to slam the veranda doors safely shut.

He invents a game to test their self-control.

Suspense mounts. Will the cobra strike?

Now I know why I needed a clear picture of the scene.

"You were right, Colonel!" the host exclaims. "A man has just shown us an example of perfect control."

The host interprets the incident as a victory for the colonel's position.

"Just a minute," the American says, turning to his hostess. "Mrs. Wynnes, how did you know that cobra was in the room?"

There is one piece of unexplained business.

A faint smile lights up the woman's face as she replies: "Because it was crawling across my foot."

The ending of the story resolves the conflict in a surprising, yet totally acceptable way. How has the author prepared me for this ending?

---

4. **forfeit** (fôr'fĭt): give up, as a penalty.
5. **rupees** (roo-pēz', roo'pēz): The rupee is the basic monetary unit of India, like the dollar in the United States.

Commentary on "The Dinner Party"

"The Dinner Party" is clearly a story of plot rather than character. Although two of the characters show remarkable courage and self-control, we are not interested in them as people as much as we are in the situation that confronts them. It is not surprising that only one character is given a name; the author realizes that it is the exciting and suspenseful plot that will hold the reader's interest.

The opening paragraph gives us all the background information we need. The setting is India in the days before independence. The scene is the home of a colonial official. The spacious dining room that opens onto a veranda seems to belong to a large, imposing house. The characters are all, with one exception, associated with the military and the civil service. The exception is an American naturalist. His profession, it turns out, is of great importance to the events of the story.

The action gets under way when two of the guests take opposing positions on the subject of women's reactions to crises. One of the guests, a young girl, argues against the stereotype of female timidity. Her opponent, a colonel, takes the position that a man has superior nerve control. It is this conflict that sets in motion the major action of the story.

At first, the events seem to bear out the truth of the colonel's statement. The American, trained by his profession to be a close observer, notes a strange expression on his hostess' face. He watches her summon the native boy. The communication is obviously significant, for the boy's eyes show concern. When the bowl of milk is placed on the veranda, the naturalist knows that there is a cobra in the room. After looking all over the room, he realizes that it must be under the table.

As the story builds to its climax, the naturalist behaves exactly as the colonel has said a man would behave in a crisis. He maintains masterful control over his own emotions, and he takes command of the situation. He knows that any movement might cause the cobra to strike. To ensure the safety of everyone at the table, he must bring all activity to a dead halt. He achieves this by challenging the others to a test of self-control. For five minutes, no one is to move a muscle. He begins counting to three hundred. Suspense mounts. When the time is almost expired, he sees the cobra moving toward the bowl of milk. Once again he acts quickly, shutting the veranda doors behind the snake.

Just as the reader is on the verge of agreeing with the colonel—that in a crisis men can be counted on to exercise self-control—the tables turn. We learn that quite simply and undramatically, a woman has shown incredible control, maintaining complete composure while a snake was crawling across her foot. Realizing her own danger and the danger of everyone else at the table, she averted a panic by setting bait—a bowl of milk—to draw the cobra toward the open porch.

While the ending comes as a delightful surprise, contrasting with the reader's expectations, the author has planned for it carefully. The earlier events now fall into place: the strange expression on the hostess' face, the contracting of her facial muscles, her whispered instructions to the native boy, his expression of alarm. Because the author has laid these clues, we are prepared to accept the outcome of events. We do not feel that we have been tricked. On the contrary, we find the conclusion wholly satisfying.

This analysis of "The Dinner Party" tells more than the events of the story as they happen. It analyzes the *structure* of the story, making apparent the interconnection between setting, characters, and events. It explains how the major action of the story—the naturalist's demonstration of "perfect control"—is related to the conflict between the guests at the dinner table. It demonstrates how events build toward a point of great intensity—the climax. It shows how the ending of the story resolves the conflict in an unexpected way, by overturning the colonel's prejudice.

The purpose of this exercise has been to demonstrate what is meant by the *close reading* of a story. When you read a story carefully, you read actively, responding to clues, anticipating outcomes, seeking to understand how different elements are related to the overall structure of the story.

With practice you can develop skill in reading and analyzing a literary work. Here are some guidelines for reading fiction.

Guidelines for Reading Fiction

1. *Look up unfamiliar words and references.* In Mona Gardner's story, the word *naturalist* (which is defined in a footnote) is a key word. It lets the reader know that the American is a trained observer. In this way you are prepared for the American's actions. If you feel uncertain about the meaning of a word and cannot get the meaning from context clues, be sure to check in a standard dictionary or other reference work.

2. *Learn to draw inferences.* The author does not tell you directly that the twenty people remain motionless for almost five minutes. However, you are told that the naturalist is counting to 300 seconds. Since there are 60 seconds to the minute, nearly five minutes have elapsed when he reaches 280.

3. *Actively question the author's purpose and method.* Ask yourself what significance there might be to details that the author gives you. In the opening paragraph of the story, for example, Mona Gardner gives the reader a clear picture of the dining room, emphasizing details that she will return to later in the story. Very early on, she indicates that the conflict of the story will have something to do with self-control. This alerts you, the reader, to anticipate what is coming.

4. *Probe for the central idea or point.* "The Dinner Party" is an example of literature that is written wholly for entertainment. Other stories that you will read in this book offer more than an entertaining and clever plot. They also have something to say about life or human nature. This underlying meaning, which is called *theme,* is seldom stated directly. Generally it must be inferred from the characters and their actions.

Practice in Close Reading

The following passage is the opening of a well-known short story. The passage is accompanied by a set of questions. Read carefully before answering the questions. If you need to, look up unfamiliar words or references.

On December the third the wind changed overnight and it was winter. Until then the autumn had been mellow, soft. The leaves had lingered on the trees, golden-red, and the hedgerows were still green. The earth was rich where the plough had turned it.

Nat Hocken, because of a wartime disability, had a pension and did not work full time at the farm. He worked three days a week, and they gave him the lighter jobs: hedging, thatching, repairs to the farm buildings.

Although he was married, with children, his was a solitary disposition; he liked best to work alone. It pleased him when he was given a bank to build up, or a gate to mend at the far end of the peninsula, where the sea surrounded the farmland on either side. Then, at midday, he would pause and eat the pasty that his wife had baked for him, and, sitting on the cliff's edge, would watch the birds. Autumn was best for this, better than spring. In spring the birds flew inland, purposeful, intent; they knew where they were bound, the rhythm and ritual of their life brooked no delay. In autumn those that had not migrated overseas but remained to pass the winter were caught up in the same driving urge, but because migration was denied them followed a pattern of their own. Great flocks of them came to the peninsula, restless, uneasy, spending themselves in motion; now wheeling, circling in the sky, now settling to feed on the rich new-turned soil, but even when they fed it was as though they did so without hunger, without desire. Restlessness drove them to the skies again.

Black and white, jackdaw and gull, mingled in strange partnership, seeking some sort of liberation, never satisfied, never still. Flocks of starlings, rustling like silk, flew to fresh pasture, driven by the same necessity of movement, and the smaller birds, the finches and the larks, scattered from tree to hedge as if compelled.

Nat watched them, and he watched the sea birds too. Down in the bay they waited for the tide. They had more patience. Oyster catchers, redshank, sanderling, and curlew watched by the water's edge; as the slow sea sucked at the shore and then withdrew, leaving the strip of seaweed bare and the shingle churned, the sea birds raced and ran upon the beaches. Then that same impulse to flight seized upon them too. Crying, whistling, calling, they skimmed the placid sea and left the shore. Make haste, make speed, hurry and begone; yet where, and to what purpose? The restless urge of autumn, unsatisfying, sad, had put a spell upon them and they must flock, and wheel, and cry; they must spill themselves of motion before winter came.

Daphne du Maurier
from "The Birds"

FOR STUDY AND DISCUSSION

1. The first sentence of this story establishes the precise date of the action. Why is this fact significant?

2. What difference is noted in the behavior of birds during the spring and during the autumn?

3. What details in the passage help to build up a mood of apprehension or uneasiness?

Close Reading of a Poem

Poetry has a special language and structure. Poets rely on the suggestive power of language and choose words for their emotional effect as well as for their literal meaning. Through images and figures of speech poets appeal to the mind and to the senses. Poets also make use of patterns of sound, such as rhyme and rhythm; special forms, such as haiku; and unusual arrangements of words on a page.

In order to express themselves in effective and imaginative ways, poets take liberties with language. They do not always use complete sentences or complete thoughts. They may reverse the normal order of words. They may choose not to use conventional punctuation.

It is a good idea to read a poem several times, and aloud at least once. Often it is helpful to write a prose paraphrase of a poem, restating all its ideas in plain language (see page 604). A paraphrase is no substitute for the "meaning" of a poem, but it helps you clarify and simplify the author's ideas and language.

Read the following poem several times. Then read the explication that follows. An *explication* is a line-by-line examination of the content and technique of a work.

May Day   Sara Teasdale

A delicate fabric of bird song
  Floats in the air,
The smell of wet wild earth
  Is everywhere.

Red small leaves of the maple   5
  Are clenched like a hand,
Like girls at their first communion°
  The pear trees stand.

Oh I must pass nothing by
  Without loving it much,   10
The raindrop try with my lips,
  The grass at my touch;

For how can I be sure
  I shall see again
The world on the first of May   15
  Shining after the rain?

7. **first communion** (kə-myoōn′yən): Girls traditionally wear white for this religious ceremony.

Explication of "May Day"

The title of Sara Teasdale's poem refers to the first day of May, a holiday traditionally marked by the celebration of spring. Teasdale expresses her pleasure in the natural beauty of the season, a pleasure intensified by the knowledge that she must enjoy beauty fully while she can.

The poet responds to the glory of nature with all her senses. In the first stanza she tells us what she hears and what she smells. The birds seem to be awakening to the season. They do not produce a full-throated stream of sound but a "delicate fabric of bird song" that "floats in the air," a metaphor that suggests beautifully fine, light singing. The earth, still in its "wild," or natural, uncultivated state, smells of the rain.

In the second stanza, the poet notes what she sees. New leaves, red and small, are appearing on maple trees. The lobed leaves give the impression of a tightly closed fist. Looking at the pear trees abloom with white blossoms in umbrella-like clusters, the poet thinks of girls standing in white frocks at their first communion.

At the opening of the third stanza, the poet says she wishes to make the most of her opportunities—to experience everything with love. She involves two additional senses in her appreciation of nature. She must "try," or taste, the raindrop on her lips; she must touch the grass to feel its texture.

The poem ends on a sobering note, explaining the poet's sense of urgency about the passing of time. She feels compelled to take in everything, for there is no surety that she will ever again experience such a day. What she has for certain is the memory of the immediate moment—the beauty of the world on a spring day, "shining" after the rain.

Guidelines for Reading a Poem

1. *Read the poem aloud at least once, following the author's clues for phrasing.* Commas, semicolons, periods, and other marks of punctuation tell you where to pause. Sara Teasdale does not expect the reader to pause at the end of each line. In the last stanza, she signals no pause until the end of the poem, signifying that she wishes no break in thought.

2. *Look up key words and references.* If you did not understand the reference to "first communion" in line 7, you might miss the meaning of the simile in lines 7–8. In poetry, a word often has special connotations, or associations. The word *floats,* in line 2, for example, has the denotative meaning of "drifts or moves slowly on the surface of a fluid." In the context of the poem, however, it suggests a sound that is so light and exquisite that it seems to be supported by air in the way that a buoyant object is supported by water.

3. *Write a paraphrase of any lines that need clarification or simplification.* A paraphrase helps a reader understand imagery and figurative language. A paraphrase of the first two lines might look like this: "The notes of the song are fitted together into a pattern the way threads are woven into cloth. The sound is so soft and gentle that it seems suspended in air, as if it were lifted up and carried along." A paraphrase also supplies connections in thought where words have been omitted. A paraphrase of line 11 might read: "The poet says she must taste or sample the raindrops with her lips."

4. *Arrive at the central idea or meaning of the poem.* Try to state this theme in one or two sentences: *In "May Day," Teasdale seems to be saying that since life is short, one ought to fill time with the enjoyment of natural beauty.*

Practice in Close Reading

Read the following poem carefully; then answer the questions that follow.

Canis Major°   *Robert Frost*

The great Overdog,
That heavenly beast
With a star in one eye,
Gives a leap in the east.

He dances upright   5
All the way to the west
And never once drops
On his forefeet to rest.

I'm a poor underdog,
But tonight I will bark   10
With the great Overdog
That romps through the dark.

° **Canis Major** (kā′nĭs mā′jər): the Great Dog, a constellation of stars containing the Dog Star, Sirius, the brightest star in the heavens.

FOR STUDY AND DISCUSSION

1. Find the line in the poem that tells you where this constellation rises. What does the word *leap* suggest about the way the stars rise?
2. What line refers to the Dog Star? How do you know?
3. What movement is described in lines 5–6?
4. Explain the two meanings of the word *underdog* in the poem.

Close Reading of a Play

While many of the elements studied in connection with short stories and poetry are relevant to the study of drama, there are several additional elements that need to be taken into account. Dramatists frequently make use of stage directions to create setting and to give players instructions for acting. Sound effects are often important in creating setting and mood. Sometimes, a dramatist may use a narrator to comment on the action, as Pearl Buck does in *The Big Wave* (page 356). Generally, however, dialogue is the dramatist's most important device for presenting character and for moving the action along.

The following passage is the opening scene of a one-act play by Milton Geiger, called *In the Fog.* Read the passage several times, and aloud at least once. Then turn to the commentary on page 559.

from In the Fog   *Milton Geiger*

Sets: *A signpost on Pennsylvania Route 30. A rock or stump in the fog. A gas station pump.*

Night. At first we can only see fog drifting across a dark scene devoid of[1] detail. Then, out of the fog, there emerges toward us a white roadside signpost with a number of white painted signboards pointing to right and to left. The marker is a Pennsylvania State Route—marked characteristically "PENNA-30." Now, a light as from a far headlight sweeps the signs.

An automobile approaches. The car pulls up close. We hear the car door open and slam, and a man's footsteps approaching on the concrete. Now the signs are lit up again by a more localized, smaller source of light. The light grows stronger as the man, offstage, approaches. The Doctor enters, holding a flashlight before him. He scrutinizes[2] the road marker. He flashes his light up at the arrows. We see the legends on the markers. Pointing off right there are markers that read: York, Columbia, Lancaster; pointing left the signs read: Fayetteville, McConnellsburg, Pennsylvania Turnpike.

The Doctor's face is perplexed and annoyed as he turns his flashlight on a folded road map. He is a bit lost in the fog. Then his flashlight fails him. It goes out!

Fog and darkness create an eerie mood.

Setting is a roadside in Pennsylvania, with signposts pointing in different directions.

Automobile indicates that the action takes place in recent times.

Doctor is checking his location; presumably, he is lost.

What is the significance of these place names?

Total darkness creates a sense of danger.

---

1. **devoid** (dĭ-void′) **of:** without.
2. **scrutinizes** (skrōōt′n-īz′əz): examines carefully.

Doctor. Darn! (*He fumbles with the flashlight in the gloom. Then a voice is raised to him from offstage.*)

Eben (*offstage, strangely*). Turn around, mister. . . .

[*The* Doctor *turns sharply to stare offstage.*]

Zeke (*offstage*). You don't have to be afraid, mister. . . .

[*The* Doctor *sees two men slowly approaching out of the fog. One carries a lantern below his knees. The other holds a heavy rifle. Their features are utterly indistinct as they approach, and the rifleman holds up his gun with quiet threat.*]

Eben. You don't have to be afraid.

Doctor (*more indignant than afraid*). So you say! Who are you, man?

Eben. We don't aim to hurt you none.

Doctor. That's reassuring. I'd like to know just what you mean by this? This gun business! Who *are* you?

Zeke (*mildly*). What's your trade, mister?

Doctor. I . . . I'm a doctor. Why?

Zeke (*to* Eben). Doctor.

Eben (*nods; then to* Doctor). Yer the man we want.

Zeke. Ye'll do proper, we're thinkin'.

Eben. So ye'd better come along, mister.

Zeke. Aye.

Doctor. Why? Has—anyone been hurt?

Eben. It's for you to say if he's been hurt nigh to the finish.

Zeke. So we're askin' ye to come along, doctor.

[*The* Doctor *looks from one to another in indecision and puzzlement.*]

Eben. In the name o' mercy.

Zeke. Aye.

Doctor. I want you to understand—I'm not afraid of your gun! I'll go to your man all right. Naturally, I'm a doctor. But I demand to know who you are.

Zeke (*patiently*). Why not? Raise yer lantern, Eben. . . .

Eben (*tiredly*). Aye.

[Eben *lifts his lantern. Its light falls on their faces now, and we see that they are terrifying. Matted beards, clotted with blood; crude head bandages, crusty with dirt and dry blood. Their hair, stringy and disheveled. Their faces are lean and hollow-cheeked; their eyes sunken and tragic. The* Doctor *is shocked for a moment—then bursts out——*]

Chilling effect of voices coming out of the darkness.

Strangers are menacing, despite their claim that they mean no harm.

Note archaic character of strangers' speech.

Imagine the sudden, dramatic effect of seeing these faces surrounded by darkness.

Doctor. Good heavens!—

Zeke. That's Eben; I'm Zeke.

Doctor. What's happened? Has there been an accident or . . . what?

Zeke. Mischief's happened, stranger.

Answers are evasive.

Eben. Mischief enough.

Doctor (*looks at rifle at his chest*). There's been gunplay—hasn't there?

Zeke (*mildly ironic*). Yer tellin' us there's been gunplay!

Doctor. And I'm telling you that I'm not at all frightened! It's my duty to report this, and report it I will!

Zeke. Aye, mister. You do that.

Doctor. You're arrogant about it now! You don't think you'll be caught and dealt with. But people are losing patience with you men. . . . You . . . you moonshiners![3] Running wild . . . a law unto yourselves . . . shooting up the countryside!

Doctor assumes that Eben and Zeke are making and selling whiskey unlawfully.

Zeke. Hear that, Eben? Moonshiners.

Eben. Mischief's happened, mister, we'll warrant[4] that. . . .

Doctor. And I don't like it!

They neither affirm nor deny the charge.

Zeke. Can't say we like it better'n you do, mister. . . .

Eben (*strangely sad and remote*). What must be, must.

Why are they sad?

Zeke. There's no changin' or goin' back, and all 'at's left is the wishin' things were different.

Eben. Aye.

What do they regret?

Doctor. And while we talk, your wounded man lies bleeding, I suppose—worthless though he may be. Well? I'll have to get my instrument bag, you know. It's in the car.

[Eben *and* Zeke *part to let* Doctor *pass between them. The* Doctor *reenters, carrying his medical bag.*]

Suspense mounts. Whom is the Doctor going to attend? What will happen to him?

Doctor. I'm ready. Lead the way.

[Eben *lifts his lantern a bit and goes first.* Zeke *prods the* Doctor *ever so gently and apologetically, but firmly with the rifle muzzle. The* Doctor *leaves.* Zeke *strides off slowly after them.*]

---

3. **moonshiners:** people who distill liquor illegally.
4. **warrant** (wôr′ənt, wŏr′): declare positively.

Commentary on Scene from *In the Fog*

The dramatist of *In the Fog* has taken care to make the setting specific. The legends on the signpost tell us that the action takes place at a junction on Route 30 in southern Pennsylvania.

The opening scene arouses and sustains a foreboding mood. It is night, and dense fog makes it difficult for drivers to read the road signs. It is a lonely, dismal place to be lost.

A solitary car approaches and comes to a stop. A motorist enters carrying a flashlight. When the man, a doctor, starts to examine his road map, his flashlight goes out, and the stage is plunged into complete darkness and silence.

Suddenly we are startled by voices coming out of the darkness. Then two men enter. Because one of them is carrying a lantern below his knees, we cannot make out their faces, but there is sufficient light to see that the second man is holding a rifle. When the lantern is raised, we see two bloody, terrifying figures. Not only their appearance is frightening. The men speak in a strangely archaic way and answer the Doctor's questions evasively. Within moments the dramatist has created a menacing, suspenseful situation.

Guidelines for Reading a Play

1. *Note any information that establishes the setting and the situation.* The setting of *In the Fog* is a roadside on a foggy night. The signpost on the stage identifies the site as a junction on Pennsylvania State Route 30. It is apparent that the main action of the play will grow out of the Doctor's encounter with the two strangers.

2. *Note clues that tell you what the players are doing or how the lines are spoken.* Stage directions indicate that the Doctor's voice is "indignant." His expression, as he looks at the strangers, is puzzled and indecisive. Even though their appearance is menacing, the two strangers speak "patiently" and "mildly"; their voices are "strangely sad and remote."

3. *Anticipate the action that will develop out of each scene.* The strangers do not deny or affirm the charge that they are moonshiners. From their archaic speech and their evasive answers, we get the sense that this is no ordinary case the Doctor is asked to attend.

4. *Be alert to the mood of the play.* An eerie mood is created immediately by the fog and the darkness. This note of foreboding is sustained by the mysterious character of the strangers.

Practice in Close Reading

Here is the conclusion of *In the Fog.*

A wounded man is lying against a section of stone fence. He, too, is bearded, though very young, and his shirt is dark with blood. He breathes but never stirs otherwise. Eben *enters, followed by the* Doctor *and* Zeke.

Zeke. Ain't stirred a mite since we left 'im.
Doctor. Let's have that lantern here! (*The* Doctor *tears the man's shirt for better access to the wound. Softly*) Dreadful! Dreadful . . . !
Zeke's voice (*off scene*). Reckon it's bad in the chest like that, hey?
Doctor (*taking pulse*). His pulse is positively racing . . . ! How long has he been this way?
Zeke. A long time, mister. A long time. . . .
Doctor (*to* Eben). You! Hand me my bag.

[Eben *puts down lantern and hands bag to* Doctor. *The* Doctor *opens bag and takes out a couple of retractors.*[1] Zeke *holds lantern close now.*]

Doctor. Lend me a hand with these retractors. (*He works on the man.*) All right . . . when I tell you to draw back on the retractors— draw back.
Eben. Aye.
Zeke. How is 'e, mister?
Doctor (*preoccupied*). More retraction. Pull them a bit more. Hold it. . . .
Eben. Bad, ain't he?
Doctor. Bad enough. The bullet didn't touch any lung tissue far as I can see right now. There's some pneumothorax[2] though. All I can do now is plug the wound. There's some cotton and gauze wadding in my bag. Find it. . . .

[Zeke *probes about silently in the bag and comes up with a small dark box of gauze.*]

Doctor. That's it. (*Works a moment in silence*) I've never seen anything quite like it.

---

1. **retractors** (rĭ-trăk′tərz): surgical instruments for holding back the flesh at the edge of a wound.
2. **pneumothorax** (nōō′mō-thôr′ăks, -thôr′ăks′, nyōō′): air or gas in the chest cavity.

Eben. Yer young, doctor. Lot's o' things you've never seen.
Doctor. Adhesive tape!

[Zeke *finds a roll of three-inch tape and hands it to the* Doctor, *who tears off long strips and slaps them on the dressing and pats and smooths them to man's chest.* Eben *replaces equipment in* Doctor's *bag and closes it with a hint of the finality to come. A preview of dismissal, so to speak.*]

Doctor (*at length*). There. So much for that. Now then—(*Takes man's shoulders*) give me a hand here.
Zeke (*quiet suspicion*). What fer?
Doctor. We've got to move this man.
Zeke. What fer?
Doctor (*stands; indignantly*). We've got to get him to a hospital for treatment; a thorough cleansing of the wound; irrigation.[3] I've done all I can for him here.
Zeke. I reckon he'll be all right 'thout no hospital.
Doctor. Do you realize how badly this man's hurt!
Eben. He won't bleed to death, will he?
Doctor. I don't think so—not with that plug and pressure dressing. But bleeding isn't the only danger we've got to——
Zeke (*interrupts*). All right, then. Much obliged to you.
Doctor. This man's dangerously hurt!
Zeke. Reckon he'll pull through now, thanks to you.
Doctor. I'm glad you feel that way about it! But I'm going to report this to the Pennsylvania State Police at the first telephone I reach!
Zeke. We ain't stoppin' ye, mister.
Eben. Fog is liftin', Zeke. Better be done with this, I say.
Zeke (*nods, sadly*). Aye. Ye can go now, mister . . . and thanks. (*Continues*) We never meant a mite o' harm, I can tell ye. If we killed, it was no wish of ours.
Eben. What's done is done. Aye.
Zeke. Ye can go now, stranger. . . .

[Eben *hands* Zeke *the* Doctor's *bag.* Zeke *hands it gently to the* Doctor.]

Doctor. Very well. You haven't heard the last of this, though!
Zeke. That's the truth, mister. We've killed, aye; and we've been hurt for it. . . .
Eben. Hurt bad.

---

3. **irrigation:** here, flushing out a wound with water or other fluid.

[*The* Doctor's *face is puckered with doubt and strange apprehension.*]

Zeke. We're not alone, mister. We ain't the only ones. (*Sighs*) Ye can go now, doctor . . . and our thanks to ye. . . .

[*The* Doctor *leaves the other two, still gazing at them in strange enchantment and wonder and a touch of indignation.*]

Eben's voice. Thanks mister. . . .
Zeke's voice. In the name o' mercy. . . . We thank you. . . .
Eben. In the name o' mercy.
Zeke. Thanks, mister. . . .
Eben. In the name o' kindness. . . .

[*The two men stand with their wounded comrade at their feet — like a group statue in the park. The fog thickens across the scene. Far off the long, sad wail of a locomotive whimpers in the dark.*

The scene now shifts to a young Attendant *standing in front of a gasoline pump taking a reading and recording it in a book as he prepares to close up. He turns as he hears the car approach on the gravel drive.*

The Doctor *enters.*]

Attendant (*pleasantly*). Good evening, sir. (*Nods off at car*) Care to pull 'er up to this pump, sir? Closing up.
Doctor (*impatiently*). No. Where's your telephone, please? I've just been held up!
Attendant. Pay station inside, sir. . . .
Doctor. Thank you! (*The* Doctor *starts to go past the* Attendant.)
Attendant. Excuse me, sir. . . .
Doctor (*stops*). Eh, what is it, what is it?
Attendant. Uh . . . what sort of looking fellows were they?
Doctor. Oh — two big fellows with a rifle; faces and heads bandaged and smeared with dirt and blood. Friend of theirs with a gaping hole in his chest. I'm a doctor, so they forced me to attend him. Why?
Attendant. *Those* fellers, huh?
Doctor. Then you know about them!
Attendant. I guess so.
Doctor. They're armed and they're desperate!
Attendant. That was about two or three miles back, would you say?
Doctor (*fumbling in pocket*). Just about — I don't seem to have the change. I wonder if you'd spare me change for a quarter . . . ?
Attendant (*makes change from metal coin canister at his belt*). Certainly, sir. . . .

Doctor. What town was that back there, now?

Attendant (*dumps coins in other's hand*). There you are, sir.

Doctor (*impatient*). Yes, thank you. I say—what town was that back there, so I can tell the police?

Attendant. That was . . . Gettysburg, mister. . . .

Doctor. Gettysburg . . . ?

Attendant. Gettysburg and Gettysburg battlefield. . . . (*Looks off*) When it's light and the fog's gone, you can see the gravestones. Meade's men . . . Pickett's men, Robert E. Lee's.[4] . . .

[*The* Doctor *is looking off with the* Attendant; *now he turns his head slowly to stare at the other man.*]

Attendant (*continues*). On nights like this—well—you're not the first those men've stopped . . . or the last. (*Nods off*) Fill 'er up, mister?

Doctor. Yes, fill 'er up. . . .

---

4. **Meade's men . . . Lee's:** The Battle of Gettysburg was a turning point in the Civil War. On July 1–3, 1863, the Confederacy's forces, under Robert E. Lee, met the Union forces, under George Gordon Meade. The climax of the battle came when 15,000 Confederate soldiers, led by George Pickett, charged Cemetery Ridge and were repelled. The North suffered about 23,000 casualties; the South about 20,000.

FOR STUDY AND DISCUSSION

1. The identity of Eben and Zeke remains a mystery until the end of the play. Who are these men?

2. What clues does the playwright give you to their identity before the last scene?

3. What significance does the setting have in this play?

WRITING ABOUT LITERATURE

The Writing Process

We often refer to writing an essay as a *process*, which consists of three key stages or phases: **prewriting, writing,** and **revising.** In this process, much of the crucial work precedes the actual writing of the paper. In the prewriting stage, the writer makes decisions about what to say and how to say it. Prewriting activities include choosing and limiting a topic, gathering ideas, organizing ideas, and arriving at a *thesis*—the controlling idea for the paper. In the next stage, the writer uses the working plan to write a first draft of the essay. In the revising stage, the writer rewrites the draft, several times perhaps, adding or deleting ideas, rearranging order, rephrasing for clarity, and proofreading for errors in spelling, punctuation, and grammar. The steps in the process are interdependent. For example, as ideas are developed on paper, the writer may find that the central idea of the paper needs to be restated or that a different organization is needed.

The amount of time devoted to each stage will vary with individual assignments. During a classroom examination, you will have limited time to plan your essay and to proofread your paper. For a term paper, you may have weeks or months to prepare your essay.

On the following pages the steps in this process are illustrated through the development of several model essays.

Answering Examination Questions

Often you may be asked to show your understanding of a literary work or topic by writing a short essay in class. Usually, your teacher will give you a specific question to answer. How well you do will depend not only on how carefully you have read and mastered the material, but on how carefully you read and interpret the essay question.

Before you begin to write, be sure you understand what the question calls for. If a question requires that you give three reasons for a character's actions, and you supply only two, your answer will be incomplete. If the question asks you to *contrast* two settings, be sure that you point out their differences, not their similarities. Don't use essays or short stories if the question calls for poetry. Always take some time to read the essay question carefully in order to determine how it should be answered.

Remember that you are expected to demonstrate specific knowledge of the literature. Any general statement should be supported by evidence. If you wish to show that a character changes, for example, you should refer to specific actions, dialogue, thoughts and feelings, or direct comments by the author, in order to illustrate your point. If you are allowed to use your textbook during the examination, you may occasionally quote short passages or refer to a specific page in order to provide supporting evidence.

At the start, it may be helpful to jot down some notes to guide you in writing your essay. If you have four main points to make, you may then decide what the most effective order of presentation will be. You might build up to your strongest point, or you might present your points to develop a striking contrast. Aim for a logical organization.

Also remember that length alone is not satisfactory. Your answer must be clearly related to the question, and it must be presented in acceptable, correct English. Always take some time to proofread your paper.

The key word in examination questions is the *verb*. Let us look briefly at some common instructions used in examinations.

ANALYSIS

A question may ask you to *analyze* some aspect of a literary work. When you analyze something, you take it apart to see how each part works. In literary analysis you generally focus on some limited aspect of a work in order to better understand and appreciate the work as a whole. For example, you might analyze the technique of suspense in "The Tiger's Heart" (page 196); you might analyze the role of moonlight in "The Highwayman" (page 452); you might analyze Thurber's use of exaggeration in "The Night the Bed Fell" (page 148).

COMPARISON CONTRAST

A question may ask that you *compare* (or *contrast*) two characters, two settings, two ideas. When you *compare*, you point out likenesses; when you *contrast*, you point out differences. Sometimes you will be asked to *compare and contrast*. In that event, you will be expected to deal with similarities and differences. You might, for instance, compare and contrast the characters of Emily Vanderpool and Lottie Jump in "Bad Characters" (page 64). You might compare and contrast two versions of a fable, "The Fox and the Crow," by Aesop (page 530), and by Thurber (page 539). Sometimes, the word *compare* is used to include both comparison and contrast. Always check with your teacher to make sure that you understand how the term *compare* is being used.

DESCRIPTION   If a question asks you to *describe* a setting or a character, you are expected to give a picture in words. In describing a setting, include not only details that establish the historical period and locale, but those details that evoke a mood. In describing a character, you should deal with methods of direct and indirect characterization (see pages 594–595). You might describe the scene in "Stopping by Woods on a Snowy Evening" (page 424); you might describe each of the Christmas spirits in "A Christmas Carol" (page 291).

DISCUSSION   The word *discuss* in a question is much more general than the other words we've looked at. When you are asked to discuss something, you are expected to examine it in detail. If you are asked to discuss the images in a poem, for example, you must deal with all major images; if asked to discuss the use of dialect in a story or poem, you must be sure to cover all significant examples. If your assignment asked you to discuss Helen Keller's sensitivity to nature in the selection from her autobiography (page 192), you would be obligated to deal with not only her feelings of nature's benign influence, but also her experience of nature's treachery.

EXPLANATION   A question may ask you to *explain* something. When you explain, you give reasons for something being the way it is. You make clear a character's actions, or you show how something has come about. For example, you might explain how Humaweepi is prepared for his role as warrior priest (page 180); you might explain what happens to the *Hesperus* and its crew (page 186); you might explain Holmes's plan for recovering the Mazarin Stone (page 324).

ILLUSTRATION   The word *illustrate, demonstrate,* or *show* asks that you provide examples to support a point. You might be asked to give examples of musical devices in "Annabel Lee" (page 440). You might be asked to illustrate peculiarities of Jean Kerr's pets in "Dogs That Have Known Me" (page 393). You might be asked to select and demonstrate instances of natural dialogue in *The Pussycat and the Expert Plumber Who Was a Man* (page 340).

INTERPRETATION   The word *interpret* in a question asks that you give the meaning or significance of something. You might, for example, be asked to interpret "The Listeners" (page 426), a poem that is famous for its mysterious meaning.

At times it will be useful to combine approaches. In discussing a subject, you may draw upon illustration, explanation, or analysis. In comparing or contrasting two works, you may rely on description or interpretation. However, an examination question generally will have a central purpose, and you should focus on this purpose in preparing your answer.

On the following pages, you will find some sample examination questions and answers for study and discussion.

I

QUESTION   *The boy in Ernest Hemingway's story "A Day's Wait" (page 253) mistakenly believes that he is going to die. Why is he confused? Explain in a single paragraph.*

METHOD OF ATTACK   This question calls for reasons. Before writing, jot down some notes to guide you:

The boy is familiar with the Celsius scale.
The doctor uses a Fahrenheit thermometer.
Boy has a temperature of 102°.
On a Celsius thermometer, a temperature of 44° would be fatal.

In the opening sentence of your answer, state your *thesis*, your main point, wording it in such a way that you restate the key words of the question.

ANSWER
Main Idea

Supporting Statements

The boy in Hemingway's "A Day's Wait" is confused about two systems of temperature measurement. Because he has gone to school in France, he is familiar with the Celsius scale of temperature. The normal temperature on the Celsius scale is 37°. A temperature as high as 44° would be fatal. The doctor who examines the boy uses a Fahrenheit thermometer on which the normal reading is 98.6°. The boy thinks that the doctor has used a Celsius thermometer. When he learns that his temperature is 102°, he assumes he is going to die.

Length: 93 words

Reading and Writing About Literature   567

II

QUESTION

QUESTION   *What is the role of the narrator in Pearl Buck's* The Big Wave *(page 356)? In your analysis, refer to specific passages in the play.*

ANSWER
Main Idea

The narrator in Pearl Buck's *The Big Wave* helps us to understand and appreciate the meaning of the characters' experiences. Like the omniscient ("all-knowing") narrator of a short story or novel, he fills us in on the background of events, provides a bridge between different episodes of the play, and comments on the action. Although he does not play an active role in the drama, he knows what every character does and thinks.

Present evidence in a logical sequence.

In Act One, the narrator introduces us to Kino and his family. He tells us how Kino and his ancestors have lived in the Japanese fishing village. At the opening of Act Two, he describes life in the village. He tells us how the villagers spend their days at work and at play. He even describes the foods that they eat. In Acts Three and Four, the narrator comments on the events of the play, noting how the big wave has brought change to the village and its inhabitants. In the final act, the narrator condenses the events of eight years so that we see a new generation of villagers confronting life.

Length: 185 words

III

QUESTION   *What makes T. J. a natural leader of the boys in "Antaeus" (page 212)? Discuss his qualities of leadership, using specific references to the story.*

METHOD OF ATTACK

Notes
T. J. had a slow, gentle voice, but he was no sissy (page 212).
He was not insecure with strangers; he reserved his opinions (page 212).
He was not ashamed of being different (page 213).
He was self-assured, not easily bullied (page 213).
He had pride in his accomplishments (page 213).
Boys were attracted to his "stolid sense of rightness and belonging" (page 213).
His imagination excited other boys (page 213).
T. J. persisted in his project, keeping others interested (page 214).
He was intelligent (page 215).
He made others share his goal (page 215).
He knew when to compromise (page 216).

There is a great deal of information to organize here. You might try grouping the notes so that you can present the evidence under three categories: perhaps self-confidence, imagination, and persistence.

ANSWER

Main Idea

First Quality

Supporting Statements

T. J., a character in "Antaeus," is a natural leader because of his self-confidence, imagination, and persistence. Although he is a stranger, he is not ashamed of being different. He feels secure about himself. He does not get upset or angry when the boys in the gang begin to tease him. When Blackie laughs at him because he comes from Alabama, T. J. remains calm and assured. When Charley kids him about his name, T. J. replies without hesitation or shame. He doesn't allow himself to be bullied, and he doesn't lose his temper because he has a "stolid sense of rightness and belonging."

Second Quality

Supporting Statements

T. J. has imagination, and his ideas appeal to the other boys. He starts them thinking about a roof garden, and whenever their enthusiasm begins to wane, he renews their interest in the project. He talks to them about raising watermelons, flowers, grass, and trees. Because he is intelligent, he knows when to give in. Although he wants to grow corn and vegetables, he compromises on his dream and agrees to grow a grass lawn.

Third Quality

Supporting Statements

T. J. perseveres throughout the winter. He gives the boys direction and organization. Even though the others become distracted, T. J. persists in carrying earth up to the roof. He works harder than any of the other boys to fulfill their mutual goal, and he inspires the others by his example.

Length: 230 words

Writing on a Topic of Your Own

Choosing a Topic

At times you may be asked to choose a topic of your own. Often it will be necessary to read a work more than once before a suitable topic presents itself.

A topic may focus on one element or technique in a work. If you are writing about fiction, you might concentrate on some aspect of plot, such as conflict. Or you might concentrate on character, setting, or theme. If you are writing about poetry, you might choose to analyze imagery or figurative language. A topic may deal with more than one aspect of a work. You might, for example, discuss several elements of a short story in order to show how an idea or theme is developed.

Once you have a topic in mind, your object is to form it into a *thesis,* a controlling idea that represents the conclusion of your findings. You would then need to present the evidence supporting your position. It may be necessary to read a work several times before you can formulate a thesis. Here are some examples:

"The Brain and I" (page 8)

Topic   Contrasting the roles of Harvey and Chip as business partners
Thesis   In this story, Harvey supplies the brains of the partnership, and Chip supplies the muscle.

"Guinea Pig" (page 44) and "The Night the Bed Fell" (page 148)

Topic   Comparing the humor in these essays
Thesis   In both essays, humor results from situations in which people's intentions misfire.

"Last Cover" (page 158)

Topic   Contrasting attitudes toward nature of Colin and his father
Thesis   Although Colin and his father both love nature, Colin shows a greater instinct for understanding the woods and wild things.

"Humaweepi, the Warrior Priest" (page 180)

Topic   Describing Humaweepi's education for warrior priest
Thesis   To prepare for his role as warrior priest, Humaweepi learns to live in harmony with nature.

"Rip Van Winkle" (page 270)

Topic   Comparing the characters of Rip and Dame Van Winkle
Thesis   Both Rip and Dame Van Winkle are treated as comic stereotypes.

"A Christmas Carol" (page 291)

Topic   Analyzing the change in Scrooge's character
Thesis   During the visit of each Christmas spirit, Scrooge gets valuable insights into his own character, which help to change him from a hardhearted miser into a kind and charitable man.

The Big Wave (page 356)

Topic   Interpreting the theme of *The Big Wave*
Thesis   The statement "Life is stronger than death," which occurs at several important points in the play, may be taken as the theme, or underlying meaning, of the work.

Gathering Evidence

It is a good idea to take notes as you read, even if you do not yet have a topic in mind. Later on, when you have settled on a topic, you can discard any notes that are not relevant. Some people prefer a worksheet, others index cards. In the beginning, you should record all your reactions. A topic may emerge during this early stage. As you continue to read, you will shape your topic into a rough thesis.

When you take notes, make an effort to state ideas in your own words. If a specific phrase or line is so important that it deserves to be quoted directly, be sure to enclose the words in quotation marks. When you transfer your notes to your final paper, be sure to copy quotations exactly.

In working with a short poem, you may cite phrases and lines without identifying the quotations by line numbers. If you cite lines in a long poem, you should enclose the line numbers in parentheses following the quotation. The following note, which is for Longfellow's poem "The Wreck of the *Hesperus*" (page 186), shows you how to do this:

> When the *Hesperus* struck the breakers, the rocks "gored her side/Like the horns of an angry bull" (lines 71–72).

The slash (/) shows the reader where line 71 ends and line 72 begins.

If you cite three or more lines of a poem, you should separate the quotation from your own text in this way.

> Longfellow compares the *Hesperus* to a frightened horse that trembles, then springs from the ground when the storm strikes:
>
> Down came the storm, and smote amain
>   The vessel in its strength;
> She shuddered and paused, like a frightened steed,
>   Then leaped her cable's length.
>
> (lines 25–28)

Let us suppose you have chosen to compare the following poems:

The Wind   *James Stephens*

The wind stood up, and gave a shout;
He whistled on his fingers, and

Kicked the withered leaves about,
And thumped the branches with his hand,

And said he'd kill, and kill, and kill;
And so he will! And so he will!

The Wind Tapped like a Tired Man

Emily Dickinson

The wind tapped like a tired man,
And like a host, "Come in,"
I boldly answered; entered then
My residence within

A rapid, footless guest,   5
To offer whom a chair
Were as impossible as hand
A sofa to the air.

No bone had he to bind him,
His speech was like the push   10
Of numerous hummingbirds at once
From a superior° bush.

12. **superior:** here, high up.

His countenance° a billow,
His fingers, as he passed,
Let go a music, as of tunes   15
Blown tremulous° in glass.

13. **countenance** (koun′tə-nəns): face, expression.

16. **tremulous** (trĕm′yə-ləs): vibrating, quivering.

He visited, still flitting;
Then, like a timid man,
Again he tapped—'twas flurriedly°—
And I became alone.   20

19. **flurriedly** (flûr′ē-əd′lē): excitedly.

Obviously there is common ground for comparison of these poems. You might work out a chart of this kind for taking notes, letting the letter A stand for "The Wind," and B for "The Wind Tapped like a Tired Man":

Similarities	Differences
The subject of both poems is the wind.	In A, the wind is a strong gale. The "withered leaves" suggest autumn. In B, the wind is a gentle breeze.
The poets compare the wind to a person.	In A, the poet describes the wind as a furious man. In B, the poet describes the wind as a shy visitor.
Both poems describe the wind in terms of human feelings and characteristics.	In A, the wind is angry and violent. It shouts and whistles. It kicks the leaves and thumps the branches. It is determined to kill.
	In B, the wind is timid. Its movements are light and rapid. It flits and taps timidly, "like a tired man." It has no visible form—no feet ("footless") and no bones, yet has speech, a face, and fingers. Its speech is like the sound of hummingbirds. Its face ("countenance") is a billow. Its fingers produce music like the sound that comes from a reed instrument. It is shy, "like a timid man," and taps "flurriedly."
Both poems suggest that nature has something in common with human beings.	

You might find at this point that a thesis statement has begun to emerge. *Although the poems are quite different in their treatment of the wind, both convey the special character of the wind by representing it as having human qualities.* You would continue to study the poems, gathering additional evidence and refining your thesis statement. The next step is organizing the material.

Organizing the Material

Before you begin writing, organize your main ideas into an outline. Your outline should provide for an introduction, a body, and a conclusion. The introduction should identify the author(s), the work(s), or the problem that is under study. It should contain a statement of your thesis as well. The body of your paper should present the evidence supporting your thesis. The conclusion should bring together your main ideas.

This is one kind of outline you might use for a short paper. It indicates the main idea of each paragraph.

INTRODUCTION

Paragraph 1   *Thesis*   Although the poets describe different aspects of the wind, both choose to convey the special character of the wind by representing it as having human qualities.

BODY

Paragraph 2   Stephens' poem represents the wind as an angry, violent man, whose object is destruction.

Paragraph 3   Dickinson's poem represents the wind as a visitor with a gentle, shy temperament.

CONCLUSION

Paragraph 4   In treating the wind in terms of human feelings and characteristics, the poets make us aware of certain resemblances between nature and human beings.

Writing the Essay

Here is a model essay developing the thesis statement.

TITLE   A COMPARISON OF JAMES STEPHENS' "THE WIND" AND EMILY DICKINSON'S "THE WIND TAPPED LIKE A TIRED MAN"

INTRODUCTION
Identify works and
authors.
   "The Wind" by James Stephens and "The Wind Tapped like a Tired Man" by Emily Dickinson deal with very different types of wind. Stephens' wind is a strong blast, perhaps a gale; Dickinson's

wind is a light, gentle breeze. *Although the poets describe different aspects of the wind, both choose to convey the special character of the wind by representing it as having human qualities.*

Thesis

BODY
Use quotations wherever apt.

Stephens' wind is a violent, raging figure. From the reference to "the withered leaves" in line 3, we can infer that it is late autumn, when powerful gusts are common. Stephens treats the characteristics of the wind—its sounds and its movements—as if they were produced by a human voice, human limbs, and human feelings. The "shout" is the sudden roar of the wind as it sweeps over the land. As it moves, it makes a high, shrill sound, its "whistle." The wind appears to be acting in fury as it lifts and scatters the leaves and pounds the branches of the trees. The wind's rage mounts as it builds to gale proportions. The repetition of the words *kill* and *will* in the concluding lines of the poem emphasizes the destructive intent of the storm.

Transition Sentence

While Stephens presents his wind as a threatening figure that shouts, whistles, kicks, and thumps, Dickinson gives us a gentle ghost of a wind. This wind is timid: it taps softly, "like a tired man." It has no visible form. Since it is "footless" and has no "bone," or skeleton, it cannot be seated. Its speech is a low, continuous humming, like that produced by the vibration of humming-

Give evidence of close reading

birds' wings. Its face ("countenance") is a great swelling or surging of air. The sound the breeze makes is attributed to the fingers of the wind, making music like that produced by glass reeds that vibrate when air is blown over them. The wind's movements are light and rapid; it flits, and shyly, "like a timid man," taps "flurriedly" and leaves.

CONCLUSION

By choosing to describe the wind in terms of human feelings and characteristics, the poets seem to be saying that nature has a great deal in common with human beings. The poets make us conscious of similarities we might never have discovered for ourselves.

Length: 374 words

Revising Papers

When you write an essay in class, you have a limited amount of time to plan and develop your essay. Nevertheless, you should save a few minutes to read over your work and make necessary corrections.

When an essay is assigned as homework, you have more time to prepare it carefully. Get into the habit of revising your work. A first draft of an essay should be treated as a rough copy of your manuscript. Chances are that reworking your first draft will result in a clearer and stronger paper.

When you revise your paper, examine it critically for awkward sentences, inexact language, errors in capitalization, punctuation, and spelling. Rewrite any passages that are unclear or incomplete.

Here are some guidelines for revision.

Guidelines for Revising a Paper

1. *Check to see that your major point, a thesis, is clearly stated.* In a short essay, the thesis should be stated in the first sentence. In a longer composition, the thesis generally should appear in the introductory paragraph.

2. *Follow a logical organization.* A long composition should have an introduction, a body, and a conclusion. Each part of the essay should be clearly related to the thesis.

3. *Make sure that ideas are adequately developed.* Support any generalization with specific evidence.

4. *Check for errors in capitalization, punctuation, spelling, and sentence structure.*

Here is an early draft of the model essay on pages 574–575, showing
how it was revised for greater clarity, accuracy, and conciseness.

"The Wind" by   *"The Wind Tapped like a Tired Man" by*

~~In their poems,~~ James Stephens and ∧ Emily Dickinson deal with

types of wind.
very different ~~forces of nature.~~ ~~In~~ Stephens' ~~poem, the~~ wind is a

perhaps a gale;
strong blast. Dickinson's wind is a light, gentle breeze. Although

poets describe   *aspects   the*
the ~~poems deal with~~ different ~~kinds~~ of wind∧, both ~~poets~~ choose to

convey the special character of the wind by representing it as

having human qualities.

Stephens' wind is a violent, raging figure. ⟨Stephens treats

the characteristics of the wind--its sounds and its movements--as

if they were produced by a human voice, human limbs, and human

⟨*From the reference to "the withered leaves" in line 3, we can infer that it*⟩
feelings. | ~~The season~~ is late autumn, when powerful gusts are common.

The "shout" is the sudden roar of the wind
∧As it sweeps over the land∧, ~~the wind roars. This is its shout.~~

As it moves, it makes a   *its "whistle."*
~~Its "whistle" is the~~ high, shrill sound∧ ~~it makes as it moves.~~ The wind

appears to be acting in fury as it lifts (the leaves) and scatters ~~them,~~

and pounds the branches of the trees. ∧The repetition of the words

kill and will in the concluding lines of the poem emphasizes the

destructive intent   *rage*
~~fury~~ of the storm. | The wind's ~~fury~~ mounts as it builds to gale

proportions.

While Stephens presents his wind as a threatening figure
that shouts, whistles, kicks, and thumps,
Dickinson gives us a gentle ghost of a wind. This wind is timid:

it taps softly, "like a tired man." It has no visible form.
Since it is "footless" and has no "bone," or skeleton,
It cannot be seated. Its speech is a low, continuous humming, like
                    the vibration of
that produced by ∧hummingbirds' wings. Its face ("countenance") is a
                                    the breeze maker
great swelling or surging of air. The sound is attributed to the
                                      ∧

fingers of the wind, making music like that produced by glass reeds
that vibrate
∧when air is blown over them. The wind's movements are light and
                                    "like a timid man," taps "flurriedly"
rapid; it flits, and ~~leaves~~ shyly∧   and leaves.
)

By choosing to describe the wind in terms of human feelings and

characteristics, the poets seem to be saying that nature has a
                        The poets make us
great deal in common with human beings. ~~We become~~ conscious of

similarities we might never have discovered for ourselves.

ADDITIONAL SELECTIONS

Humpty Dumpty   *Lewis Carroll*

Humpty Dumpty was sitting, with his legs crossed like a Turk, on the top of a high wall —such a narrow one that Alice quite wondered how he could keep his balance—and, as his eyes were steadily fixed in the opposite direction, and he didn't take the least notice of her, she thought he must be a stuffed figure, after all.

"And how exactly like an egg he is!" she said aloud, standing with her hands ready to catch him, for she was every moment expecting him to fall.

"It's *very* provoking," Humpty Dumpty said after a long silence, looking away from Alice as he spoke, "to be called an egg— *very!*"

"I said you *looked* like an egg, Sir," Alice gently explained. "And some eggs are very pretty, you know," she added, hoping to turn her remark into a sort of compliment.

"Some people," said Humpty Dumpty, looking away from her as usual, "have no more sense than a baby!"

Alice didn't know what to say to this: it wasn't at all like conversation, she thought, as he never said anything to *her*; in fact, his last remark was evidently addressed to a tree—so she stood and softly repeated to herself:

Humpty Dumpty sat on a wall:
Humpty Dumpty had a great fall.
All the King's horses and all the King's men
Couldn't put Humpty Dumpty in his place
   again.

"That last line is much too long for the poetry," she added, almost out loud, forgetting that Humpty Dumpty would hear her.

"Don't stand chattering to yourself like that," Humpty Dumpty said, looking at her for the first time, "but tell me your name and your business."

"My *name* is Alice, but—"

"It's a stupid name enough!" Humpty Dumpty interrupted impatiently. "What does it mean?"

"*Must* a name mean something?" Alice asked doubtfully.

"Of course it must," Humpty Dumpty said with a short laugh: "*my* name means the shape I am—and a good handsome shape it is, too. With a name like yours, you might be any shape, almost."

"Why do you sit out here all alone?" said Alice, not wishing to begin an argument.

"Why, because there's nobody with me!" cried Humpty Dumpty. "Did you think I didn't know the answer to *that*? Ask another."

"Don't you think you'd be safer down on the ground?" Alice went on, not with any idea of making another riddle, but simply in her good-natured anxiety for the queer creature. "That wall is so *very* narrow!"

"What tremendously easy riddles you ask!" Humpty Dumpty growled out. "Of course I don't think so! Why, if ever I *did* fall off—which there's no chance of—but *if* I did——" Here he pursed up his lips, and looked so solemn and grand that Alice could hardly help laughing. "*If* I *did* fall," he went on, "*the King has promised me*—ah, you may turn pale, if you like! You didn't think I was going to say that, did you? *The King has promised me—with his very own mouth*—to —to——"

"To send all his horses and all his men," Alice interrupted, rather unwisely.

"Now I declare that's too bad!" Humpty Dumpty cried, breaking into a sudden passion. "You've been listening at doors—and behind trees—and down chimneys—or you couldn't have known it!"

"I haven't indeed!" Alice said very gently. "It's in a book."

"Ah, well! They may write such things in a *book*," Humpty Dumpty said in a calmer tone. "That's what you call a History of England, that is. Now, take a good look at me! I'm one that has spoken to a King, *I* am: mayhap[1] you'll never see such another: and, to show you I'm not proud, you may shake hands with me!" And he grinned almost from ear to ear, as he leaned forwards (and as nearly as possible fell off the wall in doing so) and offered Alice his hand. She watched him a little anxiously as she took it. "If he smiled much more the ends of his mouth might meet behind," she thought: "And

then I don't know *what* would happen to his head! I'm afraid it would come off!"

"Yes, all his horses and all his men," Humpty Dumpty went on. "They'd pick me up again in a minute, *they* would! However, this conversation is going on a little too fast: let's go back to the last remark but one."

"I'm afraid I can't quite remember it," Alice said, very politely.

"In that case we start afresh," said Humpty Dumpty, "and it's my turn to choose a subject——" ("He talks about it just as if it was a game!" thought Alice.) "So here's a question for you. How old did you say you were?"

Alice made a short calculation, and said "Seven years and six months."

"Wrong!" Humpty Dumpty exclaimed triumphantly. "You never said a word like it!"

"I thought you meant 'How old *are* you?'" Alice explained.

"If I'd meant that, I'd have said it," said Humpty Dumpty.

Alice didn't want to begin another argument, so she said nothing.

"Seven years and six months!" Humpty Dumpty repeated thoughtfully. "An uncomfortable sort of age. Now if you'd asked *my* advice, I'd have said 'Leave off at seven'—but it's too late now."

"I never ask advice about growing," Alice said indignantly.

"Too proud?" the other inquired.

Alice felt even more indignant at this suggestion. "I mean," she said, "that one can't help growing older."

"*One* can't, perhaps," said Humpty Dumpty; "but *two* can. With proper assistance, you might have left off at seven."

"What a beautiful belt you've got on!" Alice suddenly remarked. (They had had quite enough of the subject of age, she thought: and, if they really were to take turns in choosing subjects, it was *her* turn now.)

---

1. **mayhap:** perhaps (archaic).

"At least," she corrected herself on second thoughts, "a beautiful cravat, I should have said—no, a belt, I mean—I beg your pardon!" she added in dismay, for Humpty Dumpty looked thoroughly offended, and she began to wish she hadn't chosen that subject. "If only I knew," she thought to herself, "which was neck and which was waist!"

Evidently Humpty Dumpty was very angry, though he said nothing for a minute or two. When he *did* speak again, it was in a deep growl.

"It is a—*most*—*provoking*—thing," he said at last, "when a person doesn't know a cravat from a belt!"

"I know it's very ignorant of me," Alice said, in so humble a tone that Humpty Dumpty relented.

"It's a cravat, child, and a beautiful one, as you say. It's a present from the White King and Queen. There now!"

"Is it really?" said Alice, quite pleased to find that she *had* chosen a good subject after all.

"They gave it me," Humpty Dumpty continued thoughtfully as he crossed one knee over the other and clasped his hands round it, "they gave it me—for an un-birthday present."

"I beg your pardon?" Alice said with a puzzled air.

"I'm not offended," said Humpty Dumpty.

"I mean, what *is* an un-birthday present?"

"A present given when it isn't your birthday, of course."

Alice considered a little. "I like birthday presents best," she said at last.

"You don't know what you're talking about!" cried Humpty Dumpty. "How many days are there in a year?"

"Three hundred and sixty-five," said Alice.

"And how many birthdays have you?"

"One."

"And if you take one from three hundred and sixty-five what remains?"

"Three-hundred and sixty-four, of course."

Humpty Dumpty looked doubtful. "I'd rather see that done on paper," he said.

Alice couldn't help smiling as she took out her memorandum book, and worked the sum for him:

$$\begin{array}{r} 365 \\ \underline{1} \\ \underline{364} \end{array}$$

Humpty Dumpty took the book and looked at it carefully. "That seems to be done right——" he began.

"You're holding it upside down!" Alice interrupted.

"To be sure I was!" Humpty Dumpty said gaily as she turned it round for him. "I thought it looked a little queer. As I was saying, that *seems* to be done right—though I haven't time to look it over thoroughly just now—and that shows that there are three hundred and sixty-four days when you might get un-birthday presents——"

"Certainly," said Alice.

"And only *one* for birthday presents, you know. There's glory for you!"

"I don't know what you mean by 'glory,'" Alice said.

Humpty Dumpty smiled contemptuously. "Of course you don't—till I tell you. I meant 'there's a nice knock-down argument for you!'"

"But 'glory' doesn't mean 'a nice knock-down argument,'" Alice objected.

"When *I* use a word," Humpty Dumpty said, in rather a scornful tone, "it means just what I choose it to mean—neither more nor less."

"The question is," said Alice, "whether you *can* make words mean so many different things."

"The question is," said Humpty Dumpty, "which is to be master—that's all."

1. Why does Alice have difficulty carrying on a conversation with Humpty Dumpty?
2. Alice thinks that Humpty Dumpty talks about language "just as if it was a game." How does Humpty Dumpty "play" with language?
3. Do you agree that an "un-birthday" present is better than a birthday present?

SUGGESTIONS FOR WRITING

1. Explain why Humpty Dumpty's use of the word *glory* puzzles Alice.
2. Lewis Carroll was interested in the meanings of words. Analyze the conversation between Alice and Humpty Dumpty. In your essay, focus on their problems with language and communication.

You Can't Take It with You   *Eva-Lis Wuorio°*

There was no denying two facts. Uncle Basil was rich. Uncle Basil was a miser.

The family were unanimous about that. They had used up all the words as their temper and their need of ready money dictated. Gentle Aunt Clotilda, who wanted a new string of pearls because the one she had was getting old, had merely called him Scrooge[1] Basil. Percival, having again smashed his Aston Martin[2] for which he had not paid, had declared Uncle Basil a skinflint, a miser, tightwad, churl, and usurer with colorful adjectives added. The rest had used up all the other words in the dictionary.

"He doesn't have to be so parsimonious,[3] that's true, with all he has," said Percival's mother. "But you shouldn't use rude words, Percival. They might get back to him."

"He can't take it with him," said Percival's sister Letitia, combing her golden hair. "I

need a new fur but he said, 'Why? it's summer.' Well! He's mingy,[4] that's what he is."

"He can't take it with him" was a phrase the family used so often it began to slip out in front of Uncle Basil as well.

"You can't take it with you, Uncle Basil," they said. "Why don't you buy a sensible house out in the country, and we could all come and visit you? Horses. A swimming pool. The lot. Think what fun you'd have, and you can certainly afford it. You can't take it with you, you know."

Uncle Basil had heard all the words they called him because he wasn't as deaf as he made out. He knew he was a mingy, stingy, penny-pinching screw, scrimp, scraper, pinchfist, hoarder, and curmudgeon[5] (just to start with). There were other words, less gentle, he'd also heard himself called. He didn't mind. What galled him was the oft repeated

---

°**Eva-Lis Wuorio** (ā′vä-lēs wôr′ē-ō).
1. **Scrooge:** the most famous miser in literature. See Dickens' "A Christmas Carol," page 291.
2. **Aston Martin:** a very expensive sports car.
3. **parsimonious** (pär′sə-mō′nē-əs): stingy.

4. **mingy** (mĭn′jē): mean and stingy.
5. **curmudgeon** (kər-mŭj′ən): ill-tempered, disagreeable person.

warning, "You can't take it with you." After all, it was all his.

He'd gone to the Transvaal[6] when there was still gold to be found if one knew where to look. He'd found it. They said he'd come back too old to enjoy his fortune. What did they know? He enjoyed simply having a fortune. He enjoyed also saying no to them all. They were like circus animals, he often thought, behind the bars of their thousand demands of something for nothing.

Only once had he said yes. That was when his sister asked him to take on Verner, her somewhat slow-witted eldest son. "He'll do as your secretary," his sister Maud had said. Verner didn't do at all as a secretary, but since all he wanted to be happy was to be told what to do, Uncle Basil let him stick around as an all-around handyman.

Uncle Basil lived neatly in a house very much too small for his money, the family said, in an unfashionable suburb. It was precisely like the house where he had been born. Verner looked after the small garden, fetched the papers from the corner tobacconist, and filed his nails when he had time. He had nice nails. He never said to Uncle Basil, "You can't take it with you," because it didn't occur to him.

Uncle Basil also used Verner to run messages to his man of affairs, the bank, and such, since he didn't believe either in the mails or the telephone. Verner got used to carrying thick envelopes back and forth without ever bothering to question what was in them. Uncle Basil's lawyers, accountants, and bank managers also got used to his somewhat unorthodox[7] business methods. He did have a

fortune, and he kept making money with his investments. Rich men have always been allowed their foibles.

Another foible of Uncle Basil's was that, while he still was in excellent health he had Verner drive him out to an old-fashioned carpenter shop where he had himself measured for a coffin. He wanted it roomy, he said.

The master carpenter was a dour countryman of the same generation as Uncle Basil, and he accepted the order matter-of-factly. They consulted about woods and prices, and settled on a medium-price, unlined coffin. A lined one would have cost double.

"I'll line it myself," Uncle Basil said. "Or Verner can. There's plenty of time. I don't intend to pop off tomorrow. It would give the family too much satisfaction. I like enjoying my fortune."

Then one morning, while in good humor and sound mind, he sent Verner for his lawyer. The family got to hear about this and there were in-fights, out-fights, and general quarreling while they tried to find out to whom Uncle Basil had decided to leave his money. To put them out of their misery, he said, he'd tell them the truth. He didn't like scattering money about. He liked it in a lump sum. Quit bothering him about it.

That happened a good decade before the morning his housekeeper, taking him his tea, found him peacefully asleep forever. It had been a good decade for him. The family hadn't dared to worry him, and his investments had risen steadily.

Only Percival, always pressed for money, had threatened to put arsenic in his tea but when the usual proceedings were gone through Uncle Basil was found to have died a natural death. "A happy death," said the family. "He hadn't suffered."

They began to remember loudly how nice

---

6. **Transvaal** (trăns-väl′, trănz-): a province of the Republic of South Africa, formerly known as South African Republic.
7. **unorthodox** (ŭn′ôr′thə-dŏks′): not customary or traditonal.

they'd been to him and argued about who had been the nicest. It was true too. They had been attentive, the way families tend to be to rich and stubborn elderly relatives. They didn't know he'd heard all they'd said out of his hearing, as well as the flattering drivel they'd spread like soft butter on hot toast in his hearing. Everyone, recalling his own efforts to be thoroughly nice, was certain that he and only he would be the heir to the Lump Sum.

They rushed to consult the lawyer. He said that he had been instructed by Uncle Basil in sane and precise terms. The cremation was to take place immediately after the death, and they would find the coffin ready in the garden shed. Verner would know where it was.

"Nothing else?"

"Well," said the lawyer in the way lawyers have, "he left instructions for a funeral repast to be sent in from Fortnum and Mason.[8] Everything of the best. Goose and turkey, venison and beef, oysters and lobsters, and wines of good vintage plus plenty of whiskey. He liked to think of a good send-off, curmudgeon though he was, he'd said."

The family was a little shaken by the use of the word "curmudgeon." How did Uncle Basil know about that? But they were relieved to hear that the lawyer also had an envelope, the contents of which he did not know, to read to them at the feast after the cremation.

They all bought expensive black clothes, since black was the color of that season anyway, and whoever inherited would share the wealth. That was only fair.

Only Verner said that couldn't they buy Uncle Basil a smarter coffin? The one in the garden shed was pretty tatty, since the roof leaked. But the family hardly listened to him. After all, it would only be burned, so what did it matter?

So, duly and with proper sorrow, Uncle Basil was cremated.

The family returned to the little house as the housekeeper was leaving. Uncle Basil had given her a generous amount of cash, telling her how to place it so as to have a fair income for life. In gratitude she'd spread out the Fortnum and Mason goodies, but she wasn't prepared to stay to do the dishes.

They were a little surprised, but not dismayed, to hear from Verner that the house was now in his name. Uncle Basil had also given him a small sum of cash and told him how to invest it. The family taxed[9] him about it, but the amount was so nominal they were relieved to know Verner would be off their hands. Verner himself, though mildly missing the old man because he was used to him, was quite content with his lot. He wasn't used to much, so he didn't need much.

The storm broke when the lawyer finally opened the envelope.

There was only one line in Uncle Basil's scrawl.

"I did take it with me."

Of course there was a great to-do. What about the fortune? The millions and millions!

Yes, said the men of affairs, the accountants, and even the bank managers, who finally admitted, yes, there had been a very considerable fortune. Uncle Basil, however, had drawn large sums in cash, steadily and regularly, over the past decade. What had he done with it? That the men of affairs, the accountants, and the bank managers did not

---

8. **Fortnum and Mason:** a well-known store that supplies food for parties.

9. **taxed:** expressed disapproval of; criticized.

know. After all, it had been Uncle Basil's money, ergo,[10] his affair.

Not a trace of the vast fortune ever came to light.

No one thought to ask Verner, and it didn't occur to Verner to volunteer that for quite a long time he had been lining the coffin, at Uncle Basil's behest, with thick envelopes he brought back from the banks. First he'd done a thick layer of these envelopes all around the sides and bottom of the coffin. Then, as Uncle Basil wanted, he'd tacked on blue sail-cloth.

He might not be so bright in his head but he was smart with his hands.

He'd done a neat job.

---

10. **ergo** (ûr′gō, âr′-): therefore.

FOR STUDY AND DISCUSSION

1. How does Uncle Basil manage to take his vast fortune with him when he dies?
2. How do the greed and selfishness of his family assist Uncle Basil in carrying out his plan?
3. Although Uncle Basil is a miser, he provides well for Verner and for his housekeeper. Why does he treat these two people with consideration?

4. A conclusion is satisfying when it grows out of the events in the story. How are you, the reader, prepared for the ending? Find clues that the author supplies throughout the story.

SUGGESTION FOR WRITING

Write a plot summary of the story, showing how the pattern of events grows out of a conflict. (For a model, refer to the plot summary on page 548.)

How Ijapa°, Who Was Short, Became Long

Retold by Harold Courlander

Ijapa the tortoise was on a journey. He was tired and hungry, for he had been walking a long time. He came to the village where Ojola[1] the boa lived, and he stopped there, thinking, "Ojola will surely feed me, for I am famished."

Ijapa went to Ojola's house. Ojola greeted him, saying, "Enter my house and cool yourself in the shade, for I can see you have been on the trail."

Ijapa entered. They sat and talked. Ijapa smelled food cooking over the fire. He groaned with hunger, for when Ijapa was hungry he was more hungry than anyone else. Ojola said politely: "Surely the smell of my food does not cause you pain?"

° **Ijapa** (ē-jä′pä).
1. **Ojola** (ō-jō′lä).

From *Olode the Hunter and Other Tales from Nigeria*, copyright © 1968 by Harold Courlander. Reprinted by permission of Harcourt Brace Jovanovich, Inc.

Ijapa said: "Surely not, my friend. It only made me think that if I were at home now, my wife would be cooking likewise."

Ojola said: "Let us prepare ourselves. Then we shall eat together."

Ijapa went outside. He washed himself in a bowl of water. When he came in again he saw the food in the middle of the room and smelled its odors. But Ojola the boa was coiled around the food. There was no way to get to it. Ijapa walked around and around, trying to find an opening through which he could approach the waiting meal. But Ojola's body was long, and his coils lay one atop the other, and there was no entrance through them. Ijapa's hunger was intense.

Ojola said: "Come, do not be restless. Sit down. Let us eat."

Ijapa said: "I would be glad to sit with you. But you, why do you surround the dinner?"

Ojola said: "This is our custom. When my people eat, they always sit this way. Do not hesitate any longer." The boa went on eating while Ijapa again went around and around trying to find a way to the food. At last he gave up. Ojola finished eating. He said: "What a pleasure it is to eat dinner with a friend."

Ijapa left Ojola's house hungrier than he had come. He returned to his own village. There he ate. He brooded on his experience with Ojola. He decided that he would return the courtesy by inviting Ojola to his house to eat with him. He told his wife to prepare a meal for a certain festival day. And he began to weave a long tail out of grass. He spent many days weaving the tail. When it was finished, he fastened it to himself with tree gum.

On the festival day, Ojola arrived. They greeted each other at the door, Ijapa saying, "You have been on a long journey. You are hungry. You are tired. Refresh yourself at the spring. Then we shall eat."

Ojola was glad. He went to the spring to wash. When he returned, he found Ijapa already eating. Ijapa's grass tail was coiled several times around the food. Ojola could not get close to the dinner. Ijapa ate with enthusiasm. He stopped sometimes to say: "Do not hesitate, friend Ojola. Do not be shy. Good food does not last forever."

Ojola went around and around. It was useless. At last he said: "Ijapa, how did it happen that once you were quite short but now you are very long?"

Ijapa said: "One person learns from another about such things." Ojola then remembered the time Ijapa had been his guest. He was ashamed. He went away. It was from Ijapa that came the proverb:

"The lesson that a man should be short
    came from his fellow man.
The lesson that a man should be tall also
    came from his fellow man."

FOR STUDY AND DISCUSSION

1. A *folk tale* is an anonymous story concerned with the traditions, beliefs, and customs of a people. What does this tale reveal about the importance of hospitality?
2. Examine the proverb at the end of the story. What wisdom does it express about human behavior?

SUGGESTIONS FOR WRITING

1. A wide variety of folk tales involve an animal character who is a trickster. Explain how Ijapa gets even with Ojola.
2. Briefly develop this thesis statement. *Thesis* The theme of this tale is that an individual may repay one ungenerous action with another.

A ballad *is a story told in verse and usually meant to be sung. The following ballad is an American version of an English sea ballad about a ship called the* Golden Vanity. *In older texts it is known as the* Sweet Trinity, *which supposedly was the name of Sir Walter Raleigh's flagship.*

The Golden Vanity

'Twas all on board a ship down in a southern sea,
And she goes by the name of the *Golden Vanity;*
I'm afraid that she'll be taken by this Spanish crew,
   As she sails along the Lowlands,
   As she sails along the Lowlands low.   5

Then up speaks our saucy cabin boy, without fear or joy,
Saying, "What will you give me, if I will her destroy?"
"I'll give you gold and silver, my daughter fine and gay,
   If you'll destroy her in the Lowlands,
   If you'll sink her in the Lowlands low."   10

The boy filled his chest and so boldly leaped in,
The boy filled his chest and then began to swim;
He swam alongside of the bold Spanish ship,
   And he sank her in the Lowlands,
   And he sank her in the Lowlands low.   15

Some were playing cards and some were playing dice,
And some were in their hammocks sleeping very nice;
He bored two holes into her side, he let the water in,
   And he sank her in the Lowlands,
   And he sank her in the Lowlands low.   20

The boy then swam back unto our good ship's side,
And being much exhausted, bitterly he cried;
"Captain, take me in, for I'm going with the tide,
   And I'm sinking in the Lowlands,
   And I'm sinking in the Lowlands low."   25

"I will not take you in," our captain then replied,
"I'll shoot you and I'll stab you and I'll sink you in the tide,
    And I'll sink you in the Lowlands,
    And I'll sink you in the Lowlands low."

The boy then swam around next the larboard° side,   30   30. **larboard** (lär′bərd): the
And being more exhausted, bitterly he cried,   port side, the left-hand side
"Messmates, take me in, for I'm going with the tide,   of the ship.
    And I'm sinking in the Lowlands,
    And I'm sinking in the Lowlands low."

They hove the boy a rope and they hoisted him on deck,   35
They laid him on the quarter deck, the boy here soon died;
They sewed him up in a canvas sack, they hove him in the tide,
    And they buried him in the Lowlands,
    So they buried him in the Lowlands low.

FOR STUDY AND DISCUSSION

1. The cabin boy is described as *saucy* in line 6. How does he show that he is high-spirited and bold?

2. What does the word *her* in line 7 refer to? How do you know?

3. No explanation is given for the captain's treachery. What do you suppose is his reason for betraying the cabin boy?

4. How do you know that the narrator is an eyewitness to the events recounted in the poem?

5. A *folk ballad*, also known as a *popular ballad*, was passed from generation to generation by word of mouth. What devices in the poem show that it was meant to be sung?

6. *Repetition* is a characteristic of folk ballads. A word, phrase, line, or group of lines repeated regularly in a poem is called a *refrain*. Sometimes the refrain is repeated exactly the same way, and sometimes it is varied slightly. What is the refrain in "The Golden Vanity"? How do the variations advance the story?

SUGGESTION FOR WRITING

Show how any *three* of the following characteristics of ballads are revealed in "The Golden Vanity":

1. The story concerns something out of the ordinary.

2. The poem deals concisely with one incident.

3. The storyteller does not offer an opinion of the events or judge the characters.

4. The language is plain.

5. Repetition is used as a musical device and for dramatic effect.

The Governess   *Neil Simon*

Based on a Short Story by Anton Chekhov°

Mistress. Julia! (*Calls again*) Julia!

[*A young governess,* Julia, *comes rushing in. She stops before the desk and curtsies.*]

Julia (*head down*). Yes, madame?
Mistress. Look at me, child. Pick your head up. I like to see your eyes when I speak to you.
Julia (*lifts her head up*). Yes, madame. (*But her head has a habit of slowly drifting down again.*)
Mistress. And how are the children coming along with their French lessons?
Julia. They're very bright children, madame.
Mistress. Eyes up . . . They're bright, you say. Well, why not? And mathematics? They're doing well in mathematics, I assume?
Julia. Yes, madame. Especially Vanya.
Mistress. Certainly. I knew it. I excelled in mathematics. He gets that from his mother, wouldn't you say?
Julia. Yes, madame.
Mistress. Head up . . . (*She lifts head up.*) That's it. Don't be afraid to look people in the eyes, my dear. If you think of yourself as inferior, that's exactly how people will treat you.
Julia. Yes, ma'am.
Mistress. A quiet girl, aren't you? . . . Now then, let's settle our accounts. I imagine you must need money although you never ask me for it yourself. Let's see now, we agreed on thirty rubles[1] a month, did we not?
Julia (*surprised*). Forty, ma'am.
Mistress. No, no, thirty. I made a note of it.

(*Points to the book*) I always pay my governesses thirty . . . Who told you forty?
Julia. You did, ma'am. I spoke to no one else concerning money . . .
Mistress. Impossible. Maybe you *thought* you heard forty when I said thirty. If you kept your head up, that would never happen. Look at me again and I'll say it clearly. *Thirty rubles a month.*
Julia. If you say so, ma'am.
Mistress. Settled. Thirty a month it is . . . Now then, you've been here two months exactly.
Julia. Two months and five days.
Mistress. No, no. Exactly two months. I made a note of it. You should keep books the way I do so there wouldn't be these discrepancies.[2] So—we have two months at thirty rubles a month . . . comes to sixty rubles. Correct?
Julia (*curtsies*). Yes, ma'am. Thank you, ma'am.
Mistress. Subtract nine Sundays . . . We did agree to subtract Sundays, didn't we?
Julia. No, ma'am.
Mistress. Eyes! Eyes! . . . Certainly we did. I've always subtracted Sundays. I didn't bother making a note of it because I always do it. Don't you recall when I said we will subtract Sundays?
Julia. No, ma'am.
Mistress. Think.
Julia (*thinks*). No. ma'am.
Mistress. You weren't thinking. Your eyes

° **Chekhov** (chĕk′ôf′): a major Russian writer (1860–1904).
1. **rubles** (rōō′bəlz): The ruble is the Russian unit of money, like the dollar in the United States.

2. **discrepancies** (dĭs-krĕp′ən-sēz): disagreements.

were wandering. Look straight at my face and look hard . . . Do you remember now?

Julia (*softly*). Yes, ma'am.

Mistress. I didn't hear you, Julia.

Julia (*louder*). Yes, ma'am.

Mistress. Good. I was sure you'd remember. . . . Plus three holidays. Correct?

Julia. Two, ma'am. Christmas and New Year's.

Mistress. And your birthday. That's three.

Julia. I worked on my birthday, ma'am.

Mistress. You did? There was no need to. My governesses never worked on their birthdays . . .

Julia. But I did work, ma'am.

Mistress. But that's not the question, Julia. We're discussing financial matters now. I will, however, only count two holidays if you insist . . . Do you insist?

Julia. I did work, ma'am.

Mistress. Then you *do* insist.

Julia. No, ma'am.

Mistress. Very well. That's three holidays; therefore we take off twelve rubles. Now then, four days little Kolya was sick, and there were no lessons.

Julia. But I gave lessons to Vanya.

Mistress. True. But I engaged you to teach two children, not one. Shall I pay you in full for doing only half the work?

Julia. No, ma'am.

Mistress. So we'll deduct it . . . Now, three days you had a toothache and my husband gave you permission not to work after lunch. Correct?

Julia. After four. I worked until four.

Mistress (*looks in the book*). I have here: "Did not work after lunch." We have lunch at one and are finished at two, not at four, correct?

Julia. Yes, ma'am. But I——

Mistress. That's another seven rubles . . . Seven and twelve is nineteen . . . Subtract . . .

that leaves . . . forty-one rubles . . . Correct?

Julia. Yes, ma'am. Thank you, ma'am.

Mistress. Now then, on January fourth you broke a teacup and saucer, is that true?

Julia. Just the saucer, ma'am.

Mistress. What good is a teacup without a saucer, eh? . . . That's two rubles. The saucer was an heirloom. It cost much more, but let it go. I'm used to taking losses.

Julia. Thank you, ma'am.

Mistress. Now then, January ninth, Kolya climbed a tree and tore his jacket.

Julia. I forbid him to do so, ma'am.

Mistress. But he didn't listen, did he? . . . Ten rubles . . . January fourteenth, Vanya's shoes were stolen . . .

Julia. By the maid, ma'am. You discharged her yourself.

Mistress. But you get paid good money to watch everything. I explained that in our first meeting. Perhaps you weren't listening. Were you listening that day, Julia, or was your head in the clouds?

Julia. Yes, ma'am.

Mistress. Yes, your head was in the clouds?

Julia. No, ma'am. I was listening.

Mistress. Good girl. So that means another five rubles off. (*Looks in the book*) . . . Ah yes . . . the sixteenth of January I gave you ten rubles.

Julia. You didn't.

Mistress. But I made a note of it. Why would I make a note of it if I didn't give it to you?

Julia. I don't know, ma'am.

Mistress. That's not a satisfactory answer, Julia . . . Why would I make a note of giving you ten rubles if I did not in fact give it to you, eh? . . . No answer? . . . Then I must have given it to you, mustn't I?

Julia. Yes, ma'am. If you say so, ma'am.

Mistress. Well, certainly I say so. That's the point of this little talk. To clear these matters up . . . Take twenty-seven from forty-one, that leaves . . . fourteen, correct?

Julia. Yes, ma'am. (*She turns away, softly crying.*)

Mistress. What's this? Tears? Are you crying? Has something made you unhappy, Julia? Please tell me. It pains me to see you like this. I'm so sensitive to tears. What is it?

Julia. Only once since I've been here have I ever been given any money and that was by your husband. On my birthday he gave me three rubles.

Mistress. Really? There's no note of it in my book. I'll put it down now. (*She writes in the book.*) Three rubles. Thank you for telling me. Sometimes I'm a little lax with my accounts . . . Always shortchanging myself. So then, we take three more from fourteen . . . leaves eleven . . . Do you wish to check my figures?

Julia. There's no need to, ma'am.

Mistress. Then we're all settled. Here's your salary for two months, dear. Eleven rubles. (*She puts the pile of coins on the desk.*) Count it.

Julia. It's not necessary, ma'am.

Mistress. Come, come. Let's keep the records straight. Count it.

Julia (*reluctantly counts it*). One, two, three, four, five, six, seven, eight, nine, ten . . .? There's only ten, ma'am.

Mistress. Are you sure? Possibly you dropped one . . . Look on the floor; see if there's a coin there.

Julia. I didn't drop any, ma'am. I'm quite sure.

Mistress. Well, it's not here on my desk and I *know* I gave you eleven rubles. Look on the floor.

Julia. It's all right, ma'am. Ten rubles will be fine.

Mistress. Well, keep the ten for now. And if we don't find it on the floor later, we'll discuss it again next month.

Julia. Yes, ma'am. Thank you, ma'am. You're very kind, ma'am. (*She curtsies and then starts to leave.*)

Mistress. Julia! (Julia *stops, turns.*) Come back here. (*She crosses back to the desk and curtsies again.*) Why did you thank me?

Julia. For the money, ma'am.

Mistress. For the money? . . . But don't you realize what I've done? I've cheated you . . . *Robbed* you! I have no such notes in my book. I made up whatever came into my mind. Instead of the eighty rubles which I owe you, I gave you only ten. I have actually stolen from you and still you thank me . . . Why?

Julia. In the other places that I've worked, they didn't give me anything at all.

Mistress. Then they cheated you even worse than I did . . . I was playing a little joke on you. A cruel lesson just to teach you. You're much too trusting, and in this world that's very dangerous . . . I'm going to give you the entire eighty rubles. (*Hands her an envelope*) It's all ready for you. The rest is in this envelope. Here, take it.

Julia. As you wish, ma'am. (*She curtsies and starts to go again.*)

Mistress. Julia! (Julia *stops.*) Is it possible to be so spineless? Why don't you protest? Why don't you speak up? Why don't you cry out against this cruel and unjust treatment? Is it really possible to be so guileless,[3] so innocent, such a—pardon me for being so blunt— such a simpleton?

Julia (*the faintest trace of a smile on her lips*). Yes, ma'am . . . it's possible.

[*She curtsies again and runs off. The* Mistress *looks after her a moment, a look of complete bafflement on her face. The lights fade.*]

---

3. **guileless** (gīl′lĭs): simple; without deceit.

FOR STUDY AND DISCUSSION

1. The *turning point* of a play occurs when there is a decisive change or turn in the action. What is the turning point in *The Governess?*

2. What is the "lesson" Julia's mistress wishes to teach her? Do you think she is successful?

3. This play is based on a short story called "A Nincompoop." A *nincompoop* is a person who is easily deceived. Do you believe Julia gives in so easily because she is stupid, or do you think there is another explanation for her meekness?

SUGGESTION FOR WRITING

A *theme* is the basic meaning of a literary work. It is an idea about life or an interpretation of experience. Discuss the theme of *The Governess* in a short essay.

ABOUT THE AUTHORS

Lewis Carroll (1832–1898) was the pen name of Charles Lutwidge Dodgson, who was a professor of mathematics at Oxford University in England. *Alice in Wonderland* (1865) and *Through the Looking-Glass* (1871), his two most famous books, were written to entertain the children of friends. Carroll's books are great fun, but they are also subtle and complex works that have fascinated readers for more than a hundred years.

Eva-Lis Wuorio (1918–) was born in Finland. At the age of eleven, she emigrated to Canada. She began her writing career working for newspapers in Toronto. Among her books are two novels about World War II: *Code Polonaise,* set in Poland, and *To Fight in Silence,* about the Dutch underground. She has also written a number of children's books. In 1962 *The Island of Fish in the Trees* was chosen by the *New York Times* as one of the Best Illustrated Children's Books of the Year. "You Can't Take It with You" is from a collection of tales called *Escape If You Can.*

Harold Courlander (1908–) was born in Indianapolis. A folklorist, he has collected tales from Africa, the Caribbean, the United States, and the Far East. Courlander has served as press officer with the United States Mission to the United Nations. Some of his collections of African folk tales are *The King's Drum and Other African Stories; The Hat-Shaking Dance and Other Ashanti Tales from Ghana;* and *The Fire on the Mountain and other Ethiopian Stories.*

Neil Simon (1927–) was born in New York City and studied engineering at New York University and the University of Denver. Before his first play, *Come Blow Your Horn,* opened on Broadway, in 1961, Simon wrote scripts for television shows. He is best known for his comedies, including *Barefoot in the Park, The Prisoner of Second Avenue,* and *The Sunshine Boys.* He has adapted many of his plays for film, and he has also written original screenplays. His comedy *The Odd Couple* was made into a movie and also inspired a television series. *The Governess* is one of nine scenes in *The Good Doctor.*

Guide to Literary Terms and Techniques

ALLITERATION *The repetition of a sound in a group of words usually related in meaning.* Alliteration occurs in many common phrases and expressions: "wild and woolly West," "brown as a berry," and so on. Alliteration is usually confined to consonants, but vowels are sometimes alliterated too. Most alliteration occurs at the beginning of words, but sometimes writers like to alliterate in the middle and at the end of words as well.

One of the uses of alliteration seems to be to gain emphasis and to make a group of words meaningful to us. This is why many advertising jingles depend on alliteration. Manufacturers use alliteration in naming their products as an aid to memory.

Politicians often use alliteration. When we are asked to put up with hardship, we are asked to "Tighten our belts," or to "Bite the bullet." Abraham Lincoln once said, "Among free men there can be no successful appeal from the ballot to the bullet."

Poets use alliteration to the most obvious and memorable effect. Some examples of alliteration in poetry are:

> Blue were her eyes as the fairy flax,
> Her cheeks like the dawn of day, . . .
>> Henry Wadsworth Longfellow
>> "The Wreck of the Hesperus"

> The angels, not half so happy in heaven
> Went envying her and me:
>> Edgar Allan Poe
>> "Annabel Lee"

> I remember, I remember
> The roses, red and white,
> The violets and the lily cup—
> Those flowers made of light!
>> Thomas Hood
>> "I Remember, I Remember"

These are serious examples, but sometimes alliteration is used simply for fun. One poet, Algernon Charles Swinburne, actually wrote a poem that made fun of his own style. He had been criticized for using too much alliteration. So he composed "Nephelidia" (little clouds), which is complicated and funny nonsense. It starts this way:

> From the depth of the dreamy decline of the dawn through a notable nimbus of nebulous noonshine,
> Pallid and pink as the palm of the flag-flower that flickers with fear of the flies as they float, . . .

Swinburne makes the point that heavily alliterated poetry can seem to mean more than it does.

Prose writers use alliteration, too, but they have to be careful not to sound too artificial. Some of the most memorable expressions from the King James translation of the Bible are alliterated: "Let there be light: and there was light" (Genesis). Even the famous quotation from Ecclesiastes uses alliteration: "There is no new thing under the sun."

See **Repetition**.
See also page 442.

ALLUSION *A reference in one work of literature to another work of literature or to a well-known event, person, or place.* Allusion is used to best effect when the reference calls up appropriate associations.

Literature contains many allusions to the Bible. Characters will sometimes be described as having the patience of Job, who was noted for his patience. Allusions to the literature of ancient Greece and Rome are also common in literature. The great writers of years past were carefully trained to read both Latin and Greek. Often literature makes allusions to famous events. When someone points out that a character has "met his Waterloo," the allusion is to the battle at which Napoleon was finally defeated by the English. Allusions to battlefields are common because much of history was decided by the outcome of battles. "Black Monday" is a reference to the day the stock market on Wall Street collapsed—referred to universally as "The Crash"—and the world was plunged into the Great Depression of the 1930's.

Allusions to the media are growing more and more common, though these are not as lasting as allusions to the Bible and classical literature. In the story "Bad Characters," Emily alludes to a character in the comic strip "Katzenjammer Kids" when she compares Lottie's hat to the Inspector's hat.

See page 531.

ANECDOTE *A very short story with a simple, usually amusing point.* Many jokes are anecdotes. Often short stories are expanded anecdotes. In the essay "Dogs That Have Known Me," Jean Kerr includes several anecdotes that illustrate the amusing peculiarities of her pets. One dog she tells about insisted on swimming with a fancy overhand stroke instead of using the dog paddle; another made a habit of collecting and hiding lettuce; still another enjoyed hopping on and off the piano.

See page 171.

BALLAD *A story told in verse and usually meant to be sung.* Ballads use regular patterns of rhythm and strong rhymes. A common element is the *refrain*. Most ballads are full of adventure, action, and romance. The earliest ballads, known as *folk ballads*, were composed anonymously and transmitted orally for generations before they were written down. A popular ballad like "Bonny Barbara Allan" has many different versions, since the story changed as it was passed down through the years. *Literary ballads* are composed by known writers who imitate the folk ballad.

See **Refrain.**
See also page 588.

BIOGRAPHY *The story of a person's life.* When a person writes his or her own biography, it is called an **autobiography.** Biography and autobiography are two of the most popular forms of **nonfiction,** and most libraries have a section set aside for these books. Almost every famous person has been the subject of a biography. One of the greatest biographies ever written is *The Life of Samuel Johnson* by James Boswell. Another is Carl Sandburg's six-volume biography of Abraham Lincoln. Well-known autobiographies include *The Story of My Life* by Helen Keller, *The Autobiography of Lincoln Steffens,* and *The Autobiography of Mark Twain.*

CHARACTERIZATION *The methods used to present the personality of a character in a narrative.* A writer can create a character by: (1) giving a physical description of the character; (2) showing the character's actions and letting the character speak; (3) revealing the character's thoughts and feelings; (4) revealing what others think of the character; and (5) commenting directly on the character. The first four methods are *indirect* methods of characterization. The writer shows or dramatizes the character and allows you to draw your own conclusions. The last method is *direct* characterization. The writer tells you directly what a character is like.

In "Rip Van Winkle," Washington Irving develops Rip's character through direct and indirect means. In this passage, for example, the author first comments on Rip's character and then lets Rip reveal himself through his actions.

> Rip Van Winkle, however, was one of those happy mortals, of foolish, well-oiled dispositions, who take the world easy, eat white bread or brown, whichever can be got with least thought or trouble, and would rather starve on a penny than work for a pound. If left to himself, he would have whistled life away in perfect contentment; but his wife kept continually dinning in his ears about his idleness, his carelessness, and the ruin he was bringing on his family. Morning, noon, and night, her tongue was incessantly going, and everything he said or did was sure to produce a torrent of household eloquence. Rip had but one way of replying to all lectures of the kind, and that, by frequent use, had grown into a habit. He shrugged his shoulders, shook his head, cast up his eyes, but said nothing. This, however, always provoked a fresh volley from his wife; so that he would take to the outside of the house — the only side which, in truth, belongs to a henpecked husband.

Animals can be characterized through the same techniques. Here is a description of Wolf, Rip's dog:

> True it is, in all points of spirit befitting an honorable dog, he was as courageous an animal as ever scoured the woods — but what courage can withstand the terrors of a woman's tongue? The moment Wolf entered the house his crest fell, his tail drooped to the ground or curled between his legs, he sneaked about with a gallows air, casting many a sidelong glance at Dame Van Winkle, and at the least flourish of a broomstick or ladle, he would fly to the door, yelping.

Characterization can be sketchy, particularly if the character does not play an important role in the piece. Or, it can be extraordinarily full, as when the character is the main focus of a piece.

We often describe characters as being "flat" or "round." A "flat" character is merely sketched out for us. There is no full development. Dame Van Winkle in "Rip Van Winkle" is a flat character because she is represented as a shrew. She is never really given a chance to speak for herself or to be further characterized.

"Flat" characters are often stereotypes. Harry Thorburn, in "The Erne from the Coast," is an example of a "round" character, since we see him under many different circumstances and we watch him grow and change.

See **Description, Narration, Point of View.**
See also pages 269, 284.

CONFLICT *The struggle that takes place between two opposing forces.* A conflict can be between a character and a natural force, like a bear or a hurricane; between two characters; or between opposing views held by separate characters or groups of characters. Such conflicts are *external* conflicts. Conflict can also be *internal*—it can exist within a character and be a psychological conflict.

Usually a conflict arises from a blocking of desires. In "The Highwayman," King George's men intend to kill the highwayman when he comes to visit his sweetheart. They literally block him from achieving his goal.

There may be more than one conflict in a work. In *The Big Wave* by Pearl Buck, the characters are involved in a struggle against the hostile forces of nature that threaten their lives and their homes. There is also an internal conflict within Jiya, the main character, who must decide what kind of life he wishes to lead. In Jean Stafford's story "Bad Characters," Emily has conflicts with her friends and with members of her family. She also has internal struggles. She is torn between her desire to be Lottie's friend and guilt over her own actions.

See **Plot.**
See also page 252.

DESCRIPTION *Any careful detailing of a person, place, thing, or event.* We associate the term with prose, both fiction and nonfiction, but poems also use description, if a bit more economically.

Description appeals to the senses. In this passage from Charles Dickens' "A Christmas Carol," note how the description of the Christmas pudding appeals to both smell and sight:

Hallo! A great deal of steam! The pudding was out of the copper. A smell like a washing day! That was the cloth. A smell like an eating house and a pastry cook's next door to each other, with a laundress' next door to that! That was the pudding! In half a minute Mrs. Cratchit entered—flushed but smiling proudly—with the pudding, like a speckled cannon ball, so hard and firm, blazing in half of half a quartern of ignited brandy, and bedight with Christmas holly stuck into the top.

Some description is simple, direct, and factual. But more often, description is used to establish a mood or stir an emotion. When Dickens describes the Ghost of Christmas Yet to Come, he emphasizes the shadowy and frightening appearance of the phantom:

The phantom slowly, gravely, silently approached. When it came near him, Scrooge bent down upon his knee; for in the air through which this spirit moved it seemed to scatter gloom and mystery.

It was shrouded in a deep black garment, which concealed its head, its face, its form, and left nothing of it visible save one outstretched hand.

See **Mood.**
See also page 93.

DIALECT *A representation of the speech patterns of a particular region or social group.* Dialect often is used to establish local color. Some of the regional dialects in America are the Down-east dialect of Maine, the Cajun dialect of Louisiana, the Southern and Western dialects, and, in some of the writings of the early twentieth century, a city-slang.

Mark Twain often has his characters speak in dialect. This line of dialogue appears in *The Adventures of Huckleberry Finn*, which is set in a region of the Mississippi River more than a hundred years ago:

"I've seed a raft act so before, along here . . . 'pears to me the current has most quit above the head of this bend durin' the last two years."

Twain increases local color by having his character speak ungrammatically (by traditional grammar standards) and clip the "g's" off some of his words.

See **Dialogue.**
See also page 458.

DIALOGUE *Talk or conversation between two or more characters.* Dialogue usually attempts to present the speech of characters in a realistic fashion. It is used in almost all literary forms: biography, essays, fiction, poetry, and drama. Dialogue is especially important in drama, where it forwards all the action of the play. Dialogue must move the plot, set up the action, reveal the characters, and even help establish some of the mood.

When dialogue appears in a play, there are no quotation marks to set it apart, since besides stage directions—there is nothing but dialogue. When dialogue appears in a prose work or in a poem, it is customary to set it apart with quotation marks.

Biographies often include dialogue. In most cases the dialogue is imagined and presented as it would have sounded if it really had been delivered. Biographers take many such liberties because the use of dialogue helps to liven up their presentations.

The use of dialogue in fiction is one of the ways a writer makes a story come alive. A short story that uses dialogue extensively will seem more realistic. The following passage was written by Sarah Orne Jewett, an American writer well known in the late 1800's. It is part of a story called "A White Heron":

"So Sylvy knows all about birds, does she?" he exclaimed, as he looked round at the little girl who sat, very demure but increasingly sleepy, in the moonlight. "I am making a collection of birds myself. I have been at it ever since I was a boy." (Mrs. Tilley smiled.) "There are two or three very rare ones I have been hunting for these five years. I mean to get them on my own ground if they can be found."

"Do you cage 'em up?" asked Mrs. Tilley doubtfully, in response to this enthusiastic announcement.

"Oh no, they're stuffed and preserved, dozens and dozens of them," said the ornithologist, "and I have shot or snared every one myself. I caught a glimpse of a white heron a few miles from here on Saturday, and I have followed it in this direction. They have never been found in this district at all."

The author is able, in this brief piece of dialogue, to clarify character, set the stage for the next action, and to build suspense.

See **Dialect.**
See also page 374.

DRAMA *A story acted out, usually on a stage, by actors and actresses who take the parts of specific characters.* The word *drama* comes from a Greek word meaning "act." In reading a drama it is best to try to imagine real actors as they would play their parts onstage. We usually think of two main kinds of drama: **tragedies,** serious plays generally ending in suffering and death, like William Shakespeare's *Macbeth;* and **comedies,** lighter plays that are often funny, like Shakespeare's *Twelfth Night.*

Drama involves the use of **plot,** the sequence of related events that make up the story. The plot pits characters against one another or against forces that are powerful and sometimes greater than they are. The characters carry forward the plot by means of **dialogue.**

Most playwrights include **stage directions,** which tell the actors and actresses what to do or how to feel when certain lines are spoken. The stage directions are useful to the director, who must help the actors and actresses interpret their lines correctly. The director decides such things as the timing of a line, the speed of delivery, the way the players stand or move when speaking their lines, and what they do when they are not speaking their lines. In many productions the director is as important as the author of the play.

Most plays are presented on stages with **sets.** A set is a realistic representation of the room, landscape, or locale in which the play takes place. **Props** (short for *properties*) are representations of important items in the drama, such as telephones, radios, flashlights, working automobiles, or other objects that figure in the action. **Lighting** helps to establish the desired moods. Or, instead of establishing mood, lighting can help establish the time of day or the season.

A drama usually begins with **exposition,** which explains the action that has already occurred. It then introduces the **conflict** or difficulties that the characters must overcome. All this happens at the same time the audience is getting to know the characters. Each act may be composed of several scenes. The end of each act often includes a **climax**, which is designed to keep the audience in suspense so it will come back after the intermission. The final act of the drama usually builds to a climax or crisis greater than any that has gone before. The end of the drama involves the **resolution** of the climax, usually by death in a tragedy or by marriage in a comedy.

See **Dialogue, Plot.**
See also pages 338, 339, 355, 376.

ESSAY *A piece of prose writing that discusses a subject in a limited way and that usually expresses a particular point of view.* The word *essay* means "an evaluation or consideration of something." Therefore, most essays tend to be thoughtful observations about a subject of interest to the author. Most essays are *expository* in nature, which means simply that they explain a situation, circumstance, or process. They often go on to consider the results or consequences of what they have explained. Edwin Way Teale's "Animals Go to School" is a good example of an expository essay.

See **Exposition.**

EXPOSITION *A kind of writing that explains something or gives information about something.* Exposition can be used in fiction as well as in nonfiction. The most familiar form it takes is in **essays.** A typical piece of exposition is this passage from Henry David Thoreau's *Walden:* "It is not all books that are as dull as their readers. There are probably words addressed to our condition exactly, which, if we could really hear and understand, would be more salutary than the morning or the spring to our lives, and possibly put a new aspect on the face of things for us. How many a man has dated a new era in his life from the reading of a book."

Exposition is also that part of a play in which important background information is revealed to the audience. At the opening of *The Mazarin Stone,* Holmes provides the audience with essential information when he tells Watson his plan for recovering the diamond.

See **Essay.**
See also page 222.

FABLE *A brief story with a moral, written*

in prose or poetry. The characters in fables are often animals who speak and act like human beings. The most famous fables are those of Aesop, who was supposed to have lived around the sixth century B.C. Almost as famous are the fables of the seventeenth-century French writer Jean de La Fontaine (là fôn-tĕn′).

See page 527.

FANTASY *A form of fiction, poetry, or drama that takes place in an imaginary world and makes use of unrealistic elements.* It involves combinations of an impossible sort—animals that think and talk like people, plants that move or think, or circumstances that are highly fanciful, like worlds and societies beneath the sea. Fantasy has been popular in almost all ages and among people of most cultures.

Time travel is one of the favorite themes in fantasy. In Mark Twain's novel *A Connecticut Yankee in King Arthur's Court*, a man from the nineteenth century suddenly finds himself back in the Middle Ages. In H. G. Wells's *The Time Machine*, a man builds a machine that can take him into the past and into the future.

See page 355.

FICTION *A prose account that is invented and not a record of things as they actually happened.* Much fiction is based on personal experience, but involves invented characters, settings, or other details that exist for the sake of the story itself. Fiction generally refers to short stories and novels.

FIGURATIVE LANGUAGE *Any language that is not intended to be interpreted in a strict literal sense.* When we call a car a "lemon," we do not mean it is a citrus fruit, but that its performance is "sour," or defective. When we hear someone refer to another person as a clown, a brick, a prince, or an angel, we can be sure that the person is none of those things. Instead, we understand that the person shares some quality with those other things. Figurative language makes use of comparisons between different things.

The main form of figurative language used in literature is **metaphor.** Metaphor draws a comparison between two unlike things. The opening stanza of "The Highwayman" contains a number of metaphors. The road is called "a ribbon of moonlight"; the moon "a ghostly galleon"; the sky is referred to as "cloudy seas." Longfellow compares himself to a castle in "The Children's Hour" and expresses his affection for his daughters through the metaphor of imprisonment:

I have you fast in my fortress,
    And will not let you depart,
But put you down into the dungeon
    In the round tower of my heart.

Similes are easier to recognize than metaphors because they do have a special language to set them off. That language is: *like, as, as if, than, such as,* and other words that make an explicit comparison. When Robert Burns says, "My love is like a red, red rose," he is using a simile. Like metaphor, the simile does not use all the points of comparison for its force. It uses only some. For instance, the comparison of "my love" to a rose does not necessarily mean that the loved one is thorny, nor that she lives in a garden, nor that she has a green neck. Rather, it means that "my love" is delicate, fragrant, and beautiful as the flower is.

Similes in everyday language are common: "He was mad as a hornet"; "He roared like a bull when I told him"; "Louie laughed like a hyena"; "Float like a butterfly, sting like a bee"; "Be as firm as Gibraltar and as cool as a cucumber"; "She's like Wonder Woman"; "She sang like a bird."

See **Metaphor, Simile.**
See also page 421.

FLASHBACK *An interruption of the sequence of a narrative to relate an action that happened at an earlier point in time.* The flashback is an effective technique because it is usually unexpected. A plot generally moves in chronological order: it starts at a given moment, progresses through time, and ends. A flashback interrupts that flow by suddenly shifting to past time and narrating important incidents that make the present action more intelligible.

See page 165.

FOLK TALE *A story that was not originally written down, but was passed on orally from one storyteller to another.* Folk tales often exist in several forms because they are carried by storytellers to different parts of the world. Many fairy tales, such as the story of Cinderella, are folk tales that originated in Europe, and versions of them later appeared in the Appalachian Mountains of the New World. Folk tales often involve unreal creatures, like dragons, giants, and talking animals. In the United States, folk tales have grown up about such figures as the lumberjack Paul Bunyan, the riverboatman Mike Fink, and the frontiersman Davy Crockett.

See page 585.

FORESHADOWING *The use of hints or clues in a narrative to suggest what action is to come.* Foreshadowing helps to build **sus-pense** in a story because it alerts the reader to what is about to happen. It also helps the reader savor all the details of the buildup. Foreshadowing is common in short stories, novels, and drama. Of drama, it is often said that if a loaded gun is presented in Act One, it should go off before Act Five. In other words, presenting a loaded gun or a potentially dangerous or interesting opportunity early in a literary work is an effective kind of foreshadowing.

See **Plot.**
See also pages 81, 240.

HAIKU *A three-line poem with five syllables in the first line, seven syllables in the second line, and five syllables in the third line.* It is a Japanese verse form that adapts to English fairly well. Haiku draw their power from clearly defined images that imply considerable meaning.

See pages 434, 436.

HERO/HEROINE *The chief character in a story.* In older heroic stories, the hero or heroine often embodies the best or most desirable qualities of the society for which the story was written. The hero or heroine in such stories is usually physically strong, courageous, and intelligent. Often the conflict involves the hero or heroine with a monster or with a force that threatens the entire social group. Nowadays, we use the term *hero* or *heroine* simply to mean the main character in any narrative. Occasionally, the main character is an animal, like the mongoose-hero in "Rikki-tikki-tavi."

IMAGERY *A description that appeals to any one or any combination of the five senses.* Most images tend to be visual in nature, but they may also suggest the way things sound, smell, taste, or feel to the touch. In "A Christmas Carol," Charles Dickens associates the Ghost of Christmas Present with images that appeal not only to the visual sense but to the sense of taste: "Heaped upon the floor, to form a kind of throne, were turkeys, geese, game, brawn, great joints of meat, suckling pigs, long wreaths of sausages, mince pies, plum puddings, barrels of oysters, red-hot chestnuts, cherry-cheeked apples, juicy oranges, luscious pears, immense twelfth-cakes, and great bowls of punch." Dickens heralds the entrance of Marley's ghost with images of noise. First Scrooge hears every bell in the house ringing. Then he hears "a clanking noise, deep down below as if some person were dragging a heavy chain over the casks in the wine merchant's cellar."

Not all writers use imagery extensively. Those who do, use it in an effort to make an experience in literature more intense for us. Good images involve our sensory awareness and help us be more responsive readers.

See pages 109, 420.

INFERENCE *A reasonable conclusion about something based on certain clues or facts.* Often the author of a literary work does not tell us everything there is to tell, but gives us the pleasure of drawing an inference about the characters, the situation, or the meaning of the work. The process of drawing an inference is pleasurable because we are actually making a discovery on our own.

In "Rip Van Winkle," Washington Irving expects his readers to grasp the truth about his hero's long sleep before it becomes evident to Rip. When Rip awakens, he is puzzled by what he finds, but the reader can infer what has happened from different clues:

He looked round for his gun, but in place of the clean, well-oiled fowling piece, he found an old firelock, lying by him, the barrel incrusted with rust, the lock falling off, and the stock wormeaten.

As he rose to walk, he found himself stiff in the joints.

As he approached the village, he met a number of people, but none whom he knew, which somewhat surprised him, for he had thought himself acquainted with everyone in the country round. Their dress, too, was of a different fashion from that to which he was accustomed. They all stared at him with equal marks of surprise, and whenever they cast their eyes upon him, invariably stroked their chins. This gesture induced Rip to do the same, when to his astonishment, he found his beard had grown a foot long!

See page 124.

INVERSION *A reversal of the usual order of words to achieve some kind of emphasis.* For example, in this line from "How They Brought the Good News from Ghent to Aix," Robert Browning inverts the subject and predicate: "At Aershot, up leaped of a sudden the sun." The device usually appears in poetry, but it occurs in prose and in speech as well. Its effect is to give special importance to a phrase or thought.

Sometimes it is not just the order of words but the actual sequence of events which is inverted. One of the most common uses of this kind of inversion in everyday language occurs in the expression, "Wait until I put on my shoes and socks." We all know that socks go on first—then come the shoes! But it is not only more effective to invert the order, but for many people more natural. We do not think of the sequence as an inversion.

A more usual kind of inversion is that which appears in Alfred, Lord Tennyson's poem "Sir Galahad":

When down the stormy crescent goes,
A light before me swims,
Between dark stems the forest glows,
I hear a noise of hymns.

It would be more normal to write: "When the stormy crescent goes down, a light swims before me; the forest glows between dark stems, and I hear a noise of hymns." But Tennyson liked the stateliness, the slightly unexpected quality he achieved by inverting these lines. The inversion is also designed to produce effective rhyme.

See pages 387, 433.

IRONY   *A contrast between what is stated and what is really meant, or between what is expected to happen and what actually does happen.* Irony is used in literature for different effects, from humor to serious comments on the unpredictable nature of life. A good example of irony is found in the short story "The Landlady." Impressed by appearances, Billy Weaver thinks he has found a cheap, attractive place to live in, whereas he is actually in grave danger.

LIMERICK   *A comic poem written in three long and two short lines, rhymed in the pattern aabba.* No one knows if the limerick was actually invented in Limerick, Ireland, but the form of the poem is very popular throughout that country. Writing limericks is also a popular pastime in our country.

Sometimes writers twist the spellings of rhyme words to build more humor into limericks. The following Irish limerick plays on the spelling of a town south of Dublin: *Dun Laoghaire*, pronounced "dun leery."

An ancient old man of Dun Laoghaire
Said, "Of pleasure and joy I've grown waoghaire.
   The life that is pure,
   Will suit me I'm sure,
It's healthy and noble though draoghaire."

The pattern of rhythm for lines 1, 2, and 5 is the same:

$$\smile\prime\smile\smile\prime\smile\smile\prime$$

The pattern for lines 3 and 4 is also the same:

$$\smile\smile\prime\smile\smile\prime$$

See page 438.

METAMORPHOSIS   *A change, mainly of shape or form.* In literature, it usually involves the miraculous change of a human or god into an animal or tree or flower. The most famous examples of metamorphosis are found in classical myths. In the myth of Arachne, the goddess Minerva transforms Arachne into a spider. In the myth of Daphne and Apollo, Daphne is transformed into a laurel tree, which thereafter becomes sacred to Apollo. Classical myths often employ metamorphosis to suggest a close relationship among gods, humans, and the world of nature. The goddess Aphrodite, for instance, sprang from the foam of the sea. The goddess Athene appeared to the Greek hero Odysseus in the form of a mist. She also assumed the form of an owl when it suited her. In the myths metamorphosis reflects a sense of wonder about the nature of the world: the shapes of things are not necessarily reliable indications of what the things are. If an owl could be a goddess, then it was only wise for a Greek to be cautious of the owl and to respect it. Such respect typifies other mythologies as well: American Indian myths express the same kind of respect for the natural world.

Metamorphosis is found in many popular European folktales. In "The Princess and the Frog," the frog metamorphoses into a handsome prince, and in "Beauty and the Beast," a prince is metamorphosed into an animal.

See page 491.

METAPHOR *A comparison between two unlike things with the intent of giving added meaning to one of them.* A metaphor is one of the most important forms of **figurative language**. It is used in virtually all forms of language, from everyday speech to formal prose and all forms of fiction and poetry.

When one says, "He was a gem to help me like that," the metaphor lies in calling a person a gem. Gems are stones; they glisten; they are usually quite small. But these are not the qualities that the metaphor above wants us to consider. The metaphor relies on our understanding that it is the person's gemlike or jewel-like value that is referred to. Thus, we see that metaphors use selected points of comparison that are supplied by the context.

Should we say, "The miser had a heart of flint," we do not mean that his heart is small, black, bloodless, and nonfunctioning. Rather, we mean he has no capacity to feel emotionally for someone else.

Unlike a **simile**, a metaphor does not use a specific word to state a comparison. The difference is illustrated in this pair of sentences. The first expresses a simile, the second a metaphor.

Life is like a dream.
Life is a dream.

See **Figurative Language, Simile**.
See also page 421.

MOOD *The emotional situation that a piece of literature tries to establish.* The mood of a piece of literature might be described in a single word: somber, gay, strange, comfortable, easy, happy, hopeful, or reflective. But more complex moods, such as those of apprehension, fear, and excitement will be harder to describe. Mood is achieved often by description. But it can be achieved by skillful **dialogue** as well. The uses of **foreshadowing** and of **suspense** can help establish a variety of moods.

Edgar Allan Poe is a master of mood in poetry. In "To Helen," he uses vowel sounds, such as the open **o** sound and the long **e** sound to set the mood. He then uses an unusual amount of **alliteration**. His intention is to connect Helen with the beauties of classical Greece by using language that is musical in sound. He also describes classical beauty by referring to classical ships (Nicaean barks):

Helen, thy beauty is to me
  Like those Nicaean barks of yore,
That gently, o'er a perfumed sea,
  The weary wayworn wanderer bore
  To his own native shore.

On desperate seas long wont to roam,
  Thy hyacinth hair, thy classic face,
Thy naiad airs have brought me home
  To the glory that was Greece,
  And the grandeur that was Rome.

See **Foreshadowing, Suspense.**

MYTH *An ancient story often serving to explain a natural phenomenon and generally involving supernatural beings.* Sometimes myth, like legend, seems to have a general rooting in some historical event, but, unlike legend, myth concentrates far less on history than it does on stories that include supernatural elements. Myths explaining the origin of specific events, such as the ways in which the seas or the mountains came into being, exist in almost every culture. Likewise, almost every culture has myths that explain the beginnings of the world.

Classical mythology is the name given to the myths developed by the ancient Greeks and the Romans. Most classical myths are about the gods and goddesses of Olympus.

NARRATION   *The kind of writing or speaking that tells a story (a narrative).* Any narrative must be delivered by a narrator, whether it is the author or a character created by the author. The narrator's **point of view** can sometimes color the narration. In one famous mystery story by Agatha Christie, the reader does not realize until the last page that the narrator is the murderer. And the narrator's point of view is such that he thinks of himself as innocent.

See **Point of View.**
See also page 155.

NONFICTION   *Any prose narrative that tells about things as they actually happened or that presents factual information about something.* One of the chief kinds of nonfiction is a history of someone's life. When a person writes his or her own life story, we call it **autobiography.** When someone else writes a person's life story, we call it **biography.** In each case, the purpose of the writing is to give an accounting of a person's life. Presumably, it is a true and accurate accounting. When someone writes about personal observations on some subject—as Jean Kerr does in "Dogs That Have Known Me"—the result is an **essay.** Essays are among the most common forms of nonfiction and appear in most of the magazines we see on the newsstands. Another kind of nonfiction is also to be found on

newsstands: the newspaper itself. Travel stories, personal journals, and diaries are also forms of nonfiction.

See **Biography, Essay.**
See also pages 379, 414.

NOVEL   *A fictional narrative in prose, generally longer than a short story.* The novel allows for greater complexity of character and plot development than the short story. The forms the novel may take cover a wide range. For example, there are the *historical novel,* in which historical characters, settings, and periods are drawn in detail; the *picaresque novel,* presenting the adventures of a rogue; and the *psychological novel,* which focuses on characters' emotions and thoughts. Other forms of the novel include the detective story, the spy thriller, and the science-fiction novel.

PARAPHRASE   *A summary or recapitulation of a piece of literature.* A paraphrase does not add anything to our enjoyment of a literary work. It merely tells in the simplest form what happened. A paraphrase of "The Highwayman" might go this way.

The highwayman tells his sweetheart Bess that he will return to her with the gold he plans to steal that very night. Tim, a stableman who is in love with Bess, overhears this conversation and tells the British soldiers of the lovers' plan. A troop of soldiers comes to the inn and waits for the highwayman to return. Bess is gagged and bound to her bed, but she is able to reach the trigger of a musket. When she hears the sound of horse hoofs in the distance, she pulls the trigger and warns the highwayman with her death. After he learns how Bess has died, the highwayman rides back for revenge, and is shot down on the highway. There is a legend that the lovers can still be seen and heard at the old inn on winter nights.

This summary gives us some essential information and is useful for checking to see just what did happen. But it is also clear that such a paraphrase is no substitute for the charm and beauty of the original poem.

See page 429.

PLOT *The sequence of events or happenings in a literary work.* We generally associate plot with short stories, novels, and drama. Plot differs from narrative in that it is not merely a record of events as they happen, but an ordering of events in such a fashion as to bring them to a strongly satisfying conclusion. The use of **foreshadowing**, surprise, **suspense,** and carefully worked out **conflict** produces a tight pattern of action. Plot implies a step-by-step working out of events, in which each step takes us perceptibly closer to the unraveling of the action.

The major element in plot is **conflict,** or struggle of some kind. Sometimes the conflict is *external*: it takes place between characters and their environment—whether that be nature, the gods, or other characters. Often, the conflict is *internal,* or within the character's own mind. A plot will slowly reveal the nature of the conflict, the source of the conflict, illustrate its effects on the characters, then show us how the conflict is resolved. If the conflict is not resolved, the plot will point toward changes in the lives of the characters that will be necessary to accommodate the conflict.

In most plots there is a point at which the intensity of the action rises to such a height we must consider it a point of **climax.** In Charles Dickens' "A Christmas Carol," the point of climax comes when Scrooge sees a vision of a tombstone bearing his name, and resolves to become a better man.

The **resolution** is the moment in the plot when the conflict ends. Not all plots have a resolution as such. In older stories, there generally is a resolution. In "A Christmas Carol," the conflict is resolved when Scrooge changes from a hardhearted miser to a warm and generous man. But many modern stories end without a resolution. They provide us with enough information so that we may draw our own inferences as to how the conflict will be resolved.

See pages 240, 252, 339.

POETRY *Traditional poetry is language arranged in lines, with a regular rhythm and often a definite rhyme scheme. Nontraditional poetry does away with regular rhythm and rhyme, although it usually is set up in lines.* There is no satisfactory way of defining poetry, although most people have little trouble knowing when they read it. Some definitions offered by those concerned with it may help us. The English poet William Wordsworth called it "the spontaneous overflow of powerful feelings." He also called it "wisdom married to immortal verse." Matthew Arnold, an English writer and poet of the nineteenth century, defined it in this fashion: "Poetry is simply the most beautiful, impressive, and widely effective mode of saying things."

Poetry often employs lines set up in **stanza** form. It uses **rhyme** in order to build the musicality of the language or to emphasize certain moods or effects. It uses **imagery** and **figurative language** widely. Techniques like **alliteration, repetition,** and **inversion** are often considered specifically poetic. Poetry depends heavily on strong **rhythms,** even when they are not regular.

See the terms noted above.
See also page 468.

POINT OF VIEW *The vantage point from which a work is told.* Writers may choose a totally unlimited point of view or a narrow, limited one. In some cases the point of view will be of great importance, since we will be expected to draw inferences about the nature of the narrator. In other cases, the point of view will be of less importance, since it will have been chosen only to give us all the details of the story in the most direct way possible.

In the *third-person* point of view, the story is told by an outside observer. In the following passage, we are told that a character, Hester Martin, has made a decision. She is referred to in the third person ("she"), which is how this point of view gets its name:

Hester Martin could let the insult get her down. She could reply rudely or call for the man's manager and make a formal complaint. But she decided against both courses. Instead, she took the man aside and explained to him what it felt like to have someone who was a total stranger say something cruel, even if the man did not intend to be insulting. Whether he intended to be insulting or not, once Hester told him how she felt, he changed his manner entirely. She had done the right thing. She had educated him.

This is an example of the *omniscient,* or all-knowing, point of view. The author tells us things that Hester Martin does not directly think or observe. The author speculates on whether the man was consciously rude, just as the author ultimately tells us that Hester made the right decision. She does not know whether it was right or not. The author tells us so.

A *limited third-person* narrative tells only what one character sees, feels, and thinks. The same scene written from a limited third-person point of view might go this way:

Hester Martin felt her face flush. Did he notice it, too? Should she go to his manager? Should she insult him back? She took a moment to bring her emotions back under control, but when she collected herself she drew the man aside and lectured him carefully and patiently on the subject of insulting a patron. His apologies and his extraordinary politeness and caution gave her a small measure of satisfaction.

The *first-person* point of view tells everything from the "I" vantage point. Like the third-person limited point of view, this point of view tells only what the narrator knows and feels. We cannot be told what any other character thinks, except when the narrator may speculate about the character's feelings or thoughts. It is a very limited point of view, but its popularity is secure since we all identify with "I" in a story. The scene above, in the first-person narrative might go this way:

I felt my face burn with the insult. I wondered if he noticed it. Should I go to his manager? No, I thought. And I won't stoop to his level and return the comment. When I thought I could control myself, I took the man aside and I told him in no uncertain terms that I did not like being insulted by a stranger. The only satisfaction I got was watching him try to squirm out of it, telling me he didn't mean it as an insult. But at least I got him to admit he was wrong. Maybe he learned a lesson.

See **Narration.**
See also pages 255, 318.

606 *Guide to Literary Terms and Techniques*

PROVERB *A wise saying, usually quite old and usually of folk origin.* Proverbs are related to **morals,** the concluding lessons that are often attached to fables. A proverb like "A stitch in time saves nine," "A rolling stone gathers no moss," or "A new broom sweeps clean" could easily be the moral tag on a fable. Benjamin Franklin was one of the most prolific of modern proverb writers. His publication *Poor Richard's Almanac* always included at least one proverb per issue. One of Franklin's most famous sayings is, "A penny saved is a penny earned."

See page 535.

QUATRAIN *A four-line stanza, usually rhymed.* Sometimes an entire poem will be in the form of a quatrain, while at other times the poem will be broken up into stanzas of quatrain length. One of the most famous quatrains in poetry is that of Edward Fitzgerald in his translation of Omar Khayám's *The Rubáiyát:*

A book of verses underneath the bough,
A jug of wine, a loaf of bread—and thou
  Beside me singing in the wilderness—
O, Wilderness were paradise enow!

See page 437.

REFRAIN *A word, phrase, line, or group of lines that is repeated regularly in a poem or song, usually at the end of each stanza.* One of the delights in refrains is in anticipating their return. Many ballads use refrains. Sometimes the refrain is repeated exactly the same way and sometimes it is varied slightly for effect.

See page 449.

REPETITION *The return of a word, phrase,* *stanza form, or effect in any form of literature.* Repetition, in all its forms, is probably the most dependably used literary device. **Alliteration,** repeating sounds at the beginning, middle, or end of words, is one of the most common kinds of repetition in poetry. **Rhyme** is also a form of repetition. The **refrain** in ballads and songs is a form of repetition. Once we realize that these are forms of repetition, we can begin to appreciate how important the device is. We do not wholly understand how it affects us, since the device is very complex. We do know that a stanza such as the opening quatrain in Lewis Carroll's "Jabberwocky" reads at first as if it were a foreign language:

'Twas brillig, and the slithy toves
  Did gyre and gimble in the wabe;
All mimsy were the borogoves,
  And the mome raths outgrabe.

After the entire story of the boy's adventurous slaying of the Jabberwocky is told, the stanza is repeated. Then it seems much clearer and much easier to read. It also takes on the odd quality of being comforting to us.

One of the great masters of repetition is Edgar Allan Poe. He actually worked out theories of how poetry affects a reader. His conclusion was that simple repetition was one of the most important and functional devices a poet could use. His poem "Annabel Lee" is filled with repetitive references to her name, since it was for him an immensely musical name. He also repeats in its entirety the phrase "kingdom by the sea." Such repetitions are not only pleasurable—they build emotional tension in his poems. In one of his poems, "Annie," Poe tries to build a sense of feverish intensity. The subject of the poem is Annie's death. In one stanza, Poe repeats himself almost nervously:

A holier odor
  About it, of pansies—

A rosemary odor,
   Commingled with pansies—
With rue and the beautiful
   Puritan pansies.

Sometimes a poet will repeat a formula line with slight differences each time. Christina Georgina Rossetti, an English poet of the nineteenth century, wrote this stanza in her poem "A Birthday":

My heart is like a singing bird
   Whose nest is in a watered shoot;
My heart is like an apple tree
   Whose boughs are bent with thick-set
      fruit;
My heart is like a rainbow shell
   That paddles in a halcyon sea;
My heart is gladder than all these,
   Because my love is come to me.

See **Alliteration, Refrain, Rhyme.**
See also page 442.

RHYME   *The repetition of sounds in words, usually, but not exclusively, at the ends of lines of poetry.* One of the primary uses of rhyme is as an aid to memory. Rhyme is used for this purpose in certain rules, such as: "Thirty days hath September, April, June, and November," and "*I* before *e* except after *c.*"

The most familiar form of rhyme is **end rhyme.** This simply means the rhymes come at the end of the lines. The following passage is from a long poem on the muse of music by the English poet Alexander Pope. He is trying to recreate the sounds of the underworld when Orpheus sang there in order to rescue his beloved wife, Eurydice:

What sounds were heard,
What scenes appeared,
   O'er all the dreary coasts!
      Dreadful gleams,
      Dismal screams,

Fires that glow,
Shrieks of woe,
Sullen moans,
Hollow groans,
And cries of tortured ghosts!

Each of these rhymes was an **exact rhyme** for Pope, although we now pronounce *heard* differently from *appeared*. (We call this a **partial rhyme**—the final consonant sounds are the same, but the vowel sounds are different.) The rhyme of *coasts* and *ghosts,* separated by six lines, is a marvelous example of **distant rhyme.**

Exact rhyme insists that the two words rhymed sound exactly the same. The most common form of exact rhyme is **strong rhyme.** Strong rhyme refers to words of one syllable that rhyme: *place/space.* It also refers to words of more than one syllable where the rhyme occurs on the stressed syllable: *approve/remove.* In **weak rhyme,** there are two or more syllables that rhyme, but the accent does not fall on the last syllable: *sínging/clínging; wéarily/dréarily.* The terms *strong* and *weak* do not have anything to do with the qualities of the sounds themselves. The first two rhymes in John Gay's poem "Song" are weak. The next two are strong:

O ruddier than the cherry!
O sweeter than the berry!
   O nymph more bright
   Than the moonshine night.

Rhyme that occurs within a line is called **internal rhyme.** Usually, the rhyme word appears in the middle of a line and rhymes with an end rhyme from the line above or from its own line. One of the masters of this technique is Edgar Allan Poe, who begins the first line of "The Raven" with the internal weak rhyme *eerie:* "Once upon a midnight dreary, while I pondered, weak and weary." Clearly, the reasons for rhyming in these poems go far beyond a simple memory device.

Rhymes in the work of Pope, Poe, or any other careful poet serve many purposes. One is to increase the musicality of the poem. Rhyme appeals to the ear. Another purpose is to give delight by rewarding our anticipation of a returning sound, such as the *coasts/ghosts* rhyme in Pope's poem. There is also the purpose of humor. Limericks, for instance, would not be half so funny if they did not rhyme—particularly when the rhymes are strained for comic effect.

See **Poetry, Repetition.**
See also pages 442, 451.

RHYTHM *The pattern of stressed and unstressed sounds in a line of poetry.* All language has rhythm of some sort or another, but rhythm is most important in poetry, where it is carefully controlled for effect.

The effects of rhythm are several. Rhythm contributes to the musical quality of a poem, which gives the reader or listener pleasure. Rhythm can also be used to imitate the action being described in the poem. In Robert Browning's poem, "How They Brought the Good News from Ghent to Aix," the lines actually imitate the galloping rhythm of horses' hoofs:

And there was my Roland to bear the whole
    weight,
Of the news which alone could save Aix from
    her fate,
With his nostrils like pits full of blood to the
    brim,
And with circles of red for his eye sockets' rim.

Scanning the lines—examining them for the stressed and unstressed syllables—is not easy. It requires practice. One thing to remember is that good poets usually put stress on the most important words in the line. If you say the line to yourself in a natural voice, you will hear that the most important words demand the stress.

Browning uses techniques other than just stressed and unstressed syllables to intensify his rhythm. The lines above are all one sentence and must be read in a single breath, thus building a feeling of constant motion. Even the internal rhyme of *there* and *bear* in the first line builds rhythmic intensity, since the stresses fall on those words. In the last two lines, stressed words are accented by having them also alliterate: *blood/brim; red/rim.* Such devices help build even more rhythmic pressure in a poem that depends heavily on rhythm for its effect.

Rhyme also contributes to rhythm in poetry, since it causes us to feel that a passage has come to an end. When rhymes fall close together, we have the feeling that we must pause in our reading of the lines. An extreme example is from "Endymion," a long poem by John Keats.

O sorrow!
Why dost borrow
The natural hue of health, from vermeil
    lips?—
To give maiden blushes
To the white rose bushes?
Or is it the dewy hand the daisy tips?

In addition to the rhymes, Keats uses another technique that many poets like to employ: that of asking questions in the poem. Any question has a natural rhythm of its own, so poets can capitalize on this fact and use it to their own purposes. Here, Keats is trying to have us read rhythmically in order to build in us a questioning sense of the meaning of things. He is asking in these lines why sorrow takes the healthy redness from some people's lips. Perhaps, he asks, it is to give the redness to maidens' cheeks, or to the roses and the daisies.

One of the most powerful means of building rhythm in poetry is through repetition. Consider this passage, the last lines from Edgar Allan Poe's "The Bells":

> Keeping time, time, time,
> In a sort of Runic rhyme,
>   To the throbbing of the bells—
> Of the bells, bells, bells—
>   To the sobbing of the bells;
> Keeping time, time, time,
>   As he knells, knells, knells.
> In a happy Runic rhyme,
>   To the rolling of the bells—
> Of the bells, bells, bells:—
>   To the tolling of the bells—
> Of the bells, bells, bells, bells,
>   Bells, bells, bells—
> To the moaning and the groaning of the bells.

The repetition of the words *bells, knells,* and *time* builds up a rhythm that suggests the repeated ringing of bells.

See **Alliteration, Repetition, Rhyme.**
See also page 464.

SETTING   *The time and place of action.* In short stories and novels, the setting is generally established by description. Setting can be important in poetry and nonfiction as well, and the means of establishing setting is through description, as in fiction. In dramas, the setting is usually established by stage directions and then reinforced in dialogue. Since a drama normally has sets that appear before an audience, elaborate descriptions of setting are unnecessary.

In the first sentence of "The Legend of Sleepy Hollow" Washington Irving establishes the setting of the story:

> In the bosom of one of those spacious coves which indent the eastern shore of the Hudson, at that broad expansion of the river named by the ancient Dutch navigators the Tappan Zee, there lies a small market town or rural port, which by some is called Greensburgh, but which is more generally and properly known by the name of Tarrytown.

The setting establishes not only the physical locale (Tarrytown) but also something of historical moment as well. This tells us right away that history may have something to do with the story.

Setting can be of great importance in establishing mood or building emotional intensity. Here is the famous opening passage from "The Fall of the House of Usher" by Edgar Allan Poe. Note how the italicized words help to build an atmosphere of gloom:

> During the whole of a *dull, dark,* and *soundless* day in the autumn of the year, when the clouds hung *oppressively low* in the heavens, I had been passing alone, on horseback, through a *singularly dreary* tract of country, and at length found myself, as the shades of the evening drew on, within view of the *melancholy* House of Usher.

In "The Wreck of the *Hesperus,*" Henry Wadsworth Longfellow describes the setting in highly emotional terms. Longfellow uses figurative language to intensify his description of a storm at sea:

> Colder and louder blew the wind,
>   A gale from the northeast,
> The snow fell hissing in the brine,
>   And the billows frothed like yeast.
>
>   .   .   .
>
> And fast through the midnight dark and
>   drear,

Through the whistling sleet and snow,
Like a sheeted ghost, the vessel swept
Toward the reef of Norman's Woe.

See pages 202, 283.

SIMILE *A comparison between two unlike things, using* like, as, *and similar words of comparison.* Similes are **figures of speech** and are common in everyday language and in most forms of literature. We use simile when we say: "He fought like a tiger"; "He was as mild as a dove"; and "She was cooler than a cucumber." A more poetic use of simile is this, from Lord Byron's "Stanzas for Music":

There will be none of Beauty's daughters
  With a magic like thee;
And like music on the waters
  Is thy sweet voice to me.

See **Figurative Language**.
See also page 421.

STANZA *A group of lines forming a unit in a poem.* Some poems have a single stanza. Other poems are divided into several stanzas, each of which has the same number of lines and the same rhyme scheme. Some poems do not repeat the same structure in each stanza, yet each group of lines is still referred to as a stanza. "The Broncho That Would Not Be Broken" by Vachel Lindsay has a regular pattern of five stanzas, each containing eight lines. "Annabel Lee" by Edgar Allan Poe has six stanzas. Three of the stanzas have six lines, one has seven lines, and two have eight lines.

See **Poetry**.

SUSPENSE *That quality in a literary work that makes the reader or audience uncertain or tense about what is to come next.* Suspense is a kind of "suspending" of our emotions. We know something is about to happen, and the longer the writer can keep us anticipating what will happen, the greater the suspense. The device is popular in all kinds of literature that involve plot, whether nonfiction, short stories, drama, or poetry. Suspense is possible even when the reader knows the outcome. At the opening of "Guinea Pig," Ruth McKenney tells us that she was almost drowned by a Red Cross Lifesaving Examiner and that she received a black eye in the cause of serving others. Although we know what to expect, we are still eager to find out what has led to these circumstances. Holding the reader off for as long as possible is part of the strategy of building suspense. Some writers feel it works even better when we know what is coming, so they let us know through **foreshadowing**.

See **Plot**.
See also page 240.

THEME *The main idea or the basic meaning of a literary work.* Not all literary works can be said to have a theme. Some stories are told chiefly for entertainment and have little to say about life or about human nature. But in those stories that try to make a comment on the human condition, theme is of great importance.

Because theme in fiction is rarely expressed directly, it is not always obvious to every reader. Theme is one of those qualities of a piece of literature that must be dug out and thought about. The reason for this is that writers develop their themes for thoughtful people. They expect that one of the rewards of reading for such people is the pleasure of inferring the theme on their own.

Usually, however, careful writers set up their

stories so that one can pick out passages here and there that focus on the theme. Such "key passages" point in the right direction so that we are not totally unaided in coming to understand the theme. Key passages are recognizable because they seem to speak directly to us as readers. They also make direct statements of a philosophical nature, discussing the meaning of the action and the lessons the characters may have learned. In "A Christmas Carol," one key passage that points toward the theme of the story is this speech by Marley's ghost, warning Scrooge to change his ways before it is too late:

"Mankind was my business. The common welfare was my business; charity, mercy, forbearance, benevolence, were all my business. The dealings of my trade were but a drop of water in the comprehensive ocean of my business!"

Some simple themes can be stated in a single sentence. Sometimes a literary work is rich and complex, and a paragraph or essay is needed to state the theme. When deciding upon what we think the theme of a story is, we must be careful to doublecheck our ideas against the action of the story. We must test our sense of theme to be sure the actions of the main characters are consistent with our conclusions. If their actions contradict the theme we have arrived at, we must go back, reread the story, and see if we have made a mistake, or if the author has used the contradiction to some literary purpose.

See page 290.

Glossary

The words listed in the glossary in the following pages are found in the selections in this textbook. You can use this glossary as you would a dictionary — to look up words that are unfamiliar to you. Strictly speaking, the word *glossary* means a collection of technical, obscure, or foreign words found in a certain field of work. Of course, the words in this glossary are not "technical, obscure, or foreign," but are those that might present difficulty as you read the selections in this textbook.

Many words in the English language have several meanings. In this glossary, the meanings given are the ones that apply to the words as they are used in the selections in the textbook. Words closely related in form and meaning are generally listed together in one entry (**immobile** and **immobility**), and the definition is given for the first form. Regular adverbs (ending in -*ly*) are defined in their adjective form, with the adverb form shown at the end of the definition.

The following abbreviations are used:

adj., adjective   *n.*, noun
adv., adverb   *v.*, verb

For more information about the words in this glossary, consult a dictionary.

A

abash (ə-băsh′) *v.* To embarrass. — **abashed** *adj.*

abate (ə-bāt′) *v.* To lessen.

abet (ə-bĕt′) *v.* To encourage.

abnormal (ăb-nôr′məl) *adj.* Not normal; strange. — **abnormally** *adv.*

abode (ə-bōd′) *n.* A home.

abrupt (ə-brŭpt′) *adj.* Sudden. — **abruptly** *adv.*

abundant (ə-bŭn′dənt) *adj.* Plentiful.

acclaim (ə-klām′) *v.* To greet; salute.

accommodate (ə-kŏm′ə-dāt′) *v.* To serve; oblige.

accomplice (ə-kŏm′plĭs) *n.* A partner in an activity, especially in a crime.

accost (ə-kôst′, ə-kŏst′) *v.* To meet and speak to first, often in an aggressive way.

acknowledgment (ăk-nŏl′ĭj-mənt) *n.* **1.** An admission. **2.** A sign of recognition.

adhesive (ăd-hē′sĭv, zĭv) *adj.* Sticky.

admonish (ăd-mŏn′ĭsh) *v.* To correct someone in a kindly manner.

aesthetic (ĕs-thĕt′ĭk) *adj.* Relating to principles of beauty. — **aesthetically** *adv.*

affect (ə-fĕkt′) *v.* To put on; pretend.

afflict (ə-flĭkt′) *v.* To cause to suffer. — **afflicted** *adj.*

aghast (ə-găst′, ə-gäst′) *adj.* Shocked; horrified.

agitation (ăj′ə-tā′shən) *n.* Emotional upset.

ajar (ə-jär′) *adj.* Slightly open.

alcove (ăl′kōv′) *n.* A recessed area in a room, as for a bed.

alienate (āl′yən-āt′, ā′lē-ən-) *v.* **1.** To make unfriendly. **2.** To turn away.

alist (ə-lĭst′) *adj.* Tilted.

allay (ə-lā′) *v.* To soothe, calm.

allege (ə-lĕj′) *v.* To declare or affirm.

alleged (ə-lĕjd′) *adj.* Supposed.

allurement (ə-loor′mənt) *n.* A temptation.

aloof (ə-loof′) *adj.* Unfriendly; cold.

amble (ăm′bəl) *v.* To walk in a leisurely way.

amiable (ā′mē-ə-bəl) *adj.* Friendly; agreeable.

ample (ăm′pəl) *adj.* Large; spacious.

analogous (ə-nal′ə-gəs) *adj.* Similar.

anesthetic (ăn′ĭs-thĕt′ĭk) *n.* Something that deadens physical sensations.

anguish (ăng′gwĭsh) *n.* Great suffering.

animated (an′ə-mā′tĭd) *adj.* Lively. — **animatedly** *adv.*

anoint (ə-noint′) *v.* To rub the body with oil or ointment.

anonymous (ə-nŏn′ə-məs) *adj.* Without a name.

antiquity (ăn-tĭk′wə-tē) *n.* The quality of being old or ancient.

ă pat/ā pay/âr care/a father/b bib/ch church/d deed/ĕ pet/ē fife/f fife/g gag/h hat/hw which/ĭ pit/ī pie/îr pier/j judge/k kick/l lid, needle/m mum/ n no, sudden/ng thing/ŏ pot/ō toe/ô paw, for/oi noise/ou out/o͝o took/o͞o boot/p pop/r roar/s sauce/sh ship, dish/t tight/th thin, path/th this, bathe/ ŭ cut/ûr urge/v valve/w with/y yes/z zebra, size/zh vision/ə about, item, edible, gallop, circus/ à *Fr.* ami/œ *Fr.* feu, *Ger.* schön/ü *Fr.* tu, *Ger.* über/ KH *Ger.* ich, *Scot.* loch/N *Fr.* bon.

anxiety (ăng-zī′ə-tē) *n.* Worry.

apparition (ăp′ə-rĭsh′ən) *n.* A ghost or phantom.

appease (ə-pēz′) *v.* To satisfy. — **appeased** *adj.*

appendix (ə-pĕn′dĭks) *n.* Something added on.

appraise (ə-prāz′) *v.* To judge the value of. — **appraising** *adj.*

apprehension (ăp′rĭ-hĕn′shən) *n.* Fear.

apprehensive (ăp′rĭ-hĕn′sĭv) *adj.* Uneasy; fearful.

approbation (ap′rə-bā′shən) *n.* Approval.

aquamarine (ăk′wə-mə-rēn′, äkwə-) *adj.* Pale blue-green.

aquiline (ăk′wə-līn′, -lĭn) *adj.* Curved like an eagle's beak.

ardent (är′dənt) *adj.* Enthusiastic; intense.

areaway (âr′ē-ə-wā′) *n.* A passageway between buildings.

arid (ăr′-ĭd) *adj.* Very dry.

aristocracy (ăr′ĭs-tŏk′rə-sē) *n.* The upper class.

aristocrat (ə-rĭs′tə-krăt′, ăr′ĭs-tə-) *n.* A member of the nobility; an upper-class person.

array (ə-rā′) *n.* A large display.

arresting (ə-rĕs′tĭng) *adj.* Attracting attention.

arrogant (ăr′ə-gənt) *adj.* Excessively proud; self-important.

articulate (är-tĭk′yə-lĭt) *adj.* Able to speak clearly.

asbestos (ăs-bĕs′təs, ăz-) *adj.* Made of asbestos, which is fire-resistant.

ascent (ə-sĕnt′) *n.* An upward slope.

askance (ə-skăns′) *adv.* With a side glance.

aspen (ăs′pən) *n.* A kind of poplar tree.

aspiration (ăs′pə-rā′shən) *n.* High ambition or desire.

assail (ə-sāl′) *v.* To attack.

assault (ə-sôlt′) *n.* An attack.

assess (ə-sĕs′) *v.* To determine the value of.

asset (ăs′ĕt′) *n.* An advantage.

atmosphere (ăt′mə-sfîr′) *n.* The air surrounding the earth.

atonement (ə-tōn′mənt) *n.* Satisfaction or amends for wrongdoing.

attitude (ăt′ə-tōōd′, -tyōōd′) *n.* A position of the body expressing some action or emotion.

attribute (ăt′rə-byōōt′) *n.* A quality or characteristic.

atypical (ā-tĭp′ĭ-kəl) *adj.* Unusual.

aura (ôr′ə) *n.* An air or quality that seems to surround a person.

avaricious (ăv′ə-rĭsh′əs) *adj.* Greedy. — **avariciously** *adv.*

avenge (ə-vĕnj′) *v.* To take revenge.

avert (ə-vûrt′) *v.* To prevent.

awe (ô) *n.* A feeling of great reverence for someone or something. — **awed** *adj.*

azure (ăzh′ər) *adj.* Sky-blue.

B

banish (băn′ĭsh) *v.* To force to leave.

bankrupt (băngk′rŭpt′, -rəpt) *v.* To ruin financially.

banter (băn′tər) *v.* To tease in a good-humored way.

barrette (bə-rĕt′, bä-) *n.* A clip for holding the hair in place.

bayonet (bā′ə-nĭt, -nĕt′, bā′ə-nĕt′) *n.* A daggerlike blade attached to a rifle.

beaker (bē′kər) *n.* A large container for liquids.

beckon (bĕk′ən) *v.* To motion to come forward. — **beckoning** *adj.*

begrudge (bĭ-grŭj′) *v.* To resent.

benevolence (bə-nĕv′ə-ləns) *n.* Good will.

bewilderment (bĭ-wĭl′dər-mənt) *n.* Puzzlement; confusion.

billow (bĭl′ō) *n.* A large wave.

bleak (blēk) *adj.* Cheerless.

blemish (blĕm′ĭsh) *n.* A slight defect.

bloomers (blōō′mərs) *n.* Baggy trousers once worn by women for athletics.

bootleg (bōōt′lĕg′) *v.* To produce or sell something, such as liquor, illegally. — **bootlegger** *n.*

bough (bou) *n.* A branch of a tree.

bow (bou) *n.* The front of a ship.

brand (brănd) *n.* A piece of burning wood or a hot iron.

brandish (brăn′dĭsh) *v.* To wave in a threatening way.

bravado (brə-vä′dō) *n.* False courage.

breaker (brā′kər) *n.* A wave as it breaks, especially against the shore.

bridle (brīd′l) *v.* To put a harness on a horse. — **bridled** *adj.*

brine (brīn) *n.* The sea.

bristle (brĭs′əl) *v.* To react angrily.

brood (brōōd) *n.* The young of a family.

brook (brŏŏk) *v.* To put up with; permit.

brusque (brŭsk) *adj.* Rude. — **brusquely** *adv.*

buffet (bŭf′ĭt) *v.* Hit. — **buffeted** *adj.*

burden (bûrd′n) *n.* A heavy weight.

burly (bûr′lē) *adj.* Husky.

burnish (bûr′nĭsh) *v.* To polish. — **burnished** *adj.*

butte (byōōt) *n.* A hill with steep sides.

C

cable (kā′bəl) *n.* A heavy rope or chain.

calamity (kə-lăm′ə-tē) *n.* A disaster.

calculate (kăl′kyə-lāt′) *v.* To figure out; guess.

caliber (kăl′ə-bər) *n.* Quality or worth of a person or thing.

calico (kăl′ĭ-kō) *n.* A spotted cat.

camaraderie (kä′mə-rä′də-rē, kăm′ə-) *n.* A friendly feeling among people in a group.

camisole (kăm′ə-sōl′) *n.* A woman's waist-length sleeveless undergarment.

camouflage (kăm′ə-fläzh′, -fläj′) v. To conceal; disguise. — **camouflaged** adj.

canopy (kăn′ə-pē) n. A covering.

canter (kăn′tər) v. To move at an easy pace.

capacious (kə-pā′shəs) adj. Able to hold a large quantity; roomy.

caper (kā′pər) v. To leap playfully. — **capering** n.

capital (kăp′ə-təl) adj. Excellent.

capsule (kăp′səl, -syool) n. A small container of medicine.

carcass (kär′kəs) n. The dead body of an animal.

caress (kə-rĕs′) v. To touch someone lovingly.

carrion (kăr′ē-ən) n. Dead, decaying flesh.

cascade (kăs-kād′) v. To fall in great amounts.

catapult (kăt′ə-pŭlt) v. To leap.

cathedral (kə-thē′drəl) n. A large, impressive church.

caustic (kôs′tĭk) adj. Sharp in speech.

celebrity (sə-lĕb′rə-tē) n. A famous person.

celluloid (sĕl′yə-loid′) n. A substance used for toys, film, and toilet articles.

chaff (chăf) n. The waste part of grain.

chagrin (shə-grĭn′) n. A feeling of annoyance and embarrassment.

chamois (shăm′ē) adj. Referring to a soft leather made from the hide of the chamois, a small antelope, or from the skin of sheep, deer, or goats.

champ (chămp) v. To chew on.

chaos (kā′ŏs′) n. Extreme confusion.

charger (chär′jər) n. A horse trained for battle or parade.

chasm (kăz′əm) n. A deep opening in the earth's surface.

chaste (chāst) adj. Pure.

chastisement (chăs-tīz′mənt, chăs′tīz-mənt) n. Punishment.

chivalrous (shĭv′əl-rəs) adj. Showing the gallantry and courtesy of a knight.

chops (chŏps) n. The mouth, the jaws.

churn (chûrn) v. To move or shake vigorously.

citadel (sĭt′ə-dəl, -dĕl′) n. A fort that protects a city.

civic (sĭv′ĭk) adj. Referring to a city or to a citizen.

clamber (klăm′ər, klăm′bər) v. To climb clumsily or with difficulty, usually on hands and knees.

clamor (klăm′ər) n. A loud noise.

cleave (klēv) v. To cut.

clientele (klī′ən-tĕl′) n. Customers.

clutch (klŭch) v. To hold tightly.

cobble (kŏb′əl) n. A stone used to pave streets.

colleague (kŏl′ēg′) n. A co-worker; associate.

colossal (kə-lŏs′əl) adj. Gigantic.

commission (kə-mĭsh′ən) n. A fee or percentage paid to another for doing something.

commit (kə-mĭt′) v. To bind by promise; pledge. — **committed** adj.

commotion (kə-mō′shən) n. A minor upset or disturbance.

commute (kə-myoot′) v. To travel back and forth regularly, as from one city to another.

compel (kəm-pĕl′) v. To force.

competent (kŏm′pə-tənt) adj. Skillful.

compound (kŏm-pound′, kəm-) v. To mix. — (kŏm′pound) n. A mixture. **compounded** adj.

compressor (kəm-pres′ər) n. A machine for increasing the pressure of gases.

compulsion (kəm-pŭl′shən) n. A force; an irresistable urge.

concerto (kən-chĕr′tŏ) n. A kind of musical composition.

concord (kŏn′kôrd, kŏng′-) n. Peace.

confound (kən-found′, kŏn-) v. To surprise and confuse. — **confounded** adj.

confront (kən-frŭnt′) v. To meet someone face to face, often in an unfriendly way.

congeal (kən-jēl′) v. To become solid; jell.

congenial (kən-jēn′yəl) adj. Pleasant; agreeable.

conjure (kŏn′jər, kən-joor′) v. To call upon; bring to mind.

conquest (kŏn′kwĕst, kŏng′-) n. A victory.

conservatory (kən-sûr′və-tôr′ē, -tōr′ē) n. A school of music.

consolation (kŏn′sə-lā′shən) n. A comfort.

console (kən-sōl′) v. To comfort. **consoled** adj.

conspicuous (kən-spĭk′yoo-əs) adj. Easily seen; obvious.

constrain (kən-strān′) v. To check; control. — **constrained** adj.

consume (kən-soom′, -syoom′) v. To destroy.

contemplate (kŏn′təm-plāt′) v. To look at thoughtfully.

contemplation (kŏn′təm-plā′shən) n. Meditation.

contemporary (kən-tĕm′pə-rĕr′ē) n. A person of about the same age as another.

contempt (kən-tĕmpt′) n. Scorn.

contemptuous (kən-tĕmp′choo-əs) adj. Scornful. — **contemptuously** adv.

contort (kən-tôrt′) v. To twist into unusual shapes.

contrive (kən-trīv′) v. 1. To manage to do something. 2. To scheme or plan. — **contrivance** n.

ă pat/ā pay/âr care/ä father/b bib/ch church/d deed/e pet/ē be/f fife/g gag/h hat/hw which/ĭ pit/ī pie/îr pier/j judge/k kick/l lid, needle/m mum/ n no, sudden/ng thing/ŏ pot/ō toe/ô paw, for/oi noise/ou out/oo took/oo boot/p pop/r roar/s sauce/sh ship, dish/t tight/th thin, path/th this, bathe/ ŭ cut/ûr urge/v valve/w with/y yes/z zebra, size/zh vision/ə about, item, edible, gallop, circus/à Fr. ami/œ Fr. feu, Ger. schön/ü Fr. tu, Ger. über/ KH Ger. ich, Scot. loch/N Fr. bon.

contuse (kən-tōoz', tyōoz') v. To bruise. — **contusion** n.

conventional (kən-věn'shən-əl) adj. Usual; ordinary.

converge (kən-vûrj') v. To move toward one point; to come together.

convert (kən-vûrt') v. To change.

convivial (kən-vĭv'ē-əl) adj. Good-humored; sociable. — **conviviality** n.

convulsive (kən-vŭl'sĭv) adj. Jerky.

coral (kôr'əl, kŏr'əl) n. A stonelike substance used in jewelry and other ornaments.

corroborate (kə-rŏb'ə-rāt') v. To confirm.

countenance (koun'tə-nəns) n. The face.

countinghouse (koun'tĭng-hous') n. A place where accounting and other business operations take place.

covert (kŭv'ərt, kō'vərt) n. A hiding place.

covetous (kŭv'ə-təs) adj. Greedy.

covey (kŭv'ē) n. A small flock.

crafty (krăf'tē, kräf'-) adj. Shrewd; deceitful.

crane (krān) v. To stretch.

cranny (krăn'ē) n. A crack in a wall.

crevasse (krə-văs') n. A deep crack in the earth.

crimson (krĭm'zən) adj. Deep red.

croon (krōon) v. To sing softly.

croupier (krōo'pē-ər, -pē-ā') n. A person who takes in and pays out money at a gambling table.

crucial (krōo'shəl) adj. Decisive.

crux (krŭks, krōoks) n. The most important part.

culprit (kŭl'prĭt) n. A guilty person.

cumbersome (kŭm'bər-səm) adj. Heavy and awkward.

curator (kyōo-rā'tər, kyŏor'ə-tər) n. A person in charge of a museum, library, or exhibit.

cynical (sĭn'ĭ-kəl) adj. Sneering; sarcastic.

D

dappled (dăp'əld) adj. Spotted.

decamp (dĭ-kămp') v. To leave.

deceitful (dĭ-sēt'fəl) adj. Not honest.

decipher (dĭ-sī-fər) v. To figure out.

declamation (děk'lə-mā'shən) n. A long, pompous speech.

decline (dĭ-klīn') v. To turn down; refuse.

deform (dĭ-fôrm') v. To cause to be misshapen; disfigure.

deformed (dĭ-fôrmd') adj. Misshapen.

deft (děft) adj. Skillful. **deftly** adv.

deliberate (dĭ-lĭb'ə-rāt') v. To think about carefully. — (dĭ-lĭb'ər-ĭt) adj. Intentional. — **deliberately** adv.

deluge (děl'yōoj) v. Flood. — A flood. n.

delve (dělv) v. To study something deeply.

deportment (dĭ-pôrt'mənt, dĭ-pōrt'-) n. Behavior.

depressed (dĭ-prěst') adj. Sad.

desolate (děs'ə-lĭt) adj. Deserted. — **desolateness** n.

despondency (dĭ-spŏn'dən-sē) n. Hopelessness; despair.

despotism (děs'pə-tĭz'əm) n. Tyranny; dictatorship.

destitute (děs'tə-tōot', -tyōot') adj. Extremely poor.

desultory (děs'əl-tôr'ē, -tōr'ē) adj. Aimless.

detonate (dět'n-āt') v. To make explode. — **detonation** n.

devise (dĭ-vīz') v. To plan.

dilapidated (dĭ-lăp'ə dā'tĭd) adj. In very bad condition.

dilate (dī-lāt', dī'lāt', dī-lāt') v. To become larger. — **dilated** adj.

dimension (dĭ-měn'shən) n. Size; scope.

diminish (dĭ-mĭn'ĭsh) v. To reduce.

dire (dīr) adj. Frightening.

disability (dĭs'ə-bĭl'ə-tē) n. 1. A condition that prevents someone from working. 2. A disadvantage.

disclose (dĭs-klōz') v. To reveal; to make known.

discriminate (dĭs-krĭm'ə-nāt') v. 1. To show prejudice. 2. To draw fine distinctions.

discriminating (dĭs-krĭm'ə-nā'tĭng) adj. 1. Making fine distinctions. 2. Selective.

dishearten (dĭs-härt'n) v. To discourage; depress. — **disheartened** adj.

dismay (dĭs-mā') v. To fill with alarm. — **dismayed** adj.

dispense (dĭs-pěns') v. To give out; distribute.

disposition (dĭs'pə-zĭsh'ən) n. 1. Personality; temperament. 2. The manner in which something is arranged or settled.

dispute (dĭs-pyōot') v. To argue.

disreputable (dĭs-rěp'yə-tə-bəl) adj. Not respectable; disgraceful.

dissuade (dĭ-swād') v. To persuade someone not to do something.

distract (dĭs-trăkt') v. To turn one's attention elsewhere. — **distracted** adj.

distraction (dĭs-trăk'shən) n. Anything that draws attention away from an original focus of interest.

distress (dĭs-trěs') n. Discomfort.

divert (dĭ-vûrt', dī-) v. To turn aside. — **diverted** adj.

divine (dĭ-vīn') v. To guess; to know by intuition.

domain (dō-mān') n. Territory.

domestic (də-měs'tĭk) adj. Having to do with the home.

draggle (drăg'əl) v. To make dirty. — **draggled** adj.

dram (drăm) n. A small amount of something.

drench (drěnch) v. To wet thoroughly.

E

ecstatic (ěk-stăt'ĭk) adj. Very joyful.

eddy (ěd'ē) n. A current moving against another current, usually in a swirling motion.

eerie (îr'ē) adj. Weird.

efficiency (ĭ-fĭsh′ən-sē) *n.* Ability to get things done with little effort.

elaborate (ĭ-lăb′ər-ĭt) *adj.* Complicated.

elicit (ĭ-lĭs′ĭt) *v.* To draw out.

elocution (ĕl′ə-kyōō′shən) *n.* The art of speaking well.

eloquence (ĕl′ə-kwəns) *n.* Forceful or persuasive speech.

eloquent (el′ə-kwənt) *adj.* Expressive.

elude (ĭ-lōōd′) *v.* To escape from.

emanate (ĕm′ə-nāt′) *v.* To flow out; issue.

ember (ĕm′bər) *n.* A glowing piece of coal or wood from a dying fire.

emblem (ĕm′bləm) *n.* A badge.

embolden (ĕm-bōl′dən) *v.* To make bold or courageous. — **emboldened** *adj.*

emerge (ĭ-mûrj′) *v.* To appear.

emery (ĕm′ə-rē, ĕm′rē) *n.* A substance used for grinding and polishing.

emphatic (ĕm-făt′ĭk *adj.* Definite. **emphatically** *adv.*

endear (ĕn-dîr′, ĭn-) *v.* To make dear or beloved.

endeavor (ĕn-dĕv′ər, ĭn-) *n.* An attempt.

engulf (ĕn-gŭlf′, ĭn-) *v.* To submerge; overwhelm.

enhance (ĕn-hăns′, -häns′, ĭn-) *v.* To make better.

enterprise (ĕn′tər-prīz′) *n.* An undertaking; project.

enthrall (ĕn-thrôl′, ĭn-) *v.* To hold as in a spell. — **enthralled** *adj.*

entreat (ĕn-trēt′, ĭn-) *v.* To beg.

entreaty (ĕn-trē′tē, ĭn-) *n.* A plea.

entwine (ĕn-twīn′, ĭn-) *v.* To twist around.

enumeration (ĭ-nōō′mə-rā′shən, ĭ-nyōō′-) *n.* A list of items.

envelop (ĕn-vĕl′əp, ĭn-) *v.* To cover completely.

enviable (ĕn′vē-ə-bəl) *adj.* Desirable.

envision (ĕn-vĭzh′ən) *v.* To imagine something that has not yet happened.

epidemic (ĕp′ə-dĕm′ĭk) *n.* A rapid spread of a disease.

equity (ĕk′wə-tē) *n.* Justice; fairness.

erratic (ĭ-răt′ĭk) *adj.* Irregular. — **erratically** *adv.*

essence (ĕs′əns) *n.* The essential nature of a person or a thing.

evolve (ĭ-vŏlv′) *v.* To develop gradually.

exalt (ĕg-zôlt′, ĭg-) *v.* To raise to a high position. — **exalted** *adj.*

exasperate (ĕg-zăs′pə-rāt′, ĭg-) *v.* To make angry. — **exasperating** *adj.*

exceedingly (ĕk-sē′dĭng-lē, ĭk-) *adv.* Extremely.

exhale (ĕks-hāl′, ĕk-sāl′, ĭk-sāl′) *v.* To breathe out.

exhilarate (ĕg-zĭl′ə-rāt′, ĭg-) *v.* To excite. — **exhilarating** *adj.*

exile (ĕg′zīl′, ĕk′sīl′) *n.* Separation from one's country.

exotic (ĕg-zŏt′ĭk, ĭg-) *adj.* Unusual and fascinating.

expectant (ĕk-spĕk′tənt, ĭk-) *adj.* Waiting for something to happen.

expiation (ĕk′spē-ā′shən) *n.* The act of making amends.

exploit (ĕks′ploit′) *n.* A daring act.

exposure (ĕk-spō′shər, ĭk-) *n.* Being without protection from natural forces.

exquisite (ĕks′kwĭ-zĭt) *adj.* Extremely beautiful. — **exquisitely** *adv.*

extension (ĕk-stĕn′shən, ĭk-) *n.* An extra period of time allowed for payment of a debt.

extract (ĕk-străkt′, ĭk-) *v.* To pull out.

extricate (ĕk′strĭ-kāt′) *v.* To set free.

exude (ĕg-zōōd′, ĭg-, ĕk-sōōd′, ĭk-) *v.* To give off.

exultant (ĕg-zŭl′tənt, ĭg-) *adj.* Joyful.

exultation (ĕg′zŭl-tā′shən) *n.* Great joyfulness.

F

façade (fə-säd′) *n.* The front of a building.

fain (fān) *adv.* Willingly.

falter (fôl′tər) *v.* To show uncertainty.

famine (făm′ĭn) *n.* A severe and widespread shortage of food.

fancy (făn′sē) *v.* To imagine.

fathom (făth′əm) *v.* **1.** To measure the depth of. **2.** To understand thoroughly. — A unit of measurement equal to six feet *n.*

feign (fān) *v.* To pretend.

ferocity (fə-rŏs′ə-tē) *n.* Fierceness.

fervent (fûr′vənt) *adj.* Very enthusiastic; intense.

feud (fyōōd) *n.* A bitter, prolonged quarrel between two individuals or families.

flabbergast (flăb′ər-găst′) *v.* To shock and surprise. — **flabbergasted** *adj.*

flail (flāl) *v.* To move one's arms about vigorously.

flank (flăngk) *v.* To be on either side of. — **flanked** *adj.*

flaw (flô) *n.* A defect. — **flawless** *adj.*

flax (flăks) *n.* A plant with delicate blue flowers.

fleck (flĕk) *n.* A spot. — **flecked** *adj.*

fledgling (flĕj′lĭng) *n.* A young bird.

flexible (flĕk′sə-bəl) *adj.* Capable of being bent.

flounder (floun′dər) *v.* To struggle clumsily.

ă pat/ā pay/âr care/ä father/b bib/ch church/d deed/ĕ pet/ē be/f fife/g gag/h hat/hw which/ĭ pit/ī pie/îr pier/j judge/k kick/l lid, needle/m mum/ n no, sudden/ng thing/ŏ pot/ō toe/ô paw, for/oi noise/ou out/ōō took/ōō boot/p pop/r roar/s sauce/sh ship, dish/t tight/th thin, path/*th* this, bathe/ ŭ cut/ûr urge/v valve/w with/y yes/z zebra, size/zh vision/ə about, item, edible, gallop, circus/à *Fr.* ami/œ *Fr.* feu, *Ger.* schön/ü *Fr.* tu, *Ger.* über/ ᴋʜ *Ger.* ich, *Scot.* loch/ɴ *Fr.* bon.

flush (flŭsh) v. To frighten out of a hiding place.

folly (fŏl'ē) n. Foolishness.

foolhardy (fōōl'här'dē) adj. Rash; foolishly daring.

forage (fôr'ĭj, fŏr'-) n. Food for domestic animals such as cattle, sheep, and horses.

foray (fôr'ā') n. A surprise attack or raid.

forbearance (fôr-bâr'əns) n. Patience; self-control.

forlorn (fôr-lôrn', fər-) adj. Deserted. — **forlornly** adv.

fortitude (fôr'tə-tōōd', -tyōōd') n. Courage.

foul (foul) adj. Disgusting.

frantic (frăn'tĭk) adj. Wild. — **frantically** adv.

fraudulent (frô'jə-lənt) adj. Deceitful.

fray (frā) n. A fight.

frenzy (frĕn'zē) n. Violent activity.

frothing (frôth'ĭng, frŏth-) n. Enthusiasm.

functional (fŭngk'shən-əl) adj. Practical; usable.

furtive (fûr'tĭv) adj. Sneaky; sly. — **furtively** adv.

G

garble (gär'bəl) v. To mix up; confuse. — **garbled** adj.

garland (gär'lənd) n. A wreath.

gaudy (gô'dē) adj. Flashy; lacking taste.

gazebo (gə-zē'bō, -zā'bō) n. A roofed structure serving as a shelter.

gesticulate (jĕ-stĭk'yə-lāt') v. To use gestures in place of speech.

gingerly (jĭn'jər-lē) adv. Carefully.

girth (gûrth) n. A strap that goes under the belly of an animal to secure a saddle or a pack.

glade (glād) n. An open area in a forest.

glaze (glāz) v. To apply a shiny coating. — **glazing** adj.

glower (glou'ər) v. To stare in an angry or ill-humored way.

greatcoat (grāt'kōt') n. A heavy overcoat.

greenhouse (grēn'hous') n. A glass-enclosed structure where plants are grown.

grimace (grĭ-mās', grĭm'ĭs) v. To twist or distort the face.

grizzle (grĭz'əl) v. To become gray. — **grizzled** adj.

grope (grōp) v. To feel one's way.

gross (grōs) adj. Referring to total income before deductions are made.

gruel (grōō'əl) n. Thin watery porridge, usually made of oatmeal.

grueling (grōō'ə-ling) adj. Harsh; extremely difficult.

gullible (gŭl'ə-bəl) adj. Easily deceived or cheated.

gust (gŭst) n. A rush of wind. — **gusty** adj.

gut (gŭt) v. To destroy the insides of. — **gutted** adj.

H

habitable (hăb'ə-tə-bəl) adj. Able to be lived in.

hapless (hăp'lĭs) adj. Unlucky.

hark (härk) v. To listen.

harry (hăr'ē) v. To annoy constantly. — **harried** adj.

haughty (hô'tē) adj. Proud; arrogant.

havoc (hăv'ək) n. Extreme disorder.

headland (hĕd'lənd, -lănd') n. A point of land that juts out into the water.

hearken (här'kən) v. To listen carefully.

heirloom (âr'lōōm') n. A prized family possession that is handed down from generation to generation.

helm (hĕlm) n. The steering wheel of a ship.

hemorrhage (hĕm'ə-rĭj) n. A heavy flow of blood.

hobnail (hŏb'nāl') n. A nail put on the soles of shoes to keep them from wearing or slipping.

homage (hŏm'ĭj, ŏm'-) n. To honor; respect.

hospitable (hŏs'pə-tə-bəl, hŏs-pĭt'ə-bəl) adj. Friendly toward visitors.

hostile (hŏs'təl) adj. Unfriendly.

hover (hŭv'ər, hŏv'-) v. To remain suspended in one place in the air.

hummock (hŭm'ək) n. A small hill.

hunker (hŭng'kər) v. To crouch; squat.

hurl (hûrl) v. To throw vigorously.

hysteria (hĭ-stĕr'ē-ə) n. Uncontrolled emotion.

hysterical (hĭ-stĕr'ĭ-kəl) adj. Wildly emotional.

I

ignite (ĭg-nīt') v. To set on fire. — **ignited** adj.

illuminate (ĭ-lōō'mə-nāt') v. To light up.

immobile (ĭ-mō'bəl, -bēl') adj. Not moving. — **immobility** n.

immortal (ĭ-môrt'l) n. One who will never die. — adj. Living forever.

imperceptible (ĭm'pər-sĕp'tə-bəl) adj. Barely noticeable. — **imperceptibly** adv.

imperial (ĭm-pîr'ē-əl) adj. 1. Of superior size or quality. 2. Majestic.

impiety (ĭm-pī'ə-tē) n. Lack of reverence for God; disrespect.

impish (ĭm'pĭsh) adj. Playful.

implore (ĭm-plôr', -plōr') v. To beg.

imposing (ĭm-pō'zĭng) adj. Impressive.

inaudible (ĭn-ô'də-bəl) adj. Not able to be heard.

inaugurate (ĭn-ô'gyə-rāt') v. To start officially.

incantation (ĭn'-kăn-tā'shən) n. The chanting of words to cast a magic spell.

incarnate (ĭn-kär'nĭt) adj. In the flesh; embodied.

incessant (ĭn-sĕs'ənt) adj. Continuing without interruption. — **incessantly** adv.

incompetent (ĭn-kŏm'pə-tənt) adj. Lacking needed abilities; not capable.

incomprehensible (ĭn'kŏm-prĭ-hĕn'sə-bəl, ĭn-kŏm'-) adj. Unable to be understood; baffling.

inconspicuous (ĭn'kən-spĭk'yōō-əs) adj. Attracting little notice.

incredulous (ĭn-krĕj′ə-ləs) *adj.* Unwilling or unable to believe.

indifference (ĭn-dĭf′ər-əns) *n.* A lack of concern. — **indifferent** *adj.* — **indifferently** *adv.*

indignant (ĭn-dĭg′nənt) *adj.* Angry, especially at an injustice. — **indignantly** *adv.*

indignation (ĭn′dĭg-nā′shən) *n.* Anger, especially at an injustice.

indispensable (ĭn′dĭs-pĕn′sə-bəl) *adj.* Necessary.

induce (ĭn-dōōs′, -dyōōs′) *v.* To persuade.

inert (ĭn-ûrt′) *adj.* Inactive.

inevitable (ĭn-ĕv′ə-tə-bəl) *adj.* Unavoidable.

inexplicable (ĭn-ĕk′splĭ-kə-bəl, ĭn′ĭk-splĭk′ə-bəl) *adj.* Not able to be explained.

infamous (ĭn′fə-məs) *adj.* Outrageous.

infatuated (ĭn-făch′ōō-ā′tĭd) *adj.* Characterized by a foolish attraction to someone or something.

inflated (ĭn-flā′tĭd) *adj.* Expanded; puffed up.

infringe (ĭn-frĭnj′) *v.* To trespass; violate. **Infringe on** (or **upon**).

ingenious (ĭn-jēn′yəs) *adj.* Very clever.

inhospitable (ĭn-hŏs′pĭ-tə-bəl, ĭn′hŏ-spĭt′ə-bəl) *adj.* Unfriendly toward visitors.

insensible (ĭn-sĕn′sə-bəl) *adj.* So small as to be hardly noticeable.

insolent (ĭn′sə-lənt) *adj.* Insulting.

insulation (ĭn′sə-lā′shən, ĭns′yə-) *n.* Something that prevents or reduces the passage of heat, electricity, sound, etc., in or out.

insuperable (ĭn-sōō′pər-ə-bəl) *adj.* Unable to be overcome.

intercept (ĭn′tər-sĕpt′) *v.* To seize or stop on the way; cut off.

interlude (ĭn′tər-lōōd′) *n.* An intervening period of time.

interminable (ĭn-tûr′mə-nə-bəl) *adj.* Endless or seeming to be endless. — **interminably** *adv.*

intermittent (ĭn′tər-mĭt′ənt) *adj.* Stopping from time to time; not continuous. — **intermittently** *adv.*

intimate (ĭn′tə-māt′) *v.* To hint. — **intimation** *n.*

intolerable (ĭn-tŏl′ər-ə-bəl) *adj.* Unbearable.

intrude (ĭn-trōōd′) *n.* To enter without being welcome; to force one's way in. — **intruder** *n.*

invariable (ĭn-vâr′ē-ə-bəl) *adj.* Unchanging. — **invariably** *adv.*

invective (ĭn-vĕk′tĭv) *n.* Insulting or abusive language.

invincible (ĭn-vĭn′sə-bəl) *adj.* Not able to be conquered.

involuntary (ĭn-vŏl′ən-tĕr′ē) *adj.* Done without choice or intention. — **involuntarily** *adv.*

ironic (ī-rŏn′ĭk) *adj.* Opposite to what might be expected. — **ironically** *adv.*

irresolute (ĭ-rĕz′ə-lōōt′) *adj.* Undecided.

irrevocable (ĭ-rĕv′ə-kə-bəl) *adj.* Not able to be undone or recalled.

islet (ī′lĭt) *n.* A small island.

isolation (ī′sə-lā′shən, īs′ə-) *n.* Aloneness.

J

jar (jär) *v.* To bump.

jaunty (jôn′te, jän′-) *adj.* Gay. — **jauntily** *adv.*

jeer (jîr) *v.* To make fun of.

jovial (jō′vē-əl) *adj.* Merry; jolly.

jubilant (jōō′bə-lənt) *adj.* Showing great joy. — **jubilantly** *adv.*

judicious (jōō-dĭsh′əs) *adj.* Wise. — **judiciously** *adv.*

juncture (jŭngk′chər) *n.* A point in time.

justify (jŭs′tə-fī′) *v.* To defend.

K

kiln (kĭl, kĭln) *n.* An oven for baking or firing substances, especially pottery.

knoll (nōl) *n.* A small hill.

L

lacerate (lăs′ə rāt′) *v.* To tear. — **laceration** *n.*

lance (lăns, läns) *n.* A weapon with a long shaft and a pointed tip.

languid (lăng′gwĭd) *adj.* Without energy or enthusiasm. — **languidly** *adv.*

larceny (lär′sə-nē) *n.* Theft.

lash (lăsh) *v.* To tie securely.

lavish (lăv′ĭsh) *adj.* Generous. — **lavishly** *adv.*

lethal (lē′thəl) *adj.* Deadly.

liability (lī′ə-bĭl′ə-tē) *n.* A disadvantage.

lineage (lĭn′ē-ĭj) *n.* Family background.

listless (lĭst′lĭs) *adj.* Showing no energy or interest. — **listlessly** *adv.*

lithe (līth) *adj.* Graceful.

loiter (loi′tər) *v.* To stand around idly or aimlessly.

lollop (lol′əp) *v.* To move in bounds or leaps. — **lolloping** *adj.*

loom (lōōm) *v.* To come into sight, as something fearful. — **loomed** *adj.*

lope (lōp) *v.* To move with an easy, bounding gait.

lucent (lōō′sənt) *adj.* Glowing; luminous.

lumber (lŭm′bər) *v.* To walk with a heavy, awkward step.

ă pat/ā pay/âr care/ä father/b bib/ch church/d deed/ĕ pet/ē be/f fife/g gag/h hat/hw which/ĭ pit/ī pie/îr pier/j judge/k kick/l lid, needle/m mum/ n no, sudden/ng thing/ŏ pot/ō toe/ô paw, for/oi noise/ou out/ŏŏ took/ōō boot/p pop/r roar/s sauce/sh ship, dish/t tight/th thin, path/th this, bathe/ ŭ cut/ûr urge/v valve/w with/y yes/z zebra, size/zh vision/ə about, item, edible, gallop, circus/à *Fr.* ami/œ *Fr.* feu, *Ger.* schön/ü *Fr.* tu, *Ger.* über/ KH *Ger.* ich, *Scot.* loch/N *Fr.* bon.

luminous (lo͞o′mə-nəs) *adj.* Able to glow in the dark.

lurch (lûrch) *v.* To stagger.

lurid (lo͝or′ĭd) *adj.* Glowing or shining fiery red.

M

majestic (mə-jĕs′tĭk) *adj.* Grand; stately.

malevolence (mə-lĕv′ə-ləns) *n.* Ill will.

malice (măl′ĭs) *n.* Intention to harm another person.

mania (mā′nē-ə, mān′yə) *n.* Excessive fondness; craze.

manifest (măn′ə-fĕst′) *v.* To become evident.

martial (mär′shəl) *adj.* Eager to fight; warlike.

martyr (mär′tər) *n.* One who suffers or dies for something he or she believes in.

massive (măs′ĭv) *adj.* Huge.

mast (măst, mäst) *n.* A pole used to support the sails and rigging of a ship.

mausoleum (mô′sə-lē′əm, mô′zə-) *n.* A large, grand tomb.

mawkish (mô′kĭsh) *adj.* Overly emotional.

maze (māz) *n.* **1.** A network of paths used in a laboratory to test animals. **2.** A puzzle; something that is confusing.

meander (mē-ăn′dər) *v.* To wander aimlessly.

megaphone (mĕg′ə-fōn′) *n.* A cone-shaped device to make the voice louder.

melancholy (mĕl′ən-kŏl′ē) *adj.* Sad; gloomy.

memorial (mə-môr′ē-əl, mə-mōr′-) *n.* Something, such as a monument or holiday, intended as a reminder of some person or event.

menagerie (mə-năj′ə-rē, mə-năzh′-) *n.* A zoo.

mesa (mā′sə) *n.* An elevation having steep sides and a flat top, usually found in the southwestern United States.

metabolism (mə-tăb′ə-lĭz′əm) *n.* The processes by which the body uses food or breaks it down into waste matter.

mettle (mĕt′l) *n.* Courage; worth.

microbe (mī′krōb′) *n.* A germ.

misjudge (mĭs-jŭj′) *v.* To judge wrongly.

moil (moil) *v.* To work hard.

molder (mōl′dər) *v.* To decay. — **moldering** *adj.*

monotonous (mə-nŏt′n-əs) *adj.* Lacking variety; dull because repetitious.

moony (mo͞o′nē) *adj.* Dreamy.

moor (mo͝or) *n.* A stretch of open land, often swampy.

morality (mə-răl′ə-tē, mô-) *n.* Principles of right and wrong conduct.

mortal (môrt′l) *adj.* Subject to death.

mortgage (môr′gĭj) *v.* To pledge something valuable in return for a loan.

mosaic (mō-zā′ĭk) *n.* A picture or design made from small pieces of colored material such as stone or glass.

motivate (mō′tə-vāt′) *v.* To move to action. — **motivated** *adj.*

mottle (mŏt′l) *v.* To mark with spots of various colors and shapes. — **mottled** *adj.*

mucilage (myo͞o′sə-lĭj) *n.* A type of glue.

musket (mŭs′kĭt) *n.* A shoulder gun used before the rifle was invented.

N

nonchalance (nŏn′shə-läns′) *n.* A lack of concern.

notion (nō′shən) *n.* An idea.

nurture (nûr′chər) *v.* To rear; to care for.

O

oblique (ō-blēk′, ə-) *adj.* At an angle; not straight. — **obliquely** *adv.*

obliterate (ə-blĭt′ə-rāt′) *v.* To remove completely; erase. — **obliterated** *adj.*

obscure (ŏb-skyo͝or′, əb-) *adj.* Unclear.

obstinate (ŏb′stə-nĭt) *adj.* Stubborn.

odious (ō′dē-əs) *adj.* Hateful.

ogre (ō′gər) *n.* A monster.

ominous (ŏm′ə-nəs) sinister; threatening.

onyx (ŏn′ĭks) *n.* A semiprecious stone used in jewelry and other ornaments.

opaque (ō-pāk′) *adj.* Not permitting light to go through.

opportune (ŏp′ər-to͞on′, -tyo͞on′) *adj.* Well-timed.

oppress (ə-prĕs′) *v.* To weigh down. — **oppressed** *adj.* Depressed or burdened.

option (ŏp′shən) *n.* A choice.

ordeal (ôr-dēl′) *n.* A difficult experience.

ornate (ôr-nāt′) *adj.* Very fancy.

P

pandemonium (păn′də-mō′nē-əm) *n.* Noisy confusion.

parasol (păr′ə-sôl′, -sŏl′) *n.* A small umbrella used for protection from the sun.

passel (păs′əl) *n.* A large number.

passionate (păsh′ən-ĭt) *adj.* Very affectionate.

passive (păs′ĭv) *adj.* Not participating.

patron (pā′trən) *n.* **1.** A customer. **2.** In ancient times, the god or goddess who protected a city.

patronize (pā′trə-nīz′, păt′rə-) *v.* To be a regular customer.

peaked (pēkt, pē′kĭd) *adj.* Pale.

pedagogy (pĕd′ə-gō′jē, -gŏj′ē) *n.* Teaching.

pedestrian (pə-dĕs′trē-ən) *adj.* Walking.

pedigree (pĕd′ə-grē′) *n.* **1.** Ancestry. **2.** A record of descent, particularly of purebred animals.

peer (pîr) *n.* An equal.

pelt (pĕlt) *v.* To run rapidly.

penance (pĕn'əns) *n.* Self-punishment for a sin or wrongdoing.

penetrate (pĕn'ə-trāt') *v.* To go through or into.

peninsula (pə-nĭn'syə-lə, -sə-lə) *n.* A land area almost completely surrounded by water.

peril (pĕr'əl) *n.* Danger. — **perilous** *adj.*

perimeter (pə-rĭm'ə-tər) *n.* Limits; boundary.

perpendicular (pûr'pən-dĭk'yə-lər) *adj.* Upright; vertical.

perpetual (pər-pĕch'ōō-əl) *adj.* Lasting forever or for an unlimited time.

perplex (pər-plĕks') *v.* To confuse.

perplexed (pər-plĕkst') *adj.* Confused; puzzled.

persevere (pûr'sə-vîr') *v.* To continue in some line of action or thought despite obstacles.

persist (pər-sĭst', zĭst') *v.* To continue to do something with great determination.

perverted (pər-vûr'tĭd) *adj.* Misdirected; not used properly.

pestilence (pĕs'tə-ləns) *n.* A widely spread disease.

phantom (făn'təm) *n.* A ghost.

phenomenon (fĭ-nŏm'ə-nŏn') *n.* An unusual happening.

philosophical (fĭl'ə-sŏf'ĭ-kəl) *adj.* Wise. — **philosophically** *adv.*

philter (fĭl'tər) *n.* A magic potion or charm.

pilfer (pĭl'fər) *v.* To steal small amounts of money or objects of little value.

pillar (pĭl'ər) *n.* A column.

pillbox (pĭl'bŏks') *adj.* Shaped like a small, round box.

pine (pīn) *v.* To yearn for.

placid (plăs'ĭd) *adj.* Peaceful.

plaintive (plān'tĭv) *adj.* Sad.

pliant (plī'ənt) *adj.* Easily bent; flexible.

plight (plīt) *n.* A difficult situation.

plowshare (plou'shâr') *n.* The cutting blade of a plow.

plump (plŭmp) *v.* To fall heavily.

poise (poiz) *v.* To remain balanced. — **poised** *adj.*

ponder (pŏn'dər) *v.* To think carefully about.

ponderous (pŏn'dər-əs) *adj.* **1.** Very heavy. **2.** Dull. — **ponderously** *adv.*

populous (pŏp'yə-ləs) *adj.* Having many people.

potential (pə-ten'shəl) *adj.* Possible but not yet realized. — *n.* An ability capable of development.

potter (pŏt'ər) *v. Chiefly British.* To putter; dawdle.

poultice (pōl'tĭs) *n.* A hot pack applied to a sore part of the body.

prance (prăns, präns) *v.* To rise up on the hind legs and spring forward, as a horse.

precaution (prĭ-kô'shən) *n.* Care taken in advance, as a safeguard.

precedent (prĕs'ə-dənt) *n.* An act or decision used as an example in dealing with later cases.

precipice (prĕs'ə-pĭs) *n.* A steep cliff.

precipitous (prĭ-sĭp'ə-təs) *adj.* Steep.

preliminary (prĭ-lĭm'ə-nĕr'ē) *n.* Something that comes before the main action or business.

premature (prē'mə-chōor', -tōor', -tyōor') *adj.* Happening too early; too hasty.

premonition (prē'mə-nĭsh'ən, prĕm'ə-) *n.* A feeling that something bad will happen.

prevalent (prĕv'ə-lənt) *adj.* Widespread.

prig (prĭg) *n.* A smug, pompous person.

prime (prīm) *v.* To get a gun ready for firing.

priming (prī'mĭng) *n.* Powder or other explosive material used to set off a charge in a gun.

procure (prō-kyŏŏr', prə-) *v.* To get; obtain.

profess (prə-fĕs', prō-) *v.* To claim; declare. — **professing** *n.*

profusion (prə-fyōō'zhən, prō-) *n.* A large amount.

projection (prə-jĕk'shən) *n.* Something that sticks out.

prophecy (prŏf'ə-sē) *n.* A prediction.

protrude (prō-trōōd') *v.* To stick out.

providence (prŏv'ə-dəns, -dĕns') *n.* **1.** The care and control exercised by God over the universe. **2.** (**P-**) God.

province (prŏv'ĭns) *n.* An area of duties and responsibilities.

provoke (prə-vōk') *v.* To stir up. — **provoking** *adj.*

pry (prī) *v.* To open something with difficulty.

pungent (pŭn'jənt) *adj.* Sharp-smelling.

purgative (pûr'gə-tĭv) *n.* A laxative.

pyre (pīr) *n.* A funeral pile on which a dead body is burned.

Q

quack (kwăk) *adj.* Referring to someone or something that pretends to have power to cure disease.

quarters (kwôr'tərz) *n.* The place where one lives.

quench (kwĕnch) *v.* To put an end to.

ă pat/ā pay/âr care/ä father/b bib/ch church/d deed/ĕ pet/ē be/f fife/g gag/h hat/hw which/ĭ pit/ī pie/îr pier/j judge/k kick/l lid, needle/m mum/ n no, sudden/ng thing/ŏ pot/ō toe/ô paw, for/oi noise/ou out/ōō took/ōō boot/p pop/r roar/s sauce/sh ship, dish/t tight/th thin, path/*th* this, bathe/ ŭ cut/ûr urge/v valve/w with/y yes/z zebra, size/zh vision/ə about, item, edible, gallop, circus/ à *Fr.* ami/œ *Fr.* feu, *Ger.* schön/ü *Fr.* tu, *Ger.* über/ ᴋʜ *Ger.* ich, *Scot.* loch/ɴ *Fr.* bon.

quest (kwĕst) *n.* A search.
quiver (kwĭv′ər) *v.* To tremble. — **quivering** *adj.*

R

racy (rā′sē) *adj.* Daring.
radiant (rā′dē-ənt) *adj.* Bright; glowing.
radiate (rā′dē-āt′) *v.* To send out rays of light or heat.
ramshackle (răm′shăk′əl) *adj.* Rickety; likely to fall apart.
rapture (răp′chər) *n.* A feeling of great joy.
reckon (rĕk′ən) *v.* To guess.
recitation (rĕs′ə-tā′shən) *n.* Something that is told aloud from memory.
recompense (rĕk′əm-pĕns′) *v.* To reward.
redress (rĭ-drĕs) *v.* To make up for.
reek (rēk) *v.* To give off a strong smell.
reel (rēl) *v.* To sway; stagger.
refrain (rĭ-frān′) *n.* A part of a poem or song that is regularly repeated.
refugee (rĕf′yoo-jē′) *n.* A person who flees from danger to a safe place.
reluctant (rĭ-lŭk′tənt) *adj.* Unwilling. — **reluctantly** *adv.*
remote (rĭ-mōt′) *adj.* Distant; aloof.
repentance (rĭ-pen′təns) *n.* Sorrow for wrongdoing.
repentant (rĭ-pĕn′tənt) *adj.* Showing remorse or sorrow for one's sins.
replenish (rĭ-plĕn′ĭsh) *v.* To fill again.
replica (rĕp′lə-kə) *n.* A copy.
reprimand (rĕp′rə-mănd′, -mänd′) *n.* A severe scolding.
resolute (rĕz′ə-loot′) *adj.* Determined; unyielding.
resolution (rĕz′ə-loo′shən) *n.* A decision or determination to do something.
resourceful (rĭ-sôrs′fəl, rĭ-sōrs′-, rĭ-zôrs′-, rĕzôrs′-) *adj.* Clever in finding ways to handle problems. — **resourcefulness** *n.*
retort (rĭ-tôrt′) *v.* To answer in a sharp or witty way.
revere (rĭ-vîr′) *v.* To show deep respect toward someone or something. — **revered** *adj.*
reverence (rĕv′ər-əns) *v.* To honor.
ricochet (rĭk′ə-shā′, -shĕt′) *v.* To skip off a surface after striking it at an angle.
riotous (rī-ət-əs) *adj.* Abundant; lush.
rite (rīt) *n.* A ceremonial act.
ritual (rĭch′oo-əl) *n.* A ceremony.
rivulet (rĭv′yə-lĭt) *n.* A small stream.
robust (rō-bŭst′, rō′bŭst) *adj.* Husky; healthy and strong.
rogue (rōg) *n.* A playful person.
roguish (rō′gĭsh) *adj.* Mischievous.
rowdy (rou′dē) *adj.* Rough.

rudiment (roo′də-mənt) *n.* A basic principle. Often used in the plural.
rummage (rŭm′ĭj) *v.* To search through a collection of objects. — **rummaging** *n.*

S

saffron (săf′rən) *adj.* Orange-yellow.
sagacious (sə-gā′shəs) *adj.* Wise.
sage (sāj) *n.* A wise person.
sanction (săngk′shən) *v.* To approve.
sanctuary (săngk′choo-ĕr′ē) *n.* A safe place.
sanitarium (săn′ə-târ′ē-əm) *n.* A place where one may go to rest or to recover from an illness.
saunter (sôn′tər) *v.* To walk slowly.
scabbard (skăb′ərd) *n.* A holder for a dagger or sword.
scepter (sĕp′tər) *n.* A staff a king or queen holds as a sign of authority.
schooner (skoo′nər) *n.* A kind of sailing ship having two or more masts.
scope (scōp) *n.* Reach.
scourge (skûrj) *v.* To whip.
scrawny (skrô′nē) *adj.* Skinny.
scroll (skrōl) *n.* A roll of paper or other writing material.
scuffle (skŭf′əl) *n.* A fight.
scurry (skûr′ē) *v.* To hurry. *n.* **scurry, scurrying.**
scurvy (skûr′vē) *adj.* Vile; contemptible.
scuttle (skŭt′l) *v.* To move hastily.
scuttle (skŭt′l) *n.* A container for coal.
sear (sîr) *v.* To burn the surface of something.
sensuous (sĕn′shoo-əs) *adj.* Pleasing to the senses.
sentiment (sĕn′tə-mənt) *n.* A feeling; emotion.
sentimental (sĕn′tə-mĕnt′l) *adj.* Acting from feeling rather than from reason.
servitude (sûr′və-tood′, -tyood′) *n.* Slavery.
shaft (shăft, shäft) *n.* A ray of light.
sheepish (shēp′ĭsh) *adj.* Embarrassed. — **sheepishly** *adv.*
shorn (shôrn, shōrn) *adj.* Deprived.
shroud (shroud) *v.* To wrap in a burial garment.
shuttle (shŭt′l) *n.* A device used in weaving.
sidle (sīd′l) *v.* To move sideways cautiously or stealthily.
silhouette (sĭl′oo-ĕt′) *v.* To outline. — **silhouetted** *adj.*
simultaneous (sī′məl-tā′nē-əs, sĭm′əl-) *adj.* Happening at the same time. — **simultaneously** *adv.*
sinister (sĭn′ĭ-stər) *adj.* Threatening.
skein (skān) *n.* A length of yarn wound in a coil.
skeptical (skĕp′tĭ-kəl) *adj.* Doubting; questioning.
skitter (skĭt′ər) *v.* To move quickly over water.
skulk (skŭlk) *v.* To move in a quiet, fearful way.
slack (slăk) *adj.* Weak.

slander (slăn′dər) *n.* Spoken statements damaging to another person's character or reputation.

slither (slĭth′ər) *v.* To slide.

slobber (slŏb′ər) *v.* To drool.

sluice (slōōs) *n.* An artificial channel for water.

smolder (smōl′dər) *v.* To burn without a flame. — **smoldering** *adj.*

snappish (snăp′ĭsh) *adj.* Irritable; apt to speak sharply.

snigger (snĭg′ər) *v.* To laugh in a sneaky way. Same as *snicker*.

socket (sŏk′ĭt) *n.* An opening into which something can fit.

sodden (sŏd′n) *adj.* Thoroughly soaked.

solder (sŏd′ər, sôd′-) *v.* To mend with solder, a metal alloy, which when melted can be used to connect metal parts. — **soldered** *adj.*

souse (sous) *n.* Pickled pork.

sow (sō) *v.* To plant seeds. — **sower** *n.*

span (spăn) *v.* To stretch across.

spar (spär) *n.* A pole used to support a ship's sail.

spasm (spăz′əm) *n.* A fit.

specter (spĕk′tər) *n.* A ghost.

splutter (splŭt′ər) *v.* To speak in an excited, confused way.

spontaneous (spŏn-tā′nē-əs) *adj.* Not planned.

spouse (spous, spouz) *n.* A husband or wife.

spume (spyōōm) *n.* Foam; froth.

spur (spŭr) *v.* To urge a horse forward by using spurs — pointed devices attached to a rider's boots.

stark (stärk) *adj.* Rigid.

stately (stāt′lē) *adj.* Dignified.

steed (stēd) *n.* A high-spirited horse.

sterile (stĕr′əl) *adj.* Barren. — **sterility** *n.*

stigma (stĭg′mə) *n.* A mark of disgrace.

stipulate (stĭp′yə-lāt′) *v.* To state the conditions of an agreement. — **stipulated** *adj.*

stolid (stŏl′ĭd) *adj.* Unemotional.

stratagem (străt′ə-jəm) *n.* A trick or scheme.

strategic (strə-tē′jĭk) *adj.* Important to the strategy, or plan of action. — **strategically** *adv.*

strive (strīv) *v.* To try hard; struggle.

stubble (stŭb′əl) *n.* The stumps of crops remaining after a harvest.

stucco (stŭk′ō) *n.* A covering used for building surfaces, made of cement and other materials.

stupendous (stōō-pĕn′dəs, styōō-) *adj.* Overwhelming.

stupor (stōō′pər, styōō′-) *n.* A confused state; daze.

subdue (səb-dōō′, -dyōō′) *v.* To bring under control.

submerge (səb-mûrj′) *v.* To put under water. — **submerged** *adj.*

subside (səb-sīd′) *v.* To settle down.

succulent (sŭk′yə-lənt) *adj.* Juicy.

sulky (sŭl′kē) *adj.* Slow-moving; sluggish.

sultry (sŭl′trē) *adj.* Hot and humid.

summerhouse (sŭm′ər-hous′) *n.* A small open structure in a garden.

supplicate (sŭp′lĭ-kāt′) *v.* To beg. — **supplication** *n.*

supposition (sŭp′ə-zĭsh′ən) *n.* Something thought to be true.

surfeit (sûr′fĭt) *v.* To overfeed. — **surfeited** *adj.*

surge (sûrj) *v.* **1.** To rise up or swell. **2.** To increase suddenly.

surly (sûr′lē) *adj.* Bad-tempered; rude.

surmount (sər-mount′) *v.* **1.** To climb up and over. **2.** To be at the top of.

sustain (sə-stān′) *v.* To support. — **sustained** *adj.*

swagger (swăg′ər) *v.* To walk in a bold, self-important manner.

T

tableau (tăb′lō′, tă-blō′) *n.* A striking scene.

tactful (tăkt′fəl) *adj.* Showing sensitivity to another's feelings.

talon (tăl′ən) *n.* The claw of a bird or other animal.

tantalize (tăn′tə-līz′) *v.* To tease by offering something and then withdrawing it. — **tantalizing** *adj.*

tarry (tăr′ē) *v.* To linger.

tart (tärt) *adj.* **1.** Sharp. **2.** Sarcastic. — **tartly** *adv.*

taunt (tônt) *v.* To make fun of.

taut (tôt) *adj.* Pulled tight.

tauten (tôt′n) *v.* To pull tight. — **tautened** *adj.*

tawny (tô′nē) *adj.* Tan; brownish-yellow.

teeter (tē′tər) *v.* To step or walk uncertainly.

terrarium (tə-răr′ē-əm) *n.* An enclosed container in which small plants or animals are kept.

terse (tûrs) *adj.* Brief; to the point. — **tersely** *adv.*

testy (tĕs′tē) *adj.* Touchy; irritable. — **testily** *adv.*

tether (tĕth′ər) *v.* To confine an animal's movements to a limited area by tying it to a rope or chain.

thatch (thăch) *n.* A roof covering made of straw or leaves.

thong (thông, thŏng) *n.* A leather cord.

thresh (thrĕsh) *v.* To separate grain from straw. — **threshing** *adj.*

ă pat/ā pay/âr care/ä father/b bib/ch church/d deed/ĕ pet/ē be/f fife/g gag/h hat/hw which/ĭ pit/ī pie/îr pier/j judge/k kick/l lid, needle/m mum/ n no, sudden/ng thing/ŏ pot/ō toe/ô paw, for/oi noise/ou out/ŏŏ took/ōō boot/p pop/r roar/s sauce/sh ship, dish/t tight/th thin, path/th this, bathe/ ū cut/ûr urge/v valve/w with/y yes/z zebra, size/zh vision/ə about, item, edible, gallop, circus/ à *Fr.* ami/œ *Fr.* feu, *Ger.* schön/ü *Fr.* tu, *Ger.* über/ KH *Ger.* ich, *Scot.* loch/N *Fr.* bon.

threshold (thrĕsh′ōld′, thrĕsh′hōld′) *n*. A doorway.

throng (thrŏng) *n*. A great number of people.

toil (toil) *v*. To work hard.

topple (tŏp′əl) *v*. To fall over.

torrent (tôr′ənt, tŏr′-) *n*. **1**. A fast-moving stream. **2**. An abundant or violent flow.

torso (tôr′sō) *n*. A human body without the head or limbs.

totter (tŏt′ər) *v*. To move unsteadily. — **tottering** *adj*.

trace (trās) *n*. One of the chains that connect an animal to the wagon it is pulling.

tradition (trə-dĭsh′ən) *n*. A longstanding custom or practice.

train (trān) *n*. That part of a gown that trails on the ground.

trance (trăns) *n*. A dreamlike state.

tranquil (trăn′kwəl) *adj*. Calm. — **tranquilly** *adv*.

tranquillity (trăn-kwĭl′ə-tē) *n*. Peacefulness; serenity.

transaction (trăn-săk′shən, -zăk′shən) *n*. A business dealing.

transcend (trăn-sĕnd′) *v*. To rise above.

transfix (trăns-fĭks′) *v*. To make motionless.

transient (trăn′shənt, -zhənt, -zē-ənt) *adj*. Staying only briefly.

translucent (trăns-loō′sənt, trănz′-) *adj*. Allowing light to shine through but not allowing a clear view of anything beyond.

transparent (trăns-pâr′ənt, păr′ənt) *adj*. Able to be seen through.

transplant (trăns-plănt′, -plänt′) *v*. To dig up and replant in another place.

transpose (trăns-pōz′) *v*. To change a piece of music from one key to another.

tremor (trĕm′ər) *n*. A trembling movement.

tremulous (trĕm′yə-ləs) *adj*. Trembling.

trivial (trĭv′ē-əl) *adj*. Of little value or importance.

troll (trōl) *v*. To fish by dragging a line through water.

turf (tûrf) *n*. Grass-covered soil.

turret (tûr′ĭt) *n*. A small tower.

tutor (toō-tər, tyoō′-) *n*. A private teacher.

twine (twīn) *v*. To twist.

U

uncanny (ŭn′kăn′ē) *adj*. Strange.

understate (ŭn′dər-stāt′) *v*. To express in a restrained way. — **understated** *adj*.

unique (yoō-nēk′) *adj*. **1**. Having no equal. **2**. One and only.

upsurge (ŭp′sûrj′) *v*. To rise up. — **upsurgence** *n*.

urchin (ûr′chĭn) *n*. A mischievous youngster.

V

vale (vāl) *n*. A valley.

vandalism (vănd′l-īz′əm) *n*. Intentional destruction of property, especially beautiful property.

vapor (vā′pər) *n*. A mist.

vault (vŏlt) *n*. **1**. An arched structure. **2**. The sky.

veer (vîr) *v*. To change direction. — **veering** *adj*.

vehement (vē′ə-mənt) *adj*. Showing great force or feeling. — **vehemently** *adv*.

veneration (vĕn′ə-rā′shən) *n*. Great respect or reverence.

venom (vĕn′əm) *n*. **1**. Poison. **2**. Evil; malice. — **venomous** *adj*.

veranda (və-răn′də) *n*. A porch.

vermilion (vər-mĭl′yən) *adj*. Of a vivid-red color.

vestige (vĕs′tĭj) *n*. A trace of something that once existed.

vex (vĕks) *v*. To annoy. — **vexed** *adj*.

vexation (vĕk-sā′shən) *n*. Annoyance.

vigil (vĭj′əl) *n*. A period of watchfulness.

vigilance (vĭj′ə-ləns) *n*. Alertness.

vindictive (vĭn-dĭk′tĭv) *adj*. Revengeful.

virtually (vûr′choō-ə-lē) *adv*. In effect; practically.

visceral (vĭs′ər-əl) *adj*. Very emotional.

vogue (vōg) *n*. Fashion.

vow (vou) *v*. To promise solemnly.

W

waggish (wăg′ĭsh) *adj*. Playful.

waistcoat (wĕs′kĭt, wāst′kōt′) *n*. A vest.

wan (wŏn) *adj*. Weak; pale. — **wanly** *adv*.

warp (wôrp) *n*. The threads in a fabric that run lengthwise.

wary (wâr′ē) *adj*. Cautious. — **warily** *adv*.

wharf (hwôrf) *n*. A place where ships are loaded and unloaded; dock.

wheel (hwēl) *v*. To turn around quickly.

wheeze (hwēz) *n*. A whistling sound made when breathing is difficult.

whimper (hwĭm′pər) *v*. To sob softly. — **whimpering** *adj*.

whimsical (hwĭm′zĭ-kəl) *adj*. Unpredictable; odd.

whimsy (hwĭm′zē) *n*. Strange or fanciful humor.

wickerwork (wĭk′ər-wûrk′) *adj*. Made of wicker — twigs or sticks woven together for furniture or baskets.

wicket (wĭk′ĭt) *n*. A door or gate.

wily (wī′lē) *adj*. Sly; tricky.

wince (wĭns) *v*. To make a face as in pain or embarrassment.

winnow (wĭn′ō) *v*. To blow husks away from the grain.

writhe (rīth) *v*. To twist or turn.

wrought (rôt) *adj*. Done.

Outline of Skills

Page numbers in italics refer to entries in the Guide to Literary Terms and Techniques.

Reading/Literary Skills

Index of Contents by Types

Myths, Fables, Folk Tales

Short Stories

Nonfiction

Selections from Novels

Plays

Poetry

Index of Fine Art

Photo Credits

Art Credits

Brian Cody 11, 13, 16–17
Mordi Gerstein 45, 46–47, 49, 341, 345, 348, 352–353, 438
J. J. Grandville, *The Hare and the Tortoise*, 527
Konrad Hack 234, 239
Rosekrans Hoffman 6–7, 227, 228–229, 230
Gerry A. Hoover 480, 483, 500
Harvey Kidder 186–187, 188–189, 190–191, 254, 426–427
Gordon Laite 441, 452, 453, 455, 456, 533
Richard Loehle 82–83, 85, 87, 118–119, 120, 122–123
Don Madden 167, 169, 393, 395, 396
Lyle Miller 18–19, 21, 24, 196–197, 199, 201
Carol Nicklaus 65, 67, 70, 75
Stella Ormai 192–193, 194–195, 257, 259, 262–263, 265, 267
Jan Pyk 511
Arthur Rackham 294, 295, 299, 302, 306, 310, 315
Charles Robinson 37, 39, 40–41, 42–43, 127, 128–129
Douglas Snow 28–29, 32, 34–35, 209, 210–211
Arvis L. Stewart 1, 6–7, 105, 141, 160–161, 164–165, 204–205, 329,
        333, 462–463
John Wallner 112, 114, 142–143, 270–271, 275, 276–277, 279, 282,
        284–285, 528, 529, 534–535
Bari Weissman 149, 150–151

Index of Authors and Titles

The page numbers in italics show where a brief biography of the author is located.

6
D 7
E 8
F 9
G 0
H 1
I 2
J 3